KAMIKAZE,

CHERRY BLOSSOMS,

AND NATIONALISMS

KAMIKAZE, CHERRY BLOSSOMS, AND NATIONALISMS

The Militarization of Aesthetics in Japanese History

EMIKO OHNUKI-TIERNEY

THE UNIVERSITY OF CHICAGO PRESS CHICAGO AND LONDON

Emiko Ohnuki-Tierney is the William F. Vilas Research Professor in the Department of Anthropology at the University of Wisconsin-Madison. She is the author of a number of books in English and Japanese, most recently *Rice as Self: Japanese Identities through Time* and *The Monkey as Mirror: Symbolic Transformations in Japanese History and Ritual*.

The University of Chicago Press, Chicago 60637
The University of Chicago Press, Ltd., London
© 2002 by The University of Chicago
All rights reserved. Published 2002
Printed in the United States of America
11 10 09 08 07 06 05 04 03 02   5 4 3 2 1

ISBN (cloth): 0-226-62090-5
ISBN (paper): 0-226-62091-3

Library of Congress Cataloging-in-Publication Data

Ohnuki-Tierney, Emiko.
    Kamikaze, cherry blossoms, and nationalism : the militarization of aesthetics in Japanese history / Emiko Ohnuki-Tierney.
        p.   cm.
    Includes bibliographical references and index.
    ISBN 0-226-62090-5
    1. Kamikaze airplanes. 2. World War, 1939–1945—Aerial operations, Japanese.
    3. World War, 1939–1945—Education and the war. 4. Fighter pilots—Japan.
    5. College students—Japan. I. Title.

D792.J3 O26 2002
940.54′4952′0922—dc21

                                                        2002001067

In memory of Kurata Iku

My grandmother who bore an incredible pain
throughout her life

Losing two sons to the war

Contents

Illustrations

Preface

Although I have cluttered up enough space in printed pages in the past, this project is the longest in terms of the number of years spent and the one that obsessed me, literally, the most. Not only did this book become the largest in scope I have ever undertaken, but the process of writing it involved many unexpected twists and turns. The project began as a study of cherry blossom viewing; at the time I was ignorant of the involvement of the symbolism of cherry blossoms in the *tokkōtai* (kamikaze) operation. The project resulted in this book, whose major concern became the use of aesthetics on the part of the Japanese totalitarian regime. Once started, I had no option but to push on. What sustained me through these years was the idealism and dedication to learning so evident in the pilots' diaries, which I stopped reading at night—they were too tragic and powerful, and after reading them it was difficult to fall asleep. Moreover, my rage against the forces that terminated these young brilliant minds became increasingly intense, and I felt a moral obligation to introduce them to non-Japanese readers, because they are known outside of Japan only as ultra-nationalistic zealots. I agonized over the decision to write an introduction to these young men and their writings for a broader audience vs. an analytical/interpretive book on the question of why such intelligent and intellectual young men fight in wars orchestrated by a totalitarian state. I chose the latter, since the question is not a Japanese problem or a question pertaining to the past. It is an ongoing question the world over, and the former would have had to stop short of confronting the question directly.

A project of this scope could not have been undertaken without the generous assistance of the William F. Vilas Trust Fund of the University of Wisconsin. I cannot express in words my indebtedness to it. A fellowship from the National Endowment for the Humanities at a critical juncture enabled me to engage in full-time writing. A part of the book was written in 1998 at the idyllic setting of Villa Serbelloni, for which I thank the Rockefeller Foundation, Gianna Celli, and Susan Garfield. Discussions with my colleagues at the École des Hautes Études en Sciences Sociales in 1997 and again in 1998 were most helpful, and I thank Marc

Augé for his invitations. The library research for the project started during my stay at Harvard University (1993–94) and continued at the University of Michigan (1995). I express my appreciation for the invitations and for the colleagues who shared their thoughts with me.

My thanks are due to two relatives of the tokkōtai pilots. Dr. Umezawa Shōzō, a younger brother of Umezawa Kazuyo, offered me a photo of his younger brother with branches of cherry blossoms on his uniform, and in addition provided me with invaluable information about his brother and his mother. Professor Nakao Yoshitaka at Seinan Gakuin University, and also a painter, is the brother of Nakao Taketoku, introduced in detail in chapter 6. He sent me his brother's seven-hundred-page diary, which he had edited.

My research took me into unfamiliar territories, ranging from ninth-century historical documents in Chinese, through medieval literature, the Imperial Constitution of Japan of 1889, to the diaries of pilots whose intellectual scope was far beyond my own. I was able to conduct the research only because of my good fortune of having colleagues and friends, among whom space allows me to acknowledge only a few. Irokawa Daikichi, an eminent historian of Japan, shared with me invaluable sources in his possession. Himself a student soldier from the University of Tokyo and later an almost radical historian who openly opposed the emperor system and fought tirelessly to rectify social injustices, he guided me through the project, which I began when I was without empathy for the tokkōtai pilots and had no clue as to why these brilliant young men fought in the war.

Edmund Leach long ago pointed out the ambiguities of symbolic communication. He for many years extended his warm personal support for my work. I remember Sir Edmund with profound respect and affection. Stanley Jeyaraja Tambiah has extended his moral support over the years, and his brilliant treatments of symbols and rituals, and his more recent engagement with violence involved in the ethnonationalist conflicts in his own homeland and in South Asia in general, have been an important intellectual and moral wellspring for me. Eric Wolf read an earlier version of an outline of this book and extended his comments, even when he had fallen ill and wanted to focus on his own book. I address many of the themes raised in his *Envisioning Power*. The present book is in many ways my best effort so far to meet the suggestions he made over the years in his publications, letters, and phone conversations that symbolic studies must confront power and power inequalities—a conviction coming from his personal experience and his commitment to humanity. His last letter was about his enthusiasm for tai c'hi.

John J. Kelly read an earlier version of this book and offered the most engaging and yet generous criticisms and suggestions. My understanding of the Japanese material in comparative perspective and of social theory took on far greater depth as a result. His intense engagement with my manuscript was an instance of the very best in collegiality, and from such a brilliant mind, that I have received in my long career. Tetsuo Najita read and offered encouragement and valuable comments on chapter 5. His own work on the intellectuals just before the Meiji period gave me an insight for understanding the pilots, whom I call cosmopolitan patriots and whose thoughts parallel those of Najita's intellectuals in significant ways. Pierre Bourdieu, who read the introduction and chapter 6 and patiently listened to my description of the project, perceptively identified a central question—why did the pilots "freely choose their fate." T. David Brent's work on Kant and Jung offered me the crucial step in my interpretation of the role of aesthetics in méconnaissance (misrecognition) of symbols and also of the relationship between Kant's and Berlin's thoughts on humanity. His understanding of my goal and my hope for the book as a scholarly contribution is most appreciated. George Mosse, from whose work I received much inspiration, read the introduction at a very early stage; the sudden onset of his illness forced him to cancel our dinner discussion, which would have been an invaluable experience.

H. Mack Horton shared with me his unpublished manuscript on the Silla envoy poems and invaluable indexing of cherry blossoms in *The Tale of Genji,* without which I would not have come to an understanding of the ancient imperial guards or of the *The Tale of Genji.* Ishikawa Hiroyoshi, of Seijō University, not only introduced me to his colleagues but also supplied me with valuable sources over the years. Miyake Hitoshi, of Keiō University, opened doors that enabled me to observe contemporary rituals; he also pointed out important sources on the symbolism of the flower in Japanese literature and religions. The relationship of cherry blossoms with madness came to me like a flash when Prince Mikasa (Mikasanomiya Takahito) invited me to a narrative theater which staged Sakaguchi Ango's *Sakura no Mori no Mankai no Shita* (In the forest, under cherries in full bloom) on March 30, 1996, which powerfully portrayed the subversive and playful nature of the symbolism of cherry blossoms. Hattori Shōgo, of Bōei University, is a historian of the tokkōtai operation, who led me to unpublished sources and shared his own insights.

Others who read parts of the manuscript and/or offered helpful comments and/or engaged in extensive discussions include: Karen Colvard, Louis Fusek, Haga Hideo (a prize-winning photographer), Arthur

Kleinman, Henry Smith, Jr., Yoshida Shūji (National Museum of Ethnology), Akimoto Minoru (Nōgakudō), Okuyama Keiko (Nōgakudō), Harmut O. Rotermund (École des Pratique des Hautes Études), Rudy Koshar, Eric Rothstein, Stanley Payne, John Tortorice, Jan Vansina, and Stewart Macaulay.

My special indebtedness goes to Kenji Tierney, who declined to be a co-author. This book is a product of collaboration with him at every stage of its development. With his sharp eyes for ethnographic and historical information relevant to the concerns of this book, he supplied me with invaluable information and innumerable photos. He edited an earlier draft of the key conceptual chapters, and his theoretical input vastly improved these chapters and the book in general.

The suggestions by Richard Allen, as a specialist in religions, and his excellent editing vastly improved the book. The preparation of the manuscript was facilitated by efficient help from: Louise Robins, Arai Sanae, Gregory Engle, Nemoto Yuho, Noguchi Ichirō, Suzuki Hikaru, and Hashimoto Yōko. Special thanks are due to Suzuki Keiko's dedicated assistance as well as her own expertise.

This book is dedicated to my grandmother, whose love made my childhood blissfully happy. She suffered too deeply from the loss of her sons in the war to express her grief in words. Only years later did I learn from others of her suffering. The nobility of her character made me realize her sorrow even more painfully. I dedicate this book also to my high school mathematics teacher, Ishimura Iwao, who taught me Emerson's "Hitch your wagon to a star"—both the phrase and its spirit. The phrase appears repeatedly in the diaries of the pilots. His career at the First Higher School and then at the Imperial University of Tokyo, like those of the pilots in this book, was thwarted by his illness, which also saved him from becoming a student soldier.

Chronology of Events and Publications

1839–42	Opium War
1853, 1854	Arrival of Commodore Perry

Meiji Period (1868–1912)

1868	The Meiji "Restoration"
1869	Construction of the Yasukuni Shrine
1870	Planting of cherry trees at the Yasukuni Shrine by Kido
	First navy and army uniforms with blooming cherries in their insignia
1872	Universal conscription adopted
1881	Elementary school songs (cherry blossoms as cultural nationalism)
1882	The Imperial Rescript to Soldiers *(Gunjin Chokugo)*
1883	Emergence of elementary school songs with the emperor-centered ideology
1887	More elementary school songs with the emperor-centered ideology
1889	The Constitution of Imperial Japan *(Dai-Nihon Teikoku Kenpō)*
	Tsubouchi Shōyō's school text (published 1900): Cherry blossoms as a symbol of cultural nationalism
1890	The Imperial Rescript on Education *(Kyōiku Chokugo)*
1891	Term *gyokusai* (scattering like a shattered crystal ball) appears in songs
1894–95	Sino-Japanese War
1894	"Falling Cherry Blossoms for the Emperor" (Sasaki Nobutsuna's song text)
1904–5	Russo-Japanese War
1905	Korea becomes protectorate of Japan
1908	Japanese translation of Nitobe's *Bushidō: The Soul of Japan*
1910	Korea annexed

Taishō Period (1912–26)

1914–18   World War I

Shōwa Period (1926–89)

1930   "Cherry blossom textbook" (published 1932)
1931   Manchurian Incident
1932   Manchukuo established
                Shanghai Incident
                Cogito launched (journal of Japan Romantic School)
1933–35   *The History of the Loyal Souls at the Yasukuni Shrine*
                    published
1933   Hitler's rise to power
1934   Hitler becomes führer and chancellor
1934–41   Ultra-nationalistic version of *The Forty-Seven Loyal
                    Retainers (Genroku Chūshingura)*
1935   Minobe Tatsukichi expelled from government (proponent of
                    the "organ theory" of the emperor)
1937   *Kokutai no Hongi* (Principles of the national polity) published
                "Umi Yukaba" (Die for the emperor at sea and mountains)
                Lukowkiao Incident
1938   "Dōki no Sakura" (The cherry blossoms of the same class)
                    (revised, 1942)
1941   Pearl Harbor (December 8)
1942   Film version of *The Forty-Seven Loyal Retainers* by
                    Mizoguchi
                Japan's defeat at Midway (June 5)
1943   Japan's retreat from Guadalcanal (February 5)
                First drafting of 25,000 university "graduates" (October 21)
                Drafting of 6,000 to 10,000 "student soldiers" (December)
1944   Tōjō Cabinet dissolved (July 18)
                First tokkōtai attack at the Bay of Leyte (October 25)
1945   Bombing of Tokyo (March 9, 10)
                American landing on Okinawa (April 1)
                Germany surrenders (May 7)
                Atomic Bomb on Hiroshima (August 6)
                Atomic Bomb on Nagasaki (August 9)
                Japan surrenders (August 14)

Note on Names, Dates, and Titles of Works

Following the Japanese convention, Japanese names start with the last names, followed by the first names without a comma.

When more meaningful, the days of the month are given according to Japan time, which is a day ahead of the United States; for example, the end of World War II is given as August 14, since the date is important in reference to the dates of the pilots' actions, including their deaths. Also, all the dates given in the diaries and letters are according to the dates given in the original writing/publications.

In chapters 5 and 6, in the cases in which the names of the editors, often an organization, are lengthy and the abbreviated titles are more meaningful, I use the latter in the text and in the endnotes. These are: *Cherry Blossoms of the Same Class* (1966a and b), edited by Kaigun Hikō Yobi Gakusei Dai-14-ki-kai; *Conscription of Students* (1981), edited by Mainichi Shirīzu Shuppan Henshū; *Listen to the Voices of the Sea Gods* (1949), edited by Nihon Senbotsu Gakusei Shuki Henshū Iinkai; *Listen to the Voices of the Sea Gods: The Second Collection* (1988), edited by Nihon Senbotsu Gakusei Kinenkai; *Far Off Mountains and Rivers* (1947), edited by Tokyō Daigaku Gakusei Jichikai and Senbotsu Gakusei Shuki Henshū Iinkai.

INTRODUCTION

As we reflect on the twentieth century, a profound disillusionment with the epoch looms large in the minds of many. It was a century with two world wars in addition to innumerable armed conflicts. The end of colonialism brought forth not what we hoped for but ushered in a series of gruesome international, interracial, and interethnic conflicts. As a response, nationalism, ethnicity, wars and other forms of violence became a site of scholarly productivity. Within this dialogue, the question of how and why individuals, especially intellectuals, become participants, often actively, in the developments of nationalisms or even ultra-nationalisms and wars occupies an important space. In addition, the strategic uses by nation-states of symbols, be they in rituals, monuments, or propaganda, for their political purposes became foregrounded. In particular, the aesthetics of symbols deployed for such purposes has come to light, as we reflect upon revolutionary movements, authoritarian regimes, and warfare.

A central concern of this book is the question of *how* state nationalism is developed and *how* it succeeds and/or fails to be accepted by "ordinary" individuals, who, rather than questioning let alone revolting, often embrace as "natural" basic changes in culture and society initiated by political, military, and intellectual leaders. How and why do individuals sacrifice themselves for the country? In exploring these questions, I make several distinctions. First, I differentiate between the ideology of state *nationalism* from above and the *patriotism* of the individuals who sacrifice their lives. Second, I distinguish between sacrifice for the country and sacrifice for the head of the country (king/queen, emperor, führer). The third distinction is between thought and action. When a solider "volunteers" to die for his country, does he do so both in thought and in action? Or does he sacrifice himself only in action without espousing the ideology of state nationalism in toto? If so, in what specific ways do individuals embrace state nationalism and in what ways do they fail or refuse to do so?

To address these questions, I investigate the development in Japan of a totalitarian ideology, centered on the emperor, that began in the nineteenth century and that culminated at the end of World War II in the institution of the *tokkōtai,* the "Special Attack Force," known outside of Japan as the *kamikaze,* "God's Wind." I bring in comparative perspectives when possible, since the cry *pro patria mori*—"To die for one's country"—has been part of human history ever since Horace immortalized the phrase in his ode. Moreover, there are parallels between Japan and other states that have experienced fascist, totalitarian, or authoritarian regimes.

The Japanese experience described in this book illustrates how "culture" is always *in motion*—becoming, reproducing itself even when disintegrating at the "core"and transforming, in a constant ebb and flow. If we examine the deep past of a particular culture, we realize that every culture is comprised of a series of interpenetrations as a result of the dialectic between internal developments, global and other external forces, and social agents, who are almost always cosmopolitans; for any culture, the local and the global/external have been mutually constituent (Ohnuki-Tierney 2001). We are thus compelled to question the basic assumptions of the debate over "the global and the local" that has gained currency in and out of the academy. The global and the local is a false dichotomy, as is the notion of hybridity, which presupposes a "pure culture" that never existed. While the Constitution of Imperial Japan of 1889 was drafted by German legal scholars and some sections were adopted almost verbatim, the Meiji oligarchs had the final say in the most important matters. Or, it would not be an exaggeration to say that since the beginning of the Meiji period (1868–1912), the most influential intellectual leaders were liberal or even radical Christians, who challenged both Japanese and church authorities. Yet they remained deeply patriotic. Conversely, some of the influential Japanese Romantics of the 1930s combined elements of Romanticism in Europe with their ultra-nationalism. The Weltanschauung of the tokkōtai pilots was heavily informed by these various intellectual traditions—Greco-Roman classics, Christianity, Marxism, and Romanticism, and their cross-fertilization with Chinese and Japanese intellectual traditions. *Nationalism and patriotism are born at the vibrant intersection of the global and the local,* rather than being the xenophobic expressions of a hermetically sealed people.

I approach the development of totalitarianism by focusing on the aesthetics of symbols. Symbols and their behavioral counterparts, rituals and ceremonies, are powerfully evocative, and they are often identified as the factors that move people to action. The Jacobins in the French Revolution, and Hitler, Mussolini, Mao, and many other political leaders have consciously deployed symbols and rituals for political purposes. Do they really move people, and are they more powerful than concepts, as not only Weber but "even" Durkheim proclaimed? Does the conscious, deliberate deployment of symbols and rituals, for the purpose of directing people to act, work as those deploying the symbols and rituals intend? Or do people ignore, intentionally or unintentionally, the "official meaning," and/or assign meaning(s) different from the one(s) intended by the state?

These questions led me to locate the power of symbols and rituals in *méconnaissance*, that is, the absence of communication that results when people do not share a meaning but rather derive different meanings from the same symbols and rituals. Méconnaissance can occur when the parties involved are unaware of the lack of communication (Ohnuki-Tierney 1987, 210–13), or when they intentionally disregard the meanings assigned by the other party, whether in an ordinary social context or in a systematic scheme deployed by a totalitarian regime.[1]

To examine this phenomenon, I have selected as an example the symbolism of cherry blossoms, which became the master trope of Japan's imperial nationalism at the beginning of the Meiji period—"You shall die like beautiful falling cherry petals for the emperor." Many tokkōtai pilots flew to their deaths with blooming cherry branches adorning their uniforms. Did they really embrace the emperor-centered ideology and share the meaning of the cherry blossoms that the architects of that ideology intended? Or, did they see something else in the flower?

The pilots were the intellectual crème de la crème. They were students from top universities whom the government graduated early in order to draft. Their prodigious readings and extensive diaries served as a means for soliloquy. The gold mine of writings they left behind enables us to examine the thoughts and feelings behind their actions along with the highly complex processes of penetration by state nationalism—how it was and was not translated into their patriotism.

Near the end of World War II, when the American invasion of Japan's homeland seemed imminent, Ōnishi Takijirō, a navy vice-admiral, invented the tokkōtai (kamikaze) operations, which made use of powered airplanes, gliders, and submarine torpedoes (chapter 5). None was equipped with a means of returning to base. The airplanes, best known among the tokkōtai operations, flew close to the water to avoid detection by radar. The underwater torpedoes, called "human torpedoes," were carried by submarines close to the target. After they had been launched, to avoid detection the pilots made the last stretch toward the moving American ships without the aid of periscopes. In the final analysis, Ōnishi and his right-hand men thought the Japanese soul, which had been built up to possess a unique strength to face death without hesitation, was the only means available for the Japanese to bring about a miracle when the homeland was surrounded by American aircraft carriers whose sophisticated radar systems prevented any other method to destroy them. When the operation was instituted, *not a single officer* from the military academies volunteered to sortie as a pilot; they knew too well that it was a meaningless death. Those who "chose their fate"[2] consisted of teenage pilots, mostly enlisted men, along with close to one thousand student soldiers, university students whom the government graduated early so that it could draft them.

The student soldiers—the major focus of this book—had lived in a world of idealism, seeking the aesthetics of truth and life. Most of them were single men. In the writings they left behind—each source by a single pilot consisting of several hundred pages—one sees how they were swept up in the intellectual currents of the time. They embraced modernity while trying to overcome it; they emulated the achievements of the Western high civilizations while resisting Western cultural and political hegemony. In their youthful idealism they chose to fulfill a responsibility as members of their society, even though it meant death. Yet, by the time they were drafted to the military, Japan's defeat was imminent. They had been, as it were, dropped on a roller-coaster fast descending toward its final crash. As their death was closing in on them, many realized that they had hardly lived, and their desire to live was intensified. Their writings reveal agony, ambivalence, and great contradictions—in some passages they try to convince themselves by endorsing the official ideological lines; in others they altogether negate these statements and explicitly defy the totalitarian ideology. Reading became the major means by which they engaged in soliloquy. With their voracious appetite for intellectual pursuits, these young pilots read both Japanese and Western intellectual and literary giants intensively and extensively. One pilot read some six hundred books and another five hundred, for example. Their reading ranged from Greco-Roman figures such as Aristotle, Plato, Socrates, and Zeno of Citium, the founder of Stoicism, to major nineteenth- and twentieth-century literary and philosophical figures in Japan and the West. They read authors such as Kant, Hegel, Nietzsche, Goethe, Schiller, Marx, and Thomas Mann (Germany), Rousseau, Martin du Gard, Gide, and Romain Rolland (France), and Lenin, Dostoyevsky, Tolstoy, and Berdyaev (Russia), often in the original languages.

The pressing need to understand the question of an individual's responsibility to society occupied a central place, a choice which meant life or death to them. It led them to Western and Japanese literary and intellectual figures who wrote on these issues. In this regard, the Japanese philosopher Tanabe Hajime was quite influential to them. Among the Japanese authors, he was most extensively read by the pilots. It was he who at the Imperial University of Kyoto delivered the now infamous speech on May 19, 1943 to a large audience, including the students destined for the front. Tanabe, a devout Christian, advocated the individual's involvement in society as a means to change society. For the students, his message was to go to war.

Many of the late eighteenth- through early twentieth-century figures they read, though certainly not all, espoused various kinds of Romanticism, a movement that swept through Germany, France, and Russia beginning in the late eighteenth century. In 1932, a year before Hitler rose to power, the major journal of Japan's Romantic movement, *Cogito*, which became closely tied with ultra-nationalism, was launched. The leader of Japan's Romantic movement, Yasuda Yojūrō, declared the end of Marxism and proposed that Romanticism be the bridge in the night to a new dawn. *Les liaisons dangereuses* between the intellectual and artistic community and ultra-nationalism, which often posthumously appropriated and misappropriated figures in the Romantic movement, were forming in Japan as in Nazi Germany. Of critical importance is the emphasis on aesthetics in Romanticism, which pilots projected onto their idealism and patriotism, using it to justify their sacrifice as a noble and beautiful act.

Some student soldiers were committed to Marxism—a powerful presence in Japan throughout the modern period and well into the postwar period. They found meaning in destroying even Japan as well as the United Kingdom and the United States—all of which, they felt, had been corrupted by materialism and capitalism—in order to usher in a new Japan that would, like a phoenix, rise from the ashes of the old. Some of them wished to usher in an utopia founded in the humanitarianism of Albert Schweitzer.

Others were devout Christians who carried the Bible on their final flights or who sang hymns on the last night, dangerous acts given the strict censorship on the bases. Even non-Christian pilots eagerly read about Christianity. Not only were the most influential intellectual leaders in Japan's modern times Christians, but the young men's quest for the meaning of sacrifice often led them to Christianity. They turned to Christianity also because none of the Japanese religions offered them even the slightest vision of what was to happen to them after death—to their soul and the body—a central theme in Christianity.

It would be a mistake to situate the student soldiers within a simple picture of the Japanese embracing and overcoming Western high culture.

Japan's intense intellectual engagement with the West was heavily mediated by a long history of influence by Chinese intellectual traditions. For example, Confucianism, introduced during the sixth century, and the Neo-Confucianism of Chu Hsi, which entered Japan during the twelfth century, have been most influential as systems of thought that have shaped Japan's socio-economic-political institutions. Personal loyalty was an important dimension of the conceptual-moral teaching of Chu Hsi's Neo-Confucianism, which was replaced in influence by the Wang Yang-ming (Ōyōmei) branch of Neo-Confucianism introduced into Japan during the first half of the seventeenth century. The latter's emphasis on the individual and on self-cultivation paved the way to the Japanese embrace of Kantian individualism (Bitō [1993] 1996), on the one hand, and its emphasis on intuition and moral sense over rationality had a major emphasis on the Meiji Restoration, on the other. In the 1880s the "Confucian" (in a generic sense) moral values of loyalty and filial piety were resurrected to buttress the newly created emperor system and the modern military nation, for which individual sacrifice for the state was essential.

Notwithstanding the student soldiers' desperate efforts to rationalize their actions, their diaries are full of painful expressions of their agony. Hayashi Tadao, from the University of Kyoto, repeatedly wrote, "I do not want to die! . . . I want to live!" He felt extremely lonely. In another passage he wrote in French, "Me, confusion and anarchy; it is me." In September 1942, Nakao Taketoku, from the University of Tokyo, composed a poem entitled "Silence" which begins: "How lonely is the sound of the clock in the darkness of the night." The clock was ticking away toward his death. In another poem from October 1943 he described how beautiful the moon was but then found the moon to be like a "beautiful woman gently crying." Previously, in May 1943 he had traveled from Tokyo to Kyoto to listen to the aforementioned Tanabe Hajime, whom he found to be like a congenial "grandfather from the countryside" rather than a lofty scholar. Tanabe's speech of May 19 strengthened his resolution to sacrifice himself. But two days later at Kyoto station as he was returning to Tokyo, he encountered people holding "white boxes"—empty boxes wrapped in white cloth containing only a piece of paper with the deceased soldier's name in it, instead of his remains. Nakao wrote: "The whiteness of the boxes was painful to my eyes. Were they [the deceased soldiers] able to say without hesitation, 'I will see you again at the Yasu-kuni Shrine?'"

For Hayashi Ichizō, from the University of Kyoto, a Christian, Kierke-gaard's *Sickness unto Death* and the Bible were two books with which he engaged in a soliloquy about life and death. He carried them onto his plane, together with a photo of his mother. As his final day approached, his diaries and letters became filled with cries for his mother, to whom he wrote, "I want to be held in your arms and sleep." Singing hymns at the school near the base and reading the Bible became his way of feeling close to his mother, herself a devout Christian.

Perhaps the most representative expression of the feeling of these pilots occurs in a passage in Miyazawa Kenji's *The Crow and the Great Dipper*, which Sasaki Hachirō quotes as conveying his own thoughts. It is a prayer by a crow to his guardian deity, the Great Dipper: "I pray that we will see the day as soon as possible when we welcome a world in which we do not have to kill enemies whom we cannot hate. For this end, I would not mind my body being ripped innumerable times" (Fujishiro 1981: 418–19). Miyazawa Kenji (1896–1932) was a poet and author of children's books who became highly influential among young intellectuals at the time (chapter 6).

In this book I seek explanations for the remarkable fact that these bright young men—many Marxists, or Christians, and all highly educated—did not fight against their government but were so patriotic as to sacrifice themselves for their country. In doing so, they reproduced the emperor-centered military ideology in their action, though not in their thoughts. In order to explore this phenomenon, I distinguish the patriotism of *pro patria mori*—to die for one's country—that was espoused by individual pilots, from the political nationalism that was fostered from above and that promoted *pro rege et patria mori*—to die for emperor/king and country. The state ideology of *pro rege et patria mori*, first articulated at the beginning of the Meiji period, had many dimensions. I focus on the part of the ideology that encouraged soldiers to sacrifice their lives for the emperor qua Japanese ancestral land.

I use these Latin phrases for several reasons. First of all, there are no good alternatives available. The widely used Japanese term *"tennōsei* [emperor-centered] ideology" is loaded with scholarly baggage. Furthermore, it is a label given post factum to "an ideology that must have been responsible" for the Pacific War. Although postwar intellectuals searched for what Maruyama Masao and Irokawa Daikichi famously called the "multiple layers of invisible nets" and "an enormous black box [Marx's *camera obscura*]," respectively, and eventually identified it as the tennōsei ideology, the term was never used before or during the war. Since the two major themes of my inquiry are the state's use of the emperor and of cherry blossoms, "the military ideology" is too narrow and "the imperial ideology" might be confused with the sort of imperialism that has colonial expansion as its dominant component.

The use of these Latin terms has a comparative advantage because of their extensive use in European contexts, including the Greco-Roman context and that of Christianity in the European Middle Ages, as well as that of more recent nationalistic-patriotic movements, such as Nazi Germany. Common to all is a sense of loyalty to the collective destiny of a social group—*pro domino* in Europe and Japan, and loyalty to nations and states, as well as to the vast Christian kingdom that transcends political and national boundaries. In contrast to *pro rege et patria mori, pro patria mori* does not require a central figure (*rege*—Christ, king, queen, führer, or emperor) to represent the *patria*. The distinction between the pair of Latin phrases enables us to zero in on the question of whether the Japanese soldiers died for the emperor or for their country, enabling us to assess the degree of success and failure of the state attempt at *pro rege et patria mori*.

Leaving a detailed discussion of "nation," "state," "nation-state," and "nationalism" to chapter 7, I discuss the use of a few terms here. First, fascism. Most Japanese scholars in Japan do not question that fascism was what developed in Japan, especially for the period from the 1920s through World War II. There are scholarly debates by non-Japanese historians of Japan on this issue, some of which center on the political and institutional dimensions of "fascism," rather than the ideological dimension.[3] Outside the fields of history and political science, the term has become too fashionable—a floating signifier to be used in many ways. On the other hand, "fascism" has comparative advantages. Yet the label, just like "nationalism," places various historical experiences occurring at various times in the history of each people within a grid of linear history: Japan's fascism rose not long after it shed feudalism, whereas European fascism rose in the wake of the failure of democracy; and fascism in Europe rose after monarchies were eliminated, whereas Japanese fascism developed after it reinvented an absolute constitutional monarchy. With caution, then, I use the term "fascism" to refer to a political ideology that combines *nationalism* with the *totalitarianism* that dictates that the state should have the control over all aspects of social and cultural life. The main concern of this book is a particular political nationalism which used *pro rege et patria mori* as the core of its ideological scheme, with the totalitarian goal of deploying the ideology to penetrate the quotidian lives of every "subject" of the nation.

"Ideology," invented by Antoine Destutt de Tracy (1754–1836) (Wolf 1999: 25; Althusser 1971: 158), also needs clarification. Recognizing how in modern intellectual history "the term 'ideology' has itself become thoroughly ideologized," Geertz (1973: 193, 220) offers a cultural definition of the term as "maps of problematic social reality and matrices for the creation of collective consciousness." I do not part company with Geertz, Sahlins, and others in my basic view that ideology, however one defines it, and even "economic activities," are a part of what we call "culture." I do not share Marx's view that the "mode of production in material life determines the general character of the social, political, and spiritual processes of life" (Marx and Engels [1852] 1989: 43) but concur with Sahlins (1976) that the economic system is a site of symbolic production, however dominant it may be in some Western cultures.

Nevertheless, the tasks I set forth in this book compelled me to foreground the relationship between a system of thought and political power, both internal and external, such as colonialism. This led me closer to some scholars of Marxian persuasion such as Wolf (1999: 4), who, distinguishing general ideas from ideologies, focuses his inquiry on "how ideologies become programs for the deployment of power." My question is how a system of meaning becomes a political ideology under totalitarianism, colonialism, nationalism, and various other regimes. Thus, I use the term "state" not as a homologue to "nation" but as processes, or "a privileged site of both power and struggle" (Trouillot 2001: 127), where what Foucault (1991: 102–4; see also Gordon 1991: 8) calls *gouvernmentalité* operates to penetrate every fabric of the quotidian lives of the people under a totalitarian government. How did the Japanese state or the state apparatus (Althusser 1971: 137) deliver its imperial nationalism to the people? And, were they successful, and if so, in what ways? More concretely, my task is to understand how complex and interpenetrated meanings, all embodied in the symbol of cherry blossoms with various degrees of physicality—various degrees of blooming and falling—became consolidated into "falling cherry petals as young soldiers' sacrifice for the emperor" during Japan's modern period.

Turning to the second aim of this book, I use cherry blossoms as a case to examine the power of aesthetics for political purposes. The term "aesthetics" is almost always used in relation to the arts. German and Italian fascism are known for their "aesthetics," both in the form of Wagnerian high culture and in the form of kitsch. The beauty of the Japanese cherry blossoms has been extolled in the visual, performing, and literary arts. However, the flower summoned by the military was the cherry blossom in "nature"—within the reach of farmers as well as urbanites—which made it an ideal choice for the symbol of nationalism to be espoused by the entirety of the Volk.

Since the beginning of the Meiji period, successive governments aestheticized, visually and conceptually, their military operations and the deaths of soldiers on the battlefield. The image of cherry blossoms was deployed in numerous ways but especially as a symbol of soldiers' sacrifice for the emperor qua Japan. The visual aesthetics of cherry blossoms was transferred to the "Japanese soul" *(yamato damashii)*—an exclusive spiritual property of the Japanese that endowed young men with a noble character, enabling them to face death without fear. Cherry trees, with their blossoms, representing the Japanese soul, were planted all over Japan's colonies during its imperial expansion in order to transform the colonized space into a Japanese space and the colonized into the Japanese. They were planted at the Yasukuni Shrine, where fallen soldiers had been enshrined since the beginning of the Meiji period. Originally the cherry trees were planted so that the beautiful blossoms would console the souls of fallen soldiers. As the wheel of militarization accelerated, this metaphor was extended so that falling cherry petals represented soldiers who sacrificed their lives, and blooming cherry blossoms at the Yasukuni Shrine became their metamorphosed souls. Not only was their apotheosis guaranteed, but they would be "honored" by the visits to the shrine by the emperor on special occasions.

The mobilization of the aesthetics of the flower reached its height with the tokkōtai operations. A single cherry blossom was painted in pink on a white background on both sides of the tokkōtai airplane (see plate 5), while various Japanese terms for cherry blossoms were used for the names of the corps. Cherry blossoms were in full bloom in southern Kyūshū in April 1945, and some pilots who flew from the Chiran and Kanoya airbases placed branches with blossoms on their helmets and uniforms (plate 6). Others made references to cherry blossoms in their last poems and other writings. A well-known photo shows female high-school students waving cherry branches with blooms, bidding farewell to pilots taking off on their death missions (plate 7).

As the word for "meal" also means "rice" in Japanese and Chinese, so does the word "flower" mean cherry blossoms, the queen/king of flowers in Japanese. Cherry blossoms have long been loved and enjoyed by most Japanese, rural, urban, and from all walks of life. Gorgeous full blooms covering an entire mountain range or covering the entire Japanese archipelago, starting early in the south and moving progressively northward, are seen as representative of the vitality of the Japanese. The unpredictability of the exact time of blooming and the short life of the blossoms are reasons for many Japanese in the past and today to eagerly anticipate their displays and go to view them with fervor. Under the cherry blossoms they dance, sing, masquerade, and eat and drink, becoming intoxicated, literally and figuratively. The flower also offers a medium for soliloquy. Individuals reflect upon life and death, love, and other important matters in their lives while composing poems about cherry blossoms—an integral part of the ritual of cherry blossom viewing, especially in prewar Japan.

The Japanese make minute distinctions in describing the flower not only among the wide variety of species (two to three hundred domesticated and nine wild species) (Yahiro, ed. 1995: 5–114) but also in every stage of its life cycle, from buds to petals in various stages of blooming and falling. They distinguish shades of color from white to deep red, and blossoms with a single layer of petals from blossoms with multiple layers. To the Japanese the eerie sensuality of white blossoms in the night is altogether different from the radiance of blossoms against the blue sky during the day. They appreciate blossoms on young trees but also treasure old trees which continue to produce abundant blossoms. In contrast to the importance of its fruit for many Europeans and Americans, Asians, especially the Japanese, have selectively cultivated species with beautiful blossoms for viewing.[4] All of these nuances are expressed in a vast array of meanings that the Japanese assign to the flower.

Chapter 1 examines the symbolism of cherry blossoms before the Meiji period. While the discussion is not directly related to the tokkōtai, it is crucial for an understanding of what made the symbolism of cherry blossoms such a strategic choice for the state in later years. I lay out the field of symbolism of cherry blossoms. At the level of the individual, the flower represents processes of life, death, and rebirth, and the relationships between men and women as well as production and reproduction. At a more abstract level, it represents subversions of the norm—the anti-self (madness, changes of social identity) and non-reproductive sexuality (geisha, medieval temple boys), both of which negate the reproduction of the normative society.

At the collective level, although each social group in the mosaic of Japanese society has its own tradition of cherry blossom viewing, the flower also became a dominant symbol of the Japanese as a whole by the end of the Edo period. It rose to the consciousness of the Japanese during the ninth century as a result of their discourse with the Chinese, against whom they sought to establish a distinctive identity. They chose cherry blossoms in opposition to the Chinese plum blossoms, which had been espoused by the Japanese elite. Ever since, the Japanese have made strenuous efforts to construct the flower as unique to Japan. Toward the end of the Edo period (1603–1868), the foremost authority in botany testified that the tree was unique to Japan—an opinion widely accepted at the time even though the tree is widespread outside of Japan. Cherry trees along the Potomac River, shipped in 1912 at the request of Mrs. William Howard Taft, inaugurated a long tradition of cherry trees as Japan's state gift (chapter 3). The tradition is being kept alive even today.

Cherry blossoms thus have been intensely involved in conceptions and representations of the Japanese self, both at the individual and collective levels. The symbolism, however, should not be taken as a hermetically sealed field of representation. Quite the contrary, each concept represented by the flower, such as death, has undergone changes through time as well as according to the context in which social actors assign meaning to cherry blossoms.

The second and following chapters of the book are devoted to Japan's military period, from the end of the nineteenth century through World War II. In the latter half of the nineteenth century, a global tsunami of Western colonialism was washing ashore in neighboring Asian countries. The Opium War in China (1839–42) and Britain's swift annexation of Hong Kong sent shock waves throughout Asia. Some Japanese political leaders became acutely aware of the impotence of the shogunate against this pressing external threat. Those who wished to overthrow the shogunate used as their official excuse "the return of the emperor," who had been a mere token since the end of the twelfth century. "A crystal ball in the palm"—something easily to be handled—was the metaphor for the young emperor used by the Meiji oligarchs. Although they managed to accomplish their goal in 1868, it took the oligarchs another twenty-two years (i.e., until 1889) to finalize the 1889 Constitution of Imperial Japan, which redefined the very nature of the emperor.

Originally a shaman who guaranteed a good crop of rice because of his or her power to communicate with the more powerful deities, the Japanese emperor had been one of millions of deities. The Meiji constitution elevated him to the status of an Almighty God, a concept that was and is alien to the utterly "secular" religiosity of many Japanese, who sought earthly benefits from their deities. He was made even more powerful than the European kings, who were conduits of divinity rather than divinity itself. In order to buttress the newly assigned nature of the emperor, the oligarchs adopted the advice of Lorenz von Stein, the chief German consultant, and developed the native religion of folk Shinto into a centrally orchestrated state Shinto while attempting to stamp out all "foreign" religions, including Buddhism and Christianity. While "God the father" was an utterly alien concept to the Japanese, the Meiji state adopted the pastoral model of governmentality and promoted the notion that the emperor was the father of all the Japanese people.

Most importantly, the emperor became a sovereign—the answer for the Meiji oligarchs whose primary concern was to establish a sovereign state strong enough to protect the country from its foreign enemies. Furthermore, the emperor was assigned the role of commander-in-chief of the military, mirroring the Prussian constitution. Although much of the Meiji constitution was modeled after the Prussian example, the Meiji oligarchs resisted the unanimous opposition of all the foreign consultants and placed at the very beginning of the constitution, as Article 1, a declaration of the unilinear continuity of the imperial line from time immemorial. It established the emperor and the imperial system as Japanese sui generis, and not a copy of a European monarchial model. This "invention" was facilitated by another "invention"—an imperial soul, transmitted from one emperor to the next upon the former's death, thereby guaranteeing what Kantorowicz called the "king's two bodies"— the individual emperor and the imperial system.

It was at this time that Nitobe Inazō, a devout Christian who worked for international peace at the League of Nations, refashioned the concept of the "warrior's way," or *bushidō*. His book, published originally in English in Philadelphia in 1899, opens with this statement: "Chivalry [his translation of *bushidō*] is a flower no less indigenous to the soil of Japan than its emblem, the cherry blossom." With the adoption of universal conscription in 1872, the government extended "the Japanese soul," which "enabled" them to die, or fall like cherry blossoms, for the emperor, from warriors alone to all Japanese males. Even before the promulgation of the Constitution of Imperial Japan in 1889, the government issued its Imperial Rescript to Soldiers *(Gunjin Chokuyu)*, which included the infamous clause, "the obligation is heavier than the mountains but death is lighter than a feather." The "equal right" to the Japanese soul and, consequently, to death was aestheticized by the symbolism of cherry blossoms, which successive governments used as the master trope to encourage soldiers to fight to the death.

Moreover, the "equal right" to death was extended to those who were considered not to be ethnic Japanese. At that time some leaders insisted on ethnonationalism, while others, usually more liberal, insisted that Japan was a multi-ethnic nation. The latter notion, unfortunately, was useful for Japan's colonial policy. The now infamous declaration of July 23, 1940 by Konoe Fumimaro, then prime minster, of "One hundred million Japanese as one soul must truly dedicate themselves to the Emperor" included not only the Ainu and Okinawans, both of whom were considered different from the Japanese at the time, but also over thirty million Chinese, Koreans, and others living in Japan proper and in the occupied territories of Taiwan, Korea, and Sakhalin (Ninagawa 1998: 100–101; Takahashi 1994g). In 1938, they became "eligible" to volunteer to be drafted. Mandatory conscription was imposed on Koreans in 1944 and in 1945 on Taiwanese (Ninagawa 1998: 101), with eleven Korean tokkōtai pilots (chapter 5). The state "endowed" them with the Japanese soul (yamato damashii) to face death in order to be drafted as Japanese soldiers, an act analogous to the planting of cherry trees in its colonies. The government in Tokyo made quite a fanfare about the heroic act of Ōmasu Matsuichi, who was made "the first Okinawan war deity." It was a strategy to incorporate the minorities into the war effort.

Although the state's efforts to militarize the masses began in the Meiji period, these efforts intensified during the 1920s and 1930s, after the military seized power, and continued until the end of World War II. The state relentlessly attempted to penetrate the daily lives of all Japanese via school songs and textbooks, as well as through the mass media in the form of popular songs, films, and plays. As in Germany, Russia, and many other societies at the time, gendering was used so that femininity was defined as women's capacity to "reproduce and multiply"—the infamous wartime slogan—and to raise sons to be good soldiers. Masculinity was defined in terms of men's valor in sacrificing their lives for the emperor. These processes went on while the state carried out an intensive program of censorship and thought control.

Whereas Part 2 focuses on the effort on the part of the state, Part 3 examines how the state operation was interpreted on the ground. Japan's militarization over half a century culminated, tragically, in a last-ditch effort to protect the homeland from American invasion by inventing the hitherto unknown military strategy of using airplanes and torpedoes to send young men to their deaths. I examine the circumstances in which young men "volunteered" to be tokkōtai pilots and other contextual factors involved in their act of "choosing their fate." The process began with the mandatory drafting of students. On the base, many were subjected to the brutality of corporal punishment on a daily basis. However, they had already reached the point of no return. They were like the Roman soldiers in Horace's ode—Horace's famous phrase of *pro patria mori* is followed by a warning that death would get the Roman soldiers by the backs even if they tried to run away.

The tokkōtai operation also had a tragic impact on the pilots' families and friends. Although the available material is limited, I introduce the voices of the survivors, especially those of the mothers, since most of the young soldiers were unmarried and unattached. In the military police state, any open protest by parents put these young men in danger. Family members were forced to remain silent and watch while their loved ones perished. Upon receiving notice of the deaths of their sons, many parents lost their will to live. The published writings by the pilots were primarily edited by their siblings and schoolmates at the university, with whom they had discussed issues of life and death both in philosophical and in the most immediate terms.

These contextual factors notwithstanding, the pilots did volunteer—they "chose their fate." I examine in chapter 6 the extensive writings left behind by five tokkōtai pilots in order to understand the thought processes that led them to do so. Reading occupied a central place in their lives. A list of 1,356 books that four pilots read is presented in the Appendix as a companion to chapter 6.[5] In my reading of their diaries, I attempt to distinguish between patriotism and state nationalism in order to determine whether they volunteered to die for their country or for the emperor. In addition, I try to understand the complexities—the specific ways in which state nationalism penetrated into their thinking and became transformed as part of their patriotism. As these diaries show, even the most radical espoused some elements of state nationalism, whereas many tried to embrace state nationalism but nevertheless were torn by the agony over their immanent deaths and their love for their family and friends.

Part 4 presents my interpretation of the Japanese historical experience. How did the state create such basic changes in the conceptions of the emperor and cherry blossoms without alarming the people? Were the people cognizant of the changes, or did they take them as "natural"? The concept of naturalization used by Barthes, Bourdieu, and Foucault has been widely used for understanding how cultural arbitrariness is received by people as "natural." I wish to push it further by historicizing the concept to explain historical "discontinuities" that are perceived as "continuities." I identify each of these naturalization processes as it was involved in reshaping the emperor system, building a modern military, and transforming the meaning of cherry blossoms. Moreover, I identify three specific mechanisms that facilitated the naturalization processes: (1) refashioning of the tradition; (2) aestheticization; (3) and symbolic méconnaissance.

The refashioning of tradition is a common strategy used by social agents who wish to present altered cultural institutions as "our tradition from time immemorial" so that people will accept them as "natural." The thoroughly refashioned emperor system in Meiji Japan was presented as just such a "natural" and ageless system. But drastic changes may not be accepted as natural without the deployment of other strategies. An important and common strategy is aestheticization—the process of making cultural practices and symbols appear, visually and conceptually, beautiful. Soldiers of the modern "imperial army," for example, who were literally frozen to death in trenches on the north China front, were presented as "warriors of yesteryear," endowed with the Japanese soul and symbolized by cherry blossoms. They were cloaked in the shining armor of warriors of medieval times and further aestheticized through symbolic association with cherry blossoms.

Aestheticization facilitated *méconnaissance,* a common phenomenon in symbolic communication in which actors fail to recognize that they are reading different meanings of the same symbol. The pilots endorsed the aesthetics of Japanese nature, and of cherry blossoms as a dominant symbol of nature, without realizing how these symbols were locked into the *pro rege et patria mori* ideology. Neither side—pilots or the state—was fully aware of the phenomenon. The young men found aesthetics in the purity of devotion to their country without realizing that such devotion was exactly what the state wanted so that they would die for the emperor qua Japan—not *their* Japan, but imperial Japan.

I further develop the insight of Langer and Leach on this crucial element in our symbolic communication, which hitherto has received little attention. Symbolic méconnaissance is usually facilitated by two factors. First, each symbol has a vast *field* of meanings, any one of which may be drawn on by the actor, resulting in the possibility of multiple significations coexisting in a given context. Second, méconnaissance is further facilitated by the fact that the meanings of a symbol are embedded in processes and relationships—life predicated upon death, women in relation to men, and so forth. Therefore, when a social agent moves the signification of a symbol across the field of meanings—so that, for example, the meaning of cherry blossoms shifts from life to death—the movement may go unrecognized.

In the final analysis, it was their quest for aesthetics, along with their romanticism and idealism, that doomed them to act as they did. And it was from their readings that they developed their Weltanschauung and their aesthetics. The young men would have been able to fight against the political nationalism orchestrated by the state if it had been presented to them blatantly. But when it was mediated by the lofty intellectual traditions of the West, they failed to recognize the hand of the pro-military political and intellectual leaders at work. They would have been able to resist the naked propaganda of *Ein Volk, ein Reich, ein Führer,* as we see in the diaries. However, when the "general will," transformed by the Nazi and Japanese states, was seen as the general will of Rousseau and Kant, they were disarmed and did not suspect the wicked hand of manipulation. Or, they eagerly embraced beautiful nature in the works of Rousseau, Beethoven, Goethe, or Thomas Mann, not suspecting that the Nazis also mobilized the aesthetics of nature in their motto of "Blood and Soil" *(Blut und Boden).* Like many European men who fought in World War I, the young pilots memorized Nietzsche's *Also sprach Zarathustra,* recited *Les Fleurs du mal* by Baudelaire, and expressed their agony by referring to the two souls in *Faust.* They were inspired by Emerson's "Hitch your wagon to a star," identifying the star as their intellectual and spiritual idealism, rather than as earthly ambition. Méconnaissance indeed played a critical role in this tragedy—as, unfortunately, it has in many other wars.

Although I often use the term "government" or "state" as the architect of state nationalism, it was specific historical agents, rather than an abstract structure, who were involved in the development of state nationalism. Social science literature often continues to give too much power to one side—either to institutions and "structure," or the subversive power of the oppressed. Historical causality and historical agency are far more complex. Let me here confine myself to three major points in reference to historical agency. First, rarely are individuals, be they oppressors or the oppressed, unaffected by the historical climate in which they live, whether one views the climate as an intellectual toolkit, as it were, of Lucien Febvre's *l'histoire des mentalités,* or a more unconscious "habitus," used by many, including Marcel Mauss, Erwin Panofsky, and Pierre Bourdieu. "An individual with free will" is an idealistic construct of the Western imagination, now spreading to many other societies.

The second and third points are interrelated. That is, individuals often affect the course of history. Yet, as Marx ([1852] 1989: 320–21) almost too famously warned, they "make their history," but *not* "as they please"; moreover, how they impact history becomes manifest only long after their acts. "Practice theory" in the social sciences, with its emphasis on individual actions at a synchronic slice of time, is incapable of understanding "historical" agency. Even though the Braudelian geographic time of the *longue durée* is often impractical, our study of a culture/society must be historicized so that we can understand "culture through time."

The Meiji oligarchs were cosmopolitans who instituted changes but did not anticipate the military's mobilization, in the 1920s and after, of the power they assigned to the emperor. Nitobe Inazō was a member of the League of Nations working for world peace, but he "refashioned" the warriors' way (bushidō) and contributed to the development of state nationalism without realizing it led to the militarism he strenuously opposed. Inoue Takeshi, the author of a "progressive" text book, dubbed the "Cherry Blossom Reader," was a pro-Western intellectual who fought against military encroachment on education. Yet, his well-intentioned textbook contains numerous symbols of Japanese nationalism and militarism. Tanabe Hajime was a liberal and a devout Christian, but he sent young men to their deaths by promoting the importance of an individual's engagement with the state. Historical agents also included song writers and film directors, such as those involved in the transformation of the well-known Kabuki play, *The Forty-Seven Loyal Retainers*. While the early eighteenth-century play was unabashedly opposed to the central government, that is, the shogunate, in the Meiji era it was transformed into an exemplar of *pro rege et patria mori*.

"Ordinary" people too become, to use an oxymoron, "willing" but often unknowing participants, when they are caught up by the dark forces that sweep through their country. For example, in Japan people enthusiastically responded to *The Forty-Seven Loyal Retainers* and embraced popular songs with militaristic, imperialistic, and even jingoistic contents. Yet such people are not "willing" in the sense that their willingness is qualified by the process of naturalization and of méconnaissance. However, historical agents in leadership positions in a totalitarian society, including intellectuals, possess far greater power to change the course of history, and, yet, "not as they please."[6] Nevertheless, they send more or less innocent people to their deaths usually without sacrificing their own lives, and therefore they must bear the heavy burden of an inexcusable sin against humanity.

This book benefits from a comparative perspective. From this perspective, most crucial is the stark difference between Japan and Europe in reference to the notion of sacrifice by soldiers. In Christian countries in Europe, Christ was seen to provide a model for sacrifice for others, and the major concern of Christianity in its many varieties was the life after death. In contrast, the Japanese emperor remained sacrifier (to whom the benefits of sacrifice accrue) and sacrificer (ritual specialist for the rite of sacrifice), but was never the sacrificial victim (terminology from Hubert and Mauss [1898] 1964). The only model of sacrifice in Japan had to draw from the Confucian notion of loyalty to one's parents and lord, which sometimes entailed sacrifice. A mechanical adoption of the model of emperor as protective father never succeeded. Japanese religions offered virtually no vision of, or means for, life after death. The notion of blooming cherry blossoms at the Yasukuni Shrine as metamorphosed souls of fallen soldiers remained empty. Consequently, the young pilots looked elsewhere, including to Christianity, for a meaning for their sacrifice. The sole rationale for their sacrifice was their patriotism, which did not offer any assurances of rebirth. These similarities and differences between Japan and other countries are most illuminating for an understanding of how *pro rege et patria mori* worked and failed to work in Japan.

Recent scholarship has turned to the writings of soldiers and private citizens to investigate how soldiers on the battlefields and citizens at home have experienced wars and oppressive regimes. The current controversy, brought to the fore by Goldhagen (1996), over the role of "ordinary Germans" in Nazi Germany, is part of a larger picture of paying more attention to histories from the perspectives of ordinary citizens and soldiers, as opposed to the "heroic histories" of admirals and generals—a major shift in the discipline of history in the past half century.[7] Consequently, our attention has turned to diaries and other writings left by soldiers, whether in the American Civil War or the World Wars, with a renewed interest in finding out what soldiers felt and thought in the trenches. A longer tradition of inquiry concerns the involvement of intellectuals, who, in ways similar to the Japanese pilots, fought in the Spanish Civil War, as fictionalized in Hemingway's *For Whom the Bell Tolls*, and in the World Wars, as portrayed by Paul Fussell's *The Great War and Modern Memory*, Noël Annan's *Our Age*, Marc Bloch's *Étrange défaite*, and, most recently, Mark Lilla's *Reckless Mind*.[8] I am interested in making a contribution to this tradition of deliberation with this book, by bringing together both sides—to investigate both the state's creation of an official ideology and the perspectives of individuals on the ground.

The pilots introduced in this book are examples of student soldiers. While the intellectual level of the pilots selected seems surprising, they were not exceptional among the intellectual elites of the time. Other books on the writings of student soldiers testify that many of the books read by the pilots appear in the writings of other student soldiers. However, the tokkōtai pilots also included enlisted men, many of whom did not go to higher schools or universities. They are not represented in this book, primarily because of the unavailability of their writings; only fragments pulled out of context have been published. I chose the student soldiers for this book not only because of the availability of their writing but also because, with so many liberals and even Marxists among them, they were the most unlikely group of Japanese to have reproduced the *pro rege et patria mori* ideology. Their writings are testimony both to the power and the limitations of the totalitarian ideological programming of people.

Outside of Japan, "kamikaze taxis" are recklessly driven taxis, "kamikaze drinks" are extra-potent drinks. Workers who risk exposure to radioactivity at a French nuclear power plant are called "kamikaze" (Zonabend 1993). The term has become synonymous with recklessness. In most American dictionaries, definitions of "kamikaze" refer to "suicide attack" and "suicide pilots." A book on the tokkōtai by R. O'Neill is entitled *Suicide Squads.* Yet neither the pilots themselves nor the Japanese public considered their acts to be acts of suicide. They were killed in action, just as foot soldiers were killed on the battlefield. Their deaths came as a result of ramming into American vessels in their effort to save their country. Some soldiers, especially pilots, remarked that they were going to be *murdered* by their own government. Seki Yukio from the Naval Academy was "ordered" to lead the first tokkōtai attack on Leyte when no career officer volunteered. He told a newspaper reporter that there was no hope for Japan since the navy was willing to *kill* someone like him who would otherwise be able to destroy an enemy ship and still come back alive. As we will see in their diaries, most of them wanted to live. The picture is far from a perfect reproduction of medieval warriors thrusting their swords into their stomachs to die to protect their honor.

The Japanese state played a role in constructing the tokkōtai stereotype. It put the shining armor of the warriors of yesteryear onto modern soldiers and superimposed the image of the suicide of elite samurai onto the battlefield deaths of soldiers. For Westerners, the tokkōtai has become the embodiment of the inscrutable Japanese, an icon of the utmost Otherness. The Japanese are viewed as zealots who during World War II gained a reputation for their eagerness to die, even more than to kill— an utterly irrational characteristic beyond comprehension for non-Japanese. They are thought of as the latter-day warriors of medieval Japan, like the sword-swinging characters in Mifune Toshirō's movies, an image again reflected in a book title, Denis and Peggy Warner's *The Sacred Warriors.*

The persistence of the popular image of the tokkōtai is closely related to the lack of scholarly interest in them outside of Japan. In the United States, despite the availability of countless scholarly publications on World War II, not a single scholarly work devoted to the tokkōtai has previously been published. The extensive writings left by the pilots have never been introduced in non-Japanese-language books, except for a few wills and other writings that fit the image of warriors who died for the emperor.

In Japan, their history never entered the "official" accounts in school textbooks. The tokkōtai operation began in October 1944, very late in the war, and by September 20, 1945—almost immediately after the war ended on August 15—the American occupational forces had already issued their first itemized list of passages to be deleted from textbooks. This is the famous incident referred to as "the blackened-out textbooks" (*suminuri kyōkasho*)—any passage that might encourage patriotism and militarism was literally blackened or cut out with scissors. When the Japanese were able to republish their schoolbooks, the tokkōtai incident was excluded. It was the time when topics such as the atomic bombs were also prohibited in public discourse by the occupational forces.

In the private sector in Japan, a large number of publications on the tokkōtai are available. In 1947, Nanbara Shigeru, then the president of the University of Tokyo, edited a selection from the writings left by "graduates" of the university, which lost a large number of students. The volume, the first of its kind, drew an overwhelming response, and many other publications of students' writings, including writings left by graduates of other universities, followed in its wake.

But all of these edited volumes are partial, and each reflects the political stance, right or left, of the editor who made the selections. Many "nationalistic" editors, including those in the editorial office at the Yasukuni Shrine, published books that reproduced soldiers' wills proclaiming the sentiment "I shall fall happily for the emperor like a cherry petal." We learn, however, that many of these wills were written after the men were told that their wills would be displayed on the wall as exemplars written by model soldiers. Volumes edited by liberals, conversely, omit the patriotic passages and include only the voices of defiance and mockery of the military (chapter 6).

Fortunately, a limited number of books, usually edited by a sibling of the soldier, reproduce the large corpus of writing left by individual pilots. They portray a picture far more complex—one ridden with contradictions, ambiguities, and above all agony—than the "party-line" statements extracted in many of the collections. I have chosen five of these publications for close examination (chapter 6).

In Japan today, the consequence of the exclusion of the tokkōtai operation from official history is readily apparent. This exclusion has contributed to an unfortunate phenomenon in which the sacrifice of these young soldiers during the war, let alone countless deaths of both Japanese and non-Japanese, fails to appear in public discourse as the responsibility of *all* Japanese. The memory and commemoration of the tokkōtai are now left primarily to their survivors, and, unfortunately, to members of

the extreme right wing. The latter, together with conservative government officials, are attempting to restore the previous status of the Yasukuni Shrine as the national shrine.[9] At every cherry blossom season,
boisterous crowds of young Japanese engage in drinking and merry-
making at the compound of the Yasukuni Shrine. They see no tragic
irony in their behavior, just as many Japanese, especially the young, are
completely ignorant of the horrendous death toll the war took on Saipan
and other Pacific islands, now touted by the Japanese tourist industry as
vacation "paradises." Some teachers today, on the other hand, are making an effort to bring their students to Okinawa, instead of Hiroshima
and Nagasaki, in their attempt to expose them to a more complex picture
of the war, including Japan's role as a colonizer, than the standard textbooks provide.

It is not unusual for historical events to be buried in the dustbins of
history, from which Benjamin's "angel of history" (after Paul Klee's *An-
gelus Novus*) tries to resurrect them, usually because of some contemporary interest. But outside of Japan, the case of the tokkōtai pilots is cu-
rious in terms of the inverse ratio between public interest in them as an
icon or stereotype of the Other and the stark absence of serious scholarly
interest. It is not a case of the usual form of "forgetting." It is a case of
an exile from history, and, twice at that—in and out of Japan. It has received no official space in Japanese history. Outside of Japan, this vacuum
has been occupied exclusively by a stereotypical icon. If knowledge production is mediated by geopolitics, so is exile from history. The roots
of this phenomenon are embedded in the geopolitics of World War II
and after, with Pax Americana not the least among the causal factors
(Kelly 1998a).

After the book manuscript went into production at the press, the
colossal tragedies of the World Trade Center and the Pentagon on September 11, 2001 took place. They were presented in the mass media
immediately after the event through the metaphors of Pearl Harbor,
kamikaze pilots, and the Marines' raising of the American flag on Iwo-
Jima. However, as time passed, the government and mass media warned
against racial profiling of Arabs, Muslims, Asians, etc. and pointed to the
need to understand "suicide bombers" before we exile them to the zone
of stereotypes as simple-minded "crazies." There is an enormous danger
in lumping together a wide range of phenomena, involving those individuals who sacrifice their lives for a cause and who by so doing take
a great number of lives. We must not examine histories and events
through a single set of tinted glasses.

I feel the weight of responsibility to introduce the tokkōtai pilots' writings to the world as best as I can. An extraordinarily large body of their letters, diaries, and memoirs remains as testimony to voices that are too human and too powerful to be buried for good. Not because they were Japanese but because they were humans, I find it is inexcusable to dismiss them from our knowledge and to replace them with a caricature.

While we cannot exonerate those who commit grave sins against humanity, be they Hitlers, Osama bin Laden, or Ōnishi and the others who brutally cut short the lives of young tokkōtai pilots, we must also realize our fragility, which leads us to participate in the evil operations. Above all, we must be aware of the dangers of naturalization, aestheticization, romanticization, and, above all, of méconnaissance—cultural and historical processes whereby forces of evil are hardly recognized as such. My hope is that this book will contribute toward an understanding of our frailty—the vulnerability of each one of us to historical forces that lead to human tragedies on a colossal scale.

This book is not an apologia for the deaths inflicted by the tokkōtai pilots. Nor is it meant to exonerate Japan's offenses—atrocities inflicted on its enemies and on the colonized by the Japanese military during its wars and other military aggressions.

Part 1

*THE SYMBOLISM OF
CHERRY BLOSSOMS IN
PRE-MEIJI JAPAN*

Chapter 1

THE FIELD OF MEANING,
IMAGES, AND AESTHETICS

A SYMBOL OF THE LIFE FORCE

Cherry Blossoms as Agrarian Productive Force

In ancient Japan the most sacred plant was rice. The ears of rice housed the souls of the deities, objectified as grain, and the plant thus represented agrarian productive energy. Cherry blossoms were the symbolic equivalent of the rice plant. Because of the equation, cherry blossoms also stood for life-sustaining energy.

The Japanese notion(s) of soul as well as of its relationship to the deities is both complex and ambiguous. In the myth-histories, the deities are referred to as the ear of rice plant, rather than the husked grain. My interpretation is that the husk of the rice plant is the body of the deities, whereas the grain is the soul. Since the reference for the deities must be to deities who are alive rather than dead, the myth-histories use the character for the ear, since the most important notion about the human soul is its departure, which characterizes death. The soul is often objectified as a mirror, a pebble, a rock, or even an empty space. However, Yanagita states that there is no definite historical or ethnographic evidence to claim that the Japanese conceptualize the soul as having a definite shape (Yanagita, ed. 1951: 677–78). Although not formless, the soul is extremely fluid in its mobility—it departs the body, of humans and deities,

27

and the Japanese soul may be given to non-Japanese, as we will see later in this book.

The equation of rice and cherry blossoms is clearly present in the two earliest written documents of Japan, the *Kojiki,* dated A.D. 712, and the *Nihonshoki,* dated 720,[1] which were compiled at the time of state-formation and the beginning of the ancient imperial system. These "chronicles" were commissioned by the Tenmu emperor (r. 672–86) in order to establish a Japanese identity distinct from the Chinese, whose "Great Civilization" was engulfing Japan at the time. He did so by adopting folk oral traditions in which rice, introduced from the Asian continent, was appropriated as indigenous to Japan. That is, rice was grown in heaven by Japanese deities, whose names all bear references to the ear of rice. Thus, a foreign element, rice, was turned into *the* marker of Japanese identity. This cosmogony, drawing on folk agrarian cosmologies at the time, established the official agrarian cosmology, which became the symbolic foundation of the political economy for centuries, and in fact, even today.[2]

The symbolic association between cherry blossoms and rice is articulated in the Japanese myth-histories. In a version given in the *Kojiki,* the Sun Goddess[3] sends her famous grandson (Ninigi-no-Mikoto) to transform a wilderness into a country of rice stalks with succulent ears of rice *(mizuho)* grown from the original seeds grown in heaven and entrusted to him. The grandson marries a female deity named "A Blossom on a Tree" *(Konohana-no-Sakuya-Bime).*[4]

Already present in this episode is an explicit link between cherry blossoms and a short life—a major characterization of cherry blossoms in later years. At the time of the marriage, the woman's father urges the grandson to take both this woman and her older sister, whose name refers to a rock. According to the father, if the grandson takes the older sister, he will live long like a rock, but if he takes only the younger sister, his life will be short like the blossoms. The grandson, however, refuses the older "ugly" daughter. The grandson and the younger daughter produce the imperial offspring after one night together. A passage in the *Kojiki* explains that, although emperors are supposed to live for a long time, because of the grandson's marriage to this female deity bearing the name of the short-lived cherry blossom, emperors' lives are also short. In the *Nihonshoki* version, the union between the two is the reason that humans in general do not live long.

At a more abstract level of interpretation, however, cherry blossoms gave birth to the heir to the throne, safeguarding the perpetuation of the imperial line. If so, cherry blossoms represent the reproductive force,

rather than death (Miyata 1987: 128). The marriage guarantees the rebirth of rice, which represents deities qua emperors, who in turn represent humans (Japanese) in general.[5]

The symbolic association of cherry blossoms with rice in these myth-
histories derived from folk agrarian cosmology, which involves the
mountain worship *(sangaku shinkō)* that antedated the introduction of
Buddhism to Japan from India, via China and Korea, and remained one
of the most powerful forms of belief for many Japanese until recently
(Orikuchi 1928a). Despite regional variations,[6] mountain worship centers on the belief that the Mountain Deity *(Yama-no-Kami)* is the most
powerful deity in the Japanese pantheon and that the mountains, as the
abode of the deity, are the most sacred space in the Japanese universe
(Blacker 1975; Yanagita [1947b] 1982). Cherry blossoms in ancient Japan
were exclusively mountain cherries *(yamazakura)*, providing the basis
for their symbolic association with the Mountain Deity.

Orikuchi (1928a) first proposed that both snow in early spring and
flowers, especially mountain cherry blossoms, were thought to forecast
the condition of the rice crop in the fall. If petals fell prematurely, it was
an inauspicious sign. As a way of praying for the petals to last longer,
people started to perform the flower festival *(hana-e-shiki* or *chinkasai)*,
which was first held during the eighth century and has been since held at
the imperial court as well as at various temples and shrines.[7] Although
these rituals, whether conducted specifically for cherry blossoms or for
flowers in general, have undergone many changes over time, they have
two interrelated purposes: (1) to expel by the power of "flowers of rice
plants" the evil spirits that cause epidemics, (2) to pray that the flowers
will rest and stay in bloom for a long time—an auspicious sign for the
rice crop in the fall. Because of the power of cherry blossoms to foretell
the condition of the rice crop in the fall, people began planting cherry
trees in their own yards (Orikuchi 1928a: 471–93).

Some scholars believe that the etymology of the term *sakura* (cherry
blossom) derives from the seat *(kura)* of the spirit of the deity *(sa)*,
namely, the Deity of Rice Paddies.[8] According to these scholars, in the
ancient Japanese cosmology the Mountain Deity descended to rice paddies by lodging *(yadoru)* on the petals of cherry blossoms, becoming the
Deity of Rice Paddies *(Ta-no-Kami)* in order to look after agricultural
production. Farmers therefore took the blooming of cherry blossoms as
a signal to prepare for planting rice seedlings.[9] In the fall, after being
treated by farmers to a feast at the time of harvest, the deity returned to
the mountains (Miyata 1993; Sakurai 1976; M. Suzuki 1991: 6–9). Some
scholars further suggest that *sa* in *sakura* (cherry blossoms) is the same

root as *sa* in such terms as "to prosper" *(sakaeru)*, "to be prosperous" *(sakan)*, "good fortune" *(sachi)*, and "rice wine" *(sake)*, all signifying a positive power (Saitō [1979] 1985: 45–46; Yamada Munemutsu 1977: 21). There is a logical connection between etymologies, since a major function of Japanese deities is to bring about worldly prosperity.

In contrast to the metaphor developed during the Meiji era, in which cherry blossoms represented soldiers' sacrifice for the emperor, in the imperial accession ritual it was the deity qua emperor who sacrificed himself for humans. The imperial accession ritual, which has undergone many changes in time, began as an agrarian harvest ritual. The first record of it having become the imperial accession ritual dates to the reign of the Seinei emperor (A.D. 480–84) (for details, see Ohnuki-Tierney 1993a: 48–50). On one level, the harvest ritual is a cosmic gift exchange in which a new crop of rice—a few grains of divinity—is offered to the deity as a return gift for the original seeds he gave to humans. The mode of exchange takes the form of commensality—eating together—between the deity and humans at a feast during the harvest ritual. On another level, the harvest ritual constitutes a cosmological exchange of the soul and the body. Since rice embodies the peaceful soul of the deity, by offering rice grains to humans, the deity offers his own soul—the ultimate "gift of self"—"a man gives himself" (Mauss [1950] 1966: 45). It is a sacrifice initiated by the deity who came *down* on a cherry petal from the mountains to rice paddies to offer his body-soul to humans. Humans in turn nurture the divine soul, that is, rice grains, with the rays of the Sun Goddess and make the return gift—the first crop of rice—at harvest time. It is a generalized exchange between the deity and humans. The initiator of the cycle of cosmic gift exchange was the opposite of the emperor, for whom, starting in the Meiji period and in the ideology of *pro rege et patria mori* during the military period, soldiers were told to sacrifice themselves, without his sacrifice in the first place.

Since its petals embody the Deity of Rice Paddies, the cherry tree itself was regarded as sacred. It is the sacred tree for the order of mountain ascetics *(shugendō)* (Miyake 1985: 435). Consequently, the ritual of cherry blossom viewing *(hanami)* originated as a religious ritual under cherry blossoms in the sacred mountains. The drinking of *sake* that accompanies this ritual derives from a sacred ritual during which the deity and humans drink together the sacred wine, made from the deity's body, as it were, as an act of commensality (Wakamori 1975: 180–81).[10]

The belief in cherry blossoms as the abode of the deity gave rise to a practice of wearing the blossoms on one's head in order to receive the blessing of the deities (M. Yamada 1977: 116). The practice appears already in the *Manyōshū*—the earliest collection of poems, dating from the eighth century. In one poem, the poet sings of the land of the emperor covered with the fragrance of cherry blossoms because men and women are wearing the blossoms in their hair. In another, a male poet laments the falling of the cherry petals, which he had intended to wear on his head, a gesture of courtship; obviously he was unsuccessful.[11] The practice continued until later periods as with a geisha who wears a rice stalk with grains on it, again testifying to the symbolic correlation between rice and cherry blossoms.

It is almost eerie to witness this practice adopted in the tokkōtai operation, in which single blossoms were painted on the sides of the airplanes, which were given various designations referring to cherry blossoms (chapter 5). It is easier to understand why those navy officers who invented the operation would resurrect the ancient belief and practice. However, it is hard to imagine that the tokkōtai pilots, who flew to their deaths with fully blooming cherry blossoms on their uniforms, were desperately trying to enlist a little additional assistance against the impossible. Or, did they embrace the latter-day symbolic association between warriors and cherry blossoms, as described later in this chapter?

Ultimately, the symbolic equivalence of cherry blossoms and rice rested on the aesthetics of productive power in an agrarian cosmology. In ancient Japan, both cherry blossoms and rice were beautiful because they stood for agrarian productivity, which was above all sacred: seeds of rice were thought to embody deities who grew to maturity under the rays of the Sun Goddess. Until metallic currency, introduced from China during the twelfth century, gradually replaced it between the twelfth and fifteenth centuries (Ohnuki-Tierney 1993a: 67–74; Reischauer and Craig 1978: 63), rice served as currency, but currency conceptualized in religious terms (Amino 1987), as in ancient Greece (Hocart [1952] 1970: 97–104). Thus, the character *kin* (or *kane*) refers to both money and gold. Ripe heads of rice stalks are described to have a golden luster even today.

Since the ancient period, the aesthetics of rice has been expressed in poems, essays, and visual arts, which in turn have further propagated the perception of the beauty of rice. In *In Praise of Shadows (In'ei Raisan)*, Tanizaki Junichirō (1886–1965) extols the beauty of cooked rice with an analogy of each grain to a pearl shining in a black lacquer container placed in the dark (Tanizaki [1933] 1959: 17–18). Even today brand names of rice almost always bear the character for luster in them. Like the aesthetics of mirrors, also thought to embody Japanese deities, the aesthetics of rice lies in its luster as well as in its whiteness and purity. The visual aesthetics of cherry blossoms as rice, then, ultimately derives from its religious nature. The aesthetics of the sacred that characterizes productive forces is the common thread in the symbolism of rice and cherry blossoms. It is only a short step, therefore, for these symbols to become symbols of cultural nationalism, as we see in Motoori Norinaga (1730–1801), a nativist scholar of the Edo period, who discerned the superiority of Japan and the Japanese in the superiority of its rice and cherry blossoms (Watanabe Tadayo 1989: 89).

Cherry Blossoms as Reproductive Power

The aesthetics of cherry blossoms has been extended to other "beautiful" human beings and things, including women. Like rice, women in agrarian cosmology represent both productive and reproductive power, both of which were seen as beautiful in cosmological terms. In ancient Japan production and reproduction were seen as equivalent and both were conceptualized in terms of souls. The term *musu* meant simultaneously encapsulation of a soul in a knot and both production and reproduction. The act of making a knot *(musubi)* with a string, twig, or piece of grass, as described in the *Manyōshū* poems and other literature of the time, was a ritual act to encapsulate a soul in the knot. In addition, the term *musubi* meant reproduction and production: *musu* meant reproduction and *bi* (= *hi*) meant production or growth by means of the sun (Matsumae 1977: 96–97; Orikuchi [1953] 1976).

Therefore, cherry blossoms as a symbol of women naturally follows from the symbolic equation of women's reproductive power with the productive power of rice. If rice production under the rays of the Sun Goddess is sacred and thus a beautiful activity, women with their reproductive power were also "beautiful" in a religious sense.

Cherry blossoms representing the beauty of women appear in the *Manyōshū*, which contains 4,516 poems composed during the four hundred years before 759, when it was compiled. The poets include emperors as well as farmers, beggars, and other people of "low status." Cherry blossoms do not occupy center stage in the collection, and they are overshadowed by bush clover *(hagi)* and plum blossoms *(ume)* as motifs and metaphors. When they appear in these poems, as they do in forty-seven of them,[12] cherry blossoms stand for love and women in poems by male poets.[13] Other poems about cherry blossoms praise their blooming, or, when they refer to their falling, do so without foregrounding the falling as the main theme (M. Yamada 1977: 117). In his anthology Cranston includes fourteen poems from the *Manyōshū* in which cherry blossoms appear,[14] and he declares that *"aware* [pathos over impermanence]—an important ethos in later history—has no place in these sunny glades" (Cranston 1993: 539). A poem by the well-known poet Ōtomo-no-Yakamochi (716–85) testifies to his view: "The cherry blossoms / Now are out in full splendor / In the shining palace / At sea-bright Naniwa she reigns / Grave in the flowering time" (Omodaka 1968, no. 4361 [92]; Cranston 1993: 479).

Celebrations of Love and Displays of Pomp: Cherry Blossom Viewing (Hanami)

Ultimately, cherry blossoms celebrate love itself—an intense *relationship* between a man and a woman. If men used the metaphor of cherry blossoms for women, women too used the flower in their expressions of love. The practice of wearing a cherry branch with its blossoms on one's head or of placing it on top of a bamboo pole in the yard has been recorded from ancient times as an expression of courtship by women. This custom is followed in later times by another in which a woman would tie her *kosode,* a type of garment, to a cherry tree as a sign of courtship (Miyata 1987: 123–24).

In cherry blossom viewing, *hanami,* the symbolic association between the flower and love is most conspicuously expressed. An eighth-century record, *Hitachi-no-Kuni Fudoki,* tells us that the hanami was already an established annual activity not only among the elite but also among the common folk. In this account for the Hitachi region near Tokyo, the hanami was an established annual event, as described in a passage about Mount Tsukuha (now called Tsukuba): "When the flowers [*hana*] bloom in the spring and when the leaves turn color, men and women from various regions east of Mt. Ashigara throng [at the mountain], some on foot and others on horseback, bringing food and drinks. They exchange poems and dance" (Akimoto [713] 1958: 41; my translation). An exchange of poems between men and women and their dances were the institutionalized modes of courtship at the time.[15]

In ancient Japan, singing, dancing, and music were all religious rituals. Even sexual intercourse was not singled out as purely "sexual" behavior but had religious and other dimensions. Thus, cherry blossom viewing in ancient Japan seems to have been an important spring religious rite during which women and men climbed a mountain—the sacred space—to feast and drink, while composing poetry, dancing, and making love.

The aesthetics of cherry blossoms, including their viewing, was taken over by urbanites already by the eighth century, overshadowing the rural counterpart. The political elite, including the imperial family, were people of agrarian origin who no longer tilled the soil but whose culture derived from an agrarian cosmology. These members of the urban elite incorporated the aesthetics of cherry blossoms into their high culture. By the Nanbokuchō period (1336–92), upper-class warriors were among the aristocrats for whom the display of culturedness became important. In contrast to demonstrations of military might *(bu)*, they had to cultivate "culture" *(bun,* meaning refined learning)—the ability to play musical instruments, compose poems, be well versed in Chinese and Japanese literature, and so on. Cherry blossom viewing among the elite, both aristocrats and upper-class warriors, became the occasion for the literati to demonstrate their culturedness, since composing poetry in praise of cherry blossoms and reading were the most important features of their cherry blossom viewing, along with playing music and other expressions of refined taste. These lavish aristocratic cherry blossom viewings, however, were also expressions of their political power and wealth.

Among the best-known examples of the viewing among the elite are two occasions hosted by Toyotomi Hideyoshi (1536–98), who militarily unified Japan for the first time in its history. In 1594 he held an elaborate cherry blossom viewing at Yoshino, known for cherry blossoms, with five thousand guests in attendance. The spectacle is portrayed on a famous folding screen.[16] At a directive from Hideyoshi, the daimyōs wore Portuguese attire, which was fashionable among the elite at that time and was most appropriate for the occasion, since the masquerade and other aspects of the carnival are quintessential features of cherry blossom viewings of all types. In 1598, Hideyoshi held another, even more famous hanami at Sanpōin of Daigo Temple. Again a folding screen portrays the spectacular event.[17] For this occasion, Hideyoshi ordered a series of renovations of the buildings and gardens at the temple, as well as installing thirty-three checkpoints, thereby safeguarding it from potential insurgence. This event was far more an expression of his wealth and power than was the earlier one at Yoshino, which was held in a more relaxed atmosphere (Oze Hōan [1625] 1996: 458–68, 476–84; Nishiyama 1985: 83–84; also Ogawa 1991: 114–24; Yamada [1941] 1993: 220–22).

Beyond the valuable record on eighth-century cherry blossom viewing, information about the common people for later periods is much less available than is information about the elite until the Keichō and Gen'na periods (1596–1624), when a number of paintings depicting the leisure activities of commoners appeared (Harada and Yamane, eds. 1983). In these scenes common people are enjoying their viewing at temples, shrines, and other places famous for cherry blossoms, where aristocrats are also present, although they screen themselves from the folk by putting up curtains, often with their family crests on them. Cherry blossom viewing among common people reached its zenith during the Edo period (1603–1868), when the people in Edo (Tokyo) developed a tradition of cherry blossom viewing as their major annual event—complete with masquerades and feasting, as well as the composition of poems in their own genre, as distinct from those of the high culture (Ono 1992; see also Kawasaki 1967: 66–76). How men, women, and even monks enjoyed dancing under blossoms is depicted in a well-known two-panel screen painting, entitled *Hanami Odori*, by Iwasa Matabei (1578–1650).

The Celebration of Life: Cherry Blossoms in Kabuki

Kabuki, whose golden age was the Edo period, is a performing art characterized by costumes in brilliant colors and by highly stylized dramatic movements on the part of the actors. Although it was a theater developed by the merchant class, it became popular among people from all walks of life throughout Japan, reaching out even to mountain villagers.

The first and foremost purpose of Kabuki theater is to offer entertainment to the audience. Joy of life and even tragedies and griefs must be presented in a way that appeals to and entices the audience. "The vessel of the sunny (yang) principle" *(yōno utsuwa)* has been the basic modus operandi of the theater, and the productions strive for beauty and gaiety. Cherry blossoms serve this purpose superbly (Yoshida and Hattori 1991: 219). Thus, gorgeous scenes of cherry blossoms in full bloom are often painted as the background, artificial branches of cherry blossoms are a fixture of the theater, always hung from above across the entire stage, artificial blooming cherry trees are placed on the stage, and many important scenes take place under full blooms.[18] The geisha quarters, a common setting in the plays, are symbolized almost solely by cherry blossoms—the gaiety of the quarters represented by cherry blossoms during the day, with geisha *(oiran)* clad in gorgeous multicolor kimonos, or the sensuality of the quarters represented by the eerie whiteness of cherry blossoms at night. Similarly, dancer-entertainers *(shirabyōshi)* are also popular figures in Kabuki, and their dances are often ornamented with cherry blossom motifs. "Falling flower petals" *(rakka)* is a stage technique regularly used to enhance the performance of an actor by letting cherry petals fall where he dances. In another standard technique, "flower rains" *(hana-no-ame)*, an actor dances using an umbrella, suggesting falling petals (Toita and Yoshida 1981: 50, 44). Such techniques are used for scenes at the geisha quarters, with an obvious symbolic equation between geisha and cherry blossoms. Many plays are famous because of scenes that involve cherry blossoms.[19] In these scenes cherry blossoms represent an unqualified celebration of life (Watanabe Tamotso 1989: 179).

On the other hand, since life is always predicated on death and rebirth, and vice versa, Kabuki also uses the flower in a complex way; for example, a broken branch of cherry with its blooms is a standard sign of approaching death.[20] Willows stand for the capitol, geisha, and madness—all of which are also represented by the cherry, whereas the pine is a contrasting metaphor, signifying eternity and stability.

Cherry Blossoms as Symbol of Rebirth

Since the mountain is the abode of the dead in Japanese folk cosmology, one might argue that cherry blossoms, associated with mountains, stand for death instead of life. According to Yanagita ([1946] 1982: 94–96, 123–24),[21] a fairly common folk belief was that a dead person goes to the mountains to rest and becomes "truly dead" after thirty-three years, during which time the impurity incurred by death is thoroughly removed. After thirty-three years, the individual identity of the dead merges with the collective identity of the "ancestors," represented by the aforementioned Deity of the Mountain, who comes down to the village in the spring as the Deity of Rice Paddies. In other words, according to Yanagita, the Deity of the Mountain, the Deity of Rice Paddies, and the ancestors are the same, each a transformation of the others, and collectively the protectors of humans in this life.[22]

The question is, to what extent does the association between mountains and death appear in the early literature and to what extent is this association related to the symbolism of cherry blossoms? We saw a link between cherry blossoms and a short life in the episode of the marriage of the grandson of the Sun Goddess to the cherry blossom woman in the myth-histories. However, this association was not directly linked to mountains. Moreover, the union of the two in fact symbolizes rebirth rather than death per se.

Of ninety-four songs of bereavement, called funeral songs *(banka)* in the *Manyōshū,* fifty-one refer to the soul of the dead resting on a mountain, on a rock, or in a mountain valley, whereas twenty-three identify the sky or the clouds as the resting place, and several other poems point to islands, the sea, or the wilderness (Hori 1968: 152). In other words, we can be certain that the concept of mountains as the resting place for the dead was fairly well established already in ancient Japan, especially among farmers. On the other hand, the mountains were also the place where people went for courtship. In one poem (Omodaka 1983, no. 1459 [78]) cherry blossoms are associated with the impermanence of life, though not with death. In another (no. 1425 [33–34]) the brevity of their blooming is lamented. Cherry blossoms are not symbolically associated in any direct way with the mountains or with death (Roubaud 1970). Furthermore, as the funeral songs above attest, in the past there was no one place where they believed the dead would go. In addition to the places mentioned above, some thought the dead went to the underworld *(yomi)*, while others thought they traveled to a world across the sea *(tokoyo)* where death is unknown.

Cherry blossoms never entered the iconography of Buddhism, which was introduced into Japan during the sixth century from India via China, although Buddhism is full of flowers, including the lotus flowers on which some buddhas sit or stand. Monks' robes on ordinary occasions are black, but bright colors and flower designs appear on the ceremonial attire of highly ranked monks. The Pure Land sect of Buddhism, which became popular among both the folk and aristocrats during the late Heian period (794–1185), portrayed a paradise *(gokuraku jōdo)* filled with flowers, birds, and music. Since Buddhism became the religion that took care of ancestor worship, flowers in general came to be associated with death and the afterlife, and flowers, but *never cherry blossoms*, remain important offerings at ancestral alcoves and grave sites.

Cherry trees, especially drooping trees like drooping cherry, are, however, thought to be the conduit between the world of the dead and that of the living. Yanagita links this practice to an "old" belief that spirits, including the souls of the dead, take shelter in trees, especially drooping trees. These trees are thus planted at burial grounds because of the belief that the souls of the dead travel from the sky to the earth and back again, and a drooping tree facilitates their travel. In rural Japan cherry trees, especially young ones, are planted where the dead, such as persons who died while traveling, are buried (Yanagita [1930] 1982: 215–16; 1947a: 225–26). Yanagita (1947a: 225–26) reports an oral tradition from Shinano (Nagano Prefecture) that a ghost appeared at a place considered an entrance to the world after death where an old drooping cherry tree used to stand, telling the people that those who saw the blossoms on this cherry tree during their lifetime would be spared torture after death. That is, cherry blossoms guarantee a successful transformation into an ancestor.

CHERRY BLOSSOMS AS PROCESSES AND RELATIONSHIPS

The symbolism of cherry blossoms is fluid and complex. Its meaning as a life force is embedded in a complex nesting of concepts in which life is always predicated upon death and rebirth, and vice versa. In other words, there is an extremely delicate balance in the representations of cherry blossoms—when one phase in the process of life, death, or rebirth is represented by the flower in a particular context, it is always predicated upon the other two. The representation of cherry blossoms is pregnant with the possibility that, with a delicate tip of the scale, this symbol of life and rebirth turns into a symbol of death, as happened during the military regime.

Ultimately, cherry blossoms symbolize *processes* and *relationships*. Thus, they are a symbol of the cycle of life, death, and rebirth, on the one hand, and of productive and reproductive powers, on the other—all representing processes. In addition, cherry blossoms stand for human relationships between lovers. Furthermore, cherry blossom viewing is an occasion for the collective activity for each social group within Japanese society.

Cherry trees and their blossoms have little utilitarian value.[23] It is the aesthetics of cherry blossoms that is the source of their evocative power, both conceptual and emotive. The aesthetics of cherry blossoms was originally embedded in an agrarian cosmology in which productive and reproductive powers were considered to have an aesthetic quality in a religious sense.[24] As a metaphor, cherry blossoms transfer this religious qua visual aesthetics not only to objects but to life processes and human relationships that are beautiful. The process of transference of aesthetic quality becomes *naturalized* so that it is not articulated in people's minds. In the process, some individuals and some concepts become *naturally* beautiful.

THE AESTHETICS OF PATHOS OVER EVANESCENCE: FROM BLOOMING TO FALLING CHERRY BLOSSOMS

"Falling like a beautiful cherry petal" was the metaphor the Japanese state used to promote the sacrifice of soldiers for the emperor qua state. According to the conventional wisdom, the development during the late medieval period, especially in *The Tale of Genji*, of the aesthetics of pathos over evanescence, symbolized by falling cherry blossoms, was responsible for the beautification of the death of young men and of not clinging to life, and hence for acceptance of the military motto.

The received wisdom is only partially true. The aesthetics of pathos over evanescence and its link to falling cherry blossoms did begin to surface during the latter part of the ancient period and especially during the Heian period. However, the flower's association with impermanence did not become dominant, as the cherry continued to represent the celebration of the life forces during this period and after. In addition, the association between the two was not developed in the *Genji.*

The Splendor and Impermanence of Life

While the Chinese aesthetics of plum blossoms was embraced by the elite of the ancient period, by the time of the *Kokin Wakashū,* a collection of some 1,100 poems compiled in either A.D. 905 or 914, cherry blossoms are decisively at center stage. The *Kokin Wakashū* has been dubbed the collection of poems on cherry blossoms and love, and cherry blossoms are its most frequent poetic motif, symbolizing the beauty of women and of Kyoto, the capital of Japan. A poem by the monk Sosei is often cited to convey the splendor of the capital when the cherry is in full bloom: "Seen from a distance, / willows and cherry blossoms, / all intermingled: / the imperial city, / in truth a springtime brocade" (Kubota [1960] 1968, vol. 1, no. 56 (180); H. McCullough 1985: 24). Other poems in the collection use the metaphor of blooming cherry blossoms to celebrate the vigor of life, with a tinge of sadness at their ephemerality.[25]

There is no doubt that cherry blossoms in *full bloom* are celebrated and symbolically linked to women and to the life force in the *Kokin Wakashū.* On the other hand, of the seventy poems that take on the theme of cherry blossoms, fifty focus on blossoms between their peak and their fall, whereas only twenty are about blossoms from their beginning to full bloom (Noguchi 1982: 78). Some poems link *falling* cherry petals not only with the impermanence of life[26] but also directly with death.[27] In other words, as early as the beginning of the tenth century, when the *Kokin Wakashū* was compiled, significant changes have taken place in the symbolism of cherry blossoms among the aristocrats: (1) from blooming cherry blossoms to falling petals; (2) falling petals as a metaphor for the evanescence of life; and (3) falling petals signifying death.

In comparison, *Tales of Ise (Isemonogatari),* compiled by an anonymous person most likely before A.D. 950, demonstrates that, by this time, in the Heian high culture *falling* cherry blossoms had become foregrounded and were increasingly linked to pathos over the impermanence of life and of love, although they were not directly associated with death itself.[28]

The complex symbolism of cherry blossoms refuses to follow a unilinear progression and we see next in *The Tale of Genji* a stronger presence of blooming cherry trees, representing the forces of life. This literary masterpiece was written by Murasaki Shikibu (ca. 978–1014), an insider at the imperial court serving the wife of the Ichijō emperor (r. 986–1011). It elegantly depicts the lives of the members of the imperial family, courtiers, and their relatives in the early to middle Heian period. Intricate human relationships, including power struggles and intrigues that are carried out with exquisite grace, are portrayed, with Prince Hikaru (Hikaru Genji) as the center figure. The work consists of stories of love and courtship through the exchange of poems on such occasions as viewings of the moon, plum, cherry, and wisteria blossoms, and listening to the wind. Hikaru Genji was, as his name expresses, literally the Shining Prince in the social circle at the imperial court. Women, and even men, were drawn to him because of his skills in poetry composition, his graceful dancing, and his deft playing of musical instruments, which moved both men and women to tears. He was "at the center of a golden cyclical time in which human and natural order were joined" (Field 1987: 214; see also 160–216). As instances of this joining, throughout the narrative both people and things, including the dyes used for the numerous layers of the kimono, are named after natural objects, especially plants.

It was *The Tale of Genji* that placed at the center of the Japanese ethos the aesthetics of pathos *(monono aware)*, the acute sense of the fleeting and ephemeral beauty of all living things (Field 1987: 211; Morris [1964] 1979: 207–8). Among flowers, cherry blossoms appear most often.[29] However, it is important to note that cherry blossoms are rarely associated with *aware*. Rather, cherry blossoms in the *Genji* are predominantly "sunny," with the blooming cherry representing youth, love, and courtship. For example, the chapter entitled "Cherry Blossom Viewing Ceremony" *(Hana-no-en)* describes a splendid cherry blossom viewing at the imperial court. After the initial viewing of the blossoms of the cherry tree planted in front of the Naden (the main building, also called Shishinden), the viewing ceremony was moved to Seiryōden. As it was a beautiful, cloudless day, Hikaru Genji announces: "I have drawn spring." In other words, it is he who ushered in spring. At that moment, the crown prince, heir to the emperor, remembers Genji's graceful dancing at the time of the excursion to see the colored maple leaves the previous year, and he presents to Prince Hikaru Genji a sprig of cherry blossoms. Genji, the Prince Charming, therefore, is metaphorically linked to cherry blossoms and spring. At its very beginning the chapter establishes a world of gaiety and elegance through the symbolism of blooming cherry blossoms and their viewing. In the remainder of the chapter, on a balmy spring night under blossoms in full bloom, Hikaru Genji continues to search for women, as he always and successfully does (Seidensticker 1977, 1: 150–57; Yamagishi, ed., 1958: 301–13).

Genji's position at the imperial court, however, begins to be marginalized, and he decides to leave the capital. He sends his last message to the crown prince, tying it to a branch of a cherry tree from which the blossoms have fallen, which ends with a poem: "When I shall, a ragged, rustic outcast, / See again the blossoms of the city?" (Seidensticker 1977, 1: 228; Yamagishi, ed., 1959: 27). Here the exiled Genji is contrasted with the capital with its power and pomp, symbolized by cherry blossoms. Throughout the *Genji*, Genji uses cherry blossoms as the symbol of life forces—youth, love, gaiety, and the capital.[30]

There are some instances in the *Genji* in which the ephemeral nature of cherry blossoms is pointed out, but this is seldom done only to aestheticize their short life.[31] In other words, they truly lament the brevity of blooming rather than celebrate it through aestheticization. The sentiment is sorrow rather than aestheticized pathos. Petals that fall in a gust of wind are called "weaklings," but the tree itself is not blamed (Seidensticker 1977, 2: 761). Falling cherry blossoms, just as the inevitable evanescence of life, are "resisted."

There is only one passage, describing the world after the death of Genji, in which the short life of cherry blossoms is linked to pathos over evanescence: "The cherry blossoms of spring are loved because they bloom so briefly" (Seidensticker 1977, 2: 736; Yamagishi, ed., 1962: 222). The beauty of the flower is predicated upon a short life, like that of Genji. Nevertheless, cherry blossoms are not directly linked to death.

In other words, the latter-day construction of the *Genji* as the primary source for the association of cherry blossoms with pathos over evanescence is unverifiable. It is even more so when we see the gorgeous scenes from the *Genji* in the scroll paintings produced during the early part of the twelfth century, a century after the *Genji* was published.[32] These scrolls depict the elegant court life of poetry reading, courtship, and viewing of flowers and other elements of nature, using rich colors. Although flowers of all seasons appear in the paintings, cherry blossoms are most important as an evocative symbol of love, spring, and life. These scroll paintings foreground the elegance and pomp of court life, symbolized especially by cherry blossoms, rather than pathos over evanescence.

To recapitulate, the notion of impermanence was present even in the eighth century literature of the *Kojiki,* the *Nihonshoki,* and the *Man-yōshū,* but it was hardly noticeable in these earliest collections. The "critical turn" in the symbolism of cherry blossoms took place in the late medieval period, but the three works of high literary quality of this period show us three different emphases. In the *Kokin Wakashū,* the earliest of the three, we witness the most profound changes from earlier times: *falling* cherry blossoms signify not only the impermanence of life but also death itself. The image of falling cherry blossoms to represent the evanescence of life is pronounced in *Tales of Ise,* but the symbolic link to death is not foregrounded.

In contrast, the *Genji,* both in the original novel as well as in its representation in scroll paintings, continued the tradition of "sunny" cherry blossoms in celebration of life forces, contrary to the widely held assumption that *The Tale of Genji* not only developed the notion of impermanence and evanescence but also established it through cherry blossoms as the trope for this ethos. Although the *Genji* certainly established *aware* as an important ethos in Japanese high culture, cherry blossoms were not its major trope for the ethos of pathos over the evanescence of life.

Symbols ought never to be understood as floating in the mind of social agents alone. They are always grounded in the day-to-day lives of those who use them. The notion of *aware* and its symbolic representations developed precisely because the aristocrats were enjoying the grandeur of life and yet sensing that it would not last forever. The Heian period was the last hurrah of l'ancien régime in Japan (Kitagawa 1990). Shortly after the Kanmu emperor transferred Japan's capital from Nara to Kyoto in 794, the ancient imperial system *(kodai ōchō)* reached its zenith. Pomp, gaiety, and a lavish style of life were enjoyed by the aristocrats surrounding the court, but their lives were also ridden with power struggles, as depicted in the *Genji,* whose central figure, Hikaru Genji, epitomizes the paradox. As Field (1987: 215) puts it: "Unparalleled glory and unparalleled sorrow—this is Genji's self-proclaimed motif as a hero." He has everything—intellect, musical talent, and charm for every and any woman. He is the son of an emperor, the brother of an emperor, and the father of an emperor, and yet *never* an emperor himself. His own life parallels the disintegration of the ancient imperial system, a disintegration that started to cast its long shadow over the aristocrats' lives as early as the ninth century, threatening the termination of their power and their elegant lifestyle.

The late Heian period was doomed by decay and gloom. Monks turned into weapons-carrying soldiers, and religious institutions were ridden with corruption. A series of epidemics wiped out a large proportion of the population. The time was ripe for a new Buddhist sect, the Pure Land sect *(Jōdokyō)*, which depicted a paradise overflowing with flowers blooming throughout the four seasons, and with air filled with the singing of birds and with heavenly music. It appealed to the elite, who built religious edifices for their own salvation; they envisioned the paradise as depicted by this sect as an extension of their life in this world. The common folk, too, took to this sect, but for an opposite reason—they hoped to be released from their miserable life on earth and to enjoy a better life after death.

In this context, we appreciate that the emphasis on pathos over the impermanence of life developed precisely because of the grandeur of life. Pathos over evanescence does not take on a significance unless it is predicated upon the grandeur of life, expressed as power, wealth, or the height of love. Only when one loses them does one begin to appreciate their ephemeral nature and feel pathos over the loss.[33] The mutual predication between the two holds the key to the choice of cherry blossoms as the master trope. Various aspects of nature, including flowers and autumn leaves, appear in literature as metaphors of impermanence and evanescence (Yamagishi, ed., 1959: 242; 1962: 438). Yet cherry blossoms occupy a unique role; no other flower, including plum blossoms, can compete. Thus, the evocative power of cherry blossoms as a metaphor in these works derives precisely from the way in which they bloom with such grandeur and vigor, covering entire mountainsides, temples and shrines, and river banks. Indeed, the whole capital is covered with blooms in the poem by the monk Sosei, introduced earlier. People, then as well as today, became intoxicated by the blossoms' vigor and beauty as well as by sake, an indispensable component in any cherry blossom viewing. But blooms, which usually last about two weeks, can then scatter within a few minutes in a strong wind or rain. It is this drama unfolding within a short period that gives poignancy to cherry blossoms as a metaphor for those social agents who, like cherry blossoms, rise and then fall, in power or in love.

The developments of the symbolism of cherry blossoms during the late medieval period set the course for the symbol's subsequent history. The association with the pathos of life that developed in the high culture spread throughout the rest of society. However, the new meaning never became the exclusive meaning of the flower, and different dimensions of the complex symbolism of cherry blossoms, expressed in the literary works introduced above, coexisted during the late medieval period as well as in later periods in history.

THE AESTHETICS OF ALTERNATIVE
IMAGINATIONS: BEYOND THE SELF AND SOCIETY

In order for the modern military regime to be able to manipulate the symbolism of cherry blossoms without the people detecting the hand of manipulation, or, worse yet, for the people to apparently embrace the transformed meaning of the flower, it was necessary that the symbolism of cherry blossoms constitute a vast and complex field of meaning.

The complexity of the flower's symbolism requires examination of another set of meanings that lie beyond the normative realm of imagination. The normative social order is predicated upon the identity of the self as an individual and also as a member of a social category, such as being a woman or a man, or a commoner or prince. Yet, as in almost every society, there are institutionalized, that is, culturally sanctioned, ways to subvert the ordered universe. Cherry blossoms not only symbolize these complex antitheses to the orderly universe but also aestheticize them. Aestheticization is the mechanism that firmly anchors the alternative imagination in the minds of the people, who nevertheless may not be fully conscious of these subversive forces. In other words, cherry blossoms, the very symbol of the normative order, are also a potent symbol that, by offering provocative alternatives for imagination, destabilizes the universe by calling the normative order into question.

The Aesthetics of Multiple Selves and of the Non-Self

That personhood recognizes its plurality is expressed through the symbolism of cherry blossoms, which are associated with the changing of socially defined self-identity in culturally prescribed settings as well as at the ontological level, when the person in this world moves into another through "madness."

Changing one's identity through the use of masks and masquerade is an essential feature of cherry blossom viewings, in high culture and low. We recall that in the famous cherry blossom viewing by Toyotomi Hideyoshi, he "ordered" the feudal lords to appear in Portuguese attire, thereby making a foreign element an important part of their very Japanese ritual and transforming the identity of the Japanese feudal lords into foreigners. During folk festivals, including cherry blossom viewing during the Edo period, quite common was the use of masks, including of those of a *yakko* (servant), an *otafuku* (a homely but happy woman), and of a fox, believed to disguise itself as a human. Also popular were half masks, which covered only the upper half of the face; one could become a woman with a half mask with woman's hair, or a warrior, with a warrior's helmet (Ono Sawako 1992: 175–81). A popular form of masquerade in these festivals has been cross-dressing—a man painting his face white, wearing lipstick, a woman's kimono and a wig, and often dancing as a woman, as we see even today. Women too cross-dress as men, although less frequently. Slapstick *(chaban)*, ubiquitous in cherry blossom viewings, also emphasizes changing identities. A popular theme is caricaturing the power holders (Ono 1992: 168–69).

Destabilization of the self through the use of a mask is not confined to folk festivals. It is also found in the Noh play, the classical theater of Japan since medieval times,[34] in which an actor always uses a mask, taking on the identity of the character he represents. It thus institutionalizes the nonpermanent nature of self-identity. The movements of the Noh performers are slow and subtle. A highly complex system of symbolism, in which flowers receive a major emphasis, plays a crucial role. Cherry blossoms are an important symbol in a number of Noh plays.[35] Highly stylized cherry blossoms are frequently used as the motif for Noh robes, and for the fans, lacquerware containers, and other props used on stage.

Closely related to the change of self-identity is the disclosure of the self, which again is associated with cherry blossoms. This connection with self-disclosure appears in all of the so-called three masterpieces of Kabuki theater, of which I introduce here *Yoshitsune and the Thousand Cherry Trees* (Toita et al., eds., 1968: 234–330; Jones 1993). The story is about Minamoto-no-Yoshitsune (1159–89), the legendary hero who in 1185 defeated the Taira clan in the famous final battle at Dan-no-Ura. For Japanese history the battle closed the curtain on the ancient period and inaugurated the medieval period under the shogunate established by the Minamoto clan in Kamakura. Despite his crucial contribution to his clan's victory, his relationship with his elder brother, who became the shogun, soured shortly after the battle.

Yoshitsune was forced to flee, seeking refuge in various parts of Japan. Shizuka-gozen, a *shirabyōshi* (dancer-entertainer) from Kyoto and Yoshitsune's mistress, wishes to follow him in his exile. But he will not let her do so and leaves a drum as a keepsake. At this scene, Satō Tadanobu, a faithful retainer of Yoshitsune, appears, and Yoshitsune entrusts Shizuka-gozen to him. Some time later, when Shizuka-gozen hears that Yoshitsune is in exile in the Yoshino Mountains, she and Tadanobu hurry to reach Mount Yoshino. Yoshitsune is living at the manor of

Karen Hōgan, who is in charge of Mount Yoshino, famous for "a thousand cherry trees" each at the lowest, the middle, and the highest ranges, from which the title of the play derives. To his hiding place, his faithful retainer Tadanobu arrives alone and tells Yoshitsune he has no knowledge of her. At that moment Shizuka-gozen and another Tadanobu appear. As Yoshitsune cannot understand the presence of two Tadanobus, Shizuka-gozen tells him that she might be able to solve the riddle. She takes out the drum and plays. Tadanobu, with whom she has been traveling, listens intently to the drum but then reveals himself to be a fox. Tadanobu the fox explains that the drum is made of the skin of his father and that he has disguised himself as Tadanobu in order to be close to his father. The fox apologizes for his behavior. Casting a sad eye on the drum, he tells them that he will go back to his den. Impressed by the fox's love and loyalty to its father, Yoshitsune gives the drum to the fox. Overjoyed, the fox plays with the drum as if it were a live father fox. The entire scene of Yoshino is full of cherry blossoms on the stage. But, most importantly, the fox reveals its identity under cherry blossoms (Watanabe Tamotsu 1989: 181; photo 126 in Gunji, ed. 1975).[36]

The loss of self through madness is another phenomenon associated with cherry blossoms (Watanabe Tamotsu 1989: 181), as expressed in a well-known phrase, "The flower [cherry blossoms] turns people's blood crazy."[37] Powerful expressions of this association are found in some of the best-known plays in performing arts and literature. While there are several other Noh plays in which cherry blossoms are associated with madness, *Cherry Blossom River* by Ze'ami Motokiyo (1935a) is most famous. It is about a young girl, named Cherry Blossom Child *(Sakurago)*, who can no longer bear the way her mother suffers from dire poverty. She sells herself to a "human merchant" *(hito-akindo)* from the eastern part of Japan. Asking the merchant to hand over the money and her letter to her mother, she leaves her home in Sakura-no-Baba in Hyūga in Kyushu. Reading her daughter's letter, the mother is taken by grief and sets out in search for her daughter. Three years after this incident, the young woman, who has become a nun at Isobedera in Hitachi (present-day Ibaraki near Tokyo), accompanies monks from the temple to Cherry Blossom River, which is well known for the beauty of cherry blossoms growing along its banks.

As the chief monk praises the beauty of the fully blooming cherry to a local man, the latter tells the monk to stay a while longer until a mad woman comes to dance as she scoops fallen cherry petals from the river with a beautiful net. The supposedly mad woman appears and explains that she is from Hyūga and that her guardian deity is Konohana-no-Sakuya-Bime, the "cherry blossom goddess" who married the grandson of the Sun Goddess. She explains that she came all the way from Kyushu in search for her daughter, who was named Sakurago (Cherry Blossom Child) after the goddess. She is normal until the local man tells her that a sudden wind from the mountains has blown cherry blossoms into the river. Thereupon, she begins scooping the petals out of the river before they float down the river with her net while dancing. The monk realizes that she is the mother of the young nun. The mother and daughter rejoice at the encounter. The play ends with the mother's pledge to become a nun and join her daughter.

In this play the association between falling cherry petals and madness is unmistakably linked. The mother loses herself when she loses her cherry blossom child, who is part of herself, or, even the entirety of herself. The local resident tells the monks that the way to make her become crazy (to dance) is to tell her that cherry petals have fallen into the river. This is a re-enactment of the initial loss of her child. She tries to scoop out the petals, that is, her daughter, so as *not* to lose her. The woman whose guardian deity is cherry blossoms and whose child is cherry blossoms is symbolically a cherry blossom. The falling cherry petals signify the loss of herself—madness—which is enacted in this Noh play against the background of fully blooming cherry blossoms and of the river full of cherry petals (Matsuoka 1991: 228–35; Nakanishi 1995: 259–70).

The Kabuki theater also abounds in plays in which cherry blossoms are associated with madness. An example is a play by Takeda Izumo, *Cherry Blossoms Branch Out of Reach in the Deep Mountains* (Gunji et al., eds. 1970: 121–24).[38] The stage is set against a gorgeous field of yellow mustard flowering in the spring, with a butterfly fluttering over the field, in which a lone young cherry tree stands.[39] Abe-no-Yasuna, a handsome young man, loses his mind upon the death of his love. He movingly dances under a blooming cherry tree while trying to capture a butterfly, which symbolizes his soul trying to depart from his body. Again the coterminous nature of madness and dancing is depicted. The play is another example of how cherry blossoms symbolize and aestheticize madness—a type of loss of the self.

During medieval times, the term *kuru'u* meant both "to go insane" and "to dance," and dancing in turn was an act to communicate with the deities (Ohnuki-Tierney 1987: 78–81, 104, 150, 227). Thus, those who "lose their mind" and "dance" have achieved a special religious power, gaining another identity beyond the one in this world.

In addition to their association with the plurality of the self and its nonpermanence, cherry blossoms are also linked to a permanent loss of one's self. In a Noh play by Ze'ami, *Three Mountains (Mitsuyama)* (Ze'ami Motokiyo 1935b), a woman named "Cherry Blossom Child" wins her lover only to have her rebirth prevented by her rival, the moon, who blows her petals away so that she lost not only her self in this world but in the world after death as well.

The Aesthetics of Alternative Universes

As well as representing madness and changes of self-identity—forces that subvert the self as a member of a social group—cherry blossoms also aestheticize nonnormative universes, represented by the medieval temple boys and geisha. During the medieval period, wealthy and powerful temples kept a number of young men, called *chigo*, for an average of four to five years each, until they were about fifteen to seventeen years old. During these years they applied cosmetics like women and learned flower arrangement and other forms of art for women as well as how to manage and control their bodies and behavior. The ultimate goal of the daily training was to nurture them to become like idealized court ladies. Some were made partners of older homosexual monks, who were referred to as "the fire in the abyss" *(mumyū no hi)*, whereas the boys in this situation were referred to as "the flower of truth" *(hottsushō)*, in other words, cherry blossoms. The major trope for the description of these boys was cherry blossoms, as in such phrases as "like red cherry blossoms [*benizakura*] with morning dews," and "like a willow branch waving in a soft wind and like cherry blossoms enveloping dew," and "like cherry blossoms at night whose petals are slightly closed by a spring shower."[40] Because they were associated with cherry blossoms, the chigo were an ubiquitous presence at elaborate cherry blossom viewings held at these temples, most famously depicted in *Tenguzōshi*, an illustrated scroll dated 1296 (Haruyama 1953: 211; Umezu 1978: 5).

Cherry blossoms indeed represent the beauty of chigo, who stand for the freedom to transcend normative constraints and boundaries in more than one sense. The institution of the medieval temple boys poses the most fundamental questions about gender dichotomy, the permanence of gender identity, and the assumption of the primacy of reproduction for society.

During the Edo period, the geisha and their world were also represented and aestheticized in various artforms by cherry blossoms. In addition to training in music and dancing, the geisha's lives were punctuated by numerous rituals, most importantly the cherry blossom viewing (Shibundō Henshūbu 1973). It was an event not only for themselves but also for the large number of visitors it attracted, at least as depicted in the prints if not necessarily in reality (Kumakura 1989). In Nakanochō, the most important section of Yoshiwara, a long, rectangular, elevated platform was constructed out of green bamboo fencing with dirt infill, right behind the famous gate, known as "The Large Gate" *(ōmon)* at the entrance to Yoshiwara. There cherry trees were planted every year on February 25 of the lunar calendar (Ono Takeo 1983: 34–35; Shibundō Henshūbu 1973: 84). March 3, the day of the Doll's Festival, was designated as the day for the viewing of cherry blossoms.[41]

Not unlike the Hollywood phenomenon today, the geisha and the geisha quarters, especially Yoshiwara, became an important theme in the imagination of the Japanese, both men and women, most of whom had nothing to do with either geisha or Yoshiwara or, for that matter, had ever been to Edo, let alone to the geisha quarters. This was done through the popular arts of the merchant class of the Edo period—the puppet theater, Kabuki, and woodblock prints. The "constructions" and "representations" of the world of Yoshiwara to the outside world centered on the aesthetics of the sensuality of the geisha, which was enforced by *shamisen* music and dances.[42] We have seen earlier in this chapter that the Kabuki theater played an important role in the propagation of this image, as did the puppet theater which shared a great number of texts with the Kabuki. In addition, woodblock prints, whose blocks are made from cherry tree trunks, portrayed geisha and their lives as a major theme.

The famous cherry blossoms at Nakanochō were a favorite motif of these woodblock print masters. As in the prints by Eishi, Kuniyoshi, Toyohiro, Toyokuni, Toyoharu, and, most famously, Utamaro and Hiroshige, high-status geisha *(tayū)* are often depicted with cherry blossoms in full bloom, with their preteen attendants *(kamuro)* each wearing a half tiara *(kanzashi)* made of metal replicas of cherry blossoms, often blue in color.[43] Because of the close association between cherry blossoms and geisha, the payment to the geisha is called "payment for the flower" *(hanadai)*.

No other visual image was more powerful in portraying the sensuality of the geisha world than "the night cherry blossoms at Nakanochō." The mysterious beauty of the whiteness of cherry blossoms against the dark sky became a favorite motif for masters of woodblock prints and a frequently used stage setting for the Kabuki theater. In the famous

Flowers at Yoshiwara (Yoshiwara no Hanazu) by Utamaro, dated 1794 or
1795, the glittering gaiety of Nakanochō nightlife is depicted with altogether forty-five colorfully dressed geisha and attendants under fully
blooming cherry blossoms highlighted by the glow of the full moon (Narazaki, ed. 1981: 49–50). Another famous print, *Night Cherry Blossoms
at Yoshiwara Nakanochō, Famous Place in the Eastern Capital* by Hiroshige, portrays a night scene with lanterns, geisha and their attendants,
and fully blooming cherry trees planted within the bamboo fence (Nihon
Ukiyo-e Kyōkai, ed., 1968). The eerie effect of white blossoms in the dark
is created by illumination of the blossoms by the full moon and the light
from the lanterns and from the windows of geisha houses. These lanterns
were also used by the geisha to entice guests on the street to come inside.
One of the scenes of *One Hundred Celebrated Places of Edo (Meisho Edo
Hyakkei)* by Hiroshige also includes a scene of Yoshiwara with cherry
blossoms at dawn and is entitled *Dawn at the Pleasure Quarters
(Kakuchū Shinonome)* (Gotō, ed., 1975, plate 38).[44]

The tradition of viewing cherry blossoms at night has long been observed. For example, already at the time of *The Tale of Genji*, cherry blossom viewing parties lasted well into the night (Seidensticker 1977, 1:
150–57; Yamagishi, ed., 1958: 301–14). Thus, the night cherry viewing
at Yoshiwara was not a new tradition. Even today many places are famous for night cherry blossoms, and there is more than one term for
night cherries, including "cherry blossoms at dusk" *(yoi-zakura)* and
"full moon with cherry blossoms" *(sakura mangetsu)*. But the juxtaposition of night cherries with geisha in the geisha quarters added a threatening sensuality to the symbolism of cherry blossoms at night.

My emphasis on night cherry blossoms does not altogether exclude
the daytime cherry blossoms as a symbol of geisha. There are a number
of woodblock prints depicting geisha with cherry blossoms during the
day. In fact, the image of cherry blossoms in the daylight is an important
symbol for *maiko,* young apprentices to the geisha. Today in Kyoto, for
the famous Dances of the Capital *(miyako odori)* by maiko, the main and
almost exclusive motif is cherry blossoms. The blossoms are painted over
the entire background of the stage, with blossoms hanging from the ceil-
ing and adorning the maikos' hair, and with blossoms as the design on
their kimonos. All of these cherry blossoms are depicted against a blue
sky in the bright daylight of the spring.

Though culturally sanctioned, the institution of geisha was nevertheless outside, or an antithesis to, the family *(ie)* system that was the back-
bone of Japanese society. During the Edo period Japanese society devel-

oped into a rigid society with the so-called four-caste system (warriors, farmers, craftsmen, and merchants, with the emperor at the top and two outcaste categories at the bottom).[45] The norms and values of the warrior class, including the "Victorianization" of women and arranged marriage, diffused to a large segment of society. Against the background of this reality, cherry blossoms, representing the geisha and their world, stood for the aesthetics of an alternative imagination that lay outside the normative structure of society, whose continuity rested upon marriage and women's reproductive role.

The woodblock prints depicting the geisha and their world are called *ukiyo-e*, prints of the floating world. Originally deriving from Buddhist cosmology, the "floating world" expresses the ephemerality of life in general. We recall cherry blossoms began to be associated with the pathos of evanescence during the medieval period. In the case of the geisha, however, their world is even more intensely ephemeral. The relationship may last only until the dawn; perhaps it is for this reason that dawn at Nakanochō is a favorite theme in these woodblock prints. Moreover, the world of geisha is predicated upon its own nonreproduction, individually and collectively, that is, biologically or socially.

Cherry blossoms are summoned to represent this world, which in turn reinforces the complexity of the symbolism of cherry blossoms. The aesthetics in these representations is characterized by a dual quality—threatening and enticing at the same time (Nishiyama 1985: 11). The effect of the duality is produced by blossoms in the dark of the night, but always highlighted by the full moon or lanterns, representing the geisha world.

The universe represented by cherry blossoms, then, is full of paradoxes. The flowers represent life, predicated on death, and vice versa. Pathos over evanescence derives from the juxtaposition of the height of glory and vigor of life and pomp, on the one hand, with their ephemerality, on the other. The night cherry blossoms of the geisha represent the height of "life," or "desire" in a more fashionable parlance today, underscored by its ephemerality both in the temporal sense and in the sense that it is divorced from "real" life. By representing both the temple boys and the geisha, cherry blossoms stand both for the intensely heterosexual (geisha) and the non-heterosexual (temple boys). Yet, the intensely heterosexual world of the geisha represented in Kabuki is in fact performed by all-male actors. We see multiple layers of subversion of the norm—all symbolized by cherry blossoms.

The celebration of alternative imaginations is the foundation of the

traditions of both the performing arts of Noh and Kabuki. These two traditions are called *kyōgen kigyo,* meaning "the world of make-believe"
(tsukurimono no sekai). The premise of these theatrical traditions is that
they are not realistic representations of life but are theaters for make-
believe, or, alternative imaginations.

These theatrical traditions challenge the received wisdom at the basic
ontological level, by juxtaposing the norm and its destabilization. As in
cherry blossom viewing, all sorts of practices counter to the norm are institutionalized. Yet cherry blossom viewings are occasions for heightened expressions of social stratification—not only are they occasions for
"the theatre state," to borrow Geertz's phrase, for the warriors of yesteryear but also for expressions of social stratification, with each social
group having its own tradition and its own space.[46]

That the beauty of cherry blossoms is "threatening" may be an aesthetic expression of this basic force of negativity, always reminding us
of existential instability. These antitheses are the very forces that keep
the oppositions going, keeping in check the hegemony of the normative
world and its grip on the individual.

THE RISE OF COLLECTIVE SENTIMENT
AND THE AESTHETICS OF CHERRY BLOSSOMS

While the flower represents a wide range of human experiences, including many that are paradoxical or in opposition to each other, for the Japanese it also represents their sense of collective identity, and it evokes the
sentiments associated with this sense of belonging.

Collective Sentiment among the Elite in Ancient Japan

A social group's sense of the self-identity is almost always formulated
and reformulated by the presence of, or a threat from, another social
group. In the case of the Japanese, the Chinese became the dominant
Other, and their presence prompted the Japanese to eagerly adopt and ab-
sorb the Han and Tang "high civilization," which in turn compelled them
to come to terms with their own sense of identity as distinct from that of
the Chinese (Kawasoe [1978] 1980: 253–54; Ohnuki-Tierney 1993a).

The initial development of the symbolism of cherry blossoms in ancient Japan was part and parcel of this historical experience. We recall
that in the *Manyōshū* references to cherry blossoms were far less frequent than those to other flowers. References to cherry blossoms appear

in poems by unknown poets and poets from rural Japan, indicating the importance of cherry blossoms among these people at the time when the upper-class Japanese in the capital still embraced the imported aesthetics of plum blossoms.[47] In the eighth through the ninth centuries, however, the upper classes gradually turned more toward the native aesthetics of cherry blossoms, which became the most important metaphor of the Japanese throughout their subsequent history. Thus cherry blossoms as a metaphor for the Japanese was born in the discourse with the Other.

From Plum Blossoms to Cherry Blossoms at the Imperial Palace

The imperial palace was moved in 794 to Kyoto by the Kanmu emperor (r. 737–806). Despite the overshadowing of cherry blossoms by plum blossoms in the mid-eighth-century *Manyōshū*, there are some signs that during the ninth century the imperial palace began to officially recognize the aesthetics of cherry blossoms as its own.

In 813 the Saga emperor (r. 809–23) held the first imperial viewing of cherry blossoms, called "the feast of the flower" *(hana-no-en)*, according to *Teiō Hennenki* (Kuroita and Kokushi Taikei Henshūkai, eds. 1965b: 183). The annual viewing of cherry blossoms at the imperial palace came to represent the elegance of the high culture at the court and was portrayed in many literary pieces, as in *The Tale of Genji*, and in the visual arts. This custom, although changing in form and nature through time, continued until the early 1930s (Nihon Hōsō Kyōkai, ed. 1988).

For many Japanese, integral to the image of the imperial palace are a cherry tree on the left-hand (east) side and a citrus tree (tachibana) on the right-hand (west) side in front of the South Garden of the main building.[48] The two symbolize the two divisions of the imperial guards. The image has become familiar even to children through the observation of the Dolls' Festival on March 3, celebrated at the individual home in front of a replica of the imperial court with the emperor and the empress, together with the paired plants of the cherry on the left and the citrus tree on the right, all on wooden shelves covered with red cloth.

Yet what had been thought to be the quintessential cherry tree in front of the palace was in fact a replacement, at a much later date, of the original plum tree planted when the Kanmu emperor relocated Japan's capital from Nara to Kyoto in 794. The main section of the palace *(daidairi)*, together with the plants, was repeatedly destroyed by fire.[49] Moreover, the tree on the left hand side of the imperial palace seems to have been a plum for a number of years. But by the mid-ninth century, however, the tree was permanently a cherry.[50]

The replacement of a plum tree by a cherry tree in front of the palace was not an isolated incident. The ninth century saw significant changes in the attitude of the Japanese elite toward the Chinese, including the discontinuation in 894 of the official envoys to Tang China, which had started in 630.[51] The Japanese style of painting called *Yamato-e*, which developed during the latter half of the ninth century, was a conscious effort on the part of Japanese artists to develop their own style of art in order to break free of the tradition dominated by the Chinese style of painting, *kanga*, in which cherry blossoms did not have a place. Cherry blossoms became an important and frequently used motif in Yamato-e. Again we see that cherry blossoms were chosen as a symbol of the Japanese and their art as opposed to Chinese art. The Yamato-e tradition focused on the depiction of the four seasons and the months of the year, each of which is represented by flowers and other features of nature.[52]

These historical events took place just as the Japanese were emerging from a total immersion in Chinese culture and were ready to establish their own identity. The development of the aesthetics of cherry blossoms and such signs as the abolition of the envoy to Tang China testify to the development of a shared sense of collective identity, at least among the elite.

On other hand, it is erroneous to think that this development was so strong that the Japanese abandoned all Chinese influences. Quite the contrary. Profound adoration for Chinese civilization continued. Composition of poems in Chinese characters *(kanbun)* remained an important cultural institution. For example, in the chapter on cherry blossom viewing *(Hana-no-en)* in *The Tale of Genji,* the viewing was immediately followed by composition of poems in Chinese characters. *The Tale of Flowering Fortunes (Eiga Monogatari)* of the late Heian period describes "the winding-water banquet, an imported pastime popular in the ninth century, involved reciting poems in Chinese and drinking from floating wine cups" (McCullough and McCullough 1980: 841, 843). During the Heian period, the Chinese practice of chrysanthemum viewing *(chōyō-no-sechie)* was introduced. While the emperor was viewing chrysanthemums, his body was wiped with "chrysanthemum cotton," the center part of the flower, wet with chrysanthemum dew. This annual event remained an important imperial ritual, held on September 9 of the lunar calendar, often accompanied by recitation of poems in Chinese (Fujioka 1956: 120; Niunoya 1993: 619–23).

Chinese civilization, therefore, continued to be influential among the Japanese elite, but there was no question that they began locating their own distinct identity, for which they chose cherry blossoms as their major metaphor.

Japan as the Land of Cherry Blossoms in the Edo Period

In ancient Japan mountain cherries were the only cherry trees for the Japanese, who during later periods actively planted them in their yards, along rivers, and in temples, shrines, schoolyards, and geisha quarters—literally all over Japan. They were planted for their beauty. But they were planted along the embankment of rivers and aqueducts not only for their beauty and for the practical purpose of strengthening the banks but also to purify the water, since their leaves and petals were believed to have antitoxic powers (Smith and Poster [1986] 1988: plate 42).

During the Edo period, there were a number of shoguns, including Tokugawa Ieyasu (1542–1616), Hidetada (1579–1632), Iemitsu (1604–51), and Yoshimune (1684–1751), who ordered the planting of cherry trees in various locations in Edo, whose fertile soil of volcanic ash was ideal for the tree. During the Edo period the shogunate established a system whereby regional lords and their retainers were required to reside in Edo every other year, while leaving their families behind. It was a policy designed to weaken their financial power and to prevent any move to plot a revolt in their own territory. As a byproduct of this system, many regional lords brought cherry trees from their own region to Edo, resulting in 250 to 260 varieties of cherry trees in Edo alone at that time (Hayashi Ya'ei 1982: 54–55).

The Edo capital, representing Japan, was transformed into the land of cherry blossoms, which in turn led to the construction of "Japan as the land of cherry blossoms," since Edo represented Japan. In this construction and representation of Japan, woodblock prints, developed primarily by the merchant class during this time,[53] played a powerful role. The most famous print series was *One Hundred Celebrated Places of Edo (Meisho Edo Hyakkei)* by Andō Hiroshige (1797–1858).[54] Hiroshige's work consists of 118 prints of the "places" culturally marked as famous. Among these, twenty-one "places" were chosen because of the beauty of their cherry blossoms. Plum blossoms appear only four times.[55]

Most importantly, the Japanese sought their uniqueness in cherry blossoms, as the episode involving Kaibara Ekken (1630–1714), an esteemed Confucian scholar-botanist, testifies. He declared in 1698 that according to a Chinese he questioned in Nagasaki there was no cherry trees in China. In his celebrated *Yamato Honzō*, a book on botanical species of Japan, published in 1709, the Chinese, the source of this information, was identified as Kaseiho. Since Kaibara Ekken was the most revered botanist, his proclamation excited warriors and merchants at the time, who transformed this report into "cherry blossoms are unique to Japan" (Saitō 1982: 28−29).

Given the Japanese convention in the visual arts of representing seasons and months through various flowers and given that cherry blossoms last only for a short time, it is remarkable that as many as twenty-one out of 118 places in Edo were renowned because of their beautiful cherry blossoms. In other words, the presence of cherry blossoms qualified temples, shrines, and other places as *meisho*, or celebrated places. *Both in fact and in its self-representation*, Japan became a land of cherry blossoms with their *unique* beauty.

The geisha and their world, noted earlier, is another dominant motif in the woodblock prints, and they appear quite frequently with cherry blossoms. Rice, the autumn counterpart of cherry blossoms, and activities associated with rice production also became a dominant motif in the prints.[56] Some made strenuous efforts to distinguish Japanese rice as superior to Chinese rice as evidence for the superiority of the Japanese (Ohnuki-Tierney 1993a: 104). There were other symbols chosen to represent the uniqueness of Japan and the Japanese, including Mount Fuji, which appears together with cherry blossoms in innumerable representations.[57]

Together with a few other "symbols of Japan," such as the fan and sumo wrestlers,[58] cherry blossoms, rice paddies, and Mt. Fuji became powerful symbols with which the Japanese represented themselves to Westerners who in turn saw Japan through these symbols,[59] as in the well-known 1887 painting of *Le Père Tanguy* by Vincent van Gogh (1853−90) at Musée Rodin in Paris. Here the subject of the portrait is surrounded by cherry blossoms, rice paddies in winter, Mount Fuji, two geisha figures (to the left and right of the subject), and morning glories. Through these symbols, especially cherry blossom, the Japanese wished to construct their own identity at a time when the threats of Western civilization and of modernization were encroaching upon their culture.

From the perspective of studies of symbols, cherry blossoms in Japanese culture provide us with an opportunity to engage in basic rethinking of our understanding of a symbol and its referents, or meanings. Our understanding of the symbolization process involves symbols, their meanings, their tropic functions, and the social agents who use/read them. As for the "meaning," the major focus has been on the issue of a symbol having multiple meanings, depending upon the context and the use by social agents—a major advance in anthropology pioneered by Victor Turner and his "polysemic symbols." But we must push the argument further. What cherry blossoms show us is that we must get out of our vision of a grid classifying symbols and meanings in isolation—the dog means A in one context and B in another in culture X. The rich and complex meanings of cherry blossoms constitute a matrix of interrelated concepts—not life alone, but predicated by death and rebirth; woman in relation to man; the self underscored by the destabilized self. In other words, a symbol stands for *processes* and *relationships*, not isolated concepts.[60] Furthermore, at the ontological level the flower also represents forces that challenge, undermine, and destabilize the normative world, thereby offering new possibilities.

The dynamics of a polyseme, then, does not lie in the static fact of having many meanings but in the fact of interpenetration among many meanings, including the palimpsest, as it were, of the normative world with an underlay of its subversion. This dynamics is the very site of the power of a social agent to mobilize symbols. It is precisely because cherry blossoms stand for life, predicated by death and rebirth, that the Japanese military could tip the scale in the symbolic representations by cherry blossoms and foreground death, instead of life, without people realizing that this important shift had taken place.

At the collective level, cherry blossoms stood for each social group within Japan, and also for the Japanese as a whole. The inchoate notion of the self of the Japanese was fortified as the Chinese pressed in on their space with their high civilization. After a period of intense imitation of the Chinese high culture by the elite, they began to seek an identity that was *unique*—different from various Others. Cherry blossoms' first occupation of a space in the Japanese cultural landscape took place as an important emblem of the Japanese. Ever since the Japanese have continued to reify the uniqueness of cherry blossoms as an expression of their own uniqueness.

In later history, cherry blossoms, Mount Fuji, and rice paddies became the symbols of unchanging Japan, weathering the storms of Westernization, urbanization, and modernization. They stood for Japanese space, that is, Japanese land, and Japanese time qua history. These developments before the Meiji era are crucial for later periods for paving the way for *all* Japanese to embrace cherry blossoms as their own, just as the rice agricultural cycle became the marker of seasons for all Japanese, including nonagrarian peoples. They prepared the ground for the flower to be the symbol of political nationalism. By the time Japan embarked on its course for modernization, cherry blossoms had become an important symbol at three different levels: of the individual, of social groups within Japanese society, and of Japan and the Japanese as a whole.

Part 2

THE ROAD TO PRO REGE ET PATRIA MORI: NATURALIZATION OF IMPERIAL NATIONALISM

Chapter 2

THE EMPEROR'S TWO BODIES:
SOVEREIGNTY, THEOCRACY,
AND MILITARIZATION

Part 2 of this book is devoted to the so-called modern period ushered in, as it were, by Western colonial expansion into Asia. The rallying cry of the Meiji "Restoration" of the imperial system was: "To overthrow the shogunate system *(tōbaku)* and to expel barbarians [foreigners] *(jōi)*." For many, the "restoration" was a means to achieve their goal of overthrowing the shogunate, which had been inept in preparing Japan to meet imminent threats from outside. When they achieved their goal, however, the oligarchs became advocates for opening the country in order to build Japan as a modern nation state. They sought to establish a strong sovereign nation with a modern military in order to exert internal control and to ward off foreign powers. They embarked on simultaneous industrialization and militarization, as expressed in their motto: "Enrich the Country and Strengthen the Military" *(Fukoku Kyōhei)*. Their initial goal to protect their country by building a strong military later led them far further than they initially intended; it led them down the road to totalitarian militarism, a road that finally brought the country to self-destruction on a colossal scale in World War II.

During this process of militarization, both the metaphor of cherry blossoms as the Japanese people and the complex and often contradictory meanings of the flower prepared the way for cherry blossoms to be used as a dominant and evocative trope for *pro rege et patria mori*—to die for the king/emperor qua homeland, like beautiful cherry blossoms.

In order to understand how cherry blossoms, with their vast field of meaning, were turned into the flower embedded in the imperial and colonial ideology, I make an important detour in this chapter by examining the processes of refashioning the emperor and the imperial system through the promulgation of the Imperial Rescript to Soldiers (Gunjin Chokuyu) of 1882, followed by the Constitution of Imperial Japan (Dai Nippon Teikoku Kenpō) of 1889, and the Imperial Rescript on Education (Kyōiku Chokugo) of 1890, the last two taking place twenty-one and twenty-two years after the Meiji "Restoration" of 1868, respectively.[1] My discussion of this complex topic is confined to the aspects directly relevant to the basic nature of the transformations of the emperor that laid the structural foundation for the military to carry out its program of *pro rege et patria mori* so successfully, especially during the early 1930s through World War II. It should be stressed that there was no grand plan laid out at the beginning and that the subsequent historical processes involved were by no means a unilinear progression. Numerous agents with a wide range of motivations, interests, and intentions were involved. The drafting of the constitution was a process of intense negotiation among the oligarchs and their foreign consultants. Many opposed the constitution and other structural principles of the Meiji government. Yet, the Meiji constitution was truly remarkable in establishing the structural possibilities for later developments.

My discussion starts with a brief picture of Japanese culture and society during this turbulent period. Because the chapter focuses on the structural foundation of the Meiji constitution, it is the only chapter that does not involve the symbolism of cherry blossoms.

MODERNIZATION/WESTERNIZATION: JAPAN IN THE GLOBAL TIDAL WAVE

Japan was "nominally" closed to the outside world for nearly two hundred years, although recent scholarship has challenged the received wisdom by, for example, pointing to major trade routes through which Japan had remained in contact with the outside world (e.g., Amino 1997: 122–27). Intellectual elites too had been absorbing the knowledge from the West, especially from the Dutch, to whom Japan remained open. As Najita (1998) details, in the later Edo period, Ogata Kōan (1810–63) established the Tekijuku (Tekikeisaijuku) for learning Dutch medicine in

1838, where some six hundred students registered; several times that number actually studied with Kōan, who later recognized English to be the key international language. His students included Ōmura Masujirō, Fukuzawa Yukichi, both introduced in this chapter, and other key figures of early Meiji Japan. Kōan's teaching went far beyond Dutch medicine, and he founded the epoch-making beginning of Western studies *(yō-gaku)* in Japan, which was of "fundamental importance in Japan's modern transformation" (Najita 1998).

Commodore Perry's arrival in 1853 and then again in 1854 became a catalyst for officially opening the country and also opened the floodgate for Western influence. Japanese, both intellectuals and folk, began to espouse the Western philosophy of "Civilization and Enlightenment" *(bunmei kaika)*, which they thought was at the basis of the spectacular achievements of the West in science and technology. The principle behind "Civilization and Enlightenment," as interpreted by the Japanese, was *gōrisei:* pragmatism, or, more appropriately, utilitarianism, of a crude form. The government took the lead in abandoning whatever was "useless," including some Japanese traditions.

The state adopted "new" and "modern" institutions that affected all aspects of the daily life of most Japanese, including public toilets, a postal system, and the removal of beggars from the street (Gushima 1983: 152–59). The Japanese had been quite carefree about exposing their bodies, especially men, but even women, who breast-fed in public. A new law issued in the first year of Meiji (1868) penalized these behaviors, including urination on the street, for the purpose of "correcting" the Japanese manner (Araki 1976: 35–36).[2] Among the upper-class Japanese, there was a craze for Western ballroom dancing and Western music. The Meiji emperor took the lead in the pro-Western movement in quotidian life by growing a Kaiser mustache, cutting his topknot, and adopting a Western-style haircut on March 20, 1873, and wearing a Western-style military uniform (Ohnuki-Tierney 1999). The extreme degree to which the Japanese went in for Western civilization was portrayed in satires and cartoons from this period that remain quite familiar even today. For example, one song's lyrics declared: "If you strike a head with Western-style hair *(zangiri atama)*, you hear the sound of civilization and enlightenment *(bunmei kaika)*" (Miyatake, ed. 1925: 42; see also Kanagaki Robun 1926).

From the end of the nineteenth century to the early twentieth century, with the ascendancy of Japan's imperial-colonial ambitions, political and intellectual leaders vigorously debated the problems of ethnic nationalism and multi-ethnic nationalism within the country, in relation to its colonial policy without (Doak 1997, 1998; Sakai 1997). The debates centered on the perennial question of Japan's identity as an "Asian nation." Some advocated removing Japan from the rest of Asia, especially the zone of Chinese civilization. The term *datsu-A* (Out of Asia; "A" being an abbreviation for Asia), coined by Fukuzawa Yukichi, became a powerful concept qua policy advocating *nyū-Ō* (entering Europe), Japan's affiliation with Europe. In hindsight it is quite ironic that Fukuzawa Yukichi (1835–1901), whose embrace of the Enlightenment philosophy led him to favor the dismantling of the social hierarchy of the pre-Meiji era and to champion equal rights for women, advocated the datsu-A policy and enthusiastically supported the Sino-Japanese War.

Yet, as they did with the Chinese, the Japanese strove to distinguish themselves from the Westerners with a symbolic opposition of "we vs. they." A significant example is the way in which this opposition entered into the public discourse over "rice vs. meat." A distinctive feature of the Otherness of Westerners during the early period of the Japanese encounter with them was their butchering and meat eating, as depicted in the *Yokohama-e* (Prints of Yokohama) and *Kaika-e* (Enlightenment Prints)—a series of woodblock prints depicting the foreigners who arrived in Japan (Suzuki Keiko 1997). With the pressing need to negotiate the Japanese identity, some opposed imitating the West and claimed that a rice diet and rice agriculture were evidence of Japanese superiority. Others advocated the abandonment of rice agriculture and the adoption of animal domestication. They argued that as long as the Japanese continued to eat only rice, fish, and vegetables, their bodies would never be strong enough to compete with the bodies of meat-eating Westerners (Tsukuba [1969] 1986: 109–12). In December 1871 the Meiji emperor issued an ordinance to eliminate the prohibition on meat eating in the imperial household. He ordered that the imperial kitchen should serve mutton and beef regularly, and pork, venison, and rabbit in small amounts, only occasionally (Harada 1993: 17). It was reported that the emperor ate meat himself on January 24, 1872 (Nakayama, ed. 1982a: 429; Gushima 1983: 194).[3]

The drastic change inaugurated by the emperor angered some. A most dramatic incident was the attempt by ten members of the ascetic mountain order *(shugendō),* for whom the notion of purity is of paramount importance, to enter the Imperial Palace on February 18, 1872 in order to plead with the emperor to retract the ordinance (Harada 1993: 18; Yasumaru 1980: 140–41).[4] On the other hand, Fukuzawa Yukichi, perhaps the most influential educator of the time and the founder of Keiō University, strongly advocated a meat diet.[5] Furthermore, in order to pursue the Meiji slogan of "Enrich the Country and Strengthen the Military," Western cuisine was adopted by the military from the very beginning of this period. A major reason for the military to switch to Western cuisine with dried bread *(kanpan)* and meat was to combat beriberi, caused by vitamin B deficiency resulting from a diet of polished white rice.[6]

These endorsements from above of a meat diet were effective in convincing people to try meat, which they thought was a symbol of "Enlightenment." A collection of humorous essays by Kanagaki Robun (1829–94) describing the eager adoption of meat eating at the time is entitled *Aguranabe*, "a dish one eats while sitting with one's legs crossed," rather than sitting properly on one's legs.[7] The book humorously portrays the mood of the day, when cows were seen to provide the miracle of the smallpox vaccine and their meat was not only *the* nourishment for the body but also the source of "Enlightenment." He writes: "Everyone—warriors, farmers, craftsmen, merchants, old and young, men and women, wise and foolish, poor and wealthy—all felt 'uncivilized' unless they ate beef" (Kanagaki Robun [1871–72] 1967: 77, 27, respectively). Cookbooks on meat dishes started to appear (Harada 1993: 17). Since meat stood for "Enlightenment," a new dish—sliced beef and vegetables cooked in soy sauce and placed on top of a large bowl of cooked rice and called *gyūnabe* ("beef pot") in eastern Japan and *sukiyaki* in western Japan (Endō [1910] 1968: 264)—was dubbed as the "Enlightened Bowl" (Nihon Kokugo Daijiten Kankōkai, ed., 1973a: 381).

This is quite extraordinary if we take into consideration the symbolic meaning of meat in Japanese culture during the previous centuries. The diet of the earliest inhabitants of the Japanese archipelago had no doubt consisted of animal meat, fish, and plants. As the agrarian society and its cosmology, which lay at the base of the ancient imperial system, became hegemonic, meat gradually became taboo. The process was intensified by Buddhism and Shintoism, which deemed all matters related to death, both of animals and humans, to be impure. Meat, a product of animal death, and butchering, an act of causing death, both became impure. During the medieval period meat of various wild and domestic animals was still available in cities (Harada 1993: 258). It was toward the end of the medieval period that impurity became a radical negativity (Ohnuki-Tierney 1987). By the Edo period (1603–1867) meat and butchers became "abominable." The severity of the taboo on meat is apparent when we consider that butchering was assigned to the so-called "outcaste."[8]

With the arrival of the Portuguese, toward the end of the sixteenth

century, some Japanese started to eat meat, although it remained officially taboo. Since meat was defiling, people passing in front of a meat
shop ran with their eyes closed, pinching their noses. If the procession of
a daimyō had to pass in front of a meat shop, the attendants lifted the carriage for the daimyō up in the air high enough to protect him from defilement. Recipes for beef, rabbit, and deer appeared in a cookbook with
a note cautioning that impurity lasts for one hundred fifty days after
their intake. Some who discretely enjoyed meat did so by giving the
names of flowers to animal meat, such as cherry blossoms for horse and
peony for wild boar—a custom retained even today. Just before the Meiji
period, in 1857, there were only two shops serving beef dishes in Osaka.
Their customers were shady characters with tattoos or students from
the aforementioned Tekijuku, where Dutch medicine was taught, as in
the Tokyo area, where the students from Keiō, under the influence of
Fukuzawa Yukichi, endorsed beef-eating. Shops serving beef dishes first
opened in Yokohama in 1862 and in Edo in 1867. At a shop opened in
Tokyo in 1869, customers were shady characters, some flaunting their
intake of beef as a threat—no one wanted to mess with beef-eaters.[9]

Although the concept of defilement from meat continued, from the
emperor downward the Meiji Japanese looked to meat as a source of
enlightenment.[10] Having rejected meat for centuries even though the
Chinese had been eating it, the Japanese adopted it with such gusto because it stood for "Western civilization," when the Westerners became
the Other. This was done even though meat was the marker of both the
internal Other (minority) and the dominant external Other (Westerners). The adoption of meat, initiated by none other than the emperor,
represented a real conceptual threat to the symbolic foundation of the
imperial system, which was based on the political economy of rice agriculture and an agrarian cosmology with rice at its symbolic center. Furthermore, it was a potentially subversive act not only to the symbolic but
also to the actual basis of the quasi-caste system in which those in the
agrarian sector occupied higher statuses and marginalized people were
relegated to the handling of "defiling" matters such as meat. In other
words, the introduction of meat into the daily diet of the Japanese raised
a potential threat to the imperial system, the social structure, and the
value system of a culture and society that had lasted for more than two
thousand years.

Meat as a metaphor for Westerners is not confined to the Japanese. In-
dians avidly attempted to be English, while fighting against English political and cultural colonialism. After turning away from the Anglophilia

of his early years, Gandhi expressed his resistance toward the English through vegetarianism. This diet stood for his political and ideological principle and practice against the colonialism of the "Englishman," whose meat diet made him "mighty" to rule over "the Indian small" (Gandhi 1948: 31–37, 60–71; Nandy 1995: 183–85).

The developments surrounding the adoption of the meat diet succinctly show how the historical forces at the time compelled the Japanese to articulate their collective identity and reassess their notion of their own selves. From a conceptual viewpoint, the Westerners with their dazzling achievements in science and technology became the Other, superseding the Chinese whose civilization had been eagerly adopted in earlier times. The Japanese avidly adopted Western civilization and peered "anxiously for signs of [their] own identity in the mirror of the rest of the world" (Pollack 1986: 53).

JAPAN UNDER EXTERNAL AND INTERNAL THREATS

While the Japanese, the elite and folk alike, emulated Western civilization with gusto, Western colonial powers were pressing hard. Japan's modernization effort took place in a highly tumultuous world, both within and without. Externally, threats from the Western colonial powers had been a menace for some time. The British maneuvers during the Opium War (1839–42), which resulted in the ceding of Hong Kong and the forced opening of various ports, posed a real threat to Japan. The Ansei commercial treaties of 1858 with five Western nations, including the United States, were "a humiliating assault upon Japan's sovereignty and national power," as Ogata Kōan lamented (Najita 1998: 239). Shimazu Nariakira (1809–58) advocated the enrichment and military strengthening of Japan (Haraguchi 1994), as did the samurai reformers from the Mito domain (Koschmann 1987). Commodore Perry's arrival in 1853 and then again in 1854 signaled that Japan no longer could retain its "isolation." The inability of the shogunate to cope with this new situation fueled the sentiment to overthrow the government. Internally, Japan was divided into some 260 *han* (a region controlled by a daimyō) and was not yet a nation-state, with considerable disunity among the regional lords.

Although the development of a civil society during the Edo period had provided some foundation for nation-building (Duus 1995: 4), Japan was far from being a modern state with a central government. It lacked both a national flag and a national anthem. Contrary to a commonly held assumption, both inside and outside of Japan, the rising sun flag was not chosen formally as the national flag until 1870, two years after the formal designation of the sixteen-petaled chrysanthemum as the imperial emblem. Ironically, most Japanese showed little interest in the national flag, and some even staged protests. The national flag was gradually accepted by the populace, primarily as a result of the government forcing people to welcome the emperor with the flag during his tours throughout Japan.[11]

Japan also had no national anthem in place at the time of the Meiji "Restoration." At the suggestion to create one by John William Fenton, director of the British Army Band, the government chose a poem *(waka)* by an anonymous poet in the early tenth century, from the *Kokin Wakashū*, which was later included in *Wakan Rōeishū*, edited by Fujiwara-no-Kintō and published around A.D. 1013. The composer is nominally identified as Hayashi Hiromori, a musician at the imperial court, but Oku Yoshiisa, who worked under Hayashi, is believed to have composed the music, with some rearrangement by Franz Eckert (1852–1916). The song, "Kimigayo," was first performed in 1879, and in 1893 the Ministry of Education required the singing of eight songs, including this one, at school ceremonies. It was not until 1937 that it was formally referred to as the "national anthem" in elementary school textbooks, and even to the present day there has never been formal legislation to codify it as the national anthem (Inoue [1963] 1967, 2: 212–13; Kudō 1977: 284; Murakami 1977: 128–31; Sonobe [1962] 1980: 52–55; Yui 1996).[12]

This hurriedly created anthem is amazingly short and only praises the long reign of "His Majesty," which is metaphorically expressed as "lasting until moss grows on the rock." Unlike other anthems, it contains a simple message, without including any of the codification of the emperor in the Imperial Rescript to Soldiers or the Constitution of Imperial Japan.

The fledgling start of Japan as a modern state was parallelled by the rapid development of the "Freedom and Popular Rights Movement" *(Jiyū minken undō)*, which was "spreading like wildfire" during the 1870s and 1880s. The Japanese passionately embraced democracy, individualism, and egalitarianism (Irokawa [1970] 1997: 17–19). Fukuzawa Yukichi published his famous *Encouragement of Learning (Gakumon no Susume)* between 1872 and 1876. A quotation from it, "The heaven does not create a human above another human," was enthusiastically received. But the new government took these movements as threats to its control of the population.

THE MAKING OF THE CONSTITUTION OF IMPERIAL JAPAN

The Kōmei emperor (1831–66), who preceded the Meiji emperor, strongly supported the shogunate and opposed the "Restoration." At Kōmei's death, the Meiji emperor acceded to the throne at the age of fourteen. He had been pampered exclusively by court ladies and was physically frail. In July 1864, when warriors from Chōshū fired cannon balls at the imperial palace in order to force the "Restoration," he fainted at their sound. The architects of the new government got rid of the women and undertook the "masculinization" of the emperor, who began to enjoy activities such as horseback riding. Itō Hirobumi and others had free rein to fashion any type of imperial system they wanted without resistance from the Meiji emperor. Those in the innermost circle of the government referred to the emperor as the crystal ball—easily rolled about in the palm of the hand (Inoue [1953] 1967: 21, 225–26). They made all the decisions that passed through imperial hands for legitimacy (Gluck 1985: 43). It was a clever double-entendre, since the term crystal ball had been used as a honorific prefix referring to the emperor's body, voice, etc.

Not only was the Meiji emperor manageable for the oligarchs, but the "restored" emperor system was an empty vessel which they could fill with their strategic plans. It was only after they supposedly "restored" the imperial system that they began to systematically deliberate upon how to establish a strong central government. Ultimately they chose a particular kind of constitutional monarchy and, twenty-two years after the "Restoration," codified it in the Meiji constitution.[13]

The Key Architects of the Constitution

Several of the most important members of the Meiji oligarchy went abroad to study European political systems. Yamagata Aritomo (1838–1922) traveled to Europe in 1869 and was disheartened by the decline of absolute monarchs in Europe. He strongly advocated that Japan establish an absolute monarchy (Hackett 1971: 50–89).[14] The two key figures in drafting the constitution, Itō Hirobumi and Inoue Kowashi, also traveled to Europe.[15] Itō Hirobumi (1841–1909), who fought for the Meiji "Restoration," had the most decisive role in shaping the constitution, especially in regard to the emperor. He became the first premier of the new government (1885–88), formed his second cabinet from 1892 to 1896, and the third in 1898. Inoue Kowashi (1843–95) was in charge of the actual drafting of the constitution in consultation with foreign scholars.

In 1882 Itō Hirobumi spent six months in Germany learning about the Prussian constitution from H. Rudolf von Gneist and Albert Mosse, and a little less than a month and half in Austria learning from Lorenz von Stein. Even before he began formal study with Stein, Itō met Stein and Gneist and dispatched what became a well-known letter to Iwakura Tomomi on August 11, 1882:

> Under the great teachers, Gneist and Stein, I have come to understand how to conceptualize the basic structure of the nation. The cardinal point *(dai-ganmoku)* is to strengthen the imperial foundation and *safeguard his sovereignty as indissoluble.* There is a tendency now [in Japan] to regard the writings of radical liberals in England, the United States and France as the golden threads, but they will lead our country to decline. If we establish the reasoning and strategy to reverse this situation, we can repay in a timely fashion our indebtedness to our country with our unselfish devotion *(sekishin)* and lead our efforts to fruition. I feel in my heart that I have found the eternal resting place. (Emura 1996: 485; my translation; emphasis added)

This letter makes it amply clear that the imperial system was adopted as a strategy for developing Japan into a sovereign modern state.

The key figures among foreign scholars, some of whom stayed in Japan for several years as guests of the government, were Gustave Emile Boissonade, H. Rudolf von Gneist, Albert Mosse, Carl Rudolph, Karl Friedrich Hermann Roesler, and Lorenz von Stein (Emura, ed. 1996: 262).[16]

Sovereignty: The Key Issue

Since the most important as well as urgent issue of the Meiji "Restoration" was the establishment of sovereignty in order to protect the country from Western colonial powers, the crucial question was whether sovereignty should rest with the emperor or with other state organs. At the time of the drafting of the constitution, the key figures of the oligarchy and foreign advisors were in agreement that it should rest with the emperor, as made clear in the above letter by Itō. In his lectures to Itō, Stein introduced the Prussian constitution as a model and explained the details of constitutional monarchy (Emura, ed. 1996: 265–71). In order not to reduce the emperor's sovereign authority *(tennō taiken)*, they avoided the Bonapartism of France and the parliamentary system of England, both of which, in their view, weakened both the authority and sovereignty of the king/emperor (Emura 1996: 482–84; Inada 1960: 589; Mitani 1988: 55–59).

The most serious problem in locating sovereignty in the emperor centered upon whether to spell out the rights of the emperor in the constitution. Itō Hirobumi, Inoue Kowashi, and Albert Mosse held the view that the emperor's rights should not be specified in the constitution itself. Mosse argued that the rights of the emperor should be described in general terms, since detailing them would in fact delimit the emperor's sovereign authority and endanger the principle of monarchy (Inada 1962: 8–10). He advised that some of his rights be written in the "Preamble" *(jōyu)*. Inoue Kowashi understood Mosse's point and stressed that in Japan they had a constitution because of the presence of emperor and not vice versa. Yet, Inoue had to ask the opinion of Roesler, who strenuously opposed Inoue's qua Mosse's position, which Roesler thought logical but not pragmatic. Roesler insisted that codification of the emperor's rights in the constitution itself would prevent conflicts in the future. Inoue caved in (Inada 1962: 4–13).[17]

Let me now introduce the articles relating to the issue of sovereignty and the emperor as military commander in the drafts written by three foreign scholars.

Carl Rudolph (1841–1915):

Article 2: The emperor is sacred *(shinsei ni shite)* and not to be violated *(okasu bekarazu)*. In addition he is not to be burdened with responsibilities.

Article 14: The Emperor commands the Navy and the Army.[18]

Karl Friedrich Hermann Roesler (1834–94):

Article 2: The emperor is sacred *(shinsei ni shite)* and the sovereign of the imperial nation who may not be violated *(okasu bekazaru)*.

Article 9: The emperor is the Supreme Commander of the Army and the Navy. In peace and war, he commands the soldiers and direct all matters in regard to soldiers and sailors.[19]

Lorenz von Stein (1815–90):

Article 17: The emperor is the highest commander *(mujō shuchō)* of the imperial nation. His sacred body may not be violated *(kanpan subekarazu)*.

Article 24: The emperor is the administrative commander *(gyōseiken no shuchō)* and the highest commander of the Navy and the

Army *(rikugun oyobi kaigun no saikō shireiken o yūshi).*
(Emura, ed. 1996: 265–71)

These three drafts may now be compared with the Constitution of Imperial Japan, finally issued under the name of the emperor on February 11, 1889—twenty-two years after the Meiji "Restoration." It was signed by ten government officials, including Kuroda Kiyotaka (the premier), Itō Hirobumi, and Inoue Kowashi. The constitution was issued together with the Manual of the Imperial Household *(Kōshitsu Tenpan):*

> Article 1: The emperor belongs to one line for eternity *(bansei ikkei)* and he governs Imperial Japan.
> Article 3: The emperor is sacred *(shisei nishite)* and may not be violated *(okasu bekarazu).*
> Article 11: The emperor shall command the Army and the Navy (Emura, ed. 1996: 430–34).

In comparing the official constitution of 1889 and the drafts by the foreign scholars, what is striking are the nearly identical phrasing and the notions regarding the identity of the emperor as "sacred and not to be violated" and as the "commander of the Army and Navy." This is the case especially with the draft by Roesler, which Inoue Kowashi adopted almost in its entirety.

Leaving the religious dimension to a later section, let me first point out that from the point of view of "sovereignty," Article 3 is crucial. As Mitani explicates, "the real meaning" of the article is to relieve the emperor of any political responsibility by placing him beyond or above politics. The Meiji constitution codified the emperor as the constitutional monarch and granted him imperial sovereignty, and yet at the same time it rejected the idea of direct imperial rule. Political responsibilities were placed in the hands of all organs of the state, each independent of each other and directly answerable only to the emperor. The military, reporting directly to the emperor, seized an independent power without having to clear its actions with other state organs (Emura 1996: 491–92; Mitani 1988: 60–61).

Primordiality of Kingship, Primordiality of the Japanese Self

The drafts by foreign scholars and the final constitution differ on one crucial point, however—the inclusion of Article 1, which was strenuously opposed by *all* the foreign advisors including Roesler, for whom it had no historical or legal meaning (Inada 1960: 248). However, Article 1 was crucial in the view of the oligarchs in legitimating the emperor by assigning an "infinite" antiquity to the Japanese kingship—the point also made in the Pledge which the emperor made to his ancestors before he promulgated the constitution (Satomi 1972: 160–67; see also Nagao 1995: 840). The Pledge *(kokubun)*, an address by the Meiji emperor to his "ancestors," starts with the emperor reporting to the divine soul *(shinrei)* that resided in previous emperors and now does so in himself. It was made clear in the Pledge, then, that the imperial soul was transmitted from the first emperor down the line. The antiquity of the imperial system assigned primordiality also to Japan and all Japanese as represented by the emperor.

The codification of the antiquity of the kingship through Article 1 and the Pledge would have had no impact upon the people without a series of practices implemented by the state, of which I outline three major strategies: (1) adoption of the policy of "one name for one imperial era," together with enforcement of the memorization of the names of the emperors; (2) enforcement of the performance of rituals commemorating the beginning of the imperial line; (3) use of archaic terms for the emperor and his subjects.

The government began requiring the memorization by school children of the names of all emperors, beginning with the legendary-turned-"real" first emperor, Jinmu. In addition, they adopted the "one era name for one emperor" system. The practice of naming an era was introduced from China, where the practice started in 140 B.C. during the Western Han dynasty. In Japan the practice began during the Taika Reform in A.D. 645. Names designating new eras were adopted for various reasons. Although from the Kanmu emperor through the Jun'na emperor (788 through 833), the accession of a new emperor was the reason for the change, later changes were sometimes prompted by other factors, including natural disasters, or the appearance of auspicious astrological signs. Since the Heian period (794–1185), the emperor had the authority to change the name, but during the Edo period the shogunate held de facto power. It was only with the Meiji that the "one era name for one emperor" system was officially adopted.

Basically the notion of era names derived from the cyclical notion of time. Just as the dawn returns after the night, the end of the year returns to its beginning. Similarly, the zodiac calendar, a deeply rooted system of time-reckoning among the folk, consists of a twelve-year cycle. The emperor was originally a shaman-political leader who was in charge of the timing of various agrarian rituals (Miyata 1992: 83–112). According to Orikuchi ([1935] 1976: 364–66), as the controller of time, each new emperor started a new era by offering an auspicious prayer. In fact the

imperial accession ritual enacted his/her birth, signaling a new beginning (Ohnuki-Tierney 1993a: 48–50).

Even with the Meiji proclamation of one name for one emperor, the
Japanese folk continued to use the zodiac calendar system, which oper-
ated on a twelve-year cycle irrespective of who the emperor was, as they
had done before (Murakami 1977: 122–23). After initial resistance, most
people began accepting the system, quite eagerly in fact.

The second strategy for establishing the antiquity of the imperial
system was to invent a series of imperial rituals and synchronize their
performance at the imperial palace with those at the local level, i.e., at
shrines and schools. The most elaborate was the *genshisai*, a ritual to
support Article 1 of the new constitution by enacting the mythical descent to earth of the grandson of the Sun Goddess, the first emperor,
Jinmu. The annual ritual, to be held on January 3 of every year, was inaugurated in 1870. The next in importance was the *kigensetsu*. First instituted in 1872, this was a ritual to celebrate the accession of Jinmu, the
first emperor in the Meiji military mythology. Most of the newly established rituals dealt with the imperial soul, as articulated in the Pledge. Of
the twenty-one rituals, thirteen had to be officiated by the emperor himself and the rest by the specialist of rituals at the imperial court (Murakami 1977: 76–98).

The third and perhaps the most clever strategy was the adoption of a
number of archaic terms. The oligarchs resurrected the term "Manifest
Deity," which first appeared in *Nihonshoki*, dated A.D. 720 (Takebe 1995:
339). The notion of the "human-deity" *(hitogami)* is a crucial notion
in Japanese religiosity (see below), with its continuum between humans
and deities. But the Meiji oligarchs gave it the new meaning of the emperor as God in human form, rather than the common meaning of an ordinary human who becomes a deity (Murakami 1977: 107–56). In addition, the term *chin* was adopted as a self-referential term that could be
used exclusively by the emperor in his addresses to his subjects; it appeared in such important decrees as the Imperial Rescript to Soldiers
and the Imperial Rescript on Education. The term was originally a self-
referential pronoun in China that was used regardless of the person's status. It was adopted by the Japanese and used by emperors in the ancient
period, as seen in the myth-histories of *Kojiki* and *Nihonshoki* (Gotō
1996) and the *Manyōshū* collection of poems.[20]

The major source of archaic terms for the new government was the
collection of poems by *sakimori*, the ancient imperial border guards, in
the *Manyōshū*. This collection contains ninety-nine poems composed
by border guards (Sokura 1995), of which eighty-four are in volume 20,

compiled in 755. Sakimori were peasant soldiers who were summoned, especially from the eastern part of Japan (Azuma), which was known for good soldiers, to guard north Kyūshū (Tsukushi) and Iki and Tsushima islands, then the western frontier of Japan. The system lasted from 664 to 826; even at its height, there were at most two to three thousand sakimori (Sasayama 1995b).

From these verses the Meiji government selected forms of address and reference to the emperor as well as self-referential forms. For example, it resurrected the title *kimi*, which had been used for regional political leaders before the imperial system was put in place. In 759, the imperial court banned the use of *kimi* and ordered it replaced with *kō* (Abe 1996). The ban met with little success, and the terms *kimi* or *ōkimi* (with the honorific of *ō*) were frequently used—fifteen times in the sakimori poems in volume 20.[21] During the mid-seventh century, in order to stress the religious nature of the headship of the nation, *ōkimi* was replaced by *tennō* (emperor), a term taken from China, where it had a religious meaning (Murakami 1977: 10; Ienaga 1996a: 991). The designation for the emperor was again changed to "Son of Heaven" *(tenshi)*—a Confucian term—when Neo-Confucianism was adopted by the Tokugawa shogunate (Kitagawa 1990: 157), only to revert back to *tennō*. The Meiji government adopted the term *kimi* and immortalized it by using it as the first word of the newly created national anthem, whose verse comes from a poem from *Kokin Wakashū* in which the term was used.

Another ancient designation for the emperor, *sumera mikoto*, was the first official designation for the emperor created during the seventh century (Sasayama 1995a); the term appears in the *Manyōshū*, sometimes referring to the imperial ancestor. For example, a long poem by Ōtomo no Yakamochi, who was in charge of the border guards, starts with a term, *sumeroki*, the imperial ancestor, i.e., the Nintoku emperor. In another poem by a member of the Ōtomo clan, *sumeroki* appears twice, once referring to the grandson of the Sun Goddess (Ninigi-no-Mikoto) and another time to the Jinmu emperor.[22] Adoption of these archaic terms of reference to the emperor was accompanied by use of the adjective "crystal" *(gyoku* or *tama)*, as in "the crystal body" *(gyokutai)*, to describe the emperor's body and behavior, as well as use of the prefix *kō* (imperial), as in imperial country *(kōkoku)*, imperial military *(kōgun)*, and imperial mercy *(kō'on)*.

The Meiji political leaders also chose terms for modern soldiers from the verses composed by border guards. The term *masurao*, a word for young men which foregrounds masculinity, appears twice as a term referring to a border guard himself in the above-mentioned poem by a member of the Ōtomo clan.[23] In this poem, he vows to die or fight "at the side of the emperor" *(sumerahe)*. In a poem by another border guard, the term *sumera mikusa* (imperial army) is used (Omodaka 1968: 98, no. 4370). Some border guards refer to themselves as *shiko no mitate* ("ugly shield"), which appears six times in the *Manyōshū*, including in the following poem by a border guard: "From today, I shall not look back and go to the front as an ugly shield for our Majesty."[24]

By lifting these terms and selecting a few verses, the Meiji government constructed the image of the ancient border guards as unquestionably dedicated to *pro rege et patria mori*. Yet as Horton (2003) compellingly argues, these border guard poems are full of references to their pain and sorrow at leaving behind their parents, wives, and lovers. Horton found that twenty-three of the verses mention parents and children, and thirteen more home and family. An example: "My wife must miss me terribly, Even in my drinking water I see her reflection; never will she be forgotten!" Another example: "How I wish father and mother were both blossoms! Then even on my grass for my pillow I could hold them high!" (Omodaka 1968: 42–43, no. 4322; 37–38, no. 4325; trans. Horton). Far from being unambiguously determined soldiers of the emperor, they were torn with sorrow and longing for their loved ones and they stress the fact they were drafted or commanded to be border guards. There are striking parallels between these poems and the writings left behind by the tokkōtai pilots (chapter 6).

Little is known about the context of composition of the sakimori poems, except that most were composed when the soldiers were summoned together, just as the tokkōtai pilots were summoned together to write their wills. Of 166 poems submitted by the border guards, Ōtomo-no-Yakamochi, the editor, rejected 82 and included the remaining 84 in volume 20 (Sokura 1995). There is no doubt, then, that the Meiji government's construction of the border guards was by no means a fair representation of their thoughts and feelings.

Nonetheless, the state constructed a magnificent metanarrative of times long past, which naturalized yet another aspect of its construction that the imperial line had existed in perpetuity—an effort buttressed in 1872 when the year of accession of the first emperor Jinmu was set at a date 2,600 years in the past. Not only were *Manyōshū* poems mobilized to demonstrate the antiquity of the Japanese imperial system, but, even more importantly, they were used to naturalize *pro rege et patria mori* as the Japanese tradition from time immemorial. That is, such terms as "imperial army" *(sumera mikusa)* in the *Manyōshū* naturalized the Meiji notion of the imperial army and navy with the emperor directly in control. An entirely new system was presented as if it had existed since ancient times, when Japan was hardly a nation with a central government. Furthermore, those poems provided "evidence" that Japanese soldiers had *always* put loyalty to the emperor above loyalty to their parents.

These archaic terms were used in the constitution, in both the Imperial Rescript on Education and the Imperial Rescript to Soldiers, and in prayers offered at the Yasukuni Shrine. Use of these terms would not have been effective, however, had they not also been used in school textbooks, school songs, and popular songs (see chapter 4). It was through these means, intended to militarize the masses, that these terms, together with the newly assigned concepts behind them, penetrated into the writings of World War II soldiers, including the tokkōtai pilots (chapter 6).

The strategy of constructing the antiquity of the imperial system was a powerful political move. The Meiji oligarchs attempted to unify all the Japanese under the emperor by establishing a *Volk* that had existed from time immemorial. This they did by establishing the legitimacy of the emperor through his genealogical continuity by creating "the imperial soul." The emperor was made the "Japanese emperor" sui generis—he is bound to the political unit. Furthermore, its re-invention of the emperor as the controller of time managed, internally, to control the daily *and* cosmic rhythms of the people, and, externally, to make Japanese unique by adhering to their own "Japanese time," the cyclical time, renewed at the accession of a new emperor, rather than succumbing to the Western Gregorian calendrical scheme. It is no wonder that the Meiji oligarchs insisted on Article 1—a most succinct expression of Japanese political nationalism.[25]

The Emperor as the Father

In order to mobilize the Japanese people in the name of the emperor, the emperor had to be converted into Almighty God not just in the constitution but in the minds of the people, since it was far more persuasive to the Japanese, including the soldiers, to die for the Almighty Japanese God than for one of millions of deities, as the emperor used to be before the Meiji era.

It was also important to establish the emperor as the Father to all Japanese, thereby creating legitimate kinship ties between the emperor and his subjects. That is, the state attempted to adopt "the pastoral model" of governance—a concept that Plato introduced but criticized in the *Statesman* but that was highly developed by Christianity in order to care for people's souls (Foucault [1977] 1995: 104; C. Gordon 1991: 8). The model was promoted even though none of the Japanese religions have a father figure, unlike Christianity. However, the emperor could not compete with one's parents. By this time the Confucian ethic of the *kō*, repayment to one's parents for their nurturing, and *chū*, loyalty to a regional lord, had been well established as an important moral code.[26] Loyalty to the emperor, a concept hitherto unknown to the people, had to be established in a society where there was no space for it. Not only did this new notion have no space in Japanese moral codes but, needless to say, the loyalty to the emperor, when sacrifice is entailed, often precludes the repayment to one's parents.

Therefore, the state embarked on a campaign to emblazon on the minds of the people the idea that "loyalty to the emperor equals loyalty to one's parents" *(chūkō icchi).* The motto was originally developed at the end of the Edo period by a group of samurai reformers whose goal was to "revere the emperor and expel the barbarians" (foreign enemies). In 1833 Tokugawa Nariaki spelled out this idea in his book *Kokushihen,* and such well-respected figures as Yoshida Shōin propagated it (Suzuki Eiichi 1996). The Meiji government made this idea into a decree on October 30, 1890, through the promulgation of the Imperial Rescript on Education (Kyōiku Chokugo), whose major architects were Yamagata Aritomo, Itō Kowashi, and Nakamura Masanao (Yamazumi [1990] 1996: 364–85). In the Rescript, loyalty to the emperor *(chū)* and loyalty to parents *(kō)* were defined as the spiritual flower *(seika)* of the "national body" *(kokutai,* national polity)—an expression that in later years acquired a significant meaning in the totalitarian ideology (Inoue [1963] 1967, 2: 214–25; Bitō 1997). The Japanese became one family with the emperor as the father, and loyalty to the emperor subsumed loyalty to parents. The general will of Rousseau and Kant has often been transformed into a strategic ploy by revolutionary movements, as with the Jacobins at the time of the Revolution, and by totalitarian states, as in Germany and Japan, whereby the will of the powerful was imposed upon the people. The Rescript on Education, the study of which became mandatory at every school, prescribed: "In the case of national emergency, one should sacrifice oneself courageously for the country by guarding the Imperial Throne, which is coeval with heaven and earth." Many teachers found it difficult to teach the Rescript, and other teachers opposed enforcing this rule (see Yamazumi [1990] 1996: 364, 383; Inada 1962).

If one of the state's strategies for equating loyalty to parents with loyalty to the emperor was to mandate the teaching of the Rescript in the schools, another strategy was the practice of *jungyō*—the tour of the country by the emperor to build up his image as the merciful father.[27]

The emperor visited the aged and the poor. He watched peasants in the field in order to demonstrate his appreciation of their toils. The Meiji emperor toured the country ninety-six times during his forty-five-year reign, from Hokkaido to Kyushu and from the Pacific to the Japan Sea coast (Tōyama [1988] 1996: 45–115; Taki [1988] 1990: 75–110).

By making the emperor into the father to all Japanese, the state dissolved, or at least hoped to dissolve, the apparent contradiction between loyalty to the emperor and loyalty to one's parents. The presumed "blood tie" between the Sun Goddess, the emperor, and the Japanese people was established and the Japanese were all in one family. The structure of body politic was laid down. This idea was again from von Stein, and it was put into practice by Ōkubo Toshimichi (Inoue [1953] 1967: 70–73).

The Emperor as Commander of the Military

Since the very first item on the agenda for the Meiji oligarchs was to build a military strong enough for a modern state, in Article 11 of Chapter 1 of the Constitution of Imperial Japan, the emperor was designated as Commander-in-Chief *(daigensui)* of the army and the navy, referred to as the imperial force *(kōgun)*. Before his image was replaced by that of a dragon head, the emperor always appeared in military uniform, decorated with chevrons for his military rank, army medals of stars, navy medals of cherry blossoms, and the paulownia crest symbolizing the imperial court.[28] The visualization of the emperor as the head of the military, first in woodblock prints and later in photographs, paralleled the discursive practice of using the archaic terms discussed earlier.

In ancient Japan the emperor's political power was predicated upon his religious power as the officiant of the rice-harvesting ritual, and in subsequent periods political and military power rested upon the shoguns. Thus, the new Meiji emperor took over, at least nominally, the power hitherto held by the shoguns.

THE IMPERIAL RESCRIPT TO SOLDIERS (GUNJIN CHOKUYU)

The need to build a strong, modern military resulted in the promulgation of the Imperial Rescript to Soldiers (Gunjin Chokuyu) seven years *before* the publication of the Meiji constitution. On January 14, 1882, at the Imperial Palace, the Meiji emperor delivered the document in person to Ōyama Iwao, head of the army, and Kawamura Sumiyoshi, head of the navy who was away and thus in absentia (for the delivery of the rescript, see Yui, Fujiwara, and Yoshida, eds. [1989] 1996: 172–77). The major architect of the Imperial Rescript to Soldiers was Lieutenant General Yamagata Aritomo (1838–1922), who entrusted its first draft to

Nishi Amane (1829–97) (Umetani 1996a). The most "infamous" passage from today's perspective reads:

> Do not be beguiled by popular opinions, do not get involved in political activities, but singularly devote yourself to your most important obligation of loyalty to the emperor, and realize that *the obligation is heavier than the mountains but death is lighter than a feather.* (Yui, Fujiwara and Yoshida, eds. [1989] 1996: 174; emphasis added)

With this statement, the Meiji government set out on its path of enforcing the *pro rege et patria mori* ideology. The text, however, does not have any reference to cherry blossoms.

BUILDING THE MODERN MILITARY

At the end of the sixteenth century, Hideyoshi instituted the infamous rule that separated the warrior class from that of farmers and which confiscated weapons from the latter. The policy became the bulwark of the shogunate. Premodern warriors, *bushi,* constituted the upper crust of Tokugawa society, which was legally divided into warriors, farmers, manufacturers, and merchants, in descending order. Outside the normative system were the emperor on top and the two "outcaste" groups at the bottom.

Toward the end of the Tokugawa period the internal unrest of peasant revolts and the external threat of the arrival of foreign ships necessitated strong military forces. Yet by this time the warriors, who lived in peace and isolation from the outside world, had become useless as a military force. Therefore, even before the Meiji era, regional lords began relying on so-called *nōhei* (also called *zōhyō* [miscellaneous soldiers])—farmer-soldiers, recruited from wealthy farming households *(gōnō)* (Inoue Shōsei 1993: 696–97; Kurushima 1986: 297).

Symptomatic of the changing character of soldiers in modern Japan was the Boshin War of 1868—the war that finally overthrew the shogunate and that "restored" the emperor system, thus ushering in the Meiji era. One of the major divisions of the soldiers who fought for the imperial side consisted of lower-class warriors, farmers, members of the merchant class *(chōnin),* and some members of the marginalized social group called *hisabetsu-burakumin* ("settlement people under discrimination") (S. Inoue 1993). This division won over the warriors fighting for the shogunate, revealing the military impotence of the hereditary warrior class in no uncertain terms.

The Meiji government revolutionized the military system by adopting universal conscription in 1873, well before Great Britain adopted it.[29]
This led to opposition by warriors, and in 1876 dissatisfied warriors under the leadership of Saigō Takamori revolted against the government;
they were defeated by government forces that consisted primarily of enlisted soldiers. This war, called the Seinan War, was the largest and last
of the rebellions by the warrior class against the tide of the modern era
(Inoue 197: 208–9).

A most important mission of the Meiji government was to transform
warriors who fought for regional lords into soldiers who fought for the
nation. The state coined terms such as "God's soldiers" *(shinpei)* and
"Emperor's military" *(kōgun)* to designate armies consisting of conscripts. Every Japanese male was told to repay his country with his raw
blood *(seiketsu)* for his indebtedness, presumably to be fortunate enough
to be born a Japanese. Several categories of people were exempt—most
notably, heads of households.[30]

Universal conscription in reality meant an extension of *an equal right
to death* to all males. This process *unmarked* the minorities who had
been discriminated against. As detailed elsewhere,[31] the development of
the self-identity of the dominant Japanese as agrarian involved the formation of minorities who were non-agrarian populations, such as the
Ainu and the hisabetsu-burakumin. The non-agricultural occupations of
these groups were turned into the markers of their "innate" proximity
to "beastly nature." Through a "biologizing" process (Appiah 1992a: 4),
"real" differences were constructed to *mark* the members of these minority groups, such as the supposed "hairiness" of the Ainu and the
physical "deformity" of the hisabetsu-burakumin, when in fact they
were physically indistinguishable from the so-called agrarian Japanese.

Unmarking of its minorities was not enough. While the intellectuals
debated the ethnic vs. multi-ethnic identity of the Japanese and Japanese
identity vis-à-vis other Asian nations, the imperial army and navy faced
the pressing need to recruit Koreans, Chinese, and others both in Japan
proper and in the occupied territories.

The adoption of universal conscription went hand in hand with
changes in the system of *shizoku*, the hereditary warrior class. In order
to attract commoners to enlist as "the emperor's soldiers," the government made a show of denouncing the warriors. Yet the government cleverly used the former warriors to suppress revolts by the people, while at
the same time utilizing the enlisted soldiers to fight against disenchanted
former warriors (K. Inoue 1975: 202, 206).

In reality, the officers of Japan's modern army came from the former warrior class, resulting in the retention of the stratified system with those former warriors as officers above enlisted soldiers (Kurushima 1986: 309). Some of the officers who were celebrated for their sacrifice for the emperor in the Sino- and Russo-Japanese Wars were the descendants of warriors. But by far the majority who died on the front line were enlisted soldiers. Thus there are changes and continuities between the warriors of the Tokugawa period and the modern soldiers of the imperial army. But, as we will see later, the state strategically superimposed the aestheticized image of the upper-class warriors of the past onto all the modern soldiers, including the foot soldiers.

CONSTRUCTION OF THE NATIONAL SHRINE—YASUKUNI JINJA

The Yasukuni Shrine occupies an important place in the historical processes that led to the aestheticization of the notion of *pro rege et patria mori*.[32] The Yasukuni Shrine was constructed by the Meiji government at Kudan, Tokyo, across from the northern part of the Imperial Palace, following a decree from the Meiji emperor in 1869. As indicated in the original name for the shrine, "Tokyo Shrine to Call Back the Souls of the Deceased" (Tōkyō Shōkonsha),[33] the purpose was to enshrine some 3,588 souls of deceased soldiers who had fought for the imperial "restoration" during the famous Boshin War. These soldiers were later joined by those who died during the civil wars immediately before and after the Meiji "Restoration," such as Saga-no-ran and the Seinan War, as well as those who died during Japan's invasions of Taiwan and Korea, the Sino-Japanese War, the Russo-Japanese War, World War I, and World War II. The shrine honors not only soldiers but also women and children who died in service to the country, such as women nurses caring for wounded soldiers on the battlefield. Enshrined also are three Englishmen whose ship was sunk by Russians off Okino-shima in 1904 during the Russo-Japanese war.[34] In 1979, in a little-publicized ritual, General Tōjō Hideki and other war criminals were enshrined (Japanese Philately 1996: 282). Today, of the total of 2,466,000 souls enshrined, 57,000 are women and 1,068 are "war criminals" of World War II (Yasukuni Jinja 1992).

The criteria for selecting who gets to be enshrined have, from the beginning, never been disclosed. However, the criteria must have changed over time. Initially, starting with the soldiers who died for the emperor at the time of the Meiji "Restoration," the state was primarily concerned with the need to appease the souls of the dead. This concern reflects the

Japanese belief that the souls of the dead must be properly treated lest they inflict some misfortune on the living. Thus, all souls whose living relatives cannot afford them proper treatment *(muen-botoke)*, be they English or the souls of soldiers whose relatives are unknown, are treated properly by the state, the municipal government, the village, etc. But as militarism intensified, enshrinement at the Yasukuni Shrine took on the role of celebrating war heroes as a strategy to encourage soldiers to die for the emperor.

It is hard to read the past of the Yasukuni shrine without reference to its role during Japan's military period. But its original intent was to invite the souls of the soldiers who died during the Boshin and Seinan wars and to appease and console them. It is based on the Japanese belief that survivors have a duty to commemorate the souls of the deceased, a belief that underlies an elaborate series of mortuary rituals and "ancestor worship" (Smith 1974); the latter is a misnomer in that ancestors can be one's dear little girl, rather than a patriarch of the family. Some believe that this practice is aimed at appeasing the souls of the dead so that they will not haunt the living and cause misfortunes. This basic intent explains the enshrinement of women, children, and foreigners—the souls of all the dead must be properly treated. I tend to believe that in the main the Japanese take care of the dead simply because they care for them, rather than necessarily for functional reasons. At any rate, the shrine was built at a time when many shrines throughout Japan were performing rituals for the souls of the soldiers who died in the turbulent period before and after the Meiji "Restoration." The government requested regional governments to submit lists of soldiers who died fighting for the emperor in order to console their souls at the newly erected national shrine.

The other intent of the government was to make national heroes of those fallen soldiers who fought on the side of the new government, while branding those who fought against it as *zoku* (enemies/bandits). It was a strategy to glorify the "imperial army"—an alien concept to most Japanese at the time. The shrine was built at a time when the remaining forces of the shogunate were still fighting against the new government, whose officials were often the targets of assassination attempts. There was a need to mark heroes and enemies within. The government instituted rituals called the "Ritual for Soldier-Deities" *(Gunshin-sai)* at the imperial palace for the purpose of the apotheosis of these soldiers at the shrine.

Ōmura Masujirō (1825–69), a key member of those who fought for the imperial "restoration," originated the idea of building the shrine. As the head of the newly established Ministry of the Military *(hyōbu)*, he was a major architect of the new military system of Japan. He died in 1869 from a wound inflicted by two assassins (Inoue Isao 1995). Ōmura's name heads the six-member list of officials who submitted a report to the military officials *(gunmukan)* on the decision to build a shrine at Kudan, near the Imperial Palace (Yasukuni Jinja 1983: 18). A bronze statue of Ōmura, the first statue ever to be built in Tokyo, was erected in 1893. Issued in the same year was a woodblock print entitled "The Statue of Director *(daisuke)* Ōmura at Yasukuni Shrine," which depicted his statue among cherry blossoms, with men, women, children, and soldiers strolling in the compound (Yasukuni Jinja 1984). From the very beginning the shrine was the "military shrine," under the control of the army, the navy, and the Ministry of the Interior. In reality, the army financed and held ultimate control over the shrine's operation, in contrast to all other shrines, which were controlled by the Ministry of the Interior (Ōhama 1994).

The first event took place on the afternoon of June 28, 1869, when the purification ritual and the ritual to invite the souls of the 3,588 soldiers were performed (Murakami 1974: 49). A five-day event followed, from June 29 to July 3, which started with the offering of prayers to the souls by the high priest of the shrine and the Minister on the Right *(udaijin)*.[35] The prayers extolled the virtue of those soldiers who fought for the emperor as members of the imperial army *(kōgun)* (Yasukuni Jinja 1983: 34–35). The prayers included a poem by a border guard from the *Manyōshū*, using archaic terms. The prayers were followed by a gun salute. Sumō tournaments took place for three days (June 30 through July 2), and firecrackers were set off day and night on July 3, with both the tournaments and firecrackers intended as offerings to the souls (Murakami 1974: 48–51). In 1877, many imperial soldiers died in the Seinan War, the last of the rebellions against the new government. The government felt the need to have a special large-scale ceremony for their souls. The Meiji emperor participated in the ceremony, initiating the custom of the imperial presence at subsequent special ceremonies (Yui, Fujiwara, and Yoshida, eds. [1989] 1996: 63–64).

Murakami (1993) argues that by constructing the shrine the government adopted a clever strategy to utilize the long-standing Japanese belief in the soul and in ancestor worship. The military state transformed this family-based belief and practice into a nationwide system promoting the notion that all the Japanese constitute one family under the emperor, for whose cause soldiers should die happily but be rewarded by their apotheosis at the shrine where the emperor pays his visits.

My interpretation is that the full-fledged *pro rege et patria mori* ideology was not established until much later. The social agents involved in the establishment of Yasukuni Shrine were far more concerned with the souls of their fallen comrades. As Najita (personal communication, November 1998) emphasizes, they would not have been oligarchs had their comrades not died in battle or been victims of assassination, like Ōmura himself. Ōmura was responding to the reality that a number of ceremonies were already taking place throughout Japan to appease and console the souls of those whose sacrifice made the Meiji "Restoration" possible. At the Yasukuni Shrine compound cherry trees were planted and fireworks, sumo performances, circuses, and various other forms of entertainment were put on to console the souls.[36]

Nevertheless, it was an ominous beginning, providing an opening for the shrine to play a significant role in the march toward *pro rege et patria mori*. The actors involved in the construction of the shrine were all major figures in building the new military. From the beginning, the army, which was responsible in later years for leading Japan toward imperialism and militarism, was in charge. Army officials even refused to have a regular high priest officiate at the shrine. Instead, for each ceremony, an appropriate army or navy officer was chosen to be the officiant. The prayer offered by the "Military High Priest" in his inaugural ceremony repeatedly stressed loyalty to the emperor and praised those who died in his name.

"DIVINE KING/KINGSHIP": RELIGIOUS/SYMBOLIC DIMENSIONS

Two expressions were used to describe the sovereignty of the emperor: "divine" and "inviolable" (legibus solutus; absolved from the law). As with the case of kings in Western nations who were defined as "inviolable" in their constitutions, the term "inviolable" had a definite political function—it exempted the emperor of all political responsibilities. The term "sacred/divine" *(shinsei)* was another matter. Mosse opposed including this definition of the emperor on the grounds that the king (emperor) as sacred has no legal consequence (quoted in Inada 1960: 8). Nonetheless, the codification of the emperor as sacred represented a fundamental change in the nature of the emperor.

The newly assigned sovereignty of the emperor in the Meiji constitution cannot be fully understood without consideration, first, of the nature of the pre-Meiji emperor, and, second, of the meaning of the sacred in the context of Japanese religiosity.

The Emperor in Pre-Meiji Japan

In order to overthrow the shogunate, the oligarchs used the rhetoric of the "restoration of the ancient imperial system" *(kodai ōchō)*. However, in reality they instituted an entirely new imperial system best suited for a strong central government to ward off the foreign barbarians.

The political economy of the so-called "ancient imperial system" *(kodai ōchō)* was based on wet rice agriculture, introduced to Japan around 350 B.C.[37] Drawing on folk cosmologies at the time, the Yamato state gradually established an agrarian cosmology. The early agrarian leaders, like the early emperors, were magico-religious leaders, i.e., shamans qua political leaders, whose political power rested upon an ability to solicit supernatural powers to ensure a good crop. They were human beings endowed with extraordinary power to communicate with deities. Thus, the annual harvest ritual was in fact a ritual to legitimate a local political leader, ensure the leader's symbolic rebirth, and rejuvenate his power (Murakami 1977: 4–6). For this reason many scholars consider the emperor first and foremost as "the officiant in rituals for the rice soul" *(inadama no shusaisha)* who ensures the blessing of the deities for the new rice crop on behalf of the humans (e.g. Akasaka 1988; Hora 1979, 1984; M. Inoue 1984; Miyata 1988: 193–94; Murakami 1977, 1986; Okada 1970; Yamaori 1978; Yanagita [1946] 1982: 133–34).[38] Since the mid-seventh century, if not before, and even today, the core imperial rituals officiated by the emperor, including the accession ritual, are all related to rice harvesting.[39]

The ancient imperial system definitely represented theocracy in that the emperor was both a religious and a political leader. However, one cannot overstate the point that it was not a divine kingship, for the emperor was a *kami*, a deity in the Japanese pantheon, not Almighty God.

Having reached its zenith during the eighth century, the imperial system lost its power by the end of the ancient period (300 B.C.–A.D. 1185). During the medieval (1185–1603) and Tokugawa (1603–1868) periods the emperors often could not hold the imperial rituals for financial and political reasons. Between 1464 and 1687, that is, during the reign of nine emperors, no accession ritual *(ōnamesai)* was held, and during other periods it was often held on a reduced scale (Hashimoto 1988).

What remained constant was the emperor's identity as a deity *(kami)* in the Japanese sense.[40] The kami have been both human and super-human, requiring a complex and fluid understanding of both the sacred and the profane. In Japanese cosmology, both deities and humans have dual characters and powers: good and evil, constructive and destructive, etc. (Ohnuki-Tierney 1987: 130–40). The concept of "human deity" *(hitogami)* is central in this cosmology, where humans and deities occupy a continuum (Ozawa 1987). Shamans, like emperors in early history, are considered to be humans with extraordinary supernatural power to communicate with deities and to solicit their power for the benefit of humans.

Deities have always been at the mercy of human manipulation, and the Japanese have aggressively shaped their pantheon by assigning certain functions *(goriyaku)* to them, such as ensuring a good crop of rice. Inefficacious deities are abandoned (Ohnuki-Tierney 1984: 153). Yet, the kami can and will exercise power over humans, both positively and negatively; hence the Japanese have always made sure to properly perform rituals so as not to incur their wrath.

Since the kami are like humans, emperors as kami have also been humans to most Japanese, though some did think and continue to think that they are special. Many "folktales" point out the humanness of the emperors. For example, as crown prince, Sakuramachi (r. 1735–47) acquired a taste for *soba*—noodles made of buckwheat. As emperor, he became the official guardian of the rice crops and could no longer eat other grains, which were considered inferior to rice. Nor could he receive moxibustion—the healing technique that uses lighted cones of artemisia placed on certain spots of the body—because no foreign objects could touch his "crystal body." Immediately after he abdicated his throne, he resumed these pleasurable habits (Tsumura [1917] 1970: 65). This story states in no uncertain terms that a prince is an ordinary human; a prince *becomes* an emperor who can also revert back to being a mere human.

Japanese history after the ancient period is a succession of usurpations of imperial authority by political and military leaders. Most daring was the banishing of emperors and ex-emperors by the shoguns.[41] Yet, some military leaders seemed to recognize the limitations of their strictly secular power. At the height of the Fujiwara oligarchy, Fujiwara Michinaga (966–1027), the greatest of the regents, expressed his sentiments: "Great as are our power and prestige, nevertheless they are those of the Sovereign, for we derive them from the majesty of the Throne" (Tsuchida 1983: 299; Sansom 1958: 157).[42]

Dramatic instances revealing these warriors' recognition of the power of kami occurred when they demanded apotheosis for themselves. Thus Toyotomi Hideyoshi, the military leader who in 1590 succeeded in uniting Japan for the first time, asked the imperial court to deify him as

Toyokuni Daimyōjin. His life as a deity was short-lived, however, and his descendants were unable to enjoy divine status. Upon his death, his rival, Tokugawa Ieyasu, defeated the Toyotomi clan and asked, or more accurately, ordered, the imperial court to retract the divinity previously granted to Hideyoshi. Furthermore, in his will, Tokugawa Ieyasu, the most powerful of all shoguns, asked the imperial court to deify him as Tōshō Daigongen, and his "divinity" became the bulwark of shogunate power for the next 250 years (Inoue [1963] 1967, 1: 258–59).

From the perspective of power, the normative hierarchy of beings in the universe consists, in ascending order, of humans, shaman-emperors, and deities. Hideyoshi's and Ieyasu's orders that the emperors deify them constituted an inversion of this hierarchy—these humans bestowed upon the emperor the power to create deities out of mere humans, quite an extraordinary feat. Likewise, the human architects of the imperial system during the Meiji period assigned themselves—mere humans—the power to create a bona fide deity out of an emperor. Such "inversions" of the hierarchy are, however, embedded in Japanese religiosity, where the hierarchy of supernatural beings is neither fixed nor linear. Thus, in Japanese religiosity an ordinary human can assign divinity even to a toothpick (Miyata 1975).[43]

From the perspective of the people, they had little to do with the emperor or the imperial system because the country had never been politically united by the imperial system and lacked modes of fast communication to reach the people from the center. The emperor (and a few empresses) remained an indirect figure, primarily viewed as the controller of rituals (Miyata 1992). Though never put in print, Bellah famously proclaimed that the Japanese emperor stood for the feminine principle, whereas the shoguns stood for the masculine principle, representing military matters. After the ancient period, the emperors were stripped of their political and military roles, which became the business of successive shoguns.

The Divine Emperor of the Meiji Era

It was von Stein who emphasized the need of a religion for modern Japan. He argued that since the Japanese did not have a religion comparable to Christianity, Shintoism, which had been closely associated with the imperial household since mythological times, should be transformed into a "substitute *(daiyō)* for religion." In order to foster respect for and worship of the emperor, he added, Japan must create rituals for all occasions through which the folk would unconsciously subscribe to the new imperial system, some of which were introduced above (Inoue [1953] 1967: 70; see also Inada 1962: 567–68).

While the political significance of the two key terms *shinsei* ("sacred," "divine") and *okasubekarazu* ("inviolable") in Article 3 was fairly clear cut, as they were to relieve the emperor of any political responsibility, their religious meaning is far from clear, with scholarly interpretations ranging widely in the past and at present (Satomi 1972: 652).[44] What is clear is that in religious terms, the Pledge, Article 1, and Article 3 assigned the emperor the divinity whose power surpassed that of the European monarchs, who provided a model for Japan. European monarchs, including Louis XIV, were never divine themselves. Rather, they were only a conduit for the divine power, always serving "by the Grace/Will of God." In contrast, the Japanese emperor became God by possessing *the* divine soul. The emperor was officially transformed from *a* deity (kami) in the pantheon whom people had traditionally manipulated, into *the* Deity endowed with sacredness and inviolability—a completely alien notion to the Japanese. In the constitution, Itō, Inoue, and others thus ascribed a "divinity" hitherto unprecedented, in Japan and elsewhere, to the emperor. Furthermore, through the assignment of the divine soul, the oligarchs solved the problem of the king's two bodies, as Kantorowicz famously called it, by guaranteeing the perpetuity for eternity of both the individual emperor and the imperial system, regardless of the death of individual emperors (Kantorowicz [1957] 1981). The divine emperor, however, is bound to Japan, a political unit, unlike the Christian God, who transcends political boundaries.

Although I have used the anthropological terms "divine king" and "divine kingship," my intention was not to superimpose any type of divinity on the Japanese emperor. Rather, I use the Japanese example to push the argument that the "divine," "sacred," "holy," etc. must be understood in terms of a specific religiosity. Originally developed by Frazer ([1890] 1911–15), the "divine kingship" was once a central issue in anthropology. Scholars have questioned the evidence for Frazer's proposition and its universal applicability, since it was based on the notion of God in the orthodox Judeo-Christian tradition, which, in comparative perspective, is "unique" as a notion of the sacred, as Redfield argues ([1953] 1959: 102).[45]

National Religion and National Rituals

The institutionalization of theocracy was established by elevating folk shinto into national religion. This newly institutionalized "national religion," the term I use in this book, was referred to as "State Shinto-ism" by the Occupational Forces after World War II, who viewed it as a culprit responsible for Japan's role in World War II and thus ordered the Japanese government to ban it on December 25, 1945. In postwar discourse, the Japanese have translated it as *kokka shintō* ("national shinto-ism") and have used it frequently (Murakami 1977: 132–40; Miyata 1999: 41, 48 objects to the use of this phrase).

At any rate, the government created a new religious institution. With the Ise Shrine and the Yasukuni *National* Shrine at the apex, the government placed some 170,000 shrines under the direct control of the imperial household and ordered that their rituals had to be coordinated with the grand national shrines. The creation of national shrines was accompanied by the persecution of other religious beliefs and practices. In 1870 an imperial edict was issued to promote Shintoism and to eliminate "foreign religions" *(gaikyō)* that had "plagued" the nation since the medieval period, with Buddhism as the prime target but Confucianism and Christianity as targets as well (Shibata 1978: 101–2). Although the notion of "Abolition of Buddhist Doctrines and Discarding of Buddha's Teaching" *(haibutsu kishaku)* had slowly begun to develop before the Meiji period (Tamamuro 1939), the Meiji government lent its institutional support. The government issued an ordinance prohibiting Buddhist practices such as ringing of the gong or reciting sutras. Instead, the people were told to pray to the Shinto deities (Murakami 1977: 68–69). The initial intensity for the reconstruction of the Japanese religious system, however, was not sustained, and the 1887 revision restricted state support for imperial and national shrines.

Most Japanese were not aware of these new changes until around 1900. In the euphoria over Japan's victories in the Sino-Japanese (1894–95) and Russo-Japanese (1904–5) wars, many Japanese began to become willing participants in the governmental program on religion. In 1906 the state launched a plan to control village life by officially recognizing only one shrine per village (Hardacre 1989: 33, 39) and in 1908 the state issued a manual *(Kōshitsu-saishi-rei)* that instituted a large number of imperial rituals. In addition to the rituals associated with rice, which had been almost the only rituals officiated by the emperor in the past, they established others to buttress the newly created nature of the emperor (Okada 1997; Murakami 1977: 157–66).

We recall that ritual was at the core of the characterization of the emperor in ancient Japan. However, the rituals instituted at the beginning of the Meji period were for completely different purposes. The ancient imperial rituals were intended to ensure a good harvest for the people and were not for the public to see. In fact the most crucial part of the imperial accession ritual has always been performed in secrecy, including the one for the current Heisei emperor (Ohnuki-Tierney 1993a). In contrast, the rituals instituted in the Meiji period were means to create a theocracy and to unite the Japanese into one political body. Therefore the imperial rituals were synchronized with the newly instituted rituals in villages, schools, organizations, and national shrines.[46]

OPPOSITION

Opposition from the Liberals

Before the government finalized the constitution, many outside the government, especially those involved in the Freedom and Popular Rights Movement *(Jiyū minken undō)* and other liberal movements, who were hopeful for a new Japan, actively proposed their own visions for a new constitution. There were altogether sixty-six such draft proposals, plus seven additional partial drafts (Emura 1996: 438–42). Of the eight proposed constitutions drafted by those who were not government officials, three were quite liberal and did not define the emperor as sacred and inviolable, but the remaining five chose to define the emperor in these terms.[47]

Many intellectuals also voiced opposition to the Meiji constitution. Kume Kunitake, a historian of Japan and professor at the Imperial University of Tokyo, published an article in 1891, two years after the publication of the constitution, in which he claimed that Shintoism was an old-fashioned custom. He was stripped of his professorship (Inoue [1963] 1967, 2: 214). Japanese scholars who expressed divergent opinions were ignored or even banished. The proposal by Katō Hiroyuki, who defined the emperor as a human being just like other humans, was rejected outright (Emura 1996: 462–64). Ōkuma Shigenobu, a powerful government official, founded his model on the British constitution, an alternative model available for Japan at the time. Itō and Iwakura not only rejected his proposal but ousted him from the government.

In the cities, antigovernment movements continued in the form of Freedom and Popular Rights Movements. These movements sometimes mobilized farmers, as in the case of the Chichibu incident in 1884, in which five thousand people took arms in revolt against the government (Irokawa [1970] 1997: 172–203). Many continued to harbor suspicion and antagonism toward the Meiji government, showing sympathy toward the antigovernment folk hero Saigō Takamori, who had led the last rebellion against the Meiji government in the Seinan War in 1877 (Nishizawa 1990, 2: 1989–90). These sentiments were exacerbated by famines that struck farmers in northeastern Japan six times during the Meiji period, causing many deaths from starvation. Many men left the farms to find work in the cities, and women went to work in factories or even in urban houses of prostitution (Irokawa [1970] 1997: 250–56).

Espousing the Enlightenment philosophy, those who fought for the Freedom and Popular Rights Movements were nonetheless extremely patriotic. For example, at one of their gatherings, held on February 17, 1887, at Asakusa in Tokyo, the people in the movement composed a very patriotic song that praised the Japanese soul and advised the Japanese not to imitate the West and to sacrifice themselves for the country, although not for the emperor (Nakayama, ed. 1982b: 537).

Opposition from Meiji Christian Leaders

Another type of opposition against the government and its constitution came from influential Christians (Yamaji [1906] 2000; Yamazumi [1990] 1996: 385–407). Roman Catholicism was brought to Japan in 1549 by Francis Xavier, of the Society of Jesus, while Protestantism was introduced by American missionaries only after 1858, and Greek Orthodoxy was brought by Father Nikolai (Ioan Kasatkin) of Russia in 1861. In general, the Greek Orthodox and Catholics did not disagree with national religion, but Protestants, the most influential among the Christians during the early Meiji era, opposed it on doctrinal grounds (Murakami 1970: 226–27; Ōuchi 1996).

The five most influential Christians during the Meiji period were Uchimura Kanzō (1861–1930), Uemura Masahisa (1857–1925), Ebina Danjō (1856–1937), Honda Yōitsu (1848–1912), and Nitobe Inazō (1862–1933). All came from the warrior class and had a solid education in Confucianism. All converted to Protestantism, but it is hard to categorize them in terms of denomination since most of them established their own forms of Christianity. For example, Nitobe Inazō, Uchimura Kanzō, and Honda Yōitsu were all baptized in Methodist churches, but Nitobe became a member of the Society of Friends (Quaker), whereas Uchimura turned to non-church Christianity. Uemura advocated nondenominational Christianity, and Ebina offered his own interpretation of Christianity. Honda remained a Methodist.

Uchimura taught at the First Higher School (Ikkō), where the intellectual crème de la crème at the time were educated (see Moore, ed. 1981). He was fired when he refused to bow toward the emperor's signature on the Imperial Rescript on Education when, on January 9, 1891, the school celebrated the issuance of the rescript on October 30, 1890. The incident came to be labeled "The Incident of Disrespect by Uchimura Kanzō" *(Uchimura Kanzō Fukei Jiken)*, and it caused a great deal of public reaction. The incident alerted the government, which started to persecute Christians. Many Christians began to compromise with the government and to accept the new ideology in regard to the emperor. Uchimura did not believe even in the institutionalized Christian church. He maintained that Christians must fight against and free themselves from political authority in Japan as well as from Western and Japanese church establishments. He advocated freedom from governmental authority, peers, business people, and educators. Only then could people achieve a state of mind in which they truly loved their country and translate this into the love of God. Uchimura was also vociferous in his opposition to the Russo-Japanese War and remained a staunch pacifist (Barshay 1988: 54– 59; Ōuchi 1995; Kano 1995).

His disciples kept up the antiwar spirit well into World War II. Yanaihara Tadao (1893–1961) converted to non-church Christianity under Uchimura's influence and repeatedly opposed the government's policy of colonization and most vocally opposed militarization. In 1937, he was forced to resign from the post of professor at the Imperial University of Tokyo. Nambara Shigeru (1889–1974) too was converted to non-church Christianity under Uchimura's influence and became a student of Kant and Fichte. In 1945 he became president of the newly restructured University of Tokyo. It was he who edited the first collection of the writings by the University of Tokyo students who died in the war.

Since the First Higher School produced those who later became leading intellectuals, Uchimura's legacy and intellectual influence remained powerful even among those who were not at the higher school at the time. He became a towering intellectual figure well beyond Christian circles, as testified by frequent references to him in the writings of many student soldiers, including non-Christians (chapter 6).

Another pillar of Christianity, Uemura Masahisa, fought to free Japanese Christianity both from Meiji political authority and from foreign missions. Through the journal *Fukuin Shūhō* (The Weekly Gospel), which he established in 1890, he severely criticized the government for apotheosizing the emperor through improper rituals and in the Imperial Rescript on Education. The government immediately banned his journal. The following year he renamed it *Fukuin Shinpō* (The New Report on the Gospel) and continued to oppose the government's policy of the apotheosis of the emperor (Fukuyama 1995; Yamazumi [1990] 1996:

393–96). Sekioka compellingly argues that Ebina Danjō, often criticized for his "chauvinism" *(kokusui shugi)*, too firmly believed in internationalism, denounced Shintoism as "primitive" and "chauvinistic," and did not support the apotheosis of the emperor (Sekioka 1995). Thus, all fought against the deification of the emperor, except Nitobe, the inventor of the Meiji *bushidō* (the warrior's way).

As exemplified by these major figures, most Christians in Meiji Japan, like the liberals, were patriotic. However, their patriotism did not translate into embracing the imperial ideology surrounding the apotheosis of the emperor. Nor did it lead to the endorsement of militarism. Also, their patriotism was far from any form of chauvinism. All espoused internationalism and love of humanity and simultaneously the feeling of loyalty to their country—views akin to the moral and political pluralism and nonaggressive nationalism of Herder and Berlin.

Opposition from Labor Unions and Communists

In addition to the intellectual and political elites, many common folk also continued to oppose the government even after Japan entered a period of accelerated militarism in the wake of its victorious wars against China and Russia. Although the Japanese Communist Party was illegally formed only in 1922 as a branch of the Komintern (The Third International), the labor movement and precursors of communism were quite active already around the turn of the century. Relevant to the topic of this book is that the very first May Day demonstration in Japan took place in 1901 by the newly formed labor union, called Heiminsha (Commoners' Group). An account of the event on April 2 differs in nature from an account for April 3, although both point to the involvement of cherry blossoms. On April 2, 1901, the labor union publicized a "Cherry Blossom Viewing by Laborers" *(Rōdōsha Kan'ōkai)*. The public announcement directed the members to bring their red flags and to assemble at Takeno-dai at Ueno Park, a well-known site for cherry blossom viewing, at the sound of the gun which signals noon every day. The posted announcement was designed to divert the police, which had repeatedly cracked down on the movement. It led the police to Ueno Park, while the demonstrators took to the main streets of Tokyo, starting with Ginza, Kyōbashi, Nihonbashi, Imagawabashi, and Kanda, where they beat on their large drums painted in red and waved their red flags on which were written "Hail to Socialism" *(Shakaishugi Banzai)* and "Group to Propagate Socialism" *(Shakaishugi Dendōtai)*. At Kanda they broke into small groups and headed to Ueno Park. At the sound of the gun signaling noon, they all dashed to Takeno-dai at Ueno Park, shouting "Hail to Socialism." At that point several tens of police in uniform and secret police in civilian clothes appeared. A scuffle followed, and thirty-one men were arrested and seven retained at the police station until the evening (Ōkōchi and Matsuo 1965: 159–62).

The event of the following day, April 3, is reported much differently (Wakamori 1975: 186; no source cited). About thirty newly formed labor unions in Tokyo and Yokohama gathered together under cherry blossoms, some wearing hats in the shape of sea bream. They hailed the emperor and sang the national anthem. Wakamori suggests that the tradition of cherry blossom viewing to establish ritual kinship led to this occasion during which labor union members consolidated their solidarity.

At any rate, the labor union—a radical movement purported to bring about a "revolution"—used cherry blossom viewing as the occasion for their demonstration. It was a convenient time and place, with large crowds that made their demonstration less conspicuous. Also, cherry blossom viewing has always been a space/time pregnant with possibilities (chapter 1).

THE CATALYST FOR THE DEVELOPMENT OF MILITARISM

The catalyst that transformed people's ambivalence and often strong opposition toward the state effort to build a morally and psychologically unified "national polity" *(kokutai)* was Japan's victory in two wars, the Sino-Japanese War (1894–95) and the Russo-Japanese War (1904–5) (Nishizawa 1990, 2: 1989). At the time of Japan's victory in 1895 over China, many Europeans and Americans did not even know where Japan was located or thought that it was one of the provinces of China. China possessed battleships and submarines totaling 85,000 tons, while Japan had only 59,000 tons (Nishizawa 1990, 2: 1994–95).[48] Many Japanese began to rally together, and something close to *Volksgemeinschaft* (community of people) developed.

Breaking with a long tradition of Japanese adoration of Chinese civilization, songs of the time are full of the rudest insults and ridicule of the Chinese (chapter 4), on the one hand, and, on the other, the most patriotic phrases extolling the virtues of Japanese soldiers, both alive and dead. Given that the Japanese did not believe that Japan could beat mighty China, the revered Other for centuries, Japan's victory suddenly made many of them arrogant and downright contemptuous toward the Chinese, an attitude that was orchestrated by state propaganda.

Japan's victory over China was followed by its victory over Russia in 1905, the very first victory of an Asian nation over a Western nation—for the Japanese, Russia unambiguously belonged to the West. This victory spared Japan from falling into the hands of Western colonialism. It also stirred considerable excitement and foretold the dawn of movements against Western colonial powers in Africa and many parts of Asia (Irokawa [1970] 1997: 245).

Having succeeded in blunting the forces of opposition among people through these victories, the military state was free to become another colonial power over its Asian neighbors, thus betraying the pan-Asianism spirit with which the latter had responded to the first victory by an Asian nation over a Western nation. The state took advantage of the euphoric feelings of the Japanese folk over their unexpected victories by igniting their patriotic feelings and trying to stamp out any opposition. The machinery of militarism began to pick up speed.

At the basis of the military's gaining of power was the constitution, which gave it a direct access to the emperor. However, two major issues of the Meiji constitution remained ambiguous and could have checked the power of military. They were: (1) the locus of sovereignty—whether it should be with the emperor or with the nation; and (2) the limit of the power of sovereignty. On the one hand, Hozumi Yatsuka and his heir Uesugi Shinkichi championed the view, known as the "imperial sovereign authority" *(tennō shuken setsu),* that the limitless power of sovereignty should reside in the emperor. Minobe Tatsukichi was a vociferous representative of the other view, known as the "organ theory" *(tennō kikan setsu),* which argued that sovereignty rests in the state, of which the emperor was a mere organ or mechanism. These issues, however, did not concern the liberals of the Taishō period (1912–26) who thought them to be unrelated to political realities (Duus 1988). The final victory for those in support of a monarchical sovereign was won in 1935, when Minobe was given the sentence of "irreverence to the emperor" *(fukei-zai),* which compelled him to resign from the House of Peers and other official posts. A year earlier in 1934 his publications had been banned, despite strong support for Minobe among the academics, intellectuals, and even bureaucrats (Nagao 1996). The emperor's chamberlain notes in his diary that the emperor stated that he would be comfortable with the organ theory (Toriumi 1996).

By this time the right wing and the military had gained power (see also Ienaga 1996; Nagao 1995). Even the so-called Taishō democracy—

democracy during the Taishō period (1912–26)—in fact was an "imperial democracy" (A. Gordon 1991: 5–10). Under the leadership of Tachibana Kōzaburō (1893–1974), "agricultural fascism" became active in 1927, culminating in an unsuccessful coup d'état in 1932, while in 1930 the Cherry Blossom Society was formed by young ultra-right army officers under the leadership of Hashimoto Kingorō.

Coercion and co-opting of intellectuals, including prominent literary figures, by the military state accelerated, with considerable success. Jay Rubin, a scholar and an admirer of Tanizaki Junichirō's work, was appalled by the depth of the coercion when he realized that even Tanizaki was forced to write in 1943 a piece in support of the war effort: "In order to induce a writer like Tanizaki to compose this feeble page of print, successive governments had invested countless man-hours and millions of yen in decades of legislation, committee work, police and administrative actions, trials, and schemes for indoctrinating, coddling, and brutally coercing the Japanese people" (Rubin 1984: 277–78).

THE EMPEROR AS ABSOLUTE SOVEREIGN AND MILITARY COMMANDER: THE BLUEPRINT FOR *PRO REGE ET PATRIA MORI*

After the overthrow of the shogunate, the oligarchs were groping in the dark for direction, as Najita (1979: 88–128) points out. The Meiji oligarchs were not simple-minded patriots. Like the tokkōtai pilots, they were intellectual cosmopolitans, who nonetheless identified the most critical need for Japan at the time to be the building and fortification of Japan as a modern state against Western colonialism. The final version of the Meiji constitution was nominally a result of consultation by the key Meiji oligarchs with foreign scholars. Yet far from being mere puppets of foreign scholars, Itō Hirobumi and Inoue Kowashi, together with Iwakura Tomomi, Ōkubo Toshimichi, Yamagata Aritomo, and others (Emura 1996: 482–83) were the real agents of history. Their guiding principle has always been *jōi*—expel foreign enemies—which meant to establish a strong modern state with sovereignty. Therefore, they quite decisively rejected French Bonapartism and the British parliamentary system and chose to follow the Prussian model. Their goal also led them to agree in the end with Roesler's suggestion to specify the emperor's roles in the constitution in order to avoid conflicts in the future. They also followed von Stein's suggestion to build a state religion headed by the emperor as father. That they were the historical agents is most conspicuously expressed in their rejection of the strenuous objection by every foreign consultant—not only did they instituted Article 1 but positioned it at the very beginning of the constitution, thus codifying the emperor as Japanese sui generis, rather than a copy of European monarchy.

At the time Japan was modernizing, the Meiji oligarchs established an absolute monarchical sovereignty directly in command of the military (Inoue [1953] 1967: 111). The three most important documents in this regard were the Constitution of Imperial Japan, the Pledge, and the Imperial Rescript to Soldiers. Together, they created a new emperor and a emperor system characterized by: (1) Divinity assigned to the king/emperor and the imperial system, thereby guaranteeing the emperor's two bodies (the individual emperor and the imperial system); (2) an "inviolable" emperor above politics; (3) the emperor as commander of the military; and (4) the primordiality of the kingship and thus of Japan and the Japanese.

As the new constitution served the purpose of defining the religious and military powers of the emperor, the Imperial Rescript to Soldiers, issued before the constitution, established the notion of sacrifice in which a soldier's death was as light as a feather, in contrast to his obligation to the emperor, which was as heavy as the mountains. In addition, the Imperial Rescript on Education gave the basic foundation for the later development of a polity in which the emperor was the father who reigned over the national body, requiring that care for parents be overridden by loyalty to the emperor, now the national father.

However, the Meiji oligarchs who were directly involved in the drafting of the constitution had no intention of giving the emperor unlimited power, religious, administrative, or military. The new emperor was their ultimate choice for the purpose of controlling political unrest within and Western colonialism without. Thus, their aim was simply to redefine the emperor so that *they* could control both the internal unrest and the foreign threats by using the emperor as though he were an honorable crystal ball in their palms. However, the specificities of the emperor's roles inscribed in the constitution gave legitimacy to the independence of each state organ, which had direct access to the emperor, who, by the 1930s was assigned an infinite power as "sovereign" and who was yet vulnerable to the manipulation of a state organ without checks by other state organs. The military in particular was "insulated from overt political patronage by constitutional provisions ensuring virtual independence from the civilian branches of the government" (Berger 1988: 99–100). We see a dire implication of the decision by the oligarchs to follow Roesler, instead of Mosse whose view they shared. Mosse's suggestion to place the specific roles of the emperor in the preamble would not have given such a free hand for the military and other state organs to abuse the power of the sovereign for their own advantages.

Aside from the political and military leaders as historical agents, the three emperors—Meiji, Taishō, and Shōwa—were quite different as historical agents. The topic is too complex to introduce here, but let me mention only that among scholars it is the Shōwa emperor to whom some historians assign more power of agency than to the other emperors. The Taishō emperor being feeble, he hardly mattered (see below). Inoue ([1953] 1967: 174–75, 237) argues that the Meiji emperor played a role in suppressing the liberal movements and promoting the Sino-Japanese and Russo-Japanese wars. However, he holds the Shōwa emperor to be responsible for siding with Tōjō and going to war despite opposition from Konoe, Kido, and others. He also writes that the emperor signed the Potsdam declaration only to protect his position. Irokawa (1993: 110–11) likewise puts responsibility onto the Shōwa emperor for postponing the surrender in order to save his position, thereby causing another atomic bomb to fall on Nagasaki.

From the perspective of the Japanese, emperors have always remained humans. The Meiji Japanese, who were proud of being born during the Meiji period, talked about him quite fondly in human terms. Men emulated the emperor by wearing a Kaiser mustache, and they gossiped about his liking for women of all ages. A standard joke among the people concerning Taishō, well-known to have been mentally feeble, was that he rolled up a document that a minister handed him, put it against his eye like a telescope, and looked around. To avoid further embarrassment, the crown prince, Shōwa, took over his father's official functions. The portrayals of the Japanese bowing to the ground in front of the emperor or of the imperial castle in postwar American mass media seem an unwitting reification of the propaganda by the Japanese right wingers. A conspicuous example of humanity assigned to Shōwa is the "image" of the emperor as a serious "biologist," eagerly propagated by the political leaders and mass media. They wished to promote the "modern emperor" image in accordance with the country's effort for modernization, which was epitomized, for the Japanese, in Western science and technology. Surely, from the perspective of native Shintoism and even Buddhism, the emperor's gaze into a microscope would have been an intensive examination of deified beings of nature, himself included—an interpretation which did not cross anyone's mind. He was presented as a modern man interested in science.

The Japanese daily watched on television the condition of Shōwa's health during his last months in late 1988 and in the beginning of 1989 (Ohnuki-Tierney 1984: 51–74). Repeated blood transfusions were reported as well. His "royal blood" was replaced several times, and replaced by not-so-blue blood rumored to have been "donated" by young men from the defense forces. Yet this dramatic event of the exchange of "blue blood" for common blood did not receive much attention—a clear sign of the recognition of the human emperor.

For the Japanese folk, neither the emperor nor the imperial system has ever been "divine," if the term is to imply an ascription of absolute divinity to the kingship. We are reminded that "the divine kingship" has existed for the most part in the imagination of anthropologists, and not in those African and other kingships (Feeley-Harnik 1985: 276).

Postwar scholars tried to explain the people and factors responsible for Japan's road to catastrophe. Some prominent scholars claimed the modus operandi to be the "*tennōsei* ideology" (ideology of the emperor system). Right after the war, the late Maruyama Masao, a prominent intellectual historian, proposed in a famous essay that the Japanese thought process was "a tradition without a structure" *(mukōzō no dentō)* and thus prone to accommodate any number of different traditions, including ultra-nationalism with the *tennōsei* ideology, which cast and continue to cast "multiple layers of invisible nets" over the people (Maruyama 1946). Irokawa Daikichi used Marx's camera obscura: "The emperor system as a conceptual structure is a large invisible box. The Japanese, both the intellectuals and the masses, entered this box whose four corners were invisible and died in agony without even understanding why they must suffer so much" (Irokawa [1990] 1997: 281). Nonetheless, the term *tennōsei* ideology and what it stands for, however defined, were established ex post facto (Gluck 1985: 5–6).

Above I tried to show that the Constitution of Imperial Japan, the Pledge, and the Imperial Rescript to Soldiers provided the structural base for the building of *Ein Volk, ein Reich, und ein Führer* and a road to *pro rege et patria mori*. The Imperial Rescript on Education became the major conduit for propagating the message, even though what happened in later years was not what the Meiji oligarchs intended. The early 1930s witnessed a solid consolidation of state programming for *pro rege et patria mori*, as evidenced in *The Loyal Souls at the Yasukuni Shrine*, published between 1933 to 1935, and the expulsion of Minobe who championed the "organ theory" of the emperor. In the remaining chapters in Part II, I try to elucidate a complex story of how this basic structural possibility was materialized by different actors with different intentions during extremely turbulent periods of history when the Japanese had to struggle to both modernize and westernize their country, while resisting Western colonialism, both cultural and political. A grand plan was not laid out in the beginning. Yet, the thought processes and the institutional build-up that led to *pro rege et patria mori* were neither amorphous nor mysterious.

Chapter 3

THE MILITARIZATION

OF CHERRY BLOSSOMS:

CHERRY BLOSSOMS AS THE

SOULS OF FALLEN SOLDIERS

After introducing in the last chapter the fundamental changes made in the political structure of Japan, I now return to how successive state machineries deployed cherry blossoms as the dominant political *and* military symbol. The period covered starts with the beginning of the Meiji era, when Japan began its modernization, industrialization, militarization, and Westernization, all at the same time and with great urgency. The two external wars, the Sino-Japanese War (1894–95) and the Russo-Japanese War (1904–5), managed to quench internal conflicts that were endemic at the beginning of the Meiji period and gave the military clique an opportunity to seize political power. These events had a significant impact—after all, the Japanese had won over the Chinese, the first significant Other, and the Russians, the first "Westerners" to be defeated by an Asian people. With the military seizing power and a euphoric mood over the victories among many Japanese, the military state soon began to invade and colonize other Asian nations. There was a brief period of so-called "Taishō democracy," under the leadership of Hara Takashi (known as Hara Kei), when in 1918 Hara, then the prime minister, initiated over a decade of party government. Liberalism prevailed, although Andrew Gordon (1991) cautions us regarding this interpretation by calling this period one of "imperial democracy." But in the mid-1920s, as the Shōwa period began, Japan headed for totalitarianism within and colonial expansion without, beginning with the Manchurian Incident in 1931, and its military insanity culminated in World War II.

Each section of the chapter involves the entire period. I chose this organizational scheme because the militarization of cherry blossoms simply does not follow a linear temporal progression. The picture is complex, with cherry blossoms conveying several meanings, expressed in different mediums, at any given period, with, however, a gradual shift toward the meanings defined in the context of progressive militarism, imperialism, and colonialism in a complex interplay of mutual predication. I must beg the reader's patience in going through each of these decades for each genre. The two stages of the changing meaning of cherry blossoms are the following:

Stage I: Contestation: Cherry blossoms as feudal Japan vs. new Japan in the early Meiji period

Stage II: Simultaneous presence of three meanings, all expressive of nationalism

   A. Cultural nationalism: Blooming cherry blossoms as the Japanese soul

   B1. Political nationalism: Blooming cherry blossoms as Japanese soldiers

   B2. Political nationalism: Falling cherry blossoms as fallen soldiers

Stage I is presented briefly to show how the meaning of cherry blossoms was in flux as Japan emerged from the shogunate era. The three phases in stage II do not constitute a linear sequence. Rather, after each was established, they existed simultaneously like palimpsests. It is important to recognize the profound differences among the three in order to understand the power of naturalization—even profoundly different meanings are merged together in this process.

CONTESTED SELVES OF THE "MODERN" JAPANESE: TWO MEANINGS OF CHERRY BLOSSOMS IN THE EARLY MEIJI PERIOD

Within a few years after the beginning of the Meiji period, when the government as well as the people were thrust into the "modernization" effort, cherry blossoms as a symbol of Japan became a dominant trope in public discourse. Some proponents of "modern Japan" claimed that the hitherto popular expression "Cherry blossoms among flowers and warriors among people" suggested that cherry blossoms embodied the essence of feudalism, symbolizing the undesirable past (Yamada Mune-mutsu 1977: 115). Some began chopping down and burning cherry trees. Some in the lumber business began stressing the limited utilitarian value of the tree and advocated its replacement with other trees better suited as lumber material or with the camphor tree—the manufacture of camphor was a burgeoning industry at the time.

At the same time, enthusiastic supporters of another but equally "modern" Japan went out of their way to protect cherry trees. An even stronger force was a series of developments that actively elicited cherry blossoms for the cause of political nationalism in general and military aggression in particular. The conflicting discourses surrounding cherry trees indeed tells us a story of this exciting but turbulent period.

For example, in 1871 at Yoshino—the most famous of all mountain areas for cherry trees—a man chosen to represent the residents explained to Dokura Shōzaburō, who, at age 31, was the most powerful tycoon of the lumber industry and a resident in Yoshino: "The government has decreed that we discard things of the past, resulting in fewer visitors to Yoshino and causing hardship to the villagers. A merchant from Ōsaka has offered ¥500 for all the cherry trees on the Yoshino Mountains. The villagers are all in agreement and have begun cutting down the cherry trees." The purpose of this man's visit was to request a supply of cedar and cypress seedlings to plant after the cherry trees were removed, since these trees would bring money to the villagers.

Startled, Dokura explained that now that the country had reopened, many foreigners would come to Japan, making cherry trees more important than ever. With his personal donation of ¥500, a sizable amount of money at the time, Dokura told the man to get rid of the merchant from Ōsaka.[1] Dokura was a powerful figure in business and politics, well known for his eloquent political speeches on many issues, including the importance of democracy. He was also an advocate for forestation, and he planted trees not only in Japan but, later, in 1905, in Taiwan (Suzuki et al. 1985: 48–51). In his view cherry blossoms continued to serve as Japan's national symbol. This episode not only portrays the extreme nature of the utilitarianism carried out under the banner of "Civilization and Enlightenment," but how individuals like Dokura selectively adopted aspects of Western civilization while retaining what he considered Japanese values and traditions.

With the establishment of Shintoism as the national religion and with the 1870 decree suppressing "foreign religions," the early years of the Meiji era saw a zealous effort to destroy Buddhist buildings and treasures at even the most famous temples, since they were doubly guilty—"non-utilitarian" and "foreign." In Kyoto, which has the largest number of temples, and in Nara the city governments confiscated a number of well-known temples, destroyed some, and forced others to become Shinto shrines (Saeki 1988).[2]

In this sweeping reconstitution of the religious establishment, a vast amount of land became empty. In Kyoto in 1886 what is known today as Maruyama Park was built on empty land where temples used to stand. During this process many cherry trees, some old and famous, were sold to people who in turn sold them as lumber. The famous weeping cherry tree *(shidare zakura)* that is the centerpiece in Maruyama Park today barely escaped such a fate, when Akashi Hirotaka passed by and preserved the tree by bribing the people who were about to cut it down (Kyōtoshi, ed. 1975: 274; see also Kyōtoshi, ed. 1981: 604–5).

While some people were chopping down cherry trees, others were busy planting them. In 1882 Kanda Hyōemon in Kōbe promoted the planting of cherry trees by staging a fund-raising event at Suma Temple, at which he offered out of his pocket ¥0.2 per person as the cost of planting one cherry tree. His effort received national attention and the support of prominent politicians such as Ōkubo Toshimichi, Makino Shinken, the businessman Fujita Denzaburō, and the famous navy officer Hirose Takeo (Yamada Munemutsu 1977: 115). Ōkubo was the most powerful of the Meiji oligarchs. Hirose led the Japanese assault on the Russian forces at Port Arthur *(Lüshun)* during the Russo-Japanese War and was deified after death as a "military god" *(gunshin)*. Kanda was involved in pro-Western activities and yet also served on a committee for the Imperial Navy (Naruse and Tsuchiya, eds. 1913: 3–4).

During the early Meiji era, then, while the state had already begun the militarization of cherry blossoms, even those close to the government differed in the meanings they ascribed to the flower—some held it to represent feudal Japan whereas others thought it stood for modern Japan.

CULTURAL NATIONALISMS, POLITICAL NATIONALISM, AND MILITARISM: BLOOMING CHERRIES AND FALLING PETALS

It is usually understood that Japan's militarism began to accelerate during the period between the Sino-Japanese and the Russo-Japanese wars and that it reached its height in the 1920s and 30s, setting the stage for World War II. To a large measure this is the case, but we will see that the wheel of militarization started to spin much earlier.

Before falling cherry petals came to signify the soldiers' sacrifice for the emperor, the meaning of cherry blossoms was transformed from a symbol of Japanese cultural nationalism to one of political nationalism. In these contexts, *blooming* cherry blossoms represented the soul and the beauty of the Japanese in general and of the soldiers in particular, since soldiers were made into the Japanese sui generis, embodying the Japanese soul.

The "sunny" meaning of cherry blossoms in the early Meiji period is found even in a passage from "The Moral Code of Soldiers" *(Heike Tokkō)* (Yui, Fujiwara, and Yoshida, eds. [1989] 1996: 149–62), a series of lectures given in 1878 by Nishi Amane, the major architect of the Japanese military at the time. Nishi equates cherry blossoms with the Japanese, rather than portraying them as a symbol of sacrifice. These lectures obviously were a draft of the Imperial Rescript to Soldiers of 1882, in which soldiers were told that their obligation to the country was as heavy as the mountains, but their own lives were as light as feathers (chapter 2). In these lectures, Nishi preached the importance of obedience and military hierarchy, using the French *obédience* and *hiérarchie militaire*. Despite his use of French, he emphasized that the Japanese army should not follow foreign models, and he portrayed the Japanese spirit through a reference to a very well-known poem by Motoori Norinaga (1730–1801), a prominent scholar of the Nativist School *(Kokugakusha)* and a major figure in the interpretation of *The Tale of Genji*. In this poem, written on his self-portrait when he was sixty years old (1790), Motoori ([1790] 1968: volume cover) equated the Japanese spirit with blooming mountain cherries under the morning sun: "If we are to ask about the spirit of the Japanese, it is mountain cherry blossoms that bloom fragrantly in the morning sun" (my translation). As several scholars have pointed out (e.g. Saitō [1979] 1985: 54; Toita 1982: 20; Yamada Munemutsu 1977: 117), in this poem Motoori Norinaga praises cherry blossoms as a celebration of life—the radiant beauty of mountain cherries as they bloom in the morning sun. The image has nothing to do with falling cherry petals, nor does it imply death in the slightest sense.

Some consider Motoori Norinaga to be responsible for establishing a link between cherry blossoms and the Japanese ethos of *monono aware*, the pathos of evanescence (chapter 1). However, in his voluminous work on *Genji* (e.g. Motoori [1799] 1969: 201–42), I could not find any systematic link between cherry blossoms and the ethos of pathos. His major thesis is that *monono aware* constitutes the essence of the Japanese literary and visual arts and that it is not a product either of the Buddhist world view or of Confucian doctrine (Motoori [1799] 1969: 25–26).

Returning to Nishi's lectures, we find his statement: "single-petaled cherry blossoms are unlike gaudy peonies, or pure and simple lotus flowers; cherry blossoms do no stay on the branches until rotten like camellia, or the rose of sharon; they are unlike Chinese date fruit *(yuzu)* which is not worth looking at." Given his patriotism, it is likely that Nishi intentionally referred to peonies, the emblem of China, and the rose of sharon, the emblem of Korea, as undesirable flowers; other patriotic figures of the Meiji era also expressed the superiority of the Japanese over the Chinese by using the metaphor of cherry blossoms vs. peonies. Nishi thought that Motoori's poem captured the Japanese spirit, which may be expressed in four characters: loyalty *(chū);* goodness/docility *(ryō; oto-nashiku);* straightforwardness *(eki);* and obedience *(choku).* For Nishi, these four characters represented the "unique" character of the Japanese.

A close reading of Nishi's passage indicates that although he advocated loyalty to the emperor without question, he did not emphasize "sacrifice" for the emperor as the goal. Similarly, in his metaphor of mountain cherry blossoms, it is blooming cherry blossoms that represent the Japanese virtues. However, it is noteworthy that Nishi stressed the "virtue" of cherry blossoms for "not clinging to their blooming," unlike other flowers, since to die without clinging to life *(isagiyoku shinu)* was a notion later mobilized by the state to convince soldiers to plunge into death.[3] In other words, Nishi was a major figure promoting soldiers' sacrifice for the emperor, but he did not develop the metaphor of falling cherry blossoms as a symbol of sacrifice or of blooming cherry blossoms as the souls of fallen soldiers.

My interpretation is that in the early Meiji period, cherry blossoms were invoked to stress the uniqueness of the Japanese and to develop "the Japanese soul" (yamato damashii) and thus were a powerful metaphor of cultural nationalism. Yet this is not the same as political nationalism, and it is distinct from militarism, in which falling cherry blossoms were analogous to soldiers' deaths.

The Yasukuni Shrine: From Blooming to Falling Cherry Blossoms

The Yasukuni Shrine played a key role in deploying the equation of cherry blossoms with soldiers' sacrifice for the emperor during the military period. The original purpose of the shrine on the part of the Meiji oligarchs were more benign. They wanted to console the souls of the fallen warriors who fought on the side of the "restoration."

As in other societies, the consolation of the souls of the dead often includes entertainment—performances of music, dance, etc. Thus, from the very beginning sumō wrestling, firecrackers, etc. were staged. In 1871, a French circus was performed, as depicted in a well-known woodblock print by Hiroshige III, and in 1877, 1878, and 1881 horse racing was staged, as depicted in prints.[4] Soon after the statue of Ōmura Masujirō, the major figure in promoting the construction of the shrine by the government, was erected in 1893, woodblock prints began to depict the statue surrounded by cherry blossoms in full bloom. In the prints women in kimonos, children, and officers stroll in the compound, apparently engaging in cherry blossom viewing. The best-known print, by Yōsai Nobukazu (1872–1944), was created in 1893 (reproduced in Yasukuni Jinja 1984: n.p.; see Tsubouchi 1999: 55, 57), the year before the Sino-Japanese war and the very year when Ōmura's statue was erected.

Cherry trees were planted by Kido Takayoshi (1833–77) in 1870, when the main building of the Yasukuni Shrine was constructed (Yasukuni Jinja 1992).[5] Among the Meiji oligarchs, Kido was the first to emphasize the new government's need to dissolve the feudal *han* system and to establish a strong central government (Tōyama 1996). Cherry blossoms were planted by Kido so that the beauty of the flower gave some consolation to the fallen warriors. They were not part of the plan to promote the notion of sacrifice of soldiers' lives.[6]

Despite its beginning, the shrine had become the citadel of military ideology by the time Japanese militarism reached its height in the 1930s. Between 1933 and 1935, the shrine published a five-volume history, edited by Kamo Momoki, its high priest, with both the ministries of the army and navy (Kamo, Kaigun Daijin Kanbō, and Rikugun Daijin Kanbō, eds. 1933–35). Its title, *The History of the Loyal Souls to the Emperor at Yasukuni Shrine (Yasukuni Jinja Chūkonshi)*, declares, as it were, that the character of the shrine has undergone a basic change—it celebrates loyalty to the emperor. The image of "falling cherry petals" objectifies this new character and is emblazoned on the jacket of every volume. The indigo front covers of the volumes of the original cloth edition have ten falling cherry petals in pink and the title in gold. The back covers have five falling cherry petals. On the spine are the title and the editors (Yasukuni Shrine, under the supervision of the Ministry of Army and Ministry of Navy) in gold (plate 4).[7]

That the shrine was under the strict control of the rising military, which coopted the royal family, is more than evident in the opening pages of the volumes—calligraphy by male royals, along with the character for loyalty *(chū)* in vols. 1 and 2; calligraphy by female royals in vol. 3; and in vols. 4 and 5 calligraphy by officials of the ministries of the army and navy as well as by military leaders, including Tōgō Heihachirō, the navy admiral who successfully led the Japanese navy to victory at Port Arthur during the Russo-Japanese war.

Thus the shrine as a location for inviting and consoling the souls of the fallen warriors had by this time become the space for enshrining souls loyal to the emperor. Of paramount importance is that soldiers sacrificing themselves for the emperor were symbolized as falling cherry petals. The aestheticization through cherry blossoms of *pro rege et patria mori* was now accomplished, with the Yasukuni Shrine playing the major role.

Indeed, the 1930s saw the ascendancy of unbridled militarism. It was certainly no accident that the institution of the so-called "boy pilots" was instituted in 1934.[8] In 1937, a song was composed for the navy cadets of that year, which became very popular (see chapter 4). It portrayed the cadets as scattering like falling cherry blossoms that would be reborn as blooming cherry blossoms at the Yasukuni Shrine, where the emperor would pay homage. This "brutal" song, epitomizing the military/imperial ideology, succinctly captures what the Yasukuni Shrine came to be. In other words the shrine played a major role in this development, but the state had been working extensively on the militarization of cherry blossoms in order to promote *pro rege et patria mori* at all levels, including popular songs.

Military Insignia: Cherry Blooms as Soldiers

So-called tribal warfare is known to be rich in ritual and symbolism, with warriors donning, for example, colorful feathers. Similarly, institutionalized military systems world over are rich in ceremonies and symbols, including insignia that express, usually colorfully, both the collective power of the system and the hierarchy within it. In every military, insignia are "beautiful." Military insignia are not just meaningful among soldiers but often serve an effective means to display their power to ordinary people. The function of insignia is similar to that of military pageantries; together, they play a role in constituting the "theatre state," as Geertz (1980) puts it.

In the case of Japan, under the slogan of "Enrich the Country and Strengthen the Military," the Meiji government rushed to create a "modern" military even before the constitution itself was completed. It was of symbolic importance for military men to transform their image by shedding their topknots and Japanese attire and by donning Western military uniforms. In 1870, the government issued a decree that the Japanese imperial navy be modeled after the British navy, and the imperial army after the Prussian and French armies, although in subsequent years the army came under German influence (Ōta 1980: 17, 49–50, 69).

Cherry blossoms played a central role in the insignia, many of which showed a single-petaled blossom, leaves, and buds. On October 20, 1870, the government (still called Dajōkan) promulgated an edict outlining the design of the navy uniform. The navy insignia centered on a combination of an anchor and a cherry blossom; one, for example, depicted an anchor with a rope in the center, surrounded by cherry leaves with buds and a cherry blossom on top (plate 2). They were placed on different parts of the uniform, such as the cap, collar, shoulder, sleeves, and buttons (Ōta 1980: 131).[9] Although the navy uniforms were fashioned after the those of the British, the cherry blossom motif was decisively "Japanese." The design was likely created by the well-known artists of the Kanō School of Japanese art, who were teaching at the military training school.[10]

The same 1870 promulgation also specified the design of army uniforms. The army insignia had always featured a star as the major motif. Initially, the cherry blossom was only in the motif of the button for those above the rank of second lieutenant *(shōi)* (Ōta 1980: 49; references in this paragraph are all from Ōta 1980). In later years the army started to include cherry blossoms in many other insignia: cherry blossoms with branches on the swords of generals in 1875 (58); cherry blossoms, buds, and leaves on a branch on the collar of the uniform of army police officers (83). In 1905, while Japan was still fighting in the Russo-Japanese War, an imperial decree specified designs for combat uniforms. Two cherry branches with two buds surrounding a star became the insignia for the cap for the Konoe Division (88), the division which guards the emperor and the imperial palace. New badges of honor also used the cherry blossom as the main motif: those for marksmanship, in 1906 (90, 92), and for hard work for noncommissioned officers, in 1912. In 1928, a single cherry blossom became the collar badge for noncommissioned officers *(kashisotsu)* of the Konoe cavalry division (100) that led the imperial processions. In 1934, redesigned swords had cherry blossoms and leaves prominently placed on them (101). In 1938, the design for shoulder badges added a cherry blossom (104, 106). In 1943, additional changes were made in the uniform to more conspicuously express the hierarchy. Among these changes was the creation of new badges for troop leaders *(taichō):* they showed two cherry blossoms on the top, with their buds and leaves surrounding a star in the center, all of which were placed against the background of a chrysanthemum, although with more petals than the sixteen-petaled chrysanthemum of the imperial crest. Indeed, after the 1943 changes, the cherry blossom was the most prominent motif of the army insignia (109–12).

The increasing association between cherry blossoms and the army was propagated, as in the case of the navy cadet song, via a popular song, "Song of the Foot Soldiers," composed in 1911. It began with a reference to the weeping cherry blossoms on the collar badges of the foot soldiers, who would fall like cherry blossoms at the front (chapter 4).

The intentions of those who designed these insignia are not recorded. However, the full-blooming cherry blossom in the insignia of the navy and as a motif on the buttons for army officers perhaps derived from the symbolic equation of cherry blossoms with the Japanese spirit, as in the poem by Motoori Norinaga discussed above, since both the navy and army flags have the rising sun motif. The presence of buds in the insignia is also significant in that they represented young men—a symbolic analogy that was all too frequently made in later years, when unmarried young men, including the tokkōtai pilots, became the first targets for sacrifice for the emperor.

Various medals of honor given to members of the army and the navy included other motifs. A pure gold medal with a chrysanthemum design was the highest honor, and others including designs of the rising sun, paulownia, star, etc. (Ōta 1980: 22–28; Kaigun Daijin Kanbō 1935: 95–112). The chrysanthemum and paulownia are both imperial crests. The symbolic equations are: chrysanthemum and paulownia = the emperor; rising sun = the nation; cherry blossoms and their buds = soldiers. These medals were given by the emperor (chrysanthemum and paulownia) or by the nation (the rising sun) to soldiers (cherry blossoms and their buds): the symbolism succinctly expresses the relationship between the emperor and his "imperial" army and navy.

Soldiers' Deaths as Falling Cherry Petals

While the military identified itself with blooming cherry blossoms, it soon devised ways to aestheticize soldiers' deaths through the use of falling cherry blossoms as a metaphor, especially as threat of external wars became imminent. For example, it began using the term *sange*, or to "scatter like flowers," i.e., like the petals of cherry blossoms. Not only was this term widespread in statements by the state, often issued through the media, but soldiers themselves began to refer to their own deaths as *sange*. The term *sange* derives from a Buddhist term referring to the practice of scattering flower petals in praise of Buddhas as part of a complex ritual called *shika hōyō* (Mochizuki 1958: 1495–96; Amano 1995). The military transformed the term and used it to aestheticize the soldiers' deaths as "scattering like flower (cherry) petals"—quite a departure from the original Buddhist usage.

In order to understand the military's larger scheme of aestheticization, a few examples not related to cherry blossoms will be reviewed below. One tactic was the creation of "war deities" *(gunshin)*—the apotheosis of war heroes as deities. The term "war-deities" originally referred to deities who guarded warriors. But the Meiji government refashioned the term to mean deified soldiers as a strategy to encourage soldiers to plunge to death as an honorable act and for the people not to object their sacrifice. The government first resurrected past heroes who had fought on behalf of the emperors, making them models of loyal soldiers. An example was the resurrection of Yamato Takeru-no-Mikoto, a legendary figure who was said to have conquered the Kumaso in the west and the Emishi in the northeast so that the imperial ancestors could establish political control over rival regional lords.

Kusunoki Masashige (1294–1336) was the earliest and most important real figure in this development. He fought for the Go-Daigo emperor[11] and successfully overturned the Kamakura shogunate. Later, when Ashikaga Takauji, who once fought on the side of the Go-Daigo emperor, betrayed and attempted to enter Kyoto where the emperor had established his government, Kusunoki Masashige valiantly fought against Ashikaga's force. He was first successful in defeating Ashikaga's force, but during the second advance by Ashikaga's force he was defeated in Minatogawa (Kobe), where he committed suicide as a result. Immediately after the "Restoration," in April 1868, before the era changed from Keiō to Meiji, the Meiji emperor issued an ordinance to offer "deity-title" *(shingō)* to Kusunoki Masashige and ordered the construction of the shrine at Minatogawa, which was completed in 1872 (Murakami 1970: 187–89). As a loyal hero who fought for the emperor, he became one of the most revered culture heroes among the Japanese, including Wada Minoru, one of the tokkōtai pilots (chapter 6).

The first "Ceremony for the Soldier-Deities" *(gunshin-sai)* by the state took place at the Imperial Palace on March 20, 1868, followed by a second on April 9. On May 10, the government ordered a shrine built at Higashiyama in Kyoto to ensconce the soldiers who had fallen while fighting for the imperial side (Murakami 1970: 88–89).

Those who had died more recently were even more revered as "war-deities" (Takahashi 1994d). Those who valiantly fought during the

Russo-Japanese war (1904–5) were the first to be deified, with Nogi Maresuke (1849–1912) as the most celebrated of all. He fought at Port Arthur, where many men, including his two sons, died. At the death of the Meiji emperor, as the corpse of the emperor was being taken across the Nijūbashi, the bridge that spans the moat around the Imperial Palace, he and his wife committed suicide—the practice called *junshi*, whereby someone close to a master will follow the master in death. In other words, he sacrificed both of his sons for the country qua emperor, and he and his wife followed the emperor in life and death. The state could not find a better model of *pro rege et patria mori*. Another war deity was Hirose Takeo (1868–1904), also a hero of the Russo-Japanese war. As a commanding officer of the battleship *Asahi* ("The Morning Sun"—the navy flag), he was killed as he and his men attempted to blockade Port Arthur (Shimada 1995). Two other Russo-Japanese war heroes who were made into deities were Tōgō Heihachirō (1847–1934) and Tachibana Shūta (1868–1904). The government made these men into culture heroes not simply by ensconcing them but by praising them in countless stories in school textbooks and in popular and school songs (chapter 4).

The state also aestheticized the war effort through "*beautiful* stories of the military nation" *(gunkoku bidan)* (Takahashi 1994c), in which war heroes and their activities were praised. There is a long folk tradition of storytelling *(kōdan)*, which features war stories and warrior heroes of bygone days. But the new "beautiful stories" were orchestrated by the state and disseminated from the top, especially through school textbooks and songs, rather than as a folk tradition. A famous example is the story of "The Three Brave Heroes as Human Cannons" *(Nikudan San Yūshi)*. On February 22, 1932, three privates, Eshita Takeji, Kitagawa Jō, and Sakue Inosuke, carried a three-meter bamboo tube packed with explosives and dashed into a wire-fenced Chinese fortress in Shanghai so that the army could advance.[12] The army, always competing with the navy, seized the opportunity to make the best of this incident. In March 1932, the mothers of these three "deified soldiers" were summoned to Tokyo, where they were given an envelope containing money from Araki Sadao, the Minister for the Imperial Army (Katō 1965). Throughout the country, the government erected statues of these soldiers carrying the land torpedo so that children and adults were regularly reminded to emulate them. Newspapers, radio, and other mass media told and retold the story of this heroic act. It was dramatized into a Kabuki play. Saijō Yaso, a famous composer, wrote a popular song about it entitled "The Song of the Japanese Soul" *(Yamato Damashii no Uta)*. It was also made into a school song for third and fourth graders (Matsui 1994: 136–37). The entire nation was caught up in a fervor over the heroic act. Donations of money for the families poured in. Until the end of World War II, the three brave heroes were celebrated and ingrained in the minds of the Japanese as the supreme model of patriotic self-sacrifice (Ohnuki-Tierney 1987: 121–22). Thirty-three years later, in 1965, Tanaka Takayoshi, then an army officer attached to the embassy in Shanghai, announced on television that these soldiers' lives could have been saved had the commanding officer attached a fuse one meter long, instead of one fifty cm long, to the tube: their lives had in fact been deliberately sacrificed in order to enshrine them as models, when the same military purpose could have been achieved without their deaths (Takahashi 1994c).

Similarly, the nine submarine pilots who plunged into the five vessels at Pearl Harbor (see chap. 5, note 3) were enshrined as war deities by the navy, while the tenth pilot, who was captured by the Americans, was erased from the navy record altogether (Takahashi 1994d). Katō Tateo, who led an army air attack over the Bay of Bengal on May 22, 1942, and supposedly gunned down 216 enemy planes, was another war deity, and a song in praise of his bravery became a hit (Takahashi 1994d).

A most blatant abuse of this notion of the war deity was when the government celebrated the so-called "first war deity from Okinawa." Ōmasu Matsuichi, from Yonakunijima, Okinawa, had passed the difficult entrance examination and attended the Army Officers School. After serving in southern China, he led his division in the battle on Guadalcanal and perished at age twenty-five on January 1943, together with the rest of the men in the division. The army reported that the emperor was informed of his bravery. The prefectural funeral was performed at Naha, the capital of Okinawa, where ten thousand people gathered and six thousand school children marched. A play centering on his life was performed, a song about him was made, and his biography in 136 installments appeared in the local newspaper. In addition, his younger brother, Ōmasu Shigemori had to appear at numerous events held in honor of his brother. The fanfare was a cleverly orchestrated affair by the government, which knew that Okinawa was to be the battlefield in the near future; it had to build up patriotism among the Okinawans who had been marginalized as not quite belonging to Japan (*Asahi Shinbun*, evening edition, January 7, 1999).

Another term used to aestheticize deaths on the battlefield was "a shattering crystal ball" *(gyokusai)*. The term originated in *The Chronicle of Beiqi*, a fifty-volume chronicle of the Beiqi dynasty (550–77), which was completed in 636 during the Tang dynasty in China. The term refers to the beautiful way in which a crystal ball shatters into hundreds of pieces. The Japanese military government adopted the term to encourage mass suicide when faced with a hopeless situation—an entire corps was supposed to shatter beautifully by mass suicide. The term began to appear as early as 1891 in a school song that declared that Japanese soldiers would fight until they died like a shattering crystal ball, no matter how many enemies there were (chapter 4). The most dramatic use of this term for aestheticization of soldiers' sacrifice was on May 30, 1943, when the military headquarters reported the "shattering like a crystal ball" of the soldiers who died on Attu Island, the western-most island of the Aleutians. On May 12, 1943, eleven thousand Americans landed on Attu, which was held by 2,638 Japanese. When the Japanese military headquarters decided to abandon their men on the island, which was too heavily surrounded by American ships for them to be able to send in support, the battalion commander led the remaining 150 soldiers in a suicidal attack. Except for twenty-nine who were captured, all died or committed suicide. There were 550 American casualties (Takahashi 1994e). The state repeatedly aestheticized the gyokusai on Attu as the model for all Japanese when the tide of the war already shifting hopelessly against them. During World War II, the gyokusai was carried out twelve times altogether, with the involvement of civilians in the cases of Saipan and Okinawa (Hosaka 1985: 43–45).

Refashioning "The Way of the Warrior" (Bushidō): Cherry Blossoms as the "Japanese Soul"

The social agents involved in the effort to promote patriotism and political nationalism were not exclusively politicians. Many intellectuals were also involved, in complex ways. Many opposed both militarism and imperialism, and even more opposed militarism alone, since they were less cognizant of the state scheme for imperialism. Yet most were highly patriotic, but not chauvinistic. One of them, Nitobe Inazō (1862–1933) refashioned bushidō, the "way of the warrior," through a book published in 1899. His influential book undercut his own antimilitary stance by providing ammunition for the development of *pro rege et patria mori.* Nitobe exemplifies the Japanese intellectuals from the Meiji era through World War II—most were cosmopolitan in their intellectual horizons and yet deeply patriotic, like the tokkōtai pilots, some of whom were Christians, like Nitobe.

Nitobe was converted to Christianity under the guidance of William Smith Clark, who in 1876 became the head of Sapporo Agricultural School in Hokkaido. Nitobe spent some time at Johns Hopkins University and received his Ph.D. in 1890 from Halle University (now Martin

Luther University). Married to Mary Elkinton, an American, he spent a great deal of time in the United States as well as in Germany, Canada, Ireland, Scotland, England, and the Netherlands. He became an international figure who strove for mutual understanding between Japan and the Euro-American nations, which he believed to be the prerequisite for international peace. Between 1919 and 1926, he worked closely with intellectual leaders such as Albert Einstein, Marie Curie, and Henri Bergson at the League of Nations. His most famous publication, *Bushido: The Soul of Japan,* was written in English and published in 1899 by Leeds and Biddle Company of Philadelphia. A Japanese translation appeared almost a decade later in 1908, and a revised English edition was published in 1912.

After returning to Japan in 1891, Nitobe became a significant intellectual figure and held a number of important positions: professor at Kyoto Imperial University (1903–6), head of Ikkō (The First Higher School, 1906–13), and professor at Tokyo Imperial University (1909–13). As the head of Ikkō, he opposed the government's preaching of totalitarian nationalism, advocating instead that students receive spiritual training and an education with a cosmopolitan perspective. Since the institutions at which he taught attracted young men who would be the next generation of the intellectual elite, his influence was of great significance. His educational philosophy and practice invited vocal criticisms from the ultra-right. Yet, he himself became increasingly patriotic, thus inviting criticisms from abroad.

Nitobe refashioned the bushidō of the past. Although some aspects of the way of the warriors developed during the medieval period, the term "bushidō" did not appear until the Edo period (1603–1868), when Confucian ethics provided a new moral foundation for the warriors' ethic, which was referred to as *shidō* (Sagara 1995). The most important transformation of bushidō took place during the Meiji period, when the term entered common parlance (Harashima 1991). Despite the abolition of the warrior class at the beginning of the Meiji period, by mid-Meiji the extreme nationalists had started to resurrect and refashion bushidō. Some Meiji intellectuals discovered publications from the Edo period which they used to buttress their formulation. The most important of these were *Yamaga Gorui* by Yamaga Sokō (1622–85), which became the canon for the Confucian shidō, and *Hagakure (In the Shadow of Leaves),* published in 1716, which became the canon for bushidō and remained quite influential. *Hagakure,* narrated by Yamamoto Tsunetomo and written down by Tashiro Matazaemon, was meant to be a personal memoir. Yamamoto Tsunetomo explicitly requested that it be burned after his death (Yamamoto [1716] 1969: 52). Therefore, at the time of its publication it was not read even by the warriors of the Nabeshima domain to which he belonged. Only in the Meiji period did those interested in bushidō begin reading it. Despite its identification as the canonical work of bushidō, it is a lengthy book, containing Yamamoto's opinions on all sorts of matters, including love, male homosexuality, and the behaviors of warriors of the past. Its opening sentence, which was repeated innumerable times in the discussions of bushidō, reads, "Bushidō means to die." Some argue that Yamamoto advocated death as a way to achieve spiritual nobility by transcending an attachment to life. However, a close reading of *Hagakure* reveals that Yamamoto actually emphasized death for one's master, as in the following statements: "It is more important to die on the battlefield for one's master than to kill an enemy," or, "To summarize the way of warriors, it is to give one's life to one's master without hesitation." In fact, *Hagakure* was written in part because of Yamamoto's frustration at not being able to commit suicide upon the death of his master, Nabeshima Mitsushige; this form of suicide *(junshi)* had been outlawed by the shogunate, which regarded loyalty to regional lords as a threat. In the end, what Yamamoto advocates is the purity of the devotion to one's master, rather than the necessity of avenging him. The death or sacrifice of the warrior was not a prerequisite for but a consequence of Yamamoto's bushidō.[13]

Nitobe stripped bushidō of its militaristic and antimodern elements and presented it as the most admirable aspect of Japanese tradition. His use of the term "soul" *(tamashii)* in the subtitle of his book reveals that he considered bushidō to embody the soul the Japanese. His book on bushidō frequently refers to Western philosophies and to comparable practices in Western history. In fact, in his English text he translates bushidō as "chivalry," and he compares the *hara-kiri (seppuku)* suicide to similar practices in the West, which, according to him, were considered in Western societies "instances of noblest deeds" (Nitobe [1899] 1912: 100–21). Nevertheless, he believed that bushidō was unique to Japan. His book opens as follows:

> Chivalry is a flower no less indigenous to the soil of Japan than its emblem, cherry blossom; nor is it a dried up specimen of an antique virtue preserved in the herbarium of our history. It is still a living object of power and beauty among us. (Nitobe [1899] 1912: 1)

By "indigenous," Nitobe means that the sources of bushidō were to be found in Buddhism, Shintoism, and the doctrines of Confucius and Mencius, although he regarded Shintoism—the only "indigenous" religion of Japan—to be the most important. Nitobe linked Shintoism with the patriotism and loyalty of bushidō: "The tenets of Shintoism cover the two predominating features of the emotional life of our race—Patriotism and Loyalty" (Nitobe [1899] 1912: 13).

Citing a poem by Motoori Norinaga, Nitobe establishes a metaphor between the "the soul of Japan," yamato damashii, and cherry blossoms. We recall that this poem was cited by Nishi Amane, the architect of the military codes, in 1878 to explain the beauty of the Japanese soul. Nitobe's own translation of the poem is (Nitobe [1899] 1912: 150–53): "Isles of blest Japan! / Should your Yamato spirit / Strangers seek to scan, / Say—scenting morn's sun-lit air, / Blows the cherry wild and fair." This is a cheerful and sunny picture of cherry blossoms, and thus of the Japanese soul, and without a hint of chauvinism.

In another statement, written in 1933 at the height of Japan's march toward militarism, Nitobe stresses that bushidō is about shame *(haji)* and proclaims that it is a shame for a warrior not to be loyal to the emperor *(kimi)* and for a child to be disloyal to his/her parents (Nitobe [1933] 1969: 330). This statement moves his concept of bushidō dangerously close to the emperor-centered ideology—quite remarkable for Nitobe, a devout Christian, when other Christian intellectual leaders at the time so strenuously opposed this equation. It is especially so since when writing his earlier book he apparently understood that in the West the concept of the two kingdoms (of heaven and of this world) made the idea of *pro patria mori* problematic: "God vs. the Commonwealth; heaven vs. Jerusalem; the Messiah vs. the nation itself" (Nitobe [1899] 1912: 13).

In the opening sentence of *Bushido,* quoted above, Nitobe contended that bushidō, although developed during Japan's feudal period, was still very much alive. He went on to compare it to a bright star, shining on "our moral path," leading into the future. For Nitobe, bushidō consisted of spiritual strength and beauty, residing in the soul.

In sum, Nitobe's book accomplished the transformation of bushidō and established the following symbolic equivalences:

I. Bushidō as the expression of the Japanese soul (yamato damashii):
    1. Cherry blossoms as the symbol of the Japanese soul embodied in bushidō.
    2. Transformation of bushidō to embody the soul of ALL Japanese, not just warriors.

II. Exclusive loyalty to the emperor:
    3. Transformation of the notion of loyalty to one's master in pre-Meiji bushidō into the notion of loyalty to the emperor.
    4. Equation of the emperor to the father.

5. As a corollary, loyalty to one's parents to be subsumed by loyalty to the emperor.

Still, Nitobe's cherry blossoms are "sunny," shining in the mountains under the morning sun, and his image of loyalty to the emperor does not foreground soldiers' deaths. Nonetheless, it was only a short step from Nitobe's theses to the ideology that urged young soldiers to die for the emperor.

Nitobe, a Christian, apparently found no difficulty accepting the "Emperor as God" in the Meiji constitution or approving suicide as a noble deed—a grave sin in Christianity. Likewise, he saw no contradiction between his cosmopolitan outlook, including his activities at the League of Nations, with a patriotism that went so far as to assert the superiority of the Japanese. He denigrated the work of foreign missionaries, describing them as "grossly ignorant of our history," and credited bushidō almost exclusively with the making of the New Japan, including its victories in Korea and Manchuria. He explains: "Christianity in its American or English form—with more of Anglo-Saxon freaks and fancies than grace and purity of its founder—is a poor scion to graft on Bushido stock" (Nitobe [1899] 1912: 157–58, 164–65, 173). He praises the simplicity of cherry blossoms, which he considers superior to the roses of the West. Ultimately, his chauvinism led to the decline of his influence both in Japan and abroad.

Nevertheless, Nitobe's book became a major source for non-Japanese who wished to know the secret of how Japan, a tiny, hitherto unknown Asian country, had gained victory over Russia, a mighty Western nation, in the Russo-Japanese War. The Japanese translation of Nitobe's book, published in 1908, was also widely read, especially among the intellectual elite. Some fifty years later, Nitobe's text was the major influence on Ruth Benedict's *The Chrysanthemum and the Sword*, published in 1946, which purported to unlock the Japanese personality. It led to her famous, or infamous, thesis distinguishing the cultures of guilt and of shame. Numerous postwar scholarly publications on Japan by non-Japanese followed Benedict, just as the American mass media consolidated the utter "Otherness" of the Japanese through the image of tokkōtai pilots, and, later, through the suicide in 1969 of Mishima Yukio, who published his interpretation of *Hagakure* and who advocated bushidō (Mishima 1977). In Mishima's death, some believed they found proof of bushidō as a living tradition and of the strangeness of the Japanese.

We see in Nitobe an important dimension of Japanese intellectuals since the Meiji period, who sought after Western civilization and yet acutely identified themselves as Japanese. Their thoughts embodied the turbulence created by the vertigo of modernity and of world history reaching the shores of the Japanese archipelago—always looking to the West as their model, while asserting the sense of the Japanese self and, sometimes, their superiority. We will see this pattern continue in the diaries of the tokkōtai pilots discussed in chapter 6.

Cherry Blossoms as the Souls of Fallen Soldiers

With the refashioning of the warrior's way, cherry blossoms were assigned the role of representing the souls of the Japanese—above all, of soldiers qua warriors, which "entitled" them to die without hesitation. The military construction of blooming cherry blossoms as apotheosized soldiers at the Yasukuni Shrine is most astonishing in that it represents a reverse of the ancient cosmological scheme (chapter 1). In ancient Japan the Deity of the Mountains, the most powerful of all deities, came down to the rice paddies on the petals of cherry blossoms to offer his own soul, embodied in the rice grains, to humans, who would grow the grains of rice to full maturity and give the Deity a return gift of multiplied seeds in the fall. The cosmological cycle of the "gift exchange of the self" was initiated by the Deity's sacrifice for humans. In the Yasukuni scheme, it is the humans who fall/descend and sacrifice for the emperor, the "manifest deity." The soldiers' deaths are expressed through falling cherry blossom petals; these petals then ascend to become divine cherry blossoms, which in ancient times grew only in the mountains and thus represented the Deity of the Mountains.

The newly constructed idea of sacrifice in the modern military was the opposite both of Japan's own cosmological scheme and of Christianity, in which Christ is the Savior. The model for the Meiji emperor system, then, was the emperor system of ancient Japan, when the imperial guards were defined as the emperor's shields, rather than Christianity, where God is the shield protecting humans. In addition, the purpose of the Deity's sacrifice in ancient Japan was the reproduction of seeds, that is, production, since in ancient Japan production and reproduction were conterminous (Ohnuki-Tierney 1993a: 55–57). In the modern military ideology, a most conspicuous analogy was that between cherry blossoms that fall before they bear fruit and young soldiers who die before bearing offspring. Both are stripped of reproductive capacity.[14]

It was the military state that transformed the image and meaning of cherry blossoms, such that falling blossoms represented sacrifice by the soldiers and blooming cherry blossoms were their souls. Yet, this 180-degree change in the meaning and appearance of cherry blossoms did not strike the Japanese as something odd or drastically different, since the Japanese shared a vast and rich field of meanings and images of cherry blossoms from which each could choose a meaning in a given context. The same was true of the phases of blooming: buds, slightly opening blossoms, full blooms, or falling petals—all are cherry blossoms with overlapping layers of meaning. The switch in emphasis was not consciously perceived, especially since the military simultaneously used blooming cherry blossoms as military insignia, celebrating the might of the soldiers, on the one hand, and as the metamorphosed souls of fallen soldiers at the Yasukuni Shrine, on the other. The symbolism of cherry blossoms was transformed from full blooms as a life force to falling petals as the sacrifice of soldiers, who then are reborn as blossoms at the Yasukuni Shrine. In other words, the same physicality—*blooming* cherry blossoms—came to represent both soldiers at their height of power and at their rebirth, predicated upon death.

Mapping Japanese Spaces:
Cherry Blossoms as the National, Military, and Colonial Flower

Just before the Meiji era a hybrid variety of cherry tree called the *someiyoshino* was introduced. This variety was easy to transplant and grew fast; trees were planted along rivers throughout Japan to prevent flooding, as well as in schoolyards and practically everywhere else. Japan, which had become the land of cherry blossoms through woodblock prints, became the land of cherry blossoms in actuality.

In an important development, the military undertook a systematic effort to plant cherry trees in castle grounds. With the abolition of regional lords and the wave of "Enlightenment and Civilization" sweeping through Japan, castles were seen as useless vestiges of wicked feudal Japan, ready to be turned into more useful spaces: fields in which to grow mulberry trees for silk production; sites for prisons; vegetable gardens; sites for target practice; locations for butchering to accommodate the new diet of meat eating; pasture for newly introduced dairy cows; or public parks (Yamada Yoshio [1941] 1993: 399–401). But, having resurrected the warrior's way and established the symbolic association between cherry blossoms and soldiers qua yesteryear's warriors, the state began systematically planting cherry trees in castle compounds to further bolster the symbolic association between the two. The state also promoted the folk tradition of viewing cherry blossoms by opening the castle compounds and encouraging the people to experience the symbolic association in person. It was quite a departure from the pre-Meiji tradition of castles, where pines had been the main tree used for symbolic representation. In fact, the planting of cherry trees was so sacrilegious for this tradition that former warriors openly protested when the cherry trees were planted at Hirosaki castle in 1882, charging that the former castle, an edifice sacred to the warriors, was being turned into a mere recreational playground (Takagi Hiroshi 1998: 1).

These efforts to plant cherry trees began right after the Sino-Japanese War, at the height of nationalism. Later, cherries were planted to commemorate events significant for promoting nationalism, such as the victory over Russia and the birth of the crown prince. Above all, wherever a military unit was established, including at a castle, cherry trees were planted. As Sano Tōemon, a third-generation cultivator of cherry trees recollects, cherry blossoms "marched with the military" (Sano 1998: 95–96).

Furthermore, cherry blossoms became the symbol of Japan's colonial expansion. When Japanese began colonizing other Asian countries, they either went out of their way to find native cherry trees or planted cherry trees with seedlings from Japan. This was largely an effort to symbolically stamp occupied areas as spaces for Imperial Japan, where Japanese emigrants enjoyed the Japanese way, including the viewing of cherry blossoms.

In claiming occupied territory as Japanese space, the mass media played a significant role in 1931 and 1932. Young, in her detailed portrayal of "war fever," tells us how Tōkatsu Studio did much of the filming for the "heroic" accounts of the Nen River and Qiqihar campaigns on location. The resulting films were called *Japanese Cherries!—The Fallen Blossoms of North Manchuria* and *Love in the Frozen Plain* (Young 1998: 74).

The Japanese soldiers who fought but lost the 1939 campaign against the Russians at Nomonhan, Manchuria, gave the name "Nomonhan cherry blossoms" to a flower reminiscent of cherry blossoms. The blooms are said to have consoled the soldiers.[15] A book by Kawamura (1998: 42–43) based on the travel diary of a Japanese who traveled in 1935 through Manchukuo—a puppet state from 1932 and 1945 created by the Japanese and nominally ruled by Henry Pu Yi—reported that at the end of April of that year, cherry blossoms were in full bloom everywhere, and introduced the reader to three famous sites in Manchukuo for cherry blossoms. A photo, taken by the traveler, shows a night scene of Japanese women in kimonos viewing the cherry blossoms with lanterns that have the name of the famous candy store Morinaga written on them for advertisement. There is no information as to who planted the trees.

In Korea cherry blossoms planted by the Japanese became the symbol of Japanese colonialism. The cherry trees at the Kyongbok palace in Seoul were cut down in preparation for the fiftieth anniversary of the liberation from Japanese colonialism. A plan to replace the cherry trees planted by the Japanese in the national cemetery in Seoul with the Korean national flower, the rose of Sharon, was a hotly debated issue in the general election in 1996 (*Mainichi Shinbun,* April 4, 1996, morning edition). Those planted in the south, at Chinhae and Kusan, were left alone, and some Koreans adopted the practice of cherry blossom viewing (Itō Abito, personal communication, April 1996). Koreans define the meaning of the rose of Sharon in opposition to Japanese cherry blossoms: "They blossom continuously like the Koreans, unlike cherry blossoms and the Japanese who are strong but whose strength does not last."[16]

While cherry blossoms were participating, as it were, in Japan's military and colonial missions, this polysemous flower continued to represent Japan in a benign way as well. The father of the aforementioned Sano Tōemon prepared 100,000 seedlings at the request of Ōtani Kōzui, the head monk of Honganji, who wanted to plant cherry trees along the Siberian railroad, a multinational endeavor undertaken from 1891 to 1916 in which not only the Russians but also the Japanese, Chinese, and Koreans were involved. The monk's endeavor, unintentionally chauvinistic in some sense, was not to mark the political domination of Japan but to link the Far East to Europe with cherry blossoms in order to establish peace not only between Japan, Russia, and China but throughout the world (Sano 1998: 54–55).

The practice of offering cherry trees as a state gift to other countries originated quite innocently at the request of Mrs. William Howard Taft, when she came to Japan with her husband in 1907. Six thousand forty seedlings were shipped on February 9, 1912, from Yokohama harbor, arriving in Washington at the end of March. Three thousand of them were planted along the Potomac, and the rest were sent to New York at the request of the Japanese in the city for the three-hundredth anniversary celebration of the Hudson River development initiated by Henry Hudson in 1609 (Aoki 1982: 67–71; *Asahi Shinbun,* evening edition, October 11, 1997).[17]

Today, Japanese newspapers annually report the blooming of these cherry trees in the United States, often against the background of the Capitol (e.g., *Asahi Shinbun,* January 11, 1998). A commemorative stamp issued in 1975, when the emperor and empress visited the United States, depicted an American flag in the center, with cherry blossoms clustered beneath it.

The practice of offering cherry trees continued after World War II. The Japanese Association for Flowers (Nihon Hana no Kai), a private organization, donated fifteen hundred seedlings to Bulgaria for the 1,300th anniversary of the country, five thousand seedlings to Versailles in France, to Iran, and to Hamburg, Germany (Kawai and Ōta 1982: 93). Several Japanese "sister" municipalities and private organizations pledged to plant 1,000 cherry trees along the Danube River and other sections of Vienna by the year 2,000 (*Tōkyō Shinbun*, April 30, 1996).[18]

Just as the symbolism of cherry blossoms in general began in ancient Japan as a celebration of life, the cherry blossoms reviewed in this chapter began as blooming flowers representing the Japanese soul expressed in the bushidō, leading to the long-standing tradition of their use as the state flower. Even at the Yasukuni Shrine, cherry blossoms were at first "sunny." Together with sumo, firecrackers, and a French circus, blooming cherry blossoms were used to console the souls of fallen soldiers. As military insignia, blooming cherry blossoms and their buds expressed the valor and youth of soldiers.

Yet, as the militarization of the nation accelerated and the external wars demanded greater sacrifices, even before, but certainly by the time of, the Sino-Japanese and Russo-Japanese Wars, *pro rege et patria mori* became the motto for ideal soldiers. In the process, cherry blossoms were called into duty to aestheticize soldiers' deaths on the battlefield, followed by their resurrection at Yasukuni Shrine—like cherry blossoms which fall after a brief life, the young men sacrificed their lives for the emperor but were promised to be reborn as cherry blossoms at the shrine where the emperor would pay homage. Other discursive practices, such as the "beautiful" stories of the military nation or the shattering of a crystal ball (gyokusai), were also used as strategies for the aestheticization of sacrifice. Above all, cherry blossoms played a major role in this process. The same *blooming* cherry blossoms had gone through an entire life cycle, ending up by becoming the souls of fallen soldiers. The rich and complex symbolism of cherry blossoms facilitated the "natural" progression from cultural nationalism, to political and then to military nationalisms, all the way to colonialism, representing all of these along the way.

Chapter 4

THE MILITARIZATION

OF THE MASSES

On July 23, 1940 then Prime Minister Konoe declared "One Soul for One Hundred Million People" *(Ichioku Isshin)*—that is, one soul for the entire Japanese people. The phrase became a pet phrase for members of the mass media, cabinet leaders, and other public figures. They repeatedly used it in their attempt to promote the organic unity of the people. However, by the time of Konoe's proclamation the effort for the nationalization of the masses had been going on for half a century. Such efforts were not unique to Japan. "Nationalization of the masses"—the phrase Mosse (1975) uses for the title of his book—is a prerequisite for any totalitarian state, which tries to establish a *Volk*-like community characterized by the "general will" or a "cultural soul" (Wolf 1999: 269). Of Germany, Hitler wrote in *Mein Kampf:* "The nationalization of the great masses can never take place by way of half measures, by a weak emphasis upon a so-called objective viewpoint, but by a ruthless and fanatical one-sided orientation as to the goal to be aimed at." This chapter examines how the Japanese state attempted to mobilize people for this purpose through school textbooks, songs, and theater, so that they would become "willing participants" (Goldhagen 1996). Its focus is the role of the symbolism of cherry blossoms in this process. Occasional references to Germany and Italy will be made, without the intention of disregarding the differences among these three states often lumped together under the labels of fascism, totalitarianism, and authoritarianism.

TEXTBOOKS

Although textbooks existed in Japan as early as the ancient period, the prototype for today's textbooks appeared in 1872, when the Meiji government established the new school system. At first, some textbooks were translations of French, English, and American textbooks, such as the Wilson Readers from the United States (Karasawa 1996).[1] They emphasized modernity and portrayed the past in a negative light. During the first decade of the Meiji period, school textbooks were full of Enlightenment philosophy. Fukuzawa Yukichi's well-known *Encouragement of Learning*, which proclaimed the equality of all, was widely used (Irokawa [1970] 1997: 342–56; Karasawa 1996). On the other hand, Confucianism was revived by some influential scholars and politicians in the 1880s, and the state began to take control over textbooks in 1886, adopting the Confucian principle of loyalty to that for the emperor. German textbooks provided the model.

Assessing the impact on the reader of any book, even textbooks, is an impossible task. It depends upon the individual, his/her age, etc. The most blatant ultra-nationalism on the part of the author may fall on a deaf ear, or it may make a significant and lasting impact. My task here is neither to assess the impact of school textbooks on the children nor to offer their history. Instead, I introduce two of the most important textbooks, one by Tsubouchi published in 1900 and the other by Inoue published in 1932, in order to show how even the text books authored by liberals contained numerous expressions of cultural nationalism. Sandwiched between the examination of these two textbooks is a brief discussion of textbooks published as early as 1903 that blatantly expressed political nationalism, together with the message "to die for the emperor."

1900 Textbooks: Nationalism without Militarism

In 1900, Tsubouchi Yūzō (Shōyō) (1859–1935), a very influential intellectual, wrote a series of textbooks for the elementary schools established by the Meiji government in 1886. At age six, children began the elementary school, which started out as a four-year school and which was extended to six years in 1907. At age ten or eleven, they went on to the upper-level elementary school. Tsubouchi was a renowned Shakespearean scholar, critic, novelist, and playwright, and he was a strong supporter of Enlightenment philosophy (Enomoto Takashi 1996).

The first volume of the national language textbook for the upper-level high school begins by asserting the greatness of Japan despite its small size on the map. Tsubouchi explains that Japan stands out from all other nations in the world for its people's dedication to the emperor, parents, and country, and thus they should be proud of being born in Japan. While the peony is the national flower of the Chinese, and the rose is special for Westerners, the Japanese chose cherry blossoms as the king of the flowers because they are "almost transparent, gay and yet pure" (Tsubouchi 1900: 1–5; Kaigo 1964a: 309–10). He cites the aforementioned poem by Motoori Norinaga, in which Motoori established an analogy between the spirit of the Japanese and the mountain cherry blossoms blooming in the morning sun. Tsubouchi urges: "One should fall like cherry petals without clinging if one realizes one's misbehavior" [readily admit one's mistakes]; "One's soul should be as pure and transparent as the petals of cherry blossoms"; and "Without such a soul, one is not a true Japanese." Tsubouchi's textbooks are full of patriotism and even cultural nationalism. But his "sunny" cherry blossoms are far from a symbol of *pro rege et patria mori*.

A number of textbooks printed by private presses competed with Tsubouchi's for adoption. In 1904, however, when the government established a policy of having all textbooks chosen by the Head of the Ministry of Education, Mori Arinori, Tsubouchi's textbooks became influential models (Karasawa 1996).

1903/1905 Textbooks: Militarism without Cherry Blossoms

Despite Tsubouchi's influence, the standard textbooks chosen by the Ministry of Education included texts that directly expressed the ideology "to die for the emperor/country." In volume 8 of the national language textbook for elementary schools, printed in 1903 and published in 1905—just around the time of the Russo-Japanese war—a young man and his parents are overjoyed that he has been accepted to go into the army, and he vows to his parents to fight without clinging to his life if a war should break out. The young man becomes the hero of the village and other parents become envious. This short story is followed by the statement, "Japanese soldiers do not spare their lives and their loyalty is as firm as a rock" (Kaigo 1964a: 506–7). There is no mention of cherry blossoms in the story, however. In lesson 4 in volume 1 of the textbook for the upper-level elementary school, the Yasukuni Shrine is presented as a place where the fallen soldiers who fought for the country/emperor are enshrined. The shrine is described as a park where both plum blossoms and cherry blossoms bloom beautifully, linking the flower indirectly to fallen soldiers (Kaigo 1964a: 527–28).

In these standardized textbooks, warriors and soldiers of the past were made into culture heroes because of their loyalty for the emperor *(chū)*. Other stories were morality tales that used contemporary fictional figures. "Honorable Mother" *(Kanshin na Haha)* appears in volume 1 of the textbook for the upper-level elementary school, printed in 1903 and published in 1905 (Kaigo 1964a: 528–30). It is a "beautiful story of the military nation" *(gunkoku bidan)* set during the time of the Sino-Japanese war. A sailor, who is crying over a letter, is scolded by his superior, who thought that the letter was from his lover or family, begging him to save his life. The sailor explains that the letter was from his mother, who sternly told him how ashamed and disappointed she was over his lack of military valor and who reminded him that he had to sacrifice himself for the emperor. The story attempts to establish the equivalence of loyalty for the emperor with devotion to one's parents, as embodied in the Imperial Rescript on Education, with a new twist. That is, it is now the parents who want their sons to sacrifice for the emperor. This story about the "model mother" appeared over and over in later versions of school textbooks. The plot reveals the strategy of having women join in the effort for *pro rege et patria mori* (Irokawa [1970] 1997: 350–51).

The 1932 Cherry Blossom Reader (Sakura Dokuhon): Cultural Nationalism with Cherry Blossoms

The Ministry of Education issued a new series of school textbooks for the national language in 1932, which were used from 1933 to 1940.[2] The authors of the textbooks toured the United States and Europe in order to widen their horizons. The textbooks were highly acclaimed as revolutionary because from the beginning of the first volume they used entire sentences rather than just individual words, as previous texts had done, and the first use of colored illustrations in textbooks made them exciting and pleasurable to schoolchildren.

Volume 1, for first graders, was written in the *kana* syllabic script with pictures that included cherry blossoms; a boy and a dog; marching toy soldiers; the rising sun; "hail" *(banzai)* to the rising sun flag; Tarō (a boy's name), who drew a picture of battleship, and Hanako (a girl's name that means "cherry blossom child"), who drew a picture of Mt. Fuji; and a fighter plane with silver wings (plate 3). The text ends with a children's story called "Peach Boy" *(Momotarō)* (Monbushō [Ministry of Education] [1932] 1970).

Since the series began with a color illustration of cherry blossoms for volume 1, the series was dubbed "The Cherry Blossom Readers" *(Sakura*

Dokuhon). The twelfth and last volume, for sixth graders, ends with ten poems about mountain cherry blossoms by well-known intellectuals of the Edo period. The last poem, by Takasaki Masakaze, expresses how lucky a human being is to be born in, of all the countries, the country under the sun (Japan). These poems equate mountain cherry blossoms with the soul of the Japanese (Yamazumi 1970: 8–11).

The primary author of the cherry blossom textbooks, Inoue Takeshi, was, like Tsubouchi, a progressive (Fujitomi 1985). He explicitly opposed military intervention in education and insisted on a tour of Western countries so that he could write texts based on his own observations and experiences. He was a pro-Western man, who moved to a Western-style house after his tour abroad. He played violin and had his children take piano lessons.

Yet, from the vantage point of today, the textbooks are full of symbols of cultural, political, and even military nationalism. For example, volume 1 contains: Cultural nationalism: cherry blossoms, the rising sun, Mt. Fuji; Political nationalism: the rising sun flag, "hail" to the flag, the "Peach Boy" story; and Militarism: toy soldiers, a battleship, a fighter plane, and again, the "Peach Boy" story. The "Peach Boy" (Momotarō) is a children's tale in which a boy born of a peach pit is so strong and brave that he goes off to an island inhabited by *oni* (fiends) and conquers them. There are many interpretations of the tale, but it is noteworthy that Nitobe Inazō, the author of *Bushido: The Warrior's Way*, interpreted the story as being about the spirit of the Japanese and their expedition to some Pacific islands.[3]

At the most overt level, the story carries a moral message about an ambitious boy who should be a model for all Japanese males. However, in an atmosphere of accelerated militarism, some nationalistic intellectuals used it as a justification for seeing Japanese colonial ambition as "natural." The textbook appeared just after the Manchurian Incident of 1931, in which the Kwantung Army, a Japanese army division in charge of the protection of the South Manchurian Railroad, defied orders from Tokyo and blew up the railroad just outside Mukden. The army, which claimed to have been acting in self-defense against Chinese troops, went on to overrun all of Manchuria. When the League of Nations protested, Japan withdrew from the League. In 1932, the date of publication of the Cherry Blossom Reader containing the "Peach Boy" story, Japan established the puppet state of Manchukuo. This was also the year of the Shanghai Incident, during which Japanese forces bombed an area outside of the international settlement in Shanghai. The incident led to further isolation of

Japan from the world and a worsening of the relationship with China. In other words, the textbook appeared just as the ugly head of Japan's imperial/colonial expansion dramatically surfaced.

Despite all the good intentions of the textbook authors (Fujitomi 1985), given the historical context we see that cultural nationalism, which had developed over a long period, had become so naturalized that it was not distinguishable from the political nationalism that developed at an accelerated pace starting in the mid-1920s. Even intellectuals with cosmopolitan educations and liberal opinions were not exempt from this process.

SCHOOL SONGS AND POPULAR SONGS

If textbooks became a powerful medium for promoting the ideology, school music, never a part of pre-Meiji education, was even more powerful, because it appealed to the people at an emotive level. The Meiji government sent Izawa Shūji to the United States between 1875 and 1878 to learn about music education in American schools. With his strong advocacy for music education, the Japanese government recognized the importance of music education for elementary schools in 1880 and soon after for kindergartens (Horiuchi and Inoue, eds. 1958: 240–41).[4] Songs such as "Washington," in which George Washington is extolled for liberating his country (Horiuchi and Inoue, eds. 1958: 108–9), were popular.

In the majority of the songs Japanese lyrics were added to German, Scottish, and other European folk songs, and, later, to Western-style melodies composed by Japanese. This was a time when Western civilization, including Western music, was welcomed wholeheartedly by most Japanese. Considerable energy went into creating this new genre of popular music. Yamada Kōsaku went to Germany to study music and was crucial in introducing Western musical styles, including the symphony orchestra and the opera, as well as composing popular songs that are still favorites today, such as "Red Dragonfly" *(Akatonbo)* and "Trifoliate Orange Blossoms" *(Karatachi-no-hana)*.

This was also a time of rising militarism, however, and the Japanese texts put to these Western folk songs were from the very beginning peppered with nationalism, militarism, and the *pro rege et patria mori* ideology, although, as we will see, there was a great deal of variation among them. Some of those who wrote the lyrics were well-known scholars of Japanese classical literature, including Sasaki Nobutsuna (see below).

Some popular songs that praised the patriotic bravery of soldiers made inroads into school songs. In turn, some school songs became quite popular among the general public (Takahashi 1994a: 224–26). Thus, music became an important means for the state to propagate its militarism and the *pro rege et patria mori* ideology.

Music has a special evocative power and can be a highly effective means to appeal to people. But because there are always multiple exegeses of any text, the question of how much effect the literal meaning of the lyrics had on small children in elementary school, for example, is something we cannot conclusively determine. Both children and adults may have responded to the aesthetics of the melody alone without registering the meaning of the words as intended by the authors or the state. For example, the song "Comrades" *(Senyū)* is about the painful feelings of a soldier who lost his best comrade in Manchuria. It could very well be read as an antiwar song (Horiuchi and Inoue, eds. 1958: 112–14, for text of the song; 251, as antiwar song). On the other hand, since the barrage of political messages that the state tried to disseminate through songs of all types was so overwhelming, it would be hard to say that the message had no impact. Yet, there is some decisive evidence that not all subscribed to the state agenda. Many challenged and mocked the authorities, sometimes overtly and at other times covertly.

Below I introduce some of the song lyrics that used the symbolism of cherry blossoms for ideological purposes. In particular, I show how the evocation "to fall like a beautiful cherry petal for the emperor" came to be developed in these songs. Limitations of space do not allow me to introduce lyrics in which cherry blossoms are praised without reference to nationalism and militarism.[5] However, these innocent songs nonetheless effectively helped to imprint the aesthetics of cherry blossoms so that the aesthetics of cherry blossoms in peace is "naturally" transferred to wartime cherry blossoms.

1881 School Songs: Nationalism without Militarism

In the very first music textbook for elementary schools, published in 1881, cherry blossoms appear as a symbol of cultural nationalism in two songs. The music to "Look Afar" *(Miwataseba)* was composed by Jean-Jacques Rousseau, to which the lyrics in Japanese were added. The lyrics include a stanza, "cherry blossoms and willows are weaving the tapestry for the capital," which was taken from a famous poem in the *Kokin Wakashū* (compiled in 905 or 914), which praises the beauty of the ancient capital of Kyoto. Though not militaristic, the phrase expresses cultural nationalism through an aesthetic analogy between cherry blossoms and the ancient capital of Japan. The Japanese text for "Butterflies" *(Chōchō)*, a Spanish folk song, contains a "cherry blossoms blooming in the glorious era of His Majesty," with the flower representing the emperor qua Japan (Horiuchi and Inoue, eds. 1958: 15, "Look Afar"; 18, "Butterflies").

School Songs and Others, 1883 and After: The Rise of *Pro Rege et Patria Mori*

Later songs, both school songs and others, became increasingly laden with political nationalism and militarism. "His Majesty's Country" *(Sumera mikuni)*, published in 1883 with Japanese music and lyrics, includes the use of archaic terms to establish loyalty to the emperor as a timeless tradition, equates loyalty to parents with loyalty to the emperor, and defines the duty of Japanese men to do anything for the emperor qua country (Horiuchi and Inoue, eds. 1958: 20).[6]

A kindergarten song published in 1887, "Counting Song" *(Kazo'e uta)* (Horiuchi and Inoue, eds. 1958: 28–29) was a perfectly innocent children's song in the Tokyo area during the Edo period with lyrics by an unknown writer. The original text was much altered in the 1887 school song version and includes a blatant "die for the emperor" ideology: "Mountain cherry blossoms, mountain cherry blossoms, even when they fall, it is for His Majesty." In 1872, the government designated February 11, 2,600 years ago, as the day when the legendary Jinmu emperor was supposed to have acceded to the imperial throne. In 1888, to celebrate the beginning of the emperor system, the song "The Day of Commemoration for the Founding of the Imperial System" *(Kigensetsu)* was composed, with both music and text by Japanese (Horiuchi and Inoue, eds. 1958: 30), "portraying" how people are joyful and grateful for the emperor, the Father of all Japanese, and for his reign.

Although Japan was not engaged in war at the time, during the years prior to the Sino-Japanese War a number of popular songs portrayed the Japanese valiantly fighting the enemy. "Come, Come" *(Kitaruya kitare)* starts, "Come, come enemies. We will defend His Majesty's country with all our might." Published in 1888, the lyrics were written by Toyama Masakazu (1848–1900), who studied in the United States and England, became a professor and then president of the Imperial University of Tokyo, and eventually served as head of the Ministry of Education. The text does not refer to cherry blossoms, but through the use of archaic terms, its message encourages soldiers "to die for the emperor": "Even if one dies, one should not retreat but defend the ancestral land for the imperial nation *(mikuni)* and for the emperor *(kimi)*." The lyrics of "One

Hundred Thousand Enemies" *(Tekiwa ikuman)*, which became very popular in 1891, read: "Even if enemies are one hundred thousand in number, they are like a group of birds. . . . We will fight to death even if we shatter like a crystal ball (gyokusai)." The original title of the text by Yamada Bimyōsai (1868–1910) was "Battlefield Scene, the Japanese Soul" *(Senkei yamato damashii).*[7]

The extent to which the Japanese populace was already involved in the war effort before the Sino-Japanese war may be illustrated by a dance choreographed by geisha at Shinbashi to the tune of a marching song: "The Negotiation between Japan and China" *(Nisshin Danpan)*. Not only the geisha at Shinbashi but geisha all over Japan, as well as female servants at wealthy houses, sang and danced to this military song. This song was most likely created around 1888 or 1889 in anticipation of the Sino-Japanese War even though the warship Azuma did not exist yet.[8]

In other words, even before the Sino-Japanese War, the state engaged in an intensive campaign to instill in people's minds, by various means, the notion that all Japanese, especially soldiers, must happily die for the emperor qua country. Music was a crucial tool as the *pro rege et patria mori* ideology started to take center stage and became familiar to most Japanese.

Protest Songs: The Counter-Discourse in the Mid-Meiji Period

From the very beginning of the Meiji era, not all Japanese embraced the state policy. As early as 1873 there were peasant rebellions against the "new" taxation system, which imposed as much hardship as the old one. Peasants expressed their dissatisfaction with the government through songs that pointed out that the new emperor system sounded good in words but delivered nothing of substance. Because of the spread of peasant rebellions and songs in defiance of the government, in 1873 the government banned dancing at the Bon festival, an important annual festival in commemoration of ancestors (Sonobe [1962] 1980: 46–47).

According to Irokawa, some Japanese made "subversive" statements in songs because they did not regard the emperor as the Manifest Deity. Even soldiers in the Imperial Army changed the central theme of the song "The Day of Commemoration for the Founding of the Imperial System" *(Kigensetsu)* to that of a tearful parting of a soldier from a geisha. The song was quite popular among soldiers around 1899 (Irokawa [1970] 1997: 256–57).

Those involved in the Freedom and People's Rights Movement too used songs, sometimes accompanied by dancing, as a strategy to promote their political causes. The first and best-known example is "A Dynamite Song," created around 1884, which sang of "the Japanese liver [not soul; *yamato-gimo*], polished by the tears of activists for Freedom and People's Rights," and how they "would wear the red uniforms of the prisoners for the sake of over 40,000,000 people." Each stanza ends, "If it won't work, we will throw dynamite." The song may have been made right after the famous Kabasan incident in Ibaraki Prefecture of 1884, in which a radical faction of the Liberal Party *(Jiyūtō)* took to arms in protest (Nishizawa 1990, 1: 20–22).

It is hardly remembered today that the genre of popular songs called *enka*, whose trademark today is an unfulfilled love story accompanied by a sentimental melody, originated as a genre of political protest songs that were sung by those who formed the Liberal Party in 1881—the first formally organized opposition party, founded by Itagaki Taisuke (Sonobe [1961] 1980: 48–49). Kawakami Otojirō, a prominent member of the Liberty Party, became a disciple of Katsura Bunnosuke of Osaka, a master in the art of *rakugo*, a genre of stylized storytelling often peppered with social and political satire. Kawakami made his reputation for his rakugo on his debut in Osaka in 1889 and then performed in Tokyo the next year. In his text, he recommended "liberty tea" for those who did not appreciate the rights and happiness of individuals and ridiculed people whose Western-style appearances were fancy but whose minds were devoid of political concerns (Akiba 1995). His performance gave rise to a genre called *oppekepē*, which spread widely as a means of propagating political messages by members of the Liberal Party. Other political activists, most of whom had no talent for singing, simply went to streets and parks where people would gather and sang these songs as best they could, while selling inexpensive protest texts. It was a clever tactic to use songs for protest at a time when speeches were heavily censored. Although the government imprisoned political activists, there is no record that these songs were banned (Nishizawa 1990, 1: 113–14, protest songs; 20, absence of banning).

In some ways, then, the government and the liberals engaged in "song contests": the state tried to appeal at the emotive and aesthetic level to the people in an effort to persuade them to fight and die for the emperor, whereas the liberals tried to dissuade people and emphasized the importance of individual rights and happiness. It is noteworthy that, like other liberals at the time, they were also patriotic.

Songs from the Sino-Japanese (1894–95) and
Russo-Japanese (1904–5) War Periods and After:
Falling Cherry Blossoms as Fallen Soldiers

It was Japan's double victory, first over Ch'ing China and then over Russia, that became the turning point in Japanese history that gave free rein to the state and that coopted many people who opposed the escalation of Japan's imperialism. Many Japanese were carried away with patriotic feelings, clearing a way for the state to accelerate its program of military and colonial ventures that led to its self-destruction in World War II.

The symbolic complex "to fall like cherry blossoms for the emperor/ country" began to appear frequently in song lyrics from this period. In 1894, the year when the Sino-Japanese War started, Sasaki Nobutsuna (1872–1963), a highly regarded scholar of classical poetry, composed a lengthy song entitled "The Song of the Conquest of the Chinese" *(Shina seibatsu no uta)*. The song is replete with references to mountain cherry blossoms fragrant in the morning sun and to the sacrifice of the Japanese for the country/emperor. It also repeats how Japan is helping its neighbor (China), which is still not "enlightened" (Nishizawa 1990, 2: 1987–2106, songs during the Sino-Japanese war; 2009–11, conquest of the Chinese). The term "conquest" *(seibatsu)* in the title, which is the same term used in the Peach Boy story, has a special meaning: it is used for conquests of those who deserve to be vanquished, such as ogres or barbarians.

Sasaki's song became enormously popular. Numerous other songbooks were published with such titles as *Collection of China-Conquest Songs (Seishin Kakyokushū)*, published first in 1894; *Collection of Military Songs for the Conquest of China (Shinkoku Seitō Gunka Taizen)*, published in 1894; *Military Songs to Defeat the Chinese (Tōshin Gunka)*, published in 1894; *Warship Songs (Gunkan Shōka)*, published in 1900; and *Army Songs (Rikugun Shōka)*, also published in 1900 —the list is endless (Nishizawa 1990, 2: 2018, 2028, 2014, 2017). Again, the term "conquest" appears in many of the song titles.

Military songs, already quite popular among people, reached a peak of popularity during the Sino-Japanese War (1894–95) (Sonobe and Yamazumi [1962] 1969: 64–68) and again during Russo-Japanese war (1904–5) (Horiuchi and Inoue, eds. 1958), although those of the Sino-Japanese War remained the best known and popular among them.

It is remarkable that children's songs and military songs, including the marching songs, shared the same rhythmic pattern (Sonobe [1962] 1980: 82–83, 88–89). The similarity was due in part to the fact that at the beginning of the Meiji period both school songs and military songs were produced in the context of the new energetic movement to embrace Western music, which reached its peak during the latter half of the Meiji period. Thus, a number of children's songs, whose texts were based on old children's stories, were created around 1900,[9] and they all shared the basic rhythmic pattern of military songs.

This rhythmic pattern appealed to young men who composed school songs for the higher schools (Sonobe [1962] 1980: 89–92). "Higher schools" were exclusive elite schools, like lycées in France, open only to the brightest students, who were all housed in a dormitory. The First Higher School (Dai-Ichi Kōtō Gakkō) in Tokyo and the Third Higher School (Dai-San Kōtō Gakkō) in Kyoto were at the top. Higher school graduates became the core student members of prestigious national universities, such as the Imperial University of Tokyo and Imperial University of Kyoto—the twin peaks of higher education in prewar Japan. The graduates of these "imperial universities" occupied the top positions in politics, business, and education. These students were Japan's future leaders. Many were responsible for the war and even more became its victims.

Of the songs composed by students using the same rhythmic pattern as the marching songs, the first was a "dormitory song" composed in 1901 for the eleventh anniversary of the First Higher School in Tokyo. "Blazing Colors of Flowers in Full Bloom" *(Haru ranman no hana no iro)* contains some patriotic phrases, such as "His Majesty's country of 2,000 years," supporting the state's program of naming the legendary emperor Jinmu as founder of the nation. Another dormitory song for the First Higher School, "To Receive Flower Petals in a Crystal Drinking Cup" *(Aa gyokuhai ni hana ukete)*, was composed in 1902. The term *gyokuhai* refers to a sake cup of high aesthetic quality. Using the term *hana* (flowers, cherry blossoms) repeatedly, the text establishes a metaphor between cherry blossoms and the young men at the higher school who would become protectors of the country. This text shows that the students were already under the influence of the military ideology. A school song written for the Third Higher School in Kyoto in 1906, "The Blazing Flowers on the Hill" *(Kurenai moyuru oka no hana)*, links these young men with cherry blossoms in bloom even more directly, as in the title itself. The text reads: "The young men are mountain cherry blossoms on the flanks of Mt. Fuji in a country that boasts a 2,000 year-long history." The young men are also referred to as children of the Jinmu emperor. Thus, the schools that produced future leaders as well as soldiers for the country had already embraced the military ideology by the early part of the century.[10]

Although less popular than those of the Sino-Japanese War period, the military songs of the Russo-Japanese War show that the symbolic complex of blooming cherry blossoms as souls of fallen soldiers had become firmly and systematically established. The proverb "Cherry blossoms are flowers among flowers, just as warriors are humans among humans" appeared in some of these songs, such as in the *sanosabushi* (a genre of popular songs at this time that end with a refrain, *sanosa*) and in "The Great War at the Sea of Lüshun" *(Ryojun dai-kaisen)*. It is indeed chilling to find the following lyrics in a popular song published in 1905: "Honor for the country is the honor for oneself / A Japanese male finds meaning in falling / Fragrance is for the life after death / Kudanzaka full of fragrance of cherry blossoms." "Kudanzaka" is where the Yasukuni Shrine is located. The song transforms the fallen soldiers into the everlasting fragrance of cherry blossoms. That cherry blossoms are not fragrant is irrelevant here. The song aestheticizes soldiers' deaths, immortalizes their lives, and deifies them by guaranteeing their rebirth at the Yasukuni Shrine. The song text refers to the young men with an archaic term, *masurao*, that has a strong masculine tone (chapter 2). The height of popularity of this song, called "The Bugle Song," was around 1907, but it remained quite popular even through the Taishō period (Nishizawa 1990, 2: 2469–512, songs of the Russo-Japanese period; 2476, sanosabushi; 2481, Lüshun; 2494–95, bugle song; my translation).

While these songs were widely popular among adults, the state continued their efforts to militarize the minds of the children through elementary school music education. To give just one example, "The Song of the Locomotive" *(Densha shōka)* (Horiuchi and Inoue, eds. 1958: 115–22), published in 1905, celebrates the first installation of trains in Tokyo in 1903. The railroad was a symbol of Western civilization that the Japanese eagerly adopted at the beginning of the Meiji period. As Gluck (1985: 101) observes, together with the monarch, the locomotive contributed to "the national and social integration" befitting a modern nation. The content of the song, however, tells us that it did more. Each of the fifty-two stanzas describes the view from the train and from train stations in Tokyo. The first two stanzas are about the Imperial Palace, the Tokyo government, and the Ministry of the Interior. Other locations include Ueno Park, where stands the statue of Saigō Takamori (a hero at the time of the "restoration," see chap. 2); the Sengakuji, where the forty-seven "Loyal Retainers" are enshrined (see below); the Ministry of

Law; the Ministry of Navy; the Ministry of the Army; the Military
Ground for Drills at Aoyama; and the Officers' School at Hachimangū.
The last five stanzas are about the Yasukuni Shrine, including the Yūshūkan Exhibit Hall, which displayed portraits of warriors who had died
for the nation. The last stanza describes how the souls of those who
sacrificed their lives for the emperor *(ōkimi)* are immortalized there. In
other words, the locomotives not only served to unite the *Volk;* each station represents a cog of a gigantic wheel moving people toward *pro rege
et patria mori.*

In 1907 the government, well aware of the evocative power of songs,
issued the third revision of the ordinance for music education. It stressed
that songs *(shōka)* must be easy to sing and that they should *develop aesthetics and morality* (Sonobe [1962] 1980: 105).

In 1911 candidates to be foot soldiers at the Army Officers' Training School composed the following text to the melody of a dormitory
song, "Over the Urals," from the First Higher School.[11] The song begins:
"Cherry blossoms on many hanging branches, or, is it the color of the
collar? / Cherry blossoms make a storm of petals as wind blows over the
Sumida River. / If you are born a Japanese male, scatter as flowers on
the skirmish line." Other expressions in the text include: "the soul of the
warrior strengthened over 2,000 years"; "advance, advance, and again
advance, until the human bullet reaches [the enemy]"; "this is the time
to scatter like cherry blossoms"; "the color of the badge on the collar is
reflected in the lacquer cup for wine." The song established the commonly known metaphor between "cherry blossoms on many hanging
branches" and the collar badge worn by army foot soldiers. The metaphor is grotesque—those soldiers who are supposed to be at the front
line are supposed to "scatter like cherry petals."

*Songs of the Taishō Period (1912–26) through the End of World
War II: Cherry Blossoms as Metamorphosed Souls of Fallen Soldiers*

During the Taishō period, the symbolic complex linking sacrifice for the
emperor with beautiful falling cherry petals continued to be emphasized
in song texts. The elementary school song "Lieutenant-Colonel Tachibana" *(Tachibana chūsa)* was composed in 1923. Tachibana, a hero in the
Russo-Japanese War, was posthumously made into a war deity. The song
extolls his death as "scattering like cherry petals" for the "emperor's
country" and claims that "the fragrance would remain after death" (Ho-
riguchi and Inoue, eds. 1958: 194). From the mid-1930s through World
War II, Satō Haruo (1892–1964), a poet and novelist, composed numerous poems grouped together under the titles "Songs in Praise of Japan"

(Nihon shōka), "Great East Asian War" *(Daitōa sensō)*, and "Services" *(Hōkōshishū)* (Satō 1966: 214–28, 249–59, 260–76). He wrote unabashedly jingoistic and imperialistic songs and poems on subjects such as the Special Attack Forces, War Deities, the Yasukuni Shrine, and the mass suicide on Attu Island, all of which praised and encouraged the *pro rege et patria mori* ideology. Cherry blossoms appear in innumerable places, including in one song entitled "Celebration of the Gift of Cherry Trees" *(Iōiwai)*, in which both blooming and falling cherry blossoms are repeatedly praised (Satō 1966: 219).

In 1937 Nobutoki Kiyoshi composed a melody to accompany lyrics from a long poem from the *Manyōshū* by Ōtomo no Yakamochi (716–785), who was in charge of the imperial guards (sakimori) in ancient Japan. One verse reads:

> In the sea, water-logged corpses,
>   In the mountains those corpses with grasses growing on them
> But my desire to die next to our emperor unflinching.
>   I shall not look back. (Omodaka 1984: 86–91, poem no. 4094)

Throughout this well-known song, "Umi yukaba" (In the sea), the emperor is referred to as *ōkimi*.

The resurrection of this ancient poem, however, had already taken place during the first year of the Meiji era. During the ceremony to invite the souls of the fallen soldiers and console them, held at Edo Castle in 1868 just after the "Restoration," the officiant, Ōkubo Hatsutarō, who later became an army general *(taishō)*, read a prayer in which the poem was cited (Yui, Fujiwara, and Yoshida, eds. [1989] 1996: 61–62). The officiant at the first ceremony at the Yasukuni Shrine, held the following year, also read a prayer using the poem (Yasukuni Jinja 1983: 34). In 1937, the Ministry of Education published "Principle of the National Polity" *(Kokutai no Hongi)* to spell out the national ideology for the people. Using excerpts from the eighth-century myth-histories of *Kojiki* and *Nihonshoki*, this document explains the national polity *(kokutai)* and expounds on Japan's mission in East Asia, while rejecting the individualism introduced from the West (Yamazumi 1997; Gauntlett 1949). The poem was resurrected early as part of the governmental program to indoctrinate the masses. However, it was not until Nobutoki composed his melancholy tune in 1937 that this poem became a powerful instrument for the state. Nobutoki's song was broadcast on the day Japan entered World War II; it accompanied the silent prayer for the nine war deities, the submarine pilots who rammed into American vessels at Pearl Harbor on December 8 (Japan time). The Imperial Rule Assistance

Association (Taisei Yokusankai) (Kisaka 1996), founded in 1940 by Prime Minister Konoe to mobilize people for the national effort, declared that this song was next in importance to the national anthem for the "national subjects."

The popularity of the song "Two Cherry Blossoms" *(Nirin no hana),* with its subtitle, "The Song of the Comrades,"[12] testifies to the mood of the country. In 1938, Saijō Yaso (1892–1970), a famous composer and professor of French literature at Waseda University, published the original lyrics of the song. In 1942 a navy cadet, Jōsa Yutaka, made some changes in the text and gave the song a new title, "Cherry Blossoms of the Same Class" *(Dōki no sakura).* For example, he replaced *kimi to boku* (you and me) with the masculine pronouns *kisama to ore.* The song became explosively popular among his comrades and spread throughout the navy. The new title refers to navy cadets graduating in the same year. Since the insignia of the Imperial Navy was cherry blossoms and an anchor, "cherry blossoms" refer to the cadets, who took their graduation pictures under cherry blossoms. The text (Yamaki 1986: 183–88; my translation) reads:

> You and I are two cherry blossoms. We bloom in the shadow of a pile of sand bags.
> Since we are flowers, we are doomed to fall. Let us fall magnificently for the country.
> You and I are two cherry blossoms. We bloom on the branch of the same squad.
> Though not brothers, we became good friends and cannot forget each other.
> You and I are two cherry blossoms. We both bloom for His Majesty's country.
> We stand side by side during the day and we embrace each other at night. We dream in the bed of bullets.
> You and I are two cherry blossoms. Even if we fall separately.
> The capital of flowers is Yasukuni Shrine. We meet each other in the treetops in spring.

This text embodies so clearly and in toto the symbolic complex of cherry blossoms—blooming cherry blossoms as metamorphosed souls of fallen soldiers.[13]

Military songs continued to be so popular among children that in 1935 the manufacturer of a famous candy, *Guriko,* put a seal in each box and declared that anyone collecting fifteen seals would receive a free book of military songs as a prize (Yamanaka 1989: 36). The government continued to use elementary schools for its war effort. "The Special Attack Force" *(Tokubetsu kōgekitai)* became a school song for fifth graders in 1942 (Yamanaka 1989: 113–15). The song extolled the bravery and loyalty to the country of the submarine pilots at Pearl Harbor. These pilots are described as "falling petals of young cherry blossoms." The lyrics of another schoolchildren's song, "In Praise of the Special Attack Force" *(Tokubetsu kōgekitai wo tataeru uta)*, written by Inoue Tansei, reads:

> Do not forget 1941. On December 8 for His Majesty
> They went as an ugly shield for His Majesty.
> Young cherry blossoms, Special Attack Forces
> Scattered under the morning sun.
> Lieutenant-Colonel Iwasa and eight brave soldiers.
> (Yamanaka [1975] 1985: 485)

The song is peppered with archaic terms used by the ancient border guards, such as the emperor *(ōkimi)* and His Majesty's ugly shield *(shiko no mitate)*, or brave warriors *(resshi)*, an older term referring to brave and dutiful warriors. Again, cherry blossoms serve as an analogy for the youth and beauty of these pilots who sacrificed themselves for the emperor.

The first animated film ever made in Japan was commissioned by the Imperial Navy to widely publicize its success at Pearl Harbor. A disciple of Masaoka Kenzō, the pioneer of animated films in prewar Japan, Seo Michiyo superimposed the Pearl Harbor story onto the children's tale "The Peach Boy." The film, *The Peach Boy as Sea Eagle (Momotarō no umiwashi),* became very popular among the people because of the "cute" characters in it, despite its intention to impress the populace of the navy's military success (Kōdansha Sōgō Hensankyoku 1997, 1: 24).

All the propaganda for the nine war deities at Pearl Harbor went on without disclosing that the tenth pilot was captured by the Americans—a national disgrace. The odd number of nine pilots for five submarines raised questions in the mind of even children, and the report about the tenth pilot leaked out in some quarters (Yamanaka 1986: 112–15).

The Role of Popular Songs in the Militarization

The songs described above clearly demonstrate how the whole symbolic complex of falling cherry blossoms as an analogy for the sacrifice of soldiers for the emperor qua nation was developing in the very early years of the Meiji period. The concept of cherry blossoms as souls of fallen soldiers appeared early in the Meiji period and was firmly established in the songs composed during the Russo-Japanese War. But it was in the mid-1930s that these songs became immensely popular.

The writers of lyrics constituted one set of social agents in the development of popular songs. These authors were often explicitly or implicitly encouraged by the government. Yet, like Tsubouchi, Inoue, and other authors of school textbooks, these writers were far from being simple right-wingers. The Shakespearean scholar Tsubouchi and pro-Western Inoue were liberal patriots. Saijō Yaso, a famous poet and professor of French literature at Waseda University, had studied at the Sorbonne and is known for many poems of high literary quality, including poems written for children and for the folk. As in the case of the textbook authors, however, his cosmopolitan outlook did not inform him of the depth of the danger of militarism that was developing at the time. Even Satō Haruo left novels and poems that are well respected.

Another set of social agents was the general public. Unlike the case of school textbooks, where there is little record of how children and young people reacted to them, in the case of songs, we know which songs became popular, and we know that the Japanese sang them most enthusiastically during the mid-1930s.

One is tempted to use this popularity as evidence that the state's success in coopting the people in its war effort. However, we have little evidence to reach this conclusion, since people may not have given much thought to the texts but may rather have responded to the music, since music was one of the most successful aspects of the Japanese adoption of features of Western culture. Likewise, although the navy intended in its animated film to impress the people with the submarine pilots' loyalty to the emperor, it may have been the "cute" characters to which people responded.

Nonetheless, there is no denying that both song writers and ordinary people were under the influence of state propaganda, and that they as social agents unconsciously helped the heavy wheel of militarism roll forward.

POPULAR THEATER: TRANSFORMATIONS OF *THE FORTY-SEVEN LOYAL RETAINERS (CHŪSHINGURA)*

The instruments for propagating wartime ideology included various types of popular theater in addition to songs. For the purpose of this book, one stands out above all—*The Forty-Seven Loyal Retainers (Chū-shingura)*. Numerous productions in various media have made the play an all-time hit, popular from the time of its first performance and even today. This Edo-period play underwent profound changes during the Meiji period, and it played a crucial role in the development of the *pro rege et patria mori* ideology. The play was also important for establishing the symbolic association between falling cherry petals and the suicide of modern soldiers, whose image was superimposed over that of the warrior in the original play. It is an example of the state manipulation of a popular form of entertainment for its own purposes.

The Historical Incident

The play, written in 1748, is based on a historical incident that took place on March 14, 1701, when Lord Asano Takumi-no-kami Naganori of Akō Province, who had been insulted by Kira Kōzuke-no-suke Yoshihisa (also Yoshinaka), attempted to kill Kira in Edo Castle. Drawing a sword in Edo Castle was a cardinal taboo. Shogun Tokugawa Tsunayoshi (1646–1709) (Shōgun Ashikaga Takauji, 1305–58, in the play) ordered Asano Naganori to commit seppuku suicide before the day was over and also ordered that his castle and the Akō territory be confiscated. Asano's retainers were left without a master and thus with no stipend.

Forty-six (not forty-seven, see below) of the retainers spent two years putting up a deceptive front by becoming perpetually drunk, frequenting the geisha quarters, etc. in order to disarm Kira. On the night of December 14, 1703, the retainers, led by senior retainer Ōishi Kuranosuke Yo-shitaka, managed to burst into Kira's mansion in Edo, found him hiding in a closet, and beheaded him. They then proceeded with Kira's head to Sengakuji temple in Takanawa, where the late Lord Asano was buried, in order to show that they had avenged him. Following a seven-week debate, the shogunate ordered the seppuku of the forty-six retainers who had surrendered themselves at Sengakuji. The order was carried out the same day, February 2, 1703, and their ashes were interred at Sengakugi (Watanabe Tamotsu 1991: 501–2; Keene 1971; Nihon Kokugo Daijiten Kankōkai, ed. 1972, 1: 30, 34).[14]

The Original Play and the "Historical Event"

A play based on this incident was written for the puppet theater *(jōruri)* in 1748 by three well-known playwrights, Takeda Izumo, Miyoshi Shō-raku, and Namiki Senryū.[15] Because of the government prohibition against staging of plays based on real historical events, the time of the event was changed from the Edo period under the rule of Shogun Tokugawa Tsunayoshi (1646–1709) to some three hundred years earlier at the time of Shogun Ashikaga Takauji (1305–58) during the Kamakura period (1185–1392). All of the characters' names and some facts were changed (Watanabe 1991; Nihon Kokugo Daijiten Kankōkai, ed. 1972: 30, 34; 1973b: 479).[16]

In a brief outline of the play presented below I use the real names for the characters, since they are more familiar to the Japanese audience than the stage characters in parentheses. The three most important ones are: Lord Asano Takumi-no-kami Naganori (Enya Hangan Takasada), who drew his sword in Edo Castle; Kira Kōzuke-no-suke Yoshihisa (Kō-no-Moronao), expert in court ceremonials, whom Lord Asano attempted to kill; Ōishi Kuranosuke Yoshitaka (Ōboshi Yuranosuke Yoshikane), the senior retainer of Lord Asano. These figures are referred in abbreviation: Lord Asano, Kira, and Ōishi.

Lord Asano knew that it was a capital offense to draw a sword in Edo Castle. He knew very well that he would risk losing his castle and his territory of 50,000 goku, leaving all his retainers as lordless samurai *(rōnin)*. There is no definite historical record that explains his behavior (Yagi 1989: 23). Immediately after the incident, the shogunate issued a statement proclaiming that Asano had lost his mind *(ranshin)*, despite Asano's explicit denial, which was recorded. Most people in Edo did not believe this explanation. According to Muro Kyūso,[17] Kira, who had been in charge of the office for hosting messengers of emperors and former emperors from Kyoto, became arrogant and started to demand bribes for instructions on the protocols. Asano, an inexperienced lord from a province, was assigned by the shogun to oversee the banquet for imperial emissaries. Forced to consult Kira, he was too stubborn to play up to him or offer bribes. Kira told Asano an obvious lie—that Kira, too, was ignorant and thus would not be able to help Asano. Asano, enraged by the insult, drew his sword. Muro's interpretation became a standard explanation, accepted by the people in Edo as a "historical fact."

The playwrights, however, changed the story, using the standard technique for Kabuki of including love scenes, call *nureba* (wet scenes), which always increase the appeal of the play to the audience. They retained the issue of Kira's refusal to help Asano on the protocol, but the main cause became the unsuccessful advance Kira made toward Asano's wife. Hurt and insulted, Kira thus turns his anger on Asano. In act 4, when Asano commits seppuku suicide, Asano's wife, Kaoyo, blames herself as the ultimate cause of her husband's death.

In act 7, another popular act of the play, in order to disarm Kira, who had been keeping an eye on the retainers in fear of revenge, the senior retainer Ōishi disguises himself as a perpetual drunk and habituates Gion, the famous geisha quarters in Kyoto. This is not a complete fiction, since the historical figure of Ōishi Kura-no-suke was quite talented in composing poetry, excellent in calligraphy, and also a frequent visitor to geisha quarters—far from being single-mindedly committed to avenging his lord (Nakayama 1988: 33).

Another love scene added to the play (acts 5 and 6) is about Kanpei, who would have been the forty-seventh retainer, and his lover Okaru. Kanpei commits suicide upon hearing that he had missed the opportunity to join the retainers on their attack on Kira, as he was involved in his pursuit of his love affair. The appeal for the audience of this fiction is its vivid portrayal of greed, murder, and love, which take the play over and beyond the anti-establishment theme described below (Nakayama 1988: 25).

The Antigovernment Theme:
The Basis for the Popularity of the Original Play

Interpretations of the major theme of the play emphasize either loyalty to one's master (the anti-establishment theme) or human struggles with love and greed.

Keene is a major proponent of the "loyalty to the master" interpretation. For him, the most memorable scene is when Asano, no longer able to await Ōishi's arrival, draws his sword across his stomach. At that moment, Ōishi dashes in, having arrived from Akō, some four-hundred miles southwest of Edo. Asano offers the dagger as a memento and pleads with Ōishi, "Avenge me!" Then, he thrusts the dagger into his windpipe. Ōishi "gazes at the bloodstained point and, clenching his fists, weeps tears of bitter regret. . . . Asano's last words have penetrated to his vitals" (Keene 1971: 71, 72). For Keene, this memorable scene portrays the sense of loyalty as the cardinal ethic of the warriors. In this regard, we should note that the term *chū* appears several times in the text. The title itself is *Chūshingura*, whose literal meaning is the "loyal" treasury. Yet, most scholars do not consider this play, as originally written and produced for the puppet theater, as a morality play on loyalty. According to Henry D. Smith (1990: 8), the "theme of loyalty . . . is merely a veneer to make the authorities happy."

Historical records tell us that Ōishi not only did not rush to his master, but he was not even aware of the whole event. Lord Asano was not well liked among his retainers in the first place. When the castle had to be turned over and the retainers lost their jobs, only 56 of the 308 pledged to put their lives at risk to avenge their master (Nakayama 1988: 21).

Thus, it was not their loyalty to Lord Asano that led the retainers to seek vengeance. Rather, it was the unfair treatment of Lord Asano by the shogunate that provoked them. Without investigating the matter, the government unilaterally punished Asano and left Kira without any sanction. Furthermore, the warrior who stopped Asano from thrusting his sword into Kira was rewarded handsomely by the government (Nakayama 1988: 17). The order of seppuku suicide to Lord Asano was in line with the rules among warriors at the time, but not the one-sided sanction. The rule required that both parties be penalized when they engaged in a fight in Edo Castle. In fact, in 1684, not long before the Akō incident, a warrior who drew his sword in the castle and wounded a warrior was killed instantly by a senior government officer, and his family name was discontinued. But the other party in the quarrel too was punished; he was sent to the remote countryside (Yagi 1989: 323).

Moreover, Lord Asano's retainers thought the location of Asano's suicide was unfair. The customary practice at the time was that only criminals were executed or ordered to commit suicide outside the house. High-ranking warriors did so inside the house. The historical record (Yagi 1989: 32–37) tells us that the shogunate asked Tamura Ukyōdayū of Mutsu-no-kuni to keep Lord Asano while waiting for the verdict. Shōda Shimo-usanokami Yasutoshi, the government inspector, studied the records of previous examples and the floor plan of the Tamura manor. Those at the Tamura manor suggested an alternative location inside the manor, but the inspector told them that Tsuchiya Masanao, the senior government official, instructed Asano to commit suicide in the garden on the white pebbles. The junior inspector, however, objected to this arrangement because Asano had not been demoted in rank and had been ordered to commit suicide as the lord of a castle as defined in the law of the warrior's codes, i.e., inside the manor. With other confusions, it was getting dark. Since the suicide was ordered to be done on that day, it was executed in the garden. In the play it took place inside the manor.

In other words, Lord Asano was treated quite unfairly by the shogunate, and this provoked the retainers' desire for vengeance. Their reaction to the government's treatment of the incident hit a sympathetic cord with the folk, who, also suffering under the same oppressive fifth shogun, Tsunayoshi, identified themselves with the retainers. Under Shogun Tsunayoshi, people were driven to extreme hardship. They derided him as the "Dog Shogun" *(inu kubō)* because of his capricious rules, such

as the Buddhist-inspired protection of animals, especially dogs—his favorite pets.[18] Kira represented the governmental officials whose outright
display of power repelled the people. The play had a cathartic effect upon
the audience (Nishiyama 1992: 149–50).

Loyalty to Lord Asano, let alone to the government/Japan, had little
to do with the historical event or the original play no matter how we interpret them. Even if one acknowledges the loyalty of the retainers to
Lord Asano, this loyalty to the lord was in fact disloyalty to the central
government. Unambiguously, what the retainers did was to oppose and
defy the shogunate qua the central government.[19]

The play became an immediate success, not only in Osaka, where it
was first staged, but also in Edo and throughout Japan. Nishiyama (1992:
145–86) even found records that children in Nagahama (Shiga Prefecture) had staged Ōishi in the Gion geisha quarters.[20] The popularity of
the play was in part due to the popularity of Kabuki theater in general
during the Edo period. But unlike other plays, this one was performed
everywhere, including poor villages and villages in the mountains, on
the shore, and on tiny islands, attesting to the fact that it appealed to
people of every class and region. The play became such a favorite that in
later years when a Kabuki theater went into the red, the play was staged
because of it guaranteed a crowd.

The play's popularity was expressed and in turn further enhanced by
two other genres of folk art of the Edo period. Over three thousand original woodblocks featured various scenes of the play and the Kabuki actors
who acted in it (Nishiyama 1992: 147).[21] Over twenty-five hundred senryū poems, a genre of poetry among the folk, refer to the play (Nishiyama 1992: 149).

The Symbolism of Cherry Blossoms in the Play

Both the historical records and the play certainly assigned a prominent
role to cherry blossoms. Although the play was not about the loyalty of
warriors to their master, it contributed to the idealization of warriors as
having the highest quality among humans, and cherry blossoms played
a significant role in the construction of this image through Ōishi's famously cited proverb in which warriors are equated with cherry blossoms. In act 10 the retainers decide to test the loyalty of Gihei, a merchant in Sakai (Osaka) who has been secretly supplying them weapons in
preparation for the attack on Kira's manor. Some of the retainers disguise
themselves as government officials and demand that Gihei reveal both
the contents of the box and the retainers' plot. They threaten to kill his
son if Gihei does not yield. Gihei, remaining loyal to the retainers, squats

on the box and defies the officials to kill him and his son. Ōishi is deeply impressed by Gihei and offers his admiration: "Although there is a saying, 'Cherry blossoms among flowers, warriors among men,' no samurai could match your deed." The proverb was hitherto little known and was of unknown origin, but the play transformed it into a household word. It remains well known even among contemporary Japanese (Keene 1971: 160; Saitō [1979] 1985: 53–54; Takeda [1937] 1982: 107; Yamada Yoshio [1941] 1993: 96, 215–16, 224–25, 440–41, 452). While the literary meaning of the proverb upholds the normative hierarchy and extols the virtue of warriors, given the context of the play at the time, the proverb may epitomize the subversive subtext of the play itself, which in turn testifies to the potential power of the symbolism of cherry blossoms to destabilize the universe (chapter 1). During the Edo period, warriors were losing their power and Ōishi, or the playwrights, would know how empty their image as humans among humans was.[22]

In the play, Asano's suicide is symbolically linked to cherry blossoms. The act starts with Asano's wife filling baskets with double-petaled and triple-petaled cherry blossoms fetched from the hill in order to console her husband, waiting for the verdict. His wife describes how "he spends the whole day gazing at the flowers [cherry blossoms] blooming on the hill in the garden, and his face is cheerful" (Keene 1971: 66; Takeda [1937] 1982: 42). Hiroshige's woodblock print depicts the scene of the suicide of Lord Asano with gorgeous cherry blossoms, making Asano's wife's effort to console her husband memorable to the audience (Nakau 1988: 35).

As a historical fact, after Asano was led to the garden he wrote his last poem: "Cherry blossoms that are blown off by the wind must feel reluctant to leave [the tree]. What must I do with my feelings of longing to savor spring?" Although the poem was not incorporated in the text/play, it became well known among the people (Yagi 1989: 37; cf. Nakanishi 1986: 17–19).

The Forty-Seven Loyal Retainers in the Meiji Period and After

In the Meiji period, as the warrior's way was trumpeted and the *pro rege et patria mori* ideology thrust upon the people, the play underwent a serious and basic transformation from a play embodying anti-government sentiment to one emphasizing imperial loyalty, thereby becoming an effective vehicle for state propaganda. The process of transformation came about as a result of state control of popular culture. The cutting and pasting done to copy of the play, published in 1891 and housed at the Theater Museum at Waseda University, illustrates this process. The text was censored and altered on thirteen separate occasions, as is evidenced by the government stamps—five times during the Meiji period, three times during the Taishō period, and five times during the early Shōwa. Added to this text was a scene of several female servants arranging various types of cherry blossoms in baskets to console the lord, indicating that the association between cherry blossoms and suicide was even more emphasized in this government-censored version than in the Edo-period texts for the play (Hattori Yukio, ed. 1994: 536, on censorship; 1994: 95–96, on the addition).

In 1907, right after Japan's victory over Russia, when the government had seized the opportunity to further propel nationalism among the masses, a famous version of this play by Momonakaken Kumouemon, entitled *Individual Biographies of the Loyal Retainers (Gishi Meimei-den)*, was produced. Its central theme was the loyalty of the warriors toward their master (Watanabe 1991: 501–2; 1994: 18–19). According to Smith (1990: 8), this version represents a basic shift "from the erotic to the political." I would qualify his statement by emphasizing the shift from "the erotic and antigovernmental to the progovernmental," since the original play and people's response to it were indeed "political." Another version, yet even more explicitly steeped in the imperial ideology, was written by Mayama Seika between 1934 and 1941, at the time of the escalation of militarism. The ten-part *Chūshingura of the Genroku Period (Genroku Chūshingura)*, under the guise of a faithful historical reconstruction of the event, in fact introduced "imperial loyalism into the minds of the 47 Ronin" and thus was "a product of the ideology of its own time," according to Smith (1990: 13).[23]

The cinema, newly introduced from the West, participated in this process of reproduction of *The Forty-Seven Loyal Retainers*. Counting the first film in 1907, twenty-two films were produced toward the end of the Meiji period, thirty-eight during the Taishō period, and over twenty-two during the Shōwa—altogether over one hundred films (Yamane [1985] 1991). The highly acclaimed two-part film made in 1941–42 by the famous director Mizoguchi Kenji was based on the aforementioned version by Mayama Seika, rather than the original Edo period text. Although Mizoguchi remains one of the best Japanese directors, and he was by no means a war demagogue, the film is a surprisingly explicit expression of the state ideology. Lord Asano is transformed into a model of the warrior's way, and Kira, a coward, embodies the opposite of the warrior's spirit. Mizoguchi added a fictional emissary from the Imperial Palace in Kyoto who conveys a message offering imperial support to Lord Asano and his retainers. The scene of Lord Asano's seppuku suicide occurs in the garden, and, although the act of suicide itself is not shown, the scene portrays the garden with cherry blossoms in full bloom. The symbolic analogy between the sacrifice of the warriors/soldiers and cherry blossoms is established with powerful visual impact in this film which hails the warrior's way, endorsed by the emperor. The story became a morality play par excellence in praise of *pro rege et patria mori*.[24]

POPULAR CULTURE AND MILITARISM

School textbooks, school songs and popular songs, and popular theater all became instruments for promoting the nationalism of the masses, and, more specifically, as means to lead people along the road to *pro rege et patria mori* and to the militarization of cherry blossoms. However, the ways and degrees to which the genres became instruments differed, which demonstrates that the state was not as systematic in the promotion of its ideology as one might expect. Contrary to an assumption that the state enforced the totalitarian ideology primarily through the school system, the school textbooks and school songs marched to the state's tune in different ways. What distinguishes songs from school texts is that the ideological penetration began to appear in songs much earlier and more blatantly than in textbooks. The textbooks of 1904–5 and 1932 were far more a battleground where the more liberal intellectuals fought against the encroachment of the military, although they too had embraced cultural nationalism. Although the 1881 elementary school songs embodied nationalism without militarism, expressions endorsing the "to die for the emperor" ideology appeared as early as 1883. The term *gyokusai*, to shatter like a crystal ball as it breaks, appeared in 1891. In 1894, when the Sino-Japanese War started, the entire symbolic complex of falling like cherry blossoms for the emperor appeared in a song with text written by the scholar Sasaki Nobutsuna. It was during the Russo-Japanese War that songs portrayed *blooming* cherry blossoms as souls of fallen soldiers enshrined at the Yasukuni shrine. By the 1930s, the cherry blossoms as metamorphosed souls of fallen soldiers became widespread through songs such as "Cherry Blossoms of the Same Class," composed in 1938.

From the beginning of the eighteenth century, *The Forty-Seven Loyal Retainers* has served as a hall of mirrors for the Japanese folk and later for the state. During the Edo period it expressed the desires and hopes of the folk against the oppressive government. The popularity of the play was seized upon by the Meiji state which, together with prominent playwrights, transformed it to a play embodying imperial loyalty. The "transformation" was a construction, since imperial loyalty had no place in the original play. Cherry blossoms play important roles in various versions of the play. In the original, cherry blossoms as the king/queen of flowers represented the noble character of warriors who were at the top of social hierarchy. After the play was made into a morality play extolling the virtue of imperial morality, the presence of cherry blossoms in Lord Asano's last poem, recorded in history, turns into cascade of falling cherry blossoms under which he commits suicide in the film, blatantly paralleling the state strategy to aestheticize modern soldiers' sacrifice for the emperor through the flower.

A striking parallel to other authoritarian states is the deployment of the strategy of gendering its subjects. As Foucault ([1977] 1995: 135–69) has pointed out, *biopolitique* characterizes an authoritarian state's *gouvernementalité*—the way it governs the day-to-day lives of its subjects. Its aim, especially when it anticipates a war, is to build the soldier's body for males and the reproductive body, most suited for reproducing preferably male offspring, for females—a theme that recurs in many of the writings by George Mosse. The Japanese state too began the building of the body of its people through school exercises. Whereas this topic is not covered in this book for lack of space, the school texts, songs, and popular theater amply testify that the state tried to put in discursive practices what they did in school gymnasiums.[25] Nationalist discourse in Japan, as in Germany, highlighted the masculinity of the soldiers as defenders of the country. The effectiveness of the state strategy can be seen in the adoption of the aforementioned masculine terms by the pilots in reference to themselves. The navy cadet song used *kisama* and *ore*, first-person singular pronouns that are extremely masculine, never to be used by women.[26] We saw other evidence as well that pointed to the state strategy that led these pilots and soldiers in general to think that they alone could protect women from an enemy invasion.

As a corollary, women were recast as exclusively reproductive agents whose role was to produce sons and raise them to be ideal soldiers. Japan's wartime slogan "Reproduce and Multiply" *(umeyo fuyaseyo)* parallels the Nazi emphasis on women as reproductive agents, as explicitly defined in *Mein Kampf* and instituted through awarding the bronze medal to women who bore more than four children. The Soviet government adopted a similar practice during World War II.[27]

Referential terms for the country also became gendered. In contrast to the Romance languages, the Japanese language does not have gender as a grammatical category. There is no Japanese term for fatherland, and the Japanese have always used the term "mother country" *(bokoku)* in reference to a person's native land. Yet in wartime discourse, the "mother country" receded and was replaced by the term "ancestral country" *(so-koku)* in official documents, songs, and other popular forms of discourse. Collectively, the "ancestor" in Japanese culture is conceptualized as a patriarch or as an important deceased male, even though in actuality a deceased baby girl may be psychologically the most important "ancestor" for family members. This term, ancestral land, then represents a masculinization of the country. Other designations added at the time were "imperial nation" *(kōkoku)* and "the nation of the Imperial Highness" *(sumera mikuni)*. Since the emperor too was a masculine figure by that time, these terms are also expressions of masculinization of the country.[28]

Unlike Japanese, Romance languages are constrained by gender as a grammatical category. Thus, *patria* or its equivalent (e.g., *patrie* in French) is the conventional term for one's country even in peacetime. In German, *Vaterland* (fatherland) is the same as *Heimat* (homeland) and the masculine term *Patriotismus* is patriotism, whereas the native language is the "mother tongue" *(Muttersprache)*, and "common sense" is "mother sense" *(Mutterwitz)*. Yet when "race" and its "innate quality" became connected to the nation in Germany in the nineteenth and twentieth centuries, "mother earth" *(Muttererde)* came into play, stressing the biological givens of race. In Russian, the "motherland" *(rodina)*, with its powerful evocative resonance, refers to the "birthplace," Russia. Yet, the rhetorical use of the "fatherland" in the context of military aggression came into the discourse around the time of the Napoleonic invasion and most persistently in the Soviet period. The label, the "Great Patriotic War" referring to World War II, indicates that Russia ceased to be *rodina.*

There is no denying that the Japanese state's effort was quite effective in enlisting the people into its march toward militarism—a process facilitated by the state's use of the threat of Western colonialism to fan their patriotism. The jingoism in many of these songs and the derogatory terms for the Chinese used to fan anti-Chinese sentiment were effective in offering "justification" to the Japanese people to go along with Japan's colonial expansion. On the other hand, while enthusiastically singing songs which advocated dying for the emperor, people at the same time sang sentimental love songs in which lovers pledged to be united in life and death. Did they really understand the literal meaning of cherry blossoms as the souls of fallen soldiers? Or, did they enjoy these sentimental melodies since their own lives were not at danger at the time? Popularity does not provide evidence that people understood the "message."

The militarization of the masses was a complex process. The process was not uniform and unilinear, although its general progression does confirm the received wisdom in historical interpretation that militarism first intensified in the 1920s and then gathered momentum in the 1930s, when "fascism" raised its ugly head. A major finding of this chapter is that the road to *pro rege et patria mori* began with the Meiji constitution. It did not start in the 1930s.

Plate 1

Courtesan with two attendants
under a cherry tree by Hosoda
Eishi (1756–1829), 1810.
Numerous woodblock prints
show one of the important
meanings and aesthetics assigned
to cherry blossoms—cherry
blossoms as geisha, illustrating
the vast and fluid field of
meaning of the flower. Here a
high-status geisha *(tayū)* under
cherry blossoms is depicted with
two attendants wearing half
tiaras of metal replicas of cherry
blossoms. The kimono design
also shows that the aesthetics
of the peony, introduced from
China, remained important. The
University of Michigan Museum
of Art, Margaret Watson Parker
Art Collection 1977/1.180.

Plate 2   Cherry blossom motifs in military insignia, 1870–1943. Representations made by the author. Although military insignia are many and have undergone many transformations, those in the photo show the representative insignia of the Imperial Navy and Imperial Army, both of which used cherry blossoms, leaves, and branches as major motifs.

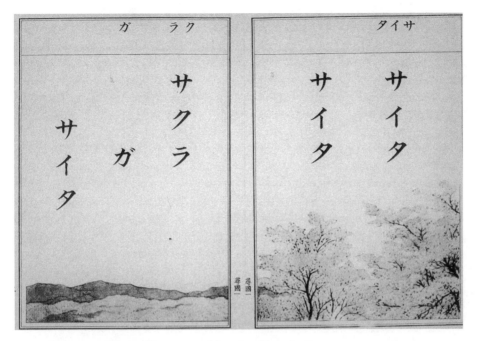

a. Pages 2–3: "Cherry blossoms are blooming, blooming"

Plates 3a–d

The Cherry Blossom Reader. Cherry blossoms, together with symbols of political nationalism and militarism, appeared in the elementary textbook for first graders published in 1932, authored by the pro-Western, anti-military Inoue Takeshi, indicating how the state nationalism penetrated even the thinking of liberal-minded intellectuals. (Page numbers refer to those in the Reader; photos were taken by the author from the original text.)

b. Page 5: "Advance, Advance, Soldiers, Advance" (toy soldiers) *c.* Pages 6–7: "The sun is red, the rising sun is red"; "The Rising Sun Flag, Banzai, Banzai"

d. Page 19: "Tarō (boy's name) drew a picture of a battleship"; "Hanako (girl's name) drew a picture of Mt. Fuji"

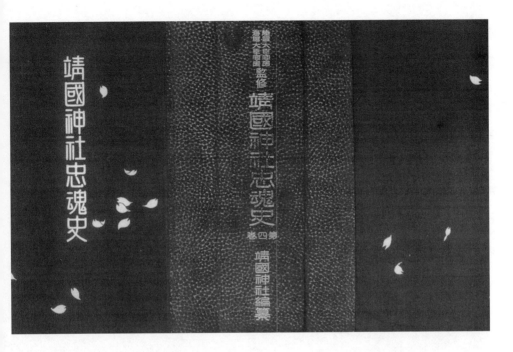

Plate 4 Falling cherry petals as metamorphoses of fallen soldiers. The cover of *The History of the Loyal Souls at Yasukuni Shrine* (1933–35). The cover shows how by this time the symbolic association had been firmly established between the "falling petals of cherry" and the fallen soldiers who sacrificed their lives for the emperor. Courtesy of Yasukuni Shrine.

Plate 5   Tokkōtai plane with a single cherry blossom painted on its side. Housed in the Exhibit Hall of Yasukuni Shrine. Photo courtesy of R. Kenji Tierney.

Plate 6 Umezawa Kazuyo, tokkōtai pilot, with branches of cherry blossoms on his uniform. Courtesy of his brother, Dr. Umezawa Shōzō.

Plate 7 Chiran High School female students waving cherry blossom branches as the tokkōtai (Shinbutai) planes take off. April 1945. Courtesy of the Mainichi Shinbunsha Photo Bank.

Plate 8 The main building of Yasukuni Shrine today. The imperial crest of the sixteen-petalled chrysanthemum is on the white cloth draped in front. A souvenir shop is on the left, selling various items, including cherry petals encased in glass (plate 9). Photo courtesy of R. Kenji Tierney.

Plate 9 Cherry petals encased in glass. The sign at the center reads, "Cherry blossoms at Yasukuni," and the one on the left reads, "Cherry blossoms as ornaments. You can keep the cherry at the shrine for a long time." Photo courtesy of R. Kenji Tierney.

Part 3

THE MAKING OF THE TOKKŌTAI PILOTS

Chapter 5

THE TOKKŌTAI OPERATION

Part 3 examines whether state propaganda was so effective that soldiers died happily for the emperor, as the stereotype of Japanese soldiers in World War II suggests. The tokkōtai pilots should provide the best "evidence" in favor of the stereotype, for they knew that their chance for survival was zero and were considered model soldiers. Furthermore, it was in the tokkōtai operation that the symbolism of cherry blossoms in the *pro rege et patria mori* ideology reached its height.

Before I turn to the writings of five tokkōtai pilots to examine the impact of the totalitarian ideology upon people (chapter 6), I begin part 3 by briefly outlining the making of the tokkōtai and the military uses of the symbolism of cherry blossoms for the operation. I introduce the voices of several pilots and their survivors here who are not selected for a detailed examination in chapter 6.

PUBLICATIONS ON THE TOKKŌTAI OPERATION

Of all wars, World War II has resulted in the largest number of publications, both academic and popular. On the Pacific front, Pearl Harbor has received a great deal of attention. It provided the basis for the perception of the Japanese as devious and untrustworthy. The tokkōtai operation at the end of the war constituted another event that fascinated non-Japanese, and the pilots became an icon par excellence of the utmost otherness of the inscrutable Japanese. While historians examine and debate the precise nature how "sudden" the Pearl Harbor attack was, neither the tokkōtai operation nor the pilots as individuals have received any scholarly attention outside of Japan. History and individuals are both replaced by the stereotype, which has been fossilized in the minds of many today.

In publications for the general audience, we see a striking example of "representation" turning into "misrepresentation." To a large extent, Americans' horror of the tokkōtai attacks is the basis of the misrepresentation. To a lesser extent it may also be due to the highly skewed selection of "Japanese sources" that have been presented as "definitive sources" for the tokkōtai operation, although it is hard to gauge the extent of the impact of these few publications on Americans. A work by Inoguchi Rikihei and Nakajima Tadashi was the first to appear in English, published in 1953 by the United States Naval Institute at Annapolis and reprinted in 1958. It was also published in French in 1955 and in Chinese in 1968 (in Taiwan) and 1969 (in Hong Kong). It appeared in Japanese in 1963. The authors were among a very small group of officers who served as right-hand men to Ōnishi Takijirō, who invented the tokkōtai operation. Although they never volunteered to sortie, they believed that they "represented" the tokkōtai pilots, and they portrayed them as the embodiment of the warrior's way—men who died happily, like falling cherry petals, for the emperor qua "God's country," in order to become a "Divine Wind" to prevent Japan from losing the war. Even during the war, Inoguchi took it upon himself to choreograph the image of the tokkōtai pilots, censoring articles submitted for publication in newspapers so that only the official line would appear. In addition to being decisively one-sided, Inoguchi and Nakajima's publication is marred by inaccuracies. For example, when citing letters and diaries, they took the liberty of combining passages written on different occasions into an entry.[1] These former officers presented their wishful portrayal as the "real" representation of the tokkōtai operation to non-Japanese readers. Another major publication in English on the tokkōtai is the translation of the 731-page diary by Vice Admiral Ugaki Matome. Published by a university press in 1991 (Ugaki 1991), it also "represents" the tokkōtai to the English-speaking world. Ugaki led sixteen young men to death *after* the war by refusing to accept Japan's defeat. The pilots flew off on August 15, 1945, and were shot down by American nightfighters. Hoyt (1983b) wrote a book about Ugaki, who, in Hoyt's view, represented all Japanese.[2] These books in English translation by Japanese contributed to the image of the tokkōtai outside of Japan as patriotic zealots who were mere puppets of the military ideology and who eagerly plunged to death.

A valuable exception is a work by a Japanese author, Naitō Hatsuho (1989), which has been translated into English. Naitō, who worked on a military base, chronicles the operation of the Thunder Gods Corps, showing the complexities of the thoughts and feelings of those involved. Another exception is an article by Hattori Shōgo (1996), which succinctly but accurately describes in English the tokkōtai operation. Edgerton's (1997) scholarly history of the Japanese military includes some coverage of the tokkōtai.

Publications on the tokkōtai operation in languages other than Japanese are primarily by journalists and specialists in military history whose use of sources in Japanese is limited. Articles in popular magazines and newspapers tend to be sensational and inaccurate.

THE CREATION AND OPERATION OF THE TOKKŌTAI

Tokkōtai is an abbreviation of *tokubetsu kōgekitai* (Special Attack Forces; *tai* means corps), which is known as *kamikaze* outside of Japan. There had been kamikaze-like attacks during the Russo-Japanese war and at other times, voluntarily executed by individuals. Although the term *tokkōtai* was used for planes and submarines at the time of Pearl Harbor, they were different in that they were expected to return, if possible, with rescuers in waiting. This was not the case with the tokkōtai operation at the end of World War II. It was the first time when the pilots were "ordered to crash themselves into the enemy" (Hattori 1996: 16–17; see also his 1991, 1993, 1994).

The tokkōtai operation was conceived by Ōnishi Takijirō (1891–1945), a navy vice admiral, and was brought into being by him along with his right-hand men, including Tamai Asaichi, Inoguchi Rikihei, and Nakajima Tadashi, with the last two being the authors of the book discussed above. It was instituted at the very end of World War II, on October 20, 1944, when the Japanese were desperate, with imminent defeat in sight. From the very beginning it was a device for defense against an American invasion of the Japanese homeland. The first attack came on October 25, 1944, when members of the Shikishima corps rammed American vessels in the Bay of Leyte. Ōnishi gave the name of *shinpū* (God's wind) to the navy tokkōtai. The underwater "torpedoes" (see below) were conceived separately by Kuroki Hiroshi, a navy lieutenant, and were first used in November 1944.

Ōnishi became interested in the nascent air force during World War I and later became the "father" of the Japanese air force, which was developed as a part of the navy and the army, rather than as a separate branch of the armed forces. He maintained to the last that Japan should not surrender. He had entertained the idea of "bodily attack" *(tai-atari)* for some time before he actually realized it as the tokkōtai operation (Bōei-chō Bōei Kenshūjo Senshishitsu, ed. 1972), which he named "God's Wind," *shinpū,* which is more colloquially pronounced as *kamikaze.* This term had been used to refer to the typhoons that overturned Mongol ships and prevented the landing of their soldiers, miraculously saving Japan from potential conquest both in 1274 and 1281, as the legend has it.[3] On August 16, 1945, the day after Japan surrendered, he committed seppuku suicide, leaving a will in which he apologized to "the heroic souls of the tokkōtai pilots."

Since the tokkōtai operation was a guarantee of death, the top military officers decided to make the operation not an official part of the Imperial Navy or Army, whose orders were issued under the name of the emperor (Morioka 1995b: 6). The corps was thus "voluntarily" formed, and men "volunteered" to be pilots. As we will see, the "voluntary basis" was only in name, and during the last few months of the war only about two-thirds were "volunteers" (Hattori 1993: 17).

The tokkōtai operation was first instituted in the navy, and the army soon joined in the effort. The equipment for the operation consisted of planes and torpedoes, neither of which had any mechanism for saving the lives of the pilots. Thus, for the first time in Japanese military history, the military manufactured war instruments that guaranteed the deaths of their own men. The "zero" single-engine fighter plane had a maximum speed of 372 miles per hour at 20,000 feet. It carried a 557 pound bomb in its nose (the figure is 1,102 lbs only in Warner and Warner 1982: 338–39). With the weight of the bomb and the high speed at which it dove, the plane was not only extremely hard to maneuver but impossible to turn around, once it began a high-speed descent (Takahashi 1994b).

The underwater *kaiten* "torpedoes" were 48 feet long and 39.37 inches in diameter. Although they were technically not torpedoes, they were nicknamed "human torpedoes" *(ningen gyorai)* because the pilot was meant to ram an enemy ship bodily. Of the four hundred made, there were three types, two of them accommodating two pilots and the other only one. The pilot(s) would crouch in the center of the nine-ton torpedo. With its 2,400-pound warhead, it traveled at thirty knots. It was attached to a mother ship which lowered it into the water when an American warship was spotted nearby. Originally, the torpedoes had a mechanism for pilots to escape, but later they were made without it. The term *kaiten* means "return to heaven," a brutal euphemism for the death of the pilot (Fukui 1997; Hattori 1996: 23; Morimatsu 1993).

Less successful gliders, boats, and other devices were also used. "Cherry blossom planes" *(ōka)* were human-guided rocket bombs (for details, see Hattori 1993: 16); they contained 1.2 tons of explosives in the nose and were released from underneath airplanes so as to ram into enemy ships. They carried enough fuel for only twenty-three miles of flying but could achieve a speed of 404 miles per hour (Ishii 1995). They were so ineffective that the Americans nicknamed them *baka*, a Japanese term for a fool. Another type of plane carried a 3-ton bomb called a "cherry blossom bomb" *(sakura-dan)*. Tokkōtai suicide boats, used by both the army and the navy, could attain a speed of seventeen knots and were equipped with 120-mm rocket launchers. American forces at harbors and ports fortified themselves so effectively that the boats, which had some limited initial success, became useless, giving rise to the use of the *kaiten* underwater torpedoes.

Although dreaded by the Americans at the time, the tokkōtai operation was quite inefficient. Planes often overshot the target vessels because of the heavy weight of the bomb, the high speed, and, possibly, the pilot closing his eyes at the last moment. After the initial phase, Japan could no longer produce mechanically functioning planes and torpedoes. Many planes could not even take off from the ground, or were forced to return shortly after takeoff because of mechanical problems. Underwater torpedoes often malfunctioned, sometimes preventing the pilots from hitting a vessel, sometimes simply sinking, trapping and suffocating the pilot inside, as in the case of Wada Minoru (chapter 6).

There were altogether 647 tokkōtai corps formed between October 21, 1944, and August 15, 1945, and three more after the end of the war (Okumura 1979: 294–305). As the following figures indicate, the first navy tokkōtai attack at Leyte on October 25, 1944, was much more successful than the overall average of attacks using planes (Hattori 1993: 23).

	Entire operation (3,300 planes)	Attack on Leyte
Hit vessel	11.6%	20.8%
Near miss	5.7%	16.7%
Shot down	5.3%	20.8%
No information	49.9%	—
No return (total of the above)	72.5%	58.3%
Return	27.5%	41.7%

Estimates of the number of American vessels sunk or damaged range between 375 and 455 (Hattori 1996: 23, 27).[4] Only one American oil tanker was sank by a kaiten submarine torpedo but others suffered damages (Fukui 1997).

The pilots consisted primarily of two types: those who were graduates from a special navy training program for pilots and those who were graduates of universities. When the Japanese military first started to build an air force, they were short of pilots and realized that training at a young age produced good pilots. In 1930 they instituted a three-year training program for pilots that was aimed at graduates of elementary school, i.e., teenagers who had completed eight years of schooling (kōtōka). They were first called "boy pilots" (shōnen hikōhei), and were renamed "navy practice pilots" (yokaren; kaigun hikō yoka renshūsei) in February 1937. In May 1937 the government also instituted another category of pilots who had completed four years of middle school, for whom the training period was one and a half years (Awaya 1994: 994; Morioka 1995b: 6). They all became enlisted men and a small number later became officers.

The other group of tokkōtai pilots consisted of graduates of universities who were drafted. Most became enlisted men first but were soon promoted to be officers.[5] In 1872, when universal conscription was instituted, male citizens of Japan were subject to the draft at the age of twenty (Kudō, ed. 1977: 275–76). A revision of the law in 1927 enabled university students to postpone the draft until age twenty-seven. In anticipation of war, the law was changed in 1939. In 1941, another revision was made by Tōjō Hideki, Minister of the Army, which shortened the period for education at universities and vocational schools (senmongakkō) by three months; in 1942 the period was shortened by six months. Finally, on October 2, 1943, special consideration for students at higher schools, universities, and vocational schools was eliminated altogether. Exemptions were made for science and education majors—two specialties the government regarded as critical for the nation. Learning, which had occupied a central place in Japanese society, was no longer protected, despite strenuous opposition from many, including the president of the University of Tokyo (Morioka 1995b: 50; Ninagawa 1998: 30–39). Students remained exempt from the draft if selected as government scientists, or if found physically unfit for military service.

In 1943, Japan was being forced to retreat from the Pacific, Admiral Yamamoto Isoroku died, and the mass suicide (gyokusai) took place on Attu Island. Italy surrendered. The drafting of students was a last-ditch effort by the Tōjō cabinet. Instead of shussei, a modern and matter-of-fact expression for being drafted, the state cloaked their draft in an archaic term, *shutsujin,* used for warriors going to the battlegrounds, painting an image of these students as yesteryear's warriors. The first "pageant" took place on October 21, 1943, when twenty-five thousand students who had been drafted gathered at the outer compound of Meiji Jingū Shrine and marched in front of Prime Minister Tōjō Hideki and Minister of Education Okabe Nagakage. During three days in December 1943 (9, 10, and 11), six thousand (ten thousand in Morioka 1995b: 51) students became soldiers, five hundred of them from the University of Tokyo. Of all those who fought in the war, the death rate was highest among the students drafted on these three days (Fujishiro 1981: 446; Ninagawa 1998: 6–16, 22, 147).

Not only was the Tōjō cabinet ready to sacrifice the intellectual cream of the crop, it also changed the law in order to recruit Koreans, Taiwanese Chinese, and the indigenous population of Taiwan *(Takasagozoku).* According to the 1940 census, of the so-called "one hundred million Japanese," about 30 percent were Koreans and Taiwanese Chinese. In 1938 they became "eligible" to "volunteer" to be drafted. In April 1944 the Tōjō cabinet instituted a mandatory drafting of Koreans, and in April 1945 Taiwanese were also forced to be drafted. At the time Japanese students were drafted, the state became relentless in pursuit of Koreans and Taiwanese, even tracking down some Korean students at Japanese universities who were on vacation in Korea. Some recent publications by Koreans who suffered from this process have detailed the brutality with which the Japanese military police recruited them and the prejudices they encountered during military life. Of 4,385 Koreans drafted as student soldiers, 640 died, and more than 400 attempted to escape to the Chinese front when they fought in China, with over half succeeding (Ninagawa 1998: 100–7; Fujitani 2000). Nagai Asami (*Daily Yomiuri,* Aug. 11, 2001) reports that eleven Koreans "volunteered" to be tokkōtai pilots.

Pilots as Cherry Blossoms

The military deployment of cherry blossoms as the embodiment of the *pro rege et patria mori,* developed since the beginning of the Meiji period, saw its most heightened expression in the state aestheticization of the tokkōtai operation. Ōnishi and his right-hand men made a systematic effort in this regard by using cherry blossoms to name the corps, planes, and bombs, except the underwater torpedoes (see below). Cherry blossoms featured prominently from the very start when Ōnishi first conceptualized the operation.[6] On October 30, 1944, after the successful attack at Leyte, he submitted a handwritten report on the first shinpū tokkōtai.[7] He had named all nine squadrons with reference to cherry blossoms: *Yamazakura-tai* (mountain cherry blossoms corps); *Hatsuzakura-tai* (first cherry blossoms corps); *Wakazakura-tai* (young cherry blossoms corps); *Hazakura-tai* (leaf-cherry blossoms corps; refers to cherry trees with green leaves, after losing their blossoms); *Ōka-tai* (cherry blossoms corps; *ōka* is another pronunciation for cherry blossoms); *Sakon-tai* (*sakon* refers to the cherry tree planted on the left side in front of the imperial palace); *Yoshino-tai* (Yoshino is the mountain chain best known for cherry blossoms, where the Go-Daigo emperor was forced into exile by Shōgun Ashikaga); *Daini ōka-tai* (second cherry blossoms corps); *Sakura-i-tai* (cherry blossom-well corps; "cherry blossom-well" refers to a famous place where Kusunoki Masashige, who fought for the Go-Daigo emperor against Shōgun Ashikaga, parted with his eldest son, Kusunoki Masatsura). In other words, all the corps symbolically stood for cherry blossoms and, in some cases, also the emperor.

Two months before Ōnishi committed suicide on the day after Japan's surrender, he composed the following poem, written in calligraphy: "In blossom today, then scattered: Life is so like a delicate flower. / How can one expect the fragrance, To last forever?" (Inoguchi and Nakajima [1953] 1958: frontispiece and xxi). The significance of the symbolism may be further elucidated when placed in a larger complex of other symbolic representations in the names given to the 647 tokkōtai corps, which fall into several interrelated categories (Okumura 1979: 294–305). The most salient ones are the following.

1. Designations/symbols of Japan: *Yamato* and *Shikishima* (both ancient terms for Japan); *Asahi* (the rising sun); *Kyokkō* (ray of the morning sun); *Kyokujitsu* (morning sun); *Fugaku* (Mt. Fuji).

2. Direct references to the emperor: *Kōkon* (imperial soul); *Shōwa* (the emperor); *Jintō* (the divine sword; the sword is one of the three treasures passed down during the imperial accession ritual); *Kusanagi* (i.e., *kusanagi no tsurugi,* another term for the divine sword).[8]

3. Spirit of the soldiers toward the emperor: *Chūyū* (loyalty and bravery); *Giretsu* (fierce morality of a warrior); *Junchū* (pure imperial loyalty); *Jungi* (pure imperial duty).

4. Terms of sacrifice of the soldiers for the emperor:

A. Cherry Blossoms: *Yamazakura* (mountain cherries); *Wakazakura* (young cherries); *Hatsuzakura* (first cherries); *Ōka* (another pronunciation for cherry blossoms); *Amazakura* (heavenly cherry blossoms); *Hazakura* (leaf cherries); *Raiō* (thunder cherry blossoms); *Kōka* (imperial flower); *Banda* (cherry tree with numerous flowering branches hanging down; the badge on the collar by army foot soldiers); *Sakon* (the imperial guards symbolized by a cherry tree planted on the left hand side of the imperial palace); *Yasukuni* (National Shrine with thousands of cherry trees; seven corps named thus).

B. Others: *Mitate* (the "shield for His Majesty" from the *Manyōshū;* for twenty-five corps); *Shinpei* (divine army); *Tenpei* (heavenly/imperial army); *Kinnō* (imperial military); *Gokoku* (protection of the country; the designation given to numerous shrines, with Yasukuni at the top, by the Meiji government); *Kikusui* (the crest composed of the iconography of chrysanthemum and water).

The *Kikusui* iconography was originally a symbol of longevity in China, but in Japan it became well known as the crest of Kusunoki Masashige, a fourteenth-century warrior loyal to the Go-Daigo emperor. It thus stood for loyalty to the emperor and it was painted on the submarine torpedoes. There are other labels that are not linked directly to the emperor. For example, the name *Shinbu,* display of military prowess, was given to many corps.

Significantly, the names given by Ōnishi to the first group of tokkōtai corps that flew on October 25 all came from a single poem by Motoori Norinaga (Hattori Shōgo 1991: 343). They are *Shikishima* (Japan), *Yamato* (Japan), *Asahi* (the rising sun) and *Yamazakura* (mountain cherries). We recall that this famous poem was cited by Nishi Amane (the major architect of the Imperial Rescript to Soldiers), Tsubouchi Shōyō (the author of the 1900 textbooks), and Nitobe Inazō (the Meiji "inventor" of the warrior's way). While all three used this poem properly, i.e., praising blooming cherry blossoms under the morning sun, as a metaphor of the radiant Japanese spirit, Ōnishi transformed the flower into falling cherry petals, a metaphor for the tokkōtai corps.

Thus, the aesthetics of cherry blossoms was objectified in the names and designs of the tokkōtai corps and planes, thereby aestheticizing the operation and its ideological basis, i.e., *pro rege et patria mori.* In the process cherry blossoms came to stand for sacrifice for the emperor. Although names of the tokkōtai corps include designations other than cherry blossoms, the centrality of cherry blossoms is undeniable when we take into account their use as the *exclusive* visual symbol for the tokkōtai operation. Thus, the military chose as a design for the tokkōtai planes a single cherry blossom in full bloom painted on the side of the plane in pink against a white background (Ebina 1977: 219) (plate 5). The pilots wore white headbands with the rising sun in red and the two characters for "God's Wind" (shinpū, kamikaze) in black calligraphy. Not only were many of the corps named "cherry blossoms," but the glider was called the cherry blossom plane *(ōka)* and the bomb, the cherry blossom bomb *(sakura-dan)*.

The symbolic strategy by the state was successful to the extent that the pilots themselves fastened branches of cherry blossoms on their uniforms and headgear, and took off on their fatal missions, as illustrated in plate 6 of Umezawa Kazuyo, who flew from Kokubun Base in southern Kyūshū (see discussion of Anazawa below; also Fujishiro 1981: 462). A work by Muranaga (1997) contains a number of pictures of tokkōtai pilots with cherry blossoms at Chiran Airbase in Kyūshū. Those who bid farewell to the pilots also did so, waving branches of cherry blossoms as in the famous picture of high school girls did so in plate 7.

THE LIVES OF THE PILOTS

Who were the Pilots?

Nominally, the tokkōtai operation involved volunteers. An astonishing fact, however, is that, when Ōnishi and others instituted the tokkōtai operation, *none* of the professional soldiers who had graduated from the naval and army academies volunteered. Embarrassed, Ōnishi and his right-hand men asked, or, rather, "ordered" some officers from the military academies to be tokkōtai pilots, as in the famous case of Seki Yukio (Morioka 1995b; Ninagawa 1998: 129–30), who led the navy tokkōtai attack on Leyte. According to Onoda Masashi (1971), who was a reporter for the Imperial Navy, Captain Seki was a skillful pilot who was well respected and liked by all, including by the student soldiers. He told Onoda: "There is no more hope for Japan, if it has to kill such a skillful pilot like myself. I can hit an aircraft carrier with a 1,102 lb. bomb and return alive, without having to make a suicidal plunge." At that time Seki had been married for only six months to a woman with whom he was passionately in love. He explained to Onoda, "If it is an order, I will go. But *I am not going to die for the emperor or for Imperial Japan*. I am going for my beloved wife. If Japan loses, she might be raped by Americans. I am dying for someone I love most, to protect her" (emphasis added). Onoda's report on the "human side" of Seki was not accepted for publication by the officers, including Inoguchi Rikihei, who was, we saw above, one of the navy officers directly involved in the institution of the tokkōtai operation (Bōeichō Bōei Kenshūjo Senshishitsu, ed. 1972) and a co-author of the only book on the operation that has been translated into English, French, and Chinese.

According to Hattori (1996: 25–26), "Except for Lt. (Jg.) Nishina, an eager promoter of kaiten, and Rear-Admiral Arima, none of the tokkōtai advocates sortied as tokkōtai and died."[9] There were, however, some compassionate officers. Commanders Minobe and Kofukuda refused to participate in the tokkōtai operation (Hattori 1996: 26, n. 3). Likewise, Abe Yasujirō (navy lieutenant) and Fujita Iyozō (navy commander) refused to send their men to be tokkōtai pilots; the former rose from the ranks of Navy Practice Pilots and the latter was a graduate of the Naval Academy (Hattori, personal communication, May 1999).

That the professional soldiers did not volunteer to sortie and, instead, sent students and navy practice pilots to death was known among the students. According to Misa (n.d., 32), one evening a student soldier at Usa Airbase, emboldened by the effect of sake, challenged his superior: "Why don't you, graduates of the Naval Academy, sortie! Day after day, only students and navy practice pilots are sent off!" The following figures indicate that the tokkōtai pilots were predominantly student officers and navy practice pilots, who constituted the majority of enlisted men. Since the numbers vary depending upon the source, I list figures provided by Morioka and put those by Ninagawa in brackets:[10]

Total deaths of pilots: 3,843 [3,349]
Navy pilots, total number of deaths: 2,514 [2,033]
    enlisted men (= navy practice pilots): 1,732 (68.9%)
    officers: 782 [769]
        (1) student soldiers: 648 (82.9%) [651 (85%)]
        (2) Naval Acad. graduates: 119 (15.2%) [118 (15%)]
Army pilots, total number of deaths: 1,329 [1,316]
    enlisted men : 708 (53.3%)
    officers: 621 [632] (46.7%)
        student soldiers: 308 (49.6%) [449 (71%)]

Point of No Return: Life on the Base

The conditions on base gave these young men little chance to opt for life in the first place. According to Irokawa Daikichi, an eminent historian who was drafted from the University of Tokyo as a student soldier and spent time at the Tsuchiura Navy Airbase, the first lesson student soldiers like himself were taught was how to use their own rifles to kill themselves, rather than to be captured alive. This included the practice of using a toe to pull the trigger and to point the gun precisely at a certain point under the chin so that the bullet would kill them instantly. They were supposed to use this technique if they were trapped in a cave or in a trench surrounded by the enemy. If they did not kill themselves but tried to escape, others would shoot them from behind anyway, since their superiors and even some comrades believed in the state dictum not to be captured by the enemy. In other words, once you are drafted, you had reached a point of no return (Irokawa, personal communication, May 1999).

Some officers were kind. For example, Wada (1972: 184) (see his diary in chapter 6) described an officer who had come up through the ranks, who beat student soldiers in the beginning but later mellowed. Wada was amused when this officer asked him if *Faust* was written by Shakespeare. Wada also reported that his superior shed tears when he gave Wada permission to volunteer to be a pilot of a submarine torpedo. Hayashi Ichizō, also introduced in chapter 6, seems also to have been treated well (Hayashi Ichizō 1995: 68–69). On the other hand, many officers acted like demons. Any minor action that irritated the professional soldiers who were above the students in rank was a cause for brutal corporal punishment, not only of the individual involved but of the entire group. Irokawa (1993: 54, see also 48)[11] offers a vivid description of the "living hell" that awaited the student soldiers:

> After I passed the gate to the Tsuchiura Navy Airbase, "training" took place day after day. I was struck on the face so hard and frequently that my face was no longer recognizable. On January 2, 1945, Kaneko (ensign) hit my face twenty times and the inside of my mouth was cut in many places. I had been looking forward to eating *zōni* [a special dish with rice cakes for the New Year]. Instead, I was swallowing blood from the inside of my mouth. On February 14, all of us were punished because they suspected that we ate at farmers' homes near the base to ease our hunger. In the midst of the cold winter, we were forced to sit for seven hours on a cold concrete floor and they hit us on the buttocks with a club. Then each of us was called into the officer's room. When my turn came, as soon as I entered the room, I was hit so hard that I could no longer see and fell on the floor. The minute I got up, I was hit by a club so that I would confess. A friend of mine was thrown with his head first to the floor, lost his consciousness, and [was] sent to a hospital. He never returned [alive]. The whole savagery was orchestrated by the corps commander named Tsutsui. I am still looking for this fellow.

Student soldiers were often targeted by professional soldiers who had come up through the ranks; they considered students as having come from privileged backgrounds that enabled them to study, when these professional soldiers could not attend higher schools, let alone universities.

"Volunteering" to be Pilots

Once on the base, soldiers were asked to "volunteer" to be pilots. In most cases, all the members of a corps were summoned into a hall. After a lecture on the virtue of patriotism and on the need to sacrifice oneself for the emperor and Japan, they were told to step forward if they were willing to volunteer to be tokkōtai pilots. It is indeed superfluous to point out how difficult it would have been to stay behind when all or many others stepped forward. Sometimes the officer in charge went through a ritual of blindfolding the young men—a gesture to eliminate peer pressure, asking them to raise their hands to volunteer. But the rustling sounds of the uniforms as they raised their hands made it obvious that many did so, leaving those hesitant without a choice but to volunteer (Hattori, personal communication, May 1999).

Even if one managed to be courageous enough not to volunteer, one's fate would have been a living hell. Some managed to say "no" in vain, as in the case of Yamada Ryū, who was "forced to volunteer to be a pilot for the inhumane tokkōtai operation." After the war, Yamada devoted his life to the ministry of the Anabaptist church in Kyushu (Yamada Ryū 1997). Kuroda Kenjirō decided not to volunteer, only to be taken by surprise, to put it mildly, when his name was called out to be a member of the Mitate navy tokkōtai corps; his superior had reported, proudly, that all the members of his corps had volunteered (Kōdansha Sōgō Henshū-kyoku, ed. 1997, 2: 5).

Writings left by the pilots reveal that an important reason for volunteering was not peer group pressure as such but they could not bear seeing their comrades and friends offering their lives while protecting their own. Thoughts, accompanied by admiration, of those who had already gone on the fatal mission frequently appear in pilots' writings. Ichijima Yasuo, who was born in 1922 and died on April 29, 1945, was a graduate of Waseda University, with the rank of navy ensign.[12] He deeply admired those who went off on the tokkōtai planes and in a letter to a friend refers to the soldiers as "falling cherry blossoms, remaining cherry blossoms also be falling cherry blossoms" (*Cherry Blossoms of the Same Class* 1966a: 124). Ichijima was a devout Christian, a member of a well-known church named the "Cherry Blossoms Church" (Morioka 1995b: 72–73). He expressed his willingness to serve his country but did not mention the emperor (Morioka 1995b: 67). If not the primary motivation, his admiration for the pilots who had already perished was a significant factor in his thought as he contemplated his own mission.

For many, it was psychologically easier to volunteer as tokkōtai pilots when they knew that, with Japan's defeat in sight, their lives were in extreme danger no matter which course of action they took (Irokawa 1993: 3). As some of them put it, if you were most likely to die anyway, you might as well die a hero. Yet, agony until the last moment over their deaths is evident in their writings and also in their responses to psychological questionnaires administered at the end of May 1945, two months after the battle for Okinawa started. In their answers, one third of the members of the tokkōtai unit of the Sixth Army Air Force corps remained undecided about the mission and were torn even after they were already in the unit (Ikuta Makoto 1977: 210 cited in Ninagawa 1998: 130–31).

After the pilots "volunteered," the officer in charge of a particular corps decided who should go on the missions and in which order. Irokawa (personal communication, May 1999) and others explain that family background and other factors kept some from ever being chosen. A son of an important political or military official, an important businessman, or a member of the royal family could volunteer without ever been chosen.[13] The oldest or the only son was often spared, honoring the primogeniture system. Soldiers who had mechanical, navigational, and other skills essential for the pilots were "favored" for selection. The criteria for selection were never disclosed publicly (Umezawa Shōzō, letter dated June 20, 1999, to the author).

Sometimes being disliked by the officer in charge of the corps was fatal for "being tapped on the shoulder." Navy Lieutenant Fujii Masaharu, a student soldier, died as a tokkōtai pilot. The officer found irritating Fujii's habit of often staring into the void at the corner of a room without a word. He "tapped" Fujii's shoulder and told him to lead the tokkōtai corps, despite the fact that no officers above the rank of lieutenant and lieutenant junior grade who were graduates of the Naval Academy were sent on tokkōtai missions. Fujii was speechless and thought it was an act of murder under the disguise of a military order. However, realizing that he had no choice, he sarcastically told the pilots in his corps: "Let's bite into the ground of Okinawa together" (Misa n.d., 29–31).

Freedom to Choose One's Fate

At the level of the individual, the question of what constitutes "volunteering" is almost too complex to narrow down to certain factors. It involves the general circumstances of society as well as the specific context. Given the patriotic fervor of the time, many young men were willing to fight for their country, especially before they experienced the reality on the base or before their deaths were imminent. However, after they were drafted and had spent some time on the base, to take the next step of vol-unteering to be tokkōtai pilots was never a clear-cut "decision." Most re-mained undecided about the step they had already taken until the last moment. "Volunteering" in the pilots' cases was far removed from such factors as motivation, intentionality, or rational decision-making in a simplistic sense.

In order to explain the complexities involved in the act of "volunteer-ing," a few cases are introduced here, while in the next chapter the thoughts and feelings of five pilots who left extensive writings will be de-scribed in detail. Umezawa Kazuyo, an ensign in the navy, died as a tok-kōtai pilot on April 28, 1945, at the age of eighteen. He had left a school for commerce before graduating, after passing the draft examination at the highest level *(kōshu)*. Despite his mother's persistent and strenuous opposition, he volunteered to be a navy practice pilot. The rationale he gave to his mother was to help her financially and fulfill the obliga-tion/loyalty *(kō)*, since his mother, a widow, was single-handedly rais-ing her children. The government provided financial incentives for re-cruits by offering higher payments for more dangerous positions and by promoting tokkōtai pilots by two ranks upon death, which sharply raised the payment *(onkyū)* to the survivors, since compensation for fallen sol-diers was determined primarily by the length of their service and their rank. Umezawa Shōzō, his brother, explained to me that a few days be-fore his brother's final flight, he returned home and cursed the navy for killing young men like himself. No doubt that patriotism, concern for his mother, and various factors must took part in his decision to be a pilot, but his thoughts were certainly complex by the time he was to sortie. He went on his death mission carrying branches of cherry blossoms (plate 6).

Anazawa Toshio, an army second lieutenant, was a student soldier from Chūō University (Morioka 1995b: 2–3, 8–9, 14–42, 45–48); he died as a tokkōtai pilot on April 12, 1945, at age twenty-three. When he was drafted, he wrote in his diary dated March 16, 1945: "Plum blossoms are celebrating the departure of a *masurao* to the front," referring to himself as *masurao*, an archaic term with a strong masculine tone (Mo-rioka 1995b: 16).[14] The last scene of Anazawa and other pilots as they took off was recorded by Maeda Shōko, then a high school student in Okinawa, in an entry in a diary now housed at the Chiran Airbase. She and her classmates came to the airfield in a car in order to see off the "di-vine eagles." They ran toward the planes, each waving a branch of cherry blossoms. She noted that he smiled and saluted them several times (Mo-rioka 1995b: 14).[15]

Yet Anazawa's diaries and letters reveal that uppermost in his thoughts during his final days was Sonoda Chieko, his love. Chieko kept following him as he was moved from base to base, hoping that they could spend at least one night together as husband and wife before his death. Their wish was never fulfilled, since the movements of the pilots were kept secret and she would arrive at a base after he had been moved to another. In his last letter to Chieko, he described deep sorrow over his brother's letter in which the brother opposed the marriage. Although his parents were influenced by his brother's objection to their marriage, he remained confident that his mother understood his love of Chieko and would allow them to marry. In his diary, discovered by Chieko after his death, he wrote: "Find happiness, Chieko. Being able to love another person is the utmost happiness. My future will be fulfilled by my wish for your happiness which is the most honorable of all my feelings" (Morioka 1995b: 42).

In the March diary entries, he uses the metaphor of plum blossoms to describe himself as a brave soldier (Morioka 1995b: 15–17). Cherry blossoms replace plum blossoms during the two weeks before his death. In his last letter to Chieko, he refers to himself as "a male who is going to fall like cherry petals," again using the term *danshi*, a masculine noun for a male. He tells her that the cherry blossoms on the base have already fallen. On April 2, 1945, ten days before his death, he composed a poem that contains the lines, "How pleased I am to have my wish to come true—to share the fate of falling cherry blossoms" (Morioka 1995b: 38, 25).

It is hard to believe that Anazawa, who was so much in love with Chieko, would be truly happy to fall like cherry blossoms. As he himself wrote, when he went into the army, he wanted to fight for the country as a Japanese male but was confident that he would return to Chieko after the war. His smile observed by Maeda Shōko must have been an expression of enormously complex feelings, for Anazawa, who knew that he had reached the point of no return, did his best to act like a man. In the published diaries and letters, despite his repeated references to falling cherry blossoms, he never refers to the emperor.

Machida Dōkyō, a graduate of the University of Kyūshū who was born in 1920 and who died in 1945,[16] clearly expressed his intense agony in his last letter to his mother, written in May from the Kanoya Navy Airbase. He repeatedly refers to his death as "falling" [of cherry petals]): "I feel torn *(kokoro nokori)* that I leave my mother, who had to struggle so hard [to raise us], and to fall like petals. . . . I feel sorry that I fall like petals without giving a good life to my mother in her old age and without repaying her for all the struggles she had endured for us. . . . After I fall like petals, please ask Seikyō [his younger brother] to take care of you" (Ebina 1977: 234–60). Cherry blossoms in Machida's thoughts had little to do with the emperor. He never swallowed the equation of the loyalty to parents with loyalty to the emperor.

Although we see expressions of agonized conflict between duty and personal feelings in the examples above, there certainly were others who were unambiguously patriotic or even expressed the pro-military ideology, at least in the passages chosen for publication. Morioka Tetsushirō, a graduate of Tokyo Agricultural University, was born on April 21, 1922 and died on April 29, 1945, with the rank of navy second lieutenant.[17] In his diary on February 14, 1944 he wrote: "I am being educated to become a soldier capable of dying for the emperor. . . . Loyalty [for the emperor] (chū) is the repayment of my spiritual debt to my parents (kō). . . . I believe that for my father it is the greatest pleasure that I die as a soldier (gunjin). I have no regret. If I fulfill chū, then I am fulfilling the kō." He cried when he read a letter from his older sister in which she wrote that at the family gathering on the previous night his father had said that Tetsushirō was looking after his parents (oyakōkō), i.e., by sacrificing himself for the emperor. In the April 2 diary entry, in which he vows to fall, he writes: "Until I die like a scattered crystal ball (gyokusai), I remain unfulfilled in the repayment to my parents. . . . I shall go [to war] with a firm belief in the glory of our family and the glory of my country." He felt particularly indebted to his father, who saved Morioka's life with his own blood when Morioka, as a child, needed a blood transfusion. He felt "lonely" when his father told him that he would write some words on a rising sun flag for him. He referred to his father more frequently than to his mother.

His poem reads: "I hope to die next to the emperor in the clouds stained by [my] bleeding corpse." His July 5, 1944 diary entry reads: "I will do my best in order to die for the emperor as soon as possible like falling cherry petals." Another entry reads: "I heard that her [the daughter at an inn frequented by the soldiers] brother perished like falling petals." Or, "I shall plunge [into the enemy vessel] and fall like petals for the emperor." In his will, he writes, "Many soldiers (senpai) are gone like falling petals," and, "I do not hesitate to sacrifice myself. I am pleased. For the emperor (ōkimi) I shall plunge [into an enemy vessel] and fall [like cherry blossoms]." There are several other references to falling cherry blossoms as a metaphor of his death. He expresses his admiration for the navy: "The navy places high value on aesthetics. Everything is beautiful. Sailors' uniforms are not ugly like the ones for the army soldiers." He proudly describes the sailors as "carrying a short gun, wearing white gloves and new shoes, with a new badge on the collar of the uniform and a shining badge on the cap" (Morioka 1995b: 77, 82).

Otherwise serious Morioka, however, obviously enjoyed drinking. His March 2 diary entry reads: "Life without sake is no life. Sake. Sake. Sake. On Sundays, I am soaked in sake" (*Cherry Blossoms of the Same Class* 1966a: 181).

Morioka's thoughts are, as far as the available material goes, almost a perfect reproduction of the ideology of *pro rege et patria mori,* including the symbolic equation of loyalty to the emperor with that to the parents and the falling cherry blossoms as soldiers' sacrifice for the emperor. Morioka is not the only one who expressed the ideology of *pro rege et patria mori* with cherry blossoms as the master trope. Furuichi Toshirō, a graduate of Keiō University, was born on September 27, 1921 and died on April 6, 1945 as a tokkōtai pilot.[18] In a letter addressed to his parents and his sibling, dated April 4, he mentions that cherry blossoms at the base are in full bloom. He also notes that when he went to Usa Shrine to pray for luck in his military duty, cherry blossoms in the shrine compound were also in full bloom. His letter ends with his poem: "This young cherry is prepared to die for the emperor. After falling its fragrance will last forever" (Ebina 1977: 239–40; *Cherry Blossoms of the Same Class* 1966b: 60–64, 181–83). In fact, there are innumerable wills left by pilots who expressed the same idea. Nonetheless, we cannot take them at face value, given the context in which wills were written.

The Night before the Final Flight

Despite published wills, photos, and films in which we see smiling pilots saluting or waving good-bye before their final mission, the following description tells a different story. It is in a letter written on June 21, 1995, by Kasuga Takeo, who was eighty-six when he wrote it, addressed to Dr. Umezao Shōzō. He was drafted into the navy and was given the assignment of looking after the meals, laundry, room-cleaning, and other daily affairs of the student soldiers at the Tsuchiura Navy Airbase. He describes the night before their final flights:

> At the hall where their farewell parties were held, the young student officers drank cold sake the night before their flight. Some gulped the sake in one swallow, others kept gulping down [a large amount]. The whole place degenerated into chaos. Some broke hanging lightbulbs with their swords. Some lifted chairs to break the windows, and tore white tablecloths. A mixture of military songs and curses filled the air.

While some shouted in rage, others cried aloud. It was their last night of life. They thought of their parents, their faces and images, lovers' faces and their smiles, a sad farewell to their fiancées—all went through their minds like a running-horse lantern. Although they were supposedly ready to sacrifice their precious youth the next morning for Imperial Japan and for the emperor, they were torn beyond what words can express—some putting their heads on the table, some writing their wills, some folding their hands in meditation, some leaving the hall, and some dancing in frenzy while breaking flower vases. They all took off with the rising sun headband the next morning. But, this scene of utter desperation has hardly been reported. I observed it with my own eyes, as I took care of their daily life, which consisted of incredibly strenuous training, coupled with cruel and torturous "corporal punishment" as a daily routine.

Kasuga Takeo has never recovered from the effect of innumerable beatings he himself received. His superiors told him that corporal punishment would instill the spirit of a soldier in him. His letter is invaluable for describing how the "volunteers" felt the night before their deaths.[19] We now understand what the smile on Anazawa's face expressed as he took off never to return to his love, and those smiles on the pilots's face used in the poster photos by the military and others.

THE VOICES OF THE SURVIVORS

The enormity of the tragedy incurred by the tokkōtai operation cannot be fathomed without considering the impact of their deaths upon their parents, wives, lovers, siblings, and, in a very few cases, children. Most were very young students who, without the government's shortening of their university career, would have still been students. As we will see more in chapter 6, the pilots' writings reveal that many have experienced some platonic love, or had women with whom they were intensely in love. A few had wives, like Seki Yukio, who led the first attack, and even fewer had children, since the military selected the unmarried first. The government sent off young men who were plucked out of their universities and young navy practice pilots who were even younger. After the war, survivors suffered from acute feelings of guilt, emptiness, and nihilism, like the historian Irokawa Daikichi who farmed on a mountainside. Some transformed their energy into editing the writings left by their friends and siblings for publication. Most parents could not face their writings, or else they were gone by the time Japan had recovered enough from the ashes of destruction to afford such publications.

The family members dreaded "the red paper" *(akagami)*, the draft notice. With its arrival, one had no choice—one would be killed by the military police unless one complied. Often, they tried to resign themselves to their fates by framing their conscription as "service for the country," as Takushima Tokujirō wrote in the preface of the writings by his son, Takushima Tokumitsu, which he edited and published, first, privately in 1961 (Takushima 1967). For seventeen years, the father kept running to the door, hearing his son's voice, "I am back home, Father," only to gaze at a plaque on which is written: "The home of the survivors of the late navy pilot Takushima Tokumitsu, Lieutenant." His brief preface ends with a poem: "My son whom I love so much; it is unbearably lonely to see Cape jasmine, the flower without a voice, beaten under rain." Cape jasmine is named the "flower without a voice" *(kuchinashi)* in Japanese because its fruit never opens (its mouth). He left Tokushima, where he owned an automobile factory, and remained in the mountains, never to be able face the city. His son was a graduate of Keiō University and died in an accident while flying at age twenty-four in April 1945.

When Umezawa Kazuyo was drafted, his mother pleaded to the Office of the Draft *(chōheika)* explaining that her three other sons had already been drafted, that she had been raising her children single-handedly since her husband's death from cancer at age forty-two, and that her life would become even more difficult without Kazuyo. They replied that she was not the only one who suffered and that she should endure her suffering until Japan's victory. When she persisted in her opposition, an officer from the draft office visited her and threatened that she would be labeled a "non-national subject" *(hikokumin)*. After this encounter, she gave up (Umezawa Shōzō, personal communication, 1996).

Some mothers wrote protest letters, describing the sheer absurdity of sending young men whom they knew would be killed (Irokawa 1993: 47–48). Others simply prayed. Just before entering the navy, Nakao Taketoku (chapter 6) found his grandmother prostrate in front of the family alcove. She explained that she was praying because she no longer could walk [to go to a shrine or temple] (Nakao 1997: 623–34).

Hayashi Matsue was the mother of Hayashi Ichizō, a pilot introduced in detail in chapter 6. Hayashi Ichizō's writings were almost exclusively about his mother. Kaga Hiroko, Hayashi's older sister and editor of his diaries and letters, also provides us with invaluable information about their mother (Hayashi 1995: 175–211). Hayashi Ichizō, a graduate of the Imperial University of Kyoto, was born to a father who firmly believed in the Meiji "Enlightenment and Civilization" and taught young people to become teachers of agriculture. He became an assistant professor in the Department of Agriculture at the University of Tokyo but died suddenly at the young age of thirty-four. Influenced by Uchimura Kanzō, a Meiji Christian (chapter 2), he became a devout Christian. Tormented by her husband's death, Hayashi Matsue, who had converted to Christianity under his influence, begged her minister to explain the death of her husband. She decided to continue her husband's ideal and began devoting herself to educating young rural women at a time when few people thought there was any need to educate peasants, let alone peasant women. Since she did not have the time to look after her children, her parents looked after them. Yet she was deeply loved and also highly respected by all her children. Despite her busy schedule, she played the *koto* whenever she had the time.

Hayashi's sister recalled that in the early spring of 1944 she accompanied her mother to a shrine in Sasebo to pray for good luck on the battlefield. There, her mother purchased an amulet. It was this amulet that Hayashi, in a letter to his mother, said he would carry with him at the time he plunged into a vessel. His sister was puzzled but understood why her mother, a Christian, would pray at a shrine and purchase an amulet; her mother had heard that an amulet from the shrine would protect a soldier from bullets (Hayashi 1995: 201–4). Yet at another time when the mother and sister went to Kudan, where the Yasukuni Shrine is located, the mother told the sister to go to the shrine alone; she herself would wait at the bottom of the slope leading to the shrine (Hayashi 1995: 205). The mother's behavior seems to be a protest against the war and the ideology of *pro rege et patria mori*. That Hayashi's mother, a Christian, who refused to pay homage to the national shrine, would purchase an amulet, tells us how desperate she was. Hayashi's mother dreamed of the day when her son would become a family man and asked him several times in her letters to consider getting married, to which he only replied that he was destined to die and thus could not consider marriage (e.g. Hayashi 1995: 120).

On the day the war ended, Hayashi's mother bitterly complained that the death from the tokkōtai operation is "the death of a dog" (*inujini*, a meangless death). According to Hanada Chiyo, another older sister of Hayashi (Hayashi 1995: 124), she shouted: "Vice-Admiral Ōnishi [the one who invented the tokkōtai operation] must die." The sister was quite shocked by the strength in her mother's voice, because ever since Hayashi's death she had become visibly weakened (Ebina 1983: 311). Hayashi Matsue died at age eighty-eight on September 10, 1981 (Hayashi

1995: 12). She was quite anxious to join her husband and her son, as she indicated in her last poem. In her poems, she left no doubt that she protested the military which sent her son to death. I translate only a few lines from the thirteen poems (Hayashi 1995: 119–23). They are entitled *My Son has Fallen like Cherry Blossoms (Wagako wa Chiriniki):* "How sad it is to be born in the era when the word loyalty governs all." "You left your mother behind and went to the war, believing that it is the way to save the one hundred million Japanese." "Knowing that crying is against my son's wish, it is unbearably lonely not to cry." "Be at peace my children, I eagerly go to Heaven where my husband and my son are waiting." The last poem was written shortly before her death.

There is little need to elaborate how she felt. Most mothers shared her feeling of desperation. When the "red paper" arrived, Irokawa and his mother went to Narita Fudōsan temple; Fudōsan temples are believed to offer protection from calamities caused by humans, such as fire, traffic accidents, and wars. She was a victim of childhood polio, and he could not remember ever having seen her run. But as they arrived at the temple she frantically ran barefoot one hundred times across the hallway of the main building at the temple (Irokawa 1993: 47, 51). Walking or running a certain course one hundred times at a temple (a practice called *ohya-kudo*) is a way of praying to a Buddha for a wish to be granted.

If Hayashi Matsue lost her will to live and spent the rest of her life after her son's death waiting to join her husband and her son in Heaven, other mothers took a different route to join their sons. Field (1997: 156–59), describing how these pilots in fact were used as beasts of burden carrying bombs, tells us about a mother who hanged herself after learning that her son had been assigned to a one-way mission. Another mother drowned herself after receiving a package containing her son's locks of hair and nail clippings. It was a customary practice to send these "remains" ahead of time since there would be no remains to send home after their deaths. Her son never sortied and had to face the tragic fact upon his return. The mothers of Shima Sumio and Itō Hidetsugu, both student soldiers who perished as navy tokkōtai pilots, became nuns at Kōyasan Temple after a ceremony commemorating the twenty-second anniversary of the end of the war at Kōyasan (Misa n.d.: 36). Even after twenty-two years, they no longer could bear the suffering.

Bridal Dolls for the Deceased Soldiers at Yasukuni Shrine

The stories of survivors were told at a special exhibition, held from April 1 to August 31, 1997, at Yasukuni Shrine's exhibition hall, Yūshū-kan. Called "Bridal Dolls Dedicated to Heroic Souls," it was a display of bridal dolls *(hanayome ningyō)*, each dedicated by a mother or a sister to the "heroic souls" *(eirei)*, including some tokkōtai pilots. In the "traditional" Japanese wedding ceremony a bride wears three different kimonos: a black kimono with designs and embroidery, a colorful kimono (usually with red as the main color), and a pure white kimono, symbolizing purity and innocence. Of the forty-four dolls in the exhibit, many had white kimonos on, with some others wearing colorful ones. The well-known folk song, "The Bride" *(hanayome goryō)*, in a tone of exaggerated sentimentality, was continuously playing over the speaker. The leaflet at the entrance explained: "Many bridal dolls were sent to the Yasukuni Shrine by the survivors. For the heroic souls who fell like cherry blossoms during a storm at night, a mother or a sister expresses her feelings toward the beloved son, younger or older brother by dedicating in tears these bridal dolls to our shrine."

Housed in the exhibition cases were the photos of the deceased soldiers, bridal and other dolls, writings and some personal belongings of the soldiers, together with writings by the survivors. No context of the writings by fallen soldiers was given, making it difficult to assess their accuracy or the nature of their representation. Of the examples of these voices introduced below, only the first is that of a student soldier who died as a tokkōtai pilot. The others were not involved in the tokkōtai operation; they are introduced here in order to offer a glimpse of the lives and thoughts of some noncommissioned soldiers who are not introduced in this book but who deserve just as much attention as the student soldiers covered in this book.

Suga Hōsō, navy lieutenant, from Tokyo and a graduate of Rikkyō University, died as a tokkōtai pilot at age twenty-four. When he was drafted as a student soldier, his mother gave him a mirror which he thought of as a part of her and carried with him on his final flight. The exhibit included an empty case for the mirror on which he had written "My Mother," and his last words, addressed to her: "I will carry the content [mirror] with me as I go to Okinawa." In 1988 his sister, Yaeko, dedicated a set of dolls that she had made—a mother and a little female child, perhaps Yaeko herself. In 1963, his father dedicated a double-petaled cherry tree to the shrine. Suga Hōsō must have been quite fond of cherry blossoms; in a letter dated April 1945 to his family, he wrote: "In contrast to spring in the human world *(shaba)*, spring at the base is peaceful. I shall write again after cherry blossoms have fallen" (Ebina 1983: 183).[20]

Satō Takekazu, from Hokkaido, was an enlisted man in the Imperial Army with the rank of sergeant *(gunsō)*. His corps was moved from the northeastern border area of Manchuria to Okinawa right after the American landing there, where he died on April 10, 1945. His mother, Nami, visited the shrine on April 15, 1981 and offered a set of large wooden carvings of a mother bear and her cub (famous Hokkaido art) together with ¥5,000,000. She visited the shrine again in December 1981 with another set of wood carvings—a mother deer and her baby. On March 28, 1982 she offered a bridal doll in a colorful kimono and ¥5,000,000, accompanied by the following letter:

> Takekazu, you were indeed great. You bravely told me to meet you at Yasukuni Shrine when you left home for the front at the age of twenty-three. . . . It is unbearable to think of you gone without taking a wife. Here is the most beautiful bride in Japan which we dedicate to you. Her name is Sakurako (Cherry Blossom Child). I am already eighty-four years old. If I continue to live, I will visit you again. Please sleep in peace. Thanking you, your Mother.

She died around 1988.[21]

Tomita Tomiei (pronunciation of his first name not certain), an army corporal, died at age twenty-five on February 28, 1945. His sister dedicated a doll in a colorful kimono with a letter which, with some deletions, was exhibited by the shrine (the one ellipsis indicates my deletion):

> I am very pleased to receive an opportunity to talk with you. I write down my thoughts that I have had in my mind for many years. It has been almost sixty years since you visited me in your army uniform. First, I have to apologize. You asked me to send some money. Not knowing what you wanted the money for, I did not send it to you. I later heard that you wanted a leather bag to hold important personal belongings. I was greatly saddened that you fell [like cherry blossoms] in the south sea [when I failed to fulfill your wish]. This time they [Yasukuni Shrine] notified us that they are going to have an exhibit of bridal dolls. We gathered together your personal belongings to send them and I added a leather bag. So, please forgive me for my failure in the past. We include the textbook for your radio correspondence course, your notebook in which you preserved pressed flowers, and a book on Noguchi Hideyo [1876–1928, an internationally known bacteriologist who, like Tomita, was from Fukushima Prefecture] which you read when you were in elementary school.
>
> While your mother was alive, she used to say how much you liked sweets and she regularly offered sweet *ohagi* and *yōkan* [to the ancestral alcove]. On the day of commemoration of your death *(meinichi)* I

too offer them without fail. I have gone four times to your tomb in the battlefield in the southern island. The last time was the fiftieth anniversary after the war. I don't think I can go to the southern island anymore. But, with my sister Kimiko I visit you at the Yasukuni Shrine twice a year and I promise to continue my visits to you.

As for your biography and the military record [perhaps requested by the shrine], I could not do justice, since we had only two to three hours to leave Dalian [a small village in northeastern China occupied by the Japanese after the Russo-Japanese war] and left many important items behind. [Deletion by the shrine.] I am now eighty-two years old. I pray not to become senile since we have no descendants to look after our ancestors. [Deletion by the shrine.] In the spring, Kimiko and I go [to the shrine] at the end of March and join the survivors of the soldiers who died in the Marshall Islands and in the summer we join in the Ceremony for the Souls of the Deceased *(mitama matsuri)* at the Yasukuni Shrine. So, do wait for us.

. . . While your mother was alive, we rebuilt our house. Last year we rebuilt our stone ancestral tomb and placed sand from Brown Island [presumably where he died] in lieu of your bones. . . . One of our nephews has been very good to us and I have asked him to take care of you. I look forward to seeing you on April 4 or 5. Please look after us. March 8, 1997. Older sister, Tomita Mitsu

The letter ended with two poems she had composed.

When I first walked into the exhibition room, I was appalled and felt a rage inside of me. How can the shrine construct such a world of illusion with which to take advantage of the survivors, whose suffering was beyond words? But then I was reminded of the widespread custom in East Asia, including Japan, especially in the northeast, where the survivors offer items like bridal dolls, photos of young women, and votive plaques *(ema)* with pictures of young women to young men who died unmarried (Matsuzaki, ed. 1993). The display therefore was based on the folk custom in the regions where some of the soldiers came from. Yet, I felt quite uneasy—is the shrine exploiting the feelings of the survivors, who must find some meaning for the death of their loved ones, for its own purposes of promoting wartime nationalism and/or of soliciting contributions? I discussed my reactions to historian Irokawa Daikichi, well known for his vocal opposition of both militarism and the emperor system, who gently pointed out to me that we who did not experience the war could not proclaim outright that the soldiers died for nothing, or "died like dogs" *(inu-jini)*. Such a proclamation is too brutal to them and to their survivors.

I then read Naitō (1989: 209), who explains that the survivors of the Thunder Gods corps annually gather at the shrine, not because they believe in what Yasukuni stands for, but because their deceased comrades' last words were "I will be waiting for you at Yasukuni Shrine." Perhaps many of these soldiers did not believe their own words, as our examples of the pilots show, but what else could they have said, given the circumstances?

Conservative members of the Diet, including some Liberal Democratic Party (LDP) members, and conservative religious organizations tried in 1969 to pass a bill to reinstate the prewar status of the shrine, so that it would be supported by the state. The LDP supports the shrine in order to get the votes of a large number of survivors who are members of the Bereavement Society (Izokukai), as well as their financial contributions. Koizumi Jun'ichirō, who took office as prime minister of Japan on April 26, 2001, immediately announced his plan to create a regular military, instead of the defense force. During his campaign, he vowed to pay homage to the shrine if he won. With protests coming from China, South Korea, and other Asian nations, Koizumi, resolute until the last moment, finally took the compromise stance and visited the shrine on August 13, instead of August 14, the day of Japan's surrender. Not only liberals within Japan, but victims of Japanese militarism and colonialism, especially the Chinese, view the shrine as the embodiment of the brutality of the Japanese military and waged a strenuous protest against his visit. Known as the Yasukuni Shrine problem (Yasukuni mondai), the controversy has surfaced time and again since the end of the war (Hardacre 1989).

The complexity of the problem lies in the feelings and wishes of these survivors, not all of whom are supporters of the Bereavement Society. They must find some meaning in the deaths of their sons, brothers, and fathers, and it is important for them to have some form of collective commemoration. Throughout its history the shrine has constituted a complex space where individuals and social groups at times contest and other times simply assign different meanings and uses, often misrecognizing each other's meanings and significations.

The tokkōtai operation was "phantasmagorical," to borrow Marx's expression. The fascist state expounded on the importance of sacrifice and created a phantasm in the air, telling young men how beautiful it was to die for the emperor/country. Many, although not all, of the professional soldiers who developed and carried out the operation tortured the soldiers on the bases and sent them off to die. None volunteered to sortie.

To make the tokkōtai operation a "forced" voluntary system instead of an imperial order seems to have been a mechanism to exonerate those who were directly responsible for the utterly insane operation. The pilots were coerced either by their superiors, by the circumstances on the base, or by the atmosphere of the society at large. It is no wonder that when the war ended some officers were shot by those below them. At the notorious Tsuchiura Navy Airbase, the officer second in command was shot by his subordinate (Irokawa, personal communication, May 1999).

We are told that these young men, who "volunteered," toasted the emperor as they drank their last cups of sake and shouted "Banzai" to him. We are shown as evidence the photos that portray smiling or determined faces with white silk scarves and the rising sun headband. These photos, some of which are circulated as "poster child" photos, conceal what really went on at the bases and what these soldiers indeed thought and felt. Many of the photos in a booklet by Muranaga ([1989] 1997) on the tokkōtai pilots who flew off from the Chiran Army Airbase are not identified with individual names. Except for a few photos of individual pilots who are identified by name, and sometimes by date, they are labeled as "members of a tokkōtai corps." The sound track of the films tells us the song "Umiyukaba" was played when each plane in a squadron took off (Onoda 1971: 15). We recall that the text of this song was an ancient poem by Ōtomo no Yakamochi, who was in charge of the border guards (chapter 4). The poem is worth recalling once again:

> In the sea, water-logged corpses,
>> In the mountains those corpses with grasses growing on them
> But my desire to die next to our emperor unflinching.
>> I shall not look back.

This last scene before their departure, complete with the headband, silk scarf, the last sake, and this music, has been repeated over and over in films as "real" documentation.

In contrast to this image, we have seen how the pilots all agonized over their fate and yet managed not to show it. We saw this in the case of Seki Yukio, who led the attack on Leyte. We saw how the student soldiers expressed their agony, created mayhem on their last night, and yet took off the next morning with the rising sun headband. We will see in diaries in chapter 6 how they attempted to come to terms philosophically with the "fate they chose."

Many saw themselves as falling cherry blossoms, and many survivors referred to them as fallen cherry blossoms. But most, including Anazawa, Ichijima, Machida, Okabe, and Hayashi Matsue (Hayashi Ichizō's mother), did not mention the emperor. Anazawa Toshio's identification as a male led him to think of himself as a cherry blossom qua warrior. Ichijima Yasuo, a devout Christian, was patriotic enough to convince himself to fight for his country. The analogy he established between cherry blossoms and the pilots may be related to the fact that his church was named Cherry Blossom Church. Like Ichijima, Hayashi Matsue, a devout Christian, was resolutely against militarism, including the ideology involving the emperor. But she too referred to her son as a falling cherry blossom. Others, like Morioka and Furuichi, thought of themselves as cherry blossoms falling for the emperor, but they are much fewer in number.[22] A sister of Ogawa Kōhei, a corporal in the Imperial Army also in the exhibit, refers to her brother as having died "a young cherry *(wakazakura)* without bearing fruit." For Satō Takekazu's mother and Ogawa's sister, their son and brother were cherry blossoms whose petals fell without bearing fruit. Each assigned a different meaning to cherry blossoms.

What is certain is that despite the songs and other means by which the state tried to indoctrinate the soldiers, few soldiers or survivors referred to cherry blossoms as the souls of the fallen soldiers. In other words, even those who saw an analogy between soldiers and cherry blossoms did not envision the men being reborn as cherry blossoms at the Yasukuni Shrine, as the military ideology had it.

Yet Suga Hōsō's father planted a cherry tree in the compound of Yasukuni Shrine in memory of his son. In fact, hanging on many cherry trees in the compound are plaques on which the name of the corps or battalion and location of the battlefield are written. They were planted for the fallen soldiers by the surviving members of the corps, who gather together to commemorate their battlefield friends *(senyū)*. Do they believe that cherry blossoms are really metamorphosed souls of their deceased comrades? I think not. The shrine and its cherry trees provide a space where they can express their feelings to their deceased comrades, which is not possible if each of them is buried separately in a family tomb. Surviving members of the family come to the shrine to collectively commemorate their sons or brothers and to feel that they died for a worthy cause but not to endorse militarism and the ultra-right—they are painfully aware what these ideologies did to their loved ones.

The importance of the souls of the deceased is at the core of the importance of Yasukuni for the survivors. Despite Japan's seemingly utterly secular religiosity, which Eisenstadt (1996: 219–77) calls the tendencies to immanentization and to a "this-worldly" emphasis, the care of the souls of the deceased, misnamed "ancestor worship," is at the heart of the Japanese religiosity (Smith 1974; also Ohnuki-Tierney 1994a, 1997b). Family members pay annual homage to the family grave at *obon, higan,* and other prescribed times with flowers and incense. At those times at cemeteries, as the Japanese would say, the cars are lined up like the beads of a rosary *(juzu-tsunagi).* Most survivors I talked to use the term *kawaisō* in expressing their feelings of sorrow over the soldiers who perished in the hope of saving Japan, and many use the phrase "to visit and talk with him." They donate cherry trees and gather at Yasukuni because they want to commemorate the loved ones, not because they think they were reborn as blossoms. The shrine remains the space for the ultraright, which includes those who regularly drive through the major cities of Japan in vans painted in camouflage or black with the chrysanthemum crest painted in gold, carrying the old army and navy flags and banners on which "Hail to the Emperor" is written. They regularly park these trucks at the outer compound of the shrine. It is indeed unfortunate that the majority of the survivors are erased from the contemporary image of the shrine.

Most unfortunate of all is that the victims of the war, the fallen soldiers, are no longer remembered by the majority of the population. They have been placed in the dustbin of history, forgotten amidst the clamor of heated discussions between the liberals and the ultra-right, rather than as a reminder for the war guilt which all and every Japanese must share.

Chapter 6

FIVE TOKKŌTAI PILOTS

Introduced in this chapter are five pilots, each of whom left a substantial corpus of writing through which one can follow their thoughts and feelings over a period of years. The two central questions I ask are, what were their thoughts behind their "volunteering," and what role did cherry blossoms play in their contemplation of death?

As a reaction against structuralism, anthropologists' interests have shifted from structures of thought to *practice*, i.e., to what social actors or agents do. Thus we now seldom differentiate between reproduction of behavior and that of an ideology or thought structure. However, it seems quite reasonable to ask: Is identifying reproduction in behavior enough for us to understand historical continuity and discontinuity? Is our quest satisfied if we find that a perfect reproduction takes place in action, even in the absence of reproduction in the thoughts and feelings of social agents? I think not. In terms of overt behavior, the tokkōtai pilots appear to have reproduced the *pro rege et patria mori* ideology. But was their behavior accompanied by the reproduction of the ideology?

I examine the diaries, letters, and other writings left behind by student soldiers in an effort to understand how the complex thoughts and feelings influencing their behavior changed over time, from the years preceding their conscription into the military to the time of their deaths. I focus in particular on the interrelationships among patriotism, nationalism, and the *pro rege et patria mori* ideology in their thoughts, and on the role of the symbolism of cherry blossoms.

I have chosen to profile student soldiers for several reasons. First, the majority of the officers who perished as tokkōtai pilots were student soldiers. Second, many of these student soldiers were liberals or even radicals and thus were the most *un*likely individuals to volunteer as tokkōtai pilots. Finally, the writings published in the volumes dedicated to single pilots are just about the only ones that are reliable on a historiographic basis (see below). For another project, a comparison of their writings with the writings by fallen soldiers from rural Japan would shed some light on the picture of war from the ground up. An invaluable collection of letters left by men from farms in Iwate Prefecture is in Iwate-ken Nōson Bunka Kondankai, ed. [1961] 1974.

WRITINGS BY FALLEN SOLDIERS

Published and Unpublished Sources

Not a single scholarly work on the writings left by these pilots has appeared in a language other than Japanese. Only small samples of their writings appear in a limited number of publications.[1] In Japanese, however, there is a wealth of published material relating to the writings left by soldiers in general, and the tokkōtai pilots in particular. In fact, soldiers' writings have received far more attention than the tokkōtai operations. Published sources are primarily collections of their writings, rather than systematic interpretations of them. Unpublished sources include the originals of wills and letters housed at the former bases, military academies, and in various archives.[2] Unpublished material is nearly impossible to use in publications due to the difficulty in locating the material and in receiving permissions from the survivors.

Selected passages of the writings by fallen soldiers have appeared in edited volumes, journals, and magazines. These published passages sometimes are inaccurate copies of the original.[3] Furthermore, the selections are necessarily influenced by the vision of editors, both liberal and conservative, regarding how to represent the pilots, which makes it difficult to establish a profile of individual pilots and to understand complexities, ambiguities, and especially contradictions in their thoughts and struggles as they faced their imminent deaths.[4]

Far Off Mountains and Rivers was the first of the edited volumes, compiled in 1947 by Nanbara Shigeru, who was then president of the University of Tokyo.[5] It includes the writings—diaries, letters, poems, wills, etc.—of thirty-seven University of Tokyo students who perished in the war, both tokkōtai and non-tokkōtai. Because of the overwhelmingly enthusiastic response to this volume, a sequel, *Listen to the Voices of the Sea Gods: Handwritten Records of the Students Who Died in the War* was published in 1949; it is hereafter referred to as *Listen to the Voices* (1949).[6] It consists of the writings of seventy-six student soldiers from several universities. The purpose of both collections was to portray the complex feelings of these young men, including ambivalence, doubts, agony, sadness, desperation, rage over and mockery of the war and the state. Nonetheless, the editors of both collections had liberal outlooks and exercised a high degree of selectivity in what they included. In fact, in *Listen to the Voices* ([1949] 1981: 1) Watanabe Kazuo, consultant for the editorial board and a highly respected scholar of French literature, explained his position about deleted passages: "Initially, I insisted that it was fair to include those passages where an extreme nationalism or praise of the war was expressed, but others disagreed." Also, little of the student soldiers' background is introduced.[7] In 1988, another collection of brief excerpts of writings by forty-seven student soldiers from various universities was published with the title *Listen to the Voices of the Sea Gods: The Second Collection;* hereafter referred to as *Listen to the Voices* (1988). This collection included texts expressing patriotic/nationalistic devotion.[8] Hakuō Izokukai, ed. (1952) includes the letters and wills of a large number of student soldiers but gives no comprehensive portrayal of individuals. Volumes edited by conservatives predictably include only the passages reproducing the *pro rege et patria mori* ideology.[9]

Editorial Selection and the Symbolism of Cherry Blossoms

From the perspective of historiography, the symbolism of cherry blossoms poses additional problems. No systematic attention to the symbolism of cherry blossoms was given by any editor. Most often, but not exclusively, soldiers thought about cherry blossoms either in the context of the ideology or when they were blooming. Consequently, there is a general patten in which those editors who wished to present the soldiers as model soldiers who died for the emperor included the passages of the writings in which cherry blossoms, as embedded in the *pro rege et patria mori* ideology, appear, whereas liberal editors mostly ignored or chose not to include them when they appeared in the context of the ideology.

In the collection of writings or volumes dedicated to single soldiers, when the entries from early April are edited out, references to cherry blossoms also appear with less frequency. On the other hand, at the time of their final flights in 1945 cherry blossoms were in full bloom on the bases in southern Kyūshū. This gave rise to frequent references to cherry blossoms in the soldiers' writings during this period and, in addition, to a number of photos of the pilots with branches with cherry blossoms fastened to their uniforms.[10]

The Contexts and Nature of Writing

The truly amazing number of lengthy diaries left by tokkōtai pilots derives from the importance of "writing" as a mode of communication in Japanese culture. In a culture in which verbal communication in the form of debates, dialogues, or oratory is little developed, writing is the most serious mode of communication and the one through which many individuals choose to express their innermost thoughts and feelings. Diaries have been an important cultural practice ever since the Heian period, during which they developed into a special genre of literature as attested by an efflorescence of diaries, especially by women. Some of them became world classics.[11] The sheer quantity of writings left by these men is due in part to this cultural practice. In part it is also due to the fact these young men were exceptionally well educated, and reading and writing were their major activities. However, even to a greater degree it was because they had to sort out their thoughts and feelings by pouring out their anguish in writing.

The volume of writing they left behind is amazing given the censorship on the bases, referred to as "scissors" by soldiers and notorious for its extensive execution. Words like "capitalism," "inflation" (Fujishiro 1981: 432), and many foreign words, such as "butter," were all taboo. Kondō Kōzaburō, a graduate of Nagoya Higher School of Business who died in the Malay Peninsula, complained in a letter to his brother from south China that he could not write what he wanted because of the "scissors" (*Listen to the Voices* 1988: 115). Takei Osamu, a graduate of the University of Kyushu who died in Burma, wrote his anti-Tōjō mockery in a toilet (*Listen to the Voices* 1949: 87–102). Irokawa Daikichi, a student soldier from the University of Tokyo, wrote his diary in big letters after the lights went off, since he was afraid of the discovery and confiscation of his writings not only by his superiors but also by his ultranationalistic comrades (personal communication, May 1999). He gave them to his father when he was allowed to visit home. Wada Minoru (profiled below) bitterly complained about censorship by his superiors. He wrapped his writings with oiled paper, hid them under a bed of rice in a lunch box, and gave them to his parents upon their visits, or asked visitors to the base to mail them from outside. Hayashi Tadao (profiled below) kept Lenin's *The State and Revolution* but threw it away page by page in the toilet as he finished rereading it to avoid having it confiscated. The authorities inspected and intercepted not only personal writings but also photos. Most photos of the tokkōtai, especially the scene of their last sake drinking just before they took off, were all stamped "not permitted" and confiscated (Itō 1998; Nishii, ed. 1998; 1999: 173–76).

As we will see, the pilots poured their thoughts and feelings out in their writings, which shows how desperate they were to express themselves even under such conditions. While their diaries are often candid, representing intense dialogues with themselves, their letters are varied. In most cases, letters addressed to fathers or to both parents tend to be formal, written along official lines. It is rather easy to identify their letters written to assure family members or friends of their well-being. They were more candid in letters addressed to their mothers, wives, and lovers. Letters to their best friends also tend to express their most candid and innermost thoughts and feelings, but they are of a more cerebral nature than those written to the women.

The last letters home and the wills are the most problematic to interpret. We saw above that Muranaga considers them to be the expressions of the pilots' true thoughts and feelings. I think otherwise. They were not written just for family members. The pilots were told that their wills and letters would be displayed as the writings by "the heroic souls" *(eirei)*. Shinta Masamichi described the conditions under which he wrote his will:

> I knew the tokkōtai pilots would die like dogs. When I was selected to be one of 36 tokkōtai out of 200 trained to be tokkōtai pilots, I sank into the depths of despair. I was told to write my will so that they can display it at the Exhibition Hall for Education *(kyōiku sankōkan)*. Of course, we could not say what we really thought and felt. So we had to lie. It was taboo to express our true thoughts *(hon'ne)*. (Matsui 1994: 117–18)

Indeed, their wills were displayed as models for others to follow. They continue to be exhibited even today at Yasukuni Shrine and elsewhere.

Therefore, the "best evidence" for the reproduction of the *pro rege et patria mori* ideology and for the symbolism of cherry blossoms as the master trope is found in these wills, which are used by the Yasukuni Shrine, Muranaga ([1989] 1997), and others as the "testimony" of the tokkōtai noble spirits.[12] However, they turn out to be unreliable sources for understanding what these young men actually thought and felt.

Diaries of the Five Pilots

Because of the extremely partial representations of the pilots' writings in edited volumes, I have chosen to focus on five published books, each devoted to a single pilot, edited by a surviving family member or a friend. Except for the one for Hayashi Ichizō, each several-hundred-page book includes the diary of a single pilot over several years. Even in these volumes, some diary entries are deleted (see Sasaki entry below). When we have a large corpus of writings, however, these deletions are not as problematic.

Diaries spanning many years are important, since the years spent at the higher school and the university are crucial for understanding the gradual process whereby the young men struggled and came to terms with the path they "chose"—"to die."

For each pilot, I examine his thoughts about life and death in relation to their idealism, and the role of aesthetics embodied in cherry blossoms. In examining their thoughts, I distinguish between patriotism, that is, the individual sentiment of love of one's country, without a political dimension, from nationalism, which is predicated upon the presence of political boundaries and thus, in turn, upon the political presence of "them," the people(s) who press the boundary, culturally or, in the case of World War II, politically. In addition, when available, I include the relationship of the pilot to his parents, since the military state tried to indoctrinate the young men to fight for the country by transferring their loyalty from their parents to the emperor.

I discuss the writings of five pilots: Sasaki Hachirō, Hayashi Tadao, Wada Minoru, Hayashi Ichizō, and Nakao Taketoku.[13] All of them were student soldiers, and all but Hayashi Tadao were tokkōtai pilots. I include the latter not only because of the availability of his writings in a single volume, but because he offers a close parallel and yet a counterpoint to Sasaki. His writings show that tokkōtai pilots were not unique among student soldiers. I chose these five pilots because they are quite different from each other in their thoughts, feelings, and experiences, thereby offering us a cross-section of tokkōtai pilots and student soldiers in general. Except for Wada, all were in the fourteenth class in the navy and are introduced in *Cherry Blossoms of the Same Class* (1966a, b).

SOLILOQUIES IN THE NIGHT:
WHAT THE STUDENT SOLDIERS READ

There is no question that reading was an important part of these young men's lives. Therefore, I treat their readings as the most important part of their diaries and letters. I include in the Appendix a list of the 1,356 identifiable works that were read primarily by three pilots (Sasaki, Hayashi Tadao, and Nakao). Although Wada's reading is included, he discusses only thirty-eight works, in contrast to the far larger numbers mentioned by the others. Since Hayashi Ichizō's sister edited his letters and diary entries with a focus on his relationship to his mother, she excluded the passages on his reading, with the exception of the frequent references to two books—the Bible and Kierkegaard's *Sickness unto Death*. Therefore I did not include his readings in the list.

The reading list embodies the Japanese historical experience of coping with the global forces that confronted Japan at the end of the nineteenth century—in other words, the struggles with modernity and overcoming modernity, and with westernization and resistance toward westernization. The French and the Japanese had some cultural affinity even before the Meiji period, but the strong French influence is remarkable considering that French was taught only at the First and the Third Higher Schools, whereas German was taught at every higher school. German cultural, medical, political, and military influences became intense at the beginning of the Meiji period. Although it was Commodore Perry who opened Japan, and American political presence in international politics was considerable, American cultural influence in Japan was minimal at that time, except for the influence of their Protestantism through the influential Meiji Christian leaders. The small number of references to Chinese authors is misleading, since Japanese intellectuals never lost their admiration for the great thinkers of China, including political philosophers as well as religious figures who brought Buddhism into the country. In part their influences were already absorbed by Japanese intellectuals, rendering it unnecessary to point them out. But it was also a sign of the times that the Japanese felt an urgency to catch up with Western civilization.

For the young men, reading was a soliloquy as well as a form of dialogue with the world's great thinkers. Why they chose certain authors and thinkers to read and how they read their works tell us a great deal about their thoughts. The student soldiers I have chosen exemplify university students and young intellectuals at the time. Regardless of their specialization, university students were immersed in world civilizations, absorbing their philosophy, literature, music, and arts. The years they spent at prestigious higher schools and universities were supposed to be a period of self-education, when they pursued their own intellectual curiosity rather than being governed by a rigid curriculum. The higher schools and universities gave them an intellectual haven in which they espoused *cogito ergo sum*, as it were, before they entered the "real world" and became saddled with practical concerns. Many of them embraced "Marxism," a form of idealism that opposed materialism and capitalism. Many read works of both fiction and nonfiction in the original languages, especially French and German. They eagerly read classics as well. They also used their favorite foreign languages to express ideas that were particularly poignant to them. Some student soldiers wrote their wills in German or French.

The pilots dreamed wishfully of a phoenix—a new Japan—rising from the ashes of Japan's destruction, rather than work pragmatically to bring about that utopia through political strategies or movements. In his interpretation of *The German Ideology*, Dumont characterizes Thomas Mann's "unpolitical individualism" as the essence of the philosophical stance of the Germans. In Mann's own words, for Germans the most flattering characterization is "inwardness," and he sees the essence of German literature as "personal cultivation [*Bildung*]" (Dumont 1994: 53). Dumont's characterization of the Germans is befitting of these young Japanese men. Emerson's "hitch your wagon to a star" was well-known in Japan, inspiring young students in higher schools and universities.

The five pilots' writings should dispel the image of the tokkōtai pilots as simple-minded ultra-nationalists who were in lockstep with the military ideology, and who happily died for the emperor. It is impossible to comment on each book or author that these pilots read, nor do I have the space to analyze how each was read by each pilot; I am forced to be very selective. Below page numbers from the major source are placed in parentheses.

SASAKI HACHIRŌ

Sasaki Hachirō was born in 1923, drafted as a student soldier from the University of Tokyo in December 1943, and volunteered to be a tokkōtai pilot on February 20, 1945. He died as a navy ensign on a tokkōtai mission on April 14, 1945, at the age of 22.

Source: The Will of a Youth: Diary and Love, in the Absence of Life by Sasaki (1981) is a 466-page book devoted to his diary, letters, essays, and poems written between 1939 and 1945. The diary starts on March 16, 1939, when he was sixteen years old, and ends on December 8, 1943, when he was twenty-one. It does not cover the last period of his life on the base (December 9, 1944 to April 14, 1945). Some letters and excerpts of his diary from this period are appended by the editor at the end of the book, and some appear also in edited volumes.[14]

The period covered in *The Will of a Youth* starts about the time of Sasaki's entrance examinations to the First Higher School (Ikkō) in March 1939. Three years later in March 1942, he entered the University of Tokyo. His career from the First Higher School to the University of Tokyo was the most successful course any Japanese male could dream of at the time. Even among the cream of the crop, he was regarded as exceptional both in his physical condition and in his brilliance. Majoring in economics with a keen interest in history, he traveled widely in Japan and his interest in other Asian countries led him also to China and Manchuria (Sasaki 1981: 38).

Sasaki was one of five hundred students from the University of Tokyo drafted during three days in December 1943. On January 28, 1944, Sasaki was sent to the Yatabe Navy Airbase, where professional soldiers known as the "demonic prison guards" *(oni no shigoki)* were waiting. Sasaki was placed in Group No. 6 under an officer nicknamed "Ishioka the Demon." With any excuse, officers inflicted corporal punishment upon student soldiers or ordered them to run around the airbase many times. Some were hit so hard that they lost consciousness. The insides of their mouths were torn and their faces were swollen from the beatings (Fujishiro 1981: 448–51). On February 20, 1945, all were summoned into a hall and were asked to write down their names if they wished to *volunteer* to be tokkōtai pilots. It was hardly a free choice (Fujishiro 1981: 455).

Personal Profile: Sasaki came from an upper-middle-class family and apparently did not experience any financial difficulties. He was or tried to be cerebral in his relationship to his parents, although in his last letters he explicitly expressed his love toward them. When he passed the entrance examination to the First Higher School, his mother ran upstairs to his room while he was still in bed, held his hand, and cried in joy, thanking him again and again for having made it (16–17).[15] He was obviously pleased by her love and respect for him, as expressed through her emotional outburst. At the time of his successful entrance to the University of Tokyo, his mother became very excited about attending the ceremony held for the new students. He was both bemused by her excitement and embarrassed by her boasting (309–10).

Almost until the time he entered the navy, Sasaki was antagonistic toward his father because for him his father was a true believer and practitioner of capitalism—the worst offense for idealistic university students at the time. His father became enraged upon hearing of his decision to join the navy. Sasaki accused his father of being happy to see others volunteer to fight and yet wanting his own son to take care of him in his old age (387–88, 393–94). However, when his father was diagnosed with an advanced case of tuberculosis, he felt extremely guilty, realizing how hard his father had worked for the family all his life. Nevertheless, he concluded: "But, I have to go to fight" (399–400). The day before his final mission, Sasaki wrote to his father, "Although I have not taken care of you at all, tomorrow I will die for Japan. . . . Although I have never said in words, since this is the last opportunity, let me say that I love you." He repeats several times his love toward his father and he noted the warmth toward himself in his father's eyes (Fujishiro 1981: 464–65).

Fujishiro, the editor of *The Will of a Youth*, believes that Sasaki was in love twice, intensely but platonically. Sasaki told Ōuchi, his friend, that he would not be able to get married unless he found a woman who would truly love him (Fujishiro 1981: 441–46).

Intellectual Profile: Sasaki had a voracious appetite for books, which ranged from Plato and Socrates, to Rousseau, to those who lived for art for art's sake, like Oscar Wilde, Tanizaki Junichrō, and Satō Haruo.[16] He read German proficiently. Though by no means exclusively, the German intellectual tradition had a profound impact on him. He listened mostly to German composers, although he also enjoyed Bartók (Hungarian), Smetana (Czech), and Sibelius (Finnish). His favorite by far was Beethoven, whose music gave encouragement and solace when needed. An abbreviated reading list includes:

Philosophy, politics, economics—German: Dilthey, Engels; Feuerbach, Fichte, Hegel, Carl Hilty, Kant, Karl Kautsky, Theodor Lipps, Marx, Nietzsche, Ranke, Erich Maria Remarque, Schopenhauer, Wilhelm Windelband; English: Sir William James Ashley, Jeremy Bentham, Alfred Marshall, John Stuart Mill, Adam Smith; Italian: Benedetto Croce; Classical: Plato, Socrates; French: Rousseau; Russian: Lenin, Trotsky; Japanese: Uchimura Kanzō.

Science—German: Albert Einstein, Max Planck; English: Isaac Newton.

Sociology—German: Max Weber; Georg Simmel.

Literature—German: Goethe, Hesse, Mann, Schiller; English: Byron, Thomas Carlyle, Lafcadio Hearn, Shakespeare, H. G. Wells, Oscar Wilde; Russian: Chekhov, Dostoyevsky, Gogol, Tolstoy, Turgenev; French: Romain Rolland; Japanese: Abe Yoshishige, Arishima Takeo, Higuchi Ichiyō, Kawabata Yasunari, Kunikida Doppo, Miyazawa Kenji, Mori Ōgai, Natsume Sōseki, Tanizaki Junichirō, Tayama Katai, Yamamoto Yūzō.

Marxism as Idealism: In his quest to understand what was happening to Japan, Sasaki read a large number of books on philosophy, political economy, history, and related subjects. He often read them as counterpoints to the Marxism of Marx, Engels, Kropotkin, Lenin, and Trotsky which, of all the philosophical schools, was most influential to him. Yet he was not a blind follower of Marx. Repeatedly calling him a "craftsman" *(kō-sakunin)*, he disapproved of Marx for scientifically measuring human happiness (331). He was impressed by the aggressive stance of Lenin and Stalin and wished that "we had someone like them in Japan" (351). To Hitler and Mussolini, he reacted negatively. He read Tanabe Hajime (1885–1962), a major figure in Japanese philosophy who attempted to transcend both Hegel and Marx (112, 115, 132, 134, 137, 156, 297). Tanabe cast a powerful spell on young university students, and in the end his famous speech of May 1943 advocating political activism for individuals to change their society unwittingly provided encouragement for them to go to war (see the introduction and chapter 7).

His diary contains frequent references to Ōuchi Tsutomu, two years senior and Sasaki's close friend at the University of Tokyo. Ōuchi became a well-known leftist scholar/professor at the University of Tokyo after the war. As a congratulatory gift upon his entrance to the University of Tokyo, Ōuchi sent him a collection of essays by Friedrich Engels in Japanese. Finding the translation tedious, Sasaki read the original in German and was deeply moved (304). He also read *Das Kapital* and wrote, "After getting into volume 2 of *Das Kapital*, my progress is very slow. It is not well organized and the writing is obtuse" (351).

In a letter to Sasaki, Ōuchi opposed the war unequivocally and unambiguously and hoped for Japan's defeat. For Ōuchi, the war was for Japan's imperialism and for its rulers, and not for the people. He told Sasaki not to die in the war, since a wish to die in such a war derived only from a sense of heroism or from momentary sentimentalism—an act of stupidity.

The crucial influence of Marxism on Sasaki was his conclusion that Japan became corrupted by capitalism and there was an urgent need to destroy it in order to bring about a new Japan—the belief/rationale which led him to his death. Disagreeing with Ōuchi (364–65), the war to him was justified because both the United Stated and England represented the evil forces of capitalism (365). He believed that the Japanese still retained some feudal elements, such as the way of the warrior (bushidō), which protected the Japanese from becoming simple prey for capitalism, although he keenly felt the danger of "illogical spiritualism" (279). The news of the American landing on Attu prompted him to engage in a long soliloquy about capitalism and Marxism and about how capitalism was going through its final stage (359–62, emphasis added):

> There is some sign of a new ethos for a new era. However, even though the material foundation for the new era is already being built, we cannot help but notice the legacy of old capitalism. If the power of old capitalism is something we cannot get rid of easily but if it can be crushed by *defeat in war, we are turning the disaster into a fortunate event.* We are now searching for something like *a phoenix which rises out of ashes.* Even if Japan gets defeated once or twice, as long as the Japanese survive, Japan will not be destroyed. It looks as though we are "carp on the cutting board" *(sojō no koi).* I am not being pessimistic, but we cannot deny reality. We have to move on, overcoming the times of difficulty.

The passage reiterates "his" patriotism, which welcomes Japan's defeat since it means the death of "old capitalism" and the birth of a New Japan free of the shackles of capitalism. He identifies his purpose of life: "At the critical juncture in history 'we' cannot let old capitalists and irrational military men cling to the old regime. We [young men] ourselves must shoulder the responsibility of bringing in the new world" (377; see also Fujishiro 1981: 439).

A "phoenix rising out of the ashes of destruction" was a favorite metaphor of the young intellectuals at the time (chapter 8). For Sasaki, the phoenix is a New Japan, brimming with love for humanity and free of the capitalistic developments that had transformed individualism into egotism (365). For him, death in the war was honorable because it bestowed honor on a young man, and he wished to die after fulfilling his duty and responsibility for the creation of a New Japan (365). His declaration to join the navy sounds decisive in tone (391–94, emphasis added):

> Finally I will join the navy on December 1. In anticipation, I have trained my body by swimming, gymnastics, and target practice. I am confident about my strength. We must now be *the shield* to protect the

eternal life of our nation by going to the front to prevent the enemy's advance as much as possible. Scholarship is important. But, our discipline [economics], which is pragmatic and socially relevant, will become even better when we are trained in the military. Even if I fall [die], society does not rely on one individual. I am not concerned and shall eagerly go to the front.

The term "shield" suggests the penetration of the state effort to resurrect the ancient term which the border guards used to refer to themselves as the shield for the emperor. Sasaki's use, however, is the shield for Japan, *pro patria mori*, rather than *pro rege et patria mori*. Had he wanted, he could have become an officer in charge of finances at the base, but he definitely preferred to be "where soldiers belong," already hinting at his volunteering to be a tokkōtai pilot.

Individual and Society — Life, or Death for Idealism: One of the major concerns Sasaki expressed time and again throughout his diary was his responsibility toward society. It was not an abstract concern for Sasaki and others, since the choice to live for themselves meant life, whereas the choice to serve society meant death. Sasaki and others chose the latter. But the choice was made only after "rationalizing" through anguished philosophical debates over happiness and death from Socrates, the Cyrenaics, the Epicureans, to the Cynics, on the one hand, and, on the other, over the notion of one's responsibility from Aristotle to Kant (188).

In the final analysis, it was their idealism that led Sasaki and others to take the course for death, through which they hoped to bring about their utopia—a New Japan. Sasaki's vision of a New Japan derived from the philosophical idealism that runs through Rousseau, Kant, Fichte, Schelling, and Goethe in *Wilhelm Meister*—all of whom he read eagerly. His idealism, therefore, was not a simple Marxian vision but a complex set of deliberations upon the nature of human being. Inspired by a lecture given by Asanaga Sanjūrō, he traces the development of the consciousness of the self: "Beginning with Socrates, it was rediscovered during the Renaissance, transformed in Kant's transcendental idealism, became the absolute self in Romanticism only to be abandoned during the latter half of the nineteenth century, and was revived by the Neo-Romanticists of southwestern Germany" (207–9). He is torn between giving priority to rationality or emotion: "Rationality, a ghost. Dessication of emotion" (118). Yet, after reading Nietzsche and Rousseau, he states: "Only after emotions subside, deliberations come through" (137).

Utopia: If Marxism provided him with a way to identify evil, Miyazawa Kenji and the humanitarianism of Albert Schweitzer shaped his vision of utopia. Sasaki wrote a long essay on Miyazawa Kenji for the last class reunion of the First Higher School on November 10, 1943. Miyazawa Kenji (1896–1932) was a poet and author of children's books who dedicated himself to helping farmers. Sasaki's essay, "Love, War, and Death: On Miyazawa Kenji's *The Crow and the Great Dipper*," centered on two passages by Miyazawa that expressed his own feelings. The first is the crow's prayer to the Great Dipper, its guardian deity, on the eve of its war against the mountain crows (Fujishiro 1981: 418–19):

> "I don't know if I am supposed to win this war but I will fight as much as I can, leaving my fate in your hands. . . . I pray that we will see the day as soon as possible when we welcome a world in which we do not have to kill enemies whom we cannot hate. For this end, I would not mind my body being ripped innumerable times."

Schweitzer also provided him with a sustaining source of inspiration and strength. While still in the higher school, he began reading Albert Schweitzer's *Aus meinem Leben und Denken* in German. He admired the motto Schweitzer wrote at the age of twenty-one: "Devote myself to scholarship and art until age thirty, and afterward devote myself to those who are unfortunate." Inspired by Schweitzer's "nonromantic humanitarianism," Sasaki felt a surge of strength inside (362–63). He quotes Schweitzer to express his determination to "recognize the value of any task and devote oneself to it with full responsibility" and to denounce heroism in one's action (376–77).

Aesthetics — Nature and Cherry Blossoms: Sasaki's quest for aesthetics was a natural part of his idealism:

> I read Schiller's poems. I find common threads between his longing for the Greeks and our quest to return to the *Manyōshū,* although I find a contrast between the sunny power of the Greek mind and the solid power of the *Manyōshū*—a contrast between the West and the East? In Hegel I sense beauty, truth, freedom, and an intuitive rationality of the Greeks. As Kierkegaard suggests, Hegel offers something more than German philosophy—Greek-like Romanticism? I read Schiller's *Die Götter Griechenlands* and *Die Künstler.* Beautiful and powerful. I feel a surge of strength in my whole body. The eighteenth and nineteenth centuries were not completely dominated by rationalism (228).

Sasaki's quest for beauty extended beyond the ideational world to nature, including cherry blossoms, either as he experienced nature directly or as it was depicted in various literary works. For an understanding of the symbolism of cherry blossoms, someone like Sasaki, an avowed Marxist, is important. The symbolism of the flower within the context of the ideology of *pro rege et patria mori* found in the writings of conservative soldiers would be predictable. It is important, then, to examine the range of meanings Sasaki assigned to the flower and to ask if the flower's meaning in the context of *pro rege et patria mori* had indeed penetrated into his thoughts.

During a 1940 bus trip along Lake Yamanaka, Sasaki became intoxicated by the spring scenery, especially Mt. Fuji and cherry blossoms (82). The following spring, he expressed his amazement over cherry blossoms that had bloomed overnight and worried that they may scatter because of a strong wind (206). A few days later he went on a trip without a fixed itinerary. On the island of Ōshima he composed two poems in both of which fallen cherry petals are a metaphor for the passing spring (209–10). At Shimoda (Shizuoka Prefecture), he appreciated how the cherry blossoms there were still blooming, unlike the mountain cherries on Ōshima which had fallen already. While referring to two famous poems by the well-known poet Bokusui which praise blooming mountain cherry blossoms, he composed his own poem expressing pathos over cherry blossoms whose blooming season was over (210–11). In March 1942, he admired mountain cherry blossoms in full bloom, which he associated with "youth," which is written in Japanese in two characters that mean the "blue spring." He noted that when he walked on the street, women in spring attire looked so attractive (308–9). Clearly cherry blossoms are a metaphor of youth, women, beauty, and himself. At the same time, cherry blossoms remind him of the fleetingness of spring and its beauty, which he associates with pathos.

Right after registering a sharp criticism of the Japanese for celebrating the Pearl Harbor attack and the apotheosis of the nine war heroes, he praised cherry blossoms enveloped in the morning mist at Shinobazu-no-ike in Ueno in Tokyo, whose petals had partially fallen. He states how refreshing they were. After accusing the government for using actresses to sell government bonds at the Imperial Theater, he praised mountain cherry blossoms that he saw from his house. He was touched by their "modest beauty" and composed two poems praising cherry blossoms that bloom by themselves in the mountains without seeking fame (311–12). A few days later, he composed another poem about how double-petaled cherry blossoms on a single tree against green nature capture the entirety of spring (312). In these passages, cherry blossoms stand for the counterpart of the Japan that was now engulfed in war fever.

Shortly before his final mission, Sasaki was given a special privilege to go back home. He confided to his best friend, Hirasawa, that he had volunteered to be a tokkōtai pilot, although he had not told his parents. Hirasawa begged Sasaki not to throw his life away but to try to fly back to the base even at the risk of facing shame. The two went to take photos and then Sasaki gave him a tuft of his hair. It was their last meeting. Sasaki later sent Hirasawa a poem in which he directly linked himself to mountain cherry blossoms whose image is reflected in the purity of snow in high mountains (Fujishiro 1981: 458).

At the time of Sasaki's final mission, cherry blossoms at the bases in southern Kyūshū were in full bloom. Fujishiro (1981: 462) notes that the pilots adorned themselves with cherry branches on their last missions but does not particularly mention if Sasaki did. In a letter to his friend Hirasawa, after describing double-petaled cherry blossoms in full bloom, he reports how one after another the tokkōtai planes had taken off—it was the time of an all-out attack. Even though his turn would come any moment, he found that it was beyond expression to describe how death as a tokkōtai pilot would be his ultimate wish as a man (Fujishiro 1981: 462). During his last days at the Kanoya Navy Airbase, Sasaki wrote a number of poems with references to cherry blossoms. In one of them, he referred to cherry blossoms which fall just as spring passes away after enveloping the "place under the sun [Japan]" with their fragrance (Ebina 1983: 185; not included in Sasaki 1981). He sent seven of his poems to Hirasawa. In one, the tokkōtai pilots taking off with cherry blossoms were described as ancient warriors. In another, after thanking Hirasawa for his friendship, he vowed to "fall like cherry blossoms" after sinking an aircraft carrier (Fujishiro 1981: 462–63). After his death, his sister composed a poem in which she referred to him as a mountain cherry blossom (Fujishiro 1981: 465).

For Sasaki, cherry blossoms represented the counterpoint to what was happening in society and were the ideal model he tried to emulate— to maintain one's own integrity and remain pure and beautiful without bending to the temptations of society and without seeking fame. More than a metaphor for himself, cherry blossoms were a transcendent mirror showing what he aspired to be, knowing very well his own weakness for fame and praise. Toward the end of his life, falling cherry blossoms served as the metaphor for the pilots, including himself, who "fall" for the country, but *without* references to the emperor or to cherry blossoms as the souls of fallen soldiers at the Yasukuni Shrine.

Just as Sasaki appreciated the beauty of cherry blossoms and of nature in general, so also was he drawn to authors who wrote about nature, such as Kunikida Doppo, whose *Musashino* famously aestheticized the ideal of nature untouched by civilization. This novel made Musashino, a Tokyo suburb, synonymous with nature and implicitly opposed it to the nearby urban center of Tokyo. Sasaki's quest for beauty, in nature and in the ideational world, explains how he became engrossed in the novels of Kawabata Yasunari, a Nobel prize-winning novelist, whose work is imbued with exquisite beauty.

After forty years of teaching at an agricultural school, Miyazawa Kenji, one of the sources of Sasaki's utopian thinking, spent the rest of his life on a farm, subsisting on the products of the farm while writing and teaching farmers how to improve their methods. Miyazawa's idealism, the purity of his spirit, and the self-sacrifice for humanity expressed in his work made him posthumously famous, and many young intellectuals became ardent followers of his work and his principles (Miura 1996: 495). Miyazawa Kenji stood for uncontaminated *Japanese* nature. As I have discussed elsewhere (Ohnuki-Tierney 1993a), in the cultural imaginations of many peoples, agriculture, the rural, and the peasant all stand for the primordial self of a people, be it in France, Germany, Russia, China, or Japan, before the contamination by urbanization, industrialization, and foreign influences.

Antiwar and Antimilitary: Like many other student soldiers, Sasaki took a firm and explicit antiwar stance (264). He was highly critical of the way the Japanese were ecstatic about the victories over China and Russia (279–80). Similarly, he was critical of World War II: "Somehow I just can't be euphoric over the news of Japanese victories. I feel anxiety. I wonder what will happen to capitalism after the war" (262). He was concerned with nonhumanitarian and unethical behavior on the part of the Japanese, and he pointed out how the military ignored "unethical" conduct, such as torturing men who refused to go to war and "training" soldiers to face death on the base (281). He was quite upset by the Japanese occupation of Singapore, which was celebrated in a frenzied manner by the Japanese. He expressed his concern over the large number of civilian casualties that the operation must have inflicted (292–93).

Beginning with his entrance to the University of Tokyo in April 1942, the tone of his diary becomes darker. On April 5, he states that spring is an annoying season—a complete turnabout from his celebration of spring on March 26 of the same year. He sees hypocrisy in the celebration of "the Japanese spirit" and "the imperial country" *(sumera mi-kuni)*. He uses exclamation marks when he writes: "The military—A Big Fool!" *(gunbu no ōbakayarō)* (310–11). He harshly criticizes the newspapers for making such fanfare about the nine deified soldiers of Pearl Harbor. He is terribly annoyed by how the media praises mothers for having raised their sons to be "splendid soldiers." He sees through the state "strategy," which misleads people into participating in the war effort by *forcing* (his word) loyalty *(chū)* to the emperor through its praise of mothers (311). He is concerned with the utilization of patriotism at the time of Japan's crisis by "the right wing" (192–93).

He heard in the news of Victor Emmanuel III's dismissal of Mussolini in July 1943. After hearing of the use of a treacherous tactic by the Germans against the British in Italy, Sasaki describes his loss of faith in Germany and envisions Germany as a country and the Germans as a people to be distasteful (380–81). He declares that it will be a matter of days before Germany and Italy surrender (381–82). His reaction to the Nazi propaganda film *Triumph des Willen* by Leni Riefenstahl is extremely negative. He is bored by its repetitiveness. He can see how one might be moved to join the Nazis because of the way they claim to represent the collective life of "one people." But he finds their techniques appalling: sanctification of labor for the "collectivity," turning people into idiots, and having them perform for the dictator. These techniques, for him, are "against humanity and against history" (301–2). His reaction to the other famous German film, *Heimat*, is not enthusiastic. He does not find "beauty" in it (182).

Patriot Critical of Japan: Despite Sasaki's critical stance he was deeply patriotic—patriotic for an idealized Japan. Even though he criticized his fellow Japanese for their joy over the victories in the Sino-Japanese and Russo-Japanese Wars, he was quite moved when he read about the mass suicide of the Japanese soldiers on Attu (363–64). The wounded who no longer could fight bowed toward the direction of the imperial palace and committed suicide, after which the rest attacked the enemy in the dark with a firm belief that their behavior would set a model for other Japanese to follow, leading to Japan's eventual victory. Sasaki was moved to tears when reading the will left by Captain Yamasaki, who led the last assault. He hoped that the war would be prolonged so that after finishing his university studies he would be able to join the military. He proclaims: "We must fight to the end so that the Japanese can create a new era by the Japanese ourselves. We cannot succumb to the 'red hair and blue eyes' *(kōmō hekigan,* term used to refer to Europeans)." Patriotism verging on nationalism is also found in Sasaki's favorite song (composer not identified), in which "the Japanese soul" (yamato damashii) is described as the motivation to act even if one knows it leads to death (Fujishiro 1981: 446).

We recall from chapter 2 that Meiji Christians had gone through a difficult time fighting against the ultra-right, while maintaining their own identity as Japanese. The struggle was exemplified by Uchimura Kanzō, the famous Christian of the Meiji period who opposed the *pro rege et patria mori* ideology. Sasaki greatly admired Uchimura for his courage in resisting the governmental pressure to worship the emperor as God (90, 113, 260).

Pro Patria Mori vs. Pro Rege et Patria Mori: Early on, Sasaki's patriotic side almost verged on *pro rege et patria mori.* When he was asked during the oral examination for the First Higher School to name the individuals he respected most, he listed Beethoven and General Nogi (15). Nogi was the general who did not spare his sons' lives during the war against Russia and who committed suicide together with his wife when the Meiji emperor's body crossed the bridge and left the Imperial Palace (see chapters 3 and 7) (Bitō [1986] 1994). When the war broke out, Sasaki wrote that since he was living a good life in this imperial nation *(teikoku)* because of the emperor's grace *(kōon no shitani),* he would not refuse the draft and would not be a coward afraid of war (263–64).

This sentiment, however, is accompanied by antimilitary statements expressing a cynical stance toward *pro rege et patria mori* ideology, especially after he entered the University of Tokyo in April 1942. He sarcastically remarks that he wishes to "personally experience" the hypocrisy of "the Japanese spirit" and "the imperial country" *(sumera mikuni)* (310–11). Referring to someone who proclaimed that he was ready to die because Prince Takamatsu talked to him in person, he declares that one does not die just to be granted a meeting *(haietsu)* with a prince or to be promoted by two ranks *(nikaikyū tokushin)* (403–4). This statement refers to two tactics the military used to encourage soldiers to die for the country/emperor: "promising" that the emperor would pay homage to their souls at Yasukuni Shrine and granting a promotion of two ranks to those who sacrificed themselves.

Loyalty toward Parents, Loyalty toward the Emperor: A major strategy of the state from the beginning of the Meiji period was to transfer the notion of love, loyalty, and indebtedness from one's parents to the emperor, who was constructed and represented to the people as their father, with the entire population of Japan constituting one family. The government policy for the posthumous promotion by two ranks increased not only the prestige that goes with a higher ranking but also the amount of compensation for the survivors. Importantly, the latter facilitated the conversion of loyalty to one's parents into loyalty to the emperor—the sacrifice for the emperor guaranteed financial support for the parents. When soldiers are faced with imminent death "anyway," this certainly offers a rationale to plunge into death, especially if the parents are not well-to-do. Sasaki was able to see through the state strategy.

His uncle had given him a great deal of money (¥1,000) as a gift upon his entrance to the University of Tokyo. After stating that he would most likely not fulfill the expectations of his uncle to become a successful man, Sasaki writes: "Although I do not want to disappoint my parents, if I must do so in my pursuit of a larger cause, I have no choice. However, I hope it will not happen." In other words, he knew that his father, his uncle, and others expected him to successful, but he was willing to serve his country even if it meant forfeiting his obligation to his parents (310). After the date for joining the navy was set, he expressed his belief that enlisting in the navy to protect his country amounted to caring for his parents (391–94). As noted above, his father became gravely ill and yet he decided not to change his mind about enlisting. In addition, he purposely chose to be a tokkōtai pilot even though he could have chosen a desk job as an accountant on the base.

On the other hand, he did not equate "his country" with the emperor, and he made explicit statements against the *pro rege et patria mori* ideology, for example, calling the concept of *chūkō icchi* (an equation of loyalty to the master/emperor and to the parents) a residue of medieval times (306). When he did not attend the ceremony commemorating the emperor's birthday *(tenchōsetsu)*, his father criticized him for not having the national spirit *(kokka seishin)*. He stated that one cannot be free from societal rules and thus he would follow the example of Socrates, but that he would not have anything to do with the national spirit (313).

In sum, Sasaki was unquestionably patriotic. For his country he was willing to forego his obligation to his parents. Despite some elements of contradiction in his statements about the *pro rege et patria mori* ideology, he was willing to sacrifice his life for his country but not for the emperor, and he knew did not believe in the equation of loyalty to the emperor with loyalty to the parents.

Agony and Ambivalence: Sasaki was deeply committed to the notion of sacrificing his life for a New Japan. Yet, he also felt great ambivalence and agony, as one might expect, as expressed in references to novels by Natsume Sōseki (1867–1916), a major intellectual figure whose literary writings were very influential. Highly educated in the English and American literary traditions, Natsume Sōseki was concerned with how to reconcile one's own integrity with one's own responsibility as a member of society. He refused to accept a doctorate in literature offered by the Ministry of Education, believing that literature and art should not be influenced by political authority.

Sasaki expressed his doubts and anxieties when writing at length about two novels by Natsume Sōseki: *Kōjin* (The Traveler) and *Kokoro* (The Soul). The solitude of human existence and the struggle for life and death are the major themes of these novels. Sasaki identifies himself with the protagonists of the novels, repeating statements such as "To die or to go insane" (from *Kōjin*) and echoing their dilemmas of whether to live according to their own convictions or to meet the demands of society. Through these references to Sōseki, Sasaki portrays his utter despair at not being able to decide which course of action he should choose. He is unable to be decisive about sacrificing himself for the war—just as he thought he was able to face death, he begins to enjoy life. He is torn and tormented by doubts. Referring to the time when he took the entrance examination to the First Higher School, he states: "At one time I even embraced General Nogi. Perhaps it is better to go to war. Things will be more clear-cut" (326). This is a statement of desperation—preferring death to the agony of indecision. Sasaki also read Mori Ōgai (1862–1922), another well-known novelist, who wrestled with the questions of modernity and of life and death in relation to one's responsibility to society.

As we will see later in this chapter, many young men shared this feeling. That is, they opted for death just to be relieved of agony of indecision. It was partly because the alternative—refusing to volunteer—was not a realistic option. They may be tortured or killed, or at the very least be ostracized. But, according to the writings of many, they simply could not refuse to volunteer when their friends and comrades had already or were offering their lives.

In his search for meaning in life, Sasaki ripped a photo of Engels from the book Ōuchi had given him and put it on his desk. He wrote that he had come to appreciate Engels, who played second fiddle to Marx all his life. In stating his envy of Engels for being able to devote himself to another person, Sasaki expressed his torment over his struggle between living for himself and dying for Japan (340). The same issue emerges in Sasaki's reaction to a stage production of *The Forty-Seven Loyal Retainers*. He was moved to tears by the singular devotion of these retainers to one cause—avenging their master (351). As we saw earlier (chapter 4), by World War II this play had been completely transformed to suit the *pro rege et patria mori* ideology and had become a morality play advocating loyalty to one's master, that is, by then, the emperor. Even though Sasaki shrewdly saw through the military state manipulation of the nine deity-soldiers of Pearl Harbor, he was moved by this morality play.

Sasaki's reaction to the news of the death of Admiral Yamamoto Isoroku (1884–1943) reveals his anguish. Yamamoto first opposed Japan's entry into the war, declaring that Japan's success would last for only six months to a year. However, he was assigned to be in charge of the Pearl Harbor attack and the battle of Midway. He was killed in a plane shot down by the Americans and became a hero. Upon hearing of his death, Sasaki felt an impulse to volunteer to be a pilot and die. But he writes, "It may give a more stable feeling," again expressing the feeling that he would rather die than go through the pain of suffering over his indecision (362–63).[17]

His ambivalence is most poignantly expressed in the following, in which he uses a well-known statement from Goethe's *Faust* ("Before the Gate") (397–98):

> *Zwei Seelen wohnen auch in Mein Herz!!* (Ah, two souls [*tamashii*] reside in my heart [*kokoro*]!!). After all I am just a human being. Sometimes my chest pounds with excitement when I think of the day I will fly into the sky [as a tokkōtai pilot]. I trained my mind and body as hard as I could and am anxious for the day I can use them to their full capacity in fighting. I think my life and death belong to the mission. Yet, at other times, I envy those science majors who remain at home [they were exempt from the draft]. Or, I think of those fellows who did not pass the draft examination [to be selected as pilots] as "having managed cleverly." I envy those who became bookkeepers or those who work at the headquarters. I am drawn by my second soul to the earth. Perhaps this is inevitable. These two souls of mine are hidden in me but each raises its head as external stimulations work on my mind. When I talk to my comrades who are also going on the mission, when I have full confidence in my body and my mind, when I visit my family and relatives who encourage me and thank me, then I become filled with spirit to protect them by becoming a *shield* for them. When they publicly announce at the base "Sasaki Hachirō, Kō Pass" [passing

with the top score], and the army tries to persuade me to quit the navy and join them, then I find meaning in my life. I become excited and wish to work as hard as possible. On the other hand, when I hear that those in bookkeeping or at the headquarters are talked about as if they are the ones with good academic records, or see those without talent becoming engineers and doctors, working at safe places and being pampered, then I realize that we are the ones who are placed at the most dangerous spot. I am reminded of workers [under the capitalistic system] who become discouraged when they realize how the management takes advantage of them. I feel like a fool to be proud of my fitness as a pilot. Those who skillfully escaped by not qualifying in the examination and took shelter in bookkeeping, engineering, and medical tasks must be the real clever ones. One of my souls looks to heaven, while the other is attracted to the earth. I wish to enter the navy as soon as possible so that I can devote myself to the task. I hope that the days when I am tormented by stupid thoughts will pass quickly.

In the end, Sasaki's doubts were so painful that he wished to join the navy and sacrifice himself as a tokkōtai just so that he could escape from the agony. In this passage, he suggests that his family supports his action, but, as we noted earlier, they were violently opposed to it.

Psychological Motivation: In addition to his cerebral "rationale" for sacrificing himself, Sasaki also shows us a state of mind that many young men experienced at the height of militarism, which penetrated the minds of even the brightest and the most critical. In wartime Japan, the state created a frenzied atmosphere in which patriotism was praised as the utmost virtue. Tokkōtai pilots were ensconced as "heroes among heroes," and their friends and people in the community lavished them with respect and praise. This praise had a powerful psychological impact on many pilots. In this atmosphere, those who considered the war effort, including the tokkōtai operation, to be futile could not voice their opinions in public.

There is no question that Sasaki enjoyed esteem from others, including the acclaim he received because of his extraordinary academic brilliance and success. He uses the German word *Ehrgeiz* to refer to the Japanese concept *kōmyōshin*, the desire for fame. He repeatedly states being torn between his own wish for *Ehrgeiz* and self-doubt (e.g., 278). In reference to the entrance examination to the University of Tokyo, he vows to pass it with the top score so that he can simply dismiss those who seek acclaim (286). In other words, because of his own weakness for praise, which he wished to get rid of, he was especially sensitive to those who performed well only to receive praise. The diary entry on the day before he entered the navy makes it clear that Sasaki derived much satisfaction and self-assurance from the praise of his friends and relatives, who held an elaborate farewell party, writing their "true feelings" on the rising sun flag. He was very much touched when former members of the Travel Club of the First Higher School came to bid farewell to him. His best friend even gave him a haircut, which moved him deeply (404–7).

One of the recurrent themes in the writings by student soldiers is their sense of identity as men. They saw their sacrifice for the country as a man's duty, which included a sense of protecting their beloved women—mostly mothers, but also wives, lovers, and young women in the abstract, since many young pilots had not had a relationship with a particular woman. Sasaki praises *kyōkaku*, a type of man during the Edo period who helps the weak and fights against the strong; they were romanticized in later periods. He wishes to live as a man and die as a man, just as a kyōkaku did. He repeatedly uses *otoko* (man), a term that emphasizes the masculinity of these figures, the ideal masculine model for him (289). The state since the Meiji era had deliberately used the strategy of appealing to young men's sense of masculinity to encourage them to take to arms and of emphasizing the reproductive role of women who produce and nurture such young men. Sasaki and many others obviously fell prey to this tactic (chapter 3).

Summary: Sasaki's writings offer us an extraordinary opportunity to understand the complex thought processes of this young tokkōtai pilot. He was deeply patriotic, but his patriotism was informed by the global intellectual currents of the time—Marxism, Romanticism, and others. His cosmopolitan intellectual horizon prevented him from entertaining a narrow vision of Japanese greatness or uniqueness. He opposed militarism and was disturbed by Japan's victories and the way they were celebrated. His Marxism was a form of idealism which made him critical of the capitalism that he saw engulfing Japan as well as its enemies. This belief led him to be determined to destroy the United States and England, and even Japan itself, in order to usher in a new era of Schweitzerian humanism and Miyazawa Kenji's idealism to Japan *and* to the world.

The idealism which doomed him to his death was part of a complex philosophical debate he engaged in with his friends, but, most importantly, with himself in his diary. It was part of his quest for understanding the individual and his will in relation to the requirements of society, as well as his quest for beauty in the ideational world through reading and personal experience.

At times his thoughts seem contradictory, at least from the vantage point of today. His basic stance was against the *pro rege et patria mori* ideology. Yet he seems to have embraced some aspects of it, especially in earlier years, as is evident in his admiration of General Nogi during his youth, his reference to bushidō as a counterpoint to capitalism, his occasional identification of loyalty toward one's parents with loyalty toward the emperor. These contradictions might suggest that the state had been at least partially successful in its effort to reproduce the *pro rege et patria mori* and military ideology even in the thoughts of such a brilliant young man and critical thinker. Yet we saw clear evidence that in the end he did not die for the emperor. Although not spelled out, his admiration for Nogi or the forty-seven retainers may have derived from his desperate quest to believe in some cause, rather than because these figures represented people who had unflinching sense of loyalty, though not necessarily for the emperor.

His quest for beauty and idealism led him to a quest for the primordial self of the Japanese as expressed in nature, before it was contaminated by capitalism. Cherry blossoms were an important "flower for thought" for Sasaki, who assigned various meanings to them. The way these meanings changed at different periods of his life is most illuminating. First, the flower embodied the spring of life, full of beauty, when Sasaki himself was celebrating his youth. Yet his cherry blossoms also held pathos for the brevity of spring and youth, as if he were anticipating his early death. When he was looking for an answer in his struggle between individual integrity and the demands of society, cherry blossoms became the mirror upholding the purity of an individual who keeps his integrity against the worldly desire for acclaim, acting as a counterpart to the war-frenzied Japanese society. Cherry blossoms were the symbol of his ideal vision. Toward the end of his short life, *falling* cherry blossoms became the metaphor for himself and his death. Of these three sets of meanings, the second one—the strength of the individual against the tide of society—came from Sasaki's imagination and yet is a meaning that other Japanese could readily understand. His identification with falling cherry petals derived more from the symbolism of cherry blossoms in Japanese culture in general than from cherry blossoms as a part of *pro rege et patria mori* ideology. For Sasaki, the cherry blossom was a powerfully evocative symbol, but it did not stand for sacrifice for the emperor or the metamorphosed soul of the fallen soldier. The flower was above all a symbol of his idealism, whose most important dimension was aesthetics.

HAYASHI TADAO

Hayashi Tadao was born in 1922. A graduate of the Imperial University of Kyoto, he was drafted as a student soldier on December 9, 1943, and in January 1944 he volunteered to be a Navy Air Force pilot for a scout plane. He was shot down in flight on duty and died on July 28, 1945, at the age of twenty-four, with the rank of navy ensign.

Source: My Life Burning in the Moonlight: Hand-Written Diary and Other Writings by Hayashi Tadao (1967) is a 239-page book edited by Hayashi's older brother, with whom he shared a great deal. The volume includes diary entries dated from April 6, 1940 to July 14, 1944, covering his years at the Third Higher School (Sankō), at the Imperial University of Kyoto, and in the navy. It also includes poems and letters written in 1945. Parts of this volume are cited in three other publications.[18]

Personal Profile: Hayashi was a western counterpart of Sasaki in that he attended the top higher school and the top university in western Japan *(Kansai).* After being drafted into the navy, he eagerly sought to be selected as a reconnaissance pilot and succeeded on May 4, 1944 (Hayashi 1967: 116, 132). Just before the end of the war, on July 27, 1945, at 11: 00 P.M., he left alone to scout for enemy vessels. At 2: 00 A.M. on July 28, he reported sighting an American aircraft carrier but was spotted by an American fighter plane, with which he began fighting. His last message came at 2: 20 A.M., before his plane was shot down off Shikoku Island (102, 221). An ironic tragedy is that his death postdates the delivery of the Potsdam Declaration to Japan on July 26, 1945 by the Allied Forces.

Hayashi was only thirteen when his father died in 1935 (Hayashi Katsuya 1967: 225–56). He was very close to his mother. In his last letter to his mother, he remembers how they talked about living together after his graduation from the university in Kyoto, which, to Hayashi, was "peaceful and plebeian" (196). He tells her that there is no longer any hope for her to live with him because of the turn of events in history. He expresses sorrow that she no longer has the past or the present in which to find meaning to live. Shortly after the war, the family received a wooden box on which was written "The Heroic Soul of the Late Ensign Hayashi Tadao." In the box, instead of his remains, there was a small paper on which "remains" *(ikotsu)* was written in calligraphy. At the news of his death, his mother lost her will to live and began to "wither" visibly. She steadily weakened until her death the following year on February 16, 1946. Hayashi's elder brother, Hayashi Katsuya, a chemist of great promise, opted to live in a remote mountain village and tutor children. His pupils built a wooden casket for his mother, in which he placed the box with his brother's "paper remains" (*Cherry Blossoms of the Same Class* 1966a: 194; Hayashi 1967: 230).

Hayashi Tadao and his elder brother, Hayashi Katsuya, did not get along during the period of abject poverty following their father's death. The elder brother pursued his university career, while Hayashi and his mother were near starvation. However, the two brothers later became very close; Hayashi Katsuya put his brother through the Third Higher School and, after his death, edited the volume of his writings. They shared a deep commitment to Marxism and a love of Western classical music. They discussed life and death, various philosophies, the war and Japan's situation, and other subjects, and enjoyed listening to recordings of symphonies at the elder brother's house (Hayashi Katsuya 1967). Katsuya openly objected to the war. Being a brilliant chemist, he was a "designated chemist" of the government and had the choice of engaging in military research, being drafted, or becoming a laborer. He chose the last, although he spit blood and lost consciousness doing the hard labor he was not used to.

Intellectual Profile: Hayashi's intellectual background is in many ways similar to that of Sasaki in that he read very widely in fields such as economics, history, and philosophy. But his heart, I think, was with literature, especially French and German. The extent of his intellectual horizon may be illustrated by his reading of Hitopadeśa, a collection of Hindi children's stories.

He used words in French, German, Italian, English, and Sanskrit to express concepts in his poems and other writings. His use of foreign languages, especially French and German, is so ubiquitous that reading the volume edited by his brother requires a basic knowledge of these languages. He kept improving his competence in languages while on the base. He explained that, even though he realized his death was imminent, his life-long assignment to himself, which he expressed in German as his *Lebensprobleme,* was to understand the relationship between European social sciences *(Sozialwissenschaft)* and European societies (137–38). He wished to pursue his quest to identify what was "European." A partial list of his reading is as follows:

Philosophy, politics, and economics—French: Descartes, Pascal, Voltaire; German: Heidegger, Marx, Nietzsche, Ranke; English: John Bagnell Bury, Christopher Dawson, Harold Laski, John Stuart Mill; Russian: Berdyaev.

Literature—French: Balzac, Flaubert, France, Loti, Martin du Gard, Maupassant, Mérimée, Rolland, Stendahl; German: Goethe, Hesse, Mann, Remarque, Rilke; English: Joyce; Russian: Dostoyevsky, Turgenev; Japanese: Izumi Kyōka, Kurata Momozō, Natsume Sōseki.

Marxism as Idealism: Like Sasaki, Hayashi was interested in economic and political history and was especially impressed by Ranke and Berdyaev. Above all, he was a staunch believer in Marxism, as he interpreted it. Before he left for the base, he begged his older brother to lend him Lenin's *State and Revolution* (1918). His brother was quite reluctant, since the book was officially banned. Hayashi told his brother that after closely reading each page in the toilet, he tore it into pieces and threw it into the toilet, or, sometimes, ate it, for fear of being caught (Hayashi Katsuya 1967: 229). While at the Ōi Airbase "at the dawn of Japan's crisis," he wrote a number of articles on "The Economic History of Modern Europe."[19]

Like Sasaki, he believed that Japan and capitalism were both at a critical phase of historical development. In one passage, after deliberating on advanced capitalism, or *Hochkapitalismus* as he called it, and the mechanization of the world, he admires a group of jailed Japanese Marxists and Communists for their courage and mental strength. He proceeds to ponder whether he can maintain the same mental fortitude on the base, since he is confronted with daily pressure to nullify or dissolve his individual *self* (112–13).

Individual and Society — Life, or Death for Idealism: In 1940, when he entered the Third Higher School (Sankō) at the age of eighteen, Hayashi had already begun to think about death. Japan was already heading for World War II, and he sensed the critical nature of the period.

After reading Plato's *Apology* and Nietzsche's *Also sprach Zarathustra*, Hayashi discusses his feelings of being threatened by the notion of his own death. He cries out in his diary (26–27): "I do not want to die! . . . I want to live. No, I don't want to die. . . . I feel lonely. I don't know why I feel so lonely—Being isolated? Feeling the poverty of the self? Homesick?"

His abiding philosophical question was the problem of life and death in relation to the fulfillment of the self, on the one hand, and of service and dedication to society and humanity in general, on the other, just as in the case of Sasaki. In exploring this question, he was heavily influenced by such writers as Romain Rolland, especially his novel *Jean-Christophe,* which was widely read in Japan for decades after its first publication. Hayashi cites a section from volume 1 in which Jean-Christophe advocates constant struggle for idealism against the temptation from within oneself and from many enemies in society—Rolland's "l'un contre l'autre" thesis. He makes numerous references to Roger Martin du Gard's *Les Thibault,* with its central theme of the self and society. This eight-volume work, for which its author received the Nobel Prize for literature in 1937, was highly influential in Japan; Hayashi read it twice in the original French. When Hayashi was driven to desperation on his base, he found solace in Jacques Thibault's cry to be left alone when confined in a penitentiary.

Although he seems to have been strongly influenced by French literature, the most important and sustained dialogue he engaged in was with Thomas Mann's work, especially *Buddenbrooks,* on which he wrote an essay. The following passage from the essay succinctly expresses Hayashi's struggle with the fulfillment of the self, which for young men in Japan at that time meant "life," as opposed to their service to society, which meant "death" (201–4):

> Mann is said to be the novelist of life and death. Or, sometimes he is said to be the novelist of decadence. It is also said that he was saved from death because of his commitment to "citizenship," which has a hundred-year history [in Germany]. . . . We have to be careful to understand that Mann uses the terms "life," "death," and "citizenship" in his own way, which is very different from the "meaning of death" of Paul Bourget. . . . What is death for Mann? And, life? What is his "citizenship" which transforms death into life and lies as the strong and steady bedrock under life? . . . Mann's "decadence" is death in the erotic state of mind.

Hayashi tries to find an answer to his agonizing question, whether to die for his country or to avoid death, by reading Mann, who, he understands, maintained that service to society and humanity at large enables one to transcend the problem of life and death.

Aesthetics and Idealism: Although he was an economic historian, as attested by a number of his essays on history, Hayashi was also an accomplished poet in quest of aesthetics. He believed that humans are not beautiful by nature, but that one should aspire to be so through self-reflection and effort (37). He read countless novels and poems, including those of Hesse, whose work is imbued with lyricism. Hayashi's writing is far more lyrical than that of Sasaki; he composed a large number of poems, some very long. Whether in poems, letters, or his diary, the word *utsukushii* (beautiful) recurs like a refrain (e.g., 37, 171, 182, 188). He sought beauty in nature, love, life and death, and human beings. While calling *Tonio Kröger* one of Mann's "most beautiful and sweet fruits," he describes his reaction to it: "My soul trembles at its tapestry, with a hint of loneliness, exquisite sensitivity, and almost threatening beauty" (148–50).

Cherry Blossoms: In a poem he composed at Miho Naval Base in 1945, Hayashi Tadao uses "falling" cherry blossoms as a metaphor for beautiful women, shortness of life, and *himself* (166–74). In another poem, blooming cherry blossoms represent his friend, while he describes himself with a metaphor of desolate wilderness (182). For Hayashi, cherry blossoms represent life, youth, and beauty, while falling cherry blossoms are a metaphor of evanescent beauty and life, and of himself facing imminent death. His references to cherry blossoms, although infrequent, are far removed from the symbolism of the *pro rege et patria mori* ideology. It is quite possible that other references to cherry blossoms occur in parts of the diary that were not published, especially since most of the diary entries from early April were excluded.

Antimilitarism: In addition to severely criticizing militarism in general, Hayashi also complained a great deal about day-to-day life at the base. For example, when he was going out on leave with *Customs and Lives in Sakhalin (Karafuto Fūbutsushō)*, a book by Taniuchi Rakubun, he was stopped and his privilege of leaving the base was revoked (122–23). The reading of books itself became prohibited, about which he comments: "What are they trying to do by issuing such a stupid prohibition? It only exposes their stupidity" (153).

His antimilitarism was deeper than his reaction to the treatment on the base per se. He believed that the military stifles the sense of individual selfhood (107–10):

> I do not avoid sacrifice. I do not refuse sacrifice of my self. However, I cannot tolerate the reduction of the self to nothingness in the process. I cannot approve it.

Martyrdom or sacrifice must be done at the climax [of self-real-ization]. Sacrifice at the end of self-annihilation has no meaning whatsoever.

In this passage, Hayashi uses the English terms, "martyr" and "climax," written in Japanese syllabary. In another passage, he writes: "The military kills passion and transforms a human into a cog in a machine" (113; see also 117–18). Both "passion" and "machine" are written in English.

Patriotism Critical of Japan: Like Sasaki, Hayashi wished imperial Japan to be destroyed in order to bring a new life to Japan. The first and last stanzas of his poem "The End of Imperial Japan" are as follows: "Ruining and crumbling / Decadence / Nothing will be left / The end of all" (188); "All will crumble / Japan will meet its finale / That taboo / Catastrophe" (189). Another poem, entitled "Finale," follows this poem after a short passage of reminiscence.

Although he predicted rightly the timing of Japan's defeat and hoped for the defeat of the old Japan, he called Japan his "ancestral land" *(sokoku)* and was deeply patriotic. Therefore, he considered it his duty to bring a new life to Japan and rebuild it (171):

The sky over southern Kyūshū is already in the hands of our enemy.
Our ancestral land, ready to crumble.
Those of us who received our lives in this country.

Why should we hesitate to give our lives [to]
Stupid Japan.
Indecisive Japan.
You, although quite foolish.
Us, who belong to this nation,
Must rise for your protection.

His patriotism, informed by his interpretation of Marxism, is similar to that of Sasaki. Both wished that a Japan plagued by capitalism and militarism would be ruined. Both fought and died for a New Japan. Hayashi did not clearly spell out a specific picture of this New Japan, but the poem cited above is replete with aesthetic references using various terms for "beautiful" *(utsukushii, uruwashii, uruwashikare)*, indicating his vision of a utopia filled with beauty.

Ambivalence: Hayashi struggled with his feelings of doubt and ambivalence. They come through when he discusses how the military stifles the sense of the individual self. He describes contradictions within himself as a struggle between Yoshida Shōin and Tonio Kröger. Yoshida Shōin (1830–59) was a scholar and politician who was deeply involved in the political struggles at the end of the Edo period. He is revered for his integrity and purity of spirit, with which he "recklessly" ventured into various activities, leading to his imprisonment a number of times and, finally, to his execution by the shogunate. Tonio Kröger is the protagonist in Thomas Mann's novel of that name. Hayashi writes that when the Tonio Kröger wins inside of him, he sinks into a deep sense of despair. But, then, the Yoshida Shōin in him cries out not to give up. He describes his struggle between the two in very abstract terms but repeatedly states that one cannot hold grudges against history and its march through time (152–56). My interpretation is that he was struggling with the options of being true to himself, like Yoshida Shōin, or of surrendering to the flow of history. In his despair, he writes in French: "Moi, cette confusion et anarchie, c'est moi." Then several lines later, he identifies himself as a "Spiritualist," and resolves his dilemma: "We do not become intimidated by the darkness but must attempt to get rid of all the Dunkelheit where materialism lies. This is the real way to live" (164–65). "Spiritualist" is written in English, "Dunkelheit" in German, and "real" in Japanese syllabary.

Summary: There is a great deal of similarity between Hayashi and Sasaki. Both attended top higher schools and universities, and both had cosmopolitan intellectual horizons. Both were heavily influenced by Marxism, which was for both a form of idealism. Both were severe critics of the situation of Japan at the time. Yet they were passionately patriotic. For both of them, love of their country was the ultimate factor for volunteering as a pilot; they hoped that their young generation would give birth to a New Japan. Yet, both saw themselves as helpless in the grand historical flow, in a somewhat different way from the historical determinism of Marx, Engels, and others.

In contrast to Sasaki, Hayashi's idealism took the form of an ardent quest for aesthetics and spiritualism, that is, the negation of materialism. Above all, he was a poet. Sasaki candidly admitted his wish to enjoy the esteem of others, whether about his academic success or his volunteering to be a tokkōtai pilot. Sasaki's struggle between two souls included the dimension of being anxious to enjoy his life on earth. The two souls of Hayashi, in contrast, were exclusively cerebral—one representing his individual self and the other a member of society, but not including the more earthly pleasures of Sasaki.[20]

A striking feature of Hayashi is that his patriotism had no relation whatsoever to any aspect of the *pro rege et patria mori* ideology. He used the image of falling cherry blossoms without any reference to the emperor or the Yasukuni Shrine. Hayashi volunteered to be a pilot in order to bring in a New Japan. But his own vision was impersonal—he saw himself caught in the tidal wave of history—revealing his painful struggle to rationalize his own death.

NAKAO TAKETOKU

Nakao Taketoku was born on March 31, 1923. A graduate of the University of Tokyo with a degree in political science, he was drafted as a student soldier in December 1943. He died on May 4, 1945 as a tokkōtai pilot.

Source: A Record of Spiritual Searching: Writings Left Behind by Nakao Taketoku, the Hand-Written Diary of a Student who Perished in the War (1997) is over seven hundred pages long and was edited by his younger brother, Nakao Yoshitaka. Among the diaries introduced in this book, not only is Nakao's the longest in terms of page numbers, but it also covers the longest period, from January 1, 1934, when he was in fifth grade in elementary school, to December 1, 1943. The diary after this date until his death was destroyed when the base burned down in an air raid. The book also includes letters to his friends, his elder brother, and his parents, written from December 18, 1942, until April 28, 1945, less than a week before his death.[21]

Intellectual Profile: Although he had an equally voracious appetite for reading, Nakao had interests different from those of Sasaki and Hayashi. Some of the books he read include:

Philosophy, politics, and economics—French: Henri Bergson, Descartes, Pascal; German: Hegel, Kant, Marx, Nietzsche; Danish: Kierkegaard; American: William James, Santayana; Classical: Aristotle, Augustine, Plato, Plutarch, Scipio, Socrates, Xenophon, Zeno; Chinese: Confucius, Mencius, Wang Yang-ming; Japanese: Kawai Eijirō, Motoori Norinaga, Nishida Kitarō, Suzuki Daisetsu, Tanabe Hajime, Watsuji Tetsurō.

Sociology and anthropology—French: Durkheim, Lévy-Bruhl; German: Simmel; English (Polish): Malinowski.

Literature—French: Balzac, Baudelaire, Paul Bourget, Dumas (both père and fils), Flaubert, France, Gide, Alphonse de Lamartine, de Maupassant, Mérimée, Montaigne, Rolland, La Rochefoucauld, Stendhal; German: Hans Carossa, Goethe, Hesse; English: Shakespeare, Marlowe, Shaw, Oscar Wilde; Russian: Chekov, Dostoyevsky, Gogol, Pushkin, Tolstoy, Turgenev; Japanese: Akutagawa Ryūnosuke, Hori Tatsuo, Izumi Kyōka, Kawabata Yasunari, Kunikida Doppo, Mori Ōgai, Mushanokōji Saneatsu, Natsume Sōseki, Shiga Naoya, Shimazaki Tōson, Yamamoto Yūzō.

Nakao read a vast amount of French literature, often in French. The most influential work on his thoughts seems to have been *Jean-Christophe* by Romain Rolland, although he also read Rolland's *Vie de Beethoven* (Nakao 1997: 444–45). The diary frequently cites poems and passages in French. Unlike Hayashi, who also read much French literature but was heavily influenced by Thomas Mann, Nakao's interest in German works was more in philosophy than in literature. Nakao read more classical literature than any other pilot, and he was deeply influenced by Chinese and Japanese philosophers, especially Dōgen, a Japanese Buddhist philosopher.

A characteristic that stands out in his reading is an interest in sociology and anthropology. While Sasaki read Weber and Simmel, Nakao read Durkheim, Lévy-Bruhl, Simmel, and Malinowski. His reading also extended to Chinese philosophy and literature, and, more than any other student soldier, his intellectual reservoir contained Japanese traditions, including the *Kojiki*, the "myth-history" of Japan, dated A.D. 712, and *The Diary of Lady Murasaki (Murasaki Shikibu Nikki)* by Murasaki Shikibu, in addition to Japanese philosophers and modern Japanese writers.

Pro Rege et Patria Mori Ideology: Although Nakao was by no means an ultra-right nationalist, there is no question that Nakao took a closer stance to the *pro rege et patria mori* ideology than any of the other student soldiers. During his first year in Fukuoka Middle School, he praised the Meiji emperor and his love of his subjects (39). After reading Mori Ōgai's *The Abe Clan (Abe Ichizoku)*, a novel which centers on the loyalty of a subject, Abe, to his master, Hosokawa Tadatoshi, Nakao was touched by Abe's unconditional loyalty (233). Nakao's case is an example of how easy it was for the state to "naturalize" the transference of loyalty toward one's master during the pre-Meiji period to loyalty toward the emperor during the modern period.

The diary for the year 1941 starts with the notation that the year is Kigen 2601—the 2601st year from the supposed beginning of the imperial line (331).[22] Nakao praises concepts involved in *pro rege et patria mori* ideology: loyalty to the emperor *(kan'nō)* as an expression of the warrior's way (bushidō), and the notion of the national body (kokutai), of which the emperor is the head. Nakao writes that respect for the national body is the cornerstone of the national spirit and that Japan is unsurpassed by other nations because of it (409). He refers to a loyal warrior who serves the emperor unconditionally (232–34). He tells how he cried when he saw a film in which a shogun prayed to the Sun Goddess, presumed ancestress of the imperial family, asking for her help to bring about victory on the battlefield (467).

Yet, a closer reading of his writings shows that he cannot be simply characterized as an unquestioning supporter of the *pro rege et patria mori* ideology. We recall from chapter 2 that the Meiji "Restoration" of the emperor had more to do with the overthrow of the shogunate and with resistance toward outside pressure than with the "return" of the emperor system per se. Nakao's heroes were not simple supporters of the emperor or of the *pro rege et patria mori* ideology, but were those who helped to overthrow the shogunate or managed to protect Japan against foreign threats. One of his heroes, Kusunoki Masashige (1294–1336) (454), who was also a hero of the other pilots, was a medieval warrior who fought against the shogunate on the side of the Go-Daigo emperor. Nakao named Saigō Takamori as the person he most admired (493–94, 601). Saigō Takamori (1827–77), also, like Nakao, from Kyūshū, played a critical role in overthrowing the shogunate during the Meiji "Restoration." Saigō managed to force the last shogun to relinquish Edo Castle (the present imperial castle in Tokyo) without shedding blood, although his later years were quite turbulent, leading him to commit suicide. Nakao admired Saigō not for his act of suicide but because of his patriotism and his integrity. Nakao also read *The Interpretation of the Constitution (Kempō Gikai)* by Itō Hirobumi, who was a major architect of the Meiji constitution (483). These figures whom Nakao admired all fought against shoguns and the shogunate government, which was incapable of coping with foreign encroachment. In fact, Nakao explicitly states his admiration for the architects of the Meiji government for having managed to overthrow the shogunate in the midst of such external pressures (485).

Resistance against external pressures was an important dimension of what on the surface seems to be support of *pro rege et patria mori* ideology. When Nakao was still at Fukuoka Higher School, he read *The History of American and British Colonial Expansion in Asia (Bei-ei Tōa Shinryaku-shi)* by Ōkawa Shūmei (1886–1957) (440), an ultra-right military and political figure who was sentenced as an A-class war crimi-

nal at the Tokyo trial. After reading the book, he became convinced that, as the strongest nation in Asia, Japan must liberate Asia from Western colonial encroachment. He believed this to be the reason for Japan's entry into World War II (440, 474–76, 497–98). After watching *A Victory Song for Asia*, a film about Japan's invasion of Bataan and Corregidor, he described how Japan made the Filipinos, who had been influenced by American culture, aware of the power of Asia (523–24). He discussed his reading of *The History of the Chinese Revolution (Shina Kakumei Gaishi)* by Kita Ikki, another ultra-right revolutionary, in relation to the need for mutual understanding between the Chinese and the Japanese for the defense of Asia against the West (605–6). In Nakao's view, the "Greater East Asia Co-Prosperity Sphere" encouraged nationalism in Asian nations and economic cooperation among them, although in the end it benefited Japan more than other Asian countries, inviting resistance against Japanese imperialism among other Asians.

On the surface, Nakao seems far less critical of the government and its strategies than Sasaki or Hayashi, and took its wartime propaganda at face value. Yet his deep commitment to social justice and to humanity at large are more than evident in his discussion of various books he read. For example, he was deeply moved by Shimazaki Tōson's novel *Hakai*, in which the protagonist, a hisabetsu-burakumin, agonizes over his identity, which he hid for a long time while he was a teacher because the profession was not open to the minority at that time. Nakao exclaims: "We throw a person into a living hell by hating him and discriminating against him just because he belongs to another social group or people" (161). Nakao's subscription to the Greater East Asia Co-Prosperity plan seems to have derived from his idealistic conviction that Japan and other Asian nations must unite against Western colonialism. His concern with the external threat to the political and cultural identity of the Japanese extended or in fact was grounded in his quest for "native" philosophical traditions. He often refers to the Buddhist monk-scholar Dōgen (1200–53) in his search for the meaning of life. He also repeatedly discusses Nishida Kitarō, a Japanese philosopher who established the Kyoto School of philosophy and engaged in a sustained dialogue with Martin Heidegger. He compares Nishida's notion of "nothingness" with "nothingness" in Buddhism (e.g., 552–53, 565–71)[23] and discusses Nishida in reference to other Japanese philosophers, such as Tanabe Hajime (see chapter 10) (564–65). Nishida and Tanabe both attempted to transcend Western philosophical traditions and to establish a Japanese tradition (598–99). Similarly, in his discussion of Chinese philosophers, Nakao emphasizes

"Asian" philosophical traditions collectively, as distinct from Western philosophical traditions.

Individual and Society: Like the other pilots, Nakao seemed to derive his patriotism and nationalism from his basic philosophical stance about human beings—that they are beings of flesh and blood who feel love toward their corporate group. He is therefore critical of Descartes and his philosophy of *cogito, ergo sum* as the essence of a human being (466–67, 476–78). His choice of readings, such as the works of Natsume Sōseki (introduced in the section for Sasaki), clearly indicates that he was tormented by the dilemma of whether to give his life for the nation or to live for himself as an individual. In addition to *Hakai,* he also read Shimazaki Tōson's *Ie* (The Household), which focuses on the problem of the individual and his/her responsibility as a member of the household, which Tōson considered as a basic kinship unit that was undergoing changes with modernity (162).

Nature and Cherry Blossoms: Nakao makes few references to cherry blossoms. When he expresses his dislike of passion, he uses "gorgeous flowers in full bloom" as a metaphor for passion. His preference is for purity and for the pathos he finds in love, expressed in cherry blossoms after their peak (132). While still in the Fukuoka Middle School, he praises plum blossoms. Because they bloom while it is very cold, he wants to emulate their spirit (39). In other passages written in 1943, he praises the beauty of blooming cherry blossoms (558–59, 661, 664, 665). Yet, at least in the collected volume of his writings, there is no reference to falling cherry petals as a sacrifice to the emperor or of blooming blossoms as the souls of fallen soldiers. The complete absence of the meaning of cherry blossoms within the *pro rege et patria mori* ideology in the writings of Nakao, who otherwise often expresses that sentiment, is quite important.

Ambivalence: Nakao's writings pose a formidable challenge for interpreters because of the subtlety in expression. On the surface he was in sympathy with the wartime ideology. In his last letter to his parents, he tells them that he is really happy, and he asks them not to be sorry but to follow his path of destroying England and the United States (666–67). Was he in fact that certain in his mind? It was only after I read and reread this long text several times that I began to appreciate the depth of meaning in the title he himself gave to his diary: *Tankyūroku* (A Record of Spiritual Searching). Indeed, the book is a record of Nakao's deliberations on life and death. If he had been so decisive about sacrificing for the emperor, he would not have engaged in such painful soul-searching.

In 1941, Nakao read Philipp Witkop's *Kriegsbriefe gefallener Studenten* (German Students' War Letters) (1928), a well-known collection of letters by German student soldiers in World War I, and he recorded his reactions extensively. He writes (365):

> Combat between human against another human, blood against blood—what else but cruelty. In the battlefield, daily witnessing friends being killed, observing grotesque slaughtering, and feeling the imminent approach of one's death. . . . Yet many of these students take their fate in stride, defending the need to fight even in the face of cruel slaughtering, sacrificing their lives to the nation, and dying while sending their blessings to their mothers and siblings. It is indeed amazing.

As time went by, his mood became even more introspective—a turn I came to realize only after reading his diaries a few times and noticed an increasing number of poems and poetic expressions. When a student at the University of Tokyo, he wrote that he would be drafted in September of the following year and that he was already psychologically prepared. He then muses on the fragility of human life—one bullet will simply destroy the body, a human being. He rationalizes that the death of an individual should not matter when it is given to the nation (490). In his poem "Silence," he writes: "How lonely is the sound of the clock in the darkness of the night" (491). Obviously, the clock is a metaphor of his life, ticking away toward his death. His musings about death take a critical turn when he begins to focus on rebirth and life after death, rather than on death itself, indicating, at least to me, that he could no longer face death as the finale. His diary entry on November 23, 1942 starts with his admiration of Socrates and his courage to calmly drink poison hemlock. Nakao's deliberation focuses on Socrates's notion of the immortal soul (511–13):

> The problem of immortality is important. However, since I have been painfully going through my life, death and immortality take on meaning only in terms of life. . . . The last writing by Socrates in which he praises the beauty of the world after death makes me want to live instead of to die.

This statement is followed by a poem in which he expresses his agony and the long sleepless night he spent without coming to terms with his death. He describes not being able to get rid of an overwhelming desire to live (511–13). The above quotation reveals that unlike Socrates, Hayashi could not find solace in the notion of immortality, but both of his heroes—Saigō and Socrates—chose death in order to fulfill their responsibilities to society.

His diary entries for 1943 are replete with references to life and death. He discusses Dante's *Divine Comedy* in relation to Christianity, and *Shōhō Genzō*, a text of Zen Buddhism, which he refers to repeatedly. However, he despairs over his inability to find peace of mind (542, 544–46). He goes back to his hero Saigō Takamori: "Saigō died because he lived. I have not even lived and thus should not be obsessed with death" (601). As the day for the physical examination nears, he states that he still does not have a firm conviction about his military duty and discusses Montaigne's thesis that it is not death itself but fear of it that makes one feel its weight (607–8). He begins to discuss God and Christianity frequently.

His diary gives the feeling that his apparent eagerness to sacrifice his life for the emperor might have been a way to convince himself of the meaningfulness of the death that he was facing, since, once drafted, the chance of escaping death was very slim indeed. He tried to convince himself that by sacrificing for a greater cause—his nation's effort in the war—his life would have a "promise" of continuing through the life of his nation. He writes that one lives for eternity by sacrificing oneself for the emperor (597). He continues his search for meaning in his death both by paying homage to Yasukuni Shrine and by reading Plato, Descartes, and Augustine. Nakao compares Augustine's Christianity with Asiatic modes of thought. His philosophical debate concludes with a poetic musing (610–15):

> The moon is beautiful tonight. As I look up at it again and again,
> The moon looks like a beautiful young woman gently crying.[24]

There is no need to spell out his sadness and longing for life and for a woman he never had. His philosophical musings begin to include frequent commentaries on the beauty of nature, as in the reference to the moon in this poem.

A passage written just before he went into the navy reveals the depth of his ambivalence about his sacrifice (625):

> At Kyōto station, and the next station and the next, remains of the soldiers were making the "victorious return" *(gaisen)*. It was painful to look at the whiteness of the box. "We shall meet again at Yasukuni

Shrine"—Do soldiers utter these words without hesitation when they are in combat?

The "whiteness of the box" refers to the white cloth wrapped over the wooden boxes that supposedly contain the ashes of cremated soldiers, although these boxes usually contained only a white piece of paper representing the remains that had not been found, as in the case of Hayashi.

Summary: Whether about literature or philosophy, Nakao's arguments are highly sophisticated, based on a thorough understanding of philosophy and social theory, both Japanese and Western, including Greek and Latin classics and even anthropology. Nakao's writings presented a most difficult challenge for me. The first time I read through the seven-hundred-page volume, I primarily picked up references that appeared supportive of the *pro rege et patria mori* and imperial ideology and more or less concluded that Nakao was a conservative or pro-nationalist. It was only the third and fourth times through that I began to understand the complexity, ambivalence, and agony that were expressed subtly and were disguised as cerebral and philosophical deliberations. Above all, his poems, hiding his deep sorrow over his fate, began to take on meaning. It is in these poems that we find the depth of his agony, which never ceased to occupy his mind until the moment of his death. He was not a simple-minded nationalist—far from it.

In many ways, Nakao's case is most revealing of the complexities involved in the success and failure of the state effort to propagate the *pro rege et patria mori* ideology. The most powerful tool the state possessed was the use and abuse of the Western threat. The Western threat, or "external pressure," was the central theme the Japanese had rallied around ever since the overthrow of the shogunate. The "Greater East Asia Co-Prosperity Sphere" was presented as a vision of all the Asians uniting against the West, rather than as a reproduction of Japan's imperialist ideology and an excuse for colonial expansion. If Nakao sounds as if he were leaning toward the *pro rege et patria mori* ideology, his underlying thought processes were far from those embraced by ultra-nationalists like Ōkawa Shūmei and Kita Ikki. In his youthful idealism, however, he offered his life, in acute pain, because service to society was his principle. The relative absence of cherry blossoms in his writing is quite significant, in that one would have expected them to appear as part of *pro rege et patria mori* ideology when he writes about his sacrifice for the emperor.

WADA MINORU

Wada Minoru was born in January 1922. A graduate of the First Higher School and the Imperial University of Tokyo, he was drafted as a student soldier in December 1943. On October 18, 1944, he volunteered to be a tokkōtai pilot for a kaiten submarine torpedo. As a navy ensign, he died on July 25, 1945, from suffocation in a malfunctioning torpedo.

Source: The Voice of the Sea Deity Shall not be Silenced: Handwritten Diary of a Kaiten Tokkōtai Pilot by Wada Minoru (1972) is a 342-page book devoted to his writings.[25]

Personal profile: Wada's published diary starts with an entry on December 12, 1940, when he was a higher school student, and ends with an entry on July 18, 1945, only a week before his death. Wada followed the same successful academic career as Sasaki: the First Higher School and the Imperial University of Tokyo, where he majored in law. He was good at playing the violin, and his father gave him a violin as a present when he passed the entrance examination to the First Higher School.

He volunteered to become a pilot for a submarine torpedo, a kaiten. These torpedoes were referred to "human torpedoes" *(ningen gyorai),* since the pilot was to strike an enemy ship while encased in the torpedo. He died on July 25, a day before the Potsdam Declaration, trapped in a torpedo that sank to the bottom of the sea, where he suffocated to death with no means of escape.[26] After the war, in mid-September, the torpedo turned up after a storm. He was found dead, squatting and looking as if he were asleep (Wada 1972: 112). Although he died gradually over a period of about ten hours, no notes were found.

Intellectual Profile: Although Wada was undoubtedly well educated in Japanese as well as in Western civilization, he referred far less often to books and music than did Sasaki and Hayashi, and those references appear mostly in the diary entries from his higher school years. He was liberal but not a Marxist. He discussed Greek philosophy extensively, without, however, referring to a particular philosopher or book. His reading included Balzac, Dumas (père), Maupassant, Hegel, Kant, Marx, Nietzsche, T. H. Green, Strindberg, Tolstoy, Turgenev, Ibsen, Dickens, and Merezhkovsky.

Individual and Society — Life and Death: As he contemplated the purpose of life, Wada confronted the question of life and death and the relationship of the individual to society. His discussion included Greek philosophers who committed suicide in order to protect individual freedom and the history of the struggle, beginning in the Renaissance, to free the individual conscience from "the bondage of Christianity" (16–18). His intellectual horizon, like others, was truly cosmopolitan.

He was not overtly critical of the military and *pro rege et patria mori* ideology. Yet he was an ardent follower of scholars of liberalism, in and out of Japan. In comparing T. H. Green and Marx, he concluded that Green reached individualistic socialism through his study of Kant and Hegel, while Marx studied Kant and Hegel, was led to Feuerbach, and reached collective socialism. He also read Kawai Eijirō, a professor at the Imperial University of Tokyo who wrote a book on Green (64–65). Kawai, a champion of liberalism, engaged in open disagreement with both Marxism and fascism and was involved in a number of political struggles against state authority. Kawai's books were banned by the government. He was arrested and suspended from his post at the university. As the war progressed, Wada read Hitler's *Mein Kampf* and studied German political philosophy since Bismarck. He expressed concern over Japan's alliance with Germany (80–82).

Antimilitary Attitude: Wada repeatedly expressed a critical view of the military. He realized that there was no critical thinking in military life but rather that one acted mechanically (122). He lamented that he used to think that student soldiers had higher goals in life. But in the navy, even minor details were so controlled that they could no longer work for their goals in life. He noted that the professional soldiers were jealous of the student soldiers, who had had the leisure to enjoy the arts and culture (126–28). He was scolded by a superior for such a minor matter as not knowing how to use a fire extinguisher (169). When one of them violated a minor rule, all of them were denied shore leave (e.g., 216–19, 227–28). He found out that his corps was named "The Divine Tide" *(kamishio)* and scoffed, "Who in the world came up with the name without our knowledge!" (283–84).

Wada repeatedly wrote about his annoyance over censorship by his superiors at the base. The bulk of his diary was kept in notebooks that were wrapped in oiled paper, hid underneath a bed of rice in a lunch box, and handed over to his parents when they visited the base (*Listen to the Voices* 1988: 273). Only those entries toward the end of the war were kept at the base and returned to the family. Soldiers were told to keep a daily log that a superior checked every now and then without warning. One day, Wada was severely scolded because he had not written down the log for the previous day (168). The next day, he became enraged because a superior censored a letter from his sister (169). He was even scolded by a superior for writing a postcard in a supposedly improper format (172). From mid-August 1944, he began using codes he devised for sending letters home—if he or his friend could get out of the base to post the letters, he would address them to his mother alone, but if the letters were mailed from the base, he would address them to his father, and the dates would be written on the third line and then slightly erased (216).

As with the others, his disdain for the military and military life became the basis for his conviction that only they, the student soldiers, could save their beloved country.

Patriotism: Despite his liberalism, Wada, like the other pilots, was passionately patriotic. He noted that he found "our love of our country to be of frightening intensity" (129). Even before volunteering to be a pilot for the kaiten torpedo, he wrote (213–14, emphasis added):

> On the human torpedo: Perhaps there is no other way to make a breakthrough [for Japan in the war] except by the human torpedo. The use of planes is so ineffective in causing damage to enemy vessels in relation to the casualties. With radar, it is now impossible to approach aircraft carriers without being detected. . . . If human torpedoes must appear in Japan . . . *there is no other group of people but us* [student soldiers] *who would become pilots.* I deliberate on this matter in a detached way. . . . When we think of it, *we are the only true navy officers.* . . . We should be more proud of ourselves.

In this passage, we see how he considered it the responsibility of student soldiers to fight for Japan, in part because of his realization of the low caliber of professional soldiers.

On October 18, 1944, he volunteered to be a pilot for a kaiten torpedo. The commanding officer wanted to make sure that his decision was not based on momentary excitement or an emotional outburst. The officer asked if Wada would regret his decision for some reason and if he could die calmly. After receiving word of Wada's firm resolution, the officer gave him permission to volunteer as a kaiten pilot. The next day, he learned that he had not been selected because he was the oldest son from a family without many male offspring, although he had a younger brother. Others selected were younger sons of families with several sons; among them was his good friend Takeda, and Wada felt left alone. The following day, he pleaded his case twice in the morning. In the evening,

the commanding officer, with tears in his eyes, notified Wada of his selection (241–42).

In preparation for his mission, he drew a chart on a piece of paper, cal-
culating the angles to use in order to maximize the accuracy of hitting
a moving enemy vessel with his torpedo (289). A person without the
courage to confront death is worthless, he writes, and he will embark
on the mission with the determination to successfully strike an enemy
ship (304).

Pro rege et patria mori ideology and *pro patria mori:* Wada's liberalism,
evident in his readings, was apparently not in contradiction with his
more sympathetic attitude toward the *pro rege et patria mori* ideology.
In late 1943, after joining the navy but well before volunteering to be a
kaiten pilot, he wrote in his diary a series of wills and poems that on the
surface endorsed the *pro rege et patria mori* ideology. In a poem he expresses his happiness to be *shiko no mitate* (the ugly/strong shield for
the emperor), a term from the *Manyōshū,* discussed earlier. In his formal will, he uses a number of phrases such as "imperial land" *(kōdo)* and
"imperial mercy" *(kō'on).* He also refers to Kusunoki Masashige (1294–
1336), who fought against the shogunate on the side of the Go-Daigo
emperor and to whom the Wada family traced their ancestry (see below).
It is hard to tell, if, for Wada, Kusunoki Masashige represented a hero
who overthrew the shogun, or a hero who supported the emperor, or
even both. It is also difficult to determine if the will, meant to be kept for
posterity, is a true expression of his thoughts and feelings. Also, the term
kō (imperial) might have been such a common expression during wartime that some individuals used it without subscribing to the *pro rege et
patria mori* ideology (107).[27]

Wada showed little rebellion against his parents, and thus there should
have been more tension in the process of transferring loyalty from his
parents to the emperor. There is no indication in his writing that his parents opposed his decision to be a kaiten pilot. He was touched when he
learned that his father had gotten off at the station where the base was
located during a trip to another destination, even though it was not the
day for visitation and he never saw his son (128). His thoughts toward his
mother were extremely tender, and he could not bear her grief over losing him (e.g., 280–82). On the day when he volunteered to be a kaiten
pilot, he expressed his torment—how he understood his parents' feelings for "their" son. He writes in his diary: "I am certain that I can shout
at the moment of my death that I am your child, Father, and I am your

child, Mother." Yet he is resolute in identifying himself as "a child of our country," whose body holds a key for the destruction of the enemy (241). In other words, he never believed in the equation of loyalty to the emperor and loyalty to the parents.

His patriotism made him critical of the military and of his fellow student soldiers. Wada criticized the student soldiers on the base for their behavior, listing their reasons for volunteering: eating well, receiving permission to leave the base for visits, and wishing to be saluted by those below them in rank (140 – 42).

Ambivalence: In February 1945, when he first engaged in a practice operation with the human torpedo, he was moved to tears, like Sasaki, as he reread Natsume Sōseki's *The Soul (Kokoro)*, a novel about the intellectual's struggle with individualism and solitude. This is a very different reaction from three years earlier, when he found Sōseki's coldness toward other humans to be alien to his thought (56). He obviously found far more meaning in Sōseki as his death approached. He was also greatly impressed by Ozaki Shirō's *The Human Theater (Ningen Gekijō)*, a long novel about a search for meaning in life, together with an appeal for patriotism, interpersonal obligations *(giri)*, and emotions *(ninjō)*. He detested the superficial consolation, encouragement, and militaristic bravos offered to him, writing, "It is quite certain that I give my life to my ancestral country. But this fact no longer has anything to do with me" (273 –75). In other words, he considered his sacrifice to be not a personal matter but an event in the historical flow. Similarly, he declares that he no longer has anything to say about his death and that he is happy with his state of mind (287). The tone in both passages is a forced detachment underneath which, as I interpret it, lie a deep sense of ambivalence and an attempt to force himself to accept the fate from which he no longer can escape, as expressed in the following (290 –91):

> Only one month is left to sum up my life. The second hand on the clock is moving. . . . Up to now I kept a calm face. But now I am frantically searching my past. I am desperately trying to find my true self without any ornament. I no longer have a self. . . . I am seen now as the bravest of the pilots in my own view and that of others. Perhaps others would shed tears at how I have been alive this long.

He felt sheer helplessness in the face of his rapidly approaching death and yet he found himself at a point of no return. His torment may also be seen in an episode of drunkenness he described in a letter to his father written sometime in mid-April, 1945. He got drunk, went into the rooms of several of his subordinates, drank water from a flower vase, preached on Johann Gottlieb Fichte, and drank ink from an ink bottle (286–87).

The last entry in the diary is most revealing of his strained effort to convince himself of the rightness of his action. Realizing that his torpedo would soon thrust itself into an enemy ship, he wished a clear marking of his "ancestral country" on his torpedo by painting a rising sun flag alongside the *kikusui* crest, already painted on the kaiten torpedoes. The crest consists of a chrysanthemum (the imperial family crest) and a stylized drawing of water (297; 143–44). This is the crest of his hero, Kusunoki Masashige, and Wada states that his family inherited the crest. His younger brother points out how odd it was for his elder brother, who had a critical mind and remained objective, to stress his family connection to Kusunoki Masashige, which was not proven, according to the younger brother (316). If I decipher it right, Wada found his identity as a Wada family member in the kikusui crest, but he wished to have his identity as a Japanese in the rising sun flag. In this statement, then, his dedication to the emperor recedes in the background.

Furthermore, immediately after this statement, he lists four women, whose names were written all in circles. For him, these women represent his ideal women, inferring that they briefly appeared in his life. They all shared determination, brightness, straightforwardness, and purity. Then he concludes: "Perhaps these women represent my ideal itself."

Cherry Blossoms: Most of the diary entries from late March or early April are not included in the collection of Wada's writings, and thus it is not possible to determine if he made references to cherry blossoms in those excluded sections of his diary and letters. However, there are two passages referring to cherry blossoms, and in both they appear in the context of the *pro rege et patria mori* ideology.

Wada's diary on May 11, 1944 starts with a poem he composed, in which he refers to himself as a cherry blossom qua Japanese male who is bravely going to war against the wind (186). The term he uses for Japanese male is *yamato danshi,* with *yamato* being an ancient term for Japan. It is a very masculine-sounding term. The other reference to cherry blossoms is where Wada cites the entire navy cadet song "Cherry Blossoms of the Same Class" *(Dōki no Sakura).* As mentioned in chapter 4, the song refers to navy cadets of the same year as "cherry blossoms of the same class." The song urges "falling" of comrades who will meet again as cherry blossoms at the Yasukuni Shrine. The most masculine of all pronouns for "you" and "I" are used in the song text. Wada states that it is their "pleasant" *(kokoro tanoshiki)* duty to go over the dead bodies of other soldiers, each one of whom became a model for the kaiten pilots, concluding, "The only real concern I have now is how I can die well" (280–82).

In the first reference, the symbolism of the cherry blossoms is that of the *pro patria mori* ideology, whereas in the second, it is that of *pro rege et patria mori*. The state strategy to appeal to the masculinity of these soldiers worked, at least on the surface. However, it is difficult to determine whether Wada understood the essence of the *pro rege et patria mori* ideology in this song, or whether he cited this popular song without giving much thought to the meaning of the text.

Summary: Wada, like other elite students, was immersed in the high cultures of the West and Japan. Although explicitly non-Marxist, his political philosophy from early on was quite liberal, influenced by the liberalism of T. H. Green and Kawai. He had a warm relationship with his parents, but his feelings toward them did not prevent him from volunteering to be a tokkōtai pilot. However, there is no explicit statement as to whether he deliberated on the relationship between loyalty toward his parents and loyalty toward the emperor. His criticism of the military is confined to day-to-day activities, rather than to the military aggression or imperialism that Sasaki and Hayashi Tadao criticized.

Wada was similar to Nakao in that his overt statements appear as if he was an unequivocal believer in the *pro rege et patria mori* ideology, including "falling like cherry blossoms for the emperor." Yet his complex thoughts, like Nakao's, were expressed in subtle ways, requiring the reader to pay close attention to his statements. Given his liberal thinking, it seems more reasonable to interpret his seeming endorsement of the *pro rege et patria mori* ideology as part of his deeper commitment to patriotism. He shared with other student pilots the belief that it was their responsibility to defend their homeland. Like others, until the end he was tormented and longed for life, rather than death.

HAYASHI ICHIZŌ

Hayashi Ichizō was born on February 6, 1922, in Fukuoka, Kyūshū. A graduate of the Imperial University of Kyoto, he was drafted as a student soldier on November 10, 1943 and became a tokkōtai pilot on February 22, 1945. He died on April 12, 1945, off Okinawa at the age of twenty-three with the rank of navy ensign.

Source: A Sun and Shield: Diary and Letters to Mother, and Other Writings Left by Hayashi Ichizō, a collection of his writings edited by Kaga Hiroko, his sister, is the major source (Hayashi Ichizō 1995). It is much shorter than the diaries of other pilots, since the purpose of the book is to portray Hayashi's extraordinarily close relationship with his mother.[28]

Personal Profile: Hayashi was the oldest son of the family; he had two elder sisters and one younger brother. Both parents had converted to Christianity and remained devout Christians. His father died when he was small, and he was raised by his mother and his maternal grandmother. Although his own choice of specialization at the Imperial University of Kyoto would have been philosophy, he chose economics, a more practical field, because it would make it easier for him to support his mother and his older sisters after graduation.

When he was young, unlike other children in wartime Japan, he did not mention that he wanted to be a soldier and never sang "I Love Soldiers *(gunjin)* Very Much," a popular children's song at the time. He and his friends went to a nearby airbase to dissuade young boys from volunteering to be pilots, telling them that they could not win the war by such an act. His mother and his sister interpreted his act as coming from being a Christian since many Christians in Japan advocated peace (Ebina 1983: 305).

When university students were called into the military, his mother and sisters begged him not to enlist in the navy since his mother believed the navy would send him outside of Japan, to an area of active fighting. However, at that time many university students thought that Japan was controlled by the army, known for its feudalistic system and brutality. The navy was viewed as Japan's internal "West" (an intriguing metaphor indeed), out of reach of the army's control. As Hayashi puts it, to enlist in the navy was like "a domestic desertion of the country." He explained to his mother and sisters: "If I did not volunteer for the navy, I would be enlisted in the army, in which case I might commit suicide since I would not be able to tolerate the bullying by the army" (Ebina 1983: 304–5). In his letters, he repeatedly apologizes to his mother for his decision to have gone against her wishes and joined the navy. In fact, after being chosen as a tokkōtai pilot, he writes: "Perhaps I should have followed your advice" (57).

To understand Hayashi, it is crucial to understand his love for his mother, his Christianity, and his patriotism, which were all closely interrelated. His diary and letters are unique in the degree of candidness with which he expresses his feelings toward his mother.

Intellectual and Spiritual Profile: While stationed in Korea, Hayashi began writing his diary on January 9, 1945, which he entitled as *A Sun and Shield (Hi nari Tate nari)*, after Psalm 84: 10–11:

> For a day in thy courts is better than a thousand elsewhere.
> I would rather be a doorkeeper in the house of my God
>   than dwell in the tents of wickedness.
> For the Lord God is a sun and shield;
>   he bestows favor and honor.

If the Bible was one intellectual and spiritual source, Kierkegaard's *Sickness unto Death* was the other. In a letter to his friend Yoshida Shōhachi, a classmate both at Fukuoka Higher School and the Imperial University of Kyoto, Hayashi reports that he has finished reading *Sickness unto Death* and feels a surge of fighting spirits for life (108). He loved to read and reread the book.

Patriotism: In the end, his patriotism was ultimately the most important factor for his volunteering. In the same letter to Yoshida Shōhachi (108), he states: "You must feel terribly angry [toward the Americans] for the bombing." He could not bear the thought of his nation being stampeded by the "dirty enemy" (28). Yet, his patriotism did not blind him from recognizing the injustices committed by the military, as when he expresses deep concern over the innocent civilians in China who fell victim to Japanese military aggression (40–41).

Pro rege et patria mori: Hayashi often uses the ancient term for the emperor, ōkimi, and states that he and others will die for the emperor (25, 27, 31, 40–41, 108, 110). The following two sentences, which appear in his diary on the same day, are most revealing (25–29): "There *must be* some peace of mind for dedicating my life to the emperor" (emphasis added). "To be honest, I cannot say that the wish to die for the emperor is genuine, coming from my heart. However, it is decided for me that I die for the emperor." The phrase "there must be," instead of "there is," and "it is decided," rather than "I have decided," reveal that he was not fully convinced of his sacrifice for the emperor. Clearly, *in the end, he did not die for the emperor* but rather did so for his country. Unlike Sasaki and Hayashi Tadao, who articulated their stance against the *pro rege et patria mori* ideology, Hayashi Ichizō tried his best to believe in the wartime ideology only to confess that ultimately he did not subscribe to it.

Cherry Blossoms: In one letter to his mother, Hayashi wrote that he should be falling like cherry blossoms at the front, when cherry blossoms at the Won-san Base in Korea where he was stationed had already fallen. In other words, identifying himself with cherry blossoms, he thinks that he should have fallen together with cherry blossoms at the front, located to the south of Korea, where the flower should have bloomed and fallen earlier than in Japan. In another, undated letter also from the Won-san Base he mentions that the cherry blossoms have already fallen and fondly envisions how those at home in Fukuoka, Kyūshū must be starting to bloom (48).

In the long letter addressed to his mother and sister from the Won-san Base, in which he discloses being selected as a tokkōtai pilot, he remarks that the cherry blossoms back home must be in full bloom. He visualizes the course which his plane will take on the final mission and tells his mother that he will be bidding farewell to cherry blossoms in full bloom as he overlooks Nishi Park from his plane (63).

In a later, undated letter to his mother from Kanoya Navy Airbase in Kyūshū, he expresses surprise that the cherry blossoms in Kyūshū are already falling, while they were still blooming in Korea (67). In another letter, he remarks that at the Kanoya Navy Airbase cherry blossoms of the Yoshino variety have fallen while the double-petaled cherry blossoms are still in bloom (76). In a poem written in the Kyūshū dialect, which he sent to his long-time friend and comrade, Doi Kentarō, he refers to cherry blossoms in full bloom at a nearby school yard, whose beauty he transfers to his friend as "beautiful" (111–13). This poem ends, "I feel lonely"; obviously he was feeling the end of his life coming close. To his young brother, he writes: "Cherry blossoms are blooming and I am going" (90). There is definitely a direct link between his approaching his death and cherry blossoms (see also 88).

Despite all these references to cherry blossoms, implicitly and explicitly linking the flower to himself, there is not even a remote link between his cherry blossoms and those in the *pro rege et patria mori* ideology.

Cherry blossoms also appear in works about him by others. In a poem written after the end of the war, his mother refers to the "falling [like cherry petals] of my son" (120). His friend, Hidemura Senzō, laments that "Hayashi's youth is fallen [like cherry petals]. Peace arrived but not the peace you wished to bring through your sacrifice; it is only in the miserable aftermath of defeat." Hidemura concludes, "Beauty appears in a sensitive vessel and life is short" (143–47).

Devotion to his Mother and to Christianity: Toward the end of Hayashi's life, his Christianity became blurred with his feelings toward his mother. He desperately wanted to be forgiven by his mother, who opposed his volunteering, and be reunited with her. His Christianity was a way for him to be psychologically close to her. He declares in his diary: "Despair, Despair is a sin." Obviously, this is a reference to Kierkegaard, it is followed by the remark that he has not received a letter from his mother (43; see also 20). His feeling of despair seems to derive more from the absence of a letter from his mother than from Kierkegaard. In a letter to his mother from Won-san Base, he tells her that he has been reading over and over the three letters he received from her (48).

After he was selected as a tokkōtai pilot, Hayashi immediately wrote a very long letter to his mother from Won-san Base in Korea. He begins the letter by addressing his mother as "okāsan," a form of address that adults use. However, in the middle of the letter, as he begins expressing his realization that his death will become real, he switches to "kāchan," a form used by children. In the letter he describes tremendous agony over his decision to have gone against her will and choose to be a tokkōtai pilot, but he also tries to persuade her that his death is honorable and that all men in Japan must die for the country (55–65).[29] He even praises her for bringing him up to become an honorable man *(rippana otoko).* Knowing full well that he is very special to his mother, he tries to console her and justifies his decision by assuring her that his younger brother will take care of her. He then tries to explain his death in terms of God, in whose hands his life and death rest, and says that he will be plunging into an enemy vessel while singing a hymn (59, 64). He cites the Bible: "Leave the dead to bury their dead" (Matthew 8: 22) and "For to me to live is Christ, and to die is gain" (Philippians 1: 21) (70, 71, respectively).[30] He tells her that he will put his Bible and hymn book in his plane (60).

In a letter written after he was moved to the Kanoya Navy Airbase in Kyūshū (66–74), he makes an obviously futile attempt to convince his mother that his death is an honorable death, while expressing deep concern about her welfare after his death. He promises her that he will strike a vessel with assurance, imagining that she is watching him and praying for him. He swears that he will see to it that the enemy ship will sink. After expressing how unreal it feels to realize that his comrades who flew off yesterday are all dead, he declares: "The enemy's action is being dulled. Victory is for us. Our mission will be the last blow to the enemy. It is splendid" (71).

In this letter he describes the attire that tokkōtai pilots wear at the time of their last mission, which includes the rising sun headband and a pure white scarf around the neck. He comments that they look like *gishi* (69), the forty-seven loyal retainers, introduced in chapter 4. He tells her that in his last flight he will also carry her picture in his bosom, with the amulet and a rising sun flag she sent him. His sister, who edited the letters, explains that his mother went to a shrine which was noted for conferring good luck on the battlefield and got him the amulet, indicating how desperate she was, and that she wrote a passage from the Bible on the flag (183): "A thousand may fall at your side, ten thousand at your right hand; but it will not come near you" (Psalm 91: 7). Hayashi ends this long letter by asking his mother to pray for him so that he will be able to enter Heaven:

> I will be going ahead of you. But, I wonder if I would be allowed to enter Heaven. Mother, please pray for me. I cannot bear the thought of going to a place where you would not join me later.

He does not explain why he is unsure about whether he will enter Heaven.

In another letter written from the Kanoya Navy Airbase he describes how he went out to a field of Chinese milk vetch *(rengesō)* and lay down, thinking about home (75–77). He tells his mother, "My friends told me that I smell of you, mother. They think that they felt the mother-son bond in me." In his letter written on March 30, he repeatedly tells her, "I still want to be loved and spoiled by you" and "I want to be held in your arms and sleep" (56–57). The last letter to his mother, written on the day before his last flight on April 12, 1945, ends by describing how he sang hymns with his friends to the accompaniment of an organ in the nearby school (78–79). The letters reveal that his Christianity is very much a part of his relationship to his mother. He tells her that he derives strength from believing in the same God that she does, writing, "I am reading the Bible every day. When I do so, I feel I am next to you, mother" (28).

Ambivalence and Agony: From the perspective of Western Christianity, it might be puzzling that neither Hayashi nor his mother conceptualized the tokkōtai action as "suicide"—the most prominent feature in the Western view of the "kamikaze" pilots, often referred to as suicide bombers. He mentions the term "suicide" twice in the diary (33–35), but not in reference to his death as a tokkōtai pilot. An extensive discussion on life and death begins with a recollection of the time when he thought of committing suicide. He explains that it was a time when he gave up the thought of happiness and devotion and was in despair *(zetsubō)*. He then switches to an expression, "Today, death is given to me," describing himself as a passive recipient of the fate, no longer in charge of his own life and death, unlike in the Japanese notion of suicide. He remarks that although he has long been aware that he was destined to die, he is now acutely feeling its immediacy. His death would make it no longer possible to pursue the path of devotion *(kōken)* and enterprise *(jigyō)* (it is not clear what he means by these words). He then identifies his attachment to life as consisting of two elements: attachment to his surroundings *(shūi eno shūchaku)* and pleasures. He is confident that he can discard the latter, but the former is more difficult, although the spiritual teachers from whom he learned in the past all encouraged him to sever the attachment to one's surroundings. He suspects that he is attracted to the notion of death in the battle *because it is an escape for him*. On the following day, he lists those things he finds difficult to give up: his mother, women, beautiful people, scenery, and honor bestowed upon him by other people (37). He does not seem to have had a particular woman with whom he was in love. He rejected his mother's urging to get married because he knew he was going to die, although he was interested in love and women.

Early in 1945, he writes in his diary, "We dreaded the approach of 'death' which is now given to us" (25). Throughout his writings, he repeats that both life and death are in the hands of God. The statement that death is given and that it is an escape certainly represent great ambivalence toward his imminent death and an effort to rationalize it by resorting to fatalism and stoicism. He is torn because life represents his mother and death represents his separation from her. His Christian rationalization to be reunited with her in Heaven is far from convincing to him. At any rate, he does not consider his approaching death as suicide.

Summary: Since Hayashi's writings were selected in order to portray the mother-son relationship, his philosophical debates are not available. In the end, from the time he volunteered to be a tokkōtai pilot his days were consumed by his agony over the separation from his mother, to whom he was extremely attached. That he volunteered against the wishes of his mother, who was strongly opposed to the war, vividly illustrates the power which the state was able exercise on idealistic youths. He was a peace-loving Christian who even tried to dissuade other children from volunteering to fight in the war. Although we do not have information about how and when he began to believe that his mission lay with the tokkōtai in order to save the country, we see how patriotism became the driving force for him as for all the young men discussed in this chapter. Like the others, in the final analysis he did not support the *pro rege et patria mori* ideology. Patriotism, buttressed by the sense of masculinity and the honor bestowed upon tokkōtai volunteers, drove them to their deaths. In contemplating his death, Hayashi used cherry blossoms as a metaphor of himself, although he never linked the flower to the *pro rege et patria mori* ideology. He wished to go to Heaven and wait for his mother. The Yasukuni Shrine never crossed his mind.

THE IDEALISM AND PATRIOTISM SHARED BY COSMOPOLITAN INTELLECTUALS

While these five pilots shared a great deal, each was very different from the others. Although Sasaki was the "rationalist" among them, he composed exquisite poems, and his readings include works that celebrate *Vissi d'arte*. He also let us have a glimpse into his emotions through his seemingly cerebral discussions and through his references to the beauty of nature. Hayashi Tadao was just as cerebral as Sasaki, but he was a poet who sought the beauty of life and human beings throughout his short life. Where Sasaki found German to be the language that best expressed his innermost thoughts, Hayashi Tadao preferred French to articulate his feelings, although his abiding interest was in Thomas Mann, and his command of German, Italian, and even Sanskrit is truly remarkable.[31] The two represent the large number of Marxists among intellectuals at the time.

Wada and Nakao were more sympathetic toward the *pro rege et patria mori* ideology. Yet neither was a puppet of the emperor-centered military ideology. They were influenced by liberal thinkers, both Japanese and Western. Their more liberal thoughts are often couched in subtle expressions so that one has to pay close attention. For example, Nakao asked if the soldiers, whose "paper remains" in the white boxes he saw on the Kyoto station, could indeed say, "let us meet at the Yasukuni Shrine," rather than directly criticizing the state which sent them to death. His poems become almost painful to read for his expressions of anguish. A complete absence of direct criticism of the state and the war becomes a powerful presence inviting the reader to read beyond the surface. Wada too never directly expressed antimilitary sentiments or opposition to the emperor-centered ideology. But his discussion of Kawai and

Green leaves no room for doubt that Wada was, like others, in the cross-currents of opposing historical forces.

Hayashi Ichizō stands out among these five pilots in that, despite his sophisticated discussion of Kierkegaard, his writings are an outpouring of his love for his mother. His struggle to reconcile Christianity with the *pro rege et patria mori* ideology gives us a unique opportunity to understand Christian pilots. His statement that in the end he could not say that he was dying for the emperor is a most definite testimony against the view that the *pro rege patria mori* ideology was successfully transmitted by the state to soldiers.

Although they all reproduced the *pro rege et patria mori* ideology *in action,* none of them reproduced it in toto *in their thoughts*. They all desperately wanted to live until the last moment.

The two most important factors for their action, as revealed in the diaries, were their idealism and patriotism. We saw that Sasaki and Hayashi Tadao both held a firm conviction that Japan, ravaged by capitalism, should be destroyed. They were willing to sacrifice their lives to destroy capitalism in Japan, the United States, and the United Kingdom in order for their dream phoenix to rise out of the ashes. In sharp contrast to the stereotype that the tokkōtai operation was a perfect reproduction of the warrior's way, their patriotism was a product of a complex interpenetration between global intellectual tides, political and military threats from the West, and their own Japanese intellectual traditions, which were themselves also the products of interactions between the local and the global. The Meiji Christians, whom all of them admired, were intensely patriotic while vocally fighting against the imperial nationalism of the state. Their patriotism has always been a response to the threat of the West, which the state skillfully used to intensify the patriotism of the Japanese.

The diaries offer an indisputable testimony that the state effort produced neither a perfect reproduction nor its outright rejection of its militarism. Being born at the time when Japan was escalating its course for military aggression, the state propaganda on behalf of imperial nationalism worked successfully on many Japanese, especially on young idealistic students, who translated it into their patriotism. The elite schools they attended were the space of intense struggle between ultra-right nationalism and various forces against it, as seen by the firings and/or resignations by a number of presidents and prominent professors of these schools.

Most frightening is the subtle ways with which the *pro rege et patria mori* ideology exercised its "symbolic violence," to extend Bourdieu's term beyond the context of reproduction of the class structure. Like fine but continuous rain, the imperial ideology penetrated primarily under the disguise of patriotism. For even those who rejected the *pro rege et patria mori* ideology, their belief in *pro patria mori* was intensified, unknowingly to them, for example, by the state effort to appeal to the masculinity of the soldiers. Sasaki stated his determination to become the *shield* for his nation, and one of the ways he uses cherry blossoms is as a metaphor for ancient warriors. Wada's use of the shield is "the shield for the emperor" *(shiko no mitate)*, straight out of the ideology, and yet he was far from being a simple right-winger.

An important finding is that even the most liberal of the pilots use cherry blossoms as a major trope. One explanation is that the flower was a complex symbol onto which soldiers assigned different meanings and feelings in relation to a variety of complex thought processes. While the flower appears *not* always a part of the *pro rege et patria mori* ideology, it is quite indicative of the power of state propaganda since the beginning of the Meiji era that even the most liberal refer to the fallen soldiers/ themselves as falling cherry blossoms, without, however, "for the emperor." It is significant to note that the fallen soldiers were referred to as "cherry blossoms in full bloom that have fallen" in the speech given in 1946 by Nanbara Shigeru, president of the University of Tokyo, commemorating the students who perished in the war (*Far Off Mountains and Rivers* 1947: 5–10). He also referred to them as *masurao*, an ancient term for men that emphasizes their masculinity. In other words, Nanbara, a Christian who fought against both the Japanese and Nazi ideologies, unconsciously perpetuated the very symbol used by the military to propagate the *pro rege et patria mori* ideology, when the purpose of the collection was to point to the utmost brutality of the state to send these young men to death and to eulogize the victims. It testifies to the power of military discourse to penetrate into popular discourse.

It was their idealism and quest for the beauty in life that led them to patriotism. But the more immediate circumstances were far from presenting a choice. Their entry to war was forced—they were drafted. On the base, they were disillusioned by some of the professional soldiers. But, they converted their disillusion into a heightened sense of responsibility for the defense of the Japanese homeland and their families at the time when the American invasion of their homeland was imminent. This sense of responsibility derives in part from the general ethos at the top higher schools and universities, which produced the future leaders of Japan. They became convinced that they, the student soldiers, had to shoulder the brunt of Japan's defense. They "chose their fate" not simply because their superiors left hardly any room but to volunteer: it was difficult for them to refuse to volunteer when they saw their friends and comrades willing to give their lives. By then they had already reached a point where there was no turning back.

When Sasaki (154) realized the political situation Japan was facing, he proclaimed, referring to Nietzsche: "Freedom is not what we choose. It is the cruel inevitability, whether we like it or not. Our free will is our fate." Patriotism and idealism were real factors motivating them to volunteer, but these perhaps became the rationale for them when they realized that they had no choice but to die when their desire for life was burning with intensity.

Part 4

NATIONALISMS,
PATRIOTISMS, AND
THE ROLE OF AESTHETICS
IN MÉCONNAISSANCE

Chapter 7

STATE NATIONALISM AND
NATURALIZATION PROCESSES

The ultimate destruction of Japan and the slaughter of its own people *and* other peoples were propelled by the twin engines of rising political nationalism and militarism. In Part 4 I offer my interpretations of the Japanese historical experience, using theoretical and cross-cultural perspectives, in order to further understand it in broader contexts. Chapter 7 focuses on Japan's nationalist ideology and its attempt to penetrate quotidian life, and chapter 8 explores how the pilots lived and experienced this extraordinary time.

NATIONALISMS

Human history is full of instances of collective self-consciousness — that is, of the awareness a people have of themselves as a people. Isaiah Berlin wrote that "consciousness of national identity may well be as old as social consciousness itself"; but nonetheless, he also believed nationalism "scarcely to have existed in ancient or classical times" (Berlin [1959] 1992: 243). In reference to the Chinese, Benjamin Schwartz (1993: 218) suggests that entities similar to nations, nationalities, or ethnic groups are "not exclusively modern."[1] Of all the terms used to refer to collective consciousness, "ethnicity" and "nationalism" have been most intensely debated among scholars. A full-fledged discussion of ethnicity and nationalism is beyond the scope of this book. My discussion is confined to a brief review of recent criticisms of Benedict Anderson because these criticisms enable us to further understand the Japanese historical experience in broader theoretical contexts. The point here is not to belittle the contribution his concept of "imagined community" has made to anthropology and to related fields.

Kelly and Kaplan struck a powerful blow to dislodge studies of nationalism from the "unnecessary and occluding punctuation of global time" by the Enlightenment schema, i.e., the lumping of all the histories of the world into one schema and the punctuation of "global time" according to the periodicity of Enlightenment historiography. In Anderson's view, nationalism is an integral part of the universal notion of modernity and of the supposed emergence of the "nation-state" (Kelly and Kaplan 2001). Anderson's "modernity" thus accrued "presumed temporal privilege" to the Western colonial powers (Kelly 1991: 242; see also 1998a). Using the example of Hindu nationalism, Kelly argues that nationalism does not have to be a "station in the human career" (Kelly 1998b: 188–89). Kelly and Kaplan's arguments are a part of a vigorous recent development that is sharply critical of the use of such terms as "nation," "nation-state," "state," "modernity," and "nationalism." These scholars have attempted to dislodge, or "rescue," to use Duara's (1995) phrase, these terms whose conceptions arose out of the understanding of history as unilinear and unilateral social evolution that developed during the European Enlightenment. Not only is nationalism *not* tied to "modernity" in the Enlightenment scheme of history, but the Western paradigm of nationalism must also be challenged by nationalist imaginations in other parts of the world (Chatterjee 1993). Critiquing Anderson's thesis that nationalism in the colonies and the third world was "largely a more or less passive or borrowed response to the European impact," Tambiah proposes "multiple modernities" and sees two distinctive yet overlapping types of nationalism: the nationalism of the nation-states, as developed especially in Western Europe, and "ethnonationalism," which originated separately in many parts of the world, including some parts of Germany, Eastern Europe, Africa, the Middle East, Latin America, and South and Southeast Asia (Tambiah 1996a: 9; 1996b: 124; see also Eisenstadt 2000; Tambiah 2000).

Proponents of nationalism as part and parcel of modernity include Gellner, an outspoken critic of constructionists like Anderson, who too follows a linear and progressive time scale. According to Gellner, a nation develops through the establishment of equality, shifting away from a hierarchically based society, and "nationalism is . . . the consequence of a new form of social organization, based on deep internalized, education-dependent high cultures, each protected by its own state" (Gellner 1983: 48; for a critique of Gellner, see Hall, ed. 1998). Hobsbawm (1990: 163) also followed the historical periodicity scheme and declared in 1990 that nationalism in the late twentieth century is "no longer a major vector of historical development," although he retracted the statement in a 1992 revised edition of his book.

Nationalism and ethnicity as strong counter forces to the so-called globalization process in the contemporary world make it hard to entertain the view that nationalism is associated with a certain historical development or period. In the so-called postcolonial era, ethnicity and nationalism have become virulent forces all over the world, including in societies that had never been colonized. This happened well before the dissolution of the USSR, putting an end to Marx's belief in his *Manifesto* that nationalism is a reactionary bourgeois ideology and that "national differences and antagonisms between peoples are daily more and more vanishing" (Marx and Engels [1852] 1989: 26). Often neglected in this era of decolonization and globalization is the force of "Pax Americana," which Ruth Benedict foresaw at the end of World War II (Kelly 1998a: 860–62) and which has been a driving force for the rise of nationalism, not just in the "Third World," but in many parts of the world.

For Anderson, nationalism is a historical product of the West and arises only after three shackles of the past have been shed: the "script-language" as the path to the truth, monarchy, and the indistinguishability of cosmology and history. Japan's political nationalism of the late nineteenth through the twentieth centuries contradicts Anderson's model on *all* three counts. Instead of shedding monarchy, Japan's "modernity" created an absolute monarchy, when the Japanese emperor system had been a politically impotent shadow under the shogunate ever since the twelfth century. Anderson calls the imperial nationalism of Japan a variant of "official nationalism," borrowing the term from Seton-Watson, which he defines as a "willed merger of nation and dynastic empire" (Anderson [1983] 1991: 86, 95–99). Anderson might have wrongly assumed that the emperor system had been a politically powerful body in pre-Meiji Japan—a common misunderstanding, based perhaps on the myth the Meiji oligarchs created. There really had been no equivalent to the Romanov dynasty in Japan.

As to Anderson's indistinguishability of cosmology and history, his view seems to rise out of the tradition of the Great Divide—one of the unfortunate legacies in anthropology which divided the world into two types: the "hot societies" of the West, governed by history, and the "cold societies" of the rest of the world, governed by myths (details in Ohnuki-Tierney 2001). This view held that societies with myth and those with "history" are in a linear developmental or even social evolutionary sequence whereby the former were seen to "evolve" into the latter. Again Japan's case goes counter to this claim. Japan's "modernity" began with the Meiji oligarchs' replacement of "history" with a "myth" about the imperial genealogy and the imperial soul. A host of other beliefs and rituals were created to transform this myth into the official history. Or, the official history of Japan entered the myth time.

Nationalism as Ideology vs. Patriotism as Individual Practice

I distinguish cultural nationalism from political nationalism. Cultural nationalism is often a collective sentiment that arises out of what Tambiah (1996a: 21) calls a "double helix": "boundary-making," on the one hand, and the "substantialization and reification of qualities and attributes as enduring collective possessions," on the other. In contrast, political nationalism is a form of *state ideology*, with "ideology" defined as "unified schemes or configurations developed to underwrite or manifest power" (Wolf 1999: 4). Thus, "ideology" is predicated upon the presence of a state, whenever it arises.

I use the term "patriotism" to refer to the feeling of loyalty to one's country as embraced and expressed by individuals, including soldiers. The term "patriotism" is often used to refer to jingoistic and chauvinistic sentiments that are hostile to all other peoples. But it need not be thus.[2]

In order to understand the central question of the book—was the pilots' patriotism conterminous with the state ideology?—I use two axes: (1) the individual perspective vs. the collective (institutional/structural) perspective; and (2) the presence or absence of a political dimension. Political nationalism is collective and institutional, orchestrated by the political and intellectual leaders, and thus is predicated upon the presence of a central political body with power, that is, the state. In reference to Japan I sometimes use the term imperial nationalism to refer more specifically to a particular kind of political nationalism developed by the state from the beginning of the Meiji period, with the *pro rege et patria mori* ideology as its strategic core. Cultural nationalism, such as the embracing of the quotidian aesthetics of cherry blossoms, lacks a political dimension but is collective, i.e., shared by most members of a society. Patriotism refers to perspectives and actions on the ground—a person's identification of him/herself as a member of a social group and resultant sentiments, often, though not always, including the sentiments of loyalty to the group.

The analytical distinction between nationalism and patriotism is important not simply for distinguishing between political ideology from above and interpretations on the ground. This distinction enables us to identify how nationalism is often disguised by the state as patriotism to make it more palatable to the people. Unless we examine *how* individuals during wartime translate or fail to translate the language of the official discourse on political nationalism into their own, we will never understand how the "general will" of a totalitarian state synecdochically becomes THE general will of the people. If we go beyond *practice* as "human action in the world" (Sahlins 1981: 6) or as "anything people do" (Ortner 1984: 149) and think of actions and behaviors as extending to the thoughts, interests, motivations, and *meanings* that social actors and agents assign to their own and others' behaviors, then our task of understanding *practice* requires a great deal more work than we have done so far in anthropology.[3] This view of practice is also important for opening up the possibility of linking culture to the individual in a real sense—the sense of the relationship of individuals' thoughts and behaviors to their culture. The distinction between nationalism and patriotism enables us to identify the successes and failures of the transmission of a nationalist ideology to individuals, and to understand in what ways individuals' patriotism was imbricated with the political nationalism orchestrated by the state.

The Global/Local Interface:
The Birthplace of Nationalism and Patriotism

The development of the selfhood of a social group is often precipitated by the need for boundary making because the Other compels a social group to come to terms with its own identity. Self/Other encounters may simply be through trade or other flows of peoples and objects. The encounters may be intense and hostile, as in the case of warfare, conquests, and colonialism, which many times result in the emergence of political nationalism among the victimized population.

Following Herder, Berlin uses the "bent twig" metaphor of Schiller and sees nationalism as stemming from "wounds, some form of collective humiliation." It lashes back and refuses "to accept the alleged inferiority." For example, German "nonaggressive nationalism" began to develop in the seventeenth century as a result of the *Volksgeist* being wounded by the perceived superiority of the high culture of the French; the Germans reacted like a "bent twig." But its boundary making was "nonaggressive" and was not based on hostility toward other peoples, although it eventually developed into the extraordinarily aggressive

Volksgeist of the Third Reich (Berlin [1959] 1992: 243–47).[4] Herder, Vico, and Berlin all see in human history a type of nationalism that was based on pluralism and respect for each other's way of life, rather than being a recipe for bloodshed (Berlin [1959] 1992: 10–11, 243–46).

According to Malia (1999), since the early nineteenth century the Russians felt that they belonged neither to the West nor to the East, and their society did not evolve according to the Hegelian vision of historical development—from medieval Christianity and feudalism to the Enlightenment from which the liberal state emerged. Feeling that they did not have a national literature in the Western sense, Russian literati were obsessed with *narodnost* (national originality), which became the sine qua non of Russian romanticism (Leighton 1985: 373; Terras 1985b: 294). Again, the presence of the Other was pivotal to the development of Russian cultural nationalism.

The presence of their own literary tradition was not as problematic to the Japanese, but the Japanese elite and the folk felt their traditions were inferior to those of the Chinese and, later, of the Westerners, whom they strove to emulate. Their cultural nationalism, based on a sense of belonging, if not loyalty, to a group beyond a local or kinship community, developed during the ninth century when the Japanese elite attempted to establish their own identity vis-à-vis the Chinese. At that time neither was Japan a state with a strong central government,[5] nor were all the inhabitants on the Japanese archipelago "imagined" to belong to one community. Their political self-identity was at an inchoate stage.

When jolted into a nascent political nationalism in reaction to the Western colonial powers, the Japanese perceived the urgent necessity of strengthening the boundary militarily and of developing political nationalism. But as with many other Asians, they succumbed to Western *cultural* hegemony—as exemplified by the Japanese pilots, they continue to regard Western high culture with awe. The double-edged sword of threat and adoration of Western civilization played a crucial role in the Japanese struggle to establish a Japanese identity. The Japanese had hardly shed their topknots before they faced their first "Western" enemy, Russia, at the time when Japan was politically and even geographically unknown to the most of the world. The Japanese felt an urgent need to be "somebody in the world," which is "at the heart of the great cry for recognition on the part of both individuals and groups" (Berlin [1958] 1969: 157). Many Japanese felt they achieved the goal by winning the war over Russia. Hardly any time passed before they were hurled into the geopolitics that escalated into World War I. In this turbulent world, many Japanese, even Christian intellectuals like Nitobe Inazō, experienced a heightened sense of their own identity as Japanese. Even though many refused to participate in imperial nationalism, choosing instead to defy the state and the military, they were patriotic, that is, they felt a sense of allegiance and even loyalty to their country and were ready to defend it from external attacks. Early Meiji liberals who were involved in the "Freedom and People's Rights" movement embraced much of Western liberalism, and yet they were ardent patriots who advocated the virtue of the Japanese soul (yamato damashii) and sacrifice for the country (chapter 2).

Political nationalism, orchestrated by the state, and patriotism, a result of individual interpretations of Japan's precarious position in geopolitics, became partially imbricated. *Hardly anyone realized the fundamental difference between the two.* For the state, anti-Western sentiment was a convenient and extremely powerful tool to utilize for enforcing its programs of political nationalism, since the sentiment was the basis of the patriotism of many individuals from the Meiji "Restoration" through World War II.

Primordiality and its Reformulation in Totalitarian Ideology

Boundary making requires substantialization. The metaphor for what is shared among the members of a social group, be it a small subaltern group or a state, could be the "will" for the Germans, the "soul" *(tama, tamashii)* for the Japanese and Russians, or "the blood tie." These metaphors express oneness of a social group based on "assumed 'givens'" (Geertz 1973: 250). Assumed blood ties, language, etc. are chosen to concretize these givens (250–69).

In this context, Article 1 of the Meiji constitution takes on a profound significance. Against the unanimous opposition of their German and Austrian advisors, the Meiji oligarchs insisted on the inclusion of Article 1, which proclaimed an unbroken imperial genealogy. This was facilitated by the imperial "soul" that was transmitted from one emperor to the next. In other words, Article 1 represented the oligarch's effort to create a unique identity by assigning primordiality to the emperor system, and thus to the Japanese. It was the crucial building block for establishing a Japanese *Volk* with a cultural soul.

"Purity" is often the most important valence attached to primordiality. In the case of the Japanese, and possibly of the Germans, "primordiality" is precisely about purity—the self, i.e., the Japanese soul, before contamination either by the Other(s) or by later historical developments such as urbanization and industrialization. The primordial German *Volk* was sought in a putative Aryan or Teutonic past with spiritual strength and purity (Wolf 1999: 236), while the Japanese located the primordiality and purity of the Japanese in an ancient past, symbolized by an imperial genealogy that stretched back to the Sun Goddess.

The construction of a unity of a *Volk* within a nation/state is almost always built upon contradiction since states are usually multi-ethnic or otherwise heterogeneous. In this context, to become a *Volk*, the dominant social group must make a special effort to purify itself. At the cosmological level, purity of the self may be maintained either by bringing in the source of purity from outside, or by purging itself of its impurity. In the case of the Japanese, they acquired the purity of deities through rituals *and/or* purged their impurity by transferring it to minority groups. The marginalization of the special status groups *(hisabetsu-burakumin)* most conspicuously expressed this process, whereby the dominant group assigned culturally defined impurity to social groups engaged in nonagrarian occupations, especially those related to human and animal deaths (Ohnuki-Tierney 1987). In Nazi Germany, a "pure" Aryan race was constructed through scapegoating Jews, gypsies, homosexuals, and the mentally retarded, to whom the Aryan Germans transferred their own impurity (Burke 1955: 407). But the Japanese construction of the self had also to do with their image of the self in relation to Westerners (Pollack 1986; S. Tanaka 1993). This led to the assignment of a different type of valence to another minority—the Ainu. As the Japanese eagerly embraced Western Enlightenment, they assigned "primitiveness" to the Ainu, who then served as the yardstick to measure the progress of the Japanese as "civilized and enlightened" (Ohnuki-Tierney 1987, 1998a).

The "anatomy of prejudice," as it were, had to be revamped once Japan entered its expansionist course, since the state needed as many bodies as possible to fight its wars. Hence, the Japanese authorities extended the Japanese soul to their own minorities as well to Chinese, Koreans, and others both in Japan proper and in the occupied territories of Taiwan, Korea, and Sakhalin, who constituted one-third of the "one hundred million" in Prime Minister Konoe Fumimaro's infamous declaration of July 23, 1940. "One hundred million, one soul" became the slogan encouraging all and every "Japanese" to "truly dedicate themselves to the emperor." It became one of the most used and abused slogans, propagated by the state through schools and mass media throughout the military period. This process led to the tragic example of ethnic Koreans flying to their deaths; Nagai Asami (*Daily Yomiuri*, August 11, 2001) lists eleven of them.

A highly influential philosopher, Tanabe Hajime (1885–1962), is immensely important in this context. Studying under Husserl at Freiburg University, he critically read Kant, Marx, and Hegel to establish his own philosophy. As professor of philosophy at the Imperial University of Kyoto, he was perhaps the most revered and influential philosopher in the 1940s. At the Imperial University of Kyoto, in his often-cited speech of May 19, 1943 in front of a large audience that included the "student soldiers" to be sent to the front, Tanabe, a devout Christian, advocated the individual's "dedication to the nation" in order to bring about changes in society. In this lecture, entitled deliberately "Death and Life" *(shisei)*, rather than life and death, he expounded on the Stoic philosophy, especially that of Marcus Aurelius, and the philosophy of Spinoza. Obviously following Spinoza, he explained: "Wise men may sacrifice for God or the founder of a religion, but it is inconceivable to think that we ordinary individuals sacrifice ourselves directly to God; it is for the country. . . . Today when our nation faces a crisis, the nation and the individual are united into one" (Tanabe 1964: 245–62). Tanabe Hajime was read by all four pilots. Nakao Taketoku, one of our pilots, rode a train from Tokyo to Kyoto—a long journey at that time—to hear the lecture, an experience that intensified his resolution to dedicate himself to the nation (chapter 6).

Tanabe's advocacy of sacrifice for one's nation had further implications. Sakai (1997) points out that Tanabe proposed that one has the free will to choose the nation to which one dedicates oneself, thereby, by extension, advocating that Chinese, Koreans, and others select Japanese nation to belong to. While giving them the right to be Japanese, the right also entailed the responsibility to be involved in the society to bring about changes (Sakai 1997). That is, their involvement called for sacrifice for Japan—indeed a chilling proposal. This lethal implication may not have been articulated in the mind of Tanabe, who, after the war, published a book in which he repented his own role during the war. It is worth noting that during the building of the Japanese puppet state of Manchukuo, many intellectuals, heavily influenced by left-wing ideas, flocked to Manchuria with revolutionary dreams of creating a new and just society that would accommodate Chinese nationalists' aspirations (Young 1998: 241–50). In other words, they misrecognized the state ideology as consistent with their own idealism. This was so even while "imperial jingoism" permeated through the mass media (Young 1998: 4).

Thus the idealism of these liberal proponents of Japan as a multi-ethnic nation unwittingly served the military goal.

While Japan's fascist state committed numerous atrocities upon other Asians, for example, the Nanking massacres and the Bataan death march, it did not engage in systematic scapegoating of its minorities in the way the Nazis did. Instead, the governments gave the "privilege" to the minorities and the colonized peoples to become "Japanese," thereby sending them all to war, that is, giving them the *equal right to death*. They even deployed the strategy to make fallen soldiers from these social groups "war deities." At the cosmological level, for the purpose of Japanese imperial expansion, the state solved the problem of maintaining the primordial purity of the "Japanese" by extending the Japanese soul (yamato damashii) to all.

A history of the "Japanese totalitarian soul" tells us a brutal story. It is a celebration of the soul as a reward for death for the emperor. The state used the absence of the body in the afterlife in Japanese folk religiosity to aestheticize mandatory death by the invention of "ethereally beautiful" cherry blossoms as postmortem souls. The Japanese state repeatedly emphasized that the Japanese soul was the quintessence of the Japanese, distinguishing them from all other peoples and enabling them to sacrifice without hesitancy. Despite some parallels between German and Japanese fascism, the Japanese emphasis was different even from the Germans, for whom to kill the enemy was the first order of business, rather than the death of their own soldiers.

HISTORICAL DISCONTINUITY NATURALIZED AS CONTINUITY

Nationalist and ethnic movements almost always involve constructions/inventions of the past of the people *and* the closing of the time between the past and the present so that the idealized past defines the essence of the people in the present. This process is often facilitated through naturalization processes which present historical discontinuities as continuities. In Japan and elsewhere, we witness these processes of naturalization as the most powerful mechanism that national leaders used in their attempt to convert state nationalism into patriotism.

The term naturalization and the concept behind it have lately become widely used in and out of academia. Foucault, Barthes, and Bourdieu used the term "naturalization" to refer to a process whereby "cultural arbitrariness" becomes "natural," that is, as "given" (Bourdieu [1972] 1977:

164). This process of culture becoming nature has been used primarily to explain cultural practices in a synchronic sense (Bourdieu [1979] 1984; Bourdieu and Darbel [1969] 1990). I wish to extend this analytical tool by historicizing it, so that it becomes a tool for understanding historical processes whereby discontinuities come to be seen as continuities, and recently altered traditions come to be perceived as traditions from time immemorial.

Refashioning of Tradition

A common mechanism for naturalization, often with powerful effect, is to present a radically altered tradition as though it were a long-cherished tradition. To describe this particular historical process, I use the phrase "refashioning of tradition."

The concept is not new at all. With Luther donning the mask of the apostle Paul as one of the examples, Marx famously described in his "Eighteenth Brumaire" how people, especially at times of anxiety such as revolutionary crisis, "conjure up the spirits of the past to their service . . . in order to present the new scene . . . in time-honored disguise" (Marx and Engels [1852] 1989: 320). Since then various terms have been used to refer to this common phenomenon. I refrain from the use of such terms as "invention of tradition" or "reification," since these terms are heavily embedded in the theoretical contexts of the scholars who introduced them. The "invention of tradition," used originally by Hobsbawm and Ranger, refers to a set of practices which, through their rules and repetition of values and norms of behavior, imply continuity with a historical past in the absence of such continuity (Hobsbawm and Ranger, eds. [1983] 1986). As the term became the rage in the 1980s and 1990s, it began to be simplified and used to imply that all traditions are inventions, or, someone's constructions, or even concoctions, like a rabbit out of a hat. But a tradition is rarely invented anew in toto, as the essays in the volume by Hobsbawm and Ranger show. For example, tartans, "invented by an Englishman after the Union of 1707" (Trevor-Roper 1983), represent a "refashioning" of the tradition at a time when the external force, the union of parliaments, necessitated the assertion of their collective self on the part of Scottish Highlanders. The term "invention of tradition" is too misleading and facile to describe historical processes which always involve both continuities and discontinuities.

The Frankfurt School's use of the term "reification" is also problematic since it derives from the Marxist theory of commodity reification, or the commodification of labor, characteristic of modernity and mass culture. The notion describes "the way in which, under capitalism, the older traditional forms of human activity are instrumentally reorganized and 'taylorized,' analytically fragmented and reconstructed according to various rational models of efficiency, and essentially restructured along the lines of a differentiation between means and ends" (Jameson 1992: 10). It emphasizes that under capitalism all human activities become sheer means or instrumentality through materialization and quantification. Jameson's application of this notion to art follows this theoretical orientation.

By using the term "refashioning," I stress first the *co-presence of both continuities and discontinuities*—the very essence of historical processes. "Refashioning" can be tied either to a particular dimension of culture, be it the imperial system or the meanings of cherry blossoms, or to culture at large. Second, while "transformations"—continuities that involve changes—are a sine qua non of historical processes, the term "refashioning" foregrounds agency. The changes are results of an active involvement by social agent(s), even though the trajectories of their refashioning seldom follow their original designs.

Rather than discussing this phenomenon in general, it is worth dissecting one particular dimension of the Japanese case in order to understand how it works and does not work. I select the refashioning of the emperor as God the Father after the model in Christianity. The idea was suggested by von Stein and adopted by the Meiji oligarchs. A brief outline of the pastoral model in European societies will highlight how the Japanese case differs fundamentally from it.

In European polities, there have been hundreds of years of conflict between religious and political authorities: the Church/Christian God vs. the State/King. According to Kantorowicz, the sense of *patria* in Europe as "an aggregate of all the political, religious, ethical, and moral values for which a man might care to live and die" (Kantorowicz [1957] 1981: 234–45), which existed in classical Antiquity, was almost obsolete by the early Middle Ages. It is important, however, that it remained in the language of the church, in which the kingdom of heaven became the patria. Throughout the early Middle Ages, monks and, later, knights were seen as "soldiers of Christ," and the killing of infidels became a virtue that guaranteed them immediate entry into heaven. The image of the Christian martyr as someone "who had offered himself up for the invisible polity and had died for his divine Lord *pro fide*" (Kantorowicz [1957] 1981: 234–35) remained until the twentieth century. The image of the martyr by the time of the crusades was a knight who died for the cause of the *Holy Land* in the service of *Christ the King:* "He that embarks to the Holy Land, He that dies in this campaign, Shall enter into heaven's bliss, And with the saints there shall he dwell" (quoted in Kantorowicz [1957] 1981: 239).[6] In this image, there is no contradiction between the religious and the secular patria. The stanza tells that the entry into heaven is at the core of this Christian belief.

By the twelfth century, Christian martyrdom had acquired some "national flavor," as demonstrated in the *Chanson de Roland* in the proclamation by Archbishop Turpin of Reims to the Frankish warriors: "For our king we have to die. Help to sustain the Christian faith. . . . I shall absolve you, heal your souls. If so you die, you shall be held martyrs. Obtaining seats high up in paradise" (quoted in Kantorowicz [1957] 1981: 240). This French epic glorifies the battles waged by Charlemagne, who supposedly conquered all of Spain except for Saragossa. Roland is described as the paragon of an unyielding warrior for his France, but the poem portrays him as a Christian martyr. By the thirteenth century the crown of martyrdom had descended on the war victims of the secular state, as Kantorowicz puts it. The entry into heaven as a "reward," as it were, remained intact throughout these periods.

During the European feudal period, when countries were divided into territories ruled by lords, the conflict between the patria in heaven and the patria on earth was further complicated by the co-presence of the patria of the feudal lord and patria of the nation. The Christian martyr may have to go against his secular lord and patria on earth in order to serve his Lord in heaven, as exemplified by Thomas à Becket (1117–70), who went against Henry II and his secular kingdom in defense of the Christian kingdom, and, two centuries later, by William of Nogaret, who struggled between dying for Christ his Lord, for the kingdom of France, and for his feudal lord (Kantorowicz [1957] 1981: 259). Yet, the patria in heaven has remained an important part of the imagination of patriotism in many European nations.

Needless to say, we cannot lump all the European nations together as having followed one historical trajectory. According to Mosse (1990: 34–35), in Germany "the revival of Christian piety had continued unbroken from the eighteenth into the nineteenth century." It gave the Germans the feeling that they were fighting for "a holy land," i.e., a Christian kingdom, and a sense of the consecration of their mission. Protestant Christianity consecrated German nationalism, giving rise to the "cult of the fallen" and the creation of martyrs. The French resisted the Christianization of the Roman *pro patria*. Nevertheless, an overlay of the kingdom of heaven on the territorialized political unit, France, cannot be ignored.

As noted earlier, war propaganda encouraging *pro patria mori* in

Germany, Italy, etc. mobilized the Christian vision, despite the contradiction that the fatherland no longer meant the Christian kingdom, *to which an enemy also belonged.* Thus, a soldier who died for Italy against Austria in World War I was seen to have been received by Christ and to have gone to heaven. Mosse argues that the "Myth of the War Experience" was constructed in retrospect in order to transform the war into "a meaningful and even sacred event," in which saints and martyrs were given significant roles: "From Germany to Poland postcards showed Christ or an angel touching a dead soldier. The design of the war cemeteries of many European countries symbolized this relationship" (Mosse 1990: 75–76). The painting, *Apotheosis of the Fallen,* at the military cemetery of Redipuglia in Italy constructed in 1938, for example, shows a soldier resting in the arms of Christ. The official postcard of the Bavarian wartime Volunteer Nurses Association, entitled "Christ at the Tomb of a Fallen Soldier," portrays Christ extending his arms to a tomb (Mosse 1990: 7–8, 76). In other words, regardless for which secular kingdom (nation/state) a soldier died, he is depicted as having died for the Christian kingdom and as having been received by Christ the Lord. Mosse (1989) tells us that in many of the anthems of Western nations, soldiers are praised for dying for their country, and their entry into heaven is guaranteed. In modern wars, the secular patria takes precedence. Nevertheless, the national anthem of the United Kingdom, for example, first appearing in print in 1745, claims "Lord" as "Our God," who would "Save the King" and "Scatter his enemies, / And make them fall" (Reed and Bristow, eds. [1960] 1997: 549–50).

The religious and political landscape of Japan is as far removed as possible from the Christian worldview. First, the Japanese folk shinto pantheon recognizes no Almighty God. Siddhartha Gautama was a human, as was Confucius. Humans easily become deities, rather than just "saints" as in Christianity. Second, the image of the emperor altogether excludes his own sacrifice. Christ sacrificed himself for humankind. It would have been unthinkable for the emperor to sacrifice himself for the Japanese. The difference is succinctly expressed by the metaphor of the shield—in the Bible it was the Lord who is shield for humans, whereas in the poems of the ancient imperial guards in Japan it was the guards who became shields to protect the emperor (chapter 2). It is indeed a tragic irony that the student soldier Hayashi Ichizō (chapter 6), a devout Christian, named his diary as "The Lord God is a Sun and Shield" when he died as a shield for the emperor. Third, there was no image of an afterlife in any of Japanese religions in modern times, and thus Japanese religiosity offered no reward of "entry into heaven." Fourth, the emperor did not preside over a kingdom overriding political boundaries.

The notions of "God the Father" in Christianity and of "the emperor as God the Father" in Japan were separated by several oceans. The two religious/political landscapes were too far apart for the Japanese emperor to be refashioned according to the pastoral model and still be recognizably the emperor the Japanese had known from "time immemorial," even with the scheme of the emperor touring all over Japan to show his concern for his subjects. Yet, they tried. First, in the absence of the notion of afterlife in Japanese religions, their strategy was the postmortem apotheosis of the soldiers, with blooming cherry blossoms at the Yasukuni Shrine as the metamorphosed souls of fallen soldiers. The exclusive concentration on the souls of fallen soldiers enabled the government and military to get around the fact that they could not recover their bodies, which in normal circumstances were necessary for the proper performance of funeral rites. Second, in the absence of the model of sacrifice for the people by the ruler, they refashioned the already existing notion of loyalty and sacrifice by means of the transference of loyalty to one's parents to the emperor *and* of the transference of loyalty to the regional lord to the emperor. The Japanese case was not unique, however. In a text from a reading primer for children published during the Nazi period before World War II, children vow love and obedience to the Führer, the Father. The text is accompanied by an illustration of a boy and a girl giving a bouquet of roses to Hitler (Hinton 1998: 10).

The refashioning thus focused on the eternity of the imperial system, especially by blocking out hundreds of years beginning with the end of the twelfth century during which the emperor retreated into the shadows. Thus, unlike other national anthems, the hurriedly composed Japanese anthem simply stated: "the emperor's reign is as long as moss grows on a rock," and *nothing else*. The state focused on its main goal—the construction of the notion of sacrifice for the emperor as an ancient tradition.

Aestheticization as a Facilitator for Naturalization

Naturalization processes are often cloaked in aesthetics. As discussed earlier, the aesthetics of assigning purity to primordiality is a key strategy in many nationalisms, which attempt to link the present directly to an imagined primordial past, while ignoring the inconvenient "impurities" introduced in the course of history. In the Japanese case, cherry blossoms played the single most important role in this process. The state resurrected the ancient imperial guards, symbolized by a cherry tree in front of the imperial palace. Upon this aestheticized and romanticized image, the state sought to model modern-day conscripts. In addition, the state attempted an "aesthetic equation" between conscripts and the upper-class warriors of pre-Meiji Japan. These upper-class warriors constituted the highest social class and were the patrons of high culture—they developed the arts of the tea ceremony, flower arrangement, Zen Buddhism, various forms of architecture, etc. When they did commit suicide, the upper-class warriors usually did so in peacetime to protect their own honor, and never during combat. It was a highly aestheticized ritual act. Seppuku (harakiri) was *not* seen as an act of aggression toward anyone, including the enemy. It was usually high-ranking warriors who performed it, as in the case of Lord Asano of *The Forty-Seven Loyal Retainers,* who owned territory and a castle, and who had a large number of retainers. Young and low-ranking warriors seldom encountered situations that required them to defend their "honor," which they rarely had. Modern soldiers of various social backgrounds, fighting with tanks and guns, and crouching in trenches, were clad in shining armor through the aesthetic label of *gunjin* (war people; warriors) that symbolically equated them with the samurai of the past.

Above all, the Japanese soul, yamato damashii, was beautified by cherry blossoms. Nitobe Inazō and other political and intellectual leaders refashioned the warrior's way (bushidō) and assigned cherry blossoms qua the Japanese soul, the exclusive possession of the warriors, to the conscripts. Suddenly, the foot soldiers from rural Japan, minorities, Koreans, and Chinese all became the *bushi* (warriors) of yesteryear, having the Japanese soul, "capable" of dying without hesitancy, falling like cherry petals.

As we saw in chapter 1, the meanings assigned to cherry blossoms in pre-Meiji Japan included processes involving life, death, and rebirth. However, blooming cherry blossoms foregrounded love and other life forces, as well as the radiant nature of the collective self of the Japanese. Initially, cherry trees were planted at the Yasukuni Shrine in order to console the souls of the fallen soldiers with their beautiful blossoms. The symbolism was subsequently refashioned by the fascist state so that these same blooming cherry blossoms came to stand for metamorphosed souls of fallen soldiers—after death. The state thus moved the meaning of the flower all the way across a rich and vast field of symbolism.

Chapter 8

PATRIOTISM: GLOBAL INTELLECTUAL
CURRENTS AS ITS SOURCE

Given the state's lack of success in instilling the *pro rege et patria mori* ideology into the minds of the tokkōtai pilots, why did they fly off to their deaths, thereby affirming the state ideology by their actions? This chapter examines and interprets the thoughts of five pilots against the broader background of the cosmopolitan intellectual currents that swept them into the idealistic flights of imagination that led to their deaths. Because there is not room enough here to discuss all the books, films, and music mentioned in the four diaries introduced in chapter 6 and in the list of readings in the Appendix, I comment only on the most salient of these. It is a hard task to discern what these young men made of the books they read not just at a different period in history but at the time of Japan's intensive militarism. I try not to inject my own views or those of contemporary revisionists.[1] Rather, I try to adhere to the way the pilots discussed these readings in their diaries.

UTOPIAN VISIONS: MARXISM, HUMANITARIANISM, AND CHRISTIANITY

Although disillusionment with communism was pervasive in Europe early in the twentieth century and in Japan by the 1930s, Marxism, especially Leninism, remained a powerful intellectual force in Japan all the way through World War II and well up into the 1980s, especially among university students and intellectuals. Even after the war, *Das Kapital* remained a bible for university students, who memorized chapter 4, "The General Formula for Capital," with its famous formulae.[2]

The pilots read extensively in Marxism. Sasaki's diary contains sustained discussions of Marx, Engels, Lenin, Kropotkin, Stalin, and Trotsky. Sasaki's and Hayashi Tadao's understandings of Marxism were quite sophisticated, locating Marxism in the broader context of political-economic history and historical materialism. For an understanding of these issues, they also read Simmel and Weber as counterpoints. Both Sasaki and Hayashi Tadao were critical but committed to Marxism, not only embracing it as a philosophical conviction alone but attempting to live up to its principles. Sasaki and Hayashi Tadao's brother fought against their own fathers whom, they thought, embraced capitalism and materialism.

Lenin's works made inroads into Japan only gradually, starting in the early 1920s (Duus 1988). Sasaki read Lenin's *Imperialism, the Highest Stage of Capitalism: A Popular Outline.* Hayashi Tadao re-read Lenin's *State and Revolution* on the base and threw page after page into the toilet for fear of discovery. Both Sasaki and Hayashi Tadao discussed the final, imperial stage of capitalism, revealing Lenin's strong influence on them. At that time Lenin's warnings against imperialism and colonialism and his advocacy for the right of nations to self-determination had a powerful influence in Asia and Africa, where Western colonialism had precipitated a strong surge of nationalism.

Despite the sophistication with which these pilots understood and critically argued about Marxism and historical materialism, Marxism was, in the end, a form of idealism that gave them a tool to fight against capitalism and materialism. After reading the works by Kawakami Hajime (1879–1946), an influential Marxist and professor of economics at the Imperial University of Kyoto, who became a member of the Communist Party, Sasaki (1981: 321) remarks that writings by Marxists are usually full of propaganda and are combative but lack sophistication in their philosophical arguments. Both Sasaki and Hayashi Tadao wanted not only to destroy the United States and England—the embodiment of capitalism—but Japan, corrupted by capitalism, as well, in order to usher in a New Japan. This hope was expressed not by these two only, but was shared by others.[3] Somewhat ironically for Marx, who disdained nationalism and hoped for a world united by the workers, Marxism was not only an expression of idealism, a spiritual fortress, for these young pilots, but was also an intellectual justification for patriotism.

For Sasaki, utopia was to be built upon the humanitarianism of Albert Schweitzer and the return to nature and agrarianism of Miyazawa Kenji. Hayashi Tadao shared a Marxian utopia with Sasaki. However, he filled his utopia with his lyricism and aesthetics.

Nakao was a serious reader of fascism and totalitarianism. But, after reading Vilfredo Pareto, Giovanni Gentile, Alfred Rosenberg, Carl Schmitt, and others, he concludes that Nazism and fascism were the "totalitarian camp which rose against liberalism and materialism" (Nakao 1997: 439–40). In other words, he interpreted fascism and totalitarianism as antidotes to the ultraliberal individualism verging on egotism and materialism which characterized modernity. He was also the one who traveled all the way from Tokyo to Kyoto to listen to Tanabe Hajime's lecture, in which Tanabe advocated young men's active involvement in their society, thereby implicitly sending them to their deaths. But that he was not a simple right-wing is clearly evident in his reaction to Osaragi Jirō's book on the Dreyfus Affair (Nakao 1997: 204–5). He was indignant at the way Dreyfus was treated and exclaimed, "The life of an innocent should never be at stake. However, for the military only its honor is at stake." After praising the Clemenceau brothers, Émile Zola, and the judge at the final trial, he declares: "Am I to enter the world of chaos in which one's partisan interests obstruct justice? I do not want to be part of the world which justifies the actions of bureaucrats and gives almighty power to the military. I prefer to be at the margin, and, like Zola, try to steer the nation toward justice and truth." He also could not understand why the hisabetsu-burakumin had to be treated with such prejudice just because they were born in that social group. Therefore, while undoubtedly succumbing to the propaganda of the right-wing intellectuals, Nakao was far from endorsing the totalitarian ideology in toto.

Christianity promised another form of utopia. Starting with Uchimura Kanzō and other Christian leaders in the early Meiji period, many Christians fought against the increasing threat of totalitarianism, although there were Christian intellectuals, such as Nitobe Inazō and Tanabe Hajime, whose patriotism, albeit unintentionally, endorsed the state ideology.[4] Japanese Christians strove to build their utopia on earth, or, to build a society based on freedom, equality, and fraternity—the goal of the Meiji "Restoration," as they interpreted it. Of the founding members of the Social Democratic Party, all but one were Christians. The party was formed in 1901—a year after the formation of the Socialist Society in 1900—but was disbanded within twelve hours of the publication of its manifesto. Except for Kinoshita Naoe, Meiji socialists, nonetheless, were critical neither of the Meiji constitution nor of the role of the emperor (Duus 1988: 659–67).

Meiji Christian leaders were highly respected throughout the twentieth century. After reading Uchimura Kanzō's *How I became a Christian* and *Consolations for Christians,* Sasaki (1981: 90–91) concluded that Christianity did not offer spiritual strength for him. Nevertheless, he was quite impressed by the purity and dedication to the search for truth Uchimura Kanzō and other Christians displayed (Sasaki 1981: 259–60).

Hayashi Ichizō and other Christian pilots struggled to sort out the complex interrelationships between Christianity, patriotism, and the *pro rege et patria mori* ideology.[5] Hayashi Ichizō went to a school to sing hymns just before his last mission and carried the Bible with him on his fatal flight. On the last night before his flight, Kumai Tsuneo, another navy tokkōtai pilot, urged other comrades to sing hymns together. He and several other pilots sang a hymn, whose words ask God to give them strength "until they meet again." Hagihara Kōtarō, one of those who joined Kumai in the singing, survived and later recalled how singing hymns could have put them in danger of punishment on the base: "Although we were not explicitly fighting Christianity and thus it was nominally permitted to sing hymns, we could have been in real danger" (Ebina 1983: 181–82). Amidst the severe censorship and the hostile attitudes of some of the career soldiers toward the student soldiers, this final act was the last celebration of the beauty of humanity in the most inhuman of circumstances, a protest against the brutality of the military aggression, or even a dirge for their impending deaths.

ROMANTICISM AND BEYOND

In most cultures, Romanticism was, like Marxism, a movement against capitalism and materialism. For this reason, Marx and Lenin held at least some elements of Romanticism in high regard. If Romanticism in Europe constituted a part of the struggle to overcome modernity, so did it in Japan. The pilots embodied Japanese historical experience in the Meiji period and after—being influenced by modernity and trying to overcome modernity/Western influence at the same time. Their experience was analogous to that of European intellectuals during the late nineteenth and early twentieth centuries, including, though not exclusively, those involved in the Romantic movement which swept through Germany, France, and Russia, and reached as far as Japan. Needless to say, it is erroneous to envision a neat package called German Romanticism that traveled from one country to the next. At any rate, these various forms of Romanticism were part of the complex picture of "overcoming modernity" in each society, on the one hand, and of confronting the increasing threats of armed conflict between nation states, which eventually escalated into the World Wars, on the other. It is easy to understand how in their soliloquies the pilots turned to the philosophers and literary figures whose central concerns involved the questions of the individual vs. society, life and death, aesthetics, and patriotism. These interrelated themes were major concerns of Romanticism, although they have also been basic and perennial questions in philosophy and literature since antiquity.[6]

The Romantic School in Japan

It has been assumed that a major intellectual influence upon the young intellectuals in the 1930s was the Japan Romantic School (Nihon Romanha). This school of thought became intimately linked to ultranationalism under its leader, Yasuda Yojūrō (1910–81), who was purged after World War II (Hashikawa 1985: 7–8). A systematic exposition of the ideological underpinnings of Yasuda was undertaken by Hashikawa Bunsō, who himself was intellectually enchanted by Yasuda in his youth (Hashikawa 1985).[7] Under the heavy influence of German Romanticism, Yasuda published his version of Japanese Romanticism in the journals *Cogito* and *Nihon Romanha* (Japan Romantic School), founded in 1932 and 1935 respectively. It is not a coincidence that Hitler rose to power in 1933 and became führer and chancellor a year later. Yasuda's writing style is seductive and opaque at the same time, liberally sprinkled with jargon and homage to Western intellectual giants. His alluring romanticism is exemplified in the opening sentences of "The Flower and Metaphysics," which starts: "Has anyone seen the flowers blooming in Plato's land? No, I don't mean those flowers in nature . . . . The eyes of those who search for the flowers are always moist with tears" (Yasuda [1932] 1984: 129–44). He keeps the reader in suspense by not revealing exactly what he means by "the flowers in Plato's land."

Yasuda declared Marxist literature to be the last stage of Japan's "Civilization and Enlightenment," and, historically, Romantic literature in Japan to be "the bridge in the night reaching toward a new dawn." He thus assigned the task of overcoming modernity to the Japanese Romantics (Yasuda [1939] 1986: 13–14). Yet Yasuda and his associates retained some aspects of Marxism and combined these with Japan's Nativist

School and German Romanticism (Hashikawa 1985: 31). Above all they juxtaposed their emphasis on a return to Japanese tradition with ubiquitous references to Western high culture.

Yasuda's master trope was "irony." For example, he wrote of "Japan as Irony," "Romanticism as Irony," and "Asia as Irony," and declared that the "foundation of Japanese Romanticism is situated in the chaos and formlessness of Japan's new spirit," "Japan's irony *simultaneously captures destruction and construction*," and that "there is an impulse for irony to capture infinite possibilities" (quoted in Hashikawa 1985: 33–34, 39–53, emphasis added). The seduction of his master trope rests, in my view, not only in its opaqueness but also in his references and allusions to high intellectual traditions of Europe. In fact his central theme of "irony" alludes to various philosophical propositions, beginning with Socrates, Hegel, Heine, Schlegel, and Schmit.

The arguments which Yasuda and his associates marshaled were antirational and anticapitalist. As alternatives, they advocated ultranationalism and a return to "nature" and "agrarianism," which supposedly embodied the purity and primordiality of the Japanese. Following the nativist tradition of the Edo period (Harootunian 1988), Yasuda preached agrarianism, especially rice agriculture (Hashikawa 1985: 69–72), which represented "Japanese nature" (for the relationship between agrarianism and the representation of Japanese nature as rice paddies, see Ohnuki-Tierney 1993a). Above all, Yasuda and other ultra-nationalists contended that the emperor system, if dislodged from politics, offered the key to a unique Japanese identity. Yasuda's vision was to attain "a revitalized Japanese identity based on the unique Japanese emperor system" (Doak 1994: xiii).

The Romantic School's emphasis on a return to Japanese tradition is apparent also in their choice of the phoenix as the emblem for their journal, *Nihon Romanha*. The emblem is a copy of the phoenix *(hō'ō)* on the roof of the so-called "Phoenix Pavilion" at Byōdō-in Temple at Uji, Kyoto.[8] The "Phoenix Pavilion" is dedicated to Amida Buddha, the principal buddha of the Pure Land sect, and the phoenix is part of the symbolism of the sect's vision of paradise. As an explanation of the emblem, Kamei Katsuichirō, a core member of the Japanese Romatic School, wrote: "We heard some criticism that the phoenix is too Buddhistic and too old-fashioned. But, this bird appears before a literary 'saint' (genius) emerges and is a symbol of a great change and is thus progressive. The bird is said to be stronger than the eagle or the hawk. . . . It is perched on the roof of Byōdō-in ('Temple of Equality'), which means 'equality,' and thus it has to be progressive" (Kamei 1935).

It is noteworthy that ever since the middle of the Heian period (794–1185) the imperial palanquin was called *hōren* or the "phoenix palanquin" because a golden figure of the phoenix was placed on its top (Suzuki Keizō 1996). When the Meiji government instituted the tours of Japan by the emperor, he was carried in this palanquin (Taki [1988] 1990: 17–36). In other words, the phoenix had long been a symbol of the emperor. It is highly likely that choice of phoenix as the emblem of the Japan Romantic School was not altogether unrelated to the bird as the royal symbol.

In the end, however, the worst sin committed by Yasuda and his associates, according to Hashikawa, was promoting a particular kind of nihilism that advocated "We must die," in sharp contrast with the slogan "We must fight" of Nazi nihilism (Hashikawa 1985: 35–36). It is commonly assumed that the "aesthetics of death," advocated by Yasuda and his associates, played a critical role in luring young men to go to war (Doak 1994: 20–27). They provided young men, who faced the imminent defeat of Japan, with a rationale to aestheticize their own deaths—if one must die, one might as well die for idealism.

According to Hashikawa, Yasuda not only led these young men to war through his "beautiful prose ridden with a painful and mysterious tone," but through becoming a "thought policeman," sniffing out, like a dog, any "smell of red" in the writings of others and reporting it to the military police (Hashikawa 1985: 8). Yet, despite his ultra-nationalism and his hymns to the "imperial army," he was antimilitary and was, as contradictory as it may sound, harshly treated by the government and military (Hashikawa 1985: 10). He hoped for victory for Germany, but he was critical of Nazism (Hashikawa 1985: 27). This is not surprising since Hitler's racism was so blatant that a translation of *Mein Kampf* could not be distributed in Japan at the time (Payne 1995: 336). It was this odd combination of perspectives that masked his more strident ultra-nationalism, managing to disarm young intellectuals who were "desperate"—torn between their embrace of democracy, individualism, and Western high culture, on the one hand, and the now evident malaise of modernity that included materialism, capitalism, and cultural and military threats from the West, on the other. Yasuda's thought exploited the idealism of young patriotic intellectuals, just as the state did.

Yasuda and other writers of the Japan Romantic School rose to literary prominence at the very time Hitler came to power. In Japan the early 1930s were the time when the middle-class Japanese intelligentsia were experiencing the pain of disillusionment over communism and the proletarian movement, which had given them a rallying point during the early phases of Japan's struggle with modernity. It was the time when Japanese "fascism" was being developed and when many right-wing individuals and organizations appropriated "agrarianism" and "Japanese nature," as exemplified by Tachibana Kōzaburō (1893–1974), the leader of "Agrarian fascism" in the late 1920s and early 1930s (Iwamoto 1996). As we have seen throughout this book, the Japanese struggle for modernity was characterized both by an adoration of and resistance to Western civilization. Not surprisingly, Yasuda embraced "pan-Asianism." This anti-Western strategy in fact served Japan's political expansion into other Asian countries.

Despite the common assumption that Yasuda was extremely influential among young intellectuals, there is no mention of his name in the diaries of the tokkōtai pilots. Since most student soldiers in World War II were in their early twenties, they may have been too young when Yasuda and the Japanese Romantic School burst onto the intellectual scene. However, works by Japanese literary figures belonging to Japan's Romantic School appear in the diaries, as do those of German literary figures and scholars who embraced German Romanticism and were influential to Yasuda and his associates. At least from their writings, it appears that the pilots went to the original German, French, and Russian sources, rather than reading through the filter of Yasuda and his associates. Furthermore, there is no indication of a systematic reading of any type of Romanticism. Rather, they read books whose themes were germane to their concerns, be they works by Greco-Roman figures or the Romantics, as literary and philosophical works, often without detecting their political implications.[9]

Individual and Society: Life, Death, and Rebirth

The intensity with which the pilots read some of these authors and the nature of the discussions in their writings leave no room but to conclude that these young men turned to these readings as an almost exclusive means to deliberate upon two crucial questions: (1) the individual and society; (2) life, death, and the afterlife. The two themes were intimately intertwined, since the answer to the first theme determined the choice between life and death in the second. That is, if one chose to uphold the primacy of the individual, then one could ignore what was going on in Japan at the time. It meant life: love, career, and enjoyment of families and friends. But, if one gave priority to one's duty as a member of society, one had to sacrifice for Japan. Patriotism meant death. Each and every pilot agonized over these two questions. Precisely because they had no choice, they all turned "choosing one's fate" into a philosophical soliloquy—perhaps the only way to ignore the fact they had reached the point of no return. Their philosophical debates over these issues were two sides of the same coin, having tragic immediacy. The clock was literally ticking, as Nakao's painful experience during one of his sleepless nights tells us. Their readings included all the major Western philosophers and literary figures who reflected on death.

The issues of the individual and society, including death for one's patria, and of life and death are the central themes of the Greek and Roman philosophers. Aristotle's works were eagerly read by Hayashi Tadao, Nakao, and Sasaki, who also read about Socrates and his teachings in the works of Plato and also in Xenophon's *Memorabilia*. They hoped to gain the courage to face their deaths by reading the story of the noble calmness and courage with which Socrates drank the poison. Socrates's death was a result of his struggle against the state and his loyalty to it (cf. Paperno 1997: 11).

Of particular importance here is Stoicism and Epicureanism of the Lucretian sort. The Stoic attitude toward death and life was expounded by the influential philosopher Tanabe Hajime (chapter 7), from whose lecture Nakao derived personal fortification. Hayashi Tadao read Zeno of Citium, whereas Sasaki read works of the Cynics and Epicureans. The Epicurean conception of the soul as being composed of atoms that disperse at death provided a sort of consolation, or, more accurately, rationale for action for the pilots who had to "choose their fate" and who had no vision of an afterlife.

They read, with equal if not more intensity, deliberations upon these issues by later Western philosophers. Although others read Hegel, it was Sasaki who engaged in sustained dialogue with him. Most of Sasaki's discussion relates to Hegel's dialectic, especially in relation to that of Marx. Sasaki found Hegel's discussions of love, life, beauty, truth, and freedom to possess a Greek spirit, and he preferred Hegel to the "Germanness" of Kierkegaard (Sasaki 1981: 195, 207, 228). As Kojève explicates, Hegel's notion of the individual and freedom was predicated upon the notion of death and immortality (Kojève 1969: e.g., 240–51)—the most urgent problem for the pilots. Kierkegaard's *Sickness unto Death* was such a standard reading among young men at the time that Hayashi Ichizō could quote the passage on "despair" without specifying its source. Fyodor Dostoevsky held a multifaceted appeal for Hayashi Tadao, Nakao, and Sasaki. His nationalism was an example of a particular type of Russian nationalism that sought a Russian identity in relation to and opposition to Western Europe. Dostoevsky's deliberations upon death and his social consciousness offered a source of inspiration to the pilots. Friedrich

Nietzsche was also highly influential among Japanese intellectuals at the time. His *Also sprach Zarathustra* was so widely read that the title in German became common parlance among them. All the pilots, especially Sasaki, read Nietzsche as they thought about death, rationality, idealism, the self, etc. The pilots often discussed Nietzsche's nihilism and his rejection of Christianity, but they did not mention "his" nationalism and "his" glorification of war, as the Nazis tried to represent him.

The pilots also eagerly read twentieth-century figures. They found Romain Rolland's political stance of "one against all" and "heroic idealism" meaningful and admired his colleagues, including Albert Schweitzer, Albert Einstein, Bertrand Russell, and Rabindranath Tagore. Rolland's *Jean-Christophe*, intensively read by Hayashi Tadao and Nakao, addresses the issue of one's moral responsibility for one's society. Sasaki refers to *Jean-Christophe* only once but, Beethoven being his favorite composer, he read Rolland's *Vie de Beethoven*, as did Nakao.

For Hayashi Tadao, notwithstanding his voracious reading of French literature, Thomas Mann (1875–55) was the most important figure. At age eighteen Hayashi wrote an essay on *Buddenbrooks*. Mann, he wrote, was an author for whom the notion of death—both death and the wish for death—was the abiding issue. Hayashi interpreted "decadence" in Mann as the state of eroticism over death, from which Mann was saved by a commitment to citizenship, as expressed in chapter 6 of *The Magic Mountain* (Hayashi 1967: 201–4). According to Hayashi, "citizenship" represented "life," leading Mann to his commitment to patriotism, even though it also led to a break from his brother Heinrich Mann, who was a strong pacifist during World War I. Mann's endorsement of patriotism touched a sympathetic cord with Hayashi. Both Nakao and Sasaki read André Gide, who emphasized individual integrity and denounced colonialism.

Their idealism was often dramatically contradicted by the brutal reality at the base. Day-to-day life on the base was often unbearable. Some superiors not only imposed petty rules and regulations but also inflicted near lethal physical blows to them on a daily basis. Many hated and despised the career officers. However, rather than giving up their idealistic vision of fighting for Japan in the face of the brutal reality at the base, they did the opposite—they became convinced that they alone could save Japan and that their sacrifice was the last hope to save the lives of their families and friends, since the career soldiers were hopeless. It is no wonder, then, that Nakao was engrossed in the reading of Philipp Witkop's *Kriegsbriefe gefallener Studenten* (German Students' War Letters) (1928). He was appalled by the brutality of the war and yet moved by their willingness to sacrifice their lives for Germany. Hayashi Tadao and Wada intensely read Erich Maria Remarque's *All Quiet on the Western Front* (1929), with its description of the experience of the soldiers in the war and its plea for pacifism. Hans Carossa's nonmilitaristic and humane writings about the war, along with his optimism for the future of humanity despite the present darkness, were appealing to Nakao, as were the themes on the spirituality of all mankind and pacifism in the works of Hermann Hesse, whom Hayashi Tadao and Sasaki also read. Like many European intellectuals, these pilots, opposed to military aggression and ultra-nationalism, were tormented by the question of how to serve their country while also fulfilling their commitment to humanity.

The absence of an articulated vision of the afterlife in Japanese religions may have been another factor which led them to Western literary sources in which the theme of rebirth and resurrection occupies a central place. Dante's *Divine Comedy*, read by Hayashi Tadao and Nakao, presents a vision of the afterlife that is absent in Japanese religions. All the pilots, including non-Christians, read intensively about Christianity, as represented in the Bible and its orthodox interpretations, rather than in the beliefs and practices of Christianity by the folk. Christian art is full of pictorial representations of devils, the damned, and the antichrist in hell, the reprobates, and of angels, the saved, and Christ in heaven. The frescoes, dated 1500–4, by Luca Signorelli at Cappella di S. Brizio in the Orvieto cathedral, depict in great detail each step from death to resurrection. They include detailed representations of "The Resurrection of the Body," in which some of the dead are coming out of the ground, although in other Christian visions they come out of tombs. Michelangelo's *Last Judgment* at the Sistine Chapel at the Vatican is too well known to detail here. The ascension of the blessed and the descent of the damned are both depicted as struggles of *bodies*, and each body is depicted as powerfully as is this master's sculpture of David.[10] Similarly, Tintoretto's *Raising of Lazarus* portrays Lazarus's body with muscular beauty.

These examples of paintings from the Italian Renaissance may not do justice to the entirety of Christian art, which varies according to the historical period, region, class, etc. In later periods, the Roman celebration of the naked body, still powerfully present at the time of Scipione Caffarelli Cardinal Borghese (1579–1633), was transformed into a grave sin. Moreover, Christian conceptions of the soul, body, and resurrection have ranged widely, as is exemplified in a study of the doctrine of purgatory by Greenblatt (2001), who charts out a complex web of beliefs and interests of the church in keeping the doctrine of purgatory, and a major change under the attack by Protestants in the mid-sixteenth century in

England, which nevertheless did not totally eradicate the longings and fears deeply instilled by the Catholic Church for centuries. Nonetheless, these Italian paintings portray death and the afterlife as central themes in Christianity, and they draw attention to the way that the body becomes the focal point in depictions of the afterlife in most forms of Christianity. As Choron states, bodily reconstitution (*resurrectionem corporis*) combined with the immortality of the soul has been "the universally accepted version of immortality in the Western world for almost two thousand years," and, indeed, the resurrection of the dead antedates Christianity (Choron 1968: 643).

Universally, the body is essential to the life *and* death of a person. It is for this reason that both the symbolic construction and destruction of persons are predicated upon a ritual enactment on the body, either through a proper treatment of the body to reassure the person's afterlife, or through disfiguring the body to deprive the person of his/her afterlife. While Shintoism, the native religion of Japan, takes care mostly of the life in this world, providing rituals for birth and marriage, Buddhism takes care of death and the afterworld. Arguably, the most important religious beliefs and practices of the Japanese in the modern period center on the aforementioned "ancestor worship," which starts with a series of Buddhistic mortuary rituals during which the dead person becomes an "ancestor." For a smooth transition from a person in this world to become an ancestor, the intactness of the body at the time of death is of paramount importance.

Yet the body is not emphasized in relation to the afterlife in Japanese religions. Toward the end of the ancient period, Buddhism preached the punishment of the sinners in hell, where sinners' bodies decay, are burnt, eaten by worms, etc. (Miya 1988). The portrayal of the hell continued during the medieval period, when, however, the Pure Land sect of Buddhism began depicting heaven where everyone went if they believed in Amida Buddha. Medieval Buddhism preached the *mujō* (impermanence) of this world and advocated a detachment from one's body, which epitomized humans' earthly desires. In their preaching, Buddhists visualized the dead as *hakkotsu* (bleached bones) and endorsed cremation, an expression of the abandonment of the attachment to one's body.[11]

Even in early visual representations of heaven and hell, the celebration of the body, as in the Italian frescoes, is completely absent in Japanese religions. Most important, the process of "embodied resurrection" has never been an element in the Japanese vision of the afterlife, even in earlier times. In later history Japanese religions, including Buddhism, as conceptualized and practiced by the people, became increasingly "this-worldly" (Eisenstadt 1996: 235), offering good health, business prosperity, and other promises for life here on earth. Earlier Buddhistic preachings and visions carried little meaning to the Japanese in modern times. Even today, most Japanese are quite observant of the care of the deceased, as discussed earlier. Nonetheless, there is virtually no vision of how their ancestors "live" in their afterlife, nor is a question of what happens to the body ever seriously deliberated by the people. That is, the immortality of the soul and the resurrection of the body—central themes of many religions, including the religion of the ancient Egyptians, with its highly developed practice of mummification, Zoroastrianism, Judaism, Christianity, and Islam—have not been a primary concern of religions in Japan for centuries.

The reasons for the non-Christian pilots' interest in Christianity included its idealism, especially the altruism for all humans advocated by early Meiji Christian leaders. But another important reason is that the pilots and other Japanese intellectuals looked for the "meaning" of their death and sacrifice in Christianity or in Western literary sources under the influence of Christianity. They found it unbearable to think that their deaths had no meaning. Yet beyond the moment of death was a void. Perhaps it was for this reason that the title of Hayashi Tadao's diary suggests an image that his life shines and burns under the moonlight only to be gone forever.

We recall how Nakao engaged in sustained deliberations over rebirth, tracing the philosophical thoughts in Western intellectual traditions dating back to Greco-Roman times. Goethe's *Faust* and *The Sorrows of Young Werther* were far more meaningful to these young men than were the Japanese classics.[12] Faust's temptation, contemplation of death, and return to life at the sound of Easter bells and singing of hymns in the spring landscape, or Werther's deliberations on suicide and his passion for the "pure" Lotte—these are precisely the themes that offered meaning and solace to Hayashi Tadao, Nakao, Sasaki, and other young men. At that time Tolstoy's *Resurrection* became quite influential, not just among the intellectuals but with the general public. A song entitled "Katyusha," sung by Katyusha in a stage production in Tokyo of *Resurrection*, became quite popular in the summer of 1914, and remained popular throughout World War II.[13] The pilots were drawn to Tolstoy's recurrent theme of death and resurrection, which, literal or figurative, appears in all of his works, including *War and Peace*.

There is a particular Western intellectual/religious tradition of "divine kingship," in which rebirth is predicated upon violent death,[14] especially involving blood sacrifice. The theme is recurrent in Western history from the myth of Dionysius, to Christianity with Christ's suffering and resurrection, through to Nietzsche's *Birth of Tragedy*, Stravinsky's *Le Sacre du printemps,* and other modern works. The more general theme of resurrection after destruction was extensively utilized by the Third Reich. Hitler and Goebbels repeatedly used the theme for his rise to power—for the "salvation" of Germany and birth of the National Socialist Germany. Goebbels enthusiastically assisted Leni Riefenstahl in the making of *The Triumph of the Will* (1934), in which the theme is played over and over again, with the ubiquitous presence of the eagle as if to imbricate the phoenix. On his final day Goebbels welcomed the bombardment of Berlin as "sanitary destruction" that would lead to the rebirth of a new Germany and new Europe without class barriers (Trevor-Roper 1962: 113–14).

The notion of violent death, intentionally inflicted upon an individual as a precondition of resurrection, is alien to Japanese religiosity.[15] However, destruction by natural disasters, especially by earthquake, as an omen of the arrival of a new society, especially an utopia, has had a long tradition.[16] Quite distinct from the folk tradition, the Japan Romantic School gave prominence to the theme of destruction and construction. Yasuda's notion of "Japan as irony" was characterized by simultaneous destruction and construction. The Romantic School chose as their emblem the phoenix, representing Buddhism and the royalty. In other words, they imbricated the Western theme of destruction and rebirth with the Buddhistic icon of the phoenix. Sasaki Hachirō and Hayashi Tadao both repeatedly hoped for the rebirth of Japan after destruction. Hayashi Tadao wrote a poem wishing for "the finale, that taboo, catastrophe." Hayashi's repeated use of chaos, destruction, and rebirth is a uncanny parallel to Yasuda's statements. Both Sasaki Hachirō and Hayashi Tadao used the metaphor of a phoenix as a new Japan, rising from the ashes of destruction of Japan, plagued by capitalism and materialism.

Although the pilots' thoughts turned to death and the afterlife, it did not cross their minds that their action would be considered suicide. In the Western religious traditions the notion of suicide has long been related to notions of "God." This complex interrelationship has been articulated in the debate over "suicide" in Western literature—whether suicide is a blasphemous act, usurping God's power over life and death of humans. The pilots read Socrates, Goethe, Nietzsche, Kierkegaard, and others who discussed suicide in their works, but they read them in order to understand death, not suicide. Neither Hayashi Ichizō nor his mother, both Christians, perceived his death as suicide. Hayashi's thoughts were deeply influenced by Kierkegaard, but not because of Kierkegaard's discussion of suicide. As we saw, the pilots, just like any other soldiers, were killed in action. Their act was not conceptualized as "suicide" either by themselves or by the Japanese in general, although they knew that their deaths were far more certain than if they fought in the trenches.

The notion of death as the moment at which the soul separates from the body, as famously described by Socrates in Plato's *Phaedo* ([1914] 1999: 363–73), is intricately intertwined with the Christian concept of the immortality of the soul in the hand of God (cf. Paperno 1997: 149). The soul is just as important in Japanese culture, and the departure of one's soul defines death (chapter 1). But life and death in Japanese culture are defined without reference to almighty God or to the presence of heaven.[17]

The pilots found profound meaning in Western literature not because the oppositions of life/death and individual/society were identical to their own conceptualizations, but because the struggles of the individuals whose wishes collided with the interests of the state in the literature offered them ways to think about their own predicaments and the meanings of their own deaths, and, the possibility of the afterlife.

Cosmopolitan Patriots: Their Idealism and "Literary Reactions"

As there were parallels between the institutional structure of state nationalism in Japan and elsewhere, there also were parallels between the intellectual profile of the young Japanese pilots and European intellectuals who fought in wars. The latter were also intensely involved in the problems of patriotism, nationalism, and pacifism, such as the pacifist Jean Jaurès, assassinated just before World War I, the English poet Rupert Brooke, who died of blood poisoning on Skyros in the war, and Thomas Mann, who with the outbreak of World War I advocated patriotism in opposition to his pacifist brother Heinrich Mann, though he repudiated his earlier patriotic view with the rise of fascism. Even a short list of those who were involved in the Spanish Civil War, though not necessarily in combat, includes prominent members of the intelligentsia in various countries: Albert Einstein, Eleanor Roosevelt, Paul Robeson, Ernest Hemingway, George Orwell, W. H. Auden, Samuel Beckett, Pablo Neruda, André Malraux. They joined the "cause" often because of their idealism, defending the Republic against fascism.

Although it was not read by any of the tokkōtai pilots, Hemingway's *For Whom the Bell Tolls*, on the Spanish Civil War and published in 1940, captures many of the themes and concerns of idealistic intellectuals,

Japanese or not, who fought in wars. They include the sense of obligation to one's country *and* humanity at large, which leads to the inevitability of one's death, as John Donne's "No man is an *Iland*," placed at the beginning of the novel, tells us. Through the character of Robert Jordan, Hemingway portrays the idealism that motivates one to fight for a "cause," disillusionment with the military and political machinery supposedly orchestrating the war operation, and the replacement of the abstract "cause" with "individuals," i.e., one's loved ones. Above all, like Robert Jordan, whose ultimate goal of the destruction of a bridge had no meaning whatsoever, the pilots plunged to their deaths in an operation, designed and executed by fanatics, which had no meaning and accomplished no military goal.

The "literary reaction" to imminent threat of death is not confined to the Japanese soldiers. In his path-breaking work on World War I, Paul Fussell ([1975] 2000) tells us in a chapter aptly entitled, "Oh What a Literary War," about Captain Oliver Lyttelton, educated at Eton and at Trinity College, Cambridge, who, looking back on a bad day, expressed his thoughts by referring to the Roman poet Ovid. General Sir Ian Hamilton's "literary reaction" to the news of the postponement of four crucial French divisions, which meant the likelihood of the failure of the Gallipoli expedition, was expressed through his reference to Keats's "Ode to a Nightingale." But, most remarkable is that Private Stephen Graham, "hardly educated at all," who referred to Shakespeare's Richard III. Fussell remarks upon "the unparalleled literariness of all ranks who fought the Great War." When they faced a crisis, or, after a "bad day," they all expressed themselves in terms of "literary reactions" (Fussell [1975] 2000: 155–90). What distinguished the Japanese pilots from these European examples is that they were cosmopolitan intellectuals in the sense of reaching out to Western intellectual traditions, while the European intellectuals read extensively, but primarily within their own traditions.

The pilots' literariness was also expressed in their ardent efforts to put their thoughts in writing. For the pilots, their diaries became the major forum for their soliloquies in which they engaged in self-confrontation, subversion of the received wisdom, and, ultimately, the location of their own selves in the cosmopolitan intellectual universe. Their diaries afforded them the opportunity to confront themselves. Or, it was through their diaries, written under the constant threat of confiscation, that they wanted to "bear witness," as Victor Klemperer (1998) did, when they had no recourse but to helplessly "witness" the inhumanity being done to them and their families. Klemperer kept his diaries even though they would have certainly led him to death if the Nazis had discovered them. Japanese Christian soldiers sang hymns knowing very well that their behavior would put them in dire jeopardy if discovered. The pilots in the depths of sorrow wrote about the moon and cherry blossoms, and sang hymns—in order to assure themselves that there was still beauty in humanity even amidst the cruellest inhumanity.

SWEET AND PROPER TO DIE FOR YOUR COUNTRY?

The importance of Romanticism and idealism for the pilots notwithstanding, it is misleading to conclude without reiterating the utterly dire circumstances in which these students "volunteered." The circumstances in which the pilots found themselves were not unique. Since Horace's phrase *Dulce et decorum est pro patria mori* has been commonly used out of context, it is worth quoting in full the two stanzas about the Roman-Parthian war of 39–38 B.C.:

> May the young Roman be toughened by experience,
> Deceptive in the field, and able to bear
> Hardship without complaint, and may he learn
> To terrify the terrifying Parthian.

> Sweet and proper it is to die for your country,
> But Death would just as soon come after him
> Who runs away; Death gets him by the backs
> Of his fleeting knees and jumps him from behind. (Horace 1997: 161)

The thesis of Horace's ode was echoed in the thoughts of Japanese soldiers, including the tokkōtai pilots, in more than one way. If the pilots did not die for the emperor, many of them died for their homeland—*pro patria mori*. Furthermore, many of them were convinced that their sacrifice for the country was indeed honorable, or that it would bestow honor on them posthumously, and on their family members. In addition, most felt that they were at a point of no return—many were forced to volunteer, and once they volunteered to be tokkōtai pilots there was no other choice but to go on the mission—death would get them from behind, as it would the young Roman soldiers, but for the Japanese soldiers, it might be at the hands of the enemy or at the hands of their own officers and comrades. Their choice was to plunge to death in the hope of saving the country and dying as heroes, or to violate the rule and turn back, most likely to be killed anyway, or at least reduced to persona non grata.

The events took place too fast, for most had not had the time to sort out in their minds why they were giving up their youthful lives.[18]

The following passage portrays succinctly how most soldiers felt "caught" in the war machinery. It comes from the epilogue of a book by Naito, who was a technician at the Navy Aeronautical Research Laboratory and the author of a book chronicling the daily experience on the base of the tokkōtai members of the Thunder Gods Corps who flew the ōka, the most inefficient of all planes used in the attacks:

> Even Emperor Hirohito, at the top of the whole system, was not charged with any responsibility. Once a program was started, the system had no way of stopping it. Instead, it converted individual insanity into organized insanity. It must be pointed out, however, that the young men who were actually called on to make the mass suicide attacks had nothing to do with the organized insanity. They experienced terrors and trauma that are beyond the imagination of anyone else. I do not believe that any of them shouted "Long Live the Emperor!" as they dived their bomb-filled planes into the enemy. They agreed to die for the sake of their families and their relatives in the firm belief that their death would contribute to their well-being. . . . The pilots knew, of course, that the spirits of those who died in the war were worshipped at Yasukuni Shrine, but they did not choose to die to be "gods." . . . They [surviving members of the corps] gather there to recall their youth, when they innocently believed that the sacrifice of their lives would make a difference. (Naito 1989: 209–10)

Naito adds:

> They [survivors] gather there because the last thing their dead comrades said to them was, "I will be waiting for you at Yasukuni Shrine."

As Naito tells us in his book and as the pilot Nakao tells us, the farewell statement about Yasukuni had a hollow echo. None of them believed that they would be reborn as cherry blossoms.

Chapter 9

THE CROOKED TIMBER
OF THE CHERRY

Reviewing the Japanese historical experiences presented so far, in this last chapter of this book I discuss the complexities of historical change and the ambiguities of historical agency.

COMMUNICATION THROUGH SYMBOLS

I start with an examination of aesthetics and symbols, and begin with two focal points of scholarly discussion of symbols—their emotive power and their polysemic nature. During the "Enlightenment period" in anthropology, scholars focused on the conceptual dimensions of symbols—what they represent. But anthropologists have always acknowledged the importance of the emotive dimension of human behavior in general and of the emotive power of symbols in particular. In *Primitive Classification*, Durkheim and Mauss ([1901–2] 1963: 85–86) exclude emotion from their analysis because it is "fluid and inconsistent." Nonetheless they recognize that it is the "emotional value" of notions that play a key role in the way ideas are connected or separated. Tambiah (1990: 153), a fine interpreter of Max Weber, reminds us that Weber "at the end of the road" realized that all forms of rationality were "ultimately grounded in subjective values, whose sources and wellsprings were non-rational, charismatic, affective and intuitive." Nondiscursive "presentational symbols," as Langer ([1942] 1980) calls them, express thought and feeling simultaneously, thereby making a Weltanschauung emotively acceptable, as Geertz phrased it in reference to sacred symbols.[1] Others assign a great deal more evocative power to symbols. For Victor Turner (1967: 30), symbols convert "the obligatory into the desirable." For Burke ([1950] 1969: 41), rhetoric has the power to "form attitude or to induce actions in other human agents." Do symbols have similar power?

Already present in the eighth-century myth-histories, the cherry blossom gradually came to be associated with the aesthetics of pathos over evanescence because of its short life and its fragility. The evocative power of cherry blossoms as a trope is based not simply on its embeddedness in the Japanese Weltanschauung but derives from its association with some of the most powerful themes of the Japanese ethos—the aesthetics of pathos over evanescence *(monono aware)* and the aesthetics of the purity of the self and idealism. Therefore, for pilots, cherry blossoms were first of all the flower to think and *feel.* Their "power" as a symbol, I think, is less about moving people to action and more about serving as a vehicle for thoughts and feelings.

The other focal point is the polysemic nature of symbols. Under the charismatic leadership of Victor Turner, anthropologists and other scholars have become well aware that most symbols have more than one meaning. We have studies that examine how, when in a given context a social actor draws on a specific signification, other actors share or do not share that signification—one sees an eagle as a bird of prey, another sees it as an endangered species, and yet another sees it as the symbol of the United States. Additionally, in the anthropological literature "dominant" symbols are usually presented as having only a limited number of meanings. However, cherry blossoms have an extraordinarily large number of meanings with complex interrelationships among them.

Rather than pursuing these lines of inquiry, I explore the roles and powers of symbols from two entirely different perspectives. Instead of assuming that individuals in symbolic communication are indeed "communicating" with each other, conceptually or emotively, I suggest that it is the lack of communication that enables the shared use, but not a specific signification, of a symbol—the phenomenon I refer to as *méconnaissance.* For this process, aesthetics plays a key role. Thus, my focus is on the aesthetics of symbols rather than on the "emotive" dimension of symbols in general.

MÉCONNAISSANCE

Discussions of symbols and their power are often based upon an assumption that a signification—a meaning of a symbol in a given context of communication—is shared by those in communication. The English term "communication" excludes any possibility of an absence of communication. This presupposition has prevented us from looking into the *absence* of communication during our "communications," verbal or nonverbal.

Langer ([1942] 1980: 79–102; see also 1953) distinguishes discursive symbols, that is, words, from nondiscursive symbols, which she called "presentational symbols," such as an object like an eagle, and stresses that the latter appeals directly to sense and is thus untranslatable, unable to directly convey generalities. In other words, an eagle does not spell out what its meaning is, i.e., what it symbolizes. In anthropology, credit must go to Leach ([1954] 1965: 86) who first urged us to realize that in their "communication" social actors in a given context often do not share a particular signification: "Two individuals or groups of individuals may accept the validity of a set of ritual actions without agreeing at all as to what is expressed in those actions."

I suggest that we extend these insights offered by Langer and Leach and realize that ambiguity and absence of shared signification and thus of "communication" in a given social context characterize our so-called communication in *all* contexts, rather than ritual contexts alone, and in *all* types of communication, using both discursive and nondiscursive symbols. It is only that the use of nondiscursive symbols and ritual contexts increase the likelihood of the absence of communication.

I use the term méconnaissance to refer to this common phenomenon. The French term *méconnaissance* conveys a more technical sense of the absence of recognition than its English equivalent, mis-reading or mis-communication. My use of méconnaissance refers to the phenomenon of "talking past each other," because symbolic communication, either by words or objectified symbols, does not force those in communication to identify to each other the particular signification he/she draws on.

In my view, there are two important factors that facilitate this phenomenon: (1) the presence of a vast field of meanings for a symbol; (2) the aesthetics assigned to the symbol.

The Field of Meaning

Méconnaissance is predicated upon the presence of a rich field of meanings for a symbol. If a symbol has only one meaning, there is no room for méconnaissance. Most symbols, especially culturally important symbols, have a rich field of meaning shared by the members of the society.

As the springtime counterpart of rice in the fall, blooming cherry blossoms across a mountain range celebrate life—they stand for both productive and reproductive power. Yet cherry blossoms are also a metaphor for a short life and then death itself. They also stand for agents of discontinuity that threaten both the self and society—for the non-reproduction of the self (geisha, and partners of homosexual monks), and for a dissolution of the social self (madness or changing identity). Young pilots were killed before they bore offspring, preventing the regeneration of their own society, like cherry petals that fall before bearing fruit.

At the collective level, the flower stood for each social group—farmers, warriors, aristocrats, and merchants, each having its own tradition of viewing cherry blossoms. Ultimately cherry blossoms have represented "the Japanese" since the ninth century, as different Others pressed the Japanese for articulation of their self-identity. The Japanese have used the flower "to represent themselves to themselves as well as to others" (Kertzer 1996: 155).

In other words, cherry blossoms stand for the most pressing concerns of an individual life, while offering a means to identity oneself as a member of a social group and ultimately as a Japanese. This ability distinguishes it from other symbols of Japan, such as Mt. Fuji, which stood for Japan but did not become a symbol in people's quotidian lives. The central problem of the pilots—and of Japanese intellectuals from the early Meiji era onward—was the tension between individual liberty and responsibility to society. In the pilots' and intellectuals' most important deliberations, cherry blossoms served as no other symbols could: the flower became the medium through which the pilots, and many other Japanese, confronted their responsibility to Japan, which meant death. The flower was the symbol at the center of sustained soliloquies on the most important issues in one's life. It was *the flower with which to think and feel.*

The transition from one meaning to another is made easy by the fact that the meanings associated with cherry blossoms do not stand for static meanings in the classificatory system. Cherry blossoms stand for life, predicated upon death; for production (as the counterpart of rice) and reproduction (young women) underscored by nonreproduction (geisha and medieval temple boys); and for women predicated upon men and vice versa—all embedded in a fluid notion of gender in Japanese culture. Therefore, a meaning can glide through the rich field of meaning to the other end, for example, from life to death, and the transformation seems natural.

A symbol's field of meaning represents neither an abstract set of meanings frozen in culture nor a linear progression through time from one meaning to the next. This field is shared by the members of a society. For example, in the diary of Sasaki, the pilot most explicitly skeptical of the war ideology and an avowed Marxist, cherry blossoms first appear as a sunny metaphor of youth, beauty, and Sasaki himself, who enjoys young women passing by. Later the flower becomes a counterpoint to the prevailing frenzied atmosphere of wartime Japan. Still later, cherry blossoms are a metaphor for an ideal society and for an ideal human being, possessing modesty and purity; they now remind him of the negative side of his earlier self, which sought after and enjoyed honor and recognition from others. Ultimately, as the time for his sortie came near, cherry blossoms became the metaphor of pilots, including himself, falling like cherry petals. At this point Sasaki directly links cherry blossoms and the soldiers' deaths, but not as part of the *pro rege et patria mori* ideology.[2]

As the example of cherry blossoms illustrates, it is often the case that social actors do not share one particular signification in a given context; rather, they draw different significations from the shared field of meanings, and rarely recognize that they do not share the same signification (Ohnuki-Tierney 1987: 210–13). "Communication" goes on among the members of a social group because they share the *field* of meaning of a symbol, but not because they share the same signification. Changes in the meaning of a symbol are made by extending what Tambiah (1981: 160) calls, "the already existing grids" of meaning. Because cherry blossoms were associated with death and rebirth in earlier periods, when the state "extended" its meaning to the souls of fallen soldiers, the Japanese, including the soldiers, did not recognize this meaning as "new" or "different." Extending the well-known statement by Geertz (1973: 12) that "culture is public because meaning is," I propose that what is "public," "shared," or "collective" is not a particular signification in a given context of communication but *the field of meaning*.[3]

Méconnaissance is a crucial mechanism which facilitates the transformation of a symbol into a symbol of mass killing, without provoking people to whom the transformation of meaning is not apparent. Rather, people take the new meaning as "natural," or they keep reading their own meanings from the symbol. This is possible precisely because the field of meaning of a dominant symbol such as cherry blossoms is so rich, complex, and vast.

In the development of its *pro rege et patria mori* ideology, the state promoted other tropes—falling petals as fallen soldiers and blooming blossoms as their metamorphosed souls. These dramatic changes did not shock people. In fact few noticed the fingerprints of those who collaborated, intentionally or not, with the state in this process, including well-respected scholars and composers as well as political leaders. It was because cherry blossoms have always stood for a set of life forces, while simultaneously symbolizing the opposite.

At first glance, it might appear that there is a disadvantage in using a well-established cultural symbol as a political symbol. When the existing meanings are deeply lodged in people's minds, assigning a new meaning would appear to be difficult. It would seem easier to adopt a new symbol, such as the Nazi swastika, which became arguably the most powerful political symbol in recent history. The swastika, which derived from Indian word "svastika" whose iconographic representation was different from the Nazi "swastika," first became connected to race theory in the nineteenth century, and Josef Goebbels's Propaganda Ministry emblazoned it as the Nazi symbol on May 19, 1933 (Quinn 1994). Its success was in many ways extraordinary, since it was not a native cultural symbol with a long tradition. The swastika was a blank slate as far as its referent, or, meaning, was concerned, unlike cherry blossoms, which have a long history of being the bearer of culturally central meanings. The Nazis packed the Nazi ideology into this hitherto unknown image, while the Japanese military had to change the meaning of cherry blossoms.

There is, however, a decisive advantage in giving a new meaning to an old symbol, whose evocative appeal has been tested through time. In the Japanese case, the state could utilize the time-honored appeal of the flower while transforming its meaning for its own military purposes. In this process, the presence of an array of meanings, some even seemingly contradictory, seems to have served as the mechanism to naturalize profound changes made during the military period.[4]

Nevertheless, the state's attempt at the transformation of meaning was less than successful, since the meanings the pilots assigned to cherry blossoms did not include the one the state intended. Had the state known that the soldiers were not identifying cherry blossoms with the *pro rege et patria mori* ideology, it would have intensified its efforts at coercion. Conversely, the pilots would have rebelled against the ideological pressure had they clearly articulated in their minds the meaning assigned by the state. Yet, the méconnaissance, facilitated by the field of meaning of the flower, prevented the confrontation, thereby leading to the ultimate tragedy.

Aesthetics

While méconnaissance could take place at any time, the aesthetics that accrues to symbols plays an important role by establishing false equations over disparate meanings—all are beautiful—just as it facilitates the naturalization of historical discontinuity as continuity. The common denominator between young women, geisha, and warriors is that all are conceptually beautiful, and death as a result of sacrifice is made as beautiful as life itself—both celebrated by cherry blossoms. Aesthetics as a facilitator of méconnaissance is far reaching, since it is a quality that is assigned to important concepts, such as "nature" as a symbol of various forms of patriotism and nationalism.

FROM EVERYDAY AESTHETICS TO POLITICAL AESTHETICS

Although Kant and a few others have not confined their deliberations of "aesthetics" to the "aesthetics of art," much of philosophical discussion is on the aesthetics of art, or, more broadly, the aesthetics of the representation of nature and/or reality, be it in art or literature. In this tradition of the aesthetics of representation, the problem of mimesis in literature and art has been an important one, ever since Plato and Aristotle discussed the problem of *imitatio*. Baudelaire, Benjamin, Adorno, Horkheimer and many others, whose work centered on the relationship between art and modernity, have also focused on the aesthetics of art, including the appropriation by art of mass-produced consumer goods.

My concern about the aesthetics of cherry blossoms in this book has concerned individuals' appreciation of the beauty of cherry blossoms in their day-to-day lives, and not the representations of cherry blossoms in art. It is a quotidian or everyday aesthetics and to a large extent is culturally construed.[5] Cherry blossoms have been represented in art and literature, both high and low brow, ever since the eighth century, and thus the ways in which the Japanese think about cherry blossoms and view "cherry blossoms in nature" are deeply influenced by their innumerable representations in art and literature. However, given the ubiquitous presence of cherry trees throughout the Japanese archipelago, appreciation of their springtime beauty is something shared by everyone, by the folk as well as by the intellectuals and other members of the elite. After World War II, the swastika was erased immediately from cultural spaces in Germany and beyond; it lived on as the symbol of the gravest sin against humanity. In contrast, after World War II, the Japanese resumed the uses of cherry blossoms as a dominant symbol. They returned to the annual ritual of cherry blossom viewing, as if they had completely forgotten the dark meaning the symbol had been assigned, even though so many of the vestiges from the war remained and continue to remain in deep suspicion (Okamoto, ed. 1999) and even the word "patriotism" *(aikokushin)* remains severely tainted.

The state deployed various means to transfer the aesthetics of cherry blossoms onto military images and actions. The conscripts were aestheticized to become warriors of the past symbolized by cherry blossoms. The deaths of soldiers in the battlefields began to be referred to as *sange* (falling like cherry petals). The badges on military uniforms bore themes of flowers, especially cherry blossoms and chrysanthemums. The Yasukuni Shrine was built to be "beautiful," with thousands of cherry trees, first to console the souls of fallen soldiers and later to represent them as their postmortem souls.

The aesthetics of cherry blossoms played a key role in masking the brutal extension of the equal right to death. The Japanese soul (yamato damashii), aestheticized by cherry blossoms, was extended from the warriors to the conscripts and from ethnic Japanese to non-Japanese, encouraging all to die for the emperor like falling cherry petals, as the warriors were supposed to have done. Then the flower "marched" with the military, moving into other Asian countries where the military planted cherry trees to mark its colonized spaces as parts of "Imperial Japan." Common to all is their beauty, both physical and spiritual. The "power" of cherry blossoms as a trope lies in its capacity to aestheticize its referents and thus make them equally beautiful—a mechanism that naturalizes méconnaissance.

AESTHETICS OF "NATURE": PATRIOTISM, AND CULTURAL AND POLITICAL NATIONALISMS

The pilots read some writers who advocated art for art's sake—*vissi d'arte,* or *l'art pour l'art.* For example, Sasaki, the rationalist, read extensively in the works of Oscar Wilde (1854–1900), Izumi Kyōka (1873–1939), a Japanese novelist whose quest for aesthetics had an otherworldly quality, Takehisa Yumeji (1884–1934), an author and illustrator whose figures of women with large eyes filled with melancholy became very influential, and Tanizaki Jun'ichirō (1886–1965), another Japanese novelist who began his career with the art-for-art's sake stance and the celebration of decadence, although he later searched for an uniquely Japanese aesthetics in the Japanese classics (Doak 1994: xxix–xxx). Kawabata Yasunari (1899–1972), the Nobel-prize-winning Japanese novelist, with his intense engagement with sensual aesthetics, was eagerly read by Nakao and Sasaki.

Among the French, Baudelaire (1821–67), including his *Les Fleurs du mal*, Balzac (1799–1850), and Flaubert (1821–80) were read by both Hayashi Tadao and Nakao. As Bell ([1980] 1991: 301) puts it, Baudelaire's conception of poetry as a secret form of knowledge and Nietzsche's insistence that only aesthetics can justify life were "doctrinal battles" against the justification of life by religion and the control of art by society. In other words, *l'art pour l'art* was deeply embedded in questions of individual liberty and of the societal restrictions upon individuals. Nonetheless, the pilots were most influenced by aesthetic theories that linked perception of the beauty of objects, symbols, and concepts to the broader social and political dimensions of life. Nakao (1997: 378) was inspired by Plato's idea that the quest for beauty transcended the physical realm and elevated it to an aesthetics of truth. He was moved by Rilke's discussion of Auguste Rodin, since Rodin's work celebrates the vigor of life and his aesthetics transcends the self in the age which exposed the "hubris" (his word in transliteration) of humans (Nakao 1997: 437–39). Kant, extensively read by Nakao and Sasaki, linked aesthetics to ethics, thereby extending it to one's conduct as a member of society. The intellectual scene in general in Japan at the time was also highly charged with the debate on aesthetics and modernity, which was in fact a central issue to Yasuda Yojūrō and the Japan Romantic School. They discussed even the Biedermeier style in Germany.

In various forms of Romanticism, aesthetics was often assigned to "nature"—the primordial space of a people or of humans in general. Some assigned purity and beauty to the primordial qua "natural" past of humans—to the "primitives," as in the "pagan Russia" of Stravinsky's *Le Sacre du printemps*, or to the "Serbian customs and folktales" of the patriotic novel *La Guzla* of Mérimée, an author Nakao read most intensively as did Hayashi Tadao and Sasaki. Theirs was a search for lost innocence, i.e., John Dryden's "noble savage," a phrase Rousseau made famous through his denunciation of the moral decadence of modern society. Sasaki read many of Rousseau's works.

Others assigned aesthetics to "nature" as a symbol of the purity and beauty of their own people. The aestheticized nature as one's homeland occupies a central place in literature and philosophy of various kinds but especially in works by Romantic writers. In these representations, not necessarily objectified in art forms but as mental constructs, idealized nature is both a spatial and temporal unit. It is "our homeland," "our space," as well as "our primordial past" without the contamination of modernity or, as in the case of Japan, also of Western influences (for the temporal-spatial axis, see Ohnuki-Tierney 1993a). Schiller's "disenchantment of the world," a phrase made well known by Weber, expresses this negative sentiment toward modernity and the longing for the pristine past. Sasaki's reading follows this line of aesthetics from Kant, to Rousseau, and to Schiller. Hayashi Tadao and Nakao read Balzac, for whom the spatial-temporal primordiality was, more parochially I might add, located in an idealized Rome, in which he saw pristine Frenchness.

Nature as a master trope for the primordial self of a people is common the world over, both in the past and at present. While agri*culture* constitutes a thorough transformation of nature by culture, it nonetheless represents "nature" in many societies whose subsistence economy in the past rested on agriculture. In the nineteenth century, peasants and shepherds (Jean-François Millet) and grain stocks (Claude Monet)—all representations of bucolic nature—became an important symbol of *temps perdu* for the French (for further discussion and examples of plant and agricultural metaphors, see Ohnuki-Tierney 1993a). The resurrection of "nature without manure and sweat" by urbanites, intellectuals or not, has been a common phenomenon among many peoples ever since the urban gave birth to the rural (Berque 1990), from Marie Antoinette's Petit Trianon at Versailles to depictions of the English countryside on the chocolate boxes of today. In Japan, wet rice agriculture has remained a powerful symbol for self-representation well after its economic and political value has been undercut by urban industrialization. Even today, when the government pays rice farmers to leave their land fallow to prevent overproduction, "rice as self" surges whenever there is outside pressure, such as the threat of importation of rice from California in 1993 (Ohnuki-Tierney 1995).

Although the pilots found in poems and novels a source of spiritual strength, music moved them even more, even though most pilots did not refer to music in their writings. Hayashi Tadao and his elder brother shared a passion for Western classical music, and the latter owned an impressive collection of records. Sasaki details his ecstatic feelings listening to Beethoven, whose music was composed to the poems of Goethe, Herder, and Schiller, in which "nature," such as moonlight or the pastoral, was central. Almost all the composers Sasaki listened to belong to the Romantic school.

"Nature" as a symbol of cultural nationalism can move easily into the realm of political nationalism. While many European Romantics upheld cultural nationalism, and not political nationalism, Fichte (1762–1814), an enthusiastic student of Kant and an influential member of the German Romantic school, developed political nationalism by transferring the concept of the Ego to the German nation, thereby elevating Germans to the status of "a primordial and unadulterated *Urvolk*" (Wolf 1999: 211). Thus, Fichte's nationalism was radically different from that of Herder, another Romantic, who saw many different peoples as being equal in principle. Wada read Fichte's most nationalistic work, *Reden an die deutsche Nation* (1808), while Sasaki and Nakao also read his work and referred to his thoughts.

In political nationalisms, an unadulterated *Volk* or *Urvolk* is often symbolized by an "unadulterated nature." The combination of "nature" and nationalism, a seemingly innocent pair, can turn lethal by becoming a part of the machinery of political nationalism, as in the case of the ultra-nationalism of Yasuda and other right-wingers during the 1930s. Mosse details the movement in late-nineteenth-century Germany in which the soil, representing agricultural communities, became the spiritual and economic source for the Volkish movement and the symbol of their utopia, the *Heimat*. The symbolic construction became an instrument of their race theory (Mosse [1964] 1981: 108–25, 155, 169; see also Koshar 1998: 26–28, 47–48, 54). It was Rudolf Darré, the Reichsminister of Agriculture, who coined *Blut und Boden* as a Nazi motto. He also pushed *Naturschutz* (protection of nature) as a state policy (Schama 1995: 81–100). Mao's Cultural Revolution did not, chronologically, take place at the time of modernization, although it shared the context of the Western threat and capitalism. Maoist slogans included those promoting the Chinese return to nature and agriculture, which led to the persecution of urban intellectuals. "Nature," purified and aestheticized, disarms people when it is turned into a political weapon.

Although nature can be represented by various symbols, many social groups choose flowers because they are "beautiful." Yet flowers are also commonly linked to the military, which then becomes aestheticized through this symbolic association. For example, Wolf (1999: 150–53) discusses the Aztec metaphors which appear in Tenochca texts, where "flowery wars" were fought by Aztec warriors from Tenochtitlan against the Tlaxcala, their neighbors. The warriors were called "dancing flowers," and their blood "flower-water," whereas the phrase "flowers of the heart" referred to the captives destined for sacrifice. A warrior who took captives in battle was a man "rich in flowers." Upon death, called "flowery death," Aztec warriors became hummingbirds or butterflies, sucking nectar from the choicest flowers, thereby metonymically becoming one with flowers. There are uncanny parallels between Aztec flowers and Japanese cherry blossoms.

Similarly, in premodern European cultures, representations of flowers were common in heraldry. The fleur-de-lis has been the emblem of the

French kings since at least 1197, as well as the symbol of Florence during the Middle Ages (Vries [1974] 1984: 193). The association of flowers with wars is readily apparent, as in the Wars of the Roses between the red rose of Lancaster and the white rose of York. Even today in European cultures flowers are used to refer to wars, battles, and deaths, such as the red poppy as the symbol of fallen soldiers on the battlefields of Flanders.[6] A wartime German postcard from World War I called "My Regiment" features a machine gun lying in a bed of roses (Mosse 1990: 67).

It was during the French revolution that the conscious manipulation of the evocative power of the aesthetics of symbols for the purpose of involving and mobilizing people was pioneered by initiating "the public use of myths and symbols as self-representations of the nation . . . which gave them a feeling of participation" (Mosse 1990: 36). A spectacular example was the June 8 festival orchestrated and presided by Robespierre (Furet [1988] 1996: 147–48; Ozouf 1988). It is well known that the Jacobins were obsessed with signs and symbols and their impact upon the people. The manipulation of symbols was a tool to make the will of the Jacobins be the "general will" of the French. Ever since, the utilization of the evocative power of myths and symbols for political and military purposes has become a standard practice all over the world. Even today the military almost everywhere is most colorfully adorned with insignia. This emphasis on political and military symbols is not confined to European nations but is seen all over the world, including Africa and the Americas.

Above all, Hitler and Mussolini were well known for their deliberate uses of political aesthetics. The Nazis went beyond purely visual aesthetics and effectively combined these with auditory aesthetics to further their cause, as in the case of Hitler's impassioned and posthumous fulfillment of Wagner's aspiration to turn his operas into the national theater and Bayreuth into the national shrine. The Nazis systematically coopted well-respected composers and musicians in order to aestheticize their endeavors through an association with German high culture (Kater 1997). Even more clever is the penetration into the seemingly quotidian aspects of life—the striking visual image and precision marching of German soldiers are accompanied by the ubiquitous sound effect of their footsteps, like hypnotic drum beats.[7] Even those who never personally witnessed the parades, festivals, and monuments have vivid memories of their images and sounds from numerous films and documentaries (Falasca-Zamponi 1997).

To reiterate, aesthetics are assigned to the symbols that stand for the most cherished values of the people—their land, their history, their idealism, and the moral codes of purity and sacrifice. People respond to aesthetics, interpreting it in terms of their own idealism and aesthetics, while the state can use the same aesthetics and symbols to coopt them.

Writing on Nazi Germany, Mosse (1975: 20) argues that "the 'aesthetics of politics' was the force which linked myths, symbols, and the feeling of the masses." Similarly but in reference to fascism and communism in general, Walter Benjamin ([1958] 1968: 242) wrote of the uses and abuses of *l'art pour l'art* by totalitarian regimes: "[Mankind's] self-alienation has reached such a degree that it can experience its own destruction as an aesthetic pleasure of the first order. This is the situation of politics which Fascism is rendering aesthetic. Communism responds by politicizing art."

My interest is in the capacity the aesthetics of symbols has to move a symbol across a wide terrain, from "innocent" cultural space to "dangerous" political space. It is a general question of the role of symbols and their aesthetics when a quotidian symbol is transformed into a political symbol whose function is to serve a state ideology. "Nature," when used as a political symbol of "our space," becomes dangerous: its idealized beauty disarms people, because they interpret "nature" in terms of old and familiar associations, while the state constructs the meaning of "nature" in terms of its ideology. It is all too easy for "nature" and nationalism to form *les liaisons dangereuses*, as has happened in many societies. The aesthetics assigned to political symbols, such as cherry blossoms and the phoenix, facilitates this process of méconnaissance, disarming those in communication who then do not suspect the presence of the evil they would otherwise perceive. As in countless other cases, méconnaissance prevented the pilots and others to come to terms with the discrepancy between what they perceived and what the state intended.

Méconnaissance is an important phenomenon for our understanding of both human communication and historical change. It enables us to understand how people replicate the state ideology in action but not in thought, because they read and assign different meanings to the symbols used by the state.

What precisely is the role of aesthetics in the process of méconnaissance beyond an explanation that the aesthetics of cherry blossoms is shared, regardless of the specific meanings assigned, and thus easily equated with them all? Most fundamentally, the role of aesthetics in this process derives from the basic nature of what Kant developed as aesthetic judgment. Kant ([1784] 2001: 306) argued that both the beautiful and the sublime are reflective judgments and do *not* depend upon a definite concept. Instead, they depend on an indeterminate reference to concepts. In other words, because they are not linked to a specific concept, they are thereby able to refer to any number of concepts, as in the case of the aesthetics of polysemic cherry blossoms. Furthermore, as Brent (1977: 125) argues, the productive imagination of aesthetics leaves room for collectivity: "Kant's identification of the lack of absolute creativity of the productive imagination does not prevent it from providing *collective* forms for empirical intuition" (italics added; underline in the original). This tension between individuation, as Jung calls it, and the possibility to link it with collectivity creates room for an object of aesthetics, such as cherry blossoms, to become "cultural," rather than universal, as Kant conceptualized it. The pilots thus could embrace the aesthetics of the flower in their own individual ways, without contradicting the fact that it also is a cultural symbol.

HISTORICAL AGENTS: THEIR CIRCUMSCRIBED POWER

In addition to méconnaissance, there are a number of other factors that make historical changes extraordinarily complex. Yet dramatic historical changes in society and culture do no take place through mysterious transformations but through the actions of specific social agents, no matter how circumscribed their power may be. In the early Meiji period, cherry blossoms as a symbol of the Japanese were at the turbulent center of the construction of Japanese identity. For some, the flower stood for the evil past of feudal Japan, while for others it was a positive symbol of a *new* Japan. The former thought that the trees should be chopped down, while the latter vigorously promoted planting more trees and initiated the long tradition of giving cherry trees as the national gift to other nations. The early Meiji discourse and counter-discourse about cherry blossoms as a symbol of Japan offers important insights into how history is made through negotiations and contestations between individuals.

A second set of examples shows how social agents seldom have control over the direction of the changes they initiate. Both the building of the Yasukuni Shrine, proposed by Ōmura Masujirō, and the planting of cherry trees in its compound by Kido Takayoshi were intended to console their comrades who had fought on their side at the time of the Meiji "Restoration." However, both the functions of the shrine and the meaning of cherry blossoms were dramatically transformed in later years. A stark example of historical agents whose actions went in a totally un-intended direction is that of the architects of the emperor system. The Meiji oligarchs did not envision that the power they accorded the emperor or the return of the emperor system itself would lead to its abuse by the military.

There are other examples in this book of individuals as historical agents, all of which point to the unpredictable and highly complex nature of their impact upon history. Marx's well-known statement starts with the "Men make history" of Heinrich von Treischke, but this affirmation is followed by many qualifications indicating that the outcomes are out of their hands (Marx [1852] 1989: 320). Some contemporary uses of "making history" stretch Marx's original conception and examine only a synchronic moment of actors' behavior without examining how individual practices impact society at large or subsequent historical developments. Historical processes examined in hindsight are full of unintended ironies, accidents, and detours. Individuals may play a role in changing the course of history but not "as they please," as Marx's sharp insight has it.

Berlin is equally measured in his assessment of the power of historical agents like Marx. His discussion of Tolstoy is, first, about "the contrast between the universal and all-important but delusive experience of free will . . . and the reality of inexorable historical determinism" (Berlin ([1953] 1978: 30). Second, it is about the inequality between social agents in their power to impact the course of history: "Napoleon may not be a demigod, but neither is he a mere epiphenomenon of a process which would have occurred unaltered without him" (Berlin ([1953] 1978: 35). The last chapter of this book examines further the complexities involved in historical changes and the nature of involvement of individuals.

A set of examples shows that social agents are "localized," that is, they are at least in part products of their cultural milieu. Yet, their "local knowledge" is a product of the "global." The tokkōtai pilots all struggled with liberalism and Romanticism, introduced from the West and espoused by the Japanese at the time, on the one hand, and patriotism, on the other, paralleling the struggle which Japan itself went through—modernizing/westernizing the nation, while coping with the external threats which turned them into patriots. While Nitobe Inazō was a Christian steeped in Western philosophy, his warrior's way supplied the spiritual force behind Japan's military aggression even though Nitobe's patriotism embraced world peace and not armed conflict. The authors of the progressive textbooks of 1900 and 1934 were the Shakespearian scholar

Tsubouchi Shōyō and the cosmopolitan Inoue Takeshi, respectively. They were both pro-Western, liberal-minded scholars who fought against the encroachment of the military into the school system. Yet, Tsubouchi's textbook was full of patriotic messages, as was Inoue's, which contained not just symbols of cultural nationalism but also symbols of political nationalism and militarism. The Sorbonne-educated Saijō Yaso, author of the text of "Cherry Blossoms of the Same Class," was also credited for introducing folk elements into Japanese popular songs.

Konoe Fumimaro's "One Soul for One Hundred Million People" has been discussed several times in this book as an example of how an endorsement of the notion of a multi-ethnic nation served Japan's colonial imperialism. Konoe, often referred to as Prince Konoe because of his aristocratic background, had a complex intellectual history. As a philosophy student at the Imperial University of Kyoto, he translated Oscar Wilde's "The Soul of Man under Socialism," in which Wilde advocated individualism and artistic freedom. Konoe's translation in the journal *Shinshichō* was banned. After graduation he entered the government. He was an enthusiastic supporter of the Manchurian Incident and the Imperial Rule Assistance Association *(Taisei Yokusankai)*, which served as an instrument of national control especially under Tōjō Hideki. But, as prime minster, he insisted that the negotiations with the United States should lead a diplomatic solution, in opposition to Tōjō Hideki. When he lost, he dissolved his cabinet. Toward the end of World War II in 1945, he pleaded to the emperor for an earlier end of the war, although some claim that he did so not necessarily for the sake of the Japanese people.[8]

These few examples show how historical agents are individuals with their own interests and motivations, while they also are the products of their local times and spaces, resulting in contradictions in their behavior. Elsewhere, I have detailed my view of historical actors as *social* agents, who, I think, are neither "demigods,"[9] empowered to make history or to invent traditions out of the blue, nor mere puppets of cultural schema (Ohnuki-Tierney 1987, 1990, 1995). In order to clarify misunderstandings of his ideas among American scholars, Bourdieu (see, e.g., 1990: 9) insists that his "agents" are not "subjects." Likewise, de Certeau (see, e.g., 1988: 59) repeatedly emphasizes the inseparability of ideas and their "social localizations."[10] The examples in this book testify beyond doubt that historical agents are *localized* in a particular socio-cultural milieu at a particular moment in history, although the local space is never hermetically sealed but is in constant motion as it interacts with global flows.

Political, business, and intellectual leaders are not the exclusive agents of history. Among these agents, in the Japanese context, are also what

Gluck (1985) aptly calls *minkan* (popular) ideologues. Many Japanese participated in this process of subtle imbrication between cultural nationalism, patriotism, and political nationalism. Although Japan's cultural nationalism had been linked to cherry blossoms since the ninth century, some of the most important seeds of cultural nationalism were planted by the folk during the Edo period (1603–1868), with the efflorescence of urban popular culture. For example, the woodblock prints of the late Edo period played a most powerful role, turning Japan into "The Land of Cherry Blossoms" in the Japanese imagination. Since the artists produced prints in response to popular demand, both the artists and their consumers throughout Japan were historical actors. However, the motif of Japan as the land of cherry blossoms enjoyed a vast popularity because of the beauty of these prints, but *not* because it was a symbol of cultural nationalism. Likewise, the Kabuki theater played an important role in making the Confucian notion of loyalty to one's parents and lord emotively compelling. It also promoted the idea that the warriors were men among men—both of these ideas became, unexpectedly of course, convenient tools for the military regime during the modern period. The patrons of the woodblock prints and the Kabuki theater were from the merchant class, which, despite its economic power, occupied the lowest stratum of the semi-caste system in pre-Meiji Japan. Ironically, then, it was the lowly merchant class which put the warriors and their way of life on an aesthetic pedestal.

The popular Kabuki play *The Forty-Seven Loyal Retainers* also shows how the folk, through their enthusiastic responses, participated in the many changes of its performance. The popularity of *The Forty-Seven Loyal Retainers* throughout the Edo period, and even today, rested on its themes of human greed and passion, on the one hand, and antigovernment sentiment, on the other. The folk responded to human frailty portrayed in the play since they saw it in themselves. But even more so, they experienced catharsis because the play was an expression of the antigovernment sentiment which they shared but could not express, given the strong governmental control of their behavior. However, since the Meiji period and especially during the 1930s, the play became a morality play in praise of the beauty of loyalty to the emperor. The enactment of the lord's suicide under the cascade of falling cherry blossoms succeeded in making sacrifice a beautiful human act. The audiences may not have articulated the message clearly in their minds, but nevertheless they too seem have been caught in war fever so as to respond to these *pro rege* versions of the play with enthusiasm.

Thus the notion of socially localized individuals as social agents applies both to the holders of power as well as to the so-called "masses." We must move beyond a simplistic picture of a historical agent as someone, oppressor or oppressed, with power to change his/her society directly or instantly. While we cannot dismiss the role of the "masses," who too participate in historical processes, it would be an injustice to gloss over power inequalities among social agents. The masses participate in and even promote the state program, but the program is orchestrated by the power holders. In the case of wars and totalitarian regimes, the power holders drive young men and countless others to death.

It is tempting to use the metaphor of the "crooked timber of the cherry," taking after Kant's "aus so krummem Holze, als woraus der Mensch gemacht ist, kann nichts ganz Gerades gezimmert werden" (One cannot fashion something absolutely straight from wood which is as crooked as that of which man is made) (Kant [1784] 2001: 124–25). It gives an image of a cherry tree bent tragically at the hands of the Japanese military. Yet the metaphor hides rather than illuminates the complexities of historical agency. Kant's vision of a society is a forest with each tree standing straight toward the sky so that each tree enjoys its freedom without destroying society with its "egotistical animal inclination." Hence, he felt the need for a master for individuals to obey—that is, for "a general will" to guide them. Isaiah Berlin ([1959] 1992: 18–19), who made Kant's phrase well known, took the crookedness of humanity as a positive source of people's resilience against "the neat uniforms" of a totalitarian state to force its people to be "straight." Neither Kant nor Berlin foregrounds the problem of agency. Both the Japanese social agents who participated in the historical process to militarize cherry blossoms and the people who did not recognize the change and/or did not protest it are all members of the human race, with its predilection for crookedness. But, in the Japanese case as well as in other fascist/totalitarian cases, the heavy weight of guilt for forcing the bending and twisting rested on those with power, who, nonetheless, were neither entirely cognizant of their behavior nor powerful enough to determine the direction of the warping.

Nevertheless, the visual image of crooked timber so vividly portrays the Japanese cherry tree, which has been shaped and reshaped as well as warped during much of Japanese history. It also evokes the warpings of what we call modernity, which has witnessed atrocities of a monstrous scale in Japan and elsewhere, rather than a smooth road toward progress "through a homogeneous, empty time" (Benjamin [1958] 1968: 261).

Just as historical agents are products of the interpenetration of the local and the global, so is what we call culture. The most intense experiences in Japanese history have been precipitated by external forces, and whatever we call "Japanese culture" has never developed through self-reproducing processes. The very rise of the cultural nationalism that selected the cherry blossom as the national flower was a result of intensive contacts with the Chinese. The 1889 Constitution of Imperial Japan was drafted by Prussian and Austrian scholars, just as a half century later the current constitution was written by Americans. The Japanese made rice, imported from the Asian continent, into the signature food for self-identity. In the early decades of this century, the state disseminated fascist and jingoistic phrases through the melodies introduced from the West. Most important, in Japan nationalism and patriotism were both born at the intersection between the local and the global, with the latter nourishing the minds of historical actors. Changes in Japanese culture, then, are neither a self-reproductive process nor a process characterized by total transformation by foreign cultures.

Every culture is a product of continuous interpenetration between the external/global and the local—the two mutually constituent forces. Each conjuncture requires a reinterpretation of the foreign elements and the process in turn transforms the local. The interpenetration of the global and the local is the sine qua non of all cultures, and it is the locus where history is made at the hands of historical agents whose Weltanschauung is cosmopolitan. Although the metaphor of culture as a hybrid, put into academic currency by Salman Rushdie, is now widely used, often with different meanings,[11] the metaphor is misleading on two grounds. First, if all cultures are historical products of the interpenetration between the global and the local, then it is a logical contradiction to propose that a culture is a "hybrid." Culture is a product of interaction between cultures, each of which is a "hybrid." Such terms as "hybrid" and "creole" are predicated upon the notion of a "pure" culture—but such a well-demarcated, essentialized, and bounded entity is a phantasm. Second, the notion of "hybrid" portrays a synchronic moment when the "global/external" meets the local, or simply points to the genealogy of some objects and features.[12] It turns our attention away from our understanding of culture as historical process.

Lastly, the role of historical agents can never be understood at the moment of their actions. The impact of the changes brought forth by historical agents in the early Meiji period expressed itself only in the 1920s and after. This finding compels us to realize that if we wish to understand the role of historical agents, snapshots of their behavior at a given historical period tell us very little. We must think in terms of "culture/society through time," or, "think with history."[13]

SUMMARY

The tragic finale for the Pacific War included the historically unprecedented tokkōtai operation, which sent thousands of young men to their deaths. Of them, 85 percent were student soldiers, many of whom were the intellectual elite. Why did these highly intelligent men, the most unlikely group of young men to endorse Japan's military and imperial mission, reproduce the military ideology in their action and fly to their deaths, when they knew that Japan was losing the war? The writings they left behind tell us in no uncertain terms that they did not reproduce the emperor-centered military ideology in their thoughts. None died for the emperor.

By no means is the question raised in this book simply a "Japanese problem." Even in extreme totalitarian regimes, top-down ideological conversions are rarely successful or unsuccessful in toto. We have a distinguished list of scholars who have attempted to understand both how the political machinery of a state can attempt to coerce people into its scheme and how people "think and feel" when they do collaborate, often without articulating in their minds the nature of the state agenda. On Nazi Germany, which has received, understandably, the most attention, we have a wide range of interpretation, including the groundbreaking work by Hannah Arendt on the "banality of evil." Lately the so-called Goldhagen controversies have now turned the terms "willing" and "ordinary" into common parlance in the United States. We are witnessing now a plethora of works on the question of whether "ordinary" people under dictatorship become "willing" participants in, if not the actual executioners of, the ghastly march toward the destruction of their own people and others. Even in Nazi Germany, Goebbels's propaganda machine was, contra Goldhagen (1996), less than perfect. Klemperer (1998) has provided us with a definitive record of the full range of human responses, thus refuting a totalizing conclusion that all Germans were antisemitic, as argued by Goldhagen.[1] The responses toward ideological pressure are highly complex, especially at the level of the individual; most individuals subjected to long-term ideological pressure are seldom completely free or completely transformed. We see that, between the imperial nationalism of wartime Japan and the patriotism of the pilots, there were at times chasms and at other times partial imbrication. We saw that even the Marxists among the pilots were not completely free of the *pro rege et patria mori* ideology, because, like fine invisible rain, many of its dimensions seeped into the fabric of the daily lives and thoughts of the people.

Yet we cannot simply end our query at this general point. Rather, we must try to identify in what ways people, even those unlikely young intellectuals, become participants in these movements and fight in wars.

This book is an attempt to understand this important question, which recurs in history the world over, by examining the Japanese case. For this reason I examined, on the one hand, the historical processes of the building of the political and military machinery and the strategies that machinery deployed to coerce the people in their march to the final destruction of their own country. On the other, I examined the writings left behind by these young men in order to understand the most incredible phenomenon—that these men "volunteered" to reproduce the ideology *in action* while defying it *in their thoughts*.

The so-called modern era was ushered into Japan at the time the Western colonial powers were reaching out to Asia at an ever accelerating pace. The Meiji oligarchs managed to overthrow the shogunate, which was day-dreaming without understanding the urgency of the danger from without. The first agenda was to build a strong and sovereign modern nation, for which these men turned to Western European models, finally settling on the Prussian model. The emperor as commander-in-chief directly in charge of the military was codified. Out of a politically impotent emperor who had been one of millions of deities in the Japanese pantheon, the oligarchs invented the emperor as Almighty God. But in order to make him the "political God" in charge exclusively of Japan, the oligarchs began the Constitution of Imperial Japan of 1889 with Article 1, which guaranteed the perpetuity of what Kantorowicz called the emperor's two bodies—the individual emperor's body and the imperial system—by inventing the notion of the imperial soul, which was supposedly transmitted from one emperor to the next in perpetuity. Furthermore, the oligarchs attempted to superimpose the "pastoral model" by making the emperor the "father" of all Japanese. This was quite an extraordinary feat. The pastoral model was predicated upon the notion of the kingdom of heaven, which transcended political boundaries, and on Christ who sacrificed himself for humanity. The emperor's "kingdom," in contrast, was solely the Japanese state, and the notion of the emperor as a sacrificer was almost an oxymoron. However, the baseline for the later political-military machinery had been set even before the promulgation of the constitution through the issuing of the Imperial Rescript to Soldiers and the Imperial Rescript on Education. In the former, soldiers were told to think of their lives as being as light as a feather and their responsibility to the nation as heavy as mountains.

One important means deployed by a number of totalitarian states is the aestheticization of the military and other political machineries. Aestheticization with its indeterminacy of referents is also a powerful weapon that can lead the people to misrecognize the motives behind state strategies. The role of aesthetics in méconnaissance is therefore crucial in facilitating the mobilization of the people.

The Japanese state extensively and intensively used the strategy of aestheticization, for which cherry blossoms took on an enormous importance. There were several important factors about the symbolism of this flower that facilitated méconnaissance. First, cherry blossoms were a quotidian symbol within reach for everyone in Japan. Second, the flower does not stand for isolated categories of meaning. Rather, it stood for life predicated by death and rebirth, and women predicated by their relationship to men. Ultimately, what cherry blossoms stood for was a concept embedded in the relationship between men and women and in the processes of life, death, and rebirth. Cherry blossoms in a particular context may foreground one meaning, but the other meanings are always present in the background. The multilayered meanings of this polyseme, then, contributed to the ease with which the military tipped the scale to use falling cherry petals as soldiers' sacrifice and fully blooming cherry blossoms as their postmortem souls. This they could do without alerting people to the profound shifts in the flower's symbolism. Third, the trope of cherry blossoms is based not simply in its embeddedness in the Japanese Weltanschauung. Its evocation derives from its association with two of the most powerful themes in the Japanese ethos—the aesthetics of pathos over evanescence and the aesthetics of purity of the self. The aesthetics of cherry blossoms went beyond visual aesthetics and was extended to represent the beauty of idealism, the purity of one's spirit, and the like, as we saw in the pilots' diaries.

These young men's responses to "Hitch your wagon to a star" doomed them in the end. What is most striking in the diaries, both of the "liberals" such as Sasaki and Hayashi Tadao, and of the "conservatives" like Nakao and Wada, is their youthful idealism/romanticism in pursuit of purity and beauty. Their pursuit was exclusively intellectual and spiritual in nature, rather than pragmatic. The writings left behind by these highly educated graduates of top universities reveal an astonishing level of sheer intelligence and dedication to learning. They lived in an intellectual world where Sasaki could refer to the two souls in German and Hayashi Ichizō could recite "despair" and others understood that their references were from Goethe and Kierkegaard. They prided themselves on their German, which was taught at all higher schools, and their French, which was taught at only the First Higher School in Tokyo and the Third Higher School in Kyoto. Higher schools and universities at that time were the embodiment of *cogito ergo sum*, as it were, where young men could simply live in their world of idealism, in search for love, purity, and beauty in life, women, and ideas (see Irokawa 1993: 45, 49). It is this idealism that led them to a point of no return. The pilots assigned aesthetics to concepts and behaviors involved in the state ideology without fully realizing that they were being coopted through ideological manipulation.

Nakao was moved by the Dreyfus affair and wished to be a Zola. But his idealism also was the basis for his favorable reaction to Mori Ōgai's novel, in which he found purity of spirit in dedicating one's life for one's lord. For many young men "loyalty" stood for this purity of spirit. We saw that most pilots did not really die for the emperor. Rather, their sense of loyalty was channeled into their sense of patriotism, which began as a choice they made to take on responsibility as members of society and of humanity at large—a moral and philosophical issue that had been a central concern to Japanese intellectuals ever since the Meiji period. There was a strong appeal of idealism in this sense of loyalty—unconditional dedication to a cause greater than their own lives. Such dedication became a means to transcend their egotistical desires and the rampant materialism they saw all around them in their beloved country, as is well articulated in the diaries of Sasaki and others. This is the danger point, as it were, where the state could bend idealistic desire into service for imperial nationalism. The state succeeded, then, not so much in transferring the sense of loyalty to parents and to one's lord into loyalty to the emperor, but in effectively channeling the sense of dedication to the country on the part of young soldiers and the masses into its own imperial agenda.

The méconnaissance of the schemes of the state was not confined to the intellectuals. Even more important than a small number of intellectuals, the masses also "misrecognized" various dimensions of the *pro rege et patria mori* ideology. The audience in the Kabuki theater reacted to the purity of spirit that the forty-seven loyal retainers supposedly held for their lord.

In this process of méconnaissance, the evocative power of the aesthetics of cherry blossoms played a critical role. The role of méconnaissance is extremely important for an understanding of the most important question of this book—why did the pilots reproduce the imperial ideology in action without reproducing its intellectual and spiritual content. The flower did not *move* them to take action, but it made them *not* confront the méconnaissance between their thoughts and the state ideology.

At an initial stage of this research, I expressed my puzzlement over why these highly intelligent men volunteered to be tokkōtai pilots to Irokawa Daikichi, an eminent historian of the Meiji period and himself a student soldier. His reply was: "We would have been able to fight against militarism and the military government. But we had no weapon to fight against idealism and Romanticism." That is, they would have fought against blatant political nationalism as orchestrated by the state. But the young intellectuals were simply powerless when the mediation was carried out through the lofty intellectual traditions of the West. They could no longer recognize the manipulative hand of the state. They would have been able to resist Japanese versions of *Ein Volk, ein Reich, und ein Führer*. But when the "general will," transformed by the Nazis and the Japanese state, was presented as the general will of Rousseau and Kant, they could not detect méconnaissance between their own vision and that of the state. Or, when the romanticization of "our nature" came from Beethoven, Goethe, or Thomas Mann, they eagerly embraced it. They were too innocent to suspect that ultra-nationalists would utilize *their* idealistic love of nature.

In Germany, the concept of the Volk became powerfully persuasive when it was cloaked in the aesthetics of a putative Aryan or Teutonic past filled with spiritual strength and purity. In Japan, this symbolic association also appeared in the works of highly revered intellectuals and novelists, such as Natsume Sōseki, Kunikida Doppo, and Miyazawa Kenji, all of which sought to establish a Japanese identity. Yet Yasuda could imbricate his "nature" onto "nature" in both the Japanese and German Romantics.

These young men struggled in a society which had plunged headlong toward a total war that was justified through appeals to the *pro rege et patria mori* ideology.[2] They lived in an extraordinary time when the waves of Western "civilization" and Western colonialism simultaneously beat on the Japanese shore. Their patriotism, an important part of their fatal decision, was a complicated product of a philosophical struggle between individual freedom, human rights, and various other liberal concepts introduced from the West, on the one hand, and capitalism, materialism, and colonialism, also introduced from the West, on the other.[3] Their struggle mirrors the process taken by the Meiji oligarchs who sought out German legal scholars to draft the constitution into which they inscribed Japanese identity sui generis. From the Meiji oligarchs to the pilots, they were intensely patriotic while equally intensely cosmopolitan in their intellectual pursuits.

If every culture is a product of the interpenetration of the local and the global, rather than a self-reproducing entity, so too are individuals whose intellectual and cultural horizons are rarely confined to the local, which is never a hermetically sealed space in the first place. In this sense, both the Meiji oligarchs and the pilots exemplify "cosmopolitan patriots," like Kwame Anthony Appiah or Edward Said. From Aristotle to Edmund Burke to Appiah, but contra Nussbaum, many scholars argue that cosmopolitanism and patriotism do not constitute antagonistic opposites. Defining nationalism as ideology and patriotism as a set of sentiments, as I do, Appiah (1992a, 1992b) argues that the cosmopolitan patriot, like himself and his father, can be "rooted," attached to cultural particularities of his or her own, while appreciating the presence of differences.

From the perspective of historiography, the pilots' diaries should speak against the scholarly sin of helping the mass media perpetuate utterly false representations of "kamikazes" as patriotic zealots. False representations, including stereotypes, constitute a powerful and most dangerous instrument not only for exiling the past but for replacing the empty space with a patina of "facts." The stereotype, which does not involve human flesh and blood, then, is a "natural" prey for commoditization. On eBay "kamikaze memorabilia," such as helmets and goggles, are regularly auctioned off as the items of "History's Lost and Found."[4]

Recent scholarship has alerted us to the politics surrounding the obliteration of "history" and how different historical agents with their own interests and motivations compete in the construction of history. However, we should pay closer attention to deliberately distorted histories and the role of geopolitics in the process. The pilots are no longer able to speak on their own. They await for the pale angel of history to awaken them and save their place in humanity and history, lest *"even the dead will not be safe from the enemy"* (Benjamin [1958] 1968: 255, emphasis in the original)—the enemy, in this case, being power inequalities in geopolitics without and political amnesia within Japan.

In any historical process, some historical agents, such as the leaders of totalitarian regimes, are far more influential than others. Their sins against humanity should never be exonerated. The pilots' diaries serve as a testimony to the monstrous acts of Japanese imperialism in driving these young men full of dreams and idealism to their deaths. This book, I hope, will serve not simply as a requiem for the pilots and countless other war victims, Japanese and non-Japanese, but as a reminder that such tragedies should never be repeated.

Appendix: List of Readings by Four Pilots

The authors are classified according to the language in which they primarily wrote, at times arbitrarily, since some authors, like Søren Kierkegaard, wrote in more than one language. Irish and Scottish authors are in "English," but "American" writers constitute a separate category. Swiss and Austrians are included in "German." Books written in Japanese but on Western scholars are listed in the appropriate Western category. When authors are well known, the pilots referred to them without naming specific publications. A category for Western music, mostly composers but also performers, is included because of its enormous impact upon the pilots and on the Japanese, although none discussed music extensively, which makes the list very incomplete. Noteworthy is that not one form of Japanese "traditional music" is mentioned by anyone, which testifies to the conspicuous decline in the popularity of Japanese music after the introduction of Western music. References to films, especially German war propaganda films, are included since they inform us of their penetration into Japan. The list is incomplete, however, because of the difficulty in identifying the titles given in Japanese translation.

I suspect that many more works were read on the days whose entries were not included in the diaries. About seventy diary entries were omitted because the references were too abbreviated or cryptic to identify the work being discussed. In the case of Sasaki, readings given by Fujishiro in the long afterword for Sasaki (1981) are added; these usually identify only the year, as no specific dates are provided. Hayashi Ichizō 1995 is excluded, since it consists primarily of letters to his mother.

The titles in French and German are given in the original, since the pilots often read books in German and French in the original languages, although errors were entered in the original titles during the editing of the published editions of the diaries. The original titles in French and German were given also for those titles in Japanese translation, since there often is more than one English translation of any given title. In the published diaries, all titles in Russian were given in Japanese translation; I have converted these to the titles by which the works are known in their standard English translations. In the identification of the titles, I used primarily Peter France 1995, Henry and Mary Garland 1997, V. Terras 1985, Simon Hornblower and Antony Spawforth 1996, and the Memorial Library catalogue of the University of Wisconsin, Madison. In listing the titles, I make no distinction between novels and short stories: all appear in italics.

	Hayashi	Nakao	Sasaki	Wada
Books				
French (187)	54	100	28	5
German (170)	41	39	78	12
English (83)	22	19	39	3
Russian (70)	11	37	19	3
Classics (42)	11	20	10	1
American (15)	2	8	4	1
Italian (14)	1	5	8	0
Other Western (36)	7	12	15	2
Chinese (9)	2	3	4	0
Japanese (731)	107	356	253	14
Total (1,356)	258	599	458	41
Western Music (37)	0	2	30	4

In the following entries, the dates are in month-day-year format and are followed by the page in the relevant diary on which the reference appears. Titles which are given in the original languages but which I have not been able to identify are followed by [*sic*]. Titles which appear in Japanese translation and which I have not been able to identify are in brackets.

French
Arland, Marcel. *L'Ordre*. Hayashi 5/15/43 (95).
Alain (Émile-Auguste Chartier). *Quatre-vingt-un chapitres sur l'esprit et les passions*. Hayashi 5/31/41 (52); 6/3/41 (53); 6/16/41 (53); 8/21/41 (59).
———. [*Stendhal*]. Nakao 10/12/40 (298).
Balzac, Honoré de. Hayashi 2/10/42 (77); Nakao 5/27/40 (261); 12/14/40 (321).
———. *Le Chef-d'oeuvre inconnu*. Nakao 8/23/39 (174).
———. *Le Cousin Pons*. Hayashi 6/27/41 (56).
———. *El verdugo*. Nakao 8/23/39 (174).
———. *Un épisode sous la terreur*. Nakao 8/18/39 (173).
———. *La Grande Bretèche*. Nakao 1/18/40 (215).
———. [*The House of Pomegranate*]. Nakao 8/23/39 (174).
———. *Le Lys dans la vallée*. Hayashi 11/6/41 (70).
———. *Le Message*. Nakao 8/17/39 (172).
———. *Une Passion dans le désert*. Nakao 8/17/39 (172).
———. *La Recherche de l'absolu*. Hayashi 5/12/41 (46); Wada 5/23/41(24).
———. [*Revenge*]. Nakao 5/27/40 (261).
———. [*Tragedy at Seaside*]. Hayashi 5/12/41 (46).
Barrès, Maurice. Hayashi 10/19/42 (93).
———. [*In Praise of Oneself*]. Hayashi 11/2/41 (67); 12/31/41 (75).
Baudelaire, Charles-Pierre. Hayashi 10/29/41 (66); Nakao 5/27/40 (261).
———. *Les Fleurs du mal*. Nakao 7/30/42 (478).
———. *Le Spleen de Paris*. Hayashi 1945 (181).
Bergson, Henri. Nakao 1/7/41 (336); Sasaki 11/8/40 (137).
Bonorr, Abél. Sasaki 1/10/41 (171).

———. [*On Friendship*]. Sasaki 3/27/41 (202); 4/2/41 (205).

Bourget, Paul. Hayashi 2/10/42 (77).

———. *Les Deux soeurs*. Hayashi 5/30/42 (85).

———. *Le Disciple*. Hayashi 9/10/41 (60); 12/31/41 (75); Nakao 8/11/41 (387); 11/3/41 (407).

———. [*The Eternal Self and Women*]. Hayashi 1/5/42 (75).

———. *Le Justicier* [*sic*]. Hayashi 2/28/42 (78).

———. *Nos Actes nous suivent*. Hayashi 9/10/41 (59).

Chinard, Gilbert. *Petite histoire des lettres françaises*. Nakao 10/4/41 (399).

Cocteau, Jean. *Les Enfants terribles*. Nakao 10/21/41 (403).

Comte, Auguste. Nakao 1/2/41 (333).

Corneille, Pierre. *Le Cid*. Hayashi 4/29/43 (95).

Daudet, Alphonse. *Les Lettres de mon moulin*. Hayashi 12/21/40 (31). Hayashi identifies the author as Marcel Pagnol.

———. *Safo*. Hayashi 10/3/41(62).

———. *Tartarin de Tarascon*. Nakao 2/20/41 (350).

Descartes, René. Hayashi 6/13/43 (99); Nakao 11/22/40 (311); 7/27/42 (476); 2/21/43 (545); 3/27/43 (556); 10/13/43 (613); 11/9/43 (624).

———. *Discours de la méthode*. Nakao 6/20/42 (466).

———. *Principes*. Nakao 7/18/42 (471).

Duhamel, Georges. *Civilisation*. Hayashi 7/8/44 (161).

———. *Scènes de la vie future*. Hayashi 7/1/44 (158); 7/8/44 (161).

Dumas, Alexandre (fils). *La Dame aux camélias*. Nakao 6/22/39 (156).

———. *La Dame aux camélias* (as film). Sasaki 1/25/42 (284); 3/24/39 (13); 3/26/39 (13).

Dumas, Alexandre (père). *Contes*. Nakao 5/8/41 (366).

———. *Homme au masque de fer*. Nakao 12/29/40 (326).

———. *Le Soldat de plomb et la danseuse de papier* [*sic*]. Nakao 4/4/41 (358).

———. *Les Trois mousquetaires*. Wada 7/17/41 (28).

Durkheim, Émile. *Éducation et sociologie*. Nakao 11/30/41 (411).

———. *Sociologie et philosophie*. Nakao 8/26/43 (594).

Fabre, Jean Henri. Sasaki 8/19/43 (385).

Faguet, Émile. *L'Art de lire*. Hayashi 1945 (175).

Flaubert, Gustave. *Un Coeur simple* (In: *Trois Contes*). Nakao 1/1/41 (331).

———. *L'Éducation sentimentale*. Hayashi 11/6/41 (70).

———. *Hérodias* (In *Trois contes*) Nakao 1/13/41 (338).

———. *La Légende de saint Julien l'hospitalier* (In *Trois Contes*) Nakao 1/6/41 (335).

———. *Madame Bovary*. Hayashi 4/22/40 (10); 6/3/41 (53).

———. *Trois contes*. Hayashi 8/31/40 (20).

France, Anatole. Hayashi 6/22/44 (150); Nakao 1/8/40 (214); 2/12/42 (435).

———. *L'Abeille*. Nakao 9/29/41 (399).

———. *Balthasar*. Nakao 9/18, 29/41 (398–99).

———. *Le Crime de Sylvestre Bonnard*. Hayashi 6/3/41 (52); 6/16/41 (53); 7/5/41 (58); 8/21/41 (59); 10/29/41 (66).

———. *Les Désirs de Jean Servien*. Hayashi 7/5/41 (58).

———. *Le Jardin d'Épicure*. Nakao 1/5/42 (418).

————. *Nos Enfants* [*sic*]. Nakao 11/14/43 (626).

————. *L'Oeuf lauge* [*sic*]. Nakao 9/29/41 (399).

————. *Thaïs.* Nakao 6/9/41 (369).

————. *La Vie en fleur.* Hayashi 11/6/41 (70).

Gauguin, Paul. *Noa Noa.* Nakao 4/2/41 (357); 4/5/41 (359).

Gide, André. Nakao 9/3/39 p.177; 9/15/39 (181–82); 9/29/39 (185).

————. *Les Caves du Vatican.* Nakao 8/14/39 (171).

————. *Les Faux-Monnayeurs.* Nakao 7/29/39 (165); 4/2/41 (357); 10/21/41 (403).

————. *L'Immoraliste.* Nakao 5/28, 30/39 (149); Sasaki 4/16/39 (20); 4/17/39 (20).

————. [*On Montaigne*]. Nakao 12/18/40 (323).

————. *Paludes.* Nakao 9/6/39 (179); 10/16/40 (299).

————. *La Porte étroite.* Nakao 5/27/39 (148); 10/31/39 (191); 7/25/40 (269);7/30/40 (271); Sasaki 4/10/39 (18); 4/12/39 (18).

————. *Prométhée mal enchaîné.* Nakao 8/13/39 (170).

————. *Retour de l'URSS.* Nakao 10/11/39 (188).

————. *Si le grain ne meurt.* Nakao 11/23/39 (199); Sasaki 4/22/39 (23).

Gilson, Étienne. [*Medieval Humanism and Renaissance*]. Hayashi 2/10/42 (77).

Gourmont, Rémy de. Wada 12/12/40 (8–9).

Jourbert, Joseph. Hayashi 1945 (177).

La Bruyère, Jean de. *Les Caractères.* Sasaki 4/4/41 (207).

La Fontaine, Jean de. *Fables.* Nakao 6/16/43 (576).

La Mettrie, Julien Offray de. *L'Homme-machine.* Sasaki 10/5/40 (113).

La Rochefoucould. François, duc de. Nakao 11/22/40 (311).

————. *Maximes.* Hayashi 4/28/44 (128).

Lamartine, Alphonse de. *Graziella.* Nakao 11/16/41 (410).

————. *Raphäel.* Nakao 11/11/41 (408).

Leblanc, Maurice. (Arsène Lupin). Sasaki Spring/35 (423).

Lévy-Bruhl, Lucien. *Les Fonctions mentales dans les sociétés inférieures.* Nakao 9/21/427 (492).

Loti, Pierre. [*American Cavalry*]. Hayashi 11/2/41 (67).

————. *Pêcheur d'islande.* Hayashi 11/6/41 (70); 5/3042 (86).

————. *Ramuntcho.* Hayashi 5/30/42 (86).

Maeterlinck, Maurice. *L'Oiseau bleu.* Nakao 5/19/41 (367).

Martin du Gard, Roger. *Confidence africaine.* Hayashi 4/30/44 (129).

————. *Les Thibault.* Hayashi 12/21/40 (31); 11/6/41 (70); 11/20/41 (74); 11/29/41 (74); 12/31/41 (75); 1/18/42 (76); 2/10/42 (77); 4/26/42 (79), 4/27/42 (80); 5/20/42 (84); 9/10/42 (91); 5/15/43 (95); 1/23/44 (113); 4/18/44 (123).

Maupassant, Guy de. Nakao 9/14/39 (181); 12/8/40 (315; four works mentioned); 1/6/41 (335); 1/18/41 (341).

————. *Apparition.* Nakao 12/14/40 (319).

————. *Les Bijoux* [*sic*]. Nakao 12/10/40 (318).

————. *Boule de suif.* Hayashi 5/30/42 (86).

————. *Les Contes du jour et de la nuit.* Nakao 12/6/40 (315).

————. *Un Coup d'état.* Nakao 12/14/39 (321).

————. *Deux amis* [*sic*]. Hayashi 8/31/40 (20); 12/21/40 (31).

————. *La Légende du Mont Saint-Michel.* Nakao 12/9/40 (316).

———. *Nos Lettres* [*sic*]. Nakao 12/20/40 (324).

———. *Le Loup* [*sic*]. Nakao 12/12/40 (318).

———. *Mademoiselle Cocotte* [*sic*]. Nakao 12/10/40 (318).

———. *Marion* [*sic*]. Nakao 12/14/39 (320).

———. *La Parte* [*sic*]. Nakao 12/17/40 (322).

———. *De Perdon* [*sic*]. Nakao 12/15/40 (322).

———. *Pierre et Jean.* Hayashi 4/17/41 (38); 5/30/41 (51); 6/3/41 (52); Sasaki 8/5/39 (37).

———. *La Reine Hortense* [*sic*]. Nakao 12/12/40 (318).

———. *Sur l'eau* [*sic*]. Nakao 2/3/41 (346).

———. *Une Vie.* Nakao 5/27/40 (260); Sasaki 4/7/39 (17); Wada 7/17/41 (28).

Maurois, André. *Sentiments et coutumes.* Nakao 12/15/41 (416).

———. *Tragédie en France.* Sasaki 2/15/41 (185).

Mérimée, Prosper. Nakao 4/5/40 (246); 5/27/40 (261); 11/11/40 (305); 11/14/40 (306); 12/14/40 (319).

———. *L'Aubépine de Veliko* [*sic*]. Nakao 11/10/40 (305).

———. *Carmen.* Hayashi 8/21/41 (59); 10/3/41 (62); Nakao 9/7/39 (179); 4/5/40 (246); Sasaki 3/27/39 (14).

———. *Colomba.* Hayashi 8/21/41 (59); Nakao 9/21/40 (296).

———. *L'Enlèvement de la redoute.* Nakao 11/2/40 (304).

———. *La Guzla.* Nakao 11/12/40 (306).

———. *Mateo Falcone.* Nakao 11/1/40 (303).

———. *La Mort de Thomas II* [*sic*]. Nakao 11/10/40 (305).

———. *Tamango.* Nakao 11/8/40 (304).

———. *La Vase étrusque.* Hayashi 8/21/41 (59); Nakao 10/31/40 (302).

Montaigne, Michel de. Nakao 11/22/40 (311); 10/8/43 (608); 10/9/43 (644).

———. *Biography of Montaigne* by Sekine Hideo. Nakao 11/2/40 (312); 12/18/40 (323).

———. *Essais* (trans. Sekine Hideo). Nakao 3/3/41 (353).

Napoléon Bonaparte. Sasaki 2/20/41 (188); 1/19/42 (280); 1/25/42 (284); 6/19/43 (368); 8/11/43 (382).

Pascal, Blaise. Hayashi 10/19/41 (65); 1/3/44 (110); Nakao 12/30/40 (327); 7/23/42 (473); 7/29/43 (584).

———. *Pensées.* Hayashi 11/29/41 (74); Nakao 1/15/42 (424).

———. *Study on the Nature of Human Beings in Pascal's Work (Pasukaru ni Okeru Ningen no Kenkyū)* by Miki Kiyoshi. Nakao 11/30/40 (311).

Poincaré, Henri. *La Science et l'hypothèse.* Wada 1/1/41 (12).

Renard, Jules. *Poil de carotte.* Hayashi 8/31/40 (20); Nakao 9/27/39 (185).

Robespierre, Maximilien. Sasaki 1/19/42 (280).

Rolland, Romain. Nakao 6/6/40 (263).

———. *Jean-Christophe.* Hayashi 1/22/42 (76); 2/10/42 (77), 2/28/42 (77–78); Nakao 2/13, 14, 18, 22/40 (229–30, 232); 3/11, 14/40 (238, 240); 4/1,2/40 (242); Sasaki Summer/38 (426); 3/30/39 (15).

———. *Vie de Beethoven.* Nakao 3/11/42 (444); Sasaki 12/12/41 (263); 12/14/41 (263).

Rousseau, Jean-Jacques. Sasaki 10/12/40 (116); 10/14/40 (118); 11/8/40 (136); 4/1/41 (204).

————. *Discours sur l'origine et les fondements de l'inégalité parmi les hommes.* Sasaki 10/5/40 (113).

————. *Émile.* Sasaki 10/20/40 (121).

————. *Rousseau* by Shima Yoshio. Sasaki 11/8/40 (137).

Saint-Pierre, Bernadin de. *Paul et Virginie.* Nakao 11/27/41 (410).

Seignobos, Charles. *Histoire sincère de la nation française.* Nakao 11/2/41 (405).

Stendhal (Henri Beyle). *L'Abbesse de Castro.* Nakao 10/15/40 (299).

————. *La Chartreuse de Parme.* Hayashi 8/21/41 (59).

————. *Le Rouge et le noir.* Hayashi 11/6/41 (70); 9/10/42 (91); Nakao 11/3/41 (406); Sasaki 5/8/41 (225).

————. *Vie de Henry Brulard.* Hayashi 8/21/41 (59).

Valéry, Paul. *Une Conquête méthodique.* Hayashi 5/30/42 (86).

————. *La Soirée avec Monsieur Teste.* Nakao 10/16/40 (299).

Vildrac, Charles. *Le Paquebot Tenacity.* Nakao 9/27/39 (185).

Vigny, Alfred de. *Le Cachet rouge* [*sic*]. Nakao 2/26/41 (351).

Voltaire. Hayashi 7/8/44 (161).

Hirose Tetsuji. *Outline of French History (Gaikan Furansu-shi).* Nakao 11/2/41 (405).

Kawamori Kōzō. *French Moralists (Furansu no Morarisuto).* Nakao 11/22/40 (310).

Takizawa Kēichirō. *Reports from France* (cont.) *(Zoku Furansu Tsūshin).* Nakao 8/20/40 (278); 8/26/40 (281).

Yoshie Takamatsu. *Essays on French Literature (Futsu-Bungaku Dansō).* Sasaki 11/19/40 (144); 11/20/40 (144).

German

Bälz, Erwin von. [*Diary of Bälz*]. Hayashi 5/30/43 (97); Nakao 2/6/43 (538).

Barth, Karl [Swiss]. *Credo.* Hayashi 1945 (168, 172, 188, 190).

Bernheim, Ernst. *Einleitung in die Geschichtswissenschaft.* Sasaki 10/12/40 (116); 10/27/40 (125); 11/6/40 (136); 11/17/40 (142).

Carossa, Hans. *Arzt Gion: Eine Erzählung.* Nakao 8/29/43 (594).

————. *Führung und Geleit: Ein Lebensgedenkbuch.* Nakao 5/29/42 (461).

————. [*The Secret of Youth*]. Could be *Geheimnisse des reifen Lebens.* Nakao 9/9–11/42 (486–87).

Dilthey, Wilhelm. *Friedrich der Grosse und die deutsche Aufklärung.* Hayashi 1/25/44 (115).

————. *Grundriss der allgemeinen Geschichte der Philosophie.* Sasaki 10/20/40 (121); 10/27/40 (127).

————. [*Man and his Worldview since the Renaissance*]. Nakao 7/23/43 (581).

————. [*Research on Weltanschauungslehre*]. Sasaki 10/20/40 (121); 10/27/40 (127).

————. [*The Structure of History*]. Could be *Aufbau der geschichtlichen Welt in den Geisteswissenschaften.* Sasaki 10/26/40 (125); 10/27/40 (127).

Eckermann, Johann Peter. *Gespräche mit Goethe in den letzten Jahren seines Lebens (Dialogue with Goethe).* Wada 7/17/41 (28).

Ehrlich, Eugen. [*Theory on the Rights and Ability*]. Nakao 8/14/42 (480).

Einstein, Albert. Sasaki 1/24/41 (178); 2/22/42 (296).

Engels, Friedrich. Sasaki 3/12/41 (196); 3/18/42 (304); 10/30/42 (339).

———. *Entwicklung des Sozialismus von der Utopie zur Wissenschaft.* Sasaki 1943 (433).

Feuerbach, Ludwig. Sasaki 10/20/40 (121); 11/1/40 (131); 11/3/40 (134); 11/9/40 (137); 12/5/40 (148); 4/4/41 (207); Wada 3/5/43 (64).

———. *Wesen des Christentums.* Hayashi 2/10/42 (77).

Fichte, Johann Gottlieb. Nakao 5/11/43 (570); 6/22/43 (576); Sasaki 10/20/40 (121); 10/27/40 (125); 11/8/40 (136); Wada 10/8/43 (101).

———. *Bestimmung des Menschen.* Sasaki 10/14/40 (118).

———. *Reden an die deutsche Nation.* Wada mid-April/45 (286).

Freyer, Hans. Sasaki 11/1/40 (132).

Fuchs, Karl Johannes. *Volkswirtschaftslehre.* Sasaki 1942 (432).

Goethe, Johann Wolfgang von. Hayashi 6/27/41 (54); 5/25/43 (97); 1945 (175); Nakao 3/19/42 (445); Sasaki 2/4/41 (183); 2/15/41 (185); 2/22/41 (190); 4/27/41 (220); 5/4/41 (222); 3/5/42 (300).

———. *Chichioya Toshite no Gēte* (Goethe as father) by Mitsui Mitsuya. Hayashi 5/25/43 (96).

———. *Dichtung und Wahrheit.* Nakao 3/30/43 (558); 8/9/43 (591).

———. *Faust.* Nakao 1/2/43 (525); Sasaki 7/3/41 (239); 4/18/42 (313); Wada 7/14/43 (78).

———. *Die Leiden des jungen Werthers.* Hayashi 5/23/44 (137); 5/31/44 (140); 6/9/44 (144); 6/12/44 (147); 7/8/44 (161); Nakao 7/30/40 (271); Sasaki 6/17/39 (30).

———. *Stirb und Werde.* Sasaki 1/28/41 (180).

———. *Wilhelm Meisters Wanderjahre, oder, die Entsagenden.* Hayashi 6/9/44 (144); 6/12/44 (147).

Droysen, Johann Gustav. Sasaki 11/1/40 (131).

Harnack, Adolph von. Hayashi 6/6/43 (98).

Hegel, Georg Wilhelm Friedrich. Nakao 1/9/41 (337); 3/10/43 (549); 5/11/43 (570); Sasaki 3/2/40 (67); 10/20/40 (121); 10/27/40 (125); 11/1/40 (132); 11/3/40 (134); 11/13/40 (141); 2/15/41 (185); 3/7/41 (192); 3/11/41 (195); 3/16/41 (200); 4/4/41 (207); 4/7/41 (209); 5/7/41 (223); 5/17/41 (228); Wada 3/5/43 (64).

———. *Hēgeru Tetsugaku to Benshōhō* (Philosophy of Hegel and the Dialectic) by Tanabe Hajime. In *Tanabe Hajime Zenshū*, vol. 3. Sasaki 12/19/40 (156).

———. *Vorlesungen über die Philosophie der Geschichte.* Sasaki 10/12/40 (116); 10/18/40 (119); 10/26/40 (124); 11/17/40 (142); 11/20/40 (144); 12/2/40 (147); 12/15/40 (154); 12/19/40 (156); 4/24/41 (218); 4/25/41 (218); 5/19/41 (228).

Heidegger, Martin. Hayashi 5/21/43 (96); 11/1/40 (130).

Heine, Heinrich. *Die Harzreise.* Sasaki 3/13/40 (70); 3/17/40 (71).

Hering, Wolfgang, ed. Julius Caesar's *Bellum Gallicum.* Hayashi 1945 (177).

Hesse, Hermann. Hayashi 12/21/40 (31); 4/30/44 (129); Nakao 6/16/39 (154–55).

———. *[Consolation for the Evening].* Nakao 5/24/40 (259).

———. *Demian.* Hayashi 4/22/40 (10); Sasaki 11/16/40 (142).

———. *Knulp: Drei Geschichten.* Sasaki 4/27/40 (90).

————. *Der Lateinschüler.* Nakao 6/15/39 (154).

————. *[The Moon and the Hay]*. Nakao 6/15/39 (154); 9/2/39 (177).

————. *Peter Camenzind.* Hayashi 1945 (182); Nakao 3/27/40 (241); Sasaki 4/23/40 (88).

————. *Schön ist die Jugend.* Sasaki 4/19/40 (87).

————. *[The Stream]*. Nakao 6/15/39 (154).

————. *Unterm Rad.* Hayashi 4/6/40 (6); 4/22/40 (9); 5/7/40 (11); Sasaki 5/2/40 (92).

————. *[Walking Travel in the Autumn]*. Sasaki 4/25/40 (89).

Hilferding, Rudolf. *Das Finanzkapital.* Sasaki 1943 (433).

Hilty, Carl [Swiss]. *[On Happiness]*. Nakao 10/8/40 (300); Sasaki 10/1/39 (42).

————. *Vom Kämpfen und Siegen.* Sasaki 7/7/43 (374).

Hitler, Adolf. Sasaki 11/11/40 (139); 2/20/41 (188); 12/11/41 (262); 1/24/42 (283); 1/25/42 (284).

————. *Mein Kampf.* Sasaki 2/14/43 (352); Wada 9/22/43 (80).

Kant, Immanuel. Nakao 1/7/41 (336); 3/28/43 (557); 5/11/43 (570); 10/13/43 (614); Sasaki 3/2/40 (67); 10/14/40 (118); 10/20/40 (121); 11/1/40 (132); 11/3/40 (134); 2/4/41 (183); 2/20/41 (188); 3/7/41 (192); 3/8/41 (193); 3/9/41 (193); 3/29/41 (202); 4/3/41 (205); 4/7/41 (209); 9/13/41 (248); 1/24/42 (284); 3/5/42 (300); 3/26/42 (309); 6/5/42 (321); Wada 3/5/43 (64).

————. *Kanto Jissen Tetsugaku no Kenkyū* (Research of Kant's Practical Reason) by Miwatari Yukio. Hayashi 8/31/40 (20).

————. *Kritik der praktischen Vernunft.* Sasaki 11/8/40 (136); 3/29/41 (202).

————. *Kritik der reinen Vernunft.* Sasaki 11/8/40 (136).

————. *[Die Metaphysik der Sitten in zwei Teilen]* (translated as *Jissen Rinri*). Nakao 6/29/39 (158).

————. *Principiorum primorum cognitionis metaphysicae nova dilucidatio* (noted simply as "Metaphysical Cognition"). Sasaki 10/12/40 (116).

————. *Prolegomena zu einer jeden künftigen Metaphysik, die als Wissenschaft wird auftreten können.* Sasaki 10/31/40 (130).

————. *Religion innerhalb der Grenzen der blossen Vernunft.* Sasaki 10/12/40 (116); 11/7/40 (136).

————. *[Study of Human Nature]*. Sasaki 3/17/40 (71).

Kautsky, Karl Johann. *[Theory of Currency] (Kaheiron).* Sasaki 1943 (434).

Lipps, Theodor. Nakao 4/28/40 (251); 8/30/40 (284); 3/11/41 (354); Sasaki 1/10/41 (171); 1/17/41 (175).

————. *Ethische Grundfragen: Zehn Vorträge.* Nakao 2/2/40 (222); Sasaki 1/13/41 (173).

List, Friedrich. *Das nationale System der politischen Ökonomie.* Sasaki 1943 (440).

Luther, Martin. *Von der Freiheit eines Christenmenschen.* Hayashi 12/2/41 (75); Sasaki 5/2/40 (92).

Mann, Thomas. Hayashi 5/20/42 (84).

————. *Buddenbrooks.* Hayashi 8/31/40 (20); his essay on it, (201–4).

————. *Enttäuschung.* Hayashi 1/1/44 (106).

————. *Tonio Kröger.* Hayashi 6/20/44 (149); 6/25/44 (155).

————. *Der Zauberberg.* Hayashi 8/31/40 (20); 1/3/44 (107).

Mannheim, Karl. Hayashi 11/8/41 (73).

Marx, Karl. Hayashi 1/25/44 (115); Nakao 1/2/41 (333); Sasaki 11/1/40 (131); 3/7/41 (192); 3/11/41 (195); 3/12/41 (196); 3/16/41 (200); 5/7/41 (223); 1/12/42 (279); 3/4/42 (300); 3/22/42 (306); 6/5/42 (321); 8/11/42 (331); 10/30/42 (340); 1/25/43 (349); 2/27/43 (354); 5/14/43 (360); 8/10/43 (381); 8/19/43 (386); Wada 3/5/43 (64).

———. *Grundrisse der Kritik der politischen Ökonomie.* Sasaki 1943 (433).

———. *Das Kapital.* Sasaki 2/9/43 (351); 8/10/43 (381); 1943 (433–34).

———. *Value, Price and Profit.* Sasaki 1943 (433).¥

———. *Wage-Labour and Capital.* Sasaki 1943 (433).

Menger, Carl. *Grundsätze der Volkswirtschaftslehre.* Sasaki 1942 (433).

Meyer-Förster, Wilhelm. *Alt-Heidelberg.* Hayashi 6/10/44 (146); Nakao 11/18/39 (195).

Mörike, Eduard Friedrich. *Mozart auf der Reise nach Prag.* Sasaki 5/19/41 (228).

Nietzsche, Friedrich. Hayashi 4/29/43 (95); 1945 (172); Nakao 11/22/40 (311); 12/9/40 (317); 12/30/40 (327); Sasaki 10/14/40 (118); 10/16/40 (119); 10/27/40 (125); 10/29/40 (128); 11/8/40 (137); 12/16/40 (154); 12/17/40 (154); 12/19/40 (156); 1/10/41 (171); 2/4/41 (183); 2/22/41 (190); 3/16/41 (200); 4/7/41 (208); Wada 10/12/41 (33).

———. *Also sprach Zarathustra.* Hayashi 11/12/40 (26); Nakao 7/19/43 (580); Sasaki 10/18/40 (120); 12/19/40 (156); Wada 12/31/41 (46).

———. *Menschliches, Allzumenschliches.* Sasaki. 10/20/40 (121).

———. *[Theory on Hygiene].* Nakao 3/22/40 (241).

———. *Vom Nutzen und Nachteil der Historie für das Leben.* Hayashi 1945 (175).

Novalis (Friedrich Freiherr von Hardenberg). *Heinrich von Ofterdingen.* Hayashi 6/25/44 (156)..

Planck, Max. Sasaki 12/10/40 (150).

Ranke, Leopold von. Hayashi 12/11/42 (94); 11/1/40 (131); Nakao 1/9/41 (337); Sasaki 11/5/40 (135); 11/9/40 (137); 2/16/41 (186).

———. *Die großen Mächte.* Sasaki 10/14/40 (118); 10/25/40 (124); 10/27/40 (125).

———. *[Questions and Answers on Politics].* Nakao 11/8/42 (508); Sasaki 5/7/41 (224).

———. *Ranke to Sekaishigaku* by Suzuki Narutaka. Hayashi 8/31/40 (20); 5/26/41 (48); Nakao 12/27/41 (417); Sasaki 10/12/40 (116); 10/14/40 (118); 10/20/40 (121); 10/26/40 (125); 10/27/40 (125).

———. *[Similarities and Differences between History and Politics].* Sasaki 5/7/41 (224).

———. *[Strengthening of the Nation] (Kyōkoku-ron).* Hayashi 8/31/40 (20).

———. *Über die Epochen der neueren Geschichte.* Hayashi 1/18/42 (76).

Remarque, Erich Maria. *Im Westen Nichts Neues.* Hayashi 6/8/44 (143); 6/22/44 (150); 6/25/44 (154); 7/1/44 (157); 1945 (172).

Rickert, Heinrich. *Kulturwissenschaft und Naturwissenschaft.* Hayashi 6/17/44 (148); 6/20/44 (149); 6/22/44 (151); 7/1/44 (158); Sasaki 10/12/40 (115); 10/20/40 (121); 10/26/40 (124).

Rilke, Rainer Maria. Hayashi 1945 (180).

————. *Der Apostel.* Hayashi 7/8/44 (161).

————. *Rodin.* Nakao 2/23/42 (437–39).

Rosenberg, Alfred. *Der Mythus des 20 Jahrhunderts.* Nakao 2/24/42 (439–40).

Schelling, Friedrich Wilhelm Joseph von. Sasaki 10/20/40 (121); 11/8/40 (136).

Schiller, Johann Christoph Friedrich von. Sasaki 2/20/41 (188); 5/17/41 (228); 5/21/41 (229); 3/5/42 (300).

————. *Die Götter Griechenlands.* Sasaki 5/17/41 (228).

————. *Kabale und Liebe.* Sasaki 2/16/41 (186).

————. *Die Künstler.* Sasaki 5/17/41 (228).

————. *Die Raüber.* Sasaki 2/12/41 (184).

————. *[Theory of Beauty and Art].* Sasaki 4/27/40 (90).

Schmidtbonn, Wilhelm. *Die Letzte.* Hayashi 7/8/44 (161); 7/9/44 (163).

Schmitt, Carl. Nakao 2/24/42 (439–40).

Schnitzler, Arthur. Hayashi 7/1/44 (158); 7/8/44 (161).

Schopenhauer, Arthur. Nakao 6/19/41 (372); Sasaki 2/22/41 (190).

Schubin, Ossip (Kirschner, Aloisra) [Czech]. *Die Geschichte eines Genies.* Translated by Mori Ōgai as *Umoregi.* Sasaki 3/30/40 (79).

Schweitzer, Albert [Alsace]. Sasaki 7/15/43 (377).

————. *Aus meinem Leben und Denken.* Sasaki 5/24/43 (362).

————. *The Warrior of Light and Love: A Biography of Schweitzer (Hikari to Ai no Senshi)* by Takeyama Michio. Sasaki 10/18/43 (396).

Simmel, Georg. Nakao 2/26/40 (235); 2/29/40 (236).

————. *[Essays].* Could be *Aufsätze 1887 bis 1890* or *Aufsätze und Abhandlungen.* Nakao 2/12/42 (435).

————. *Grundfragen der Soziologie.* Sasaki 3/29/41 (202).

————. *Schopenhauer und Nietzsche: Ein Vortragszyklus.* Nakao 10/4/42 (497).

Spyri, Johanna [Swiss]. *Heidi.* Nakao 6/7/41 (368).

Storm, Theodor. Hayashi 10/19/42 (93).

Taut, Bruno. *Nihonbi no Sai-hakken* (Rediscovery of Japanese aesthetics). Nakao 5/29/42 (461).

Thoma, Ludwig. *Lausbubengeschichten.* Hayashi 8/31/40 (20)

Tönnies, Ferdinand. Sasaki 1/12/42 (279).

Weber, Max. Hayashi 6/6/43 (98).

————. *Die protestantische Ethik und der Geist des Kapitalismus.* Sasaki 9/16/43 (389); 1943 (440).

————. *[Scholarship as Profession].* Sasaki 4/7/41 (208).

Wedekind, Frank. *Frühlings Erwachen.* Sasaki Summer/38 (426).

Windelband, Wilhelm. Wada 11/23/41 (36).

————. *[History and Natural Science].* Sasaki 10/12/40 (115).

————. *[On the Principles of Ethics].* Sasaki 4/3/41 (205).

Witkop, Philipp. *Kriegsbriefe gefallener Studenten.* Nakao 4/28/41(365).

Wittfogel, Karl August. *Scientific Research of Chinese Society.* Could be, *Die Wissenschaft der bürgerlichen Gesellschaft, eine Marxistische Untersuchung.* Sasaki 9/24/39 (40).

Kawakami Hajime. *Marukusu-shugi Keizaigaku* (Marxist economic theory.). Sasaki 4/24/41 (218).

English (including Irish and Scottish writers but excluding American writers)
Ashley, William James. Sasaki 10/14/40 (118).
―――. *The Economic Organization of England.* Sasaki 10/18/40 (119).
―――. *An Introduction to English Economic History and Theory.* Sasaki 10/12/40
   (116); 1/8/42 (278).
Bacon, Francis. [*Collected Works*]. Nakao 9/28/42 (494).
Bentham, Jeremy. Sasaki 1/12/42 (279); 1/14/42 (280).
Bury, J. B. (John Bagnell). Hayashi 10/19/42 (93).
―――. *Idea of Progress.* Hayashi 11/10/42 (93); 12/11/42 (94).
Byron, George Noel Gordon. Nakao 3/1/36 (83).
―――. [*Poetic Works of Byron*]. Sasaki 12/15/40 (154).
Carlyle, Thomas. Hayashi 7/8/44 (161); Sasaki 4/22/41 (216); 4/29/41 (221);
   11/21/41 (259); 12/19/41 (264); 1/1/42 (275); 7/15/42 (329).
―――. *Life of Schiller.* Sasaki 12/27/41 (265).
―――. *Philosophy of Clothes.* Trans. Nitobe Inazō. Sasaki 1/27/42 (286); 7/9/42
   (328).
―――. *Sartor Resartus.* Sasaki 4/18/41 (215); 4/24/41 (218); 4/25/41 (218); 12/9/41
   (262); 7/9/42 (328); 7/31/42 (331); 7/7/43 (374).
Chamberlain, Basil Hall. [*The Mouse is Still Alive*]. Sasaki 3/31/40 (79).
Dawson, Christopher. Hayashi 2/10/42 (77); 5/20/42 (84); 12/11/42 (94); 1945 (177).
―――. [*Beyond Politics*]. Hayashi 5/2/41 (42); 12/31/41 (75).
―――. *Inquiries into Religion and Culture.* Hayashi 4/26/42 (79).
―――. *Making of Europe.* Hayashi 4/26/42 (79); 4/27/42 (80).
―――. *Modern Dilemma.* Hayashi 11/3/41 (69).
―――. [*The New Leviathan*]. Hayashi 5/30/42 (86).
―――. *Progress and Religion.* Hayashi 7/5/41 (58); 8/21/41 (59); 8/31/41 (59);
   9/23/41 (60); 10/3/41 (61); 10/9/41 (62).
―――. *Religion and the Modern State.* Hayashi 6/16/41 (53); 11/29/41 (74);
   12/14/41 (75).
―――. [*St. Augustine and His Age*]. Hayashi 5/30/42 (86).
Dickinson, Goldsworthy Lowes. *A Modern Symposium.* Hayashi 4/17/41 (38);
   5/25/41 (48).
Dickens, Dickens. Wada 9/10/42 (56).
―――. *A Tale of Two Cities.* Sasaki 12/27/41 (265).
Doyle, Arthur Conan. *The Memoirs of Sherlock Holmes.* Sasaki Spring/35 (423)
Faraday, Michael. Sasaki 5/10/42 (315).
Fullarton, John. *On the Regulation of Currencies.* Sasaki 1943 (440)
Green, Thomas Hill. Wada 3/5/43 (64).
―――. *Tomasu Hiru Gurīn no Shisō Taikei* (Structure of thought of Thomas Green
   Hill) by Kawai Eijirō. Hayashi 4/22/40 (10).
Hearn, Lafcadio.Nakao 8/21/41 (390).
―――. Nakao 9/16/40 (295).
―――. *History of English Literature.* Sasaki 1/1/40 (56); 1/2/40 (56); 1/5/40 (57);
   1/31/40 (60); 3/13/40 (70); 3/17/40 (71); 3/27/40 (78).
―――. *Tōzai Bungaku Hyōron* (Comparison of literature east and west). Nakao
   9/16/40 (295).

Hogben, Lancelot (Thomas). [*Mathematics for One Million People*]. Hayashi 1945 (197).

Hudson, William Henry. *Green Mansions*. Hayashi 8/31/40 (20).

Huxley, Aldous. *Crome Yellow*. Hayashi 5/31/44 (140).

Joyce, James. *Portrait of the Artist as a Young Man*. Hayashi 5/7/40 (11); 8/25/40 (19); 8/27/40 (19).

Laski, Harold Joseph. *Political Thoughts in England from Hobbes to Bentham*. Hayashi 12/31/41 (75). Could be *Political Thought in England from Locke to Bentham*.

Lawrence, T. E. *Lawrence of Arabia*. Trans. of Lowell Thomas or Robert Graves (?) by Nakano Yoshio as *Arabia no Rōrensu*. Sasaki 7/23/41 (243).

Livingstone, David. Sasaki 12/27/41 (265).

Maine, Sir Henry James. *Summer*. Sasaki 1/12/42 (279).

Malinowski, Bronislaw. *Crime and Custom in Savage Society*. Nakao 4/9/43 (560).

Marlowe, Christopher. *Dr. Faustus*. Nakao 4/6/41 (360).

Marshall, Alfred. *Principles of Economics*. Sasaki 12/5/40 (149).

Maugham, W. Somerset. Hayashi 10/25/41 (66).

———. *The Moon and Sixpence*. Nakao 4/5/41 (358).

Mill, John Stuart. Hayashi 7/8/44 (161); Sasaki 10/14/40 (118); 11/6/40 (136); 9/13/41 (248); 1/14/42 (280); Wada 3/5/43 p.64.

———. *Autobiography*. Hayashi 5/31/44 (140); 6/12/44 (147); Nakao 3/4/43 (548).

———. *On the Subjection of Women*. Sasaki 11/15/40 (141).

———. *Principles of Political Economy*. Sasaki 1942 (433).

———. *Utilitarianism*. Sasaki 10/18/40 (120); 11/11/40 (138); 12/15/40 (153).

Newton, Isaac. Sasaki 1/24/41 (178); 2/22/42 (296).

Ricardo, David. *On the Principles of Political Economy and Taxation*. Sasaki 12/5/40 (149); 4/28/42 (313); 5/18/42 (316); 1942 (432);1/25/43 (349).

———. *Rikarudo Kachiron no Kenkyū* (Research on Ricardo's measure of value) by Mori Kōjirō. Sasaki 1942 (432).

Seeley, Sir John Robert. *The Expansion of England*. Hayashi 12/31/41 (75).

Shakespeare, William. Nakao 4/5/40 (246); 10/31/40 (302); Sasaki 10/25/40 (124).

———. *Antony and Cleopatra*. Sasaki 4/14/40 (84).

———. *Hamlet*. Nakao 1/30/40 (221).

———. *Julius Caesar*. Nakao 1/30/40 (220).

———. *King Lear*. Nakao 2/3/40 (223).

———. *Macbeth*. Nakao 2/4/40 (224).

———. *Othello*. Nakao 2/4/40 (224).

———. *Romeo and Juliet*. Nakao 2/10/40 (228); Sasaki 4/10/39 (18); 4/11/39 (18).

Shaw, George Bernard. *Back to Methuselah*. Nakao 8/16/40 (277).

———. *Man and Superman*. Nakao 8/15/40 (277); Sasaki 9/24/39 (41).

———. *Widowers' Houses*. Nakao 8/14/40 (275); 8/27/40 (283).

Shipton, Eric Earle. *Blank on the Map*. Sasaki 9/4/42 (334).

Smith, Adam. *An Inquiry into the Nature and Causes of the Wealth of Nations*. Sasaki 3/4/42 (300); 5/3/42 (314); 1/11/43 (349); 1/25/43 (349); 3/11/43 (356); 5/14/43 (361); 1942 (432).

Smith, Adam. *Smith and List* by Ōkōchi Kazuo. Sasaki 1942 (432).

Synge, John Millington. *Collected Plays.* Hayashi 8/31/40 (20)
Thomson, J. Arthur. *The Outline of Science.* Sasaki 5/10/42 (315).
Wells, H.G.. Sasaki 10/11/39 (44).
———. *Outline of History.* Sasaki 8 /24/41 (246).
Wilde, Oscar. Nakao 2/26/40 (235).
———. *The Canterville Ghost.* Sasaki 1/1/42 (276).
———. *The Model Millionaire.* Sasaki 1/1/42 (276).
———. *The Portrait of Mr. W. H.* Sasaki 1/1/42 (276).
———. *Soul of Man and Prison Writings* Nakao 2/25/40 (235); Sasaki 10/1/39 (42)

Russian
Berdyaev, Nikolai. Hayashi 1/18/42 (76); 1945 (177).
———. *The End of our Time* [sic, in English] Hayashi 1/22/42 (76).
———. *The Destiny of Man.* Hayashi 12/31/41 (75).
———. *The Meaning of History.* Hayashi 12/31/41 (75); 2/10/42 (77); 3/3/42 (78).
Chekhov, Anton Pavlovich. Nakao 5/27/40 (261); 10/31/40 (302); 12/30/40 (327).
———. *The Cherry Orchard.* Nakao 11/17/39 (194); Sasaki 11/7/41 (258).
———. *Dans le bas fond* [sic]. Nakao 7/27/40 (270); 8/14/40 (276).
———. *The Duel.* Sasaki 3/24/39 (13).
———. *Graine erante* [sic]. Nakao 8/8/40 (275).
———. *Salle 6 (Ward No. 6).* Nakao 6/24/40 (265).
———. *The Wife.* Sasaki 3/24/39 (13); 3/27/39 (13).
Dostoevsky, Fyodor Mikhailovich. Nakao 8/5/40 (274); Sasaki 10/14/40 (118); Wada 12/22/40 (9).
———. *The Brothers Karamazov.* Hayashi 8/31/40 (20); 12/11/42 (94); Sasaki 6/4/40 (105).
———. *Crime and Punishment.* Hayashi 5/30/42 (86); Nakao 11/26, 30/39 (201–2); Sasaki 3/23/39 (12); 3/24/39 (13).
———. *Dosutoefusukī no Seikatsu* (The Life of Dostoevsky) by Kobayashi Hideo. Nakao 11/24/39 (200)
———. *The House of the Dead.* Hayashi 6/16/43 (99); 1/1/44 (107).
———. *Poor Folk.* Hayashi 5/30/42 (86); Nakao 8/1/39 (166); 8/4/39 (167).
———. *[The Waves].* Nakao 8/4/39 (167).
Gogol, Nikolai Vasilievich. Nakao 5/27/40 (261).
———. *The Inspector General.* Nakao 3/28/40 (242).
———. *Nevsky Prospect.* Nakao 11/12/39 (194).
———. *The Nose.* Nakao 11/12/39 (194).
———. *The Overcoat.* Nakao 11/12/39 (194); Sasaki 2/1/41 (181).
Goncharov, Ivan Aleksandrovich. *The Frigate Pallas.* Nakao 8/8/42 (479).
Kropotkin, Pyotr Aleksyevich. *Memoirs of a Revolutionist.* Hayashi 6/16/43 (99).
Lenin, Vladimir Ilyich. Sasaki 2/9/43 (351).
———. *Imperialism.* Sasaki 1943 (433).
———. *State and Revolution.* Hayashi 7/8/44 (161). Recorded by his brother about his reading (229).
Merezhkovsky, Dmitri Sergyevich. Wada 9/10/42 (56).
———. *The Resurrection of the Gods.* Nakao 8/8/43 (590).

————. *Tolstoy and Dostoevsky*. Sasaki 10/12/40 (116); 10/13/40 (117); 10/14/40 (118).

Pushkin, Aleksandr Sergyevich. [*The Black Slaves of Peter the Great*]. Nakao 7/28/39 (165).

————. [*The Declaration*]. Nakao 7/28/39 (165).

————. *The Queen of Spades*. Nakao 7/28/39 (165).

Stalin, Joseph. Sasaki 2/o/43 (351).

Tolstoy, Lev Nikolayevich. Nakao 4/5/40 (246); Sasaki 2/4/42 (291).

————. *Anna Karenina*. Nakao 6/12/40 (652).

————. *Boyhood*. Nakao 5/13/40 (255).

————. *Childhood*. Nakao 5/2/40 (252).

————. *Collected Works of Tolstoy*, vol. 13. Nakao 8/31/40 (287).

————. *The Fruits of Enlightenment*. Nakao 7/19/40 (266).

————. [*Happiness of Marriage*]. Nakao 8/23/40 (280); Sasaki 10/20/40 (121).

————. *The Kreutzer Sonata*. Nakao 3/27/42 (446).

————. *Resurrenction*. Sasaki 8/6/39 (37); 8/8/39 (38).

————. [*The Soul*]. Nakao 6/12/39 (153); 7/22/41 (378).

————. *Tolstoy* by Mushanokōji Saneatsu. Nakao 9/21/39 (184).

————. *Twelve Lectures on Tolstoy (Torusutoi Jūnikō)*. Nakao 6/6/40 (262).

————. *Youth*. Nakao 5/20/40 (259).

————. *War and Peace*. Nakao 8/20, 24/41 (390); 6/12/40 (652); Sasaki 9/24/39 (40); 9/29/39 (42); 10/10/39 (44); Wada 2/8/42 (52).

————. *What Then Must We Do?*. Nakao 6/9/39 (153).

Trotsky, Lev Davidovich. Sasaki 1/8/41 (170).

Turgenev, Ivan Sergeyevich. Nakao 11/19/42 (198); 5/27/40 (261).

————. *Fathers and Sons*. Nakao 12/2939 (206); 8/31/40 (287); Sasaki Summer/38 (426).

————. *First Love*. Sasaki Summer/38 (426).

————. *Smoke*. Nakao 11/18/39 (196).

————. *Torrents of Spring*. Hayashi 4/22/40 (10); Nakao 12/7/39 (203).

————. *Virgin Soil*. Sasaki Summer/38 (426); 3/24/39 (13).

Classics

Aristotle. Nakao 6/20/41 (373–74); 9/3/41 (397); Sasaki 2/19/41 (188); 2/20/41 (188).

————. *Athenaion Politeia*. Nakao 8/8/41 (387).

————. *Ethica Nichomachea*. Hayashi 4/9/41 (36); 5/12/41 (46); Nakao 10/5/41. (400).

————. *Politics*. Sasaki 3/14/40 (70).

Augustine, St. (Aurelius Augustinus). *Confessions*. Hayashi 7/1/44 (158); Nakao 4/21/42 (452).

————. *Augustinus* by Matsumura Katsumi. Hayashi 12//2/41(75).

————. *Augustinus* by Mitani Takamasa. Hayashi 12/31/41 (75).

————. *Soliloquia*. Hayashi 1/25/44 (115); Nakao 10/11, 12, 13/43 (611–13).

Augustus. Hayashi 7/8/44 (161).

Cynics. Sasaki 2/20/41 (188).

Cyrenaics. Sasaki 2/20/41 (188).

Epicurus. Sasaki 2/20/41 (188).

Plato. Hayashi 5/7/40 (11).

————. *Apology (Apology of Socrates)*. Hayashi 11/12/40 (26); Nakao 4/8/40 (246); 7/19/41 (376); 11/5/42 (510).

————. *Collected Works of Plato*, vol. 3. Nakao 11/19/43 (631).

————. *Crito*. Hayashi 11/12/40 (26); Nakao 4/8/40 (247); 7/20/41 (377); 11/15/42/ (510).

————. *Euthydemus*. Nakao 11/15/42 (510).

————. *[On letters to friends]*. Nakao 7/29/41 (384).

————. *Phaedo*. Nakao 10/13/43 (613–15).

————. *Protagoras*. Nakao 4/18/40 (249); 7/22 and 25/41 (377, 379).

————. *Republic*. Nakao 9/29/40 (297); 7/23/41 (378); 8/30/41 (395); 10/6,7/41 (401).

————. *Symposium*. Hayashi 8/21/41 (59); 8/31/41 (59); Nakao 7/21/43 (581); Sasaki 5/21/41 (229); 5/24/41 (230).

————. *Theaetetus*. Nakao 7/29/41 (384).

Plutarch. *Parallel Lives*. Nakao 12/31/36 (116); 1/2/37 (118).

Scipio (C. S. Aemilianus Africanus Minor). Nakao 9/9/43 (599).

Socrates. Nakao 9/17/39 (183); 7/29/41 (384); 2/23/43 (546); 10/13/43 (615); Sasaki 11/6/40 (136); 1/6/41 (169); 2/20/41 (188); 4/7/41 (208); 8/7/41 (245); 4/29/42 (313). See also Plato.

Stephanus of Byzantium. Sasaki 10/30/42 (339).

Thucydides. Sasaki 3/5/42 (300).

Xenophon. *Memorabilia*. Nakao 3/1/43 (547).

Zeno of Citium. Hayashi 5/21/43 (96).

Hara Zuien. *Greek Myths*. Nakao 6/12/40 (264).

Greek philosophy (in general). Wada 3/24/41 (16–18).

American

Buck, Pearl S. *The Good Earth*. Hayashi 12/11/42 (94); Nakao 8/16/39 (171); Sasaki 3/24/39 (13).

————. *The Mother*. Nakao 9/4/39 (177).

Burnett, Frances Eliza Hodgson. *A Little Princess*. Sasaki 5/17/42 (316).

Chandler, Raymond. *Lady of the Lake*. Hayashi 8/31/40 (20).

Durant, Will. *Story of Philosophy*. Nakao 6/19/41 (372); 7/13/41 (375).

James, William. *Pragmatism*. Nakao 6/19/41 (373).

Franklin, Benjamin. *Autobiography*. Nakao 2/6/40 (226); Wada 7/17/41 (28).

Lincoln, Abraham. *Lincoln* by Tsurumi Yūsuke. Nakao 5/26/43 (572).

O. Henry (William Sydney Porter). *The Last Leaf*. Sasaki 4/19/39 (22)

Santayana, George. Nakao 6/19/41 (373).

Stowe, Harriet Beecher. *Uncle Tom's Cabin*. Sasaki 4/2/40 (81).

Webster, Jean. *Daddy-Long-Legs*. Nakao 11/26/43 (632).

Italian

Croce, Benedetto. Sasaki 2/16/41 (186).

————. *Croce* by Hani Gorō. Sasaki 2/6/43 (351).

————. [*Introduction to History*]. Sasaki 3/20/42 (305).

D'Annunzio, Gabriele. Sasaki 1/27/43 (350).

Dante Alighieri. *Divine Comedy*. Hayashi 1945 (172); Nakao 2/3/43 (537); 2/15/43 (542).

De Amicis, Edmondo. *Cuore*. Nakao 3/15/36 (86); Sasaki 8/12/42 (331).

Galilei, Galileo. Sasaki 1/24/41 (178); 3/21/43 (358).

Gentile, Giovanni. Nakao 2/24/42 (439–40).

Leonardo da Vinci. Book on Leonardo, trans. Yonekawa Masao. Nakao 8/8/43 (590).

Michelangelo Buonarroti. Sasaki 8/22/41 (245).

Mussolini, Benito. Sasaki 1/24/42 (283); 7/29/43 (379).

Pareto, Vilfredo. Nakao 2/24/42 (439–40).

Other Western

Andersen, Hans Christian [Danish]. *Improvizatoren*. Nakao 4/4, 5/40 (244).

Cervantes Saavedra, Miguel de [Spanish]. Hayashi 1/23/44 (114); 4/28/44 (128).

Hitopadeśa [Hindi]. Hayashi 1945 (174, 176).

Hus, Jan [Czech]. Sasaki 2/10/42 (292).

Ibsen, Henrik [Norwegian]. Wada 9/10/42 (56); 6/1/45 (301).

————. *A Doll's House*. Sasaki 10/5/40 (113).

————. *En Folkefiende*. Sasaki 10/5/40 (113).

Kierkegaard, Søren [Danish]. Nakao 12/30/40 (328); Sasaki 5/17/41 (228).

————. *The Sickness unto Death*. Sasaki 2/17/41 (187).

Meunier, Constantin [Belgian]. [*On Characters*]. Sasaki 5/4/40 (92); 10/20/40 (121).

Old Testament [Hebrew]. Nakao 1/9/42 (423); Sasaki 5/23/42 (317).

Spinoza, Baruch [Dutch]. Nakao 7/27/42 (476); Sasaki 11/8/40 (137).

————. *Tractatus Theologico-Politicus*. Nakao 8/3/42 (479).

————. *Treatise on the Improvement of the Understanding, Ethics, and Correspondence*. Nakao 7/26/42 (476).

Strindberg, August [Swedish]. Nakao 9/14/39 (180); Wada 9/10/42 (56).

————. *The Father*. Nakao 12/3/39 (202).

————. [*The Lightning*]. Sasaki 1/6/41 (169).

Works specifically on the West by Japanese

Hon'iden Yoshio. *Ōshū Keizaishi* (Economic history of Europe). Sasaki 1942 (432).

Matsubara Kan. *Seiyō Tetsugaku Monogatari* (Outline of Western philosophy). Nakao 1/17/41 (341).

Mitsukuri Genpachi. *Seiyōshi Kōwa* (Western history). Hayashi 1/28/41 (32); 2/10/41 (34); 11/29/41 (74).

Ōrui Noburu. *Seiyō Chūsei no Bunka* (Culture of the Middle Ages in the West). Hayashi 2/10/41 (34).

————. *Seiyōshi Shikō* (New research on history of the West). Hayashi 8/31/40 (20); Nakao 5/18/41 (366).

Ōtsuka Hisao. *Ōshū Keizaishi Josetsu* (Introduction to the economic history of Europe). Sasaki 1942 (432).

————. *Seiyō Kinsei Keizaishi* (Economic history of the West). Sasaki 9/16/43 (389, 440).

Sakaguchi Takashi. *Gaikan Sekai Shichō* (Outline of world intellectual currents). Hayashi 8/31/40 (20); Sasaki 12/19/40 (156).

Yamatani Shōgo. *Jesus.* Nakao 5/26/43 (572).

Chinese

Chu Hsi. [*The Art of the Mind*]. Hayashi 7/3/44 (160).

Confucius. Nakao 10/13/43 (614–15); 1/11/43 (638); Sasaki 4/24/41 (218).

Mencius. Sasaki 4/24/41 (218).

Wang Yang-ming. Nakao 12/25/42 (522).

Wu Ch'eng-en. *The Journey to the West.* Nakao 2/27/36 (83).

Ozaki Homitsu. *Gendai Shinaron* (Modern China). Sasaki 10/10/39 (44).

Tachibana Shiraki. *Chūkaminkoku Sanjūnenshi* (Thirty year history of the Republic of China). Hayashi 5/19/44 (135); 5/23/44 (138).

Takeuchi Yoshio. *Shina Shisōshi* (Intellectual history of China). Sasaki 4/24/41 (218).

Western Music

Bartók, Béla. Sasaki 5/10/39 (28).

Beethoven, Ludwig van. Sasaki 3/30/39 (15); 12/12/40 (153); Wada 12/11/41 (44).

———. The Eighth Piano Sonata ("Pathétique"). Sasaki 1/30/40 (59).

———. The Fifth Piano Concerto ("Emperor"). Sasaki 1/21/40 (58); 5/19/40 (99); 12/2/40 (147).

———. The First Piano Sonata. Sasaki 12/2/40 (147).

———. The Ninth Symphony. Sasaki 12/31/40 (159).

———. The Ninth Violin Sonata ("Kreutzer"). Sasaki 12/14/41 (263).

———. The Third Symphony ("Eroica"). Sasaki 5/10/39 (28); 1/20/40 (58); 12/14/41 (263).

———. Violin Concerto. Sasaki 11/26/40 (146); 1/12/41 (173).

Bizet, Georges. *Carmen.* Sasaki 3/27/39 (14).

Caruso, Enrico. Sasaki 3/19/39 (12).

Chopin, Frédéric François. Sasaki 3/5/42 (300).

———. Preludes. Sasaki 1/30/40 (59); 1/12/41 (173).

———. Sonata No. 2 ("Funeral March"). Sasaki 5/18/40 (99).

———. Waltz No. 1 in E-flat major ("Grande Valse brillante") Sasaki 5/18/40 (99).

Haydn, Franz Joseph. Wada 12/11/41 (44).

———. Serenade. Wada 1/4/45 (266).

Liszt, Franz. The Dance of the Dwarfs. Sasaki 1/30/40 (59).

———. Hungarian Rhapsodies, Op. 8. Sasaki 1/30/40 (59).

———. Mephisto Waltz. Sasaki 1/30/40 (59).

Mahler, Gustav. Das Lied von der Erde. Sasaki 1/23/41 (177).

Mozart, Wolfgang Amadeus. Flute Concerto. Sasaki 4/7/39 (17); 5/10/39 (28); 3/5/42 (300).

Ravel, Maurice. Bolero. Sasaki 3/20/39 (12).

Schubert, Franz Peter. Ave Maria. Nakao 3/2/40 (238).

———. Lindenbaum. Sasaki 11/19/40 (143); 11/22/40 (144).

———. Serenade. Nakao 4/22/39 (136).

———. Symphony No. 8 ("Unfinished"). Sasaki 1/23/41 (177).

————. Die Winterreise. Sasaki 1/12/41 (172).

Schumann, Robert. Sasaki 3/5/42 (300); Wada 12/11/41 (44).

————. Träumerei. Sasaki 4/13/40 (84).

Sibelius, Jean (Julias Christian). Violin Concerto. Sasaki 3/27/41 (202).

Smetana, Friedrich (Bedřich). Vltava (The Moldau). Sasaki 1/20/40 (58).

Strauss, Johann. *Die Fledermaus*. Sasaki 1/20/40 (58).

Western Films, by director

Clair, René. *The Ghost Goes West*. Sasaki 6/17/40 (107).

————. *Quatorze Juillet*. Sasaki 9/24/41 (253). (The title only given in Japanese, but the reference is obviously to the film and not to the play by Romain Rolland.)

Riefenstahl, Leni. *Fest der Schönheit*. Sasaki 1/3/41 (168); 1/4/41 (169); 3/16/41 (199).

————. *Fest der Völker*. Sasaki 1/4/41 (169).

————. *Triumph des Willens* (Triumph of the will). Sasaki 3/6/42 (301).

Western Films, by title

The Adventures of Robin Hood. Sasaki 3/20/40 (74)

La Bandéra. Sasaki 12/27/41 (265).

Bolero. Sasaki 3/20/39 (12).

Burgtheater. Sasaki 9/28/39 (41).

La Chanson de l'adieu. Sasaki 3/31/39 (15).

City Lights. Nakao 6/1/ 39 (150).

Heimat. Sasaki 2/4/41 (182).

Leise Flehen Meine Lieder. Nakao 10/25/39 (189–90).

Mazurka by Frédéric François Chopin (as a film). Sasaki 3/31/39 (15).

Mr. Smith Goes to Washington. Sasaki 10/16/41 (257).

Morocco. Nakao 10/25/39 (189–90).

The New World. Sasaki 3/13/40 (70).

The Plainsman. Sasaki 4/2/39 (16).

Poil de carotte. Nakao 9/4/39 (178).

Popeye. Sasaki 3/20/39 (12); 9/20/39 (39).

Tarzan. Nakao 3/16/35 (53).

Too Hot to Handle. Sasaki 4/2/39 (16).

Les Trois mousquetaires. Sasaki 3/13/40 (70).

Unternehmen Michael. Sasaki 4/30/40 (91).

Japanese

Abe Jirō. Hayashi 6/16/41 (53); Sasaki 10/11/42 (337).

————. *Bigaku* (Aesthetics). Sasaki 2/16/41 (186).

————. *Jinkaku Shugi*. Nakao 8/30/40 (283); 8/27/40 (282).

————. *Santarō no Nikki*. Nakao 2/27/40 (235); 4/2, 3/40 (243); 4/21, 22/40 (250–51); 12/9/40 (317); 6/21/42 (467); 4/16/43 (562).

Abe Yoshishige. Sasaki 10/14/40 (118); 10/29/40 (129); 12/9/40 (150); 12/10/40 (150); 1/21/41 (177); 2/2/41 (182); 2/12/41 (183); 2/18/41 (187); 4/1/41 (204); 5/10/41 (226); 5/24/41 (230); 6/12/41 (234); 9/12/41 (247); 12/4/41

(261); 12/9/41 (262); 1/27/42 (286); 2/2/42 (291); 5/30/42 (318); 6/27/42 (325); 9/2/42 (333); 12/12/42 (340); 5/24/43 (362); 10/15/43 (395); 11/10/43 (401).

———. *Jidai to Bunka.* Nakao 4/13/41 (362).

———. *Sanchū Zakki.* Sasaki 5/6/40 (93).

Abe Tomoji. *Fuyu no Yado.* Nakao 9/5/39 (178).

Akagi Kensuke. *Jinseiron.* Sasaki 10/18/41 (258).

Akegarasu Haya. *Da'en to En.* Nakao 11/13/41 (409).

———. *Dokuritsu-sha no Sengen.* Nakao 11/3/39 (193); 2/29/40 (237).

———. *Fukasetsuden no Ki.* Nakao 3/2/40 (238).

———. *Shinjitu ni Tsuite.* Nakao 8/10/39 (168).

Akutagawa Ryūnosuke. Nakao. 8/21/41 (390); Sasaki 10/29/40 (129); 12/19/40 (157); 1/8/42 (278).

———. *Chichi.* Nakao 7/25/39 (163).

———. *Imogayu, Shuju no Inori.* Nakao 11/12/39 (194).

———. *Itojo Oboegaki, Haguruma.* Nakao 7/26/39 (164).

———. *Kappa.* Nakao 6/24/39 (157).

———. *Mujina.* Nakao 7/25/39 (163).

———. *Ogata Ryōsai Oboegaki.* Nakao 7/25/39 (163).

———. *Saihō no Hito, Zoku Saihō no Hito, Juppon no Hari, Aru Kyūyū e Okuru Shuki.* Nakao 1/21/41 (343).

———. *Tabako to Akuma.* Nakao 5/5/40 (253); 7/19/40 (266).

Amano Teiyū. *Dōri eno Ishi.* Sasaki 10/29/40 (129).

———. *Gakusei ni Atauru Sho.* Nakao 7/23/43 (581); Sasaki 9/24/39 (41).

———. *Jissen to Shinnen.* Hayashi 1/23/44 (114).

Andō Shōeki. Sasaki 3/4/42 (299).

Anezaki Masaharu. *Konpon Bukkyō.* Nakao 4/4/42 (451).

Arakawa Yoshihiko. *Bungaku to Dentō.* Hayashi 5/30/42 (85).

Araki Kōtarō. *Kahei Gairon.* Sasaki 1943 (434).

Arakida Reijo. *Ike no Mozuku.* Nakao 3/23/41 (356).

ArishimaTakeo. *Chīsaki Mono e.* Nakao 3/3/42 (441); Sasaki 6/26/40 (109).

———. *Kain no Matsuei.* Sasaki 11/18/40 (143)

———. *Kurara no Shukke.* Sasaki 11/18/40 (143)

———. *Sengen.* Sasaki 6/26/40 (109)

———. *Umare Izuru Nayami.* Sasaki 6/26/40 (109); Nakao 3/3/42 P.441

Ayukawa Yoshisuke. *Mono no Mikata Kangae Kata.* Sasaki Summer/38 (426).

Azumi Tokuya. *Mirai eno Shuppatsu.* Nakao 6/1/38 (127).

Ban Kōkei. *Kinsei Kijinden.* Nakao 11/30/41 (413).

Daidōji Yūzan. *Budō Shoshin-shū.* Nakao 7/15/43 (579).

Date Shirō. *Kojin no Taido.* Nakao 12/30/40 (328).

Dōgen. Nakao 1/1, 3/43 (525–26); 2/21/43 (545); 3/15/43 (552); 10/13/43 (614); 1/11/43 (639).

———. *Shōbō Genzō Zuibun Ki,* Kaijō. ed. Nakao 1/28/43 (535); 2/11/43 (541); 4/8/45 (664).

Fujiki Kuzō. *Yuki, Iwa, Arupusu.* Sasaki 5/4/40 (92).

Fujimura Misao. Wada 3/24/41 (16).

Fujioka Sakutarō. Sasaki 10/20/40 (129).

————. *Kokubungakushi Kōwa.* Sasaki 6/19/39 (30).

Fujita Tōko. *Kōdōkan Kijutsugi.* Nakao 12/1/43 (634).

Fujitani Misao. *Kōkoku Nisen-roppyaku-nen-shi.* Nakao 1/16/42 (424).

Fujiwara Sakuhei. Sasaki 3/10/41 (194).

Fukada Hisaya. *Kōryō Jihō.* Sasaki 2/14/40 (64).

————. *Nise Shūdōin.* Hayashi 5/30/42 (86).

Fukai Eigo. *Tsūka Chōsetsuron.* Sasaki 1943 (434).

Fukuchi Gen'ichirō. *Bakufu Suibōron.* Nakao 9/4/42 (485).

————. *Kaiō Jidan.* Nakao 4/26/42 (455).

Fukuda Kunihiko. *Zentai to Zenki.* Nakao 3/19/43 (553).

Fukuzawa Yukichi. *Fukuō Jiden.* Hayashi 11/29/41 (74).

Futabatei Shimei. Sasaki 9/24/40 (111).

————. *Heibon.* Sasaki 6/14/40 (106).

————. *Sono Omokage.* Sasaki 6/14/40 (106)

Haga Yaichi. Sasaki 10/29/40 (129).

Hagiwara Sakutarō. Wada 12/18/41 (45).

Hamada Seiryō. *Kōkogaku Nyūmon.* Nakao 9/15/42 (490).

Hannya Shingyō Kōwa (Arai Uzen Kōjutsu). Nakao 3/22/40 (241).

Hani Gorō. *Bakumatsu ni Okeru Rinrishisō.* Sasaki 3/22/42 (306).

Hasegawa Nyozekan. *Hitai no Otoko.* Hayashi 4/22/40 (10).

Shōbō Ganzō Shakui by Hashida Kunihiko. Nakao 12/25/42 (522); 1/11/43 (638).

Hashimoto Minoru. *Hagakure Kenkyū.* Nakao 9/28/43 (603).

Hatano Kanae. *Kachi Gakusetsushi.* Sasaki 1942 (432).

————. *Kaitei Keizaigaku Nyūmon.* Nakao 4/21/42 (452).

————. *Keizaigaku Nyūmon.* Sasaki 5/9/41 (225).

————. *Keizai Kōwa.* Nakao 5/9/42 (460).

————. *Tōsei Keizai Kōwa.* Nakao 6/16/42 (465).

Hatano Seiichi. *Kirisutokyō no Kigen.* Hayashi 2/10/42 (77).

————. *Shūkyō Tetsugaku.* Sasaki 1/17/40 (57).

Hayashi Fumiko. *Hitori no Shōgai.* Sasaki 3/23/39 (12).

Hayashi Fusao. *Gokuchū-ki.* Nakao 10/8/40 (298).

————. *Saigō Takamori.* Nakao 10/13, 15, 16, 17/42 (500–3); 10/31/42 (506); 11/28/42 (514); 7/21/43 (581); 9/19/43 (601).

Heike Monogatari. Nakao 8/24/39 (174).

Higo Kazuo. *Nihon Kokka Shisō.* Nakao 1/9/41 (336); 2/10/42 (431).

————. *Nihon Shinwa Kenkyū.* Nakao 6/16/42 (465).

Higuchi Ichiyō. Sasaki 3/14/41 (198).

————. *Hanagomori.* Sasaki 4/19/40 (88).

————. *Nigorie.* Nakao 3/6/42 (443); Sasaki 2/22/40 (66).

————. *Ōtsugomori.* Sasaki 4/19/40 (88).

————. *Takekurabe.* Nakao 3/6/42 (443); Sasaki 2/22/40 (66).

————. *Yamiyo.* Sasaki 4/19/40 (88).

————. *Yuku Kumo.* Sasaki 4/19/40 (88).

Hijikata Masami. Sasaki 10/29/40 (129).

Hino Ashihei. *Ao Gitsune.* Nakao 11/9/43 (625).

————. *Utsukushiki Chizu*. Sasaki 1/4/41 (169).

Hiraizumi Kiyoshi. *Kikuchi Kin'nō-shi*. Nakao 11/12/41 (408).

Hirano Yoshitarō. *Minzoku Seijigaku no Riron*. Nakao 11/30/43 (633).

Hirayama Atsushi. Sasaki 8/26/41 (246).

Hisamatsu Sen'ichi. *Kodai Bungaku ni Arawaretaru Nihon Seishin*. In *Nihon Kokka Kagaku Taikei*. Vol. 1. Nakao 10/1/43 (604).

Hon'iden Yoshio. *Dai Tōa Keizai Kensetsu*. Nakao 10/20/42 (503).

————. *Tōsei Keizai no Riron*. Sasaki 1942 (432).

Hori Ichirō. *Nihon Jōdai Bunkashi to Bukkyō*. Nakao 4/23/41 (363).

Hori Tatsuo. *Kagerohu no Nikki*. Nakao 1/10/43 (529, 531).

————. *Moyuru Hō*. Sasaki 3/27/41 (202).

————. *Naoko*. Hayashi 5/30/42 (86).

————. *Rūbensu no Giga*. Sasaki 3/27/41 (202).

————. *Sei Kazoku*. Hayashi 5/30/42 (86).

Hozumi Shigetō. *Hanrei Hyakuwa*. Nakao 5/5/42 (459).

Ibuse Masuji. *Tajinkoson*. Sasaki 2/28/40 (67).

Ichihara Toyota. *Shikō, Ishiki, Aijō*. Hayashi 12/11/42 (94).

Ide Takashi. *Tetsugaku Izen*. Hayashi 2/10/41 (34); Nakao 5/25/40 (260); Sasaki 1/4/40 (56); 1/18/40 (58).

Ienaga Saburō. *Nihon Shisō-shi niokeru Shūkyōteki Shizenkan no Tenkai*. Hayashi 4/23/44 (138).

Igarashi Chikara. *Nihon Densetsushū*. Nakao 5/15/42 (460).

Ikari Shizan and Nakano Tōsui. *Sugiura Shigetake Zadan Roku*. Nakao 8/30/43 (595).

Ikuta Shungetsu. *Shinjitsu ni Ikiru Nayami*. Nakao 12/9/40 (316).

Inō Tadataka. Sasaki 3/11/42 (303).

Inoue Gakumaro. *Shin-taisei Kenpō Hōkan*. Nakao 9/10/43 (600).

Inoue Hiroshi. *Jinsei to Kōfuku*. Nakao 8/25/39 (174).

Inoue Kaoru. Sasaki 3/22/42 (306).

Inoue Masatsugu. *Yamato Koji*. Hayashi 5/30/42 (86).

Ishida Baigan. Sasaki 3/4/42 (299).

Ishigami Gen'ichirō. *Kurāku-shi no Kikai*. Hayashi 12/11/42 (94).

————. *Seishinbyōgaku Kyōshitsu*. Hayashi 11/3/42 (93).

————. *Tominaga Chūki*. Nakao 11/18/40 (310).

Ishikawa Takuboku. Nakao 6/5/39 (151).

Ishikawa Tatsuzō. *Kekkon no Seitai*. Nakao 1/8/40 (213).

————. *Sōbō*. Hayashi 5/30/42 (86); Nakao 1/30/40 (221).

————. *Tenraku no Shishū*. Wada 4/18/45 (288).

————. *Tsuta-kazura*. Nakao 1/30/40 (221).

Ishin Shiryō Hensan Jimukyoku. *Gaikan Ishin-shi*. Hayashi 5/13/41 (47).

Itō Hirobumi. Sasaki 3/22/42 (306).

————. *Kenpō Gikai*. Nakao 8/22/42 (483).

Iwakura Masaharu. *Sonchō Nikki*. Hayashi 1/5/42 (75).

Iwamoto Jun. Sasaki 11/21/41 (260).

Iwata Toyo'o. *Kaigun Zuihitsu*. Hayashi 5/19/44 (135).

Izumi Kyōka. Nakao 1/10/43 (531); 1/11/43 (638); Sasaki 4/1/40 (80); 3/14/41 (198).

———. *Chūmonchō, Seidan Jūnisha*. Nakao 1/4/43 (528).

———. *Fukei-zu, Muyū-ju, Obentō San'ninmae, Shunchū, Shunchū Gokoku*. Nakao 1/3/43 (525).

———. *Gion Monogatari, San'nin no Mekura no Hanashi*. Nakao 1/3/43 (527).

———. *Kaban no Kai, Nihon-bashi*. Nakao 1/3/43 (527).

———. *Kōya Hijiri*. Hayashi 12/11/42 (94); Nakao 1/19/41 (342); Sasaki 3/10/40 (69).

———. *Mayu Kakushi no Rei*. Hayashi 12/11/42 (94); Nakao 1/19/41 (342); Sasaki 3/10/40 (69).

———. *Murasaki, Tazuna, Shinsaku*. Nakao 1/5/43 (528).

———. *Shirasagi*. Nakao 1/4/43 (528); Sasaki 3/30/40 (79).

———. *Uta Andon*. Hayashi 12/11/42 (94); Nakao 1/4/43 (528); Sasaki 3/10/40 (69).

Kada Tetsuji. *Nihon Keizai Gakusha no Hanashi*. Sasaki 3/4/42 (299).

Kagawa Toyohiko. *Sono Ryūiki*. Nakao 11/3/39 (193).

Kaibara Ekken. Hayashi 4/28/44 (128).

———. *Kadō Kun*. Nakao 9/13/42 (489).

———. *Yōjō Kun*. Nakao 9/11/42 (487).

Kainō Michitaka. *Hōritsu Shakaigaku no Shomondai*. Nakao 3/2/43 (548); 7/27/43 (581).

Kaji'i Motojirō. Hayashi 10/29/41 (66).

———. *Remon*. Hayashi 11/2/41 (67).

Kakesu Katsuhiko. *Kami-nagara no Michi*. Nakao 9/28/43 (603).

———. *Kokka no Kenkyū*. Nakao 10/2/43 (604).

Kamo no Chōmei. *Hōjō-ki*. Nakao 12/19, 20, 23/40 (324–25).

Kanba Toshio. "Rekishiteki Kōi" (lecture). Sasaki 11/1/40 (131); 11/3/40 (134).

———. *Rekisi ni okeru Rinen*. Sasaki 12/19/40 (156); 2/15/41 (185).

———. *Rekishi Shugi no Kiki*. Sasaki 2/16/41 (186).

———. *Sei ni Taisuru Rekishi no Rigai*. Sasaki 2/16/41 (186).

Kanokogi Baishin. *Sentōteki Jinseikan*. Nakao 1/23/41 (344).

Katō Kanji. Nakao 7/28/40 (270).

Kawabata Yasunari. *Asakusa Kurenai Dan*. Nakao 9/29/39 (185).

———. *Dōyō*. Sasaki 4/1/40 (80).

———. *Fubo*. Nakao 10/1/39 (186); Sasaki 7/12/41 (241).

———. *Itaria no Uta*. Nakao 10/1/39 (186).

———. *Izu no Odoriko*. Nakao 9/1/39 (176); Sasaki 3/31/40 (80).

———. *Jojōka*. Nakao 9/2/39 (177); Sasaki 4/1/40 (80).

———. *Kinjū*. Sasaki 4/1/40 (80).

———. *Kore o Mishi Toki*. Nakao 10/1/39 (186); Sasaki 7/14/41 (242).

———. *Onsen* Yado. Sasaki 3/31/40 (80).

———. *Yūbae Shōjo*. Nakao 10/1/39 (186); Sasaki 7/14/41 (242).

———. *Yukiguni*. Nakao 10/1/39 (186); Sasaki 7/12/41 (241).

Kawaguchi Ekai. *Shaka no Isshō*. Nakao 8/19/39 (173).

Kawai Eijirō. Wada 3/5/43 (64).

———. *Bungaku no Shūi*. Hayashi 4/22/40 (10).

———. *Dai'ichi Gakusei Seikatsu*. Hayashi 4/22/40 (10).

———. *Daini Gakusei Seikatsu*. Hayashi 4/22/40 (10).

————. *Fashizumu Hihan*. Hayashi 4/22/40 (10).

————. *Gakusei to Dokusho (Dokusho no Igi)*. Nakao 8/8, 9, 10/39 (168); Sasaki 4/22/39 (23); 1939 (428).

————. *Gakusei to Kyōyō*. Nakao 1/11/40 (214).

————. *Gakusei to Rekishi*. Hayashi 8/31/40 (20).

————. *Kanshō to Hansei*. Hayashi 4/22/40 (10).

————. *Shakai Shisōka Hyōden*. Hayashi. 4/22/40 (10); Sasaki 1/14/42 (280); 1/22/42 (281).

————. *Shosai no Mado-yori*. Hayashi 4/22/40 (10).

————, ed. *Gakusei to Sentetsu*. Nakao 5/26/43 (572); 6/22/43 (577); Sasaki 7/20/41 (243).

Kawakami Bizan. *Kan'non Iwa*. Sasaki 3/12/40 (70).

Kawakami Hajime. Sasaki 4/25/41 (218); 5/30/42 (319); 6/5/42 (321).

————. *Marukusu-shugi no Kisoriron*. Sasaki 1942 (432).

————. *Shihonron Nyūmon*. Sasaki 1942 (433).

Kawazu Susumu. *Kaitei Keizai Genron*. Nakao 8/14/42 (479).

Kihira Masami. *Chi to Gyō*. Nakao 1/24/42 (425); 6/27/42 (428).

Kikuchi Kan. *Nihon Bushōdan*. Nakao 3/3/42 (442).

————. *Onshū no Kanata ni*. Nakao 2/16/35 (42).

Kishida Kunio. *Danryū*. Hayashi 10/28/40 (22).

Kita Ikki. *Shina Kakumei Gaishi*. Nakao 10/3/43 (605).

Kobayashi Hideo. Sasaki 2/15/41 (185).

Kobayashi Issa. Nakao 10/6/41 (401).

Kōda Rohan. *Gojū-no-tō*. Nakao 10/29/39 (191).

Koizumi Shinzō. Sasaki 10/14/40 (118); 12/5/40 (149).

————. *Keizai Genron*. Sasaki 1942 (432).

Kojiki. Nakao 11/19/40 (310); Sasaki 5/21/41 (229); 3/4/42 (300).

Komiya Toyotaka. *Natsume Sōseki*. Sasaki 2/27/43 (354); 3/10/43 (355); 8/29/43 (388).

Konishi Shirō. *Nihon Kindaishi*. Hayashi 12/11/42 (94).

Kōsaka Masaaki. *Minzoku no Tetsugaku*. Nakao 10/6/42 (497).

————. *Rekishiteki Sekai*. Hayashi 8/31/40 (20); 2/10/41 (34); 8/21/41 (58); Sasaki 12/19/40 (156); 1/20/41 (177).

————. *Rekishi Tetsugaku to Seiji Tetsugaku*. Hayashi 8/31/40 (20); Nakao 1/26/41 (345).

Koyama Iwao. *Bunka Ruikeigaku Kenkyū*. Hayashi 8/31/40 (20).

Kōzu Seiji. *Wakaki Tetsugakuto no Shuki*. Nakao 8/27/42 (484); 9/30/42 (495).

Kubota Mantarō. His work (unspecified) in. *Bungakkai* (October issue). Hayashi 12/11/42 (94).

————. *Hagi Susuki*. Hayashi 12/11/42 (94).

————. *Suegare, Ōdera Gakkō*. Hayashi 12/11/42 (94).

Kudō Gishū. *Jinsei no Seika*. Nakao 8/26/39 (175).

Kunikida Doppo. Nakao 8/24/37 (123).

————. *Akuma*. Nakao 6/3/39 (150–51).

————. *Azamukazaru no Ki*. Nakao 9/5/43 (597); 10/20/43 (616).

————. *Bajō no Tomo*. Sasaki 2/28/40 (67).

————. *Gyūniku to Bareisho.* Nakao 4/11/40 (248); 6/17/41 (371); Sasaki 2/28/40 (67).

————. *Hibon Naru Bonjin.* Sasaki 2/28/40 (67).

————. *Hinode.* Sasaki 2/28/40 (67).

————. *Hiru no Kanashimi.* Sasaki 2/28/40 (67).

————. *Jonan.* Nakao 6/17/41 (371–72); Sasaki 2/28/40 (67).

————. *Musashino.* Sasaki 3/10/40 (69).

————. *Oka no Shirakumo.* Nakao 7/22/40 (267).

————. *Shōjikimono.* Nakao 6/17/41 (371–72); Sasaki 2/28/40 (67).

————. *Shuchū Nikki.* Nakao 6/3/39 (150–51); Sasaki 2/28/40 (67).

————. *Tanpenshū.* Sasaki 2/12/40 (62).

————. *Tomioka Sensei.* Nakao 6/17/41 (371–72); Sasaki 2/28/40 (67).

————. *Unmeironsha.* Nakao 6/3/39 (150–51); Sasaki 2/28/40 (67); 2/7/42 (292).

Kurano Kenji. *Kojiki no Kenkyū.* Nakao 1/21/41 (343).

Kurata Momozō. Nakao 8/5/40 (273).

————. *Ai to Ninshiki tono Shuppatsu.* Hayashi 4/22/40 (9); 8/31/40 (20); Nakao 8/3/40 (272); 11/25/40 (311).

————. *Chichi no Shinpai.* Nakao 1/25/40 (218).

————. *Fuse Taishi no Nyūzan.* Nakao 7/27/39 (164).

————. *Shukke to Sono Deshi.* Hayashi 5/17/44 (134); 5/19/44 (135); Nakao 12/23/39 (206); 1/13/40 (215); Sasaki Summer/38 (426); 6/2/42 (320).

Kuroda Satoru. *Kaitei Nihon Kenpōron.* Nakao 11/3, 5/42 (507).

Maide Chōgorō. *Keizan Gakusetsushi Gaiyou.* Sasaki 1942 (432).

————. *Keizai Genron.* Sasaki 1942 (432).

Manyōshū. Sasaki 5/21/41 (229).

Maruyama Kaoru. *Namida Shita Kami.* Hayashi 5/31/44 (140).

————. *Tenshō Narutokoro.* Hayashi 5/10/44 (133); 5/23/44 (138).

Maruyama Sadao. Sasaki 5/28/42 (318).

Masamune Hakuchō. Sasaki 3/14/41 (198).

————. *Bikō.* Sasaki 6/3/40 (105).

————. *Irie no Hotori.* Sasaki 6/3/40 (105).

————. *Umazarishi Naraba.* Sasaki 6/3/40 (105).

Masaoka Shiki. Sasaki 3/27/41 (201).

Masuya Fumio. *Bukkyōron.* Nakao 8/22/40 (279).

Matsuda Michio. *Kekkaku.* Nakao 10/7/41 (401).

Matsuo Bashō. Hayashi 1/1/44 (106).

Meiji Tenno. Nakao 2/8/35 (39).

Miki Kiyoshi. Sasaki 10/26/40 (125).

————. *Rekishi Tetsugaku.* Hayashi 2/10/41 (34); 11/29/41 (74); Nakao 11/30/41 (412); Sasaki 10/23/40 (122); 11/3/40 (134).

————. *Tetsugaku Nyūmon.* Nakao 2/7/42 (431).

Minamoto no Sanetomo. *Kinkai Wakashū.* (Saitō Mokichi ed.,) Nakao 2/9/43 (540).

Minobe Tatsukichi. *Gyōseihō I.* Nakao 3/17/43 (553); 8/11/43 (591).

————. *Gyōseihō II.* Nakao 3/19/43 (553).

————. *Gyōseihō Sōsoku.* Nakao 8/14/43 (591).

————. *Nihon Gyōseihō.* Nakao 9/11/43 (600).

Mitani Takamasa. Sasaki 2/20/41 (188); 1/12/42 (279); 3/26/42 (309); 4/29/42 (313); 5/13/42 (316); 6/5/42 (321).

———. *Kokka Tetsugaku.* Sasaki 10/21/41 (258).

Mitsuda Iwao. *Nihon no Kōryō.* Nakao 9/24/43 (601).

———. *Shōwa Fū'un Roku.* Nakao 8/15/43 (592).

Miyake Shōtarō. *Saiban no Sho.* Nakao 5/22/43 (572).

Miyazawa Kenji. Sasaki 2/11/43 (352).

———. *Gusukōbudori no Denki.* Sasaki 2/11/43 (352).

———. *Karasu no Hokuto Shichisei.* Sasaki 6/26/43 (369).

———. *Matsuri no Ban.* Sasaki 6/26/43 (370).

Mori Ōgai. *Abe Ichi Zoku.* Nakao 2/23/40 (233).

———. *Fumizukai.* Sasaki 5/18/40 (99).

———. *Gan.* Nakao 5/11/40 (254); Sasaki 1/3/41 (168).

———. *Goji'in-gahara no Katakiuchi.* Nakao (233).

———. *Ita Sekusuarisu.* Sasaki 3/19/43 (357).

———. *Maihime.* Sasaki 6/18/40 (99).

———. *Ōshio Heihachirō oyobi Furoku.* Nakao 2/24/40 (234).

———. *Utakata no Ki.* Sasaki 5/18/40 (99).

Mōri Kikue. Sasaki 5/28/42 (318).

Motoori Norinaga. Nakao 5/20/43 (641); Sasaki 2/12/41 (183); 3/4/42 (300).

———. *Gyojū Gaigen.* Nakao 7/2/42 (470).

———. *Isonokami Shishuku Gen.* Nakao 7/19/42 (471).

———. *Kojiki-den.* Nakao 12/24/40 (325).

———. *Suzuya Mondō Roku.* Nakao 5/2/42 (457).

———. *Tamakatsuma.* Nakao 5/31/42 (462).

———. *Uiyamafumi.* Hayashi 12/11/42 (94); Nakao 5/2/42 (457).

Muraoka Noritsugu. *Nihon Bunkashi Gaikan.* Nakao 3/11/41 (354).

———. *Nihon Bunkashi Gaisetsu.* Nakao 2/11/42 (432).

———. *Nihon Seishinron.* (in. *Nihon Kokka Kagaku Taikei. Vol.1*) Nakao 10/1/43 (604).

———. *Nihon Shisōshi Kenkyū.* Nakao 2/1/42 (428).

———. *Zoku Nihon Shisōshi Kenkyū.* Nakao 4/28/42 (455).

Murasaki Shikibu. *Murasaki Shikibu Nikki.* Nakao 12/29/40 (326).

Murase Sachiko. Sasaki 5/28/42 (318).

Murobushi Takanobu. ed.. *Gendai Gakusei wa Nanio Nasubekika.* Nakao 5/19/41 (367).

Murou Saisei. *Waga Tomo.* Nakao 11/21/43 (631).

Mushanokōji Saneatsu. Sasaki 4/30/41 (221); 7/17/42 (330).

———. *Aiyoku.* Nakao 6/9/39 (152).

———. *Daisan no Inja no Unmei.* Nakao 7/24/39 (163).

———. *Jinrui no Ishi ni Tsuite.* Hayashi 6/23/40 (14); Nakao 1/23/40 (217).

———. *Jinseiron.* Sasaki 6/19/39 (30).

———. *Kōfuku-mono.* Nakao 8/8/39 (168).

———. *Kōfukunaru Kazoku.* Hayashi 5/30/41 (51).

———. *Ningen Banzai.* Sasaki 6/19/39 (30).

———. *Saigō Takamori.* Nakao 9/22/42 (493).

————. *Shaka.* Nakao 5/30,31/39 (149–50).

————. *Sono Imōto.* Nakao 6/18/39 (155); Sasaki 4/1/40 (80).

————. *Yūjō.* Nakao 6/14/39 (154); Sasaki Summer/38 (426).

Mutai Risaku. *Shakai Sonzairon.* Nakao 2/22/42 (436).

————. *Zentai Shugi Gairon.* Nakao 2/24/42 (439).

Mutō Sanji. Nakao 8/12/37 (119).

Mutsu Munemitsu. *Ken Ken Roku.* Hayashi 1/28/41 (33); 5/13/41 (47); Nakao 4/9/42 (451).

Nagai Kafū. Hayashi 10/3/41 (62); 10/25/41 (66).

————. *Ude Kurabe.* Sasaki 1/2/41 (168).

Nagatsuka Takashi. *Tsuchi.* Nakao 5/21/39 (146); 5/24/39 (147).

Nagayo Yoshirō. *Mutsu Naojirō.* Nakao 7/23/39 (162).

————. *Nagayo Yoshirō-shū.* Sasaki 2/22/41 (190).

————. *Seidō no Kirisuto.* Nakao 7/23/39 (162); Sasaki 3/13/41 (197).

————. *Taitei Kōki.* Sasaki 7/20/41 (243).

————. *Takezawa Sensei toiu Hito.* Nakao 9/13/40 (292); Sasaki 9/29/41 (253).

Naitō Arou. Sasaki 5/28/42 (318).

Naitō Torajirō. Nakao 12/10/41 (415).

Naka Kansuke. Sasaki 1/31/42 (288); 2/4/42 (291); 5/31/42 (320); 3/10/43 (356); 6/14/43 (366).

————. *Gin no Saji.* Sasaki 7/10/42 (329); 7/17/42 (330).

————. *Hichō.* Sasaki 9/9/42 (334).

Nakagawa Yoichi. Wada 12/18/41 (45).

————. *Ten no Yūgao.* Hayashi 8/31/40 (20); Sasaki 1/2/41 (168); 10/2/41 (255); 9/9/42 (334).

Nakagawa Zen'nosuke. *Nihon Shinzoku-hō.* Nakao 3/7/43 (548).

Nakamoto Takako. *Wakaki Ai no Hi.* Sasaki 4/12/41 (214); 4/14/41 (214).

Nakamura Kichiji. Sasaki 10/6/42 (336).

Nakamura Takaya. *Kindaishi ni Arawaretaru Nihon Seishin.* (In. *Nihon Kokka Kagaku Taikei.* Vol.1) Nakao 10/1/43 (604).

Nakaya Ukichirō. *Zoku Yuki no Hana.* Sasaki 12/28/41 (266).

Nakayama Ichirō. *Kōsei Keizaigaku.* Nakao 8/24/43 (594).

Naniwada Haruo. *Kokka to Keizai.* Sasaki 1/11/43 (349).

Naoki Sanjūgo. Wada 6/7/43 (74).

————. *Kusunoki Masashige.* Nakao 4/26/42 (454).

Nasu Hiroshi. *Kōseinaru Kosaku-ryō.* Nakao 7/5/43 (578).

Natsume Sōseki. Nakao 10/31/39 (191); Sasaki 4/1/40 (80); 5/6/40 (93); 1/11/41 (172); 3/27/41 (201); 4/4/41 (206); 3/10/43 (356); Wada 9/10/42 (56).

————. *Bocchan.* Nakao 8/19/43 (594); Sasaki 3/11/43 (356).

————. *Garasudo no Naka.* Nakao 3/4/42 (442); Wada 5/30/45 (299).

————. *Gubijinsō.* Nakao 5/17,18/39 (144–45); Sasaki 3/29/41 (202); 3/19/43 (357).

————. *Higan-sugi Made.* Sasaki 4/1/41 (204); 4/4/41 (206).

————. *Kōjin.* Hayashi 7/16/40 (16); Nakao 5/9/39 (141); 5/16/39 (144); Sasaki 6/27/42 (324); Wada 5/31/45 (300).

————. *Kokoro.* Hayashi 12/11/42 (94); Nakao 4/23/39 (136); 10/25, 28/39 (189–90); Sasaki 7/1/42 (325); Wada 2/1/45 (274).

———. *Koto no Sorane*. Hayashi 8/1/40 (17).

———. *Kusa-makura*. Sasaki 4/28/39 (25).

———. *Meian*. Hayashi 7/27/40 (15); Nakao 4/15/39 (133); 5/9/39 (141).

———. *Michikusa*. Hayashi 12/11/42 (94); Nakao 5/4/39 (140); 5/9/39 (141).

———. *Mon*. Hayashi 7/27/40 (16); Nakao 6/12/41 (370).

———. *Sanshirō*. Nakao 5/2, 3, 4 /39 (139–40); 8/28/39 (175); Sasaki Summer/38 (426); 4/2/41 (205).

———. *Shumi no Iden*. Hayashi 8/1/40 (17).

———. *Sorekara*. Hayashi 7/27/40 (16); Nakao 5/4/39 (140); Sasaki 4/6/41 (207).

———. *Sōseki Zenshū*. Ed. by Amano, Abe, and Nagayo. Hayashi 4/22/40 (10); Sasaki 2/22/41 (190).

———. *Wagahai wa Neko de Aru*. Hayashi 8/1/40 (17); 8/31/40 (20); 12/11/42 (94); Sasaki 3/25/40 (76).

———. *Yōkyoshū*. Hayashi 8/1/40 (17).

Nichiren. Hayashi 4/28/44 (128).

Ninomiya Sontoku. Nakao 2/5/36 (78).

Nishida Kitarō. Nakao 11/22/40 (310); 1/7/41 (336); 4/14/43 (560); 4/16/43 (562); 5/1/43 (566); 5/5/43 (568); 5/13/43 (571); 10/8/43 (608); 5/20/43 (642); Sasaki 10/20/40 (121); 10/11/42 (337).

———. *Chishiki no Kyakkansei ni Tsuite*. Nakao 9/8/43 (598).

———. *Geijutsu to Dōtoku*. Nakao 3/22, 24/43 (554).

———. *Hataraku-mono kara Miru-mono e*. Nakao 3/29/43 (558.).

———. *Ippansha no Jikakuteki Taikei*. Nakao 4/26/43 (565).

———. *Ishiki no Mondai*. Nakao 3/21/43(553).

———. *Jikaku ni okeru Chokkan to Hansei*. Nakao 3/15/43 (552).

———. *Kokka Riyū no Mondai*. Nakao 4/27/43 (565).

———. *Mu no Jikakuteki Gentei*. Nakao 4/30/43 (566).

———. *Nihon Bunka no Mondai*. Nakao 2/19/41 (349).

———. *Shisaku to Taiken*. Nakao 4/15/39 (133); 3/26/43 (555); 3/29/43 (558).

———. *Sōda Hakase ni Kotafu* (in *Hataraku-mono kara Miru-mono e*.) Nakao 3/28/43 (557).

———. *Tetsugaku no Konpon Mondai*. Nakao 7/29/43 (584).

———. *Tetsugaku no Konpon Mondai Zokuhen*. Nakao 7/31/43 (585).

———. *Tetsugaku Ronbun-shū*, vol. 1: *Tetsugaku Taikei eno Kizu*. Nakao 8/1/43 (586).

———. *Tetsugaku Ronbun-shū*, vol. 3. Nakao 8/4/43 (589).

———. *Tetsugaku Ronbun-shū*, vol. 4. Nakao 8/6/43 (589).

———. *Zen no Kenkyū*. Hayashi 2/10/41 (34); 8/21/41 (59); Nakao 2/21/43 (545); 3/10/43 (549); Sasaki 1/20/40 (58).

———. *Zoku Shisaku to Taiken*. Nakao 4/20/43 (563).

Nishida Naojirō. *Kokushi ni okeru Eien no Shisō*. Nakao 3/16/43 (553).

Nishinuma Shigeki. *Nihon Dōtokuron*. Nakao 1/6/42 (419).

Nishitani Keiji. *Kongenteki Shutaisei no Tetsugaku*. Hayashi 2/10/41 (34).

———. *Sekaikan to Kokkakan*. Nakao 10/18/41 (403); 1/13/43 (532).

Nitobe Inazō. Sasaki 4/22/41 (216); 11/21/41 (260).

Nogami Toyoichirō. Sasaki 1/8/42 (278).

———. *Hon'yaku-ron*. Sasaki 1/2/40 (56).

Ochikubo Monogatari (unknown author). Nakao 12/13/40 (318).

Odaka Tomo'o. *Jitteihō Chitsujoron*. Nakao 5/2/43 (567).

———. *Kokka Kōzōron*. Hayashi 11/29/41 (74); Nakao 4/15/43 (562).

———. *Kokka Tetsugaku*. Nakao 5/11/43 (570).

Ogawa Masako. *Kojima no Haru*. Hayashi 8/31/40 (20).

Oguchi Tamichika. *Kaigun*. Hayashi 5/19/44 (135).

Ogura Kin'nosuke. *Kakei no Sūgaku*. Nakao 11/20/43 (631).

Okakura Tenshin. Nakao 1/29/43 (535).

———. *Nihon no Mezame*. Nakao 4/8/41 (361).

Okamoto Kidō. *Shuzen-ji Monogatari*. Nakao 3/8/42 (443).

Ōkawa Shūmei. *Eibei Tōa Shinryakushi*. Nakao 2/25/42 (440).

———. *Nihon Nisen-roppyaku-nen-shi*. Nakao 1/3/42 (418).

Ōkōchi Kazuo. *Sumisu to Risuto*. Sasaki 9/16/43 (389).

Ōkushi Toyo'o. *Zentaisei no Seiji*. Nakao 3/13/43 (550).

Onda Moku. *Higurashi Suzuri*. Hayashi 5/30/42 (85).

Ōrui Noburu. *Shigaku Gairon*. Sasaki 12/19/40 (156); 3/15/41 (199).

Osaragi Jirō. *Dorefyusu Jiken* (The Dreyfus affair). Nakao 12/12/39 (204–5).

Ōtake Yasuko. *Byōinsen*. Hayashi 8/31/40 (20).

Ōtsuka Hisao. Sasaki 10/6/42 (336).

Ozaki Kihachi. Sasaki 5/28/42 (318).

Ozaki Kōyō. *Futari Nyōbō*. Sasaki 4/39/40 (92).

———. *Tajō Takon*. Sasaki 5/18/40 (99).

Ozaki Shirō. *Jinsei Gekijō*. Wada 2/1/45 (274); 6/20/45 (307).

Ozaki Yukio. *Kindai Kaiketsu Roku*. Nakao 4/5/42 (451).

Ryōzan Masamichi. *Seijishi*. Nakao 9/3/42 (485).

Saigō Takamori. Hayashi 4/28/44 (128); Nakao 3/7/35 (48); 9/27/36 (113). See also
     Hayashi Fusao. *Saigō Nanshū Ikun*.

———. *Saigō Nanshū Ikun* (Yamada Jun Ed.,). Hayashi 12/14/41 (75); Nakao
     2/23/40 (232); Sasaki 8/14/42 (332).

Sakaeda Yoshiki. *Gottoru no Keizaigaku*. Nakao 10/6/43 (607).

Sakakiyama Jun. *Rekishi*. Hayashi 6/25/44 (155).

Sanbukyō. Nakao 4/16/39 (134).

Sasaki Sōichi. *Kenpō Gyōseihō Enshū*. Vol.1. Nakao 9/18 (601).

———. *Kenpō Gyōseihō Enshū*. Vol.2. Nakao 10/4/43 (606).

Satō Haruo. *Hoshi*. Sasaki 3/29/41 (202).

Satō Kōroku. *Eiyū Kōshin Kyoku*. Nakao 11/14/36 (113).

———. *Shōnen Kōshin Kyoku*. Nakao 8/12/37 (120).

Satō Nobuhiro. Sasaki 3/4/42 (300).

Satō Takafusa. *Miyazawa Kenji*. Sasaki 6/14/43 (366).

Satō Yoshiaki. *Ikiru Chikara*. Nakao 3/22/40 (241).

———. *Kōjō no Michi*. Nakao 1/5/40 (211).

Satomi Ton. *Ibara no Kanmuri*. Sasaki 7/16/41 (242).

———. *Tajō Busshin*. Hayashi 4/19/41 (38).

Sawagata Hisataka. *Man'yōshū Kōwa*. Nakao 8/5/43 (589).

Seki Takakazu. Sasaki 3/11/42 (304).

Serizawa Kōjirō. *Inochi Aru Hi.* Wada 5/30/45 (299).

Shiga Naoya. Sasaki 3/18/40 (72); 4/1/40 (80).

―――. *An'ya Kōro.* Hayashi 8/25/40 (18); Sasaki 3/19/40 (74); 3/25/40 (76).

―――. *Aru Otoko, Sono Ane no Shi.* Nakao 9/29/ 39 (185); Sasaki 3/13/40 (70).

―――. *Kozō no Kamisama.* Sasaki 4/29/40 (91).

―――. *Tanpen (Kozō no Kamisama* Hoka 10 Pen). Nakao 9/8/39 (180).

―――. *Wakai.* Nakao 9/26/39 (184); Sasaki 3/11/40 (69).

Shimaki Akahiko. *Kadō Shōken.* Sasaki 3/17/42 (304).

Shimaki Kensaku. *Chihō Seikatsu.* Hayashi 9/10/42 (91).

―――. *Seikatsu no Tankyū.* Nakao 1/14/40 (215).

―――. *Unmei no Hito.* Hayashi 5/30/42 (86).

Shimamura Hōgetsu. Sasaki 4/13/40 (83).

Shimazaki Tōson. Nakao 11/19/39 (198).

―――. *Bōsei.* Nakao 3/28/40 (242).

―――. *Hakai.* Nakao 7/20/39 (161).

―――. *Ie.* Nakao 7/22/39 (162).

―――. *Oitachi no Ki.* Nakao 3/28/40 (242).

―――. *Sakura no Mi no Jukusuru Toki.* Nakao 1/5/40 (210).

―――. *Tōhō no Mon.* Nakao 10/14/43 (616); 10/13, 14/43 (615–16).

―――. *Yoakemae.* Hayashi 4/17/41 (38); 5/29/41 (49); 5/29/41 (50).

Shimomura Kojin. *Jirō Monogatari.* Nakao 4/28/42 (457); 12/20, 21/42 (520, 522).

―――. *Rongo Monogatari.* Nakao 8/2/43 (587).

―――. *Satō Nobuhiro.* Nakao 11/16/43 (627).

Shinran. Nakao 1/1/43 (525); 4/14/43 (561).

Suehiro Gentarō. *Hōsō Manpitsu.* Sasaki 3/17/42 (304).

―――. *Hōsō Zatsuwa.* Nakao 5/2/42 (458).

―――. *Saiseki Kakuron.* Nakao 2/8/43 (539).

Suganuma Tēhū. *Shin Nihon no Zu Minami no Yume.* Nakao 2/7/43 (539).

Sugawara Takasue no Musume. *Sarashina Nikki.* Nakao 1/2/41 (332).

Sugi Masatoshi. *Kyōshūki.* Hayashi 4/27/42 (80); Nakao 12/30/40 (326); 12/6/42 (516); Sasaki 11/4/40 (135).

Sugita Genpaku. *Rangaku Kotohajime.* Hayashi 11/20/41 (74); Nakao 2/17/43 (543).

Suzuki Daisetsu. *Kindai ni okeru Zendō no Igi.* Nakao 3/24/43 (555).

―――. *Mushin to Iu Koto.* Nakao 8/20/42 (480).

―――. *Zen to Nihon Bunka.* Nakao 4/4/42 (451); Sasaki 7/11/41 (241).

Suzuki Hideo. *Jikurareshi Hana.* Nakao 9/14/42 (489).

Suzuki Miekichi. Sasaki 3/14/41 (198).

―――. *Kotori no Su.* Sasaki 3/13/41 (197).

―――. *Kuwa no Mi.* Nakao 4/14/40 (248); Sasaki 3/13/41 (197).

Suzuki Narutaka. *Rekishiteki Kokka no Rinen.* Hayashi 12/11/42 (94); 5/19/44 (135).

Tabata Shinobu. *Hō to Seiji.* Nakao 2/16/43 (543).

Tachihara Michizō. Wada 7/14/43 (78).

Taguchi Ukichi. *Nihon Kaika Shōshi.* Nakao 12/7/41 (413); Sasaki 4/28/41 (220).

Taihēki. Nakao 12/4/42 (516).

Takada Yasuma. Sasaki 12/5/40 (149).

―――. *Dai-ni Keizaigaku Gairon.* Nakao 7/3/42 (470); 8/22/43 (594).

————. *Minzoku-ron.* Nakao 10/4/42 (497).

————. *Minzoku to Keizai.* Nakao 10/9/42 (498).

Takami Jun. Sasaki 5/28/42 (318).

————. *Ikanaru Hoshi no Moto ni.* Hayashi 5/30/42 (85).

————. *Kokyū Wasureubeki.* Hayashi 8/31/40 (20); 5/30/42 (86).

————. *Watashi no Shōsetsu Benkyō.* Hayashi 5/30/42 (86).

Takamura Kōtarō. *Chieko-shō.* Sasaki 12/22/41 (265).

Takashima Yoshiya. Sasaki 1/11/43 (349).

————. *Keizaigaku no Konpon Mondai.* Sasaki 1942 (432).

Takasugi Shinsaku. Hayashi 5/14/44 (133).

Takayama Chogyū. *Takiguchi Nyūdō.* Nakao 3/27/40 (241); 3/6/42 (443).

Takayama Iwao. *Bunka Ruikei-gaku.* Nakao 1/1/41 (331); 2/15/42 (434).

————. *Nihon Bunkashi.* In. *Nihon Kokka Kagaku Taikei.* Vol.1. Nakao 10/1/43
    (604).

Takeda Yūkichi. *Seishōnen Nihon Bungaku Man'yōshū.* Nakao 8/11/43 (591).

Takehisa Yumeji. *Wasure'enu Hito.* Sasaki 11/9/40 (137).

Taketori Monogatari. Nakao 2/28/36 (83); 12/20/40 (324).

Takikawa Sējirō. *Nihon Shakaishi.* Nakao 10/10/43 (610); 10/9/43 (644).

Tanabe Hajime. Nakao 5/3/43 (567); 11/9/43 (624); 5/20/43 (642); Sasaki 11/3/40
    (134).

————. *Eien, Rekishi, Kōi.* Nakao 5/8/43 (569).

————. *Kagaku Gairon.* Sasaki 10/12/40 (115); 11/9/40 (137); 11/11/40 (138);
    11/14/40 (141).

————. *Kokkateki Sonzai no Riron.* Nakao 5/1/43 (566).

————. *Nihon Tetsugaku no Senjū.* Nakao 3/24/43 (555).

————. *Nishida Sensei no Oshie o Aogu.* Nakao 5/13/43 (571).

————. *Rekishiteki Genjitsu.* Hayashi 8/31/40 (20); 9/3/40 (20); 5/29/41 (49); Nakao
    10/19/40 (301); 5/2/43 (567); Sasaki 9/25/40 (112); 11/1/40 (132); 3/1/42
    (297).

————. *Rekishi Tetsugaku Seiji Tetsugaku.* Hayashi 8/31/40 (20).

————. *Rinri to Riron.* Nakao 5/12/43 (570).

————. *Shakai Sonzai no Riron.* Nakao 4/20/43 (563).

————. *Shōbō Ganzō no Tetsugaku Shikan.* Nakao 2/21/43 (546).

————. *Shu no Riron no Imi o Akirakanisu.* Nakao 5/5/43 (568).

————. *Shu no Riron to Sekai Zushiki.* Nakao 4/14/43 (560).

————. *Tetsugaku no Hōkō.* Nakao 8/12/41 (389); Wada 7/14/43 (78).

————. *Tetsugaku to Kagaku no Aida.* Sasaki 10/12/40 (115); 12/19/40 (156).

————. *Tetsugaku Tsūron.* In. *Tanabe Hajime Zenshū,* Vol.3. Nakao 4/6/43 (559);
    4/14/43 (560); Sasaki 10/12/40 (116).

————. *Tokusei to Shiteno Kagaku.* Nakao 4/25/43 (564).

Tanabe Shigeharu. *Yama ni Hairu Kokoro.* Sasaki 10/18/40 (120).

Tanaka Kōtarō. *Kaisei Shōhō Sōsoku Gairon.* Nakao 5/15/43 (571).

Tanigawa Tetsuzō. *Nihonjin no Kokoro. Japan.* Hayashi 4/22/40 (10).

————. *Seikatsu Tetsugaku Geijutsu.* Hayashi 4/22/40 (10).

Taniuchi Naobumi. *Karafuto Fūbutsu Shō.* Hayashi 4/2/44 (120); 4/7/44 (121);
    4/18/44 (122); 5/23/44 (138).

Tanizaki Jun'ichirō. Sasaki 3/14/41 (198).

———. *Genji Monogatari.* Sasaki 3/25/39 (13); 4/4/39 (16); 5/6/40 (93); 2/27/41 (191).

———. *In'ei Raisan.* Sasaki 2/16/41 (186); 2/27/41 (191).

———. *Neko to Shōzō to Futari no Onna.* Sasaki 1/6/41 (169).

———. *Shunkinshō.* Hayashi 11/2/41 (67); Sasaki 1/10/41 (172).

———. *Tade Ku'u Mushi.* Sasaki 1/7/41 (170).

———. *Yoshino Kuzu.* Sasaki 1/8/41 (170).

Taoka Ryōichi. *Kokusai Hōgaku Taikō.* Nakao 11/29/42 (515).

Tatsuno Takashi. *Inshō to Tsuioku.* Hayashi 5/30/42 (86).

Tatsuzawa Takeshi. Sasaki 2/20/41 (188); 5/1/41 (222); 6/15/41 (236); 1/22/42 (281).

Tayama Katai. Sasaki 3/18/40 (72); 4/1/40 (80).

———. *Futon.* Nakao 5/14/39 (143); Sasaki 3/18/40 (73).

———. *Inaka Kyōshi.* Sasaki 3/26/40 (77)

———. *Ippeisotsu.* Nakao 5/14/39 (143); Sasaki 3/18/40 (73).

———. *Sei.* Nakao 8/12/39 (170); Sasaki 3/15/40 (71); 3/18/40 (73).

Terada Torahiko. Sasaki 12/28/41 (266); 8/19/43 (386).

———. *Fuyuhiko-shū.* Sasaki 8/10/43 (381); 8/19/43 (384).

———. *Zoku Fuyuhiko-shū.* Sasaki 3/2/42 (298).

Teshigawara Sōfū. Sasaki 6/13/43 (366).

———. *Hasami-dako.* Sasaki 6/16/43 (367).

Tokuda Shūsei. *Arakure.* Nakao 7/31/39 (166); Sasaki 2/28/40 (67).

———. *Kabi.* Nakao 8/5/39 (168).

———. *Tadare.* Sasaki 2/28/40 (67).

Tokugawa Nariakira. *Kōdōkan Gakusoku.* Nakao 8/31/43 (595).

Tokutomi Roka. Sasaki 4/1/40 (80).

———. *Kuroi Me to Chairo no Me.* Hayashi 4/22/40 (9).

———. *Omoide no Ki.* Sasaki 3/31/40 (80).

Tokutomi Sohō (Iichirō). *Yoshida Shōin.* Hayashi 5/30/42 (86); Nakao 9/9/40 (289); 9/12/43 (600).

Tomita Kōkei. *Hōtoku-ki.* Nakao 6/14/42 (464).

Tomonaga Sanjūrō. *Kinsei ni okeru "Ga" no Jikaku-shi.* Hayashi 5/31/41 (52); Sasaki 3/29/41 (202); 4/7/41 (208).

Tsuboi Chūji. *Jishin no Hanashi.* Sasaki 4/24/41 (218).

Tsubota Jōji. *Kodomo no Shiki.* Nakao 5/31/40 (261).

Tsubouchi Shōyō. Sasaki 10/20/40 (121).

Tsuchiya Takao. *Nihon Keizaishi Gaiyō.* Sasaki 12/19/40 (156).

———. *Nihon Kokubō Kokka Kensetsu no Shiteki Kenkyū.* Nakao 10/7/42 (498).

Tsuda Sōkichi. *Jukyō no Jissen Dōtoku.* Nakao 3/18/41 (356).

———. *Shina Shisō to Nihon.* Nakao 12/10/41 (415).

Tsugita Jun. *Kojiki Shinkō.* Nakao 11/6/42 (507).

Tsumura Nobuo. In *Bungakkai* (October). Hayashi 12/11/42 (94).

Uchida Iwao. *Kaiga no Bi.* Nakao 11/14/43 (626).

Uchimura Kanzō. Sasaki 11/21/41 (260).

———. *Kirisuto Shinto no Nagusame.* Sasaki 4/29/40 (90).

———. *Kōsei eno Saidai Ibutsu.* Sasaki 10/5/40 (113).

————. *Yo wa Ikanishite Kirisuto Kyōto to Narishika.* Sasaki 4/29/40 (90).
Ueda Shūsei. *Ugetsu Monogatari.* Nakao 8/21/41 (390).
Uesugi Shinkichi. *Shinkō Kenpō Jutsugi.* Nakao 11/7/42 (508).
————. *Shinkō Teikoku Kenpō.* Nakao 10/20/42 (503); 10/29/42 (506).
Uji Shūi Monogatari. Nakao 3/15/41 (355.).
Uno Chiyo. *Nichiro Senbunki.* Hayashi 6/9/44 (144).
Wada Den. *Ōhinata Mura.* Nakao 9/29/39 (185).
Wakayama Bokusui. (Poems). Sasaki 4/10/41 (211); 3/4/42 (299).
Watsuji Tetsurō. Hayashi 6/16/41 (53); Sasaki 3/26/40 (78); 10/11/42 (337).
————. *Gūzō Saikō.* Nakao 4/28/40 (251); Sasaki 3/19/40 (73); 3/31/40 (79).
————. *Natsume-sensei no Tsuioku.* Sasaki 3/25/40 (76).
————. *Nihon Kodai Bunka.* Nakao 7/2/42 (469).
————. *Nihon Seishin-shi Kenkyū.* Nakao 2/9/40 (227).
————. *Ningen no Gaku Toshiteno Rinrigaku.* Nakao 10/5/42 (497); Sasaki 3/14/40
    (70); 10/12/40 (116); 2/16/41 (186).
————. *Rinrigaku.* Hayashi 7/5/41 (58);
————. *Shamon Dōgen.* Nakao 2/9/40 (227); 1/15/43 (532).
————. *Zoku Nihon Seishin-shi Kenkyū.* Nakao 2/7/42 (430).
Yajima Yōkichi. *Rinrigaku no Konpon Mondai.* Hayashi 2/10/41 (34).
Yamada Takao. *Kojiki Gaisetsu.* Nakao 6/6/42 (462).
————. *Nihon Keikokushi* (in, *Nihon Kokka Kagaku Taikei*, Vol.1). Nakao 10/1/43
    (604).
Yamada Rērin. *Zengaku Dokuhon.* Nakao 10/18 (503).
Yamaguchi Kaoru. *Zensen Eishatai.* Hayashi 5/23/44 (138).
Yamamoto Tsunetomo. *Hagakure.* Nakao 4/8/45 (665).
Yamamoto Yūzō. Nakao 2/23/40 (233); Sasaki 4/1/40 (80); 3/14/41 (198); 7/13/43
    (376).
————. *Ana.* Sasaki 1/3/40 (56).
————. *Chokorēto.* Nakao 9/8/39 (180); Sasaki 4/2/40 (81).
————. *Dōshi no Hitobito.* Nakao 10/1/39 (187); Sasaki 1/5/40 (57).
————. *Eiji Goroshi.* Sasaki 1/3/40 (56).
————. *Fushaku Shinmyō.* Nakao 1/13/40 (214); 9/29/42 (494)–as a radio drama;
    Sasaki 4/2/40 (81).
————. *Gikyokushū.* Sasaki 1/3/40 (56); 10/20/40 (121).
————. *Hanikamiya no Kurara.* Sasaki 4/2/40 (81).
————. *Honzon.* Nakao 10/1/39 (187); Sasaki 1/5/40 (57).
————. *Ikitoshi Ikerumono.* Nakao 9/10/ 39 (180); Sasaki 1/2/40 (56).
————. *Jochū no Byōki.* Nakao 10/1/39 (187).
————. *Kamon to Shichirōemon.* Nakao 10/1/39 (187).
————. *Kaze.* Sasaki 12/2/40 (147); 10/2/40 (297).
————. *Kimitachi wa Dō Ikiruka.* Sasaki 3/30/39 (15); 1/2/40 (56); 7/13/43 (375).
————. *Kobu.* Nakao 9/5/39 (178); Sasaki 4/2/40 (81).
————. *Kome Hyappyō.* Sasaki 7/6/43 (372)
————. *Koyaku.* Nakao 9/8/39 (180); Sasaki 4/2/40 (81).
————. *Kumatani Renshōbō.* Nakao 10/1/39 (187).

————. *Kyōdai.* Nakao 9/8/39 (180); Sasaki 4/2/40 (81).

————. *Nami.* Nakao 8/3/43 (587); Sasaki 1/5/40 (57).

————. *Onna no Isshō.* Sasaki 10/20/40 (121); 11/1/40 (134).

————. *Robō no Ishi.* Sasaki 1/2/40 (56); 3/7/41 (192).

————. *Sakazaki Dewa-no-kami.* Sasaki 1/3/40 (56).

————. *Seimei no Kanmuri.* Sasaki 1/3/40 (56).

————. *Shinjitsu Ichiro.* Nakao 9/20/39 (183).

————. *Tsumura Kyōju.* Sasaki 1/3/40 (56).

————. *Umihiko Yamahiko.* Nakao 10/1/39 (187); Sasaki 1/5/40 (57).

Yamanaka Minetarō. *Ajia no Akebono.* Nakao 7/20/40 (267).

————. *Hara de Iku.* Nakao 3/22/40 (241).

Yamanaka Monjuran. *Shin Shōfū Haiku Dokuhon.* Nakao 11/27/43 (632).

Yamauchi Tokuritsu. *Ningen no Porisu-teki Keisei.* Nakao 2/27/42 (441).

Yanagita Kenjūrō. *Jissen Tetsugaku toshiteno Nishida Tetsugaku.* Nakao 3/8/43 (549).

Yanagita Kunio. *Kokugo no Shōrai.* Nakao 10/12/41 (402).

Yanaihara Tadao. *Yo no Sonkeisuru Jinbutsu.* Hayashi 8/31/40 (20).

Yokoi Shōnan. Sasaki 3/22/42 (307).

Yokomitsu Riichi. *Chūbō Nikki.* Nakao 9/17/39 (182).

————. *Nichirin.* Nakao 5/19/40 (258).

————. *Ōbē Kikō.* Nakao 9/13, 14, 15/39 (180–82).

————. *Shanghai.* Hayashi 2/7/44 (118).

————. *Tanpenshū (Kikai, Jikan, Muchi, Tori, Kōkasen, Me ni Mieta Kaze, Fubo no Mane, Akuma).* Nakao 9/3/39 (177).

————. *Tokei.* Nakao 6/17/39 (155).

Yosano Hiroshi. *Nikudan San-yūshi.* Nakao 2/22/36 (82).

Yoshida Kenkō. *Tsurezure-gusa.* Nakao 8/22/43 (594).

Yoshida Shōin. Hayashi 5/1/44 (130); 6/25/44 (155).

Yoshii Isamu. *Gendai-yaku Genji Monogatari.* Nakao 11/28/43 (632).

Yoshikawa Eiji. *Sangokushi.* Nakao 8/2/43 (586); 8/6/43 (590); 8/9, 11/43 (591); 8/17, 18/43 (593–94).

Yukawa Hideki. Sasaki 10/29/42 (339).

Yumeno Kyūsaku. *Doguma Dogura.* Nakao 9/29/ 39 (185).

Zeami. *Geijutsu Ronshū.* Hayashi 11/29/41 (74).

Japanese Films, Kabuki, Jōruri (puppet plays), and Zenshinza (progressive theater)

Barukan Dengekisen. Sasaki 1/25/42 (284).

Chūshingura Kiratei Uramon no Ba (zenshinza). Sasaki 2/5/43 (351).

Fuji ni Tatsu Kage (film). Wada 3/29/45 (284).

Geidō Ichi-dai Otoko (film). Nakao 5/29/43 (573).

Ginkai Jūsō. Sasaki 1/30/40 (59).

Hadaka no Kyōkasho (film?). Sasaki 4/11/39 (18).

Hawaii, Marē Oki Kaisen (Sea battle over Hawaii and Malaysia). Sasaki 12/8/42 (340).

Himetaru Kakugo (film). Wada 12/14/44 (260).

Kagirinaki Zenshin. Sasaki 3/5/42 (300).

Kanjinchō (kabuki). Sasaki 3/26/41 (201).

Kansha no Kyōshitsu (film). Wada 9/25/44 (228).

Kaze no Matasaburō (film). Sasaki 10/13/40 (118).

Kettō Han'nyazaka (film). Wada 9/25/44 (228).

Kichi no Kensetsu (film). Wada 12/14/44 (260).

Kin'nan no Ie (film). Sasaki 3/3/42 (298).

Momiji-gari (kabuki). Sasaki 3/26/41 (201).

Muhōmatsu no Isshō (film). Nakao 11/3/43 (621).

Narukami (zenshinza). Sasaki 2/5/43 (351).

Nessa no Hate. Sasaki 4/30/40 (91).

Nihontō Dohyō-iri (zenshinza). Sasaki 2/5/43 (351).

Odorikomi Hanayome (film?). Sasaki 3/20/39 (12).

Ōinaru Hiyaku. Sasaki 11/29/41 (261).

Pari no Hyōban Onna (film?). Sasaki 4/11/39 (18).

Rozamunde. Sasaki 1/20/40 (58).

Setsuhyō? Kagaku no Yūbe. Sasaki 2/4/43 (351).

Shinsetsu (film). Wada 3/29/45 (284).

Shōgun to Sanbō to Hei (film). Nakao 6/20/42 (467).

Sugawara Denju Tenarai Kagami (kabuki). Sasaki 3/26/41 (201).

Taiiku no Gaika. Sasaki 11/29/41 (261).

Tajinkoson (film). Sasaki 1/30/40 (59).

Tanoshikikana Jinsei (film). Wada 11/4/44 (249).

Toranpu Monogatari (film?). Sasaki 3/20/39 (12).

Tōyō no Gaika (film). Nakao 12/27/42 (523).

Tsubosaka Reigenki (author unknown; jōruri). Sasaki 1/18/41 (176).

Tsuchi. Nakao 4/25/39 (137).

Wakai Hito (film). Sasaki 3/6/42 (301)

Yuki no Kesshō (film). Sasaki 9/20/39 (39).

Notes

Introduction

1. The term *méconnaissance* originated with Henri Wallon, Lacan's teacher, and is used by Lacan, whose *méconnaissance* is embedded in his thesis on the origin of selfhood in the image a child sees in the mirror. Bourdieu ([1972] 1977: 4–6) uses it in the context of gift exchange, which, according to him, is predicated upon the *méconnaissance* of the intention of the donor by the receiver because of the time lag in the structure of gift exchange. Althusser (1971: 172–73, 182–83) uses the concept but within his framework of the interpellation by ideology of the individual as subject. My use of the concept is as it applies to symbolic communication.

2. I owe this phrase to Pierre Bourdieu, who patiently listened to my description of this project in May 1998 at the Collège de France.

3. Gordon (1991: esp. 333–39) sees similarities between Japanese, German, and Italian developments, all to be considered as fascism. Payne (1995), on the other hand, thinks that two factors crucial to fascism were absent in Japan: a single party and a political leader of immense power. In contrast to Hitler, Payne contends, Tōjō was a pale shadow; he held less power than Churchill or Roosevelt, for example, and was removed from office in July 1944 without incident. Neither Tōjō nor the emperor was a "charismatic all-powerful dictator" (Payne 1995: 328–37, 335–36; Payne 2000). For detailed discussion of "Japanese fascism," see Maruyama 1964: esp. 152–70; Najita 1974.

4. The Japanese imported fruit-bearing cherry *(Cerasus avium)* for fruit consumption and called it "Western fruit cherry" *(seiyōmizakura)* (Yahiro 1995: 5–118). Like all other plants, the petals fall before the tree bears fruit. However, since the Japanese have not emphasized fruit-bearing cherries, the metaphorical equation of cherry blossoms and a short life may not be based on their observation that blossoms fall before the reproductive process completes.

5. Of the five pilots introduced in chapter 6, the editor of Hayashi Ichizō (1995) selected writings that reflect his relationship with his mother. They are thus excluded from the Appendix.

6. In this book, I therefore do not address the question of the war responsibility of the Shōwa emperor, who must shoulder the major burden of responsibility for the atrocities committed before and during the war. But, to blame a single figure, whether the Shōwa emperor, Tōjō, or any other figure, seems to be a simplistic approach to highly complex historical processes, and, moreover, contributes to whitewash the responsibility of all those involved, including the masses.

7. This is not to say that the history of great men has disappeared, as clearly evidenced by enormous popularity of David McCullough's *John Adams* (2001).

8. Fussell ([1975] 2000: 156) is careful in pointing out the "unparalleled literariness of all ranks," which includes the highly educated and hardly educated. N. Annan (1990) focuses on the Oxbridge intellectuals.

9. Visits paid to the shrine by the members of the Liberal Democratic Party, including Prime Minister Kozumi Jun'ichirō, is due in part because of block voting by members of the Bereaved Society, consisting of survivors of the war dead.

Chapter One

1. In general the *Kojiki* and the *Nihonshoki* contain many of the same episodes, although the *Kojiki* contains records that are contradictory to each other, indicating an earlier and less controlled attempt to establish the *official* history.

2. The representation of Japan as "Agrarian Japan" and of "agrarian cosmology as the Japanese cosmology" resulted in the exiling of the Japanese in nonagrarian sectors from history (Ohnuki-Tierney 1993a; 1999).

3. The Sun Goddess, the ancestress to the imperial family, did not acquire her importance until the imperial system became established (Ohnuki-Tierney 1993a).

4. On the name Konoha-no-Sakuya-Bime, see Kurano and Takeda, eds. 1958: 131–33, for *Kojiki*; Sakamoto et al., eds. 1967: 154–55, for *Nihonshoki*. Interpreting *sakuya* in her name as *sakura* (cherry blossoms), M. Yamada (1977: 121–22), M. Sakurai (1974: 25), and others link this female deity to cherry blossoms. Saitō ([1979] 1985: 39–42) objects to this interpretation.

5. The symbolic association between rice qua emperor and cherry blossoms is seen also in the episode involving the fifth-century Richū emperor (in the myth-histories, the seventeenth emperor, succeeding his father, the Nintoku emperor; no accurate dates of his reign are available). See Kurano and Takeda, eds. 1958: 283, 289, for *Kojiki*; Sakamoto et al., eds. 1967: 425–26, for *Nihonshoki*; and Ohnuki-Tierney 1998b for interpretation; see also M. Yamada 1977: 118; 1982: 4.

6. While mountain worship is found throughout Japan, the specific content of the belief system varies between social groups and according to region (Yanagita, ed. 1951: 642–44). For example, unlike farmers, hunters *(ryōshi)*, charcoal makers *(sumiyaki)*, lumberjacks *(kikori)*, and others who work in the mountains do not believe that the Mountain Deity becomes the Deity of Rice Paddies, who has no meaning for them. Among some, it is female, while among others it is male.

7. Okada [1988] 1996; M. Yamada 1977; K. Yamamoto 1982. Well-known flower rituals are at Yakushiji in Kyoto (Nihon Hōsō Kyōkai, ed. 1988); Zaōdō Temple in Yoshino (Blacker 1975; Miyake 1978: 162; 1988: 86; Miyata 1993: 5–6); and Imamiya Shrine (Yasurai ritual) in Kyoto (Imamiya Jinja Shamusho, ed. [1982] 1987; Kawane [1984] 1986: 69). I observed the latter two in April 1996.

8. These scholars include Kanzaki 1989: 77; Nishiyama 1985: 20–21; Wakamori 1975: 179–81; M. Yamada 1977: 116–22. Wakamori (1975) points to other examples in which the term *kura* is used to refer to the seat of the shaman's spirit. This etymological interpretation is criticized by some scholars on the basis of insufficient evidence (e.g., Saitō 1977).

9. Kanzaki 1994: 16. Visual representations of the connection between cherry blossoms and the planting of rice appear only later. In an eighteenth-century painting, *Agricultural Works in Four Seasons (Shiki Kōsaku-zu Byōbu)* by Kanō Eiō,

cherry blossoms are depicted alongside farmers in rice paddies (housed at the National Museum of History and Ethnography, Chiba, Japan). An almanac of the late Edo period left by the farmer Kinase Tsunenosuke of Ibaraki specifies that seedlings for rice be planted when cherry blossoms fall and yellow roses *(yamabuki; Kierria japonica)* start to bloom (Miyata 1987: 121–22).

10. Since the Nara period (646–794), at established shrines and temples, cherry blossom viewing followed a religious ritual, *sakurae* (cherry blossom meeting), during which monks and priests prayed (Sakamoto 1995).

11. These hair decorations with cherry blossoms were called *uzu* or *kazashi*. For these two poems, see Omodaka 1983, no. 1429 (39–40) and Omodaka 1984, no. 3786 (12).

12. Takagi Kiyoko 1996: 70. Saitō ([1979] 1985: 42) counts forty-four poems with cherry blossoms, whereas M. Yamada (1977: 117) counts forty. Takagi (1996: 70) lists forty-seven poems in which the term for cherry blossoms appears, with thirty-three poems directly about cherry blossoms, ten referring to cherry blossoms in passing, and four in which the term is part of a name for a place or personal name. I use Saitō's count here since it is done in comparison with other flowers: the 141 references to bush clover *(hagi)* and the 118 references to plum blossoms (Saitō [1979] 1985: 42).

13. Yamada's examples are the poem by Yamabe-no-Akahito in vol. 8 and the one by Kakinomoto-no-Hitomaro in vol. 13 (M. Yamada 1977: 118).

14. See Cranston 1993: 254, 312, 327, 384, 405, 460, 479, 539, 544, 602, 607, 610, 626, 718.

15. *Hitachi-no-Kuni Fudoki* was commissioned by the imperial court in 713 and is based on records written before 716 (Akimoto [713] 1958). It is one of a series of *fudoki*, accounts of nature and customs of inhabitants in each region. It refutes Nishiyama's (1995: 1) dating of the first cherry blossom viewing to the Heian period (794–1185) for aristocrats and to *Yamatomori Nikki* in 1673 for the common folk. The practice of the exchange of poems is usually referred to as *utagaki*, but in the *Hitachi-no-Kuni Fudoki*, it is referred to as *tanoshimi asobu* (enjoy and play) (Akimoto [713] 1958: 41). Both in *Izumo-no-Kuni Fudoki*, published in 733, and in *Harima-no-Kuni Fudoki*, it is referred to as *utage*, but written in different characters (Kanzaki 1989: 78).

16. *Yoshino Hanami-zu Byōbu* (Screen of the Cherry Blossom Viewing at Yoshino) (Harada and Yamane, eds. 1983: 145).

17. *Daigo Hanami-zu Byōbu* (Screen of the Cherry Blossom Viewing at Daigo) at Kokuritsu Rekishi Minzoku Hakubutsukan (Harada and Yamane, eds. 1983: 144).

18. Extensive use of "artificial" representations, such as those of cherry blossoms, have a long tradition. Already in the *Manyōshū*, representations of rice plants, made of tree trunks such as willow, appear (Orikuchi 1928a: 490–91; M. Yamada 1982: 38).

19. Cherry blossoms are the major motif in the so-called three greatest Kabuki plays: *Kanadehon Chūshingura, Yoshitsu Senbon Zakura,* and *Sugahara Denju Tenarai Kagami.* Other plays in which cherry blossoms are used as an important symbol are: *Kagotsurube Sato no Eizame, Sugawara Denju Tenarai Kagami, Gion Sairei Shinkōki, Edo-zakura Kiyomizu Seigen, Genrokufū Hanami Odori, Soga Moyō Tateshi no Goshozome, Wakagi no Hanasugata no Saishiki, Shin Usuyuki Monogatari, Sukeroku Yukari no Edo-zakura, Dōjōji Matamo Kaneiri, Kana Dehon Chū-*

shingura, Hiyoshimaru Wakaki no Sakura, Kyōganoko Musume Dōjōji, Dōjōji Koi ha Kusemono, Rokkasen Sugata no Irodori, Sanmon Gosan no Kiri, Sakura-hime Azuma Bunshō and *Aotozōshi Hanano Nishikie* (except for the last two, identification by Akimoto Minoru, personal communication, April 5, 1996; English translations of titles are not meaningful). For cherry blossom viewing in famous scenes, see Toita and Yoshida 1981: 40; Watanabe Tamotsu 1989: 179; and Yoshida and Hattori, eds. 1991: 219. Toita (1969) considers the scenes of cherry blossom viewing in *Shin Usuyuki Monogatari* and *Kagamiyama Kokyō no Nishiki-e* to be the two most famous cherry blossom scenes in Kabuki. Until the mid-Meiji period, the first scene (Cherry Blossom Viewing at Hasedera [*Hasedera Hanami-no-ba*]) in *Kagamiyama Kokyō no Nishiki-e* (Toshikura et al., eds. 1969: 242–78) had been a critical one, enticing the audience to feel the gaiety and sensory saturation that one experiences in cherry blossom viewings. After the mid-Meiji period, this scene has often been skipped (Toita 1969: 237).

20. For example, in the famous *Sugahara Denju Tenarai Kagami* (Toita et al., eds. 1968: 139–233), three brothers are named after plum, pine, and cherry. As the brothers quarrel, trying to hit each other with rice sacks, a cherry branch is accidentally broken off, foretelling the later death by suicide of the brother whose name bears the word for cherry tree *(Sakura-maru)* (Enomoto 1975: 181; Toita and Yoshida 1981: 18). In another play, *Imoseyama On'na Teikin,* a blossoming cherry tree branch floats down a stream, signaling the approaching tragedy of two lovers unable to be united (Toita and Yoshida 1981: 46).

21. Miyata (1993: 3–4) argues that in a fairly common folk belief the souls of the dead do not go to just any mountain but only certain ones, like Yoshino, which are endowed with spiritual power, emphasizing *reizan shinkō* (belief in the mountains with holy spirits) and that the souls of the dead rise toward the mountains, just as the smoke from cremation rises toward the mountains.

22. The interpretation of the relationship between these three super-human beings is complex as well as controversial. It is not clear whether the Deity of Rice Paddies is thought to be in the singular or plural, although the Deity of the Mountains, however, is objectified as a singular deity in various parts of Japan (Miyata personal communication).

23. Limited numbers of tree trunks are used as blocks for woodblock printmaking. Many families during the early Meiji had a charcoal heater *(hibachi),* trays, or saucers for tea cups made of cherry wood (Minakami 1982: 14). Flower petals may be floated in tea and pickled in salt, and leaves pickled in salt are used to wrap pastry.

24. Despite his insight in identifying cherry blossoms as the spring counterpart of rice, Orikuchi ([1928a] 1982: 473–74) superimposed the contemporary notion of aesthetics upon the aesthetics of the flower in the context of ancient cosmology.

25. Examples are Kubota [1960] 1968, vol. 2, no. 97 (236–37), no. 98 (237–38), and no. 103 (243–45) (McCullough 1985: 32–33).

26. Examples are Kubota [1960] 1968, vol. 2, no. 84 (218–19) (K. Takagi 1979: 58), no. 92 (228–30) (K. Takagi 1979: 18), and no. 113 (256–58) (McCullough 1985: 30, 31, and 35, respectively).

27. Examples are Kubota [1960] 1968, vol. 2, no. 71 (200–201), no. 73 (202–203),

no. 77 (208–11), and no. 112 (255–56) (McCullough 1985: 27, 28, 28, and 34, respectively; K. Takagi 1979: 134, 132, 133).

28. Examples of poems are in McCullough 1968: 82, 104, 125, and 133 (Arai [1939] 1965: 224, 460, 691, and 774).

29. The term *sakura* (cherry blossoms) appears forty times (Ikeda 1987: 227–28), and in addition there are numerous occurrences of *hana* (flower), which also refers to cherry blossoms; references to cherry blossoms thus outnumber the references to plum blossoms, which appear forty times (forty-two times, according to Kinoshita 1974).

30. Other examples include Genji's reminiscence of the lavish festival with fully blooming cherry blossoms in front of the Grand Hall (Seidensticker 1977, 1: 243; Yamagishi, ed., 1959: 48–49); Genji's reference to cherry blossoms in black as an oxymoron in the *Kokin Wakashū* (Seidensticker 1977, 1: 340; Yamagishi, ed., 1959: 231); reference to even those blooms that have passed their peak as "smiling" *(hohoemi)* (Seidensticker 1977, 1: 418; Yamagishi, ed., 1959: 396); an analogy between cherry blossoms and courtship (Seidensticker 1977, 2: 751–74; Yamagishi, ed., 1962: 251–94); Genji's reference to a young girl as a "mountain blossom" (Seidensticker 1997, 1: 97; Yamagishi, ed., 1958: 203).

31. Examples are the analogy a nun draws between Genji's thoughts of a young girl and a scattering of blossoms (Seidensticker 1977, 2: 97; Yamagishi, ed., 1958: 204); an old man's reference to an old cherry tree (Seidensticker 1977, 2: 97; Yamagishi, ed., 1958: 204).

32. Scroll paintings, in which important scenes from famous stories are lavishly illustrated, reached the height of their development in the tenth through twelfth centuries. Given the popularity of the novel, numerous scroll paintings of the *Genji* were produced. The best-known example was created by an unknown artist during the first half of the twelfth century and is now housed at Tokugawa Reimei-kai (Shinmura, ed. [1955] 1990: 770). The chapter "Bamboo River" in the *Genji*, with the two young women and a suitor, became well known because of representations of the scenes in scrolls (Akiyama, ed., 1975: plate 14, 106–7).

33. The symbolism was reinforced by the Buddhist notion of impermanence *(mujō)*. It reached the height of literary expression in the masterpieces of the late medieval period (1185–1603), especially during the Muromachi period (1392–1603). These masterpieces include, to list a few examples, *Shin Kokin Wakashū*, published in 1209, and *Essays in Idleness (Tsurezuregusa)* written by Yoshida Kenkō between 1310 and 1331; *Sankashū* and other works by Saigyō (1118–90) (LaFleur 1983; K. Takagi 1979); important Noh plays, such as *Cherry Blossoms at the Saigyō's (Saigyō zakura)*, by Zeami (1364–1443); and the linked poetry (*renga*) by Shinkei (1406–75) (Ramirez-Christensen 1994).

34. The Noh, founded by Kan'ami (1333–84) as *sarugaku* during the Kamakura period, was developed into the most cultivated form of performing art during the subsequent Muromachi period by Ze'ami (1364–1443), Kan'ami's son. Upper-class warriors became their patrons. With highly sophisticated Buddhist philosophy and metaphysics at its base, it has been an important hallmark of Japan's high culture ever since (Ohnuki-Tierney 1987: 89, 169–70).

35. In a personal communication on April 5, 1996, Okuyama Keiko of Nōgakudō identified the following: *Kochō, Shun'nōden, Shunteika, Shundeiraku, Manzairaku, Arashiyama, Ukon, Oshio, Kurama Tengu, Kōya Monogurui, Saigyō-zakura, Sakuragawa, Shiga, Suma Genji, Sumizome-zakura, Sōshiarai Komachi, Taizan Fukun, Tadanori, Tamura, Dōjōji, Futari Shizuka, Mitsuyama, Yuya, Yoshino Shizuka,* and *Yoshino Tenjin* (English translations not meaningful).

36. Other famous examples of the association between cherry blossoms and changing/disclosing of one's identity are *Dōjōji* (Gunji 1970: 16; Gunji et al., eds., 1970: 19–30; Yokomichi and Omote, eds. 1963: 129–42) and *Aotozōshi Hanano Nishikie (Shiranami Gonin Otoko)* (Gunji et al., eds. 1969: 86–136).

37. The contemporary writer Sakaguchi Ango's (1997) well-known short story is based on the association of cherry blossoms with madness and the disclosure of one's true identity.

38. Referred to also as *Yasuna*. Composed for the puppet theater in 1734, its first Kabuki production was in 1818. Productions today are based on Kikugorō VI's production in 1922.

39. The cherry tree was added in a 1922 production (Gunji 1970: 119), although, as indicated in the title, the cherry blossoms were a master trope in the play from the beginning.

40. Matsuoka 1991: 162–63; 145–49, 150–56. These young men came from the families of aristocrats and warriors, although in some exceptional cases they were members of so-called "outcaste" groups (see chap. 1, note 45). Matsuoka argues that the aesthetics and metaphysics underlying the institution of chigo expose the emptiness of the structures of quotidian life and of gender and sexuality.

41. Takigawa 1971: 141. These cherry trees were removed after blooming in April or May (S. Saitō [1979] 1985: 17). The tradition of planting cherry trees originated with the Kabuki theater (Takigawa 1971) some time between 1741 and 1749, when fully blooming cherry blossoms in daytime in Nakanochō were used as a metaphor for the ephemeral gaiety of the floating world by a famous Kabuki actor, Danjūrō II, in his role as Sukeroku, a favorite Kabuki figure, although some claim the cherry in the stage setting were night cherry blossoms in a green bamboo fence.

42. The glitteringly beautiful *representations* of the geisha and the geisha quarters in the woodblock prints and Kabuki theater were far from the reality of the majority of these women, whose lives were full of debt, ill health, and unwelcome customers. They also ignored male geisha and male prostitutes. The institution of geisha was created by the military-political leaders who legalized prostitution by gathering women into a designated area, with the first established in Osaka in 1585 by Toyotomi Hideyoshi, and another established in 1589 at Shimabara in Kyoto (T. Ono 1983: 49), possibly to destroy the spirit of warriors in order to prevent revolts by regional lords (Hasegawa 1991). My discussion here is confined to the one in Edo, where Tokugawa Ieyasu, the shogun, gave permission in 1618 to Shōji Jin'emon to gather *yūjo* in publicly recognized quarters at Moto-Yoshiwara. The quarter was moved, after a fire, to another location and called Shin-Yoshiwara.

The term *geisha* is relatively recent, appearing in Osaka during the Kyōho period (1716–36) and in Edo during the Hōreki period (1751–64) (Harashima Yōichi 1993).

Komori (1984) cites its first use in Edo at around 1803 and around 1716 in western Japan (Kansai), although judging from its use in the title of some woodblock prints, Komori's date for use in Edo is too late. For example, a well-known woodblock print by Eishi, entitled *Seirō Geishasen* (Selected Geisha in the Blue Palace Pleasure Quarter), is dated to the Kansei period (1789–1801) (the print is at Tōkyō Kokuritsu Hakubutsukan). The literal meaning of the term is a person who has *gei* (talent in the performing arts). They were trained in playing musical instruments, especially the three-stringed *shamisen*, and in singing, dancing, and other skills in order to provide entertainment at a "tea house" *(chaya)* while guests ate and drank.

The geisha belong to a category of women who were entertainers in music and dancing, including noninstitutionalized religious specialists, such as shamans, and the aforementioned *yūjo*, literally "play-women," some of whom provided sexual services outside of marriage (Amino 1994; Kumakura 1989; Miyata 1987; Miyamoto 1993). Some were called *shirabyōshi*, a term which originally referred to a special kind of music and dancing popular toward the end of the Heian period and through the Kamakura period, but which became another term for *yūjo*. The geisha of the Edo period, however, were different from these women in that the geisha no longer held religious significance.

Technically, *kuruwa geisha* referred to the geisha in the geisha quarters who entertained their clients with the skills and performing arts and also offered their bodies. The term *yūjo* and *jorō* were used to distinguish them from *machi geisha*, who were exclusively entertainers. Yet, in reality the distinction between the two types of geisha was far less clear-cut, since some of the latter too engaged in sexual services as well. Strict rules prohibiting prostitution were instituted in 1796 at Yoshiwara (Komori 1984); geisha who violated the rule were required to leave Yoshiwara, and the teahouse that provided the place for prostitution as well as the teahouses on both sides of it had to be closed. For the history of Yoshiwara, see Hanazaki 1988; T. Ono 1983: 43–49; Tsukada 1994. For a summary of the number of geisha *(yūjo)* and their ages, see Kumakura 1989. See also Seigle 1993: 170–72; 241.

43. There was a refined system of ranking and classification among geisha and their attendants, which underwent changes over time (see Seigle 1993). Examples of these prints are *Courtesan Beauties under Cherry Blossoms (Sakuranoshita Yūjo Bijin)* by Utamaro (1753–1806); *Courtesan with Two Attendants under Cherry Tree* by Eishi (1756–1829), dated 1810 (see plate 1); two sections of the five-piece panel entitled *The Main Street of the Yoshiwara in Cherry Blossom Time (Shin-Yoshiwara Sakura-no Keshiki)* by Toyokuni (1769–1825); and a three-piece panel entitled *Imitation of the Kabuki Theater in the Blue Pleasure Houses (Seirō Kabuki Yatsushi Ezukushi)* by Utamaro. Except for the first *(Courtesan Beauties under Cherry Blossoms)* by Utamaro, the rest of these woodblock prints are housed at the University of Michigan Museum of Art.

44. Cherry blossoms at night were also a major theme of a style of poetry among the folk called *senryū* (Takigawa 1971: 142).

45. For a history of the hisabetsu-burakumin, see Ohnuki-Tierney 1987; for the Ainu, see Ohnuki-Tierney 1981a; for the marginalization of these social groups, see Ohnuki-Tierney 1998a.

46. Compare the statement by Toita and Yoshida (1981: 42): "While viewing cherry blossoms, there is no distinction between the young and the old, men and women, class and age." See also Hattori Yukio 1975: 56.

47. Praise for the beauty of cherry blossoms by lesser-known poets may be interpreted as an anti-establishment stance against court life in Kyoto. However, Wakamori (1975: 172–73) and Saitō (1977: 41–45) reject the agrarian association of the flower and regard cherry blossoms as the symbol of kingship and urban aristocrats.

48. The main building, *shinden* (sleeping building) is also called *shishinden*, or *naden* (south building), also pronounced *nanten*, and its garden *dantei* or *nantei* (Fujioka 1956: 125, 126).

49. In the years 960, 976, 980, 982, 999, 1001, 1005, 1014, 1018, 1039, 1042, 1048, 1058, 1082, 1219, and 1227.

50. Although none of the available sources in Japanese trace the history of the cherry tree in front of the palace, some details are offered here. According to *Kojidan* (Kuroita and Kokushi Taikei Henshūkai, eds., 1965c: 113; see also Minamoto-no-Akikane, 1965; for a translation of *Kojidan* into contemporary Japanese, see Shimura 1980), it was originally a plum tree that was planted at the time of the Kanmu emperor's relocation of Japan's capital from Nara to Kyoto in 794. According to the *Teiō Hennenki* (Kuroita and Kokushi Taikei Henshūkai, eds., 1965b: 183), the Saga emperor, who held the first imperial cherry blossom viewing in 813, also had a cherry tree planted in front of the main building. However, other passages contradict this description. According to a later section in the *Teiō Hennenki* (Kuroita and Kokushi Taikei Henshūkai, eds., 1965b: 247) and the *Kojidan* (Kuroita and Kokushi Taikei Henshūkai, eds., 1965c: 113), the original plum tree planted at the time of the construction of the imperial palace in Kyoto died during the Jōwa period (834–48). According to *Nihon Kiryaku* (Kuroita and Kokushi Taikei Henshūkai, eds., 1965a: 371) and *Shoku-Nihon Kōki* (Kuroita and Kokushi Taikei Henshūkai, eds., 1966b: 175), in 845, when the Ninmyō emperor held a banquet at the Shishinden (main building), he adorned the hair of the crown prince and his attendants with plum blossoms. In addition, both *Nihon Kiryaku* (Kuroita and Kokushi Taikei Henshūkai, eds., 1965a: 371) and *Shoku Nihon Kōki* (Kuroita and Kokushi Taikei Henshūkai, eds., 1966b: 176, 206) refer to plum blossoms in the palace during the Ninmyō emperor's reign (833–50).

Some consider that it was the Ninmyō emperor who promoted the aesthetics of cherry blossoms (Kuroita and Kokushi Taikei Henshūkai, eds., 1966b: 176, 206). Yet the references during his reign were primarily to plum blossoms. It was after 850 and the end of his reign that references to cherry blossoms started to appear in various records. Thus, *Nihon Kiryaku* (Kuroita and Kokushi Taikei Henshūkai, eds., 1965a: 386, 389) refers to a beautiful cherry tree in 850 and again in 852—both at a manor of prominent court officials *(daijin)*, but not at the palace itself.

The definite proof of the presence of a cherry tree on the left front of the Shishinden is in *Kinpishō* by the Juntoku emperor, written between 1219 and 1222, which states that a cherry tree in front of the Shishinden withered during the Jōgan era (859–77) but was entrusted to Sakanoue-no-Takimori, who carefully restored the tree (Juntoku [1219–22] 1929: 374).

The presence of a cherry tree in front of the main building at the time of the first imperial cherry blossom viewing is dated 813 in *Teiō Hennenki*. Yet, there are other records that contradict this information. In 845 the tree in front of the Shishinden was a plum, and a cherry tree replaced it sometime between 859 and 877, suggesting that the plum had been replaced by the cherry some time after 845 and before 859 (or 877). One of the major sources of misreading is a pair of similar passages in *Kojidan* (Kuroita and Kokushi Taikei Henshūkai, eds. 1965c: 113) and *Teiō Hennenki* (Kuroita and Kokushi Taikei Henshu̅kai, eds. 1965b: 247), which describe how a plum tree was planted at the time of the Kanmu emperor's moving of the capital to Kyoto and how it withered during the Jōwa period. The description is followed by a statement that the Ninmyō emperor "planted again." Some interpret this to mean that the emperor planted a cherry tree. Yet a close reading of the text in Chinese testifies beyond doubt that what the emperor planted was another plum tree. Kubota (1990) guesses that the plum tree was replaced by a cherry tree toward the end of the Ninmyō emperor's reign in 850, whereas Nakamura (1982) places the time during the Seiwa period (858–76). Imae (1993) places the date between 845 and 874. Ponsonby-Fane's (1956: 63) estimate of 960 seems to stem from a misreading of the text.

This cherry tree, however, was burned in the fire of 960 at the palace. At the time of its reconstruction in 965 (Fujioka 1956: 116), a cherry tree, originally a mountain cherry at Yoshino that had been transplanted in the garden of Prince Shigeaki, was transplanted on the left-hand side in front of the Shishinden, as recorded in the *Kojidan* (Kuroita and Kokushi Taikei Henshūkai, eds., 1965c: 113), the *Teiō Hennenki* (Kuroita and Kokushi Taikei Henshūkai, eds., 1965b: 247) and the *Kinpishō* (Juntoku [1219–22 1929: 368]; see also Tsumura ([1917] 1970: 82).

51. Starting in 630, the envoy to Tang China (*kentōshi*) had been sent to acquire knowledge of Tang civilization and the international political situation. Toward the end some five to six hundred people crossed the sea, even though the round trip took two to three years. Sugawara-no-Michizane ordered its discontinuation in 894. Reasons for the abolition of the envoys included the high casualty rate during these voyages and the internal turmoil of Tang China, although Inoue ([1963] 1967, 1: 105–6) attributes it to the loss of curiosity about the outside world on the part of the Japanese elite. The complexities of the reasons behind it notwithstanding, the abolition of the envoy was part of the picture of ninth-century Japan, whose unquestionable admiration of Tang China was going through reassessment.

52. For Yamato-e, see Shinbo 1982. Another use of the cherry tree among the elite is found in the game called *kemari* (or *shūkiku*), during which about eight people kick a deer-hide-covered ball with leather shoes. For a passage in the *Nihonshoki,* see Sakamoto et al., eds. (1965, 2: 254–55). Having reached its popularity among the elite during the first half of the tenth century (Ōshima et al., eds. 1971: 703), the format of the game became well established by the time of the Go-Shirakawa emperor (r. 1158–62), with a court with four plants in each corner: cherry, willow, pine, and maple (Ōshima et al., eds. 1971: 704; see also Suzuki Keizō, ed. 1995).

53. Hiroshige came from a family of the warrior class (Smith and Poster [1986] 1988: 9–10; Miyao 1975: 75).

54. They were published from 1856 until his death in 1858, before which 115 were published (Smith and Poster ([1986] 1988: 9–10). Other famous prints include *Illustrated Book on the Famous Sites in Edo (Edo Meisho Zue)* by Hasegawa Settan, published between 1829 and 1836.

55. Gotō, ed., 1975: plates 11, 14, 15, 16, 17, 19, 22, 23, 24, 25, 28, 29, 31, 35, 37, 38, 40, 41, 42; Gotō ed., 1976: plates 92, 95. Plum blossoms appear in Gotō, ed. 1975: plates 27, 30, 36 and Gotō, ed., 1976: 104.

56. For example, in *Pictures of One Hundred Poems by One Hundred Poets, Explained by the Wet-Nurse (Hyakunin Isshu Uba ga Etoki)* by Katsushika Hokusai (1760–1849), twenty-six prints feature the motif of rice (Morse 1989: prints 1, 5, 8, 9, 12, 13, 14, 17, 19, 20, 22, 23, 30, 39, 44, 47, 65, 68, 70, 71, 78, 79, 83, 84, 90). Likewise they appear in Hiroshige's *Fifty-three Stations along the Tōkaidō* (Gotō, ed. 1975) and in *Kiso Kaidō Rokujū-Kyū-Tsugi* (Sixty-nine stations along the Kiso Road) (Gotō, ed. 1976), which contains prints by both Hiroshige and Keisai Eisen (1790–?) (Ōta Kinen Bijutsukan, ed. 1983). For details, see Ohnuki-Tierney 1993a: 89.

57. In the series by Hiroshige in which cherry blossoms appear twenty-one times, Mount Fuji appears eighteen times altogether (Gotō, ed. 1975: plates 1, 3, 5, 8, 24, 25, 39, 45, 48, 56, 57, 75, 77, 84; Gotō, ed. 1976: plates 95, 96, 101, 115). Hiroshige had earlier executed a famous series, *Thirty-Six Views of Mount Fuji (Fuji Sanjū-rokkei)*, as did Katsushika Hokusai in his series, similarly entitled *Thirty-Six Views of Mount Fuji (Fugaku Sanjū-rokkei)*. In terms of frequency of appearance, Mount Fuji, the most sacred of all mountains, outnumbers cherry blossoms. However, Mount Fuji is there at all times regardless of the season, and is seen even from afar, in contrast to cherry blossoms, which bloom only for a short time, although often the two appear in the same print, as in those at Yoshiwara and at Koganei in Hiroshige's Mount Fuji prints.

58. The Japanese government chose sumo wrestlers to demonstrate the strength of the Japanese toward the very end of the Edo period, when Commodore Perry came knocking on the door to open the country. The Westerners were not impressed but were rather bemused, seeing in sumo the exotic and primitive Japanese (Tierney n.d.)

59. When Dan Rather reported on the funeral of the Shōwa emperor, a Japanese fan was displayed in the background.

60. For a detailed discussion of symbolization process, see Ohnuki-Tierney 1981b, for interpenetration of tropes ("polytrope" in my use), see Ohnuki-Tierney 1990, and for a symbol without materiality ("zero signifier" in my use), Ohnuki-Tierney 1994b.

Chapter Two

1. In 1868, the government already issued, under the emperor's name, the *Outline of the Political System (Seitaisho)*. For a discussion of the political system *(seitai)* and the national polity *(kokutai)*, see Eisenstadt 1996: 30–33; Gluck 1985: 144–45; Tanaka Akira 1996. Some argue that the *seitaisho* made the emperor remain apolitical, while Tanaka (1996) argues how it in fact contributed to the establishment of a strong central government with the emperor at the top.

2. Both urination by men and breast-feeding by women in public spaces continued into the 1960s (Ohnuki-Tierney 1997a: 176).

3. A woman from the imperial kitchen was sent to France to learn the French cuisine, and ever since French cuisine has been the standard for public banquets at the imperial court (Harada 1993: 19).

4. Clad in white, which they believed to repel bullets, they came to the palace to

appeal to the emperor to return to the prohibition of meat-eating. They ended in a scuffle with the palace guard, resulting in four deaths, one seriously injured, and the arrest of the remaining six.

5. In 1882 Fukuzawa wrote an article explaining why meat should not be prohibited on nutritional grounds. In 1890 he wrote that Japan was not suited for rice cultivation and thus the people should eat meat and rely on foreign rice (Harada 1993: 20–22).

6. The navy first adopted Western cuisine, successfully reducing the incidence of beriberi but inviting complaints from the sailors who were not used to Western cuisine. Mori Ōgai, a medical doctor and well-known novelist, advocated in 1885 a return to the rice diet, proclaiming how for nutrition, rice was all right as long as it is consumed together with fish, meat, and vegetables. His proposal was defeated, but the army found the solution to combat beriberi by adopting a diet of rice, mixed with wheat, meat, fish, and vegetables (Harada 1993: 22–23).

7. To eat while squatting signifies a major breach of proper eating manners. To sit on one's legs *(seiza)* was and still is the proper way to eat. Thus, meat-eating brought forth a drastic change in manners (Ohnuki-Tierney 1997a).

8. Butcher shops were called "beast shops" (*kemonoya; kemono* literally means "creatures with hair") or *momonjiya* (*momonji,* a derogative term for creatures with tails and hair/hide), and were located in marginal areas, such as the other side of a river from the major part of the city. Even today one sees a *momonjiya* across from Ryōgoku Bridge in Tokyo. The area beyond this bridge used to be a specially marked space where the marginalized people engaged in their stigmatized occupations.

9. For the pre- and early Meiji meat diet, see Endō [1910] 1968: 264; Gushima 1983: 188–97; Harada 1993: 258–59. For: the daimyō procession, Gushima 1983: 189; the cook books, Harada 1993: 259; the names of flowers for meats, Kanagaki Robun [1871–72] 1967: 27; the 1857 information, Harada 1993: 21; Keiō students, Gushima 1983: 191–92; the stores in Yokohama and Edo, Endō [1910] 1968: 264; the shop opened in Tokyo in 1869, Gushima 1983: 193–94.

10. Even during the early Meiji era, when the Japanese started to eat meat, the inns which served meat to foreigners destroyed and threw away all the cooking utensils and dishes with which they cooked and served meat, since they were permanently defiled. This practice made their hotel bills quite expensive, resulting in foreigners' complaints (Gushima 1983: 188–89). When Nakagawaya Kahei, eager to make money on beef with its growing popularity, wanted to set up a slaughterhouse in Tokyo, he could not find anyone willing to lend their land for the purpose. After setting up his shop at his relative's yard, he became afraid of the defilement from the slaughtering and performed a purification ritual (Gushima 1983: 192–93).

Although many began eating meat at these shops, cooking and eating meat at home did not become common until the Taishō period (1912–26) in eastern Japan (Kantō) (Endō [1910] 1968: 264).

11. By the end of the Edo period, the rising sun flag was fairly well known and was used by various social groups. For example, the Satsuma clan's request in 1853 to the shogunate to fly the rising sun flag on their ship headed abroad so as to identify it as a Japanese ship led to the government's adoption of the rising sun flag as the flag for Japanese ships. During the war for the Meiji "Restoration," those supporting

the shogunate and those attempting to overthrew it both carried the rising sun flag. After the adoption of the rising sun flag by the Meiji government as the national emblem, the army adopted the flag as it was, i.e., with the circular red sun in the center of a white background. The navy adopted another iconic representation of the rising/morning sun flag, which showed rays radiating from a red sun in the center (Murakami 1977: 179, on the emblem; 127–29, on the flag).

12. Murakami (1977) gives 1880 as the year of the first performance, and Inoue ([1963] 1967, vol. 1) gives 1896 as the year when the Ministry of Education required the eight songs to be sung at elementary school ceremonies. Shigeshimo (1991) offers a somewhat different account of the development of the national anthem. Today the absence of formal adoption of the anthem gives a weapon to individuals who oppose the current government's attempt to legislate its mandatory singing at schools. Even the label *Nihon* (the base where the sun rises) was originally a designation for Japan by the Chinese, from whose geographic perspective Japan was situated at the base of the place where the sun rose (Amino, personal communication).

13. From the perspective of personal interest, Iwakura Tomomi (1825–83), the major architect of the Meiji era, was a courtier who, by the "Restoration," could hope to gain access to the decision-making processes from which the courtiers had been excluded during the shogunate (Harootunian 1988: 391). Some of the figures who brought about the "Restoration" and those who were involved in the building of Meiji Japan were personally devoted to the idea of the emperor system (Hackett 1971; Gluck 1985) or to the Meiji emperor in particular. However, they were political figures for whom the emperor system met their personal and political goals.

14. For the rivalry between Yamagata and Itō, who shared the conviction of the need of a very strong central government but differed in visions for its execution, see Hackett 1971: esp. 243–44.

15. Others most involved are: Ōkuma Shigenobu, Iwakura Tomomi, Kido Takayoshi, Ōkubo Toshimichi, Yamagata Aritomo, and Mori Arinori (Emura, ed. 1996: 215–60; Najita 1979: 102–8).

16. Lorenz von Stein (1815–90), a professor at the University of Vienna, a German legal, economic and government scholar (Umetani 1995), was most influential to Itō Hirobumi when he visited Austria. Citing his age, he declined the Japanese government's invitation to stay in Japan, but he gave a series of lectures which was edited by Kawashima Jun, who went to Germany with Itō and learned from Stein in 1882, and again in 1886 through 1887 (Emura, ed. 1996: 265–66). At the request of the Japanese government, Karl Friedrich Hermann Roesler (1834–94), a German legal and economic scholar, came to Japan in 1878 and stayed until 1893, advising Itō Hirobumi on the drafting of the constitution, the Manual for the Imperial Household *(Kōshitsu Tenpan)*, Laws for the Diet, and Laws for Commerce (Emura, ed. 1996: 271; Umetani 1996b). H. Rudolf von Gneist (1816–95), a German legal scholar, was an expert on British constitutional history and advised Itō Hirobumi (Inada 1996). Albert Mosse (1846–1925), Gneist's student and a German legal expert, also lectured on the German constitution to Itō for five months in 1882 while Itō visited Germany. He stayed in Japan as the government consultant between 1886 and 1890. He made extensive comments and criticisms of the drafts written by his fellow German scholars. He drafted laws governing the basic structure of the regional governments and

was widely acclaimed as the father of regional self-governance (Umetani 1996c). While Itō Hirobumi visited Germany to learn about the government, Bismarck recommended Carl Rudolph (1841–1915), who came to Japan as a consultant for the Japanese government between 1884 and 1887. He advised Itō and others not only about the constitution but also about regional governments and the police system (Emura, ed. 1996: 263–65). Gustave Emile Boissonade (1825–1910), a professor at the University of Paris, was a legal expert who was invited to Japan between 1873 to 1895 to consult on the civil and criminal laws.

17. See also Roesler's letter of March 24, 1890 in Itō, ed. [1970] 1980: 484–88.

18. His draft was dated January 5, 1886 (Emura, ed. 1996: 263–65).

19. His draft was presented on April 30, 1887 in German, "Entwurf einer Verfassung für das Kaisertum Japan" (Emura, ed. 1996: 271–79).

20. The character for *chin* was initially pronounced as *ware* or *are*, but later changed to *chin* (Gotō 1996). For *Manyōshū* poem 4293 (vol. 20), Saitō ([1938] 1971: 168) uses the character for *chin*, with the pronunciation *ware* added, whereas Omodaka (1968: 12) uses two characters, with the pronunciation *ware* added.

21. These poems are (the number corresponds to the number which is assigned to each poem in the collection): 4328, 4331 (twice), 4358, 4373, 4393, 4394, 4398, 4403, 408 (twice), 4414, 4472, 4509, and 4510 (Omodaka 1968).

22. The two poems are 4360 and 4465 (Omodaka 1968: 87–92; 204–10).

23. Number 4465 (Omodaka 1968: 204–10). The term also appears in 4320, 4331, and 4456 (Omodaka 1968: 33, 51, 193).

24. Omodaka 1968: 103–4, no. 4373, trans. by this author. There is a scholarly controversy over the interpretation of the term *shiko* in *shiko no mitate*. Omodaka (1968: 103–4) argues that it is a self-referential term that is used out of modesty, while others interpret it as meaning "strong" instead of "ugly," while still others even argue that the phrase refers to "the damned shield," expressing a disguised note of resistance (Horton n.d.).

25. In reference to the pre-Meiji nativists' strategy for the "Restoration" of the *ancient* imperial system, Harootunian (1988: 374–75) argues that the "sign of antiquity" gave "the greatest degree of flexibility and the least amount of binding associations," and thus the oligarchs sought to place the foundation of the state in the legendary Jinmu emperor and in "a conception of authority unmediated by either history or recent institutional experience."

26. The *chū* sometimes included the sacrifice of one's own kin, as expressed by the term *migawari*, which refers to someone who sacrifices himself or his/her dear kin in order to save his master. This is the theme of *Sugawara Denju Tenarai Kagami*, one of the three most popular Kabuki plays (Toita et. al. eds., 1968: 139–233), where a man sacrifices his own son to save his master's son.

27. For an insightful history of the play of visibility and invisibility of the Meiji emperor in the government's effort for his representations, see Taki [1988] 1990, who emphasizes the visualization of the emperor since the Meiji. Murakami (1977: 182) in contrast emphasizes how in fact the emperor was a remote and invisible figure to the Japanese. I might add there that the father figure in Japanese culture and social imagination has never been a warm and caring figure.

28. As the deification of the emperor intensified, any physical representation of

the emperor became taboo. Instead of his portrait, coins carried the head of a dragon, following the practice in ancient China in which the face of a dragon was a metaphorical representation of emperor's face. In addition, a number of linguistic conventions were instituted, including forms of address and reference. Thus, his body and behaviors were referred to as, for example, the crystal (*gyoku* = *tama* = crystal) voice, crystal face, crystal body, crystal gate, etc. (Murakami 1977: 176–78). While the term *gyokutai* (crystal body) had been used to refer to the body of an emperor (see Miyata 1989; Tsumura [1917] 1970: 615), the ordinance by the Meiji government expanded the repertoire and enforced its usage by the people.

29. The expression "blood tax" created strong fear among the people and resulted in a number of revolts, often led by disgruntled former warriors (Iijima 1943: 376, 413–26). The original conscription underwent some changes in subsequent years (Iijima 1943: 427–33). For the entire text issued in 1872, see Iijima 1943; for exemptions, see Iijima 1943: 428–29.

30. The Meiji government had adopted a primogeniture system that enforced the kinship system based on the ideology, called the *i'e* system, in which the emperor is the father for all Japanese and each household is headed by a male who is in turn succeeded by the first-born male. Because of this system, all Japanese wars were fought by males other than the firstborn, responsible for the care of their parents, until World War II when they could not spare even the firstborn, although such consideration persisted to a certain degree.

31. See Ohnuki-Tierney 1998a for a conceptual model of the dialectic formation of the Self (the agrarian Japanese) and various external Others and internal Others (minorities).

32. For histories of the Yasukuni Shrine, see Kamo 1933–35; Murakami 1988, 1993; Mure 1988; Ōhama 1994; Sakamoto 1992; Yasukuni Jinja 1976, 1983, 1984, 1992; and Yui, Fujiwara, and Yoshida, eds. [1989] 1996: 60–64.

33. The *shōkonsha* (*shōkon* = to invite the souls of the dead; *sha* = shrine) were built throughout Japan to appease/console the souls of fallen soldiers. Originally pronounced as *yasuguni*, the term originated in a Chinese document and means to appease and peacefully govern the nation (Yui, Fujiwara, and Yoshida, eds. [1989] 1996: 64).

34. The first woman, Yamashiro Miyo from Akita Prefecture, was enshrined in 1869 and twenty-four others were enshrined in 1891. The English men, enshrined in 1907, were on a Japanese ship, *Hitachimaru*, whose captain was John Campbell (Miyata 1999: 51).

35. The new government was not yet established and the Dajōkan, the older form of the cabinet, was still in operation and was in charge of the imperial guard.

36. Sumō, Noh, and various other performing arts are regularly dedicated to the souls of the dead at shrines and temples, in the past as at present. In addition to the sumō performance during the ceremony in 1869, during the summer festival of the same year the most highly ranked sumō wrestlers (*yokozuna*) were featured in the matches (Tierney n.d.). The practice has continued, with some wartime interruptions, until today, when it is held at the height of the cherry blossom season in April, attracting some 10,000 people (Yasukuni Jinja 1992).

37. The origin of wet rice agriculture is still hotly debated. It came to Japan and

spread northeastward from northern Kyūshū in three successive waves. The Yamato state was established almost six centuries after the introduction of rice agriculture.

38. These scholars' emphasis on the religious-ritual nature of the Japanese kingship, held even by Marxist scholars like Murakami, deemphasizes the exclusively political nature of the Japanese kingship before the Meiji era. The religious qua political qua economic nature of these agrarian rituals of early leaders, including the emperors, is clearly expressed in the concept *matsurigoto* which means "the country where food for deities is made" (Orikuchi [1928b] 1975: 159–61; [1928c] 1975: 175–82; [1947] 1983: 271–80; for details, see Ohnuki-Tierney 1991; 1993a: 44–62).

39. They are: *niinamesai, ōnamesai (daijōsai),* and *kannamesai.* The annual harvest ritual of *niinamesai* becomes the *ōnamesai* at the time of the accession of a new emperor and is held as the last of three accession rituals, following the *senso* (including *kenji togyo*) and the accession ritual *(sokui no rei).* For the historical changes of various rituals, see Ohnuki-Tierney 1993a: 47. For imperial rituals, see Nihiname Kenkyūkai, ed. 1955; Ohnuki-Tierney 1993a; Sakurai 1988; Tanaka 1988; Ueda 1988; Yamamoto and staff, eds. 1988: 224–231; Yokota 1988; those in English are: Ebersole 1989; Ellwood 1973; Holtom [1928] 1972; and Mayer 1991.

40. Although the term *kami* usually refers to Shinto deities, I use it here to refer to all the "superhumans," including buddhas and even deities originating in Taoism. The Japanese do not make a clear-cut distinction between various religions, which many of them espouse simultaneously (Ohnuki-Tierney 1984: 145–55).

41. They include: ex-emperors Sutoku (r. 1155–58), Go-Toba (r. 1184–98), and Juntoku (r. 1210–21), and the Go-Daigo emperor (r. 1318–39) (Kitagawa 1990: 144, 147, 150). Kitagawa (1990) gives numerous instances of how the de facto military leaders held power over emperors.

42. Shoguns at times did not support, financially and otherwise, the execution of imperial rituals during the medieval and Edo periods. However, perhaps indicating their realization of the emperor's religious power, none dared take over the role of officiant in the rituals for the soul of rice. Likewise, some attended the imperial rituals wearing hoods *(zukin)* over their heads (Miyata, personal communication)—perhaps an admission of their "blasphemous" presence.

43. These individual instances expressing the dynamic characterization of the kami in Japanese religion are paralleled by the fluidity with which the Japanese "adopted" various foreign religions. When Buddhism was introduced from India via China and Korea, it was embraced eagerly by the elites, including the imperial family. But "most people in Japan at that time [the sixth and the seventh centuries] probably thought of the Buddha as just another kami" (Kitagawa 1990: 136). Officially, the Japanese tried to reconcile the two religious, by claiming that the kami are manifestations of the buddhas and bodhisattvas—a theory known as *honji suijaku.* Equally with ease, the Tokugawa Japanese, especially the elites, adopted Neo-Confucianism with its emphasis on the natural law and the Way of Heaven (Kitagawa 1990). Astonishing, for Westerners perhaps, the Meiji government enforced "'non-religious Shintō' which was to be adhered to by every Japanese subject, regardless of his or her personal 'religious' affiliation" (Kitagawa 1990: 161). Most Japanese today are at least nominally both Buddhist and Shintoist at the same time, usually without personal conviction (Eisenstadt 1996; Ohnuki-Tierney 1984: 145–49).

44. The term *shinsei* consists of two characters: *shin* (deity) and *sei* (sacred). The *kan* (Chinese) pronunciation of these characters indicates that it is a relatively new term. Importantly, other than in the constitution, it is most often used in reference to events in the West that are "holy," such as the Holy War of ancient Greece, Holy Roman Empire, Holy Alliance of 1815 in Austria. The term *okasubekarazu* was also a new term at the time, somewhat alien to the Japanese even today.

45. Ray (1991: 22–53) points out that Frazer's original formulation was based only on the classical example of the slaying of the priest-king of Diana at Nemi, but that Frazer himself and others nevertheless used it as a universal model. Some scholars of the Japanese emperor system consider the Japanese emperor system to constitute Frazerian divine kingship. Orikuchi ([1928b] 1975) first proposed this interpretation. Contemporary followers of Frazer via Orikuchi include Ebersole (1989) and Yamaori (1990a; 1990b). For "divine kingshp," see Dumont [1966] 1970; de Heusch 1985; Hocart [1927] 1969; [1936] 1970; Feeley-Harnik 1985; Geertz 1980: 121–46; Ohnuki-Tierney 1991; 1993a: 44–62; Sahlins 1985; and Tambiah 1976. Valeri (1985) uses the term "diarchic kingship."

46. Imperial rituals also underwent significant changes under the Meiji ordinance. With the adoption of the Gregorian Calendar, the date for the *niinamesai* was fixed on November 23, rather than the traditional date in the lunar calendar, and the *mitama shizume* ritual began to be performed for the souls of the emperor's wife and children (Murakami 1977: 70–71).

47. The drafts, liberal in nature, are nos. 6, 7, and 8; others are nos. 1, 2, 3, 4, and 5 (Emura 1996: 96–213).

48. This is from the report of Matsuoka Yōsuke when he went to the United States a year before the beginning of the Sino-Japanese war at the age of fourteen. He later became the wartime foreign minister and an A-class war criminal, who died of an illness during the trial.

Chapter Three

1. Nihon Hōsō Kyōkai Sābisu Sentā, ed. 1993: 21–22. Dokura's wife dates the incident to 1868 (Dokura 1966: 164–65).

2. For example, the buildings of Kōfukuji, the famous temple in Nara, were destroyed. The storage house was also destroyed, and Buddhist statues, sutras, and all other treasures were simply thrown away. The famous five-story pagoda was sold to a person, called Yasaburō, for ¥250. Yamada Yoshio ([1941] 1993: 400) gives the figure of ¥50, instead of ¥250, the figure quoted in Murakami, Tsuji, and Washio (1970: 172), whereas Saeki (1988: 160–62) puts the price at ¥25. The man wanted to melt it down for scrap metal, but the residents in the area objected for fear of fire spreading to their houses (Murakami, Tsuji and Washio, eds. 1970: 103–5, 171–72; Ōta 1979: 164; Saeki 1988: 160–62; Yamada Yoshio [1941] 1993: 400).

3. Some argue that cherry blossoms were chosen as a trope for short life after the creation of the *somei yoshino* variety just before the Meiji "Restoration." A gardener at Somei in Tokyo crossed a species called *edo higan zakura* with *ōshima zakura* from the Izu Peninsula, and the new species was named *somei yoshino* in Meiji 5 (Yamada Munemutsu 1977: 116). This variety proved to be easy to plant and fast growing.

Thus, it was planted all over Japan and became numerically the dominant species of cherry (Yahiro, ed. 1995: 5–114). However, as we saw earlier (chapter 1), even in the eighth-century myth-history the short life of cherry blossoms was noted by the Japanese, and most species of cherry blossoms fall after a brief blooming period.

4. Tsubouchi 1999: 29 and book jacket, for the circus; 69, 73, for horse racing. The circus was also performed at Asakusa Temple (Tōkyōto Edo Tōkyō Hakubutsukan 1993: 106).

5. The official histories of Yasukuni (Kamo 1933–35; Yasukuni Jinja 1983, 1984) do not mention who planted the trees, but a billboard at the shrine today identifies Kido. According to Nakajima Shigeko, wife of a Meiji politician, Kido had transplanted cherry trees from his villa in Somei (a Tokyo suburb), a neighborhood known for cherry trees (Ōmura Masujirō Sensei Denki Kankōkai 1944: 858–59). There is no record that Kido consulted Ōmura on the transplantation. The biography of Ōmura, published in 1944, states the appropriateness of cherry blossoms at Yasukuni, since "cherry blossoms are the mirror of bushidō" (the warrior's way) and are "appropriate for consoling the soul of Ōmura," but this is a latter-day association.

6. Despite the importance of cherry blossoms for the shrine, as an imperial shrine its crest was the imperial crest of the sixteen-petaled chrysanthemum. After World War II, on May 24, 1946, the shrine officially was allowed to adopt a crest in which a cherry blossom is superimposed over the chrysanthemum.

7. I thank Ms. Tomoda Junyo at Yasukuni Shrine for supplying me with the information about the original five-volume edition (her letters dated September 14 and October 8, 2000). According to her, they were published both in cloth and in leather, with the leather covers having no designs. My inquiry to her was prompted by my discovery that a copy of vol. 4 at the Far Eastern Library at the University of Chicago, donated by Yamazaki Tōji, has a cover with a design of falling cherry petals. But no other volumes have the design. None of the five volumes at the University of California, Berkeley, donated by the Mitsui family, has the cherry petal design. Given that the illustrations on the pages immediately after the title page are different in the Chicago and Berkeley volumes, my guess is that these pages were replacements of the original ones.

8. These boy air force soldiers were admitted in the army at Tokorozawa army air base. First called *shōnen kōkūhei* ("boy air force soldiers"), the term was changed to *shōnen hikōhei* ("boy flying soldiers") in 1942. Morimatsu 1993: 534–35.

9. There were some precursors. In 1869, Sakura (written with different characters from the one for cherry blossoms) domain had a cherry blossom as a design on the cap (Ōta 1980: 43) and the navy that fought on the side of the shogun also had an insignia with an anchor in the center, surrounded by cherry leaves, and a cherry blossom at the top (Ōta 1980: 127).

10. Ōta 1980: 134, for the artists; 16–17, 131–78, for insignia. Kaigun Daijin Kanbō 1935: 20, 22, 26–31, 37, 41–42, 46–47, 49–52, 59–61, 94.

11. The part of the government effort was to establish the so-called Nan-chō, the southern imperial line, as the legitimate imperial line (Murakami 1970: 187–88). During the Nanbokuchō era (1336–92), there were two rival imperial courts—the north and the south—with the Go-Daigo emperor establishing the southern imperial line.

12. The Japanese attribute this event to the so-called Manchurian Incident of 1931 (Smith and Wiswell 1982: 232).

13. Yamamoto [1716] 1969: 134, 253–54 (love); 42 (male homosexuality); 58, 152 (death); 111, 125 (devotion to one's master). He explains that homosexuality in the context of bushidō expressed an absolute bondage between the master and his follower/retainer (113–16, 134). According to him, heterosexual love is basically functional—reproduction of offspring. Referred to as *shūdō*, or *danshoku*, homosexual love between warriors, according to him, is pure and yet intense, although he considers that a warrior's love should be kept strictly hidden as *shinobu koi* (love that should be restrained).

14. Michael Silverstein, personal communication, Nov. 1999.

15. A dried plant is encased at the Yūshūkan Exhibition Hall, at the Yasukuni Shrine. The information is from the explanation attached to the case.

16. Bak Sangmee, personal communication, December 1994.

17. The initial shipment of two thousand young trees by Ozaki Yukio, the mayor of Tokyo, did not pass inspection due to insects among them. At the mayor's request, the second shipment of trees were grown by Mr. Kumagai Yatozō, a graduate of the agricultural school of the Imperial University of Tokyo and the head of the Agricultural Experiment Division of the Department of Agriculture and Commerce of the Japanese government.

18. The European Union banned both commercial and "friendship" donations of Japanese cherry trees until Japan opened its market to foreign agricultural products (*Daily Yomiuri*, May 8, 1997).

Chapter Four

1. The Wilson Readers are: *Nature Study in Elementary School: A Manual for Teachers* (1897), *Nature: First Reader* (1897), and *Nature: Second Reader* (1898), by L. L. W. Wilson (1864–1937), an American educator. New York: Macmillan.

2. The first volume of *Shōgaku Kokugo Dokuhon* was published in 1932 and the last, vol. 12, was published in 1938 (Kaigo 1964b: 539). For discussion of the socioeconomic and political context of textbooks, see Kaigo 1964b: 609–14.

3. Nitobe believed that many of the ancestors of the Japanese came from the Pacific islands, especially Malaysia (Nitobe [1907] 1970: 186–96). Yanagita (1933) offered the first of many interpretations of this tale. See also Antoni 1991.

4. The government published the first music textbook in 1881, the second in 1883, and the third in 1884. A book of songs for kindergartners was published in 1887.

5. For example, "Moon for Four Seasons" *(Shiki no tsuki)*, published in 1884, which praises "cherry blossoms in the mountains in full bloom" (Horiuchi and Inoue, eds. 1958: 23).

6. Examples of the archaic terms are: the Majesty's country *(sumera mikuni)* and warriors *(mononofu)*. A song to celebrate the emperor's birthday, composed in 1893, also uses the archaic term of ōkimi (Horiuchi and Inoue eds., 1958: 42).

7. "Come, Come" in *Songs of the Meiji Era (Meiji Shōka)* (Horiuchi and Inoue, eds. 1958: 32–33); "One Hundred Thousand Enemies in Songs" in *The Songs for the National Subjects (Kokumin Shōkashū)* (Horiuchi and Inoue, eds. 1958: 40–41).

8. In an essay "Kimono" by Hasegawa Shigure, quoted in Nishizawa 1990b: 2005; for the year of composition, Nishizawa 1990b: 1999–2001.

9. Examples are "Hanasaka Jijii," "Urashima Tarō," "Momotarō," "Usagi to Kame," "Hatopoppo," and "Oshōgatsu."

10. These dormitory songs are (in the order of appearance in the text): Horiuchi and Inoue, eds., 1958: 76–77, 104–5, 128–29. *Kurenai* (red) refers to the pinkish color of cherry blossoms, and *hana* (flowers) specifically refers to cherry blossoms (Yoshida Shūji, personal communication, May 1998).

11. Rikugun Chūō Yōnen Gakkō (later Rikugun Shikan Gakkō Yoka). Nominal author of the text is given as Katō Meishō. Yamaki 1986: 120–21.

12. The composer of the music, Ōmura Nōshō, did not even notice its popularity and did not bother to identify himself as the composer until 1980, when an old recording was discovered that identified him as the composer (Nishizawa 1990, 2: 2464–67; Takahashi 1994a).

13. Saijō Yaso wrote another song, "Tōkyō Ondo," which may also have a subtext of endorsing Japan's military expansion into the Pacific (Takahashi 1994f).

14. The dates in this section are given according to the lunar calendar; they are the dates used even in contemporary productions. The date of the retainers' killing of Kira actually took place on December 15, but December 14 is the date used in the Kabuki texts from various periods and film productions. For the chronology of the historical incidents, see Nakayama 1988: 58–59.

15. For this comparison with historical records, I used the original script for the 1748 production (Takeda [1937] 1982; English translation, Keene 1971). A most comprehensive study of the historical event is found in Yagi 1989. The play was first staged in the puppet theater (jōruri) on August 14, 1748, at the Takemotoza theater in Osaka and then adapted for the Kabuki theater in December of the same year (Urayama 1997: 458; Takeda 1937: 3).

16. Before this play was staged, there were other attempts to portray the Akō incident on stage under disguise. For example, *Akebono Soga no Youchi* (Night attack at dawn by the Soga), staged at the Nakamura Theater in Edo, presented the incident under the pretext of describing the celebrated night attack of the twelfth century Soga brothers. Another is *Goban Taiheiki* (A Chronicle of great peace played on a chess-board), written in 1706 by Chikamatsu Monzaemon. See Keene 1971: 3–5; Smith 1990.

17. Muro, a Confucian scholar who served Shogun Tokugawa Yoshimune (reigned 1716–45), wrote *Akōgijinroku* (The honorable warriors of Akō) (Yagi 1989: 23–15).

18. "Law for Mercy for All Beings" *(Shōrui Awaremi no Rei).* Reischauer and Craig 1978: 112–13.

19. While the interpretation by Keene (1971), the dean of Japanese literature, is puzzling, it is not surprising that Benedict ([1946] 1967: 163–64, 199–205, 217) was given the version of the play as transformed during Japan's totalitarian periods. For an original reading of Benedict as she foresaw the coming of the age of Pax Americana, see Kelly 1998a: 851–53, 860–63.

20. Smith (1990: 7) suggests that the sustained popularity was found more in Kyoto and Osaka, but not in Edo.

21. Nakau notes that these woodblock prints were produced most actively toward the end of the Edo period and estimates the number to be well over ten thousand. Nishiyama thinks that every woodblock-print artist who became famous after the first production of the play depicted one or more scenes and actors from the play. Utagawa Kuniyoshi (1797–1861), a master of the genre of warrior prints, created a series of prints on the forty-seven retainers, such as the *Seichū Gishi-den* (1847–48) and its sequel under the same title (1848) (Weinberg 2000).

22. John Kelly urged me to interpret the proverb beyond its literary meaning.

23. In Mayama's *Genroku Chūshingura*, the scene of Lord Asano's suicide was switched from the manor back to the yard.

24. The film was produced in 1941–42 by Kōa Eiga Co., with Shirai Shintarō as executive producer, screenplay by Hara Ken'ichirō and Yoda Yoshikata, and starring Kawarazaki Chōjūrō, Nakamura Kanemura, and Arashi Yoshisaburō. An English version available in video was produced in 1988. Recognizing how the play served as a powerful means to propagate the state ideology, the American Occupational Forces banned the staging of the play at the end of the war, but it resurfaced in 1952 in disguise. It remains popular even today.

25. See detailed discussions in Tierney (n.d.) and Yamanaka ([1975] 1985). Yamanaka examines the program for building the body at elementary schools.

26. In Japanese there are over thirty grammatical forms that serve as pronouns. Some are exclusively for men and others for women, while some are used by women in most contexts but by men only in formal contexts.

27. For Germany, Mosse 1990: 72–73 and Wolf 1999: 239; and for Russia, J. Kornblatt personal communication, February 17, 1999. Judith Kornblatt (personal communication on September 11, 1998) points to the complexity of the concepts of nationalism and patriotism in Russia, where the loyalty involved in nationalism and patriotism was divided: toward the tsars, who were all foreign trained or often foreign born, vs. *narod*, that is, the Russian soil or the Russian soul. She uses these terms in a reverse way from mine, using nationalism to refer to "a more amorphous love of the country, and patriotism as the sentiment linked toward the institution. The former is for 'motherland' or 'Mother Russia,' and the latter for 'fatherland.'" Garon's (1997) treatment of postwar Japan includes a discussion of how, since the 1920s, the state persistently attempted to mobilize women in the war effort.

28. In his well-known lecture which was never published, Bellah (1967) pointed out that the emperor represented the feminine principle and the shoguns the masculine principle.

Chapter Five

1. For example, see the case of Okabe Heiichi, which appears in Inoguchi and Nakajima 1963: 180; 1975: 235–37. Or see the three letters from Hayashi Ichizō (1995: 66–79), which are presented as two letters, with multiple deletions from each (Inoguchi and Nakajima 1967: 231–35).

2. Hoyt, who has written a great deal on Japanese operations during World War II, has written two books on the tokkōtai operation, one (1983b) on Ugaki and the other on the operation in general (1983a), neither of which uses Japanese sources

extensively. He believes the Japanese would have kept fighting, even after the atomic bombs and the "holocaust" brought about by the B-29 bombers, had it not been for the emperor's announcement of defeat, which brought the "salvation of Japan" and saved the lives of millions of American and Allied troops (Hoyt 1983a: 302–3).

3. The Mongols were well equipped with poisoned arrows and guns, which the Japanese did not have. They had a force of 900 ships and 30,000 men the first time, and over 4,400 ships and 140,000 men the second time. If not for "God's wind," the Japanese could have been defeated. Ōnishi's father was an instructor of Japanese fencing *(kendō)* and named his practice hall *(dōjō) Shinpū* (Hattori Shōgo, personal communication, May 1999). Ōnishi's use of *Shinpū* for the navy tokkōtai derives from his family background as well as from his wish that God's wind in the form of the tokkōtai would repeat the miracle of saving Japan. Ōnishi's photo and his last poem in calligraphy are on the frontispiece and the two characters in calligraphy for "God's Wind" are on the title page of Inoguchi and Nakajima 1958.

4. Ninagawa's (1998: 127) figures (the source unidentified) are: 32 vessels sunk; 368 vessels damaged. On the Okinawa operation Coox (1988: 367) reports that the Americans counted 896 raids against Okinawa and another 1,000 against the fleet, especially against destroyer and escort pickets and anchored aircraft carriers. For the entire operation, Coox's figures are: 36 ships sunk; 386 damaged; 763 planes knocked out by all causes, with 7,830 Japanese aircraft downed by the Americans. According to the record kept by the Allied Forces: hitting the target: 383 planes; near miss: 180 planes; shot down: 174 planes (quoted in Ninagawa 1998: 127).

5. Translations of the ranks of navy practice pilots and students soldiers were from Hattori Shōgo (letter dated April 26, 2000).

6. None of biographical information tells much about Ōnishi's idea in reference to cherry blossoms, except for noting his fondness for flowers in general (Kusayanagi 1972: 250–55). For a very sympathetic/partisan biography, see Ko Ōnishi Takijirō Kaigun Chūjō-den Kankōkai, ed. 1957; Moji 1989.

7. The handwritten report, which Hattori Shōgo let me examine, is kept at the Senshi-shitsu (War History Room) of the Japanese Defense Force Library.

8. The sword was believed to be used by the legendary Yamato Takeru-no-Mikoto during his expedition to conquer the eastern region of Japan. The sword is the "divine body" enshrined at the Atsuta Jingū in Nagoya, a major national Shinto shrine from the Meiji era until the end of World War II. It enshrines the Sun Goddess and other legendary deities ancestral to the imperial family.

9. Another grotesque "exception," I might add, is Admiral Ugaki, Commander in Chief of the Fifth Naval Air Fleet, who sortied as a private tokkōtai pilot from Ōita, Kyushu, to Okinawa after hearing the emperor's announcement of surrender, killing himself and sixteen young followers (Ugaki 1991). Besides Ugaki, there were two others who flew off after the declaration of the end of the war by the emperor (Okumura 1979: 305).

10. The figures are from Morioka (1995b: 11, 50–59) and Ninagawa (1998: 127–280). The figures provided by Fujishiro (1981: 455) are almost identical with those provided by Ninagawa. Hattori (personal communication, May, 1999) warns that these figures are only approximations, since they include deaths from accidents, etc.

11. Sasaki Hachirō also was at this base, but his diary does not include the last days.

12. For Ichijima Yasuo, the sources are: Ebina 1983: 142–43, 189, 272, 275–282; *Cherry Blossoms of the Same Class* 1966a: 13–17, 115–25; 1966b: 225; *Drafting of Students* 1981: 108; Morioka 1995b: 59–60, 67–73. 81, 85; *Listen to the Voices* 1988: 241–44. Ebina (1983: 275) lists his rank as navy second lieutenant.

13. According to the Meiji constitution, male imperial family members must serve in the military, taking turns between the army and navy, with the first born male in the army.

14. In his March 19, 1945 diary entry, he composed four poems with plum blossoms as the central trope. In his diary entry of March 26, he briefly mentions camellia and peach blossoms.

15. This scene or a scene similar to this is captured by a cameraman from the Mainichi Newspaper Company (plate 7). The photo has been circulated and appears in a number of places, including at the special exhibit of the "Fiftieth Anniversary of the Students Going to the Front" *(Gakuto Shutsujin Gojūshūnen)* at Yūshūkan at Yasukuni Shrine. Sonoda Chieko married after the war. After her husband's death, she made available to various individuals Anazawa's diary and letters, which she had entrusted to someone during her marriage. Some were displayed at the above-mentioned special exhibit at the Yasukuni Shrine.

16. Sources: Ebina 1977: 234–360; 1983: 32–33, 36, 76, 146, 195–97; 199–200; *Cherry Blossoms of the Same Class* 1966a: 57–60, 101–4, 177–79; 1966b: 90–94; Morioka 1995b: 79–92, 96–97, 100.

17. Except for the entry on his drinking, passages quoted are from Morioka 1995b: 60, 73–79, 82–99, 104–6, 110–14, 117–54, 163, 174–77. See also: Ebina 1983: 41, 142–43, 169–171, 177–78; *Cherry Blossoms of the Same Class* 1966a: 60–64, 181–83; 1966b: 95–97.

18. Sources: Ebina 1977: 239–40; 1983: 77, 80, 134, 157–58; *Cherry Blossoms of the Same Class* 1966a: 95–101; 1966b: 81–83.

19. Mr. Kasuga's permission to publish his letter was given to me in his letter dated September 8, 2000.

20. Suga is introduced in Ebina 1983: 142, 181–83; Inoguchi and Nakajima 1963: 182–83; 1975: 238–239; *Cherry Blossoms of the Same Class* 1966a.

21. The information about Satō Nami and her letter were posted in the exhibition case as well as printed in the newsletter, *Yasukuni*, published by the shrine (Yasukuni Jinja 1982). The latter was sent to me by Ms. Itonaga Motoko of the Advertisement Department at the shrine.

22. See also Ōtsuka Koreo, who was born in 1922, graduated from Chūō University and died on April 28, 1945 (sources: Ebina 1983: 217; *Listen to the Voices* 1949: 222–26). He refers to cherry blossoms without linking them to *pro rege et patria mori*, whereas Ōhira and Ōkita refer to them in relation to the *pro rege et patria mori* ideology. Ōhira Seishi was born in 1922, graduated from Hōsei University, and died as an army tokkōtai pilot on April 12, 1945 (sources: Morioka 1995b: 9, 14, 22–23, 35–36, 42–44). Ōkita Kei was born on June 23, 1921, graduated from Nihon University and died on April 12, 1945 as a navy tokkōtai pilot (sources: Ebina 1983: 137, 160; *Cherry Blossoms of the Same Class* 1966b: 21–22).

Chapter Six

1. A few letters or passages from diaries appear here and there, but without context, in Cook and Cook 1992, Morris 1975, and Inoguchi and Nakajima 1958. An English translation of *Listen to the Voices* was published in 2000 (Yamanouchi 2000).

2. They were donated by the survivors to the Yasukuni Shrine, some of which are displayed at the Yūshūkan Exhibition Hall at the shrine. Original wills and other writings are housed at former army and navy academies and tokkōtai bases, including: Kyōiku Sankōkan at the former Naval Academy in Edajima (Hiroshima Prefecture); the former kaiten underwater torpedo training center at Ōtsushima (Yamaguchi Prefecture); the former army tokkōtai airbase in Chiran (Kagoshima Prefecture); and the former navy tokkōtai airbase at Kanoya (Kagoshima Prefecture). Copies of the wills *(ishotsuzuri)* are housed at the Library of the Research Institute of the Defense Ministry (Bōeichō Bōei Kenkyūjo Toshokan). According to Hattori Shōgo, Research Professor at the Library of the Defense Research Center and a specialist on the tokkōtai, Ōmi Ichirō meticulously hand-copied the writings housed at the former military academies and bases and deposited over three hundred double-sided pages at the Defense Ministry Library. I was not allowed to look at them in May of 1999 on the grounds that the library had not received permission for public viewing from all the survivors.

3. When Morioka Kiyomi (1995a: 3–6) checked some published material against the originals stored at the former tokkōtai bases and other archives, he discovered numerous discrepancies and errors. He was therefore forced to narrow down his selection to those writings whose accuracy he could verify. He identified the only reliable sources as those left by university student soldiers. More specifically, his selection came from the tokkōtai pilots from one army corps (the 20th Shinbu Corps, which flew from the Chiran Army Airbase) and from the Jinpū Navy tokkōtai corps (consisting of Shichishō-tai; Shōwa-tai; Tsukuba-tai), who took off from the Kanoya Navy Airbase (Morioka 1995b: 5–6).

4. I began my research by attempting to establish a profile of each pilot covered in a number of edited books. However, when I read volumes on individual pilots who were also cited in the edited books, I realized that the latter were almost totally unusable because the editors, although well intentioned, selected mostly the passages that fit their vision. Beyond brief remarks in their prefaces and postscripts, the editors, except Morioka, rarely spelled out their method of selection. In general, however, editors with liberal inclinations excluded nationalistic passages, while conservative editors did the opposite.

5. The title in Japanese: *Harukanaru Sanga ni.* Tōkyō Daigaku Gakusei Jichikai and Senbotsu Gakusei Shuki Henshū Iinkai, eds. 1951.

6. The title in Japanese: *Kike Wadatsumi no Koe: Nihon Senbotsu Gakusei no Shuki*, Nihon Senbotsu Gakusei Shuki Henshū Iinkai, ed. [1949] 1952. The term *wadatsumi* is an ancient term from the *Manyōshū*, referring to the God in charge of the sea. For English translation, see Yamanouchi 2000.

7. Brief introductions to the excerpts include only their name, birth date, major at the university, date of entry into the military, and date and place of death.

8. The title in Japanese: *Kike Wadatsumi no Koe: Dai-Ni-shū*, Nihon Senbotsu Gakusei Kinenkai, ed. [1988] 1995. An example of the inclusion of expressions of

military ideology is the writings of Kido Rokurō (237–40), which was excluded from the *Far Off Mountains and Rivers* (1947). Kido proudly announced that a feeling of devotion to military causes filled the air at Waseda University and referred to the presence and activities of ultra-right organizations at several universities. Some alterations of the original texts by the editors were pointed out by the NHK, the national broadcasting company and then in an article by Hosaka Masayasu, a well-known nonfiction writer, published in *Bungei Shunjū*, a highly respected monthly magazine. Hosaka (1985) pointed out how the revised version of *Listen to the Voices* (1949) still contained the alterations (see *Shūkan Bunshun*, August 1997). According to historian Irokawa Daikichi, who wrote his own memoir as a student soldier (Irokawa 1993), these alterations are mostly minor additions of words that give the text a liberal slant, and they represent less than 2 percent of the corpus (personal communication, May 1999).

9. For example, a two-volume set was published in 1996, *Ah, Cherry Blossoms of the Same Class: Writings of the Youth Never to Return (Aa Dōki no Sakura: Kaezarazu Seishun no Shuki)*, edited by Kaigun Hikō Yobi Gakusei Dai-14-ki-kai; hereafter referred to as *Cherry Blossoms of the Same Class* (1996a and b). The first volume, 1996a, was originally published under the same title by Mainichi Shinbun. The second volume, 1996b, includes the material that was left out of 1996a. This set contains writings by the pilots as well as recollections by their surviving family members and comrades. Another collection, *Conscription of Students: Portraits of Youth Who Faced Death (Gakuto Shutsujin: Shi to Taiketsu shita Seishun no Gunzō)*, edited by the Mainichi Shirīzu Shuppan (1981) (hereafter referred to as *Conscription of Students*) is even less systematic in representing these student soldiers than those discussed above.

Morioka's two works (1993; 1995b) are helpful not only because of his scrutiny of sources but because of his inclusion of soldiers' personal backgrounds. Each pilot appears in a number of separate sections of narratives that are arranged according to the sequence of events. This provides some context that is not evident in the writings of a single pilot, such as the phase of the war or the information on a particular base. However, only a small portion of the corpus of writing of each individual is included, and it appears in a number of places, which renders it hard to establish a profile of a particular pilot and to understand the complexities and contradictions in his thoughts. For example, the statement by Hayashi Ichizō (profiled in this chapter) that he will die for the emperor and his later retraction of that statement are some forty pages apart in Morioka's book (Morioka 1995b: 117 and 157), and the reader is not alerted to the contradiction. Similarly, the portrayal of Sasaki Hachirō (profiled in this chapter) consists primarily of a summary of Sasaki's philosophical debates with his friends and leaves aside the complex and often contradictory dimensions of his thoughts.

Publications by Ebina, although consisting of excerpts, are also helpful, since he presents passages not included in the volumes on the single pilots as well as remarks by family members that portray how they, too, struggled with their doubts about the war (Ebina 1977, 1983).

If liberals have represented these pilots through their own lens, so have those on the right. A large number of publications, mostly non-scholarly, consist of collections of letters, wills, etc., taken out of context and emphasizing patriotic/nationalistic themes. The publications by the Yasukuni Shrine are dedicated to the validation of the *pro rege et patria mori* ideology, with cherry blossoms as the master trope (Yasukuni Jinja 1994, 1995a, 1995b, 1996). The subtitle of one of their publications (1995a), which derives from the title of their exhibit, refers to World War II as "The Great Asian War." Not only are the writings of fallen soldiers taken out of context, but they are reproduced in such a way that it is difficult to judge their authenticity. For example, as we saw in chapter 5, on the day of Japan's defeat on August 15, Hayashi Ichizō's mother shouted, "Vice-Admiral Ōnishi [the inventor of the tokkōtai operation] must die." But in the publication by the Yasukuni Shrine (1994: 71), his mother is reported to have sent the following statement to an unidentified magazine: "If it had been a peaceful time, Ichizō would have become a gentle family man with his wife and children. But it was his fate to have been born when the whole nation was involved in the war. When the motherland is in danger, you cannot simply watch it. Those who must go [to the war] must go." In one of her poems she laments how the whole society is governed by the notion of "loyalty," but, even if she did indeed write this letter expressing resignation or rationalization, it is not introduced in the context of her anguish and defiance. Similarly, in a section called "Last letters home," Inoguchi and Nakajima ([1953] 1958: 196–208) include only one letter from Hayashi Ichizō to his mother that suited the purpose of the book.

10. Cherry blossoms appear only rarely in the three collections *Far Off Mountains and Rivers* and *Listen to the Voices* (1949, 1988). Yet, the passages referring to cherry blossoms by the same soldiers appear elsewhere. For example, excerpts of writings by Ichijima Yasuo, introduced in chapter 5, are included in *Listen to the Voices* (1949), Morioka (1995b) and *Cherry Blossoms of the Same Class* (1966a, 1966b). On the other hand, sections with references to cherry blossoms appear only in *Cherry Blossoms of the Same Class* (1966a: 116, 117), which, however, does not contain information about his Christianity, an extremely important aspect of Ichijima's thought. Morioka (1995b) includes Ichijima's Christianity but excludes Ichijima's references to cherry blossoms.

The absence of references to cherry blossoms in these three collections may be due to their exclusion of nationalistic passages as well as passages that contain more affective dimensions, in which cherry blossoms are more likely to appear. *Far Off Mountains and Rivers* contains only one reference to cherry blossoms, in a passage by Moriwaki Funio, a graduate of the University of Tokyo who was an attache to the Japanese Embassy in Germany (*Far Off Mountains and Rivers* 1947: 58–61). Through a window he gazes at cherry blossoms beaten down by cold rain, trembling and clinging to the branches. He considers them ugly and thinks it is much more beautiful to fall without hesitation—a reminder that he and his comrades should fall beautifully. *Listen to the Voices* (1949) also edits out ultra-nationalistic writings, but it contains a few more references to cherry blossoms. *Listen to the Voices* (1988) contains scarcely any. Similarly, neither volume of *Cherry Blossoms of the Same Class* includes many passages concerning cherry blossoms, their titles notwithstanding. Yet the same soldiers in these two volumes refer to cherry blossoms in passages that appear in Ebina 1983 and Morioka 1995b.

Where the editors' own beliefs are closer to the *pro rege et patria mori* ideology, not only cherry blossoms in other contexts but cherry blossoms as the symbol of soldiers' sacrifice for the emperor/country are the central focus of the books, as in the case of publications by the Yasukuni Shrine. The whole 125-page booklet by Muranaga ([1989] 1997), who edited and published some of the wills left at the Chiran Airbase, is full of patriotic phrases containing references to cherry blossoms—a perfect reproduction of the *pro rege et patria mori* ideology. On page after page we read how happy the soldiers were to fall like cherry blossoms for the emperor/country, and we are shown numerous photos of smiling young tokkōtai pilots, although some of the faces in the group photos certainly reveal anxieties. This booklet might even convince the reader that they all believed in the *pro rege et patria mori* ideology and were happy and honored to perish. Muranaga, who was himself a student soldier in the navy, declares, "It is foolish to say that the wills and letters do not tell the truth because of the censorship and that they were forced to write in a certain way. How in the world would you think that these brave soldiers facing death would be afraid of censorship?" (Muranaga [1989] 1997: 124). However, the wills and last letters to the parents were meant to be part of the "public" record, and the soldiers were told so before they wrote them.

11. For the importance of writing as the mode of communication, see Ohnuki-Tierney 1984: 65. For the importance of diaries, see Hashimoto 1990; Keene 1984: 10–14. Keene's interest in this genre of "diary literature" originated during World War II, when he was assigned the job of translating the diaries of Japanese soldiers left on the battlefields. Some soldiers even wrote their messages in English addressed to American soldiers who, they hoped, would find their diaries after their death (Keene 1984: 14–18).

12. For example, *Riku-Kaigun Tokubetsu Kōgekitai Ieishū*, no. 1, a collection of last poems by tokkōtai pilots, edited by Tokkōtai Senbotsusha Irei Heiwa Kinen Kyōkai (mimeograph, no date of publication), is full of references to themselves as young cherry blossoms, often with reference to the emperor and/or to the Yasukuni Shrine. This organization is also referred to as Eirei ni Kotaeru-kai (Organization to Respond to the Heroic Souls), which is associated with Nihon Izokukai (The Organization of the Survivors). This nation-wide organization has, through its publications and public statements, been pushing for the return of Yasukuni Shrine as the national shrine with the annual visits by the prime minister, cabinet members, defense army staff, and foreign guests. On the anniversary of the end of the war on August 15, 1998, it made a public statement denouncing former Prime Minister Obuchi's failure to pay an official visit to the shrine as the grounds for considering Obuchi not qualified to be prime minister (*Asahi Shinbun*, evening edition, August 15, 1998). The organization also published a booklet which portrays the war as an exercise in self-defense and which exonerates Tōjō, the Shōwa emperor, etc. Nihon Kaigi is a similar organization. These three organizations seem to sanction/promote the wartime ideology, while always stressing peace as their goal.

13. The first names of Hayashi Tadao and Hayashi Ichizō are added only when the context does not indicate which Hayashi is referred to.

14. Sasaki is introduced briefly in: Mainichi Shirīzu Shuppan 1981: 108; Ebina 1983: 138, 184–86, 272, 295–97; *Far Off Mountains and Rivers* [1947] 1951: 13–17; *Listen to the Voices* 1949: 113–22; *Cherry Blossoms of the Same Class* 1966a: 20–

23, 137, 1966b: 225; Morioka 1995b: 59–67, 72–73, 81, 85. His lengthy essay on Miyazawa Kenji is mentioned only briefly and his last poem, composed on April 11, 1945, is not in Sasaki 1981, but both are reproduced in *Listen to the Voices* 1949 and in Ebina 1983, respectively. Ebina also has some excepts of his diary on the base until his death. A lengthy essay on Sasaki's life by Fujishiro, editor of Sasaki (1981), at the end of the book is most helpful. Fujishiro's own life is almost identical except the end—like Sasaki he went both to the First Higher School and the Imperial University of Tokyo, and became a student soldier in the navy.

15. This is not an unusual relationship between mother and son in Japan, where a mother takes a nonauthoritarian, and at time subordinate, position to her male child when he achieves his adulthood, which starts around the time of higher school.

16. Satō Haruo, introduced in chapter 4, wrote some pro-war jingoistic poems. However, he also wrote many novels and poems of various kinds. Sasaki read *The Star (hoshi)* and found it "beautiful" and its "art for art's sake" premise convincing (Sasaki 1981: 202).

17. See also the diary entries for October 14, 15, 18 and 19, 1943. The government's construction of Yamamoto Isoroku as the model of Japanese soldier was questioned by his own men who saw him otherwise (Umezawa Shōzō, personal communication).

18. Ebina 1983: 42–43, 46–47, 87–89, 272, 298–303; *Cherry Blossoms of the Same Class* 1966a: 48–56, 86–92, 174–76, 194–97, 205–7; 1966b: 149, 206; *Conscription of Students* 1981: 26–27, 108, 114–15, 157.

19. He began writing on February 26, 1945. The last essay, marked as "unfinished," was written on March 11, 1945 (Hayashi 1967: 205–15).

20. Note that Hayashi's notion of the two souls resonates with the Japanese notion of *konpaku*. As Miyake (1985: 222–23) points out, a person is born with a soul *(tamashii, kon)* but another soul *(haku, paku)* must be nurtured after birth and this is done by the consumption of rice. Since rice embodies the soul of deities, a human becomes complete with both souls *(konpaku)* as he/she partakes in rice consumption.

21. Short passages about Nakao appear also in Ebina 1983: 145; *Far Off Mountains and Rivers* 1947: 165–66; *Listen to the Voices* 1949: 129–30; and *Cherry Blossoms of the Same Class* 1966a: 83, 166.

22. In 1870 the Meiji government turned the mythical origin of Japan, accession to the throne by the Jinmu emperor, into a "historical fact" and established the Japanese calendar year beginning in that year.

23. There has been a scholarly controversy over Nishida's philosophy in reference to the nationalist ideology at the time and his link to Heidegger.

24. In the poem, he uses the name Kaguyahime, which I translated as a beautiful woman. Kaguyahime is a protagonist in a Japanese fairy tale of the Heian period who was born of a bamboo and raised by an old man. Although she was exceptionally beautiful and was courted by many noble men, including the emperor, she rejected them all and went up to the moon on August 15.

25. The title in Japanese is *Wadatsumi no Ko'e Kieru Koto-naku: Kaiten Tokkōtai-in no Shuki*. As noted in the text, the term *wadatsumi* means a deity of the sea, but has been used in the title of the well-known collection of writings left by tokkōtai pilots and became a metaphor for these pilots who died in the sea. Some parts from

Wada (1972) are also reproduced in *Far Off Mountains and Rivers* 1947: 125–36, *Listen to the Voices* 1949: 228–35, and *Listen to the Voices* 1988: 273–310.

26. Mechanical problems occurred regularly. On May 28, 1945, he took off for the mission, but was forced to return on June 28 because of mechanical problems.

27. The will written on December 8, 1943 (Wada 1972: 108–9).

28. The title in Japanese is *Hi nari Tate nari: Nikki, Haha eno Tegami, Hayashi Ichizō Ikōshū.* It consists primarily of letters to his mother and others. Unfortunately, the letters in Hayashi Ichizō (1995) are not dated. Dates to these letters are offered in other sources for Hayashi, but they are not reliable when cross-checked against his movements and events during his last months. Therefore, I did not use them. Thus only the page numbers are cited in most cases. His diary and letters were first published in *Listen to the Voices* 1949, but the passages, including those containing references to cherry blossoms, were edited out. A more extensive coverage was published in Ebina 1977: 227; 1983: 137, 173–74, 224–28, 272, 303–12 and in Morioka 1995b: 114–17; 128, 140–42, 154–59, 163–69, 172. The following sources also include coverage of Hayashi: Inoguchi and Nakajima 1963: 177–180; 1975: 231–35; *Cherry Blossoms of the Same Class* 1966a: 171–74; 1966b: 66–69, 136–37; *Conscription of Students* 1981: 138–41; *Listen to the Voices* 1949: 215–18. Itō Kazuyoshi (Hayashi Ichizō 1995: 161) points out that Hayashi's letter to his mother is the only one written by a Japanese published in *Letters to Mother*, edited by Charles Van Doren (1959). A letter by Hayashi is also included among the letters by tokkōtai pilots in *Sturm der Götter*, published in Germany (Hayashi 1995: 161).

29. He entrusted this letter of March 30, 1945 to his friend Umeno to be delivered to his mother. He wanted her to burn all of his diary and other writings after she read them; they were meant only for her and not for anyone else. Also in Hayashi Ichizō 1995: 27.

30. The second quotation in English appears in his letter to Tsuchii Kentaō, his friend with whom he went the Fukuoka Higher School and the Imperial University of Kyoto (Hayashi Ichizō 1995: 111).

31. There are many others who used foreign languages extensively. To give one more example, Kirihara Saburō wrote his will in German: "Wir leben nur zum Zweck des Sieges. Wenn nicht wollen und können nicht leben" (Ebina 1977: 183).

Chapter Seven

1. An appropriate label to refer to this collective sentiment is hard to find. The terms "national culture" (Marriott 1963) or, "nationalist ideology" (Fox, ed. 1990; Handler 1988) do not solve the problems involved in the term "nation," a political entity whose emergence is never clear and those developments are often erroneously linked to a particular historical period, such as nineteenth-century "modernity" or the rise of new states during the post-colonial period.

2. What I call cultural nationalism is Gellner's patriotism (Gellner 1983: 138), and it predates his nationalism, which I call political nationalism. Explaining the use of "patriots," Fenton states: "The word 'patriot' means in this context not some flag-waving jingoist, not someone who wishes to assert the rights of his own country over the interests of some other country, but someone who loves his country enough to wish to defend it against tyranny" (Fenton 1998: 39).

3. I assign "social/historical agents" power to impact the culture/society, while "social actors" is a term which stresses the individual as a member of the society but not necessarily with power.

4. Henry Hardy, the editor for Berlin 1999, notes that "Schiller's bent twig" is found neither in Diderot, to whom Berlin ascribed it in Berlin 1999, nor in Schiller to whom he ascribed in writing (Berlin [1959] 1992: 246). Hardy suggests that the image may be Berlin's own invention (Berlin 1999: 161).

5. As with other "nations" (Anderson [1983] 1991), it is hard to determine when Japan became a nation.

6. "Illuc quicumque tenderit, / Mortuus ibi fuerit, / Caeli bona receperit, / Et cum sanctis permanserit."

Chapter Eight

1. Because of their involvement in Nazism, the assessments today of not only Heidegger but also of Wagner, Goethe, and other German scholars, composers, and literary figures are complex.

2. This is the key chapter in *Das Kapital*, in which Marx develops the well-known model of M-C-M and C-M-C (Marx [1867] 1967: 145–53). For an explication of socialism, liberalism, and Marxism during the first three decades of the twentieth century, see Duus and Scheiner 1998.

3. An example is Okabe Heiichi, who was born in February 1923, and who graduated from Taihoku University, a Japanese university in occupied Taiwan. He died as a navy tokkōtai pilot in 1945. Sources: Ebina 1983: 137, 169–70, 173–74; Inoguchi and Nakajima 1963: 180, 1975: 235–37; Kaigun 1966a: 128–29, 1966b: 195; Morioka 1995b: 110–14, 125, 137–38, 142, 153, 154–55, 160–61, 172.

4. Most Japanese Christians became Christians through personal conversion, as was the case with all the Meiji Christians, and also with Hayashi Ichizō and his parents. They are known for their strong moral convictions, with which they lived a disciplined life, for example by abstaining from alcohol.

5. Christian soldiers include: Ichijima Yasuo (see chapter 5), Kumai Tsuneo (Ebina 1983: 97, 142, 181–82; *Cherry Blossoms of the Same Year* 1966b: 41, 218–19); and Ōi Eikō (not a tokkōtai pilot; *Far Off Mountains and Rivers* [1947] 1951: 18–31; *Listen to the Voices* [1949] 1952: 8–12).

6. My remarks on Romanticism in various countries are very broad, only pointing out the characteristics most relevant to the discussion. For German Romanticism, see Mosse 1988: 29–64, 237–49; Garland and Garland, eds. 1977; for French, Crossly 1995; for Russian, Leighton 1985; Malia 1999; France, ed. 1995; and Terras, ed. 1985a.

7. See Doak (1994) for the Japan Romantic School against the backdrop of what he calls Japan's "ethnic nationalism," which other prominent scholars at the time, including Nishida Kitarō and Watsuji Tetsurō, promoted. See also Pincus (1996) who examines Kuki's notion of *iki* (a particular kind of beauty) and argues that "aesthetic modernism" went hand in hand with political fascism. Hayashi's (1999) Introduction to the articles by Kaneko Chikushi in *Taiyō* focuses on "neo-idealism" and naturalism, another influence from Germany.

8. The phoenix is an important symbol in East Asia, including China, Korea, and

Japan. The iconic representation of the phoenix is somewhat different from the one originated in Egypt and diffused far and wide.

9. According to Hashikawa (1985: 48, 56), the way Wada passionately studied how best to direct his own body against an enemy ship is an enactment of Yasuda's metaphysics of death. There is no mention of Yasuda and his associates in Wada's diary. Note that Takushima Tokumitsu, who was not a tokkōtai pilot, declared that he was born to pursue Romanticism and freedom and that Romanticism was his religion (Takushima 1967: 163, 175).

10. Personal observation of the frescoes by Signorelli and by Michelangelo in May, 2000 and of David by Michelangelo in November of 1998.

11. Cremation was in practice before the eighth century and became common among the elites during the Nara (646–794) and the Heian (794–1185) periods. The cremation and subsequent scattering of the ashes of the Junna emperor in 840 (Jōwa 7) are well known, although at that time the prototypical burial was still *dosō* (burying the dead body in the ground). When the government began to collect statistics on cremation in 1925, cremation constituted only 43.2 percent of funerals. During the decade between 1935 and 1945, cremation became more common than internment. Although the rate of cremation dropped right after World War II, in 1990, 97.5 percent of all funerals involved cremation (Fujii 1992: 292–95). Although interpretations of the meaning of cremation vary, some consider that cremation has become the most prevalent mode in part because it guaranteed the intactness of the dead body until the moment of cremation, thus eliminating the precarious stage of deterioration during which the body may lose its intactness. For details of the notion of death and the body in relation to Japanese religions, see Ohnuki-Tierney 1994a, 1997b.

12. "Werther fever" swept through Europe in the 1820s, with some speculative assertions of it being a cause for a suicide epidemic (Paperno 1997: 13). As far as I know, the enthusiastic reception of Werther in Japan was not accompanied by a suicide epidemic, real or imaginative.

13. The lyrics for the song were composed by Shimamura Hōgetsu and Sōma Gyohū and the music by Nakayama Shinpei (Shinmura [1955] 1990: 466).

14. In contrast, in Japanese kingship, there was not even the element of ritual sacrifice common in the divine kingship of Europe, Africa, and elsewhere. In Japanese kingship, sacrificial elements were discontinued after the eighth century (Macé 1985) at the time when the ancient imperial system reached its zenith of power and splendor. Ever since, the imperial accession ritual involves the exchange of the soul, embodied in rice grains, between deities and humans, rather than animal sacrifice (for a restricted practice of animal sacrifice, see Ohnuki-Tierney 1991, 1993a).

Although I have used the term "sacrifice," its equivalent in Japanese *(gisei)* does not appear often in the pilots' diaries or in the writings and statements of political and intellectual leaders during and after the Meiji period. Such terms as loyalty *(chū)*, service *(hōshi)*, and dedication *(kenshin)* are used instead.

15. Natural death is the ideal, and an important reason for the reluctance for organ transplantation from the brain dead derives from the view that surgical removal of organs from the dead constitutes "violence" to the dead body (Ohnuki-Tierney 1994a).

16. The most famous expression of this folk belief is a series of woodblock prints

of catfish by folk artists that appeared right after the 1855 earthquake in Edo. The people of Edo had long suffered from the shogunate's incompetent rule. The government was incapable of coping with foreign pressure, with the first British ship appearing in 1847 at Uraga, followed by the first visit by Commodore Perry in 1853. When the earthquake took place, the folk assigned a dual role to the catfish, the causal agent of the quake (the catfish breaks the mud over it when coming out of hibernation) and the savior, who destroys the wicked feudal society and ushers in a utopia. One of these prints depicts a catfish forcing two wealthy men from whose mouth and anus gold coins are flowing out. See Miyata and Takada, eds. 1995; Ouwenhand 1964.

17. Japanese Buddhism, especially during the late ancient and medieval periods, visually portrayed heaven and hell.

18. A student in law at the University of Tokyo, put the question as: "Do I pick up the gun for the emperor? Or, for my ancestral country? Or, my parents? Or, the [beautiful] nature of Japan which has always been my ancestral land? However, I have not resolved the question of why I am putting my life on the line" (Irokawa 1993: 43; the identity of the student is not given).

Chapter Nine

1. See Geertz's (1973: 126) well-known explication: "the ethos is made intellectually reasonable . . . [by] world view . . . and the world view is made emotionally acceptable by [ethos]."

2. "In contrast to spring in the human world, spring at the air force base is peaceful. I shall write again after cherry blossoms have fallen. . . . Cherry blossoms eagerly fall after their blooming. It is a good time for me to do the same. . . . As we eagerly compete for a chosen spot to fight and [perish] like falling cherry petals, we find meaning in life" (quoted in Ebina 1983: 183, 184).

3. In my earlier work, using the monkey as a polysemic symbol in Japanese culture through time, I elaborated how a historical actor pulls out, as it were, from the *field* of meaning of the monkey—mediator, scapegoat, clown, etc.—and how in a given ritual context of a monkey performance, actors draw different meanings (Ohnuki-Tierney 1987: 210–13).

4. The use of a metaphor, as opposed to a logo, manages to create a phenomenon whereby the space between the symbol and the referent gets narrowed. From Aristotle on, a metaphor is by definition based on "the similarity *in dissimilars*" (Aristotle *Rhetoric* [1932] 1960: e.g., 212–15 [3, 1412a–b]). For further discussion of trope vs. individual belief, see Ohnuki-Tierney 1990, 1995. Because humans and flowers belong to two distinct denotative domains, cherry blossoms were able to function as a metaphor but they do not become humans. The pilots and others did not believe that they were falling cherry blossoms or that they would be reborn as cherry blossoms. In other words, the flower remained a metaphor. However, since the Meiji period, the state had engaged in systematic and intensive "education" of the people to fuse the two by removing the space between cherry blossoms as a metaphor and cherry blossoms as the Japanese in reality, just like the metaphor of "being at daggers drawn," which was used as a hollow threat around 1900, which became a metaphor to mystify the realities of military technology during World War I, and which, finally, was brought back to reality in the knives and daggers used by the SS

in Nazi Germany (Timms 2000). The swastika, in contrast, could not become its referent, i.e., the Nazi Germans.

5. Thus my approach is more Hegelian than empiricist in that the aesthetics of cherry blossoms as described in this book is a product of the Japanese *Geist*. Contra Kant's universality of aesthetic judgment, aesthetics in my use is to a large degree, but not entirely, a product of a given culture.

6. Goody (1993), whose focus is not on symbolism, only briefly discusses the relationship of flowers to sacrifice and war/peace. For example, when garlands as offerings to the dead are replaced by flowers, he interprets it as a shift from icons of war to those of peace, without questioning the possibility that the flowers may indeed have been metaphorically associated with wars and warriors (Goody 1993: 71).

7. The marching of German soldiers and the sound of their footsteps were already in place before World War II. In Jean Renoir's highly acclaimed film of the First World War, *Grand Illusion* (1937), a French prisoner of war (Jean Gabin) tells a fellow prisoner that it is the sound of footsteps by the German soldiers that really affects him.

8. After the war, the occupation force first asked Konoe to participate in the revision of Japan's constitution, but later changed its mind about him and named him a war criminal. He committed suicide by taking poison at age 55 (Itō 1997).

9. A derisive term used by Braudel ([1958] 1980: 10) to oppose Heinrich von Treitschke's "Men make history." Braudel's *longue durée* erases the traces of individuals involved in historical processes.

10. Geertz (1995: 51) too is interested in "not the individuals" but *dramatis personae*. He emphasizes the acting out by individuals as members of a culture, although characteristically, does not emphasize their role in the reproduction or transformation of their cultures.

11. See for example, Latour [1991] 1993.

12. For the notion of "genealogy," see Friedman, cited in Sahlins 1999. For arguments about the global and the local, see Harrison 1999, Napier 1992, Sahlins 1999, and Tambiah 2000. Ohnuki-Tierney (2001), presents a fuller discussion of this issue.

13. The first phrase comes from the title of Ohnuki-Tierney, ed. 1990, and the second from the title of the book by Schorske 1998.

Summary

1. See Browning (1992) for an earlier argument against the Goldhagen thesis. There are also a number of non-Jewish Germans who helped the Jews during the Nazi regime, including the White Rose members, Maria Paasche and others. See also Schneider 2000.

2. Watanabe Kazuo, a highly respected scholar of French literature who was involved in the editing of the *Listen to the Voices*, points out that these young students were forced to naturalize that which was so utterly unnatural—plunging to their death for a war they could not really fathom (*Listen to the Voices* 1949: 2).

3. Whether there is more than one form of capitalism and whether "Japanese capitalism" was introduced from the West is a debatable issue. Metallic currency was introduced from China (see Ohnuki-Tierney 1993a).

4. I thank Kenji Tierney for alerting me to this commoditization on eBay.

References

For articles, Japanese translations of the titles are given only for the articles, not for journals, edited books, etc. Some of the Japanese titles are meaningless in translation. Personal names and other proper nouns are left without translation. The place of publication for works in Japanese is Tokyo, unless specified otherwise.

Abe Takehiko. 1996. Kimi (His Majesty). *Kokushi Daijiten* 4: 209. Yoshikawa Kōbunkan.

Akasaka Norio. 1988. *Ō to Tennō* (King and emperor). Chikuma Shobō.

Akiba Tarō. 1995. Oppekepē-bushi ("Oppekepē" songs). *Kokushi Daijiten* 2: 866–67. Yoshikawa Kōbunkan.

Akimoto Kichirō. [713] 1958. Hitachi-no-Kuni Fudoki (The folkway in Hitachi). In *Fudoki*, edited by Akimoto Kichirō, 33–92. Iwanami Shoten.

Akiyama Mitsukazu, ed. 1975. *Genji Monogatari Emaki* (Scroll paintings of "The Tale of Genji"). *Shinshū Nihon Emakimono Zenshū*. Vol. 2. Kadokawa Shoten.

Althusser, Louis. 1971. *Lenin and Philosophy.* New York: Monthly Review Press.

Amano Denchū. 1995. Shika Hōyō (Shika Hōyō ritual in Buddhism). *Kokushi Daijiten* 6: 682. Yoshikawa Kōbunkan.

Amino Yoshihiko. 1980. *Nihon Chūsei no Minshūzō* (Portrait of the folk in medieval Japan). Iwanami Shoten.

———. 1987. Chūsei no Futan Taikei (System of levy in the medieval period). *Miura Kobunka* 41: 1–11.

———. 1994. *Chūsei no Hinin to Yūjo* (The "Non-Humans" and the "Play Women" in the medieval period). Akashi Shoten.

———. 1997. *Nihon Shakai no Rekishi* (History of Japanese society). Vol. 2 (Ge). Iwanami Shoten.

Anderson, Benedict. [1983] 1991. *Imagined Communities.* London and New York: Verso.

Annan, Noël. 1990. *Our Age.* New York: Random House.

Antoni, Klaus. 1991. Momotarō (The Peach Boy) and the Spirit of Japan. *Asian Folklore Studies* 50: 155–88.

Aoki Kei'ichirō. 1982. Washinton e Okutta Sakura (Cherry trees sent to Washington). *Nihon Jishin* 23: 67–71.

Appiah, Kwame Anthony. 1992a. *In My Father's House.* New York: Oxford University Press.

———. 1992b. Cosmopolitan Patriots. In *For Love of Country*, edited by M. Nussbaum and J. Cohen, 21–29. Boston: Beacon Press.

Arai Mujirō. [1939] 1965. *Hyōshaku Ise Monogatari Taisei* ("The Tale of Ise" with annotations). Osaka: Yukawa Kōbunsha.

Araki Masayasu. 1976. *Shinbun ga Kataru Meijishi* (Meiji Restoration as reported in newspapers). Vol. 1. Hara Shobō.

Aristotle. [1932] 1960. *The Rhetoric of Aristotle.* Trans. L. Cooper. New York: Appleton-Century-Crofts.

Awaya Kentarō. 1994. Yokaren (Navy pilots in training). *Nihonshi Daijiten* 6: 994. Edited by Shimonaka Hiroshi. Heibonsha.

Barshay, Andrew E. 1988. *State and Intellectual in Imperial Japan.* Berkeley and Los Angeles: University of California Press.

Bell, Daniel. [1980] 1991. *The Winding Passage.* New Brunswick: Transaction Publishers.

Bellah, Robert N. 1967. The Japanese Emperor as a Mother Figure: Some Preliminary Notes. Lecture presented at the Colloquium of the Center for Japanese and Korean Studies, University of California at Berkeley, October 11, 1967.

Benda, Julien. 1955. *The Betrayal of the Intellectuals.* Boston: Beacon Press.

Benedict, Ruth. [1946] 1967. *The Chrysanthemum and the Sword.* New York: New American Library.

Benjamin, Walter. [1958] 1968. *Illuminations.* New York: Schocken Books.

Berger, Gordon M. 1988. Politics and Mobilization in Japan, 1931–1945. In *The Cambridge History of Japan,* edited by P. Duus, 6: 97–153. Cambridge: Cambridge University Press.

Berlin, Isaiah. [1953] 1978. *The Hedgehog and the Fox.* Chicago: Ivan R. Dee.

———. [1958] 1969. Two Concepts of Liberty. In *Four Essays on Liberty,* 118–72. New York: Oxford University Press.

———. [1959] 1992. *The Crooked Timber of Humanity.* New York: Random House.

———. 1991. Two Concepts of Nationalism. *New York Review of Books* (Nov. 12): 19–23.

———. 1999. *The Roots of Romanticism.* Edited by Henry Hardy. New Jersey: Princeton University Press.

Berque, Augustin. 1990. *Nihon no Fūkei, Seiō no Keikan, soshite Zōkei no Jidai.* Kōdansha.

Bitō Masahide. [1986] 1994. Junshi (Suicide following one's master). *Kokushi Daijiten* 7: 416–417. Yoshikawa Kōbunkan.

———. [1993] 1996. Yōmeigaku (Wang-Yang-ming). *Kokushi Daijiten* 14: 351. Yoshikawa Kōbunkan.

———. 1997. Kokutairon (Theories on national polity). *Kokushi Daijiten* 5: 670–71. Yoshikawa Kōbunkan.

Blacker, Carmen. 1975. *The Catalpa Bow.* London: George Allen & Unwin.

Bloch, Marc. 1946. *Étrange défaite.* Paris: Société des Éditions Franc-tireurs.

Bōeichō Bōei Kenshūjo Senshishitsu, ed. 1972. *Fuirippin-oki Kaisen* (The battle off the Philippines). *Kaigun Shōgō Sakusen.* Vol. 2. Asagumo Shinbunsha.

Bourdieu, Pierre. [1972] 1977. *Outline of a Theory of Practice.* Cambridge: Cambridge University Press.

———. [1979] 1984. *Distinction.* Cambridge, Mass.: Harvard University Press.

————. 1990. *In Other Words*. Stanford: Stanford University Press.

Bourdieu, Pierre, and Alain Darbel. [1969] 1990. *The Love of Art*. Stanford: Stanford University Press.

Bourdieu, Pierre, and Loïc J. D. Wacquant. 1998. Sur les ruses de la raison impérialiste. *Actes de la recherche en sciences sociales*, 121/122: 109–18. English translation by L. Wacquant.

————. 1992. *An Invitation to Reflexive Sociology*. Chicago: University of Chicago Press.

Braudel, Fernand. [1958] 1980. *On History*. Chicago: University of Chicago Press.

Brent, T. David. 1977. Jung's Debt to Kant: Kant's Transcendental Method and the Structure of Jung's Psychology. Ph.D. diss., University of Chicago.

Browning, Christopher R. 1992. *Ordinary Men*. New York: Harper Collins.

Burke, Kenneth. [1950] 1969. *A Rhetoric of Motives*. Berkeley and Los Angeles: University of California Press.

————. 1955. *A Grammar of Motives*. New York: George Braziller, Inc.

Chatterjee, Partha. 1993. *The Nation and its Fragments*. Princeton: Princeton University Press.

Choron, Jacques. [1968] 1973. Death and Immortality. *Dictionary of the History of Ideas* 1: 634–46. New York: Charles Scribner's Sons.

Cook, Haruko T., and Theodore F. Cook. 1992. *Japan at War: An Oral History*. New York: The New Press.

Coox, Alvin. 1988. The Pacific War. In *The Cambridge History of Japan*, edited by P. Duus, 6: 315–82. Cambridge: Cambridge University Press.

Cranston, Edwin A. 1993. *A Waka Anthology*. Vol. 1. Stanford: Stanford University Press.

Crossley, C. 1995. Romanticism. In *The New Oxford Companion to Literature in French*, 714–16. Oxford: Clarendon Press.

de Certeau, Michel. 1988. *The Writing of History*. New York: Columbia University Press.

de Heusch, Luc. 1985. *Sacrifice in Africa*. Bloomington: Indiana University Press.

Doak, Kevin Michael. 1994. *Dreams of Difference*. Berkeley and Los Angeles: University of California Press.

————. 1997. What is a Nation and Who Belongs? National Narratives and the Ethnic Imagination in Twentieth-Century Japan. *The American Historical Review* 102 (2): 283–309.

————. 1998. Culture, Ethnicity, and the State in Early Twentieth-Century Japan. In *Japan's Competing Modernities*, edited by Sharon Minichiello, 181–205. Honolulu: University of Hawaii Press.

Dokura Shōko. 1966. *Hyōden Dokura Shōzaburō* (Biography of Dokura Shōzaburō). Asahi Terebinyūsu Shuppankyoku.

Duara, Prasenjit. 1995. *Rescuing History from the Nation*. Chicago: University of Chicago Press.

Dumont, Louis. [1966] 1970. *Homo Hierarchicus*. Chicago: University of Chicago Press.

————. 1994. *German Ideology*. Chicago: University of Chicago Press.

Durkheim, Emile, and Marcel Mauss. [1901–2] 1963. *Primitive Classification.* Chicago: University of Chicago Press.

Duus, Peter. 1988. Socialism, Liberalism, and Marxism, 1901–1931. In *The Cambridge History of Japan,* edited by P. Duus, 6: 654–710. Cambridge: Cambridge University Press.

———. 1995. *The Abacus and the Sword.* Berkeley and Los Angeles: University of California Press.

Duus, Peter, and Irwin Scheiner. 1998. Socialism, Liberalism, and Marxism, 1901–31. In *Modern Japanese Thought,* ed. B. T. Wakabayashi, 6: 147–206. Cambridge: Cambridge University Press.

Ebersole, Gary L. 1989. *Ritual Poetry and the Politics of Death in Early Japan.* Princeton: Princeton University Press.

Ebina Kenzō. 1977. *Kaigun Yobi-Gakusei* (Navy student reserve). Tosho Shuppansha.

———. 1983. *Taiheiyōsensō ni Shisu — Kaigun Hikō Yobi Shōkō no Sei to Shi* (To die in the Pacific War—Life and death of the Navy Aviation Reserve Officers). Nishida Shoten.

Edgerton, Robert B. 1997 *Warriors of the Rising Sun.* New York: W. W. Norton.

Eisenstadt, S. N. 1996. *Japanese Civilization.* Chicago: University of Chicago Press.

———. 2000. Multiple Modernities. *Daedalus* 129 (1): 1–162.

Eksteins, Modris 1989 *Rites of Spring.* New York: Doubleday.

Ellwood, Robert S. 1973. *The Feast of Kingship.* Sophia University Press.

Emura Eiichi. 1996. Bakumatsu Meiji Zenki no Kenpō Kōsō (Drafts for the Constitution during the late Tokugawa and early Meiji periods). In *Kenpō Kōsō. Nihon Kindai Shisō Taikei* 9: 436–92. Iwanami Shoten.

———, ed. 1996. *Kenpō Kōsō* (Drafts for the Constitution). *Nihon Kindai Shisō Taikei.* Vol. 9. Iwanami Shoten.

Endō Motoo. [1910] 1968. Gyūnabe (Beef pot). In *Meiji Jibutsu Kigen Jiten,* 264. Shibundō.

Enomoto Takashi. 1996. Tsubouchi Shōyō. *Kokushi Daijiten* 9: 804. Yoshikawa Kōbunkan.

Enomoto Yukio. 1975. Sandai Kessaku no Seiritsu (The Development of the three masterpieces). In *Sandai Kabuki,* edited by Gunji Masakatsu, 171–95. Mainichi Shinbun.

Falasca-Zamponi, Simonetta. 1997. *Fascist Spectacle.* Berkeley and Los Angeles: University of California Press.

Feeley-Harnik, Gillian. 1985. Issues in Divine Kingship. *Annual Review of Anthropology* 14: 273–313.

Fenton, James. 1998. Keats the Radical. Review of *John Keats and the Culture of Dissent* by Nicholas Roe. *The New York Review of Books* 15 (8): 39–41.

Field, Norma. 1987. *The Splendor of Longing in the "Tale of Genji."* Princeton: Princeton University Press. Reprint, University of Michigan Press, 2001.

———. 1997. *From My Grandmother's Bedside.* Berkeley and Los Angeles: University of California Press.

Foucault, Michel. [1977] 1995. *Discipline and Punish.* New York: Random House.

———. 1991. Governmentality. In *Foucault Effect,* edited by G. Burchell, C. Gordon, and P. Miller, 87–104. Chicago: University of Chicago Press. Detailed on the recording, *De la gouvernementalité sound recording* (Paris: Editions du Seuil, 1989).

Fox, Richard G., ed. 1990. *Nationalist Ideologies and the Production of National Cultures*. Washington, D.C.: American Ethnological Society.

France, Peter, ed. 1995. *The New Oxford Companion to Literature in French*. Oxford: Clarendon.

Frazer, James G. [1890] 1911–15. *The Golden Bough*. 2 vols. London: Macmillan.

Fujii Masao. 1992. Nōshi to Zōkiishoku (Brain death and organ transplanation). In *"Nōshi" to Zōkiishoku*, edited by Umehara Takeshi, 284–304. Asahi Shinbunsha.

Fujioka Michio. 1956. *Kyōto Gosho* (Kyoto imperial palace). Shōkokusha.

Fujishiro Hajime. 1981. Kaisetsu Sasaki Hachirō no Shōgai (Introduction to life of Sasaki Hachirō). In *Sasaki Hachirō Seishun no Isho*, edited by Fujishiro Hajime, 421–66. Shōwa Shuppan.

Fujitani Takashi. 2000. The Masculinist Bonds of Nation and Empire. In *Japanese Civilization in the Modern World*, edited by Umesao Tadao, Fujitani Takashi, and Kurimoto Eisei, 133–61. Osaka: The National Museum of Ethnology.

Fujitomi Yasuko. 1985. *Sakura-Dokuhon Tsuisō* (Reflections on the Cherry Blossom Textbook). Kokudosha.

Fukui Shizuo. 1997. Kaiten (Underwater torpedoes). *Kokushi Daijiten* 3: 79–80. Yoshikawa Kōbunkan.

Fukuyama Toshio. 1995. Uemura Masahisa. *Kokushi Daijiten* 2: 36–37. Yoshikawa Kōbunkan.

Furet, François. [1988] 1996. *The French Revolution 1770–1814*. Cambridge, Mass.: Blackwell.

Fussell, Paul. [1975] 2000. *The Great War and Modern Memory*. Oxford: Oxford University Press.

Gandhi, Mahatma K. 1948. *Gandhi's Autobiography*. Washington, D.C.: Public Affairs Press.

Garland, Henry, and Mary Garland, eds. 1977. *The Oxford Companion to German Literature*. Oxford: Oxford University Press.

Garon, Sheldon. 1997. *Molding Japanese Minds*. Princeton: Princeton University Press.

Gauntlett, John O., trans. 1949. *Kokutai no Hongi*. Cambridge, Mass.: Harvard University Press.

Geertz, Clifford. 1973. *The Interpretation of Cultures*. New York: Basic Books.

———. 1980. *Negara*. Princeton: Princeton University Press.

———. 1995. *After the Fact*. Cambridge, Mass.: Harvard University Press.

Gellner, Ernest. 1983. *Nations and Nationalism*. Ithaca: Cornell University Press.

Gluck, Carol. 1985. *Japan's Modern Myth*. Princeton: Princeton University Press.

Goldhagen, Daniel Jonah. 1996. *Hitler's Willing Executioners*. New York: Knopf.

Goody, Jack. 1993. *The Culture of Flowers*. Cambridge: Cambridge University Press.

Gordon, Andrew. 1991. *Labor and Imperial Democracy in Prewar Japan*. Berkeley and Los Angeles: University of California Press.

Gordon, Colin. 1991. Governmental Rationality. In *Foucault Effect*, edited by G. Burchell, C. Gordon, and P. Miller, 1–51. Chicago: University of Chicago Press.

Gotō Shigeki, ed. 1975. *Tōkaidō Gojū-San Tsugi* (Fifty-three stations along the Tōkaidō). Shūeisha.

———. 1976. *Kiso Kaidō Rokujū-Kyū Tsugi* (Sixty-nine stations along the Kiso Road). Shūeisha.

Gotō Shirō. 1996. Chin (Self-referential term for the emperor). *Kokushi Daijiten* 9: 678. Yoshikawa Kōbunkan.

Greenblatt, Stephen. 2001. *Hamlet in Purgatory.* Princeton: Princeton University Press.

Gunji Masakatsu. 1970. Kaisetsu Yasuna (Explanation of "Yasuna"). In *Meisaku Kabuki Zenshū*, edited by Gunji Masakatsu, 19: 118–20. Tōkyō Sōgen Shinsha.

———, ed. 1975. *Sandai Kabuki* (The three great masterpieces of the Kabuki). Mainichi Shinbun.

Gunji Masakatsu et al., eds. 1969, 1970. *Meisaku Kabuki Zenshū* (Collection of Kabuki masterpieces). Vol. 11 (1969), Vol. 19 (1970). Tōkyō Sōgen Shinsha.

Gushima Kanesaburō. 1983. *Bunmei eno Dappi* (Exodus toward civilization). Kyūshū: Kyūshū Daigaku Shuppankai.

Hackett, Roger F. 1971. *Yamagata Aritomo in the Rise of Modern Japan, 1838–1922.* Cambridge, Mass.: Harvard University Press.

Hakuō Izokukai, ed. 1952. *Kumo Nagaru Hate-ni* (Where clouds float). Nihon Shuppan Kyōdō Kabushiki Gaisha.

Hall, John A., ed. 1998. *The State of the Nation.* Cambridge: Cambridge University Press.

Hanazaki Seitarō. 1988. Yoshiwara. *Nihon Daihyakka Zensho* 23: 604–5. Edited by Tetsuo Sōga. Shōgakkan.

Handler, Richard. 1988. *Nationalism and the Politics of Culture in Quebec.* Madison: University of Wisconsin Press.

Harada Nobuo. 1993. *Rekishi no Naka no Kome to Niku* (Rice and meat in history). Heibonsha.

Harada Tomohiko and Yamane Yūzō, eds. 1983. *Yūraku* (Leisure activies). *Kinsei Fūzoku Zufu.* Vol. 2. Shōgakkan.

Haraguchi Torao. 1994. Shimazu Nariakira. *Kokushi Daijiten* 7: 113–14. Yoshikawa Kōbunkan.

Harashima Tadashi. 1991. Bushidō (The way of warriors). *Kokushi Daijiten* 12: 150–152. Yoshikawa Kōbunkan.

Harashima Yōichi. 1993. Geisha. *Nihonshi Daijiten* 1: 1188–89. Edited by Shimonaka Hiroshi. Heibonsha.

Hardacre, Helen. 1989. *Shintō and the State, 1868–1988.* Princeton: Princeton University Press.

Harootunian, Harry. 1988. *Things Seen and Unseen.* Chicago: University of Chicago Press.

Harrison, Simon. 1999. Cultural Boundaries. *Anthropology Today* 15 (5): 10–13.

Haruyama Takematsu. 1953. *Nihon Chūsei Kaigashi* (History of painting in medieval Japan). Asahi Shinbunsha.

Hasegawa Takuya. 1991. Kōshō Seido (System of licensed prostitution). In *Taishū Bunka Jiten*, edited by Ishikawa Hiroyoshi et al., 252–53. Kōbundō.

Hashikawa Bunsō. 1985. *Hashikawa Bunsō Zenshū* (Collected articles by Hashikawa Bunsō). Vol. 1. Chikuma Shobō.

Hashimoto Yoshihiko. 1988. Ōnamesai no Chūzetsu (Interruption of the imperial accession ritual). In *Zusetsu Tennō no Sokuirei to Ōnamesai*, edited by Yamamoto Hikaru, Satō Minoru, and staff, 38–39. Shinjinbutsu Ōraisha.

———. 1990. Nikki (Diaries). *Kokushi Daijiten* 11: 39–41. Yoshikawa Kōbunkan.

Hattori Shōgo. 1991. Kamikaze Tokkōtai no Kōgeki (Attacks by Kamikaze Special Attack Forces). *Rekishi to Tabi* (Rinji Zōkangō 50: Taiheiyō Senshi Sōran): 342–45.

———. 1993. Teikoku Rikukaigun Tokubetsu Kōgekitai no Jittai Bunseki (Analyses of the operation of the Special Attack Forces of the Imperial Navy and Army). *Kikan Gunjishigaku* 113: 19–29.

———. 1994. Kōkū Tokkō (Airplane Special Attack Forces). In *Sensō to Jinbutsu*, edited by Ushijima Yoshikatsu and Deguchi Noriki, 12: 86–95. Ushio Shobō.

———. 1996. Kamikaze. *Air Power History* 43 (1): 14–27.

Hattori Yukio. 1975. Kabuki no "Hanami" (Cherry blossom viewing in Kabuki). *Engekikai* 33 (4): 56–57.

Hattori Yukio, ed. 1994. *Kana Dehon Chūshingura* (The Forty-seven loyal retainers). *Kabuki On Stēji*. Vol. 8. Hakusuisha.

Hayashi Ichizō. 1995. *Hi nari Tate nari* ([The Lord is] a sun and shield). Edited by Kaga Hiroko. Fukuoka: Tōka Shobō.

Hayashi Katsuya. 1967. Kaisōni Ikiru Hayashi Tadao (Hayashi Tadao in my memory). In *Waga Inochi Getsumei ni Moyu*, edited by Hayashi Katsuya, 217–30. Chikuma Shobō.

Hayashi Masako. 1999. Taiyō ni okeru Kaneko Chikusui no "Shin-Risōshugi" ("New Idealism" of Kaneko Chikushi in Taiyō [journal]). *Nihon Kenkyū* 19: 335–85.

Hayashi Tadao. 1967. *Waga Inochi Getsumei ni Moyu* (My life burning in moonlight). Edited by Hayashi Katsuya. Chikuma Shobō.

Hayashi Ya'ei. 1982. Kinsei Saibaishi (Horticulture in the early modern period). *Nihon Jishin* 23: 53–55.

Hinton, Alex. 1998. Why did the Nazis Kill? *Anthropology Today* 14 (5): 9–15.

Hobsbawm, Eric. 1990. *Nations and Nationalism since 1780*. Cambridge: Cambridge University Press.

Hobsbawm, Eric, and Terence Ranger, eds. [1983] 1986. *The Invention of Tradition*. Cambridge: Cambridge University Press.

Hocart, A. M. [1927] 1969. *Kingship*. Oxford: Oxford University Press.

———. [1936] 1970. *Kings and Councilors*. Chicago: University of Chicago Press.

———. [1952] 1970. *The Life-Giving Myth*. Edited by Lord Raglan. London: Methuen.

Holtom, D. C. [1928] 1972. *The Japanese Enthronement Ceremonies*. Monumenta Nipponica.

Hora Tomio. 1979. *Tennō Fushinsei no Kigen* (Origin of the apolitical nature of the emperor system). Azekura Shobō.

———. 1984. *Tennō Fushinsei no Dentō* (Tradition of the apolitical nature of the emperor system). Shinjusha.

Horace (Quintus Horatius Flaccus). 1997. *The Odes of Horace*. Bilingual edition. New York: Noonday Press.

Hori Ichirō. 1968. *Folk Religion in Japan*. Chicago: University of Chicago Press.

Horiuchi Keizō and Inoue Takeshi, eds. 1958. *Nihon Shōkashū* (Collection of Japanese songs). Iwanami Shoten.

Hornblower, Simon, and Antony Spawforth, eds. 1996. *The Oxford Classical Dictionary*. Oxford: Oxford University Press.

Horton, H. Mack. 2003. Tra/versing the Frontier: The Silla Envoy in Man'yōshū. Cambridge, MA: Harvard University Press. Forthcoming.

Hosaka Masayasu. 1985. *Haisen Zengo* (Before and after the defeat in the war). Asahi Shinbunsha.

Hoyt, Edwin P. 1983a. *The Kamikazes*. New York: Arbor House.

———. 1983b. *The Last Kamikaze*. Westport, Conn.: Praeger.

Hubert, Henri, and Marcel Mauss. [1898] 1964. *Sacrifice*. Chicago: University of Chicago Press.

Ienaga Saburō. 1996a. Tennō (The emperor). *Kokushi Daijiten* 9: 991–95. Yoshikawa Kōbunkan.

———. 1996b. Tennō Shuken Setsu (Theory on the imperial sovereighty). *Kokushi Daijiten*. 9: 1007. Yoshikawa Kōbunkan.

Iijima Shigeru. 1943. *Nihon Senpeishi* (History of conscription in Japan). Kaihatsusha.

Ikeda Kikan. 1987. *Genji Monogatari Jiten* (Dictionary of "The Tale of Genji"). Tōkyōdō Shuppan.

Ikuta Makoto. 1977. *Rikugun Kōkū Tokubetsu Kōgekitaishi* (History of the Special Attack Forces of the Army Air Division). Bijinesusha.

Imae Hiromichi 1993. Sakon no Sakura Ukon no Tachibana (The cherry blossoms on the left and the mandarin orange on the right [hand of the Imperial Palace]). *Nihonshi Daijiten* 3: 614. Edited by Shimonaka Hiroshi. Heibonsha.

Imamiya Jinja Shamusho, ed. [1982] 1987. *Imamiya Jinja Yuisho Ryakki* (Outline of the history of Imamiya Shrine). Kyoto: Imamiya Jinja Shamusho.

Inada Masatsugu. 1960. *Meiji Kenpō Seiritsushi* (History of the development of the Meiji constitution). Vol. 1 (Jō). Yūhikaku.

———. 1962. *Meiji Kenpō Seiritsushi* (History of the development of the Meiji constitution). Vol. 2 (Ge). Yūhikaku.

Inoguchi Rikihei and Nakajima Tadashi. 1951 *Kamikaze Tokubetsu Kōgekitai* (Special Attack Forces). Shuppan Kyōdōsha.

———. 1963. *Shinpū Tokkōtai no Kiroku* (Record of the Shinpū Special Attack Forces). Sekkasha.

———. 1967. *Shinpū Tokubetsu Kōgekitai* (Shinpū Special Attack Forces). *Taiheiyō Senki*. Vol. 4. Kawade Shobō Shinsha.

———. 1968. *Jih-pen shen feng t'e kung tui* (The Japanese Divine Wind Special Attack Forces). San-ch'ung shih: Cheng wen ch'upan she.

———. 1975. *Taiheiyō Senki* (4): *Shinpū Tokubetsu Kōgekitai* (The Pacific War record, no. 4: Shinpū Special Attack Force). Kawade Shobō Shinsha.

Inoguchi Rikihei and Nakajima Tadashi, with Roger Pineau. 1953. *The Divine Wind*. Annapolis: United States Naval Institute. Reprinted New York: Ballantine, 1958.

Inoue Isao. 1995. Ōmura Masujirō. *Kokushi Daijiten* 2: 700. Yoshikawa Kōbunkan.

Inoue Kiyoshi. [1953] 1967. *Tennōsei* (The emperor system). Tōkyō Daigaku Shuppankai.

———. [1963] 1967. *Nihon no Rekishi* (History of Japan). Vol. 1 (Jō), Vol. 2 (Chū). Iwanami Shoten.

———. 1975. *Nihon no Gunkoku Shugi* (Japan's militarism). Vol. 1. Gendai Hyōronsha.

Inoue Mitsusada. 1984. *Nihon Kodai Ōken to Saishi* (The kingship and ritual in ancient Japan). Tōkyō Daigaku Shuppankai.

Inoue Shōsei. 1993. Nōhei (Peasant soldiers). *Nihonshi Daijiten* 5: 696–97. Edited by Shimonaka Hiroshi. Heibonsha.

Irokawa Daikichi. [1970] 1997. *Meiji no Bunka* (Culture of Meiji Japan). Iwanami Shoten.

———. 1993. *Wadatsumi no Tomo e* (For my friends, the sea deities). Iwanami Shoten.

Ishii Kō. 1995. Ansei Gakakoku Jōyaku (The Ansei Treaty with the five nations). *Kokushi Daijiten* 1: 383. Yoshikawa Kōbunkan.

Itō Hirobumi, ed. [1970] 1980. *Teikoku Gikai Shiryō* (Records of the imperial diet). Vol. 2 (Ge). *Meiji Hyakunen-shi Sōsho*, vol. 117. Hara Shobō.

Itō Takashi. 1997. Konoe Fumimaro. *Kokushi Daijiten* 5: 950. Yoshikawa Kōbunkan.

Itō, Terī. 1998. Kōiu Jidai wa Sugumatakuru (Soon this type of era will come again). In *Mainichi Shinbun Hizō Fukyoka Shashin*, edited by Nishii Kazuo, 1: 206–8. Mainichi Shinbun.

Iwamoto Yoshiteru. 1996. Tachibana Kōzaburō. In *Kokushi Daijiten* 9: 190. Yoshikawa Kōbunkan.

Iwate-ken Nōson Bunka Kondan-kai, ed. [1961] 1974. *Senbotsu Nōmin Heishi no Tegami* (Letters from the fallen peasant soldiers). Iwanami Shoten.

Jameson, Fredric. 1992. *Signatures of the Visible*. New York: Routledge.

Japanese Philately, ed. 1996. *Japanese Philately*. 51 (6).

Jones, Stanleigh H. Jr., trans. 1993. *Yoshitsune and the Thousand Cherry Trees*. New York: Columbia University Press.

Juntoku Emperor [1219–22] 1929. Kinpishō. In *Gunsho Ruijū*, edited by Hanawa Hoki'ichi, 26: 367–418. Gunsho Ruijū Kanseikai.

Kaigo Tokiomi, ed. 1964a. *Kokugo (3)*. (The national language) *Nihon Kyōkasho Taikei*, vol. 6 (Kindaihen). Kōdansha.

———. 1964b. *Kokugo (6)*. (The National Language). *Nihon Kyōkasho Taikei*, vol. 9 (Kindaihen). Kōdansha.

Kaigun Daijin Kanbō. 1935. *Kaigun Shoreisoku* (The rules for the navy). Vol. 4. Bunjudō.

Kaigun Hikō Yobigakusei Dai-14-kikai, ed. 1966a. *Aa Dōki no Sakura* (The cherry blossoms of the same class). Honhen (Vol. 1). Dōbunkan Shuppan.

———. 1966b. *Aa Dōki no Sakura* (The cherry blossoms of the same class). Bessatsu (Vol. 2). Dōbunkan Shuppan.

Kamei Katsuichirō. 1935. Henshū Kōki (Postscript from the editor). *Nihon Romanha* 1 (2): 90.

Kamo Momoki, Kaigun Daijin Kanbō, and Rikugun Daijin Kanbō, eds. 1933–35.

Yasukuni Jinja Chūkonshi (History of the loyal souls at the Yasukuni Shrine). Vol. 1 (1935), Vol. 2 (1934), Vol. 3 (1934), Vol. 4 (1935), Vol. 5 (1933). Yasukuni Jinja Shamusho.

Kanagaki Robun. [1871–72] 1967. *Aguranabe* (The dish to eat while squatting). Iwanami Shoten.

———. 1926. *Seiyō Dōchū Hizakurige* (Shanks' mare to the western seas). Shūhōkaku.

Kano Masanao. 1995. Uchimura Kanzō Fukei Jiken (The incident of the disrespectful behavior toward the emperor by Uchimura Kanzō). *Kokushi Daijiten* 2: 123–124. Yoshikawa Kōbunkan.

Kant, Immanuel. [1784] 2001. *Basic Writings of Kant*. Edited by Allen W. Wood. New York: Random House.

Kantorowicz, Ernst H. [1957] 1981. *The King's Two Bodies*. Princeton: Princeton University Press.

Kanzaki Noritake. 1989. Monomiyusan no Minzoku (Custom of viewing and playing in the mountains). In *Nihonjin to Asobi, Gendai Nihon Bunka ni okeru Dentō to Hen'yō, vol. 6*, edited by Moriya Takeshi, 76–91. Domesu Shuppan.

———. 1994. Hitobito wa Naze Yama ni Asondanoka (Why did people play in the mountains). *Mahora* 1: 8–20.

Kaplan, Martha. 1995. *Neither Cargo nor Cult*. Durham and London: Duke University Press.

Karasawa Tomitarō. 1996. Kyōkasho (The school textbooks). *Kokushi Daijiten* 4: 280–82. Yoshikawa Kōbunkan.

Kater, Michael H. 1997. *The Twisted Muse*. New York: Oxford University Press.

Katō Hidetoshi. 1965. Bidan no Genkei (The Proto-type of the "Beautiful Stories"). *Asahi Jānaru* (April): 74–78.

Kawai Ryōichi and Ōta Yōai. 1982. Nihonjin no Kokoro no Furusato (The primordial space for the Japanese soul). *Nihon Jishin* 23: 89–93.

Kawamura Minato. 1998. *Manshū Tetsudō Maboroshi Ryokō* (A dream journey on the Manchurian railroad). Nesuko.

Kawane Yoshiyasu. [1984] 1986. *Chūsei Hōken Shakai no Shuto to Nōson* (The capital and the rural villages in medieval feudal society). Tokyo Daigaku Shuppankai.

Kawasaki Fusagorō. 1967. *Edo Fūbutsushi* (The folk customs of Edo). Tōgensha.

Kawasoe Taketane. [1978] 1980. *Kojiki no Sekai* (The world of Kojiki). Kyōikusha.

Keene, Donald, trans. 1971. *Chūshingura*. New York: Columbia University Press.

———. 1984. *Hyakudai no Kakyaku* (One hundred generations of travelers). Vol. 1 (Jō). Asahi Shinbunsha.

Kelly, John D. 1991. *A Politics of Virtue*. Chicago: University of Chicago Press.

———. 1998a. Time and the Global. *Development and Change* 29 (4): 839–71.

———. 1998b. Aspiring to Minority and Other Tactics Against Violence. In *Making Majorities*, edited by D. Gladney, 173–97. Stanford: Stanford University Press.

Kelly, John D., and Martha Kaplan. 2001. Nation and Decolonization. *Anthropological Theory* 1 (4).

Kertzer, David I. 1996 *Politics and Symbols*. New Haven: Yale University Press.

Kimura Takeshi. 1970. Bunmei Kaika (Civilization and enlightenment). *Shakai Kagaku Daijiten* 16: 249–50. Edited by Shakai Kagaku Daijiten Henshū Iinkai. Kashima Kenkyūjo Shuppankai.

Kinoshita Masao. 1974. *Genji Monogatari Yōgo Sakuin* (Index for terms in "The Tale of Genji"). 2 vols. Kokusho Kankōkai.

Kisaka Jun'ichirō. 1996. Taisei Yokusankai. *Kokushi Daijiten* 18: 790–91. Yoshikawa Kōbunkan.

Kitagawa, Joseph M. 1990. Some Reflections on Japanese Religion and its Relationship to the Imperial System. *Japanese Journal of Religious Studies* 17 (2–3): 129–78.

Klemperer, Victor. 1998. *I Will Bear Witness*. New York: Random House.

Kōdansha Sōgō Hensankyoku, ed. 1997. *Nichiroku Nijūseiki* (The daily record of the twentieth century). 2 vols. (nos. 21 and 22). Kōdansha.

Kojève, Alexandre. 1969. *Introduction to the Reading of Hegel*. Assembled by R. Queneau. New York: Basic Books.

Komori Takashi. 1984. Geisha. *Kokushi Daijiten* 5: 38. Yoshikawa Kōbunkan.

Ko Ōnishi Takijirō Kaigun Chūjō-den Kankōkai, ed. 1957. *Ōnishi Takijirō*. Ko Ōnishi Takijirō Kaigun Chūjō-den Kankōkai.

Koschmann, J. Victor. 1987. *The Mito Ideology*. Berkeley and Los Angeles: University of California Press.

Koshar, Rudy. 1998. *Germany's Transient Past*. Chapel Hill: University of North Carolina Press.

Kubota Jun. 1990. Nanden no Sakura (Cherry Blossoms in the South Garden [of the Imperial Palace]). *Bungaku* 1 (1): 34–48.

Kubota Utsubo. [1960] 1968. *Kokin Wakashū Hyōshaku* (Interpretation of Kokin Wakashū). [3 vols.; ch. 1, note Z.] Vol. 1 (Jō). Tōkyōdō Shuppan.

Kudō Hiroshi, ed. 1977. *Meiji, Taishō, Shōwa Sesō to Jiken Zatsugaku Jiten* (Dictionary of folk life during the Meiji, Taishō, and Shōwa periods). Mainichi Shinbunsha.

Kumakura Isao. 1989. Yūjo to Yūkaku (The "play women" and the pleasure quarters). In *Nihonjin to Asobi*, edited by Moriya Takeshi, 198–215. Domesu Shuppan.

Kurano Kenji and Takeda Yūkichi, eds. 1958. *Kojiki Norito* (Kojiki and Norito). Iwanami Shoten.

Kuroita Katsumi and Kokushi Taikei Henshūkai, eds. 1965a. Nihon Kiryaku (Zenpen). In *Kokushi Taikei* 10: 1–546. Yoshikawa Kōbunkan.

———. 1965b. Teiō Hennenki. In *Kokushi Taikei* 12: 1–456. Yoshikawa Kōbunkan.

———. 1965c. Kojidan. In *Kokushi Taikei* 18: 1–132. Yoshikawa Kōbunkan.

———. 1966a. Nihon Kōki. In *Kokushi Taikei* 3: 1–138. Yoshikawa Kōbunkan.

———. 1966b. Shoku Nihon Kōki. In *Kokushi Taikei* 3: 1–246. Yoshikawa Kōbunkan.

Kurushima Hiroshi. 1986. Kinsei no Gun'eki to Hyakushō (The military duty and peasants during the early modern period). In *Nihon no Shakaishi*, edited by Asao Naohiro et al., vol. 4 (Futan to Zōyo): 276–317. Iwanami Shoten.

Kusayanagi Daizō. 1972. *Tokkō no Shisō* (The philosophy of the Special Attack Forces). Bungei Shunjūsha.

Kyōtoshi, ed. 1975. *Kyōto no Kindai* (Kyōto during the modern period). *Kyōto no Rekishi*, vol. 8. Kyoto: Gakugei Shorin.

————. 1981. *Shigai Seigyō* (Streets and livelihood). *Shiryō Kyōto no Rekishi.* Vol. 4. Heibonsha.

LaFleur, William R. 1983. *The Karma of Words.* Berkeley and Los Angeles: University of California Press.

Langer, Susanne K. [1942] 1980. *Philosophy in a New Key.* Cambridge, Mass.: Harvard University Press.

————. 1953. *Feeling and Form.* New York: Charles Scribner's Sons.

Latour, Bruno. [1991] 1993. *We Have Never Been Modern.* Cambridge, Mass.: Harvard University Press.

Leach, Edmund. [1954] 1965. *Political Systems of Highland Burma.* Boston: Beacon Press.

Leighton, Lauren G. 1985. Romanticism. In *Handbook of Russian Literature,* edited by V. Terras, 372–76. New Haven: Yale University Press.

Lenin, Vladimir I. [1918] 1992. *The State and Revolution.* New York: Penguin.

Lilla, Mark. 2001. *The Reckless Mind.* New York: New York Review Books.

Macé, François. 1985. Genmei Dajō Tennō no Sōgi ga Imisuru Maisō Gireishijō no Danzetsuten (A break in the history of the funeral rituals as indicated by the funeral for the Empress Genmei). *Shūkyō Kenkyū* 266: 55–77.

Mainichi Shirīzu Shuppan Henshū, ed. 1981. *Gakuto Shutsujin: Shi to Taiketsu shita Seishun no Gunzō* (Conscription of students). Mainichi Shinbunsha.

Malia, Martin. 1999. *Russia under Western Eyes.* Cambridge, Mass.: Harvard University Press.

Marriott, McKim. 1963. Cultural Policy in the New States. In *Old Societies and New States,* edited by Clifford Geertz, 27–56. New York: Free Press of New York.

Maruyama Masao. 1946. Chōkokkashugi no Riron to Shinri (Theory and psychology behind the ultra-nationalism). *Sekai* (May): 2–15.

————. [1964] 1968. *Gendai Seiji no Shisō to Kōdō* (Thought and behavior in modern Japanese politics). Miraisha.

Marx, Karl, and Friedrich Engles. [1852] 1989. Excerpts from The Eighteenth Brumaire of Louis Bonaparte. In *Basic Writings on Politics and Philosophy,* edited by Lewis S. Feuer, 318–48. Garden City: Doubleday.

————. [1867] 1967. *Das Kapital.* Edited by Frederich Engels. Vol. 1. New York: International Publishers.

Matsui Kakushin. 1994. *Gakuto Shutsujin Gojū-nen* (Fifty years after the drafting of students). Asahi Sonorama.

Matsumae Takeshi. 1977. *Nihon no Kamigami* (Japanese deities). Chūōkōronsha.

Matsuoka Shinpei. 1991. *Utage no Shintai* (The body of the feast). Iwanami Shoten.

Matsuzaki Kenzō, ed. 1993. *Higashi Ajia no Shiryō Kekkon* (The marriage of the dead soul in eastern Asia). Iwata Shoin.

Mauss, Marcel. [1950] 1966. *The Gift.* London: Cohen and West.

Mayer, Adrian C. 1991. Recent Succession Ceremonies of the Emperor of Japan. *Japan Review* 2: 35–61.

McCullough, David. 2001. *John Adams.* New York: Simon and Schuster.

McCullough, Helen Craig, trans. 1968. *Tales of Ise.* University of Tokyo Press.

————. 1985. *Kokin Wakashū.* Stanford: Stanford University Press.

McCullough, William H., and Helen Craig McCullough, trans. 1980. *A Tale of Flowering Fortunes* (trans. of *Eiga Monogatari*). Vol. 2. Stanford: Stanford University Press.

Minakami Tsutomu. 1982. Oizakura ni Haru naki Kuni (A country without spring for old cherry trees). *Nihon Jishin* 23 (March): 10–16.

Minamoto-no-Akikane. 1965. *Kojidan*. Kuroita Katsumi and Kokushi Taikei Henshūkai, eds. *Kokushi Taikei*. Vol. 18. Yoshikawa Kōbunkan.

Misa Tokikazu. n.d. Misa Shiryō, No. 4: Ichi Yobi Shikan no Mita Kaigun, No. 2 (Misa date, no. 4: A view of the navy seen by a student-officer, no. 2). Unpublished, handwritten manuscript.

Mishima Yukio. 1977. *The Way of the Samurai*. New York: Basic Books.

Mitani, Taichirō. 1988. The Establishment of Party Cabinets, 1898–1932. In *The Cambridge History of Japan*, edited by Peter Duus, 6: 55–96. Cambridge: Cambridge University Press.

Miura Hitoshi. 1996. Miyazawa Kenji. *Kokushi Daijiten* 13: 840–44. Yoshikawa Kōbunkan.

Miya Tsugio. 1988. *Rokudō-e* (Paintings of the Six Worlds of Wanderings). *Nihon no Bijutsu*, vol. 12, no. 271. Shibundō.

Miyake Hitoshi. 1978. *Shugendō* (The mountain ascetic religion). Kyōikusha.

———. 1985. *Shugendō Shisō no Kenkyū* (Research on the mountain ascetic religion). Shunjūsha.

———. 1988. *Ōmine Shugendō no Kenkyū* (Research on the ascetic religion at Mt. Ōmine). Kōsei Shuppansha.

Miyamoto Yukiko. 1993. Yūjo (The "play women"). *Kokushi Daijiten* 14: 272–74. Yoshikawa Kōbunkan.

Miyao Shigeo. 1975. Hiroshige to Meisho Edo Hyakkei (Hiroshige and the One Hundred Famous Places in Edo). In *Meisho Edo Hyakkei* (I). Edited by Gotō Shigeki. *Ukiyoe Taikei* 16: 74–80. Shūeisha.

Miyata Noboru. 1975. *Kinsei no Hayarigami* (Popular deities during the early modern period). Hyōronsha.

———. 1987. *Hime no Minzokugaku* (Folklore of princesses). Seidosha.

———. 1988. *Reikon no Minzokugaku* (Folklore of the soul). Nihon Editā Sukūru Shuppan.

———. 1989. Nihon Ōken no Minzokuteki Kiso (Ethnographic basis of Japanese kingship). *Shikyō* 18: 25–30.

———. 1992. *Hiyorimi* (The control of the calendar). Heibonsha.

———. 1993. *Yama to Sato no Shinkō* (Belief in the mountains and the village). Yoshikawa Kōbunkan.

———. 1999. Kokka Shintō (National Shintoism). In *Shūkyō to Seikatsu*, edited by Aoki Tamotsu et al. *Kindai Nihon Bunka-ron* 9: 39–54. Iwanami Shoten.

Miyata Noboru and Takada Mamoru, eds. 1995. *Namazu-e* (The catfish paintings). Ribun Shuppan.

Miyatake Gaikotsu, ed. 1925. *Meiji Kibun* (Reports about the Meiji period). Vol. 2. Hankyōdō.

Mochizuki Shinkyō. 1958. Sange (Buddhist ritual). *Mochizuki Bukkyō Daijiten* 2: 1495–96. Seikai Seiten Kankō Kyōkai.

Moji Chikanori. 1989 *Kaisō no Ōnishi Takijirō* (Memory of Ōnishi Takijirō). Kōjinsha.

Monbushō. [1932] 1970. *Shōgaku Kokugo Dokuhon* (Elementary school reader for the national language). Vol. 1. Osaka: Ōsaka Shoseki. Reissued in 1970 by Akimoto Shobō in Tokyo.

Moore, Ray A., ed. 1981. *Culture and Religion in Japanese-American Relations.* Stanford: Stanford University Press.

Morimatsu Toshio. 1993. Tokubetsu Kōgekitai (Special Attack Squad [Kamikaze Squad]). *Nihonshi Daijiten* 5: 181–82. Edited by Shimonaka Hiroshi. Heibonsha.

Morioka Kiyomi. 1993. *Kesshi no Sedai to Isho* (The generation that faced death and their wills). Yoshikawa Kōbunkan.

———. 1995a. Kenkyū Shiryō toshiteno Senbotsusha no Kikanshuki (Published handwritten records of the fallen soldiers as documents). *Shukutoku Daigaku Kenkyū Kiyō* 29: 311–27.

———. 1995b. *Wakaki Tokkō Taiin to Taiheiyō Sensō* (Young kamikaze pilots and the pacific war). Yoshikawa Kōbunkan.

Morris, Ivan. [1964] 1979. *The World of the Shining Prince.* New York: Penguin Books.

———. 1975. *The Nobility of Failure.* New York: Noonday Press.

Morse, Peter. 1989. *Hokusai.* New York: George Braziller.

Mosse, George L. [1964] 1981. *The Crisis of German Ideology.* New York: Schocken Books.

———. 1975. *The Nationalization of the Masses.* Ithaca: Cornell University Press.

———. 1988. *The Culture of Western Europe.* Boulder: Westview Press.

———. 1989. National Anthems. In *From Ode to Anthem,* edited by R. Grimm and J. Hermand, 86–99. Madison: University of Wisconsin Press.

———. 1990. *Fallen Soldiers.* Oxford: Oxford University Press.

Motoori Norinaga. [1790] 1968. *Motoori Norinaga Zenshū* (Complete works by Motoori Norinaga). Edited by Ōno Susumu. Vol. 1. Chikuma Shobō.

———. [1799] 1969. *Genji Monogatari Tama no Ogushi* (Research and interpretation on "The Tale of Genji"). In *Motoori Norinaga Zenshū,* edited by Ōno Susumu, 4: 173–523. Chikuma Shobō.

Murakami Senjō, Tsuji Zennosuke, and Washio Junkei, eds. 1970. *Meiji Ishin Shinbutsu Bunri Shiryō* (Records of the separation between Buddhas and deities at the time of the Meiji Restoration). Vol. 2. Meicho Shuppan.

Murakami Shigeyoshi. 1970. *Kokka Shintō* (State Shintoism). Iwanami Shoten.

———. 1974. *Irei to Shōkon* (The consolation and summoning of souls). Iwanami Shoten.

———. 1977. *Tennō no Saishi* (Imperial rituals). Iwanami Shoten.

———. 1986. *Ten'nō to Nihon Bunka* (The Emperor and Japanese culture). Kōdansha.

———. 1988. Yasukuni Jinja Mondai (The Yasukuni Shrine problems). *Nihon Daihyakka Zensho* 23: 169. Edited by Sōga Tetsuo. Shōgakkan.

———. 1993. Yasukuni Jinja (The Yasukuni Shrine). *Kokushi Daijiten* 14: 53. Yoshikawa Kōbunkan.

Muranaga Kaoru. [1989] 1997. *Chiran Tokubetsu Kōgekitai* (The Special Attack Forces at Chiran). Kagoshima: Japuran.

Mure Hitoshi. 1988. Yasukuni Jinja (The Yasukuni Shrine). *Nihon Daihyakka Zensho* 23: 168–169. Edited by Sōga Tetsuo. Shōgakkan.

Nagao Ryūichi. 1995. Dainihon Teikoku Kenpō (The constitution of Imperial Japan). *Kokushi Daijiten* 8: 840–44. Yoshikawa Kōbunkan.

———. 1996. Minobe Tatsukichi. *Kokushi Daijiten* 13: 450. Yoshikawa Kōbunkan.

Naitō Hatsuho. 1989. *Thunder Gods*. Kodansha International.

———. 1999. *Kyokugen no Tokkōtai Ōka* ("Cherry Blossoms"—The Special Attack Forces). Chūōkōronshinsha.

Najita Tetsuo. [1974] 1980. *Japan*. Chicago: University of Chicago Press.

———. 1979. *Meiji Ishin no Isan* (The heritage of the Meiji Restoration). Chūōkōronsha.

———. 1998 Ambiguous Encounters. In *Osaka*, edited by J. L. McClain and Wakita Osamu, 213–40. Ithaca: Cornell University Press.

Nakamura Hiroshi. 1982. Sakura no Gogen (The etymology of cherry blossoms). *Nihon Jishin* 23: 59–61.

Nakanishi Susumu. 1986. *Jisei no Kotoba* (The last words). Chūōkōronsha.

———. 1995. *Hana no Katachi* (The forms of the flower). Vol. 1 (Jō, Koten), Vol. 2 (Chū, Kindai). Kadokawa Shoten.

Nakao Taketoku. 1997. *Tankyūroku* (Record of spiritual searching). Edited by Nakao Yoshitaka. Fukuoka: Tōka Shobō.

Nakau Ei. 1988. *Chūshingura Ukiyoe* (Woodblock prints of the forty-seven loyal retainers). Ribun Shuppan.

Nakayama Mikio. 1988. Chūshingura Monogatari (The story of the forty-seven loyal retainers). *Ukiyoe Kabuki Shirīzu* 3: 168–69. Kyoto: Gakugei Shorin.

Nakayama Yasumasa, ed. 1982a. *Shinbun Shūsei* (Compilation of the newspapers). Vol. 1. Honpō Shoseki.

———. 1982b. *Shinbun Shūsei* (Compilation of the newspapers). Vol. 6. Honpō Shoseki.

Nandy, Ashis. 1995. *The Savage Freud and Others Essays on Possible and Retrievable Selves*. Princeton: Princeton University Press.

Napier, A. David. 1992. *Foreign Bodies*. Berkeley and Los Angeles: University of California Press.

Narazaki Muneshige, ed. 1981. *Utamaro*. Vol. 6 of *Nikuhitsu Ukiyoe*. Shūeisha.

Naruse Rin and Tsuchiya Shūtarō, eds. 1913. *Dainihon Jinbutsushi* (Biographies of Imperial Japan). Hakkōsha.

Nihiname Kenkyūkai, ed. 1955. *Nihiname no Kenkyū* (Research on the Nihiname). Yoshikawa Kōbunkan.

Nihon Hōsō Kyōkai, ed. 1988. *Nihon no Bi* (Beauty of Japan). NHK Shuppan.

Nihon Hōsō Kyōkai Sābisu Sentā, ed. 1993. *Yoshinoyama Sakura Monogatari* (Stories of cherry blossoms on Mount Yoshino). Yoshino-chō: Nara-ken Yoshino-chō Keizai Kankōka.

Nihon Kokugo Daijiten Kankōkai, ed. 1972. *Nihon Kokugo Daijiten* (Dictionary of the Japanese language). Vol. 1. Shōgakkan.

————. 1973a. *Nihon Kokugo Daijiten* (Dictionary of the Japanese language). Vol. 4. Shōgakkan.

————. 1973b. *Nihon Kokugo Daijiten* (Dictionary of the Japanese language). Vol. 5. Shōgakkan.

Nihon Senbotsu Gakusei Kinenkai, ed. [1988] 1995. *Kike Wadatsumi no Koe* (Listen to the voices of the sea gods: The second collection). Iwanami Shoten.

Nihon Senbotsu Gakusei Shuki Henshū Iinkai, ed. [1949] 1981. *Kike Wadatsumi no Koe* (Listen to the voices of the sea gods). Tōkyō Daigaku Kyōdō Kumiai Shuppanbu. Republished in 1952 by Tōkyō Daigaku Shuppankai.

Nihon Ukiyo-e Kyōkai, ed. 1968. *Edo Meisho* (Famous places of Edo). Yamada Shoin.

Ninagawa Jukei. 1998. *Gakuto Shutsujin* (Conscription of student-soldiers). Yoshikawa Kōbunkan.

Nishi Amane. [1989] 1996. Heike Tokkō (Moral codes of soldiers, 1878). Guntai Heishi, edited by Yui Masaomi, Fujiwara Akira, and Yoshida Yutaka. *Nihon Kindai Shisō Taikei,* vol. 4, 149–62. Iwanami Shoten.

Nishii Kazuo, ed. 1998. *Mainichi Shinbun Hizō Fukyoka Shashin* (Photos suppressed by the military and kept in secret at the Mainichi Newspaper Co.). Vol. 1. Mainichi Shinbunsha.

————. 1999. *Mainichi Shinbun Hizō Fukyoka Shashin* (Photos suppressed by the military and kept in secret at the Mainichi Newspaper Co.). Vol. 2. Mainichi Shinbun.

Nishiyama Matsunosuke. 1985. *Hana to Nihon Bunka* (Flowers and Japanese culture). *Nishiyama Matsunosuke Chosaku-shū,* vol. 8. Yoshikawa Kōbunkan.

————. 1992. *Yomigaeru Edo Bunka* (The cultural history of the Edo period). NHK Shuppan.

————. 1995. Edo no Hanami (Cherry blossom viewing in Edo). *Hongō* 2: 1.

Nishizawa Sō. 1990. *Nihon Kindai Kayōshi* (History of popular songs in modern Japan). Vol. 1 (Jō). Vol. 2 (Ge). Ōfūsha.

Nitobe Inazō. [1899] 1912. *Bushidō.* Philadelphia: Leeds and Biddle. 18th edition, 1912, Teibi Publishing.

————. [1907] 1970. Momotarō no Mukashibanashi (The old folk tale of the Peach Boy). In *Nitobe Inazō Zenshū* 5: 186–96. Kyōbunkan.

————. [1933] 1969. Bushidō to Shōnindō (The way of warriors and the way of merchants). In *Nitobe Inazō Zenshū* 6: 324–36. Kyōbunkan.

Niunoya Tetsuichi. 1993. *Nihon Chūsei no Mibun to Shakai* (Status and society in medieval Japan). Hanawa Shoten.

Noguchi Takehiko. 1982. Utsurou Hana (Flowers losing their color). *Nihon Jishin* 23: 77–80.

Ogawa Kazusuke. 1991. *Sakura no Bungakushi* (Cherry blossoms in literature). Asahi Shinbunsha.

Ōhama Tetsuya. 1994. Yasukuni Jinja (The Yasukuni Shrine). *Nihonshi Daijiten* 6: 805. Edited by Shimonaka Hiroshi. Heibonsha.

Ohnuki-Tierney, Emiko. 1981a. *Illness and Healing among the Sakhalin Ainu.* Cambridge: Cambridge University Press.

————. 1981b. Phases in Human Perception/Conception/Symbolization Process. *American Ethnologist* 8 (3): 451–67.

————. 1984. *Illness and Culture in Contemporary Japan.* Cambridge: Cambridge University Press.

————. 1987. *The Monkey as Mirror.* Princeton: Princeton University Press.

————. 1990. Monkey as Metaphor? *Man* n.s. 25: 399–416.

————. 1991. The Emperor of Japan as Deity (Kami). *Ethnology* 30 (3): 1–17.

————. 1993a. *Rice as Self.* Princeton: Princeton University Press.

————. 1993b. Nature, pureté et soi primordial. *Géographie et Cultures* 7: 75–92.

————. 1994a. Brain Death and Organ Transplantation. *Current Anthropology* 35 (3): 233–54.

————. 1994b. The Power of Absence. *L'Homme 130 (avril–juin)* 34 (2): 59–76.

————. 1995. Structure, Event and Historical Metaphor. *Journal of the Royal Anthropological Institute* 30 (2): 1–27.

————. 1997a. McDonald's in Japan. In *Golden Arches East,* edited by James Watson, 161–82, 230–34. Stanford: Stanford University Press.

————. 1997b. The Reduction of Personhood to Brain and Rationality? In *Western Medicine as Contested Knowledge,* edited by A. Cunningham and B. Andrews, 212–40. Manchester: Manchester University Press.

————. 1998a. A Conceptual Model for the Historical Relationship between the Self and the Internal and External Others. In *Making Majorities,* edited by D. Gladney, 31–51, 287–94, 309–13. Stanford: Stanford University Press.

————. 1998b. Cherry Blossoms and Their Viewing. In *The Culture of Japan as Seen Through its Leisure,* edited by Sepp Linhard and Sabine Frühstück, 213–36. Albany: State University of New York Press.

————. 1999. We Eat Each Other's Food to Nourish Our Body. In *Food in Global History,* edited by Raymond Grew, 240–72. Boulder: Westview Press.

————. 2001. Historicization of Culture Concept. *History and Anthropology* 12 (3): 213–54.

————, ed. 1990. *Culture through Time.* Stanford: Stanford University Press.

Okada Shōji. 1970. *Kodai Ōken no Saishi to Shinwa* (Ritual and myth of the ancient emperor system). Hanawa Shobō.

————. [1988] 1996. Chinkasai (The ritual to appease the flowers). *Kokushi Daijiten* 9: 679. Yoshikawa Kōbunkan.

Okada Yoneo. 1997. Kōshitsu Saishirei (The imperial rituals). *Kokushi Daijiten* 5: 367–68. Yoshikawa Kōbunkan.

Okamoto Atsushi, ed. 1999. Tokushū Hinomaru Kimigayo eno Shiten (Perspectives on the rising sun flag and the national anthem). *Sekai* (no. 662; special issue).

Ōkōchi Kazuo and Matsuo Hiroshi. 1965. *Nihon Rōdō Kumiai Monogatari* (The story of Japanese labor unions). Chikuma Shobō.

Okumura Kōtarō. 1979. Rikukaigun Kōkū Tokkōtai Shutsugeki Nenpyō (The chronology of the Attack Forces of the Army and Navy Air Divisions). In *Tokubetsu Kōgekitai,* edited by Okumura Kōtarō, *Nihon no Senshi,* Bekkan (special issue) 4: 294–305. Mainichi Shinbunsha.

Omodaka Hisataka. 1968. *Man'yōshū Chūshaku* (Interpretation and annotation of the "Manyōshū"). Vol. 20. Chūōkōronsha.

————. 1983. *Man'yōshū Chūshaku* (Interpretation and annotation of the "Manyōshū"). Vol. 8. Chūōkōronsha.

———. 1984. *Man'yōshū Chūshaku* (Interpretation and annotation of the "Man-yōshū"). Vol. 16. Chūōkōronsha.

Ōmura Masujirō Sensei Denki Kankōkai. 1944. *Ōmura Masujirō*. Hajime Shobō.

O'Neill, Richard. 1981. *Suicide Squads*. London: Salamander House.

Ono Sawako. 1992. *Edo no Hanami* (Cherry blossom viewing in Edo). Tsukiji Shokan.

Ono Takeo. 1983. *Yūjo to Kuruwa no Zushi* (Illustrated history of the "play women" and their quarters). Tenbōsha.

Onoda Masashi. 1971. *Kamikaze Tokkōtai Shutsugeki no Hi Ningen Seki Taii no Shin'ō ni Fureta Tada Hitori no Hōdōhan'in* (A Journalist who came to know Lieutenant Seki as a human being on the day he flew as a kamikaze pilot). *Taiheiyō Sensō Dokyumentarī*, vol. 23. Kyō no Wadaisha.

Orikuchi Shinobu. [1928a] 1982. Hana no Hanashi (On cherry blossoms). In *Orikuchi Shinobu Zenshū* 2: 467–93. Chūōkōronsha.

———. [1928b] 1975. Shintō ni Arawareta Minzoku Ronri (Ethnographic interpretation of Shintoism). In *Orikuchi Shinobu Zenshū* 3: 145–173. Chūōkōronsha.

———. [1928c] 1975. Ōnamesai no Hongi (The meaning of the Ōnamesai). In *Orikuchi Shinobu Zenshū* 3: 174–240. Chūōkōronsha.

———. [1935] 1976. Norito (Blessing). In *Orikuchi Shinobu Zenshū* 12: 340–67. Chūōkōronsha.

———. [1947] 1983. Matsuri no Hanashi (On festivals). In *Orikuchi Shinobu Zenshū* 15: 271–80. Chūōkōronsha.

———. [1953] 1976. Sanrei no Shinkō (Belief in the soul at birth). In *Orikuchi Shinobu Zenshū* 20: 253–60. Chūōkōronsha.

Ortner, Sherry B. 1984. Theory in Anthropology since the Sixties. *Comparative Studies in Society and History* 26 (1): 126–66.

Ōshima Takehiko et al. eds. 1971. *Nihon o Shiru Jiten* (Dictionary of Japanese customs). Shakai Shisōsha.

Ōta Hirotarō. 1979. *Nanto Shichidaiji no Rekishi to Nenpyō* (History and chronology of the seven great temples at Nanto). Iwanami Shoten.

Ōta Kinen Bijutsukan, ed. 1983. *Jojōeshi Hiroshige Gagyōten* (The artist with feeling: Exhibition of the artistic career of Hiroshige). Ōta Kinen Bijutsukan.

Ōta Rin'ichirō. 1980. *Nihon no Gunpuku* (Japanese army uniforms). Kokusho Kankōkai.

Ōuchi Saburō. 1995. Uchimura Kanzō. *Kokushi Daijiten* 2: 122. Yoshikawa Kōbunkan.

———. 1996. Kirisutokyō (Christianity). *Kokushi Daijiten* 4: 443–47. Yoshikawa Kōbunkan.

Ouwehand, Cornelis. 1964. *Namazu-e and Their Themes*. Leiden: E. J. Brill.

Ozawa Hiroshi. 1987. Minshū Shūkyō no Shinsō (The thought structure of the folk religions). In *Nihon Shakaishi*, edited by Asao Naohiro et al., 8: 296–332. Iwanami Shoten.

Oze Hōan. [1625] 1996. *Taikōki* (The record of the reign of Toyotomi Hideyoshi). *Shin Nihon Koten Bungaku Taikei*, vol. 60. Iwanami Shoten.

Ozouf, Mona. 1988. *Festivals and the French Revolution*. Cambridge, Mass.: Harvard University Press.

Paperno, Irina. 1997. *Suicide as a Cultural Institution in Dostoevsky's Russia.* Ithaca: Cornell University Press.

Payne, Stanley G. 1995. *History of Fascism, 1914–1945.* Madison: University of Wisconsin Press.

———. 2000. Historical Fascism and the Radical Right (review article). *Journal of Contemporary History* 35 (1): 109–18.

Pincus, Leslie. 1996. *Authenticating Culture in Imperial Japan.* Los Angeles: University of California Press.

Plato. [1914] 1999. *Phaedo.* In *Plato,* translated by Harold N. Fowler, 193–403. Loeb Classical Library 36. Cambridge, Mass.: Harvard University Press.

Pollack, David. 1986. *The Fracture of Meaning.* Princeton: Princeton University Press.

Ponsonby-Fane, R. A. B. 1956. *Kyoto.* Kyoto: The Ponsonby Memorial Society.

Pound, Roscoe. 1957. *The Development of Constitutional Guarantees of Liberty.* New Haven: Yale University Press.

Quinn, Malcolm. 1994. *The Swastika.* London: Routledge.

Ramirez-Christensen, Esperanza. 1994. *Heart's Flower.* Stanford: Stanford University Press.

Ray, Benjamin C. 1991. *Myth, Ritual, and Kingship in Buganda.* Oxford: Oxford University Press.

Redfield, Robert. [1953] 1959. *The Primitive World and Its Transformations.* Ithaca: Cornell University Press.

Reed, W. L. and M. J. Bristow, eds. [1960] 1997. *National Anthems of the World.* London: Cassell.

Reischauer, Edwin O., and Albert M. Craig. 1978. *Japan.* Boston: Houghton Mifflin.

Roubaud, Jaques. 1970. *Mono no aware.* Paris: Gallimard.

Rubin, Jay. 1984. *Injurious to Public Morals.* Seattle: University of Washington Press.

Saeki Etatsu. 1988. *Haibutsu Kishaku Hyakunen* (One hundred years of expulsion of Buddhism and the Buddha's teaching). Miyazaki: Kōmyakusha.

Sagara Tōru. 1995. Bushidō (The way of warriors). *Kokushi Daijiten* 2: 150–52. Yoshikawa Kōbunkan.

Sahlins, Marshall. 1976. *Culture and Practical Reason.* Chicago: University of Chicago Press.

———. 1981. *Historical Metaphors and Mythical Realities.* Ann Arbor: University of Michigan Press.

———. 1985. *Islands of History.* Chicago: University of Chicago Press.

———. 1999. Two or Three Things that I Know about Culture. *Journal of Royal Anthropological Institute* n.s. 5 (3): 399–421.

Saigō Nobutsuna. [1967] 1984. *Kojiki no Sekai* (The world of Kojiki). Iwanami Shoten.

Saitō Mokichi, ed. [1938] 1971. *Man'yōshūka* (Superb poems from the "Man'yōshū"). Vol. 2 (Ge). Iwanami Shoten.

Saitō Shōji. 1977. *Hana no Shisōshi* (History of concepts associated with flowers). Kyōsei.

———. [1979] 1985. *Shokubutsu to Nihon Bunka* (Plants and Japanese culture). Yasaka Shobō.

———. 1982. Futatabi Sekai no Sakura e (Once again cherry blossoms of the world). *Nihon Jishin* 23: 25–30.

Sakaguchi Ango. 1997. In the Forest, Under Cherries in Full Bloom. Translated by J. Rubin. In *The Oxford Book of Japanese Short Stories*, edited by T. W. Goossen, 187–205. Oxford and New York: Oxford University Press.

Sakai Naoki. 1997. Nihonjin de Arukoto (To be "the Japanese"). *Shisō* 882: 5–48.

Sakamoto Koremaru. 1992. Yasukuni Jinja (The Yasukuni Shrine). In *Nihon "Jinja" Sōran*, 86–87. Shinjinbutsu Ōraisha.

Sakamoto Masayoshi. 1995. Sakura-e (A Buddhist ritual). *Kokushi Daijiten* 6: 323. Yoshikawa Kōbunkan.

Sakamoto Tarō, Ienaga Saburō, Inoue Mitsusada, and Ōno Susumu, eds. 1965. *Nihonshoki* (The chronicle of Japan). Vol. 2 (Ge). Iwanami Shoten.

———. 1967. *Nihonshoki* (The chronicle of Japan). Vol. 1 (Jō). Iwanami Shoten.

Sakurai Katsunoshin. 1988. Ōnamesai to Kannamesai (Ōnamesai and Kannamesai). In *Zusetsu Tennō no Sokuirei to Ōnamesai*, edited by Yamamoto Hikaru and staff, 32–34. Shinjinbutsu Ōraisha.

Sakurai Mitsuru. 1974. *Hana no Minzokugaku* (The folklore of flowers). Yūzankaku.

Sakurai Tokutarō. 1976. *Minkan Shinkō to Sangaku Shūkyō* (Folk beliefs and the belief in the mountains). Meicho Shuppan.

Sano Tōemon. 1998. *Sakura no Inochi Niwa no Kokoro* (The life of cherry blossoms, the soul of the garden). Sōshisha.

Sansom, George. 1958. *A History of Japan to 1334*. Stanford: Stanford University Press.

Sasaki Hachirō. 1981. *Seishun no Isho* (The will of a youth). Edited by Fujishiro Hajime. Shōwa Shuppan.

Sasayama Haruo. 1995a. Ōkimi (His majesty). *Kokushi Daijiten* 2: 537. Yoshikawa Kōbunkan.

———. 1995b. Sakimori (The imperial guards). *Kokushi Daijiten* 6: 301. Yoshikawa Kōbunkan.

Satō Haruo. 1966. *Satō Haruo Zenshū* (Complete works of Satō Haruo). Vol. 1. Kōdansha.

Satomi Kishio. 1972. *Tennō-hō no Kenkyū* (Research on the laws of the emperor system). Kinseisha.

Schama, Simon. 1996. *Landscape and Memory*. New York: Vintage Books.

Schneider, Peter. 2000. Saving Konrad Latte. *The New York Times Magazine* (February 13): 52–57.

Schorske, Carl E. 1998. *Thinking with History*. Princeton: Princeton University Press.

Schwartz, Benjamin I. 1993. Culture, Modernity, and Nationalism: Further Reflections. *Daedalus* 122 (3): 207–26.

Seidensticker, Edward G., trans. 1977. *The Tale of Genji*. 2 vols. New York: Alfred A. Knopf.

Seigle, Cecilia Segawa. 1993. *Yoshiwara*. Honolulu: University of Hawaii Press.

Sekioka Kazushige. 1995. Ebina Danjō ni okeru Sekaishugi to Nihonshugi (The cosmopolitanism and nationalism of Ebina Danjūrō). *Kirisutokyō Shakai Mondai Kenkyū* 44: 26–48.

Shibata Dōken. 1978. *Haibutsu Kishaku* (Expulsion of Buddhism and the Buddha's teaching). Kōronsha.

Shibundō Henshūbu. 1973. *Senryū Yoshiwara Fūzoku Ezu* (Illustrated customs at Yoshiwara as expressed in senryū poems). Shibundō.

Shigeshimo Kazuyoshi. 1991. Kimigayo (The national anthem of Japan). In *Taishū Bunka Jiten*, edited by Ishikawa Hiroyoshi et al., 191. Kōbundō.

Shimada Kinji. 1995. Hirose Takeo. *Kokushi Daijiten* 11: 1096. Yoshikawa Kōbunkan.

Shimura Kunihiro, trans. 1980. *Kojidan* (The stories of ancient times). Kyōikusha.

Shinbo Tōru, ed. 1982. *Yamato-e no Shiki* (The four seasons of the Yamato style of painting). *Kachō-ga no Sekai* (The world of paintings of flowers and birds), vol. 1. Gakushū Kenkyūsha.

Shinmura Izuru, ed. [1955] 1990. *Kōjien* (Dictionary). Iwanami Shoten.

Shūkan Bunshun, ed. 1997. "Kike Wadatsumi no Koe" ni Kaizan Giwaku (Suspicion of alterations in "Kike Wadatsumi no Koe"). *Shūkan Bunshun* 39 (31): 232–35.

Smith, Henry D. II. 1990. Rethinking the Story of the Forty-Seven Rōnin. Paper presented at the Modern Japan Seminar, Columbia University. Unpublished manuscript.

Smith, Henry D. II, and Amy G. Poster. [1986] 1988. *Hiroshige*. New York: George Braziller.

Smith, Robert J. 1974. *Ancestor Worship*. Stanford: Stanford University Press.

Smith, Robert, and Ella L. Wiswell. 1982. *The Women of Suyemura*. Chicago: University of Chicago Press.

Sokura Takeshi. 1995. Sakimoriuta (Poems of the ancient imperial guards). *Kokushi Daijiten* 6: 301. Yoshikawa Kōbunkan.

Sonobe Saburō. [1962] 1980. *Nihon Minshū Kayōshikō* (Research on the popular songs of Japan). Asahi Shinbunsha.

Sonobe Saburō and Yamazumi Masami. [1962] 1969. *Nihon no Kodomo no Uta* (Children's songs of Japan). Iwanami Shoten.

Suzuki Eiichi. 1996. Chūkō Icchi (The equation between the loyalty to the emperor and loyalty to parents). *Kokushi Daijiten* 9: 482. Yoshikawa Kōbunkan.

Suzuki Keiko. 1997. Yokohama-e and Kaika-e Prints. In *New Directions in the Study of Meiji Japan*, edited by H. Hardacre and A. L. Kern, 676–87. Leiden: E. J. Brill.

Suzuki Keizō, ed. 1995. *Yūsoku Kojitsu Daijiten* (How to understand ancient customs). Yoshikawa Kōbunkan.

———. 1996. Hōren (The imperial carriage). *Kokushi Daijiten* 12: 681. Yoshikawa Kōbunkan.

Suzuki Masamune. 1991. *Yama to Kami to Hito* (Mountains, deities, and humans). Kyoto: Tankōsha.

Suzuki Ryō et al. eds. 1985. *Nara-ken no Hyakunen Kenmin Hyakunenshi* (History of one hundred years of Nara Prefecture, one hundred years of the people of the prefecture), vol. 29. Yamakawa Shuppan.

Takagi Hiroshi. 1998. Sakura to Nashonarizumu (Cherry blossoms and nationalism). In *Seiki Tenkanki ni okeru Kokusai Chitsujo no Keisei to Kokumin Bunka no Hen'yō*, edited by Nishikawa Nagao and Watanabe Kōzō, 1–15. Kashiwa Shobō.

Takagi Kiyoko. 1979. *Sakura Hyakushu* (One hundred poems about cherry blossoms). Tanka Shinbunsha.

————. 1996. *Sakura* (Cherry blossoms). Chūōkōronsha.

Takahashi Nobuo. 1994a. Gunka (Military songs). In *Taishū Bunka Jiten*, edited by Ishikawa Hiroyoshi et al., 223–24. Kōbundō.

————. 1994b. Tokkōtai. In *Taishū Bunka Jiten*, edited by Ishikawa Hiroyoshi et al., 564. Kōbundō.

————. 1994c. Gunkoku Bidan (Heroic stories of a military nation). In *Taishū Bunka Jiten*, edited by Ishikawa Hiroyoshi et al., 224–25. Kōbundō.

————. 1994d. Gunshin (War-deities). In *Taishū Bunka Jiten*, edited by Ishikawa Hiroyoshi et al., 226. Kōbundō.

————. 1994e. Gyokusai (Scattering of a shattered crystal). In *Taishū Bunka Jiten*, edited by Ishikawa Hiroyoshi et al., 204. Kōbundō.

————. 1994f. Tōkyō Ondo (The song of Tokyo). In *Taishū Bunka Jiten*, edited by Ishikawa Hiroyoshi et al., 546. Kōbundō.

————. 1994g. Ichioku Isshin (One million people, one soul). In *Taishū Bunka Jiten*, edited by Ishikawa Hiroyoshi et al., 48. Kōbundō.

Takebe Toshio. 1995. Arahitogami (The manifest deity). *Kokushi Daijiten* 1: 339. Yoshikawa Kōbunkan.

Takeda Izumo. [1937] 1982. *Kanadehon Chūshingura* (The forty-seven loyal retainers). Iwanami Shoten.

Taki Kōji. [1988] 1990. *Tennō no Shōzō* (Portraits of the emperor). Iwanami Shoten.

Takigawa Masajirō. 1971. *Yoshiwara no Shiki* (The four seasons at the Yoshiwara geisha quarters). Seiabō.

Takushima Tokumitsu. 1967. *Ikō Kuchinashi-no-Hana* (The writings left behind: The flower without voice [cape jasmine]). Daikōsha.

Tamamuro Taijō. 1939. *Meiji Ishin Haibutsu Kishaku* (The expulsion of Buddhism and the Buddha's teachings at the time of the Meiji Restoration). Hakuyōsha.

Tambiah, S. J. 1976. *World Conqueror and World Renouncer*. Cambridge: Cambridge University Press.

————. 1981. A Performance Approach to Ritual (Radcliffe-Brown Lecture, 1979). *Proceedings of the British Academy* 65: 113–69.

————. 1990. *Magic, Science, Religion and the Scope of Rationality*. Cambridge: Cambridge University Press.

————. 1996a. *Leveling Crowds*. Berkeley and Los Angeles: University of California Press.

————. 1996b. The Nation-State in Crisis and the Rise of Ethnonationalism. In *The Politics of Difference*, edited by E. N. Wilmsen and P. McAllister, 124–43. Chicago: University of Chicago Press.

————. 2000. Transnational Movements, Diaspora, and Multiple Modernities. *Daedalus* 129 (1): 163–94.

Tanabe Hajime. 1964. *Tanabe Hajime Zenshū* (Complete works of Tanabe Hajime), vol. 8. Takuma Shobō.

Tanaka Akira. 1996. Seitaisho (The ordinance on political organizations). *Kokushi Daijiten* 8: 232–33. Yoshikawa Kōbunkan.

Tanaka, Stephen. 1993. *Japan's Orient*. Los Angeles: University of California Press.

Tanaka Takashi. 1988. "Niiname" kara "Ōname" e (From the Niiname to the Ōname).

In *Zusetsu Tennō no Sokuirei to Ōnamesai,* edited by Yamamoto Hikaru and staff, 28–30. Shinjinbutsu Ōraisha.

Tanizaki Jun'ichirō. [1933] 1959. In-ei Reisan (In praise of shadows). *Tanizaki Jun-ichirō Zenshū* 22: 2–41. Chūōkōronsha.

Terras, Victor, ed. 1985a. *Handbook of Russian Literature.* New Haven: Yale University Press.

———. 1985b. Naródnost'. In *Handbook of Russian Literature,* edited by Victor Terras, 293. New Haven: Yale University Press.

Timms, Edward. 2000. Draining the Swamp. *Times Literary Supplement,* April 2, 2000.

Tierney, Kenji. n.d. Wrestling with Tradition. Book manuscript in preparation.

Toita Michizō. 1982. Ōka Kanashiki (Sorrow of the cherry blossom). *Nihon Jishin* 23: 17–21.

Toita Yasuji. 1969. *Kaisetsu Kagamiyama Kokyō no Nishikie* (Title of a puppet play). Edited by Toshikura Kōichi et al. *Meisaku Kabuki Zenshū,* vol. 13. Tōkyō Sōgen Shinsha.

Toita Yasuji and Yoshida Chiaki. 1981. *Shashin Kabuki Saijiki* (Photo illustrations of the seasons in the kabuki plays). Kōdansha.

Toita Yasuji et al., eds. 1968. *Meisaku Kabuki Zenshū* (Collection of Kabuki masterpieces). Vol. 2. Tōkyō Sōgen Shinsha.

Tokkōtai Senbotsusha Irei Heiwa Kinen Kyōkai, ed. n.d. *Riku-Kaigun Tokubetsu Kōgekitai Ieishū* (Poems left by fallen soldiers of the Army and Navy Special Attack Forces). No. 1.

Tōkyō Daigaku Gakusei Jichikai and Senbotsu Gakusei Shuki Henshū Iinkai, eds. [1947] ([1951] 1980). *Harukanaru Sanga ni* (Far-off mountains and rivers). Tokyo Daigaku Shuppankai.

Tōkyō-to Edo Tōkyō Hakubutsukan. 1993. *Hakuran Toshi Edo Tōkyō* (Exhibition of the cities of Edo/Tokyo). Edo Tōkyō Rekishi Zaidan.

Toriumi Yasushi. 1996. Tennō Kikansetsu Mondai (The problem of the organ theory of the emperor). *Kokushi Daijiten* 9: 1004–6. Yoshikawa Kōbunkan.

Toshikura Kōichi et al. eds. 1969. *Meisaku Kabuki Zenshū* (Masterpieces of the Kabuki). Vol. 13. Tōkyō Sōgen Shinsha.

Tōyama Shigeki. [1988] 1996. Chihō Jungyō (The imperial visits to various regions). In *Tennō to Kazoku. Nihon Kindai Shisō Taikei* 2: 45–115. Iwanami Shoten.

———. 1996. Kido Takayoshi. *Kokushi Daijiten* 4: 170–71. Yoshikawa Kōbunkan.

Tresidder, Jack. 1997. *Dictionary of Symbols.* San Francisco: Chronicle Books.

Trevor-Roper, H. R. 1962. *The Last Days of Hitler.* New York: Collier Books.

———. 1983. The Invention of Tradition. In *The Invention of Tradition,* edited by E. Hobsbawm and T. Ranger, 15–41. Cambridge: Cambridge University Press.

Trouillot, Michel-Rolph. 2001. The Anthropology of the State in the Age of Globalization. *Current Anthropology* 42 (1): 125–38.

Tsubouchi Shōyō (Yūzō). 1900. *Kokugo Dokuhon* (The national language textbook). Vol. 1. Fuzanbō.

Tsubouchi Yūzō. 1999. *Yasukuni.* Shinchōsha.

Tsuchida Naoshige. 1983. *Ōchō no Kizoku* (The aristocrats at the imperial court). *Nihon no Rekishi,* vol. 5. Chūōkōronsha.

Tsukada Takashi. 1994. Yoshiwara (The Yoshiwara geisha quarters). *Nihonshi Daijiten* 6: 1039–40. Edited by Shimonaka Hiroshi. Heibonsha.

Tsukuba Tsuneharu. [1969] 1986. *Beishoku, Nikushoku no Bunmei* (Civilizations of rice consumption and meat consumption). Nihon Hōsō Shuppansha.

Tsumura Masayoshi. [1917] 1970. *Tankai* (A name of a collection of essays). Kokusho Kankōkai.

Turner, Victor. 1967. *The Forest of Symbols.* Ithaca: Cornell University Press.

Ueda Kenji. 1988. Ōnamesai Seiritsu no Haikei (The background of the establishment of the Ōnamesai). In *Zusetsu Tennō no Sokuirei to Ōnamesai,* edited by Yamamoto Hikari and staff, 31–32. Shinjinbutsu Ōraisha.

Ugaki Matome. 1991. *Fading Victory.* Pittsburgh: University of Pittsburgh Press.

Umetani Noboru. 1995. Shutain (Lorenz von Stein). *Kokushi Daijiten* 7: 384–85. Yoshikawa Kōbunkan.

———. 1996a. Gunjin Chokuyu (The imperial rescript to soldiers). *Kokushi Daijiten* 4: 1036–37. Yoshikawa Kōbunkan.

———. 1996b. Rēsutoru (Roesler). *Kokushi Daijiten* 14: 704–5. Yoshikawa Kōbunkan.

———. 1996c. Mosse (Albert Mosse). *Kokushi Daijiten* 13: 827. Yoshikawa Kōbunkan.

Umezawa Shōzō. 1997. Umezao Kazuyo. Essay on his late brother, sent to the author, originally posted in the exhibition case for his brother at the Yasukuni Shrine in 1997.

Umezu Jirō. 1978. Tengu Zōshi ni tsuite (About the tengu stories). In *Shinshū Nihon Emakimono Zenshū,* edited by Umezu Jirō, 27: 3–14. Kadokawa Shoten.

Urayama Masao. 1997. Kanadehon Chūshingura (The Forty-Seven Loyal Retainers). *Kokushi Daijiten* 3: 458. Yoshikawa Kōbunkan.

Valeri, Valerio. 1985. *Kingship and Sacrifice.* Chicago: University of Chicago Press.

Vlastos, Stephen. 1989. Opposition Movements in Early Meiji, 1868–1885. In *The Cambridge History of Japan,* edited by Marius B. Jansen, 367–431. Cambridge: Cambridge University Press.

Vries, Ad de. [1974] 1984. *Dictionary of Symbols and Imagery.* Amsterdam: North-Holland Publishing Company.

Wada Minoru. 1972. *Wadatsumi no Koe Kieru Koto Naku* (The voices of the sea deity shall not be silenced). Kadokawa Shoten.

Wakamori Tarō. 1975. *Hana to Nihonjin* (Cherry blossoms and the Japanese). Sōgetsu Shuppan.

Warner, Denis, and Peggy Warner. 1982. *The Sacred Warriors.* New York: Van Nostrand Reinhold.

Watanabe Tadayo. 1989. Nihonjin to Inasaku Bunka (The Japanese and rice culture). *Nikkan Āgama* 103: 81–91.

Watanabe Tamotsu. 1989. *Kabuki.* Shin'yōsha.

———. 1991. Chūshingura (The forty-seven loyal retainers). In *Taishū Bunka Jiten,* edited by Ishikawa Hiroyoshi et al., 501–2. Kōbundō.

———. 1994. *Butai toiu Shinwa* (The myth of the stage). Shinchōsha.

Weinberg, David R. 2000. *Kuniyoshi*. Leiden: Hotei Publishing.

Wolf, Eric. 1994. Perilous Ideas. *Current Anthropology* 35 (1): 1–12. Reprinted in *Pathways of Power*, 398–412. Berkeley and Los Angeles: University of California Press.

———. 1999. *Envisioning Power*. Berkeley and Los Angeles: University of California Press.

Yagi Tessen. 1989. *Chūshingura* (The forty-seven loyal retainers). Edited by Akōshi Sōmubu Shishi Hensanshitsu. Vol. 1. Akō: Hyōgo-ken Akō-shi.

Yahiro Shūtō, ed. 1995. *Shokubutsu no Sekai* (The world of plants). *Shūkan Asahi Hyakka*, vol. 1008. Asahi Shinbunsha.

Yamada Hideo. 1995. Nengō (The names of the eras). *Kokushi Daijiten* 11: 330. Yoshikawa Kōbunkan.

Yamada Munemutsu. 1977. *Hana no Bunkashi* (The cultural history of flowers). Yomiuri Shinbunsha.

———. 1982. Ōshigi (The review of the history of symbolism of cherry blossoms). *Nihon Jishin* 23: 32–38.

Yamada Ryū. 1997. Watakushi no Anabaputizumu tono Deai (An essay on anabaptism: My encounter with Anabaptism). No. 3. Unpublished manuscript. Courtesy of Prof. Yamashita Sanpei of Kyūshū University.

Yamada Yoshio. [1941] 1993. *Ōshi* (History of the flowering cherry in Japan). Edited by Yamada Tadao. Kōdansha.

Yamagishi Tokuhei, ed. 1958. *Genji Monogatari* (The Tale of Genji). Vol. 1. *Nihon Koten Bungaku Taikei*, vol. 14. Iwanami Shoten.

———. 1959. *Genji Monogatari* (The Tale of Genji). Vol. 2. *Nihon Koten Bungaku Taikei*, vol. 15. Iwanami Shoten.

———. 1962. *Genji Monogatari* (The Tale of Genji). Vol. 4. *Nihon Koten Bungaku Taikei*, vol. 17. Iwanami Shoten.

Yamaji Aizan. [1906] 2000. *Essays on the Modern Japanese Church*. Stanford: Stanford University Press.

Yamaki Akihiko. 1986. *Gunka Saijiki* (Collection of military songs). Hyūman Dokyumentosha.

Yamamoto Hikaru and staff, eds. 1988. *Zusetsu Tennō no Sokuirei to Ōnamesai* (Illustrated accounts of the imperial accession ritual and the Ōnamesai). Shinjinbutsu Ōraisha.

Yamamoto Kenkichi. 1982. Hana (Flowers). *Nihon Jishin* 23: 73–76.

Yamamoto Tsunetomo. [1716] 1969, 1971. *Hagakure Kikigaki* (Title of a book on the warriors' way). Edited by Naramoto Tatsuya. Chūōkōronsha.

Yamanaka Hisashi. [1975] 1985. *Mitami, Ware: Bokura Shōkokumin* (We, your Majesty's subjects: Young national subjects). Vol. 2. Keisō Shobō.

———. 1986. *Kodomotachi no Taiheiyō Sensō* (The Pacific war for children). *Kokumin Gakkō no Jidai*. Iwanami Shoten.

———. 1989. *Bokura Shōkokumin to Sensō Ōenka* (We, the young national subjects, and songs in support of the war). Asahi Shinbunsha.

Yamane Sadao. [1985] 1991. Chūshingura Eiga (Films of "The forty-seven loyal retainers"). In *Daihyakka Jiten*, edited by Shimonaka Hiroshi, 883–884. Heibonsha.

Yamanouchi, Midori. 2000. *Listen to the Voices from the Sea* (trans. of *Kike Wada-tsumi no Koe*). Scranton: University of Scranton Press.

Yamaori Tetsuo. 1978. *Tennō no Shūkyōteki Ken'i towa Nanika* (What is the religious authority of the emperor?). San'ichi Shobō.

———. 1990a. Kakureta Tennōrei Keishō no Dorama (Hidden drama of the imperial Succession). *Gekkan Asahi* (February): 80–85.

———. 1990b. *Shi no Minzokugaku* (Folklore of death). Iwanami Shoten.

Yamazumi Masami. 1970. *Kyōkasho* (School textbooks). Iwanami Shoten.

———. [1990] 1996. *Kyōiku no Taikei* (Outline of education). *Nihon Kindai Shisō Taikei*, vol. 6. Iwanami Shoten.

———. 1997. Kokutai no Hongi (Principles of the national polity). *Kokushi Daijiten* 5: 670. Yoshikawa Kōbunkan.

Yanagita Kunio. [1930] 1982. Shidare-zakura no Mondai (On the weeping cherry). *Yanagita Kunio-shū* 22: 213–19. Chikuma Shobō.

———. 1933. Momotarō no Tanjō (The birth of the "Peach Boy"). *Yanagita Kunio-shū* 8: 1–314. Chikuma Shobō.

———. [1946] 1982. Senzo no Hanashi (On the ancestors). *Yanagita Kunio-shū* 10: 3–152. Chikuma Shobō.

———. [1947a] 1982. Shinanozakura no Hanashi (On the Shinano cherry blossoms). *Yanagita Kunio-shū* 22: 220–27. Chikuma Shobō.

———. 1947b. Yamamiya-kō (Thoughts on the mountains as shrines). *Yanagita Kunio-shū* 11: 299–358. Chikuma Shobō.

Yanagita Kunio, ed. 1951. *Minzokugaku Jiten* (Ethnographic dictionary). Tōkyōdō.

Yasuda Yojūrō. [1932] 1984. Hana to Keijijōgaku to (The flower and metaphysics). *Cogito* 5: 129–44.

———. [1939] 1986. Bunmei Kaika no Riron no Shūen ni tsuite (On the end of the theory of "civilization and enlightenment"). *Yasuda Yojūrō Zenshū* 7: 11–21. Originally appeared in *Cogito,* no. 80 (1939).

Yasukuni Jinja. 1976. *Yasukuni Jinja* (The Yasukuni Shrine). Yasukuni Jinja.

———. 1982. *Yasukuni,* May 1, 1982.

———. 1983–84. *Yasukuni Jinja Hyakunenshi* (History of one hundred years of the Yasukuni Shrine). Vol. 1 (1983); Vol. 2 (1984). Yasukuni Jinja.

———. 1992. *Yasukuni Daihyakka* (Encyclopedia of the Yasukuni Shrine). Yasukuni Jinja.

———. 1994. *Iza Saraba Ware ha Mikuni no Yamazakura* (Farewell, we are the mountain cherries of our country). Tentensha.

———. 1995a. *Eirei no Koto no Ha* (Words of the souls of the heroes). Vol. 1. Yasukuni Jinja Shamusho.

———. 1995b. *Sange no Kokoro to Chinkon no Makoto* (The souls of falling cherry petals and the sincerity of the appeasement of the souls). Tentensha.

———. 1996. *Eirei no Koto no Ha* (Words of the souls of the heroes). Vol. 2. Yasukuni Jinja Shamusho.

Yasumaru Yoshio. 1980. *Kamigami no Meiji Ishin* (The Meiji Restoration and the deities). Iwanami Shoten.

Yokomichi Mario and Omote Akira, eds. 1963. Dōjōji (A name of a play). In *Yō-*

kyokushū, vol. 2 (Ge). *Nihon Koten Bungaku Taikei* 41: 129–42. Iwanami Shoten.

Yokota Ken'ichi. 1988. "Ōnamesai no Seiritsu Jidai" Hosetsu (Additional explanation for the age of the establishment of the Ōnamesai). In *Zusetsu Tennō no Sokuirei to Ōnamesai*, edited by Yamamoto Hikaru and staff, 27–29. Shinjinbutsu Ōraisha.

Yoshida Chiaki, and Hattori Sachio, eds. 1991. *Kabuki Iroha Ezōshi* (Illustrated stories of the Kabuki). Kōdansha.

Young, Louise. 1998. *Japan's Total Empire*. Berkeley and Los Angeles: University of California Press.

Yui Masaomi. 1996. Kimigayo (The national anthem). *Kokushi Daijiten* 4: 210. Yoshikawa Kōbunkan.

Yui Masaomi, Fujiwara Akira, and Yoshida Yutaka, eds. [1989] 1996. *Guntai Heishi* (Armies and soldiers). *Nihon Kindai Shisō Taikei*, vol. 4. Iwanami Shoten.

Ze'ami Motokiyo. 1935a. Sakuragawa (A Noh play). In *Kaichū Yōkyoku Zenshū*, edited by Nogami Toyoichirō, 3: 323–40. Chūōkōronsha.

———. 1935b. Mitsuyama (A Noh play). In *Kaichū Yōkyoku Zenshū*, edited by Nogami Toyoichirō, 3: 309–22. Chūōkōronsha.

Zonabend, Françoise. 1993. *Presqu'île au nucléaire*. Paris: Editions de la maison des sciences de l'homme. *The Nuclear Peninsula*. Translated by J. A. Underwood. Cambridge: Cambridge University Press, 1993.

Index